A COMPANION
TO ROMAN ITALY

BLACKWELL COMPANIONS TO THE ANCIENT WORLD

This series provides sophisticated and authoritative overviews of periods of ancient history, genres of classical literature, and the most important themes in ancient culture. Each volume comprises approximately twenty-five and forty concise essays written by individual scholars within their area of specialization. The essays are written in a clear, provocative, and lively manner, designed for an international audience of scholars, students, and general readers.

A COMPANION TO ROMAN ITALY

Edited by

Alison E. Cooley

WILEY Blackwell

This edition first published 2016
© 2016 John Wiley & Sons, Ltd.

Registered Office
John Wiley & Sons, Ltd, The Atrium, Southern Gate, Chichester, West Sussex, PO19 8SQ, UK

Editorial Offices
350, Main Street, Malden, MA 02148-5020, USA
9600 Garsington Road, Oxford, OX4 2DQ, UK
The Atrium, Southern Gate, Chichester, West Sussex, PO19 8SQ, UK

For details of our global editorial offices, for customer services, and for information about how
to apply for permission to reuse the copyright material in this book please see our website at
www.wiley.com/wiley-blackwell.

Library of Congress Cataloging-in-Publication data applied for

ISBN: 9781444339260 (hardback)

A catalogue record for this book is available from the British Library.

Cover image: Map of Roman Italy © Getty Images/DEA Picture Library

Set in 9.5/11.5pt Galliard by SPi Global, Pondicherry, India
Printed and bound in Malaysia by Vivar Printing Sdn Bhd

1   2016

Contents

List of Illustrations

List of Tables

Notes on Contributors

Clifford Ando is Professor of Classics, History and Law in the College at the University of Chicago, USA and Research Fellow in the Department of Classics and World Languages, University of South Africa.

Rebecca R. Benefiel is Associate Professor of Classics at Washington and Lee University, USA and teaches Latin literature and Roman archaeology, with research focusing on Latin epigraphy and Roman social history. She is Director of the Herculaneum Graffiti Project, contributor to EAGLE Europeana and the Oplontis Project, and co-editor of *Inscriptions in the Private Sphere in the Greco-Roman World* (Brill, in press).

Joanne Berry is an honorary research associate in the Department of History and Classics, Swansea University, UK. She is the author of *The Complete Pompeii* (Thames and Hudson, 2007), and co-author of *The Complete Roman Legions* (with Nigel Pollard, Thames and Hudson 2012).

Edward Bispham is Fellow and Tutor in Ancient History at Brasenose and St Anne's Colleges, Oxford, UK. He teaches and researches in Roman republican history, and its intersections with archaeology and epigraphy; he also co-directed the Sangro Valley Project landscape archaeology project in Adriatic Central Italy between 1999 and 2010. His publications include *From*

Asculum to Actium: the municipalization of Italy from the Social War to Augustus (Oxford University Press, 2007).

Neil Christie is Reader in Archaeology at the School of Archaeology and Ancient History at the University of Leicester, UK. His main research areas cover Italy, late Roman and early medieval urbanism, and defense; he has worked on various field and excavation projects in Italy, including in the central Italian Cicolano and Sangro regions. His main publications include *From Constantine to Charlemagne: an archaeology of Italy, AD 300–800* (Ashgate, 2006), and, edited with A. Augenti, Vrbes Extinctae. *Archaeologies of Abandoned Classical Towns* (Ashgate, 2012).

Alison E. Cooley is Professor in the Department of Classics and Ancient History, University of Warwick, UK. Her research focuses upon epigraphy, Roman Italy, and the early Principate. Her recent books include *Pompeii and Herculaneum: a sourcebook* (Routledge 2014, with M.G.L. Cooley); *The Cambridge Manual of Latin Epigraphy* (CUP 2012); *Res Gestae Divi Augusti* (CUP 2009).

Janet DeLaine is Lecturer in Roman Archaeology at the University of Oxford, UK. Her research focuses upon Roman architecture, art, and urbanism in the Mediterranean, especially the Roman building industry, Roman baths, and the urban development of Ostia.

Elizabeth Fentress is an independent scholar who excavated at Cosa between 1991 and 1997 on behalf of the American Academy in Rome.

Penelope J. Goodman is Lecturer in Roman History at the University of Leeds, UK. She is the author of *The Roman City and its Periphery: from Rome to Gaul* (Routledge, 2007), as well as articles on sacred and urban space in Roman Gaul and Italy.

Emma-Jayne Graham is Lecturer in Classical Studies at the Open University, UK. Her research focuses on funerary ritual, treatment of the body, identity and bodily experience. She is author of *Death, disposal and the destitute: the burial of the urban poor in Italy in the late Roman Republic and early Empire* (BAR, Oxford, 2006).

Valerie M. Hope is Senior Lecturer in Classical Studies at the Open University, UK. Recent books include *Roman Death. The dying and the dead in Ancient Rome* (Continuum 2009); *Death in Ancient Rome: a sourcebook* (Routledge 2007) and *Memory and Mourning: studies on Roman Death*, jointly edited with J. Huskinson (Oxbow, 2011).

Elena Isayev is Senior Lecturer in Ancient History, Dept of Classics and Ancient History, University of Exeter, UK. Her publications include *Inside Ancient Lucania: dialogues in history and archaeology* (BICS Supplement, 2007) and, with Guy Bradley and Corinna Riva, *Ancient Italy: Regions Without Boundaries* (Exeter University Press, 2007).

Simon Keay is Professor of Archaeology at the University of Southampton, UK and Research Professor and Director of Archaeology at the British School at Rome. His research focuses upon archaeology of the Roman Empire, particularly Iberia, Italy, and Roman commerce. He directs the Portus Project and the ERC funded Portuslimen (RoMP) Project. Recent publications include

Rome, Portus and the Mediterranean (British School at Rome, 2013) and (with L. Paroli) *Portus and its hinterland: recent archaeological research* (British School at Rome, 2011).

Margaret L. Laird is a Lecturer in the Department of Foreign Languages and Literatures at the University of Delaware, USA. She has published on the art made by and for the *Augustales*, which is also the subject of her forthcoming book, as well as the history of the lands of an abbey in Lazio.

Ray Laurence is Professor of Roman History and Archaeology at the University of Kent, UK. He has published on a wide range of topics including Roman cities, especially Pompeii, ageing in the Roman world and other topics of social history dealing with the family, and the geographical, political, and economic impact of roads in Italy.

Kathryn Lomas is an Honorary Senior Research Associate in archaeology at University College London, UK, and has research specialisms in the history and archaeology of early Italy and the Western Mediterranean, ethnic and cultural identities in the ancient world, and the development of literacy in the ancient Mediterranean. She is the author of *Rome and the Western Greeks* and *Roman Italy, 338 BC – AD 200* (Routledge, 1993), and the editor of several volumes of collected papers, and has published numerous articles on her areas of interest.

Martin Millett is Laurence Professor of Classical Archaeology at Cambridge University and a Fellow of Fitzwilliam College, Cambridge, UK. He has undertaken field-work and research in Italy and across the western Roman Empire. He currently co-directs field projects at Interamna Lirenas (Pignataro, FR) in Italy and at Isurium Brigantum (Aldborough, North Yorks) in the UK.

John R. Patterson is University Senior Lecturer in Classics at the University of Cambridge, UK, and Director of Studies in

Classics at Magdalene College. He is the author of *Samnites, Ligurians and Romans* (Comune di Circello, 1988), *Political Life in the City of Rome* (Bristol Classical Press, 2000), and *Landscapes and Cities: Rural Settlement and Civic Transformation in Early Imperial Italy* (Oxford University Press, 2006). With Emmanuele Curti and Emma Dench he reviewed recent publications on Roman Italy in *Journal of Roman Studies* 86 (1996), 170–89.

Phil Perkins is Professor of Archaeology in the Department of Classical Studies, The Open University, UK. He became involved in Etruscan archaeology during the 1980s field surveying in the Ager Cosanus /Albegna Valley in Tuscany, excavating the first ever Etruscan farm at Podere Tartuchino and studying ceramics. He has published the bucchero in the British Museum and is currently excavating and studying bucchero at Poggio Colla.

Jonathan S. Perry is Associate Professor of History at the University of South Florida—Sarasota-Manatee, USA. He is the author of *The Roman Collegia: the modern evolution of an ancient concept* (Brill Academic Press, 2006), which explores the evaluation of an ancient Roman institution in modern societies from Mommsen through Fascist Italy to the present. He is engaged in writing another monograph on international opinion concerning Augustus in the 1930s.

Nigel Pollard is Associate Professor in the Dept of History and Classics, Swansea University, UK. His research studies forms of interaction between the ruling elites of the Roman Empire and its subjects, especially in the eastern provinces. He has a wide experience of fieldwork and has also worked on museum collections and archives.

Rafael Scopacasa is research fellow at the Department of Classics and Ancient History, University of Exeter, UK. His most recent publications include *Thinking Ancient Samnium: settlement, culture and identity between history and archaeology* (Oxford University Press, 2014) and "Gender and ritual in ancient Italy: a quantitative approach to grave goods and skeletal data in pre-Roman Samnium" (*American Journal of Archaeology*: 118.2, 2014). He is interested in bringing together historical, epigraphic, and archaeological evidence as a means of constructing alternative histories of pre-Imperial Italy.

Celia E. Schultz is Professor of Classical Studies at the University of Michigan, USA. She is the author of *Women's Religious Activity in the Roman Republic* (University of North Carolina Press, 2006) and co-editor with Paul B. Harvey, Jr. of *Religion in Republican Italy* (Cambridge University Press, 2006). She is working on a study of Cicero's *De Divinatione*.

Robert Witcher is Senior Lecturer in Archaeology at Durham University, UK. His principal research interests are landscape and Roman archaeology. He has worked on landscape field surveys in Lazio, Sicily, and the Sangro valley, researching ancient agriculture, economy, and demography. Recent publications include "'That from a long way off look like farms': the classification of Roman rural sites," in Attema and Schörner, eds, *Comparative Issues in the Archaeology of the Roman Rural Landscape* (*JRA* Suppl. 88, 2012).

Acknowledgements

I would like to thank all of the contributors to the volume for their immense patience in waiting for this book to take its final form, especially those contributors who delivered their typescripts in time for that first deadline several years ago. Along the way, Al Bertrand, Galen Young, Haze Humbert, and, most recently Allison Kostka, at Blackwell-Wiley have kept faith with the project. Initial plans for the volume included chapters on the environment and landscape, sanctuaries, colonization, *municipia*, Capua and the *ager Campanus*, imperial estates, and non-urban settlements. I would like to thank particularly Jonathan Perry and Rafael Scopacasa for stepping in as contributors at a late stage. Although I regret not being able to achieve the ambitious outline first planned, I am happy to refer readers to other Wiley-Blackwell Companions (such as *A Companion to the Roman Republic*, *A Companion to the Roman Empire*), where some of these topics have already found a home, notably Tesse Stek's, 'Monumental Architecture of Non-Urban Cult Places in Roman Italy' in *A Companion to Roman Architecture*. I would also like to thank Benet Salway for super-fast comments on a draft of chapter 7.

Warwick, May 2014

INTRODUCTION

Setting the Scene

CHAPTER 1

Italy Before the Romans

Elena Isayev

1.1   Introduction

The spread of Roman hegemonic power was not itself responsible for the creation of an entity called Italy (Figure 1.1). In the end it was the result of a newly formed method of organization, an overarching structure that by the late Republic bound all those inhabiting the peninsula to each other through the central authority based in Rome; an authority that became the director of resources both human and material, shaping the Italian landscape to orient itself around the center (Morley, 1996). Yet we can argue for an Italy even before this moment. Already in the early 2nd century BC Cato could treat the peninsula as if it was his high street, noting the best places to get provisions for running a farm: if purchasing an olive press, best to go to the yard of Rufrius in Pompeii (*De agricultura*: 22). Interregional connections which developed rapidly in the Hellenistic period led to the formation of a single organism. Prior to such a moment, Italy the peninsula was multi-polar, and not only in a physical sense. A number of overlapping organizational forces operated simultaneously, and competed in controlling the resource base. These forces were not restricted by the coastline; Italy was not their container: rather, they drew on networks that criss-crossed the Mediterranean and reached beyond it (Horden and Purcell, 2000; van Dommelen and Knapp, 2010). In the Archaic period a merchant from Veii in Etruria probably had more in common with another such trader from Carthage, Corinth, or Massilia than with one living in the region of Messapia in the heel of Italy. There was more chance that the two Italians would meet at a festival abroad, a port at one of the trading hubs such as Corinth, a boat captured by pirates, or as part of a mixed mercenary force fighting for a Greek tyrant, than on the peninsula itself. It is also plausible that they might find it easier to communicate with each other in Punic or Greek, rather than in any Italic language, of which there would have been at least a dozen at the time (cf. Lomas, ch.11 this vol.). That does not mean that there were no links, common socio-political worries, interest in economic opportunities, or shared modes of cultural expression that ran along the length of Italy's spine, but rather that such ties were not necessarily stronger simply because those who were bound by them shared the landscapes of the peninsula as their home.

Narratives of pre-Roman Italy usually begin by outlining its broad regional divisions, where each territorial section overlaps with a particular ethnic group's sphere of influence, its

A Companion to Roman Italy, First Edition. Edited by Alison E. Cooley.
© 2016 John Wiley & Sons, Ltd. Published 2016 by John Wiley & Sons, Ltd.

Figure 1.1   Map of Italy with sites cited in the text (modern names in italics). Drawing: Antonio Montesanti.

associated language, and its other distinguishing cultural characteristics. These tend to include the following: most prominently the Etruscans with a base in Etruria who extended to Campania in the south and the Po Valley in the north; they edged the territory of Cisalpine Gaul, which encompassed Liguria, the Veneto, the Insubres and also a number of Celtic groups; in a central position reaching to the west coast was Latium; the length of Italy's spine was the main home to the speakers of Osco-Umbrian or Sabellic languages associated mostly with the Umbrians, Samnites, and Lucanians, stretching into the toe of Bruttium, and Campania on the west coast; these were edged on the east coast by Picenum, and further south the Apulian region incorporated Daunia and Messapia on the Salento peninsula; ringed around the south coast, the Greek colonies which appeared from the eighth century BC onward are also usually taken as a group. Such an overview is helpful for categorizing information, but also has the danger of lending cohesion to areas where it did not exist, while overlooking ties beyond them. Even the homogeneity of the Greek colonies has been questioned. Scholars point to the mixed nature of such settlements and show that their beginnings have the characteristic of being small group ventures rather than any state-initiated enterprise (Osborne, 1998; Hurst and Owen, 2005; Bradley and Wilson, 2006). A regional approach to Italy begins to break down once the focus shifts onto individual sites and networks of connectivity that ran through them (Bradley, Isayev, and Riva, 2007). This chapter looks at the organizational possibilities that were prevalent in Italy before it gained a cohesive form, at a time when her shores were fluid. How these were transformed and super-seded, and which of them continued to exist in a Roman *Italia*, is in part what the rest of this volume is about.

1.2 Forces of Centralization – Interpreting Settlement Patterns

The single settlement is often seen as the most concrete organizational unit, whether it is a city, town, or village. But its relationship to a particular community is less straightforward. We may take the most obvious case of the Roman citizen body, which extended well beyond the group who inhabited the physical city. Those born in Rome who held the citizenship could choose to live abroad, while those born outside the city could gain the citizenship through various means, such as the carrying out of services for the state (Sherwin-White, 1973). Eventually whole settlements, such as colonies, held Roman citizen status, and in 89 BC it was granted to all communities south of the Po. We know little about how other Italic member-ships functioned, but there is enough to indicate fluidity between members of different communities who were of the same high social standing, including those from outside Italy. It is such fluidity and openness that allowed Rome to experiment with different forms of membership status and inter-community ties that some see as the key to its success in Italy and the Mediterranean (Eckstein, 2006: ch. 7).

The question is how we interpret the diverse settlement patterns across the peninsula that existed simultaneously, and what do the structures on the ground tell us about community and state- formation (Bradley, Isayev, and Riva, 2007; Terrenato and Haggis, 2011; Cornell, 1995; Riva 2010a)? Landscape archaeology has allowed for a wide-reaching sweep of the peninsula (Attema, Burgers, and van Leusen, 2010; Patterson, 2004; Carter, 2006). The material shows two key points of transformation which, although varying in scale and rates of change, affect the whole of Italy: centralization in the early centuries of the first millennium BC, and a filling in of habitation in the countryside in the early Hellenistic period. A shift to nucleated settlements occurs in the period between the Final Bronze Age and the Iron Age. It is most visible in Etruria, Umbria and northern Latium, in what was already a densely populated landscape characterized by a multiplicity of small sites of circa 1–15 hectares throughout the Bronze Age. Within only a few centuries there was a process of amalgam-ation, which led to the rise of fewer but substantially larger settlements, some of 100–200 hectares, occupying broad plateaus that could accommodate populations in the thousands (Attema, Burgers, and van Leusen, 2010; Smith, 2007b). The most prominent communities that continued to flourish and exert power throughout the eighth–sixth centuries BC were Tarquinii, Caere, Veii, Volsinii, Vulci, Orvieto, Chiusi, Arezzo, and arguably Rome.

Just to the south of these hubs in the Pontine region of Latium, the transformations resulted in a different pattern. Here, sites such as Satricum and Lanuvium also show centralizing tendencies, but the sites are significantly smaller, 20–50 hectares and they are distributed more evenly through the landscape, especially around the Alban Hills (Attema, Burgers and van Leusen, 2010: 112–17). A similar pattern of site distribution is evident in the south of

Italy. Nucleating forces in the Salento peninsula privileged the creation of equally modest sites of 30–50 hectares, such as Oria (Attema, Burgers, and van Leusen, 2010: 132). In the north of Italy, a region such as the Veneto saw both the creation of substantial towns such as Este and Padua, and smaller sites in the mountainous hinterland (Lomas, 2007), which was also characteristic of Liguria in the east (Häussler, 2007).

Comparative settlement sizes and distribution patterns are a starting point for ascertaining how sites related to each other and their surrounding territories. One way to analyze the data is through the model of *peer polity interaction* (Renfrew and Cherry, 1986). It proposes that change is initiated by the interaction and competition between a large number of independent and initially equally matched polities. This explanatory framework seems suited to the inhabited landscapes of Latium's Pontine region and the Salento peninsula in the Iron Age and Archaic periods. Forces that transformed this balance are particularly visible in Latium, where the significant rise of Rome led to a more hierarchical system of power relations oriented around a prominent central place (Attema, Burgers, and van Leusen, 2010: 140–43). At this point a different model of *core and periphery* may be more suitable, according to which change is driven by unequal interacting parts of single systems (Rowlands, Larsen, and Kristiansen, 1987). Both of the models are supported by rank-size studies that theoretically position a site within a hierarchy, and project the extent of its territorial control. The results can then be visualized through the use of cartographic techniques such as Thiessen polygons, and the more advanced XTENT model (Renfrew and Level, 1979; Redhouse and Stoddart, 2011; Attema, Burgers, and van Leusen 2010: 26–29). These methods are helpful in providing indicative results of territorial divisions and hierarchies, but they cannot be taken as evidence of political or territorial dependency on their own, as the bonds between center and hinterland varied over time, and clear evidence of their interaction is still hard to produce (Attema, Burgers, and van Leusen, 2010: 151–52).

One of the issues is that size alone does not mean that a settlement necessarily functioned as a coherent autonomous polity, such as a city or state, which exerted power over a significant territory. Other signs are necessary, especially that of communal action, that would point to the presence of a central authority, with decision-making power and institutions that could enact these decisions by harnessing shared resources. Conversely, it is not necessary to have a model urban center for such communal action to take place, or, put another way, the community that shares its resources and socio-political structures can encompass a number of settlements, which its members inhabit. Hence, attempts at locating settlements in ancient Italy, on a spectrum which employs model definitions of city and state, have struggled, since the parameters are too rigid to encompass the variety of organizational forms. We may take the example of the settlement of Arpi, in Puglia, ancient Daunia, which Strabo (6.3.9) noted as once being one of the largest *poleis* in Italy. Remains of a substantial earthwork, which are still visible around the settlement, would seem to support this statement, but the archaeological material of the early phases of the site presents a more complex picture (Herring, 2007, 286–90). The site was occupied already in the eighth century BC, and by the sixth century BC it was encircled by the large earthwork structure. Whether it was defensive is debatable as its perimeter is far too long to secure efficiently. This monumental project is the main evidence of any communal enterprise at the site. Otherwise it has been shown that until the Hellenistic period there is no evidence of public areas, structures, or any organized approach to the use of space. The habitation within the enclosure was of a dispersed nature, suggesting a number of small villages and farmsteads, with their own cemeteries and agricultural land, with little evidence that they formed a coherent unit. A similar pattern of semi-nucleated settlement is evident in other parts of the region, such as at Tiati and Ordona.

As a comparison we may consider the development of Veii on the north side of the Tiber. Veii's impressive remains allow for an investigation of the workings of the centralizing forces through which a single city unit materialized. Recent re-evaluation of the material from the Tiber Valley survey has shown the way that Archaic Veii emerged from distinct village-type settlements of the Early Iron Age, positioned around the tufo plateau. A total of sixteen separate necropoli which encircle the site, containing thousands of burials of the tenth–fourth centuries BC, are believed to be testament of the earlier distinct groups (Patterson, 2004; Murray, 2011; Riva, 2010a: 26–27). Communal efforts between these groups are evident on a large scale from the sixth century BC: construction of a fortification circuit around the plateau, the creation of *cuniculi* – a sophisticated system of water distribution- and the monumentalization of sacred precincts, such as the Portonaccio sanctuary, complete with Tuscan temple and water pool (Colonna, 2002; Colonna and Ambrosini, 2009). There is also a contemporaneous interest in the division of land that may be recognized through the remains of furrows at Piazza d'Armi, which point to an orthogonal division of space, along with erection of boundary walls and the construction of elite residences. An internal hierarchical organization is also apparent from the funerary evidence: tomb assemblages are full of banqueting equipment representing commensality, and other forms of elite display. The pride of the town's elite was not limited to the private domain: Veii's elaborate architectural displays and art works were well known, and according to tradition it is to Veii that Rome looked when seeking top artists to design the sculpture of Jupiter for the Capitoline Temple (Pliny the Elder, *Natural History*: 35.157).

The key features of centralization and communal decisions visible at Veii, and evident at other sites across Italy, include the creation of public spaces, fortification circuits, land division, spatial planning, and the building of sacred structures. Other signs of early collective action may be added to this list, for example specialization of production and the control of common resources such as grazing lands, although the latter is difficult to show. In the material record, where epigraphic texts are lacking, what we see are the products rather than the process of such decision-making, which is associated with state formation. The question is, did state formation precede such joint ventures or were they the catalysts for it? At the center of such a debate is the creation of the Roman forum, which some see as a major initiative that led to state formation. Others argue that necessary reclamation of the marginal land on which it was positioned in 600 BC would have required that some form of state already existed to make the decisions for the organization of resources and substantial manpower to drain and infill the area (Ammerman, 2011). A further issue for this early period is to understand the way in which a central authority emerged through a negotiation of dominant individuals and varied competing kinship and other groups, visible in the funerary sphere (C.J. Smith, 2007a; Terrenato and Haggis, 2011). What prompted them into this joint action to begin with? The idea that such transformations were necessarily a response to foreign stimuli, such as Greco-Phoenician merchants and settlers coming from the East, is now being challenged, as there is enough evidence to support that they were a result of long-established internally motivated trajectories (Izzet, 2007: 232–33). Engagement with foreign culture, individuals and knowledge was part of the process but not its initiator, in that, by joining together, these disparate groups could exploit wider mutually beneficial networks.

The impact and role of newcomers to the peninsula has been most critically tested in south Italy, which by the sixth century BC housed a substantial number of Greek colonial schemes. Prior to this period those who arrived at such sites as Pithekoussai, just off the Italian coast – mostly Greek and Phoenician merchants and laborers – were part of small group ventures that sought out lucrative opportunities around the Mediterranean. Some of them came to rest at Pithekoussai because it allowed them to take part in the exchange and distribution of goods, especially metals, from the coastal regions of Italy such as Etruria and Campania (Osborne, 1998; Cuozzo, 2007; Bradley and Wilson, 2006). Increasing material visibility allows us to track the newcomers as they settled down and integrated into existing settlements or established ones *ex novo*. These early interactions were not the kind of state-initiated colonial enterprises that appeared by the end of the sixth century BC. The motivation for these later ventures was to establish power bases in competition, not so much with their Italic neighbors, but with the Greek rivals of the founders, as may be seen by Kroton's takeover of Achaean Sybaris in 510 BC and the eventual Athenian creation of the new site of Thurioi in 446/444 BC in its place.

The story of Sybaris as a city wielding a south Italian empire is well attested, yet its early history and the position of the first Greek arrivals are less well understood. According to tradition, Sybaris was an Achaean colony founded in the eighth century BC which exerted a hegemonic influence until its destruction in 510 BC. Strabo (6.1.13) states that it ruled three tribes and twenty-five towns. Of the original colony, other than a few archaic houses at Stombi, little remains due to the alluvial deposits covering earlier habitation layers near the coastline. What evidence there is comes from the territory further inland. At sites such as Timpone della Motta, some thirty km. away, there is evidence of Archaic houses with similar style and technique as at Stombi. The site also has remains of a sanctuary with Greek material, as does Torre Mordillo. The latter also has a settlement that shows centralizing tendencies in the Iron Age. Other sites in the area, such as Amendolara, also have evidence of Greek material dating from the early seventh century BC. For those who subscribe to the traditional narrative, these pieces of evidence provide further support of Greek hegemony from the start (Guzzo, 1987: 373–79; de Polignac, 1984; Osanna, 1992: 122–32, 157–66; Greco, 1993: 467). Early Greek material in the surrounding territory could be read as a sign of Sybarite expansion, while Timpone della Motta and Torre Mordillo may be interpreted as frontier sanctuaries created to defend the early colonial territory. These suppositions have supported the notion that the Greek influence not only triggered centralization in the surrounding indigenous communities during the colonial period, but also settlement transformation in the preceding phase (Guzzo, 1987). While such interpretations match the literary evidence, they do not explain other features of the material record that challenge this view. Centralization at Torre Mordillo shows prominent aristocratic houses with cult activities, centered on a weaving deity. These preceded the Greek-style temple complex on the site in the seventh century BC. Instead, once there is evidence of Greek material it appears in the cemeteries alongside indigenous material, and suggests the presence of Greek migrants who may have been integrated into the community. The evidence shows that indigenous elite were prominent in the period of site transformation and that Greek influence developed slowly, without necessarily initial aggression or violence. How Sybaris then extended to play a major role in the seventh century BC remains unclear (Kleibrink, 2001; Attema, Burgers, and van Leusen, 2010: 103–05, 119–23).

The initially slow infiltration of Greek settlers from the East Mediterranean is similarly witnessed slightly later in the Salento peninsula, with the founding of key centers at Taras and Metapontion. Here, too, evidence for a centralizing settlement pattern points to local internal factors, which may have drawn on and used the connections with foreign networks, but were not dependent on them for triggering change. Replacement of huts with houses in the Iron Age need not be a sign of destruction, but rather an upgrading of structures, which was a phenomenon witnessed across Italy (Brandt and Karrlson, 2001; Attema, Burgers, and van Leusen, 2010: 104–05). In the Salento peninsula, as in the Sibaritide area, there are remains of cohabitation and Greco-Indigenous integration at sites such as L'Amastuola (Burgers and Crielaard, 2007; 2011). There is no evidence that early colonial Greek objects proliferate in these indigenous contexts. Most Greek artefacts in the Salento were obtained from overseas as a result of trans-Adriatic exchange networks between Greeks and Italians. There is also no evidence to suggest that the Greeks dominated this exchange network; rather, it is the local elite that increasingly appropriated Greek culture for prestige, and integrated it into existing local value systems (Osborne, 2004; Burgers, 1998: 179–94; Attema, Burgers, and van Leusen, 2010:

131; Whitehouse and Wilkins, 1989). The nature of the evidence points to a framework of cooperation rather than domination in relation to early Greek-Indigenous encounters.

Far-reaching exchange networks allowed for an increase in the economic potential created by surplus goods, through the exploitation of natural resources and the access to a wide market base and its distributive framework. The economic zones that existed in the Mediterranean and its surrounding regions were built on small group exchange (Horden and Purcell, 2000) but had wide remits and required communal treaties and military forces to deal with common menaces such as pirates and enemy states (Bederman, 2001). Some groups were more successful in exploiting these than others, and it is the products of their energies that are inscribed on the Italian landscape. Tombs and cemeteries with assemblages of prestige objects are one sign of success; another is the spread of influence and power visible in the proliferation of cultural models such as urbanism. When Cato speaks of the early history of Italy he states that it was under Etruscan authority (Cato, *Origines*: F72 = Peter, *HRR*: 62). Critias points to some of the resources that fuelled this expansion by noting that they became important redistributors of metals and famous also in Greece for their metallurgical skills in gold and bronze (Critias cited in Athenaeus, *Deipnosophistae*: 1.28b–c). Etruscan settlements proliferated from the center of Italy to the Po Valley in the north, with such sites as Felsina (Bologna), and south into Campania with the foundation of Capua. Prior to the rise of Rome, Etruscans were depicted as the most active colonizers, with such sites as Marzabotto, and Hatria (Livy: 5.33.8–10) in Italy, and Alalia/Aleria on Corsica (Diodorus Siculus: 5.13.3–5). The idea of an Etruscan empire and its extent through colonization is one way that ancient authors understood the variety of encounters of these Italic groups, but, as in the Greek context, colonization may not be an appropriate term (Riva, 2010b: 214–16). Other narratives of site foundation that were not labelled as colonies could be articulated through such myths as the *ver sacrum* – the sacred spring that culminated in the sending out of a group of youths to establish a new site (Dench, 1995: 189–93; Livy: 22.9.10; 24.44; Strabo: 5.4.12; Dionysius of Halicarnassus, *Roman Antiquities*: 1.16). This was associated with the spread of the peoples from the Central Apennines, which later authors preferred to depict as tribal communities and more primitive than their urban counterparts. Their portrayal in ancient texts as lacking sophistication and complex community structures is questionable: archaeology tells a different but equally compelling story of their mountainous landscape.

Outside the heavily urbanized environment of Etruria and Latium, the rugged terrain of the Apennines, including the regions of Samnium and Lucania, sustained a substantial Oscan-speaking population that inhabited numerous small- and medium-sized sites on high plateaus and intermountain plains (Bispham, 2007b; Isayev, 2007). These are most prominently visible from their fourth-century BC remains and fortified circuits enclosing territories of 30–50 hectares, with some, such as Serra di Vaglio, already a major settlement in the sixth century BC, easily double that size. But, as noted above, size is not necessarily the main determining factor. A fortified center may have been just one of the elements of a wider settlement network that had outlying satellite sites. Roccagloriosa, a substantial center in the west coast highlands, had both villages and defensive towers positioned in its surrounding territory, which was interspersed with habitation complexes of varying sizes (Gualtieri and Fracchia, 1990; 2001). From what we know about the layout of these settlements, few have anything resembling recognizable public spaces or monumental structures. Where there are such open spaces within the fortifications they are small and have few, if any, structural features. At Roccagloriosa it has been argued that the houses of the elite – some with substantial courtyards and votive shrines – were used for public activities (Fracchia and Gualtieri, 1989), as was the elite dining room complex at another fortified site of Civita di Tricarico (de Cazanove, 2008). Primitivism, however, is not what these patterns represent, but a different value given to the settlement than that found among their urban-based contemporaries.

The potential of communities within this region to accumulate wealth, and to be active members of the cultural networks that pervaded Italy, is visible in the funerary evidence. It is also exemplified in the ancient literature which records that groups from these territories posed a serious threat, and were sought after as allies. The Samnite Wars with Rome are the most prominent, but also Lucanian alliances with the tyrants of Syracuse, and other polities. For investment in the public sphere within these communities, we need to look elsewhere in the landscape other than the settlement sites, where space may have been restricted by the mountainous terrains. The rise of rural sanctuary complexes may be the main areas of investment and focus for communal action in the fifth–third centuries BC. It is in this period that these Oscan communities exhibit the widest extent of power and influence, which is evident in the spread of material culture, and particularly in the use of Oscan language that infiltrated pre-existing settlements, including the Greek *poleis* in Italy. The transformations are noticeable in the Greek city of Poseidonia, particularly in the funerary sphere, with the appearance of a new trend of painted tombs, showing warriors sporting "Italic" forms of armor, such as the Samnite belt and the three-disk breastplate (Figure 1.2). Oscan inscriptions appear both in the private context of the tombs, and also in the most public platform in the city, painted on a stele, found in the center of the *ekklesiasterion* (Isayev, 2010; Crawford, 2006a). At this time historical narratives present these Oscan groups as the key competitors for resources on the peninsula along with Rome and other major centers such as Taranto.

Figure 1.2 Warrior returning home, from Andriulo Necropolis, Tomb 5340, Poseidonia (Paestum). Fourth century BC. Photograph: Elena Isayev.

By the early Hellenistic period we can identify four rival power hubs operating in Italy simultaneously. In part they replaced the authority previously held by Etruscan communities, which was already waning by the fifth century BC. To some extent the change arose from a re-centering of internal networks and alliances, allowing new actors onto the stage. When the Romans defeated Etruscan Veii in 396 BC, and as a result doubled their territory (Livy: 5.24; 30–31), Etruscan communities did not come to the aid of this powerful city. Rome's successful campaigns in this period allowed it to take over leadership of networks previously controlled by Etruscan polities, particularly in relation to Carthage, the other major operator in the Western Mediterranean. The treaties between Rome and Carthage that define each power's sphere of influence are recorded by Polybius (3.22–25), with the earliest dating to 509/8 BC. These may have been similar to those that Carthage had with other Italian polities such as Etruscan Caere (Serrati, 2006). The second and more substantial treaty of 348 BC includes clauses restricting Rome from founding cities on the far side of the Fair Promontory, at Mastia, Tarseum, Sardinia and Libya (Polybius: 3.24.4; 3.24.11), which gives a sense of the rapidly spreading Roman interests beyond Italy.

The shrinking of Etruscan power in the north of Italy provided the opportunity for increasing Gallic influence that spanned the Alpine mountain range. The Gallic sack of Rome in 389 BC (Livy: 5.35–55) may be one of the signs of this growing power, which suggests a new hostile incomer, with little history on the peninsula (e.g. Livy: 5.24; 5.33–35). Such a scenario is challenged by the material record from the northern regions. In the Veneto and Liguria, archaeological evidence points to the presence of these groups within Italic settlements visible already from the seventh century BC (Häussler, 2007: 45; Lomas 2007: 36). In Padua, a mixture of Celtic and Venetic names, such as Tivalos Bellenios, appears on inscriptions (Prosdocimi, 1988: 288–92), and funerary stelai exhibit Celtic motifs in the iconography (Fogolari, 1988: 102–03). The history of the early interaction of these groups is similar to that of Greek and local integration at sites in the south of the peninsula. In the heel of Italy, by the fourth century BC Taranto had successfully taken over the position that had previously been held by Kroton, and sustained it with the help of Italic allies and overseas connections, exploiting the ambitions of foreign generals from Macedon and Epirus. At the same time Oscan communities of the Central Apennines drew their power from other links, especially through their connections with the tyrants of Syracuse, who had their own agendas and used Italian allies and manpower to achieve them. Areas of earlier Etruscan influence in Campania were now taken over by Oscan speakers, who appear prominently at such sites as Neapolis, Capua, Pompeii, and Poseidonia.

These competing spheres of influence led to interregional links across the peninsula, gradually tying it into a single web. In so doing it increased the opportunities for knowledge-sharing that contributed to the other major peninsula-wide change in the settlement pattern: the infilling of the countryside through the proliferation of rural settlements. This phenomenon has been in part attributed to the development of agricultural technologies coupled with colonizing strategies that led to a more intensive exploitation of the landscape and reclamation of marginal territories (Attema, Burgers, and van Leusen, 2010: 161–65). While there were local variations and diverse causes for this spread it was evident in all the regions of Italy. It could be that such dense populating of the landscape focused attention on Italy as a single landmass with a finite territory available for exploitation. Such a perception is implied in the Roman agrarian laws and the second-century BC land reform policies of the Gracchi that aimed at redistribution and placed limits on land-holding. All these forces within and outside Italy – some emanating from urban centers, others operating from a more diffuse base – were brought together in the period that followed, culminating in a series of conflicts out of which Rome emerged as the lead polity overseeing the many interconnected networks that rapidly extended its power across the Mediterranean.

1.3   Single Communities – Cemeteries

So far our focus has been on the formation of polities and interactions between them. On the level of individual communities, the funerary material and the layout of cemeteries provide our best evidence for understanding the way that individuals related to each other and the internal groupings they formed. The spectrum of such relationships and hierarchies, as we understand them, includes princely (and princessly) society, clan- and kin-based factions, and egalitarian elements, all of which need not be mutually exclusive. The archaeological material provides opportunities for understanding the societal structures and their transformation, as well as challenges, due to the nature of the evidence base. For the early periods we know much more about the cemeteries than the settlements with which they were associated, particularly in the Apennine regions, but there is a sharp drop in the amount of funerary evidence across the whole peninsula from the fourth century BC. It is furthermore difficult to know how representative any cemetery is of the community which used it, as burial may have been reserved only for certain groups and individuals, perhaps only elites or adults. In the Salento peninsula, which is considered exceptional in the South Italian Iron Age, we have no burial evidence until the sixth century BC, and then only a few examples. The communities of this region honored and disposed of their dead in archaeologically untraceable rituals, which only become visible when certain members of society had access to a more materially based form of burial (Attema, Burgers, and van Leusen, 2010: 126). In the following discussion a number of funerary cases primarily from Apennine Italy, will be used to explore the diverse forms of internal organization and the investigative process that informs our interpretations.

The most visually impressive funerary evidence is to be found in the lavish Iron Age and Archaic chamber tombs of Umbria (Bradley, 2000: 92ff.), Etruria (Riva, 2010a), Campania (d'Agostino, 1988; Horsnaes, 2002; Cuozzo, 2007), Picenum (Colonna, 1992; Riva, 2004), and Latium (Fulminante, 2003). Many of these are lined with masonry walls and built into round earth tumuli that rise monumentally like small hills above the ground. They often contain multiple burials, with sarcophagi for inhumations and cinerary urns for cremations. These are accompanied by grave good assemblages that can include imported fine-wares, such as Attic black and red figure vases, bronze vessels, and banqueting implements, as well as jewelry, armor, and, most impressively, chariots. One such tomb at Monteleone di Spoleto in Umbria, contained a sixth-century BC chariot, whose bronze fittings depict what appears to be a scene from the myth of Achilles (Bradley, 2000: 94). It is not surprising that they are known as "princely" tombs, although to what extent they reflect a "princely" society, and what that would mean in this context is another matter (Morris, 1999; Ruby, 1999; Cuozzo, 2007). The extent to which such a princely led group may have differed from an organization that was centered on the clan or band is debatable (Smith, 2007a). What is clear is that such tombs represent an aristocratic culture that chose these funerary monuments as a way to display their wealth and power. Funerary assemblages, including imported goods as well as local ones, attest to extensive intercultural networks, connectivity that formed part of the power base that controlled resources and access to them. In a later period, such display moved from the personal to the civic and sacred sphere.

In the central Apennines – the region associated with Samnium by ancient authors – funerary evidence has been employed to establish the existence and the nature of a Samnite *ethnos* (Salmon, 1967; Torelli, 1988). Inscriptions from the area with the self-referential term *safin-*, appearing from the fifth century BC, were believed to confirm the existence of such a cohesive ethnic group (La Regina, 1980; 1981; 1984). Its characteristically austere warrior mentality, of which later authors wrote when describing Roman wars with the Samnite enemy, was thought to be detectable within the burials. However, rather than cohesion within the material record, what has been highlighted instead is the diversity of burial forms within the same region, and the extent of shared traits with other parts of Italy and links across the Mediterranean (Scopacasa, 2010; 2015). Rather than showing that the inhabitants of the region were essentially organized as an ethnic or "national" entity as described in ancient texts, the mortuary evidence points to a variety of other groupings that were the basis for community organization. Ethnicity may have had little role in inter-community ties and joint action. The extent to which any ethnic signifiers, as opposed to cultural traits, can be recognized in the material record becomes even more difficult to sustain (Shennan, 1994).

In the region of Samnium, lavish chamber tombs of the kind noted above are lacking, although some wealthy tombs do exist. One example is the so-called "grave of the princess" in Bisaccia, in which the inhumed body was covered in jewelry including amber beads and accompanied by bronze vessels (De Juliis, 1996a; Rathje, 2000). There are nevertheless other similarities in funerary practice which the region shares with those adjoining it (Scopacasa, 2015). Bronze disks that formed part of the armor, as displayed on the terracotta statue of the "Capestrano Warrior," are comparable to those found in ninth-century contexts in Umbria and Picenum. Similarities in the deposition of "Samnite belts" show cultural links with regions further south: Campania, Daunia, and Lucania. Other characteristics are shared across all Samnium and most of the surrounding regions. There is a common approach to the distribution of grave goods, with apparel such as jewelry and armor placed on the body, with objects such weapons and knives alongside it and vessels at the head or feet (Scopacasa, 2015). Another preference for supine burial in rectangular trenches is highlighted by the notable difference in the burying culture of neighboring Daunia, where crouching inhumations in circular pits was favored (Lo Schiavo, 1984; De Juliis, 1996b; Herring, 2000; 2007).

Cemeteries in Samnium may not have chamber tombs that provide a demarcated space to enclose a specific clan or kin unit. Nevertheless, the distribution of burials within a number of the cemeteries in Samnium, especially around the Sangro valley, suggests a similar interest in distinguishing the coherence of particular burial groups, often encircling a central grave that appears more prominent by its deposits (Scopacasa, 2015; Figure 1.3, Figure 1.4 and Figure 1.5). It is from such patterns that we surmise that bands or clans were a key societal organizing method, where familial links may or may not have been a deciding factor. This cemetery organization differed from contemporaneous cemetery layouts that were associated with the Greek colonies, such as Poseidonia. Here the graves were not organized in groups nor with any clear hierarchical relationship that would suggest group enclaves, although individual burials could stand out, such as the painted tomb of the diver in Poseidonia. The distribution of burials in Greek colonial cemeteries may represent a more egalitarian society, or a disinterest in signaling power through the funerary sphere, but it should not be simply viewed as a difference between Greek and Italic communities. A number of cemeteries on the Adriatic coast of Samnium, such as at Porticone and Larino, are similarly organized without clear hierarchical structuring of burials (Scopacasa, 2015).

In those regions of Samnium where burials were organized hierarchically, the central-most prominent figure of each group need not have been male (Scopacasa, 2010). Women too were buried with the symbols of power, including banqueting and drinking equipment, chariots, and even weapons. The high position that was held by women is also notable in other regions. Wealthy burials are prevalent at Campanian sites such as Pontecagnano (e.g. tomb 2465) (Cuozzo, 2003; 2007) and in Etruria, where communal feasting between men and women is depicted on tomb paintings. Such practices differed significantly from those of the Greek sphere, consequently coming under scathing comment by the Hellenistic author Theopompus (*Philippica*: 43, cited in Athenaeus, *Deipnosophistae*: 12.517–18). It is notable that in the cemeteries of the Greek colonies of Poseidonia and Locri Epizephyrii, drinking equipment is primarily deposited with male burials and not female ones, suggesting a more

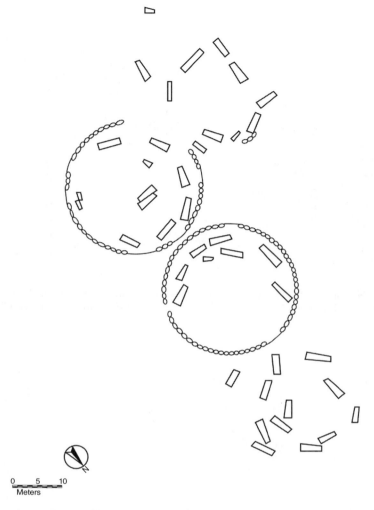

Figure 1.3 Necropolis of Alfedena. Redrawn by Antonio Montesanti after L. Mariani, 1901. "Aufidena." *Monumenti Antichi dell'Accademia Nazionale dei Lincei* 10: 225–638, tav.II.

male-dominated society (Scopacasa, 2010; Rathje, 1990; 2000; Spivey, 1991; d'Agostino, 1993; Bartoloni, 2003). Evidence for the powerful position of some Italic women may also be seen by inclusion of female names on curse tablets, such as that of the Etruscan Turana found in the Sicilian city of Selinus, dated to the fifth century BC (*SEG* IV, 38 (inv. s.n.); Heurgon, 1972–73; Tagliamonte, 1994: 93–94). Whoever she may have been, she had lived long enough in Sicily and held a high enough status there to have made enemies.

Whoever may have been the central figure within a burial group, whether male or female, a further question is how these groups interacted. Where no nearby settlement is known it is even difficult to tell whether a cemetery was used by a single centralized settlement or by a number of villages. In Latium at the prominent cemetery of Osteria dell'Osa, where 600 graves have been excavated, it is unclear whether the two Iron Age burial groups, which are distinguished by the nature of the pottery techniques, were representative of two kinship

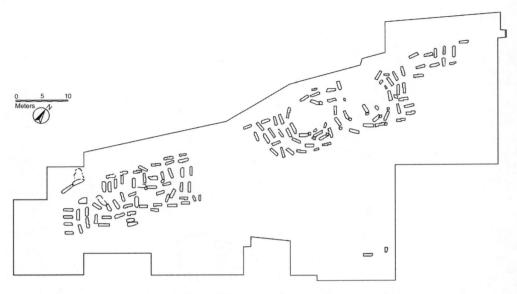

Figure 1.4 Necropolis of Alfedena – Campo Consolino. Redrawn by Antonio Montesanti after F. Parise Badoni and M. Ruggeri Giove, 1981. *Alfedena: la necropoli di Campo Consolino.* Chieti, Fig. 17.

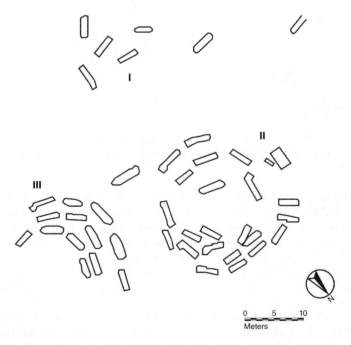

Figure 1.5 Necropolis of Opi – Val Fondillo. Redrawn by Antonio Montesanti after G. Tagliamonte, 1996. *I Sanniti. Caudini, Irpini, Pentri, Carricini, Frentani.* Milan, Fig. 4.

groups or two settlements. Within both of these the internal organization is in clusters, where central cremations were surrounded by inhumations (Smith, 2007b). There is no straightforward model for how to read these sites, as demonstrated by the difference between two nearby settlements of Este and Padua in north Italy, which lie a mere thirty kilometers distance from each other (Lomas, 2007: 30–32). From the seventh century BC the settlement at Este has a number of burial areas, each associated with a concentration of houses, implying that it was a community which maintained a division along sub-groups. At Padua, in contrast, a single burial area on the east side of the city served the whole settlement. Nevertheless, the cemeteries of both of these sites expressed status difference through wealth and the distribution of the graves, with burials organized in clusters either in the open or within communal earth tumuli. As in Samnium either the clan or a non-kinship based group appears as the main unit of organization.

Hierarchical structures that were based on differential deposits or positioning of graves in the Iron Age began to change in the following period, with a rapid decline in the amount of wealth in the graves. At the same time, across the peninsula there is increasing evidence for investment in fortification walls, monumental architecture, and public works, whether in settlements or rural sanctuaries, some of which sported the latest Italic and Hellenistic styles. Wealth display appears to have shifted from a person-centered to a more commune-centered context, as we saw with the development of Veii. In the north Italian settlements of Este and Padua, by the fourth century BC the large clustered burials gave way to smaller tombs for individuals or just the nuclear family (Lomas, 2007: 31). Is this a sign of a more egalitarian society or rather a distribution among a wider elite group? The change may represent an interest of the elite in contributing to the well-being of a community rather than a focus on individual status; alternatively, it may be a shift to a wider platform on which to display one's power base. What the burial evidence shows is that on the whole it is difficult to identify clear regionally based trends that would suggest that they operated as coherent homogeneous units. Any such perspective is negated by diversity of practices within regions and by peninsula-wide phenomena that take effect almost simultaneously. By the third century BC there is very little funerary evidence anywhere in Italy.

1.4   Individual Networks and Mobility

From stories of characters such as Demaratus we can get a sense of wide-reaching networks and the multiplicity of backgrounds among community members. According to tradition, at some time in the eighth or seventh century BC, Demaratus and his band of followers from Corinth came to the shores of Italy (Livy 1.34–35; Dionysius of Halicarnassus, *Roman Antiquities*: 3.46–49; Strabo, 5.2.2; Polybius: 6.11a.7; Cornell, 1995: 122–30). Hospitality greeted them at the wealthy Etruscan town of Tarquinii, where Demaratus married a local girl, and their offspring Lucumo became the king of Rome under the name Lucius Tarquinius Priscus. Demaratus is depicted as an exile escaping tyranny, a merchant and a craftsman, as well as the bringer of new technologies and ideas to Italy. It is also not by chance that Tarquinii was the chosen landing point: it was one of the vibrant and well-connected nodes of the Mediterranean that offered opportunities for the energetic looking for successful ventures. The prominent groups in Tarquinii, in their turn, would have benefited from the latest knowledge, expertise, and contacts that the likes of Demaratus would have brought, extending their networks and power base. It is also conceivable that they knew each other already. While many details of the Demaratus story are questionable, it is a very plausible scenario. The archaeological and epigraphic records from Italy for this period show substantial cultural contact and trade between Corinth and Etruria, with trajectories extending through Campania and Latium (Cornell, 1995: 124–26; Osborne, 2004). We also know that the emporium and sanctuary at Gravisca, which is associated with Tarquinii, was a major cosmopolitan hub in the sixth century BC, and possibly a regional center for the export of wine *amphorae* (Peña, 2011: 190–91; Riva, 2010b: 220–21; Cristofani, 1996). It was only one of a number of such dynamic hubs, including the port sanctuary at Pyrgi, associated with the powerful city of Caere. Embodied in the character of Demaratus is a successful member of the mobile aristocratic community of the Mediterranean who could establish himself through his network of elite personal connections, which were powerful enough to place his offspring onto the Roman throne.

Traces of such personal networks that operated in a domain external to any community organization are recognizable through the institution of guest friendship and gift exchange. They were embodied in objects, records of mutual friendship that acted as a binding contract extending over geographic distances and generations. The object itself, at times known as the *tessera hospitalis*, could be in a myriad shapes and designs, a ram or a lion for example (Figure 1.6 and Figure 1.7), and made out of a variety of materials, including ivory, metal, and terracotta. It consisted of two parts, each of which was kept by the parties whose names it recorded. We know how the object was used because Hanno the Carthaginian, a character in Plautus's play *The Carthaginian* (1047–55), carries one with him. As he arrives in Calydon, in Northern Greece, he presents it as proof of identity to the son of his now dead friend Agorastocles, who had the matching half of the *tessera* as a sign of the bond which they once had, and which the offspring would honor. We are also fortunate to have surviving examples of such objects from Italy and Rome and from other parts of the Mediterranean, attesting to links with individuals of Italic background (Arnott, 2004: 82; Cristofani, 1990: 21 no. 1.6, pl. 1; Turfa and Steinmayer, 2002: 21). One half of an ivory plaque of the sixth century BC, from a cemetery in Carthage, is carved in the shape of a boar (Figure 1.8 and Figure 1.9), and proclaims in Etruscan: *Mi puinel karthazie els q[---]na*; "I (am) Puinel from Carthage…" (Prag, 2006: 8–10; Rix, 1991: Af 3.1; Messineo, 1983; Acquaro, 1988: 532–37). It is testament of a link between a Carthaginian and his Etruscan-speaking guest-friend. These objects would have

Figure 1.6 Ivory Lion, sixth century BC from Sant'Omobono, side A. Inv. AC 27878, Capitoline museum, Rome. Photo copyright: Musei Capitolini, Rome.

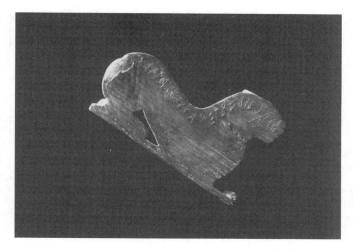

Figure 1.7 Ivory Lion, from Sant'Omobono, side B. Name inscribed in Etruscan: *Araz Silqetenas Spurianas*. Inv. AC 27878, Capitoline Museum, Rome. Photo copyright: Musei Capitolini, Rome.

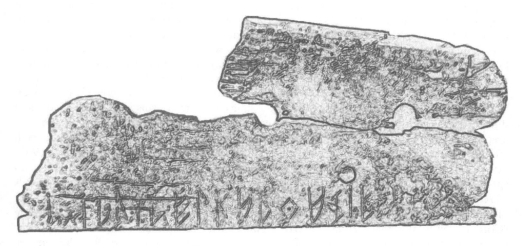

Figure 1.8 Ivory Boar, sixth century BC from a necropolis near ancient Carthage, side B. Drawing: Antonio Montesanti after E. Peruzzi, 1970. *Origini di Roma: La. Famiglia*, vol. 1, Florence: Valmartina, tav. I.

formed part of a wider system of private contracts and hospitality on which the Mediterranean network was based. The remains of banqueting and commensality that would have been crucial to maintaining these ties are found in the elite burials of both men and women. Scenes of such activities – banqueting, games, and processions – are also found on tomb paintings and depicted on vessels from the northern regions of the peninsula (Frey, 1986; Lomas, 2007: 33). They represent an elite culture not dissimilar to that of the Homeric world, which they could have easily fitted into, and perhaps to which they, along with their other Mediterranean compatriots, aspired (Malkin, 1998; 2002).

Figure 1.9   Ivory Boar, from a necropolis near ancient Carthage. Close up of inscription on side B, inscribed in Etruscan: *Mi puinel karthazie els q[---]na* (I (am) Puinel from Carthage…). Drawing: Antonio Montesanti after E. Peruzzi, 1970. *Origini di Roma: La Famiglia*, vol. 1, Florence: Valmartina, tav. II.

1.5   Community Organization Beyond Territory

When we picture early Italy through the mytho-histories of ancient writers, kingship appears quite prominently, and we are most familiar with it from the colorful exploits of the Etruscan kings of Rome (Cornell, 1995). As an institution, however, it is by no means straightforward, not least because in the Roman case for several generations the position was held by elected non-Roman elites. The so-called Tarquin dynasty, of which Demaratus's offspring may have been the initiator, came to rule over the *populus Romanus*, a community not its own. Tradition then depicts vibrantly how the dynasty was overthrown in 509 BC by that same community to be replaced by a republican system headed by two elected Roman consuls (Wiseman, 2008: chs 16–18). It is still unclear how these kings and the consuls who superseded them differed from the superior magistrates in other parts of Italy whom we know about from epigraphic evidence. These include the *meddix touticus*, a supreme Oscan magistrate, well attested in the central Apennines, (Bispham, 2007b; Dench, 1995: 135–36; La Regina, 1989: 304), the *uhtur* in Umbria (Bradley 2000: 178–83) and the *zilath* from the Etruscan sphere. Were these leading individuals the descendants or successors of those whose burials were at the center of chamber tombs and burial clusters in the earlier period? The complexity of institutional development is well attested within the urban environment of Rome (Cornell, 1995; Wiseman, 2008; Forsythe, 2005), with its annually elected consuls, later supported by the tribunes of the plebs and a series of other magistracies, such as the censors. The system for making decisions and pooling resources on behalf of the community operated using the mechanisms of the senate, the military and civic assemblies, and alongside them priestly colleges. As far as we know, other Italic communities had versions of these forms of organization as well.

Beyond urban-based polities we have epigraphic evidence for deliberative bodies and processes not dissimilar to the model at Rome, but what defined the community which they served is more difficult to pinpoint, as it may not have been based around a single settlement. Here we will focus on community forms that were represented by the Oscan term for the largest socio-political grouping, the *touta*. It is most prevalent in the Central Apennines, where it is also written as *tota* and associated with *trifu* in the Umbrian context (Bradley, 2000: 181), and *teuter* in the Veneto (Pellegrini and Prosdocimi, 1967: 264–68). It could be used to represent either an individual settlement-based community (Letta, 1994), or a combination of these that might form a unified people (La Regina, 1981: 129–37). While there is some overlap with the terms *nomen* and *populus* in Latin, they are not exact substitutions, partly because the Latin terms also changed over time. One of the earliest instances of *touta* dates from the sixth/fifth century BC, as part of a dedication on a ceramic vessel from Castelluccio (Crawford, 2011: Lucania/NERLULUM 1, p.1340). The inscription, *toutikem dipoterem*, is written in what may be early Oscan using the Achaean alphabet. Its meaning is controversial but generally taken to be an offering made to the deity of the community, possibly Jupiter (Arena, 1972). There is no indication as to what the name of the "community" may have been, nor does it give us any sense of the constituency of the group. Other instances of the term, mainly dating from the Hellenistic period, are found in dedications and legal texts. *Touta* appears on a fragmentary *lex*, dated circa 300 BC, inscribed on a bronze tablet from the settlement of Roccagloriosa (Gualtieri and Poccetti, 2001: 239–40, Side B, 4). It reads: *[… p]oust touteikaiß aut […]*, which is a reference either to the people or the public good, the *populus* or *res publica* in Latin. The term appears in similar contexts in a much later Oscan legal text of the early first century BC *Lex Osca Tabulae Bantinae* (*RS* I, 13).

These texts indicate the presence of a bounded community with a central authority which had decision-making powers and jurisdiction over its members. Such membership, as citizenship, implies that those who did not hold it were excluded. In Umbria, a unique text on the *Tabulae Iguvinae* records the ritual ceremonies for the purification of the Iguvine *poplo* and includes those who were banished, such as the Tadinates and the Etruscans (Rix, 2002: ST Um 1; Sisani, 2001: 216; Bradley, 2000: 181–83; Weiss, 2010). The Tadinates, for example, would have had their own internal membership, but as a community or tribe they also belonged to a wider grouping that in Latin may be called a *nomen*. *Touta*, *nomen*, and *poplo* represent units of membership with intentionally created frameworks of belonging that could be delimited along socio-political as well as other constructed boundaries, including religious, military and ethnic. How quickly these were superseded by new Roman frameworks of belonging is questionable. These corporate designations may have continued to exist even after Roman citizenship was extended to the whole of the peninsula in 89 BC. They could have functioned alongside the system of colonies and *municipia*, which represented the new vehicles through which one was officially tied to a particular community and one's citizenship rights were enacted (Bispham, 2007a; Sherwin-White, 1973: 134).

1.6 Supra-Community Organization

This chapter began with the image of fluid borders, and ties that stretched beyond them. In most ancient narratives early Italy and its communities are presented as the static receivers of knowledge and culture which they then absorbed and mediated. To redress the imbalance within ancient literature, epigraphic and other evidence has been used to stress the active involvement of Italic communities within the Mediterranean trade networks, and especially that of the Etruscans who are the most visible in the material record (Cristofani, 1996; Naso, 2001; Bonfante, 2003; Izzet, 2007: 215–23). Etruscan cities, such as Caere, had strong links and rivalries with centers overseas, Massilia and Carthage among them. Finds of Etruscan-produced wine *amphorae* in the south of France are a testament to the commercial activities of these Italic groups with the Gauls in that region, which pre-existed the Greek foundation of Massilia (Riva, 2010b: 213–14; Dietler, 2005: 46–47; Gori and Bettini, 2006). It may even be the case that, as recorded by Diodorus Siculus, Gaulish elites traded slaves for wine in this period (Diodorus Siculus: 5.26.3). Possibly the availability of this human resource may have allowed for the construction projects and embellishment of sites such as Veii in the sixth century BC. Shipwrecks, such as the Archaic Giglio Campese that sank fifteen kilometers. off the Italian coast, most likely en route to Massilia, reveal the variety of Italian products traded around the Mediterranean (Peña, 2011: 184–89). Its cargo included numerous *amphorae* from Vulci with pine pitch, olives and maybe wine, as well as stone anchors, and copper and lead ingots probably from Giglio itself. Etruscan craftsmanship was sought-after even in Greece as indicated by Critias (Critias cited in Athenaeus, *Deipnosophistae* 1.28b–c). These economic activities coupled with traces of overseas expansion at such sites as Alalia on Corsica, are evidence that Italic communities, especially the Etruscans, were a maritime power already in the sixth century BC (Riva, 2010b: 214–16; Cristofani, 1996; Izzet, 2007).

  In order to maintain a successful trading environment among the competitors and keep it free from pirates, many of whom were Etruscan, it was necessary to establish cooperative modes of understanding with other powerful polities that had shared interests (Bederman, 2001). The most visible of these is the relationship between the Etruscans and Carthaginians. An inscription on gold plaques at the Caeretan port sanctuary of Pyrgi includes a dedication to the Punic deity Astarte by the king of Caere, inscribed in Phoenician and Etruscan (Heurgon, 1966; Bonfante and Bonfante, 2002: 64–68). The far-reaching power of the Etrusco-Carthaginian alliance was important enough to have been recorded by Aristotle (*Politics*: 3.5.10–11). Herodotus (1.166–67) provides further insight into their joint ventures, and an alliance to counteract the influence of the Phocaeans, which culminated in the Sardinian sea battle of 540 BC (Riva, 2010b: 214). The Etrusco-Carthaginian success secured the Etruscan hold on the trading zone in the north Tyrrhenian, but could not prevent Massilia from developing into a Greco-Celtic power base. The competition between Massilia and the formidable Etruscan city of Caere was not only evident on the Western Mediterranean seas; both of these polities, and their elites, also had presence on a more global stage, through the erection of treasuries at the sanctuary of Delphi (Laroche and Nenna, 1992; Jacquemin, 1999; Caeretan treasury, Strabo 5.2.3; Massiliote treasury, Diodorus Siculus: 14.93.3; Plutarch, *Life of Camillus*: 8). A couple of centuries later, once Rome emerged as a substantial power and took over the network from Caere and other leading Etruscan cities, it replaced them as the key partner with Carthage, and also developed long-standing good relations with the Massiliotes (DeWitt, 1940). When the Romans won their victory over Veii and wanted the success marked globally, in 394 BC they dedicated a golden bowl to be deposited at Delphi in the Massiliote treasury. The story recounted by ancient authors describes how the Roman ship delivering the bowl to Delphi got waylaid by patrolling Lipareans, who mistook them for Etruscan pirates (Strabo: 6.2.2). It implies that the Romans were at this point newcomers to this international stage, but not for long.

1.7   Sanctuaries as *Fora*

Sanctuaries such as Delphi are well known to have been more than just the intersections of the human and divine: they were also relatively neutral inter-community meeting spaces. In that capacity they acted as platforms for state displays of power and provided a civic frame for ostentatious dedications by wealthy citizens (Neer, 2004). In Italy extra-mural sanctuaries and sacred groves had similar roles and were used as emporia and political meeting centers. They were a significant part of the mechanism through which multi-settlement and supra-community ties were negotiated and action was organized. Ancient texts record the use of rural sacred sites for gatherings, such as that of the Latins on the Alban Mount for the festival of the *Feriae Latinae* (Livy: 32.1.9; 37.3.4), or the more military assembly of Etruscans at the shrine of Voltumna (Livy: 4.23.5–4.25.6-8; 5.17.6–8; 6.2.2). The two major Etrurian sanctuaries already mentioned – Pyrgi and Gravisca – were dynamic cosmopolitan hubs that acted as in-between spaces for locals and outsiders serving the cities of Caere and Tarquinii, respectively. One way that their role has been understood is through the concepts of hybridity and the Middle Ground, where distinct cultures come together and through interaction form a new cultural entity (Malkin, 2002). While such sites may have been exceptionally cosmopolitan, the mixed population they sustained was also comparable to any successful coastal or inland port city, and hence the idea of a gateway or intersection may be more relevant in describing their role.

In the more mountainous landscapes of Samnium and Lucania it is plausible that the rural sanctuaries, which gained permanent structures in the fifth and fourth centuries BC, had the additional role of acting as a forum would in a city. Such public spaces could be shared by a number of settlements, perhaps the remit of a *touta*. In Rome, temples were also multi-purpose structures, used for meetings and as galleries to exhibit the spoils of victorious generals. So too in Samnium the sanctuary of Pietrabbondante displayed the armor of Romans and others over whom victories were won (Stek, 2009: 39). Despite their substantial remains, Italic sacred sites are rarely mentioned by ancient authors and then often only in passing (Figure 1.10). The extant literary sources make no reference to the impressive temple-theater complex at Pietrabbondante in Samnium (Stek, 2009; Bispham, 2007b; Wallace-Hadrill, 2008: 137–43), or the monumental court-sanctuary at Rossano di Vaglio, in Lucania (Cracolici and Nava, 2005; Isayev, 2007; 2010). We have little understanding of who was responsible for their creation and whether it was through the efforts of small groups and elites or the joint initiatives of several communities. These sites do not represent any straightforward expression of territoriality, nor are they the materialization of borders, as may be the case in more urban environments. In the Veneto, the sacred precincts of Este developed on the perimeter of the city's territory, while at Padua, those that were further from the town appear to have been located on the border between its territory and that of Este. In the higher hinterland of the

Figure 1.10 Sanctuary at Pietrabbondante, view from the theater to the valley. Photograph: Elena Isayev.

Veneto, sanctuaries were positioned in the midst of rural territory away from centers (Lomas, 2007: 26), along a pattern that is not dissimilar to that of the rural sanctuaries in the Apennines.

It is not a given that all communities and polities occupied space bordering on others, which is only one model based on complete territorial occupation. Instead, a number of these rural sacred sites appear to be located in the midst of resource landscapes, such as pasture land, or at the center of crossing transhumance routes and other trajectories (Stek, 2009; Crawford, 2003: 62–63). Such positioning may be distinguished from those of extra-urban sanctuaries that are located immediately outside a specific settlement, such as for example that of Iguvium. The *tabulae Iguvinae* delimited the *poplo*, and it also outlined the rite for sanctifying the sacred grove, and the rituals within it (Weiss, 2010). In this case the primary role of the rituals and the sanctuary, which may not have been permanent, was to create and entrench a shared identity through practice and repetition. In this sense it has more in common with the festival of the *Feriae Latinae* in which the Latins took part on the Alban Mount.

In the case of Pietrabbondante and Rossano di Vaglio, the diversity and wealth of material from the sites suggest that these sanctuaries attracted a more global audience than that of a single settlement or group. From the fourth century BC newly built permanent structures drew on a mixture of the latest fashions, which at the time must have rivaled other such monuments on the Italian peninsula. As noted in the discussion on cemeteries, it is precisely at this

Figure 1.11   Pietrabbondante theater, *cavea* seating with carved griffin. Photograph: Elena Isayev.

Figure 1.12   Pietrabbondante theater, telamon supporting the parodos retaining wall. Photograph: Elena Isayev.

point that we see the disappearance of funerary evidence and a shift of wealth investment from individual burials to the communal sphere. The resulting products of this new use of resources were such gems as the Pietrabbondante theater complex. It may not be the most impressive in its size but it is in the attention to detail in its architecture and positioning. It showcases Italic trends in temple construction and combines them with Hellenistic features in the theater design. The rows of seating in the *cavea* are guarded by carved griffins (Figure 1.11), while kneeling telamons support the retaining wall of the parados (Figure 1.12). Under the shadow of the temple, these creatures stare at each other across the auditorium which, from its high perch on the hillside, faces an uninterrupted breathtaking view of the valley. The environment that was created by this site is similar to that of the later first-century BC terraced sanctuary of Fortuna at Praeneste in Latium, with its dramatic views.

No such monumental structures survive at the sanctuary of Rossano di Vaglio, which has a different architectural tradition. The site is centered on a large paved court area or piazza with fountains on the sides and a central altar of considerable proportions, stretching to some nine meters. Surrounding this open area are buildings, some with porticos and large rooms, which may have been used for ritual dining and votive deposition. Although it does not have a stone theater, slanting into the piazza is a natural bowl-shaped terrace that could easily have formed a theater environment, which still has the remains of a central stone entrance flanked by the two fountains. The lack of a temple at the site relates to the particular architectural and ritual context of the region, where many of the sanctuaries use a similar layout of buildings around a courtyard, rather than having the temple as the focus of sacred activity. What Rossano di Vaglio shares with Pietrabbondante is its pattern of rise and decline. Both sites received substantial structures in the fourth century BC, which were then embellished in the following two centuries. By the first century BC the level of activity at these sites had severely diminished, and they were no longer operational by the time of the early Empire.

Rossano di Vaglio and Pietrabbondante both have rich material remains, in the form of votives that include sculpture, jewelry, and coins, and a large number of inscriptions, a substantial number of which are in Oscan. They indicate that Mefitis was the primary deity worshipped there among others, including Jupiter, Mamers and Venus (Lejeune, 1990; Isayev, 2010). The rich epigraphic evidence records the patrons who contributed to the embellishment of the sites and refers to magistrates, deliberative bodies, and other institutional frameworks which operated through them, or at least encompassed the sanctuaries in their business. What makes the collection of epigraphic texts stand out is the otherwise small number of inscriptions dating prior to the first century BC which have been recovered from any one site in the regions where these sanctuaries were based. They are testament to the wide-ranging audience that frequented these sites over several centuries and the important position they held. Their decline is paralleled by the Roman-induced spread of the organizational model which used the public spaces of the urban framework, including the *municipia* and the colony, for any display and gathering. The rural sacred sites, no longer functional in their capacity as centers for communal gathering and display, and increasingly distant from new road networks, were abandoned. Their sacred rituals were apparently secondary to their other socio-political roles.

1.8   Free Agents and Organization of Instant Communities

This final section looks at organizations and operators that existed outside community structures. Pirates were one such group, and, although a menace, they were also key distributors of resources around the Mediterranean that could be enlisted to help or hinder opponents (De Souza, 2002; Horden and Purcell, 2000: 386–87). Etruscan pirates were well known and operated over a wide area, as demonstrated by the capture of the Roman ship, mistaken for pirates, on its way to Delphi. Other well-known Italic pirates are attributed as originating from the Volscians and the Samnites (Livy: 8.26.1; 8.13.5; 3.1.5–7; Thiel, 1954: 8; Patterson 2006: 194–95, 199). Piratical activities bound a disparate group of people into a mobile community. They created connectivity not only amongst themselves but also, inadvertently, through encouraging joint state action in an attempt to stop them. By the end of the Republic they were a substantial enough group to be used as a tool in Roman political competitions, especially when it came to Pompey (Cicero, *On Duties*: 3.49; De Souza, 2002: 177). It also became convenient to label marginal groups as pirates, or as harboring pirates, to justify their suppression.

Operating outside any single community structure, another powerful group was created through the mercenary recruitment system. Mercenary armies formed some of the most visibly mobile groups in the Mediterranean, possessing a certain degree of independent agency both as individuals and as units. Soldiers from Italic communities made up just one fraction of a heterogeneous mass that was hired for military operations in the employ of tyrants and states at least as early as the archaic period (Tagliamonte, 1994). The literary sources are most vocal about the activities of the Campanian cavalry hired by the Syracusan tyrants from the fifth century BC onward (Diodorus Siculus: 13.44.1–2). Their infamy was not simply due to their success, but their supposed brutality, fickleness, and powerful persistent presence in Sicily, which took on the form of autonomous communities. They infiltrated Sicilian settlements, when in the employ of Dionysius I of Syracuse, who is said initially to have engaged some 1200 Campanians for his cause (Frederiksen, 1968; Nicolet, 1962). The archaeological evidence from the Sicilian towns of Entella and Messana reflects the deep penetration of these military incomers, and the powerful positions which they occupied. They created an instant community, which minted its own coinage with legends KAMPANON and MAMERTINON (Tagliamonte, 1994: 243ff; Säström, 1940; I. Lee 2000; Crawford, 2006b; 2011, Sicilia/ MESSANA 1, p. 1511). They also introduced their own socio-political structures. Inscriptions attest to the use of the Oscan language and the application of Italic institutional forms with references to magistrates as *meddices* and the community as *touta* through the third century BC. On the architrave of the temple of Apollo at Messana, a dedication using the Greek alphabet gives the names of two *meddices*, Stenius Calinius Statis and Maras Pomptius Numsedis, of the *touta* Mamertina (Crawford, 2006b; Tagliamonte, 1994: 258–59; Crawford, 2011, Sicilia/ MESSANA 4, p. 1515–16). From the onomastic evidence at Messana, it is evident that the Mamertines, whose origins are still disputed, were a heterogeneous group, with roots not only in Campania but spanning across much of central and southern Italy, whose members even included such well-known *gens* names as the Claudii (Crawford, 2011, Sicilia/MESSANA 6, p. 1519–20; Tagliamonte, 1994: 260).

As Roman hegemony spread across the Mediterranean, opportunities for free agents to choose their military career paths became much more constrained. Within Italy the supply of military contingents was by then determined by the hierarchical status of different communities in their relationship to Rome, whether as *socii* (allies) or as citizens with or without the vote (*civitas sine suffragio*). Therefore, any mercenary troops upon which Rome itself would depend came from those communities that lay outside the system. In this way Rome made use of the Celtiberians in the Second Punic War (Livy: 24.49.7; 25.32) and Cretan archers against Philip of Macedon in 197 BC (Livy: 33.3.10). The network of alliances that was progressively centered on Rome required that communities took responsibility for the external military actions of their members, which were severely curtailed.

1.9 Conclusion

At what point can we talk about Italy as more than just a landmass projecting into the Mediterranean? Was it when Hannibal forced the communities to choose sides and hence recognize the extent to which their histories and fates were interconnected? Or were the forces of cohesion already evident in the fourth century BC in the treaties and alliances that bound polities, and in the shared knowledge that allowed the exploitation of marginal lands and resources, hence leading to the infilling of the countryside? Cato's work the *Origines* is an expression of the interconnectedness of the various peoples who, along with the Romans, came to share the peninsula. Without doubt, by the time of the Social War, *Italia* had gained a new meaning. *Italia* was the legend that appeared on the coins of the *socii* who challenged the hegemonic regime led by Rome, and with the culmination of the war the reality of this coherent entity was cemented in the extension of the Roman citizenship to all those in Italy who lived south of the Po in 89 BC. The shores were no longer fluid, but became the edges of a sphere that rotated around Rome, or at least that is what the leaders in the capital hoped. A century later, Lucan, writing in Nero's Rome, consciously questioned Rome's fixity and centrality: Rome did not depend on its urban fabric or site, but could exist wherever good Romans were (Lucan, *Pharsalia*: 5.27-30; Masters, 1992; Bexley, 2009; Edwards, 1996: 64–66).

FURTHER READING

The works cited here are those, primarily in English, which have been published since the survey by Curti, Dench, and Patterson 1996. The most recent review of ancient Italy is the volume edited by Bradley, Isayev, and Riva 2007 which includes references to more detailed regional studies. Other major collections on Italian themes include: on connectivity, mobility, and colonization – Horden and Purcell 2000, Harris, ed, 2005, Hales and Hodos, eds, 2010, van Dommelen and Knapp, eds, 2010; G. Bradley and Wilson, eds, 2006, Isayev forthcoming; on state formation and identity – Terrenato and Haggis, eds, 2011, Gleba and Horsnaes, eds, 2011, *Confini e Frontiera* 1999, Cornell and Lomas, eds, 1995, 1997, Herring and Lomas, eds, 2000, along with other volumes compiled under the auspices of *Accordia*; on culture, integration, and Romanization – Keay and Terrenato, eds, 2001, Torelli 1999, Roth and Keller, eds, 2007; on epigraphy, literacy, and language – Cooley, ed, 2000; Bonfante and Bonfante 2002 (rev. ed.); Lomas, Whitehouse, and Wilkins, eds, 2007; on landscape archaeology and spatial modelling – Attema, Burgers, van Leusen, eds, 2010, H. Patterson, ed, 2004, Camassa, De Guio, and Veronese, eds, 2000; on Italic religion and sanctuaries – Bispham and Smith 2000; de Cazanove and Scheid 2003; Stek 2009; G. Bradley forthcoming; Nava and Osanna, eds, 2005; de Grummond and Edlund-Berry, eds 2011; Whitehouse 1992; Schultz and Harvey, eds 2006; Scheid 2003; Beard, North, and Price 1998. For an Italian series focusing on Magna Graecia, see *Atti di Taranto* and *BTCGI*; on Etruscans, the journal *Studi Etruschi*. The following projects make the primary evidence base more accessible, for Italian coinages – Rutter ed, 2001; for epigraphy, language, and grammar – Untermann 2000, Rix 2002; and most recently Crawford's 2011, *Imagines Italicae*, which supplements Vetter's *Handbuch der italischen Dialekte*, 1953, and *Inscriptiones Italiae*.

REFERENCES

Acquaro, E. 1988. "Phoenicians and Etruscans." In *The Phoenicians*, ed. S. Moscati, 532–37. Milan: Bompiani.

d'Agostino, B. 1988. "Le genti della Campania antica." In *Italia omnium terrarum alumna: la civiltà dei Veneti, Reti, Liguri, Celti, Picaeni, Umbri, Latini, Campani e Iapigi*, ed. A.M. Chieco Bianchi, 531–89. Milan: Scheiwiller.

d'Agostino, B. 1993. "La donna in Etruria." In *Maschile/femminile. Genere e ruoli nelle culture antiche*, ed. M. Bettini, 61–73. Rome/Bari: Laterza.

Ammerman, A.J. 2011. "Relocating the center: a comparative study." In *State Formation in Italy and Greece. Questioning the neoevolutionist paradigm*, eds N. Terrenato and D.C. Haggis, 256–72. Oxford: Oxbow.

Arena, R. 1972. "Sull'iscrizione arcaica di Nerulum." *La Parola del Passato* 27: 322–30.

Arnott, W.G. 2004 "Alexis, Greek new comedy and Plautus' *Poenulus*." In *Studien zu Plautus' Poenulus*, ed. T. Baier, 61–92. Tübingen: Narr.

Attema, P.A.J., Burgers, G.-J.L.M., and van Leusen, P.M. 2010. *Regional Pathways to Complexity: Settlement and land-use dynamics in early Italy from the Bronze Age to the Republican Period*. Amsterdam: Amsterdam University Press.

Bartoloni, G. 2003. *Le società dell'Italia primitiva. Lo studio delle necropoli e la nascita delle aristocrazie*. Rome: Carocci.

Beard, M., North, J., and Price, S. 1998. *Religions of Rome*. Vol. 1. *A History*. Cambridge: Cambridge University Press.

Bederman, D.J. 2001. *International Law in Antiquity*. Cambridge: Cambridge University Press.

Bexley, E.M. 2009. "Replacing Rome: geographic and political centrality in Lucan's *Pharsalia*." *Classical Philology* 104: 459–75.

Bispham, E.H. 2007a. *From Asculum to Actium: the municipalization of Italy from the Social War to Augustus*. Oxford: Oxford University Press.

Bispham, E.H. 2007b. "The Samnites." In *Ancient Italy. Regions without boundaries*, eds G. Bradley, E. Isayev, and C. Riva, 179–223. Exeter: University of Exeter Press.

Bispham, E. and Smith C.J., eds, 2000. *Religion in Archaic and Republican Rome and Italy: Evidence and experience*. Edinburgh: Edinburgh University Press.

Bonfante, L. 2003. *Etruscan Dress*. Baltimore and London: Johns Hopkins University Press.

Bonfante G. and Bonfante L. 2002, rev. ed. *The Etruscan Language. An introduction*. Manchester: Manchester University Press.

Bradley, G. 2000. *Ancient Umbria. State, culture and identity in Central Italy from the Iron Age to the Augustan era*. Oxford: Oxford University Press.

Bradley, G. forthcoming *Early Rome to 290 BC: The beginnings of the city and the rise of the Republic*. Edinburgh.

Bradley, G., Isayev, E., and Riva, C., eds, 2007. *Ancient Italy: Regions without boundaries* Exeter: University of Exeter Press.

Bradley, G. and Wilson, J.-P., eds, 2006. *Greek and Roman Colonization. Origins, ideologies and interactions*. Swansea: Classical Press of Wales.

Brandt, R. and Karlsson L., eds, 2001. *From Huts to Houses: Transformations of ancient societies. Proceedings of an international seminar organized by the Norwegian and Swedish Institutes in Rome, 21–24 September 1997*. Stockholm: Paul Aströms Förlag.

Burgers, G.-J.L.M. 1998. *Constructing Messapian Landscapes: Settlement dynamics, social organization and culture contact in the margins of Graeco-Roman Italy*. Amsterdam: Gieben.

Burgers, G.-J. L.M. and Crielaard, J.-P. 2007. "Greek colonists and indigenous populations at L'Amastuola, Southern Italy." *Bulletin Antieke Beschaving* 82.1: 77–114.

Burgers, G.-J. and Crielaard, J.-P. 2011. "Communicating Identity in an Italic-Greek Community: the Case of L'Amastuola (Salento)," M. Gleba and H. Horsnaes, eds, *Communicating Identity in Italic Iron Age Communities*, 73–89. Oxford: Oxbow.

Camassa, G., De Guio, A., and Veronese, F., eds, 2000. *Paesaggi di potere: problemi e prospettive. Atti del Seminario, Udine, 16–17 maggio 1996*. Rome: Quasar.

Carter, J.C. 2006. *Discovering the Greek Countryside at Metaponto*. Ann Arbor: University of Michigan Press.

Cazanove, O. de. 2008. *Civita di Tricarico. I. Quartier de la maison du monolithe et l'enceinte intermédiaire*. Rome: École française de Rome.

Cazanove, O. de and Scheid, J., eds, 2003. *Sanctuaires et sources dans l'antiquité: les sources documentaires et leurs limites dans la description des lieux de culte*. Naples: Centre Jean Bérard/ Collège de France.

Colonna, G. 1992. "Apporti etruschi all' 'orientalizzante' piceno." In *La civiltà Picena nelle Marche:studi in onore di Giovanni Annibaldi. Ancona 10–13 luglio 1988*, ed. M. Dardari, 92–127. Ripatransone: Maroni.

Colonna, G., ed. 2002. *Il santuario di Portonaccio a Veio. 1, Gli scavi di Massimo Pallottino nella zona dell'altare (1939–1940)*. Rome: «L'Erma» di Bretschneider.

Colonna, G. and Ambrosini, L. 2009. *Il santuario di Portonaccio a Veio. 3, La cisterna arcaica con l'incluso deposito di età ellenistica: scavi Santangelo 1945–1946 e Università di Roma "La Sapienza" 1996 e 2006*. Rome: «L'Erma» di Bretschneider.

Confini e frontiera nella grecità d'Occidente: atti del trentasettesimo Convegno di studi sulla Magna Grecia, Taranto, 3–6 ottobre 1997, 1999. Taranto: Istituto per la storia e l'archeologia della Magna Grecia.

Cooley, A.E., ed. 2000. *The Epigraphic Landscape of Roman Italy*. London: BICS Suppl. 73.

Cornell, T.J. 1995. *The beginnings of Rome: Italy and Rome from the Bronze Age to the Punic Wars (c. 1000–264 BC)*. London: Routledge.

Cornell, T.J. 2013. *The Fragments of the Roman Historians*, Vols. 1–3. Oxford: Oxford University Press.

Cornell, T.J. and Lomas, K., eds, 1995. *Urban Society in Roman Italy*. London: UCL Press.

Cornell, T.J. and Lomas, K., eds, 1997. *Gender and Ethnicity in Ancient Italy*. London: Accordia Research Institute.

Cracolici, V. and Nava, M.L. 2005. "Il santuario lucano di Rossano di Vaglio." In *Lo spazio del rito: santuari e culti in Italia meridionale tra indigeni e Greci: atti delle giornate di studio (Matera, 28 e 29 giugno 2002)*, eds M.L. Nava and M. Osanna, 103–13. Bari: Edipuglia.

Crawford, M.H. 2003. "Land and People in Republican Italy." In *Myth, History and Culture in Republican Rome: Studies in honour of T.P. Wiseman*, eds D. Braund and C. Gill, 56–72. Exeter: University of Exeter Press.

Crawford, M.H. 2006a. "From Poseidonia to Paestum via the Lucanians." In *Greek and Roman Colonization. Origins, ideologies and interactions*, eds G. Bradley and J.-P. Wilson, 59–72. Swansea: Classical Press of Wales.

Crawford, M.H. 2006b. "The Oscan Inscriptions of Messana." In *Guerra e pace in Sicilia e nel Mediterraneo antico (VIII–III sec. a. C.): Arte, prassi e teoria della pace e della guerra*, Vol. II, 521–25. Pisa: Edizioni della Normale.

Crawford, M.H., ed. 2011. Imagines Italicae: *a Corpus of Italic Inscriptions*. London: BICS Suppl. 110.

Cristofani, M., ed. 1990. *La grande Roma dei Tarquini. Roma, Palazzo delle Esposizioni, 12 giugno–30 settembre 1990*. Rome: «L'Erma» di Bretschneider.

Cristofani, M. 1996. *Etruschi e altre genti nell'Italia preromana: mobilità in età arcaica*. Rome: «L'Erma» di Bretschneider.

Cuozzo, M. 2003. *Reinventando la tradizione: immaginario sociale, ideologie e rappresentazione nelle necropoli orientalizzante di Pontecagnano*. Paestum: Pandemos.

Cuozzo, M. 2007. "Ancient Campania: cultural interaction, political borders and geographical boundaries." In *Ancient Italy: Regions without boundaries*, eds G. Bradley, E. Isayev, and C. Riva, 224–67. Exeter: University of Exeter Press.

Curti, E., Dench E., and Patterson, J. R. 1996. "The archaeology of central and southern Roman Italy: recent trends and approaches." *Journal of Roman Studies* 86: 170–89.

De Juliis, E.M. 1996a. *Magna Grecia. L'Italia meridionale dalle origini leggendarie alla conquista romana*. Bari: Edipuglia.

De Juliis, E.M. 1996b. *San Severo: la necropoli di masseria Casone*. Bari: Edipuglia.

Dench, E. 1995. *From Barbarians to New Men. Greek, Roman and modern perceptions of peoples from the central Apennines*. Oxford: Clarendon Press.

De Souza, P. 1999. *Piracy in the Graeco-Roman World*. Cambridge: Cambridge University Press.

DeWitt, N.J. 1940. "Massilia and Rome." *Transactions of the American Philological Association* 71: 605–15.

Dietler, M. 2005. *Consumption and Colonial Encounters in the Rhône Basin of France: A study of early Iron Age political economy*. Lattes: *Monographies d'Archéologie Méditérranéenne*, 21.

Dommelen, P.A.R. van and Knapp, A.B., eds, 2010. *Material Connections in the Ancient Mediterranean: Mobility, materiality and identity*. London: Routledge.

Eckstein, A.M. 2006. *Mediterranean Anarchy, Interstate War, and the Rise of Rome*. Berkeley: University of California Press.

Edwards, C. 1996. *Writing Rome, Textual Approaches to the City*. Cambridge: Cambridge University Press.

Fogolari, G. 1988. "La cultura." In *I Veneti antichi. Lingua e cultura*, eds G. Fogolari and A.L. Prosdocimi, 17–196. Padua: Editoriale Programma.

Forsythe, G. 2005. *A Critical History of Early Rome: From prehistory to the first Punic War*. Berkeley and London: University of California Press.

Fracchia, H. and Gualtieri, M. 1989. "The social context of cult practices in pre-Roman Lucania." *American Journal of Archaeology* 93: 217–32.

Frederiksen, M. 1968. "Campanian Cavalry: a question of origin." *Dialoghi di archeologia* 2: 3–31

Frey, O.H. 1986. "Les fêtes dans l'art des situles." *Ktema* 2: 199–209.

Fulminante, F. 2003. *Le sepolture principesche nel "Latium Vetus": tra la fine della prima età del ferro e l'inizio dell'età orientalizzante*. Rome: «L'Erma» di Bretschneider.

Gleba, M. and Horsnaes, H., eds, 2011. *Communicating Identity in Italic Iron Age Communities.* Oxford: Oxbow.

Gori, S. and Bettini, M.-C., eds, 2006. *Gli Etruschi da Genova ad Ampurias. Atti del XXIV Convegno di Studi Etruschi ed Italici, Marseille-Lattes, 26 settembre – 1 ottobre 2002,* 2 vols. Pisa: Istituti Editoriali e Poligrafici Internazionali.

Greco, E. 1993. "L'impero di Sibari: bilancio archeologico-topografico." In *Sibari e la sibaritide: atti del trentaduesimo Convegno di Studi sulla Magna Grecia. Taranto-Sibari, 7–12 ottobre 1992,* Vol. 1, 459–85. Taranto: Istituto per la -Storia e l'Archeologia della Magna Grecia.

Grummond, N.T. de and Edlund-Berry, I., eds, 2011. *The Archaeology of Sanctuaries and Ritual in Etruria.* Portsmouth, RI: Jour*nal of Roman Archaeology* Suppl. 81.

Gualtieri, M. and Fracchia, H., eds, 1990. *Roccagloriosa I: L'abitato, scavo e ricognizione topografica (1976–1986).* Naples: Centre Jean Bérard.

Gualtieri, M. and Fracchia, H., eds, 2001. *Roccagloriosa II: L'oppidum lucano e il territorio.* Naples: Centre Jean Bérard.

Gualtieri, M. and Poccetti, P. 2001. "Frammento di tabula bronzea con iscrizione osca dal pianoro centrale." In *Roccagloriosa II: L'oppidum lucano e il territorio,* eds M. Gualtieri and H. Fracchia, 187–275. Naples: Centre Jean Bérard.

Guzzo, P.G. 1987. "Schema per la categoria interpretativa del 'santuario di frontiera'." *Scienze dell'Antichità* 1: 373–79.

Hales, S. and Hodos, T., eds, 2010. *Material Culture and Social Identities in the Ancient World.* Cambridge: Cambridge University Press.

Harris, W.V., ed. 2005. *Rethinking the Mediterranean.* Oxford: Oxford University Press.

Häussler, R. 2007. "At the margin of Italy: Ligurians and Celts in North-West Italy." In *Ancient Italy: Regions without boundaries,* eds G. Bradley, E. Isayev, and C. Riva, 45–78. Exeter: University of Exeter Press.

Herring, E. 2000. "To see ourselves as others see us. The construction of native identities in southern Italy." In *The Emergence of State Identities in Italy in the First Millennium B.C.,* eds E. Herring and K. Lomas, 45–77. London: Accordia Research Institute.

Herring, E. 2007. "Daunians, Peucetians and Messapians? Societies and settlements in southeast Italy." In *Ancient Italy: Regions without boundaries,* eds G. Bradley, E. Isayev, and C. Riva, 268–94. Exeter: University of Exeter Press.

Herring, E. and Lomas, K., eds, 2000. *The Emergence of State Identities in Italy in the First Millennium B.C.* London: Accordia Research Institute.

Heurgon, J. 1966. "The inscriptions of *Pyrgi.*" *Journal of Roman Studies* 56: 1–15.

Heurgon, J. 1972–73. "Intervento." *Kokalos* 18–19: 70–74.

Horden, P. and Purcell, N. 2000. *The Corrupting Sea.* Oxford: Blackwell.

Horsnaes, H.W. 2002. *The Cultural Development in North Western Lucania c. 600–273 B.C.* Rome: «L'Erma» di Bretschneider.

Hurst, H. and Owen, S., eds, 2005. *Ancient Colonizations: Analogy, similarity and difference.* London: Duckworth.

Isayev, E. 2007. *Inside Ancient Lucania: Dialogues in history and archaeology.* London: Institute of Classical Studies.

Isayev, E. 2010. "Unintentionally being Lucanian: dynamics beyond hybridity." In *Material Culture and Social Identities in the Ancient World,* eds S. Hales and T. Hodos, 201–26. Cambridge: Cambridge University Press.

Isayev, E. forthcoming. *Migration, Mobility and Place in Ancient Italy.* Cambridge: Cambridge University Press.

Izzet, V. 2007. *The Archaeology of Etruscan Society.* Cambridge: Cambridge University Press.

Jacquemin, A. 1999. *Offrandes monumentales à Delphes.* Paris: De Boccard.

Keay, S. and Terrenato, N., eds, 2001. *Italy and the West. Comparative issues in Romanization.* Oxford: Oxbow.

Kleibrink, M. 2001. "The search for Sybaris: an evaluation of historical and archaeological evidence." *Bulletin Antieke Beschaving* 76: 33–70.

La Regina, A. 1980. "Dalle guerre sannitiche alla romanizzazione." In *Sannio: Pentri e Frentani dal VI al I sec. a.C.*, 29–42. Rome: De Luca.

La Regina, A. 1981. "Appunti su entità etniche e strutture istituzionali nel Sannio antico." *Archeologia e Storia Antica* 3: 120–37.

La Regina, A. 1984. "Aspetti istituzionali nel mondo sannitico." In *Sannio: Pentri e Frentani dal VI al I sec. a.C. Atti del Convegno*, 17–25. Campobasso, Edizioni Enne.

La Regina, A. 1989. "I Sanniti." In *Italia omnium terrarum parens: la civiltà degli Enotri, Choni, Ausoni, Sanniti, Lucani, Brettii, Sicani, Siculi, Elimi*, 301–432. Milan: Libri Scheiwiller.

Laroche, D. and Nenna, M.-D. 1992. "Deux trésors archaïques en poros à Delphes." In *Delphes. Centenaire de la "Grande Fouille" réalisée par l'École française d'Athènes (1892–1903)*, ed. J.-F. Bommelaer, 109–24. Leiden: Brill.

Lee I. 2000. "Entella: the silver coinage of the Campanian mercenaries and the site of the first Carthaginian mint 410 – 409 BC." *Numismatic Chronicle* 160: 1–66.

Lejeune, M. 1990. *Méfitis d'après les dédicaces lucaniennes de Rossano di Vaglio*. Louvain-la-Neuve: Peeters.

Letta, C. 1994. "Dall'*oppidum* al *nomen*: i diversi livelli dell'aggregazione politica nel mondo osco-umbro." In *Federazioni e federalismo nell'Europa antica*, eds L. Foresti, A. Barzanò, C. Bearzot, L. Prendi, and G. Zecchini, 387–406. Milan: Vita e Pensiero.

Lomas, K. 2007. "Community and state in northern Italy. The ancient Veneti." In *Ancient Italy: Regions without boundaries*, eds G. Bradley, E. Isayev, and C. Riva, 21–44. Exeter: University of Exeter Press.

Lomas, K., Whitehouse, R.D., and Wilkins, J.B., eds, 2007. *Literacy and the State in the Ancient Mediterranean*. London: Accordia Research Institute.

Lo Schiavo, F. 1984. "La Daunia e l'Adriatico." In *La civiltà dei Dauni nel quadro del mondo Italico*, 212–47. Florence: Leo S. Olschki.

Malkin, I. 1998. *Returns of Odysseus: Colonization and ethnicity*. Berkeley and London: University of California Press.

Malkin, I. 2002. "A colonial middle ground: Greek, Etruscan and local elites in the bay of Naples." In *The Archaeology of Colonialism*, eds C.L. Lyons and J.K. Papadopoulos, 151–81. Los Angeles: The Getty Research Institute.

Masters, J. 1992. *Poetry and Civil War in Lucan's Bellum Civile*. Cambridge: Cambridge University Press.

Messineo, G. 1983. "Tessera hospitalis?" *Xenia* 51: 3–4.

Morley, N. 1996. *Metropolis and Hinterland: The city of Rome and the Italian economy, 200 B.C.–A.D. 200*. Cambridge: Cambridge University Press.

Morris, I. 1999. "Iron Age Greece and the meanings of 'princely tombs'." In *Les princes de la protohistoire et l'émergence de l'État*, ed. P. Ruby, 57–80. Rome: Centre Jean Bérard/ Ecole française.

Murray, C. 2011. "Constructions of authority through ritual: considering transformations in ritual space as reflecting society in Iron Age Etruria." In *State Formation in Italy and Greece. Questioning the Neoevolutionist Paradigm*, eds N. Terrenato and D.C. Haggis, 199–216. Oxford: Oxbow.

Naso, A. 2001. "Etruscan and Italic artifacts from the Aegean." In *Ancient Italy in its Mediterranean Setting. Studies in honour of Ellen Macnamara*, eds D. Ridgway, *et al.*, 193–207. London: Accordia Specialist Studies on the Mediterranean 4.

Nava, M.L. and Osanna, M., eds, 2005. *Lo spazio del rito: santuari e culti in Italia meridionale tra indigeni e Greci: atti delle giornate di studio (Matera, 28 e 29 giugno 2002)*. Bari: Edipuglia.

Neer, R. 2004. "The Athenian treasury at Delphi and the material of politics." *Classical Antiquity* 23.1: 63–93.

Nicolet, C. 1962. "Les *equites Campani* et leurs representations figurées." *Mélanges d'archéologie et d'histoire de l'École française de Rome* 74: 463–517.

Osanna, M. 1992. *Chorai coloniali da Taranto a Locri: documentazione archeologica e ricostruzione storica*. Rome: Istituto Poligrafico e Zecca dello Stato, Libreria dello Stato.

Osborne, R. 1998. "Early Greek colonization? The nature of Greek settlements in the west." In *Archaic Greece. New approaches and new evidence*, eds N. Fisher and H. van Wees, 251–70. London: Duckworth with Classical Press of Wales.

Osborne, R. 2004. "The anatomy of a mobile culture: the Greeks, their pots and their myths in Etruria." In *Mobility and Travel in the Mediterranean from Antiquity to the Middle Ages*, eds R. Schlesier and U. Zellmann, 22–36. Münster: Transaction Publishers.

Patterson, H., ed. 2004. *Bridging the Tiber. Approaches to regional archaeology in the Middle Tiber Valley*. London: Archaeological Monographs of the British School at Rome, 13.

Patterson, J.R. 2006. "Colonisation and historiography: the Roman Republic." In *Greek and Roman Colonization. Origins, ideologies and interactions*, eds G. Bradley and J-P. Wilson, 189–218. Swansea: Classical Press of Wales.

Pellegrini, G.B. and Prosdocimi, A.L. 1967. *La Lingua Venetica*. Padua: Istituto di glottologia dell'Università.

Peña, J.T. 2011. "State formation in southern coastal Etruria: an application of the Kipp–Schortman model." In *State Formation in Italy and Greece. Questioning the neoevolutionist paradigm*, eds N. Terrenato and D.C. Haggis, 179–98. Oxford: Oxbow.

Polignac, F. de. 1984. *La naissance de la cité grecque: cultes, espace et société, VIIIe–VIIe siècles avant J.-C.* Paris: Editions La découverte.

Prag, J. 2006. "Poenus Plane Est — But Who Were the 'Punickes'?" *Papers of the British School at Rome* 74: 1–37.

Prosdocimi, A.L. 1988. "La lingua." In *I Veneti antichi. Lingua e cultura*, eds G. Fogolari and A.L. Prosdocimi, 225–422. Padua: Editoriale Programma.

Rathje, A. 1990. "The adoption of the Homeric banquet in central Italy in the Orientalising Period." In *Sympotica: a Symposion on the Symposion*, ed. O. Murray, 279–88. Oxford: Clarendon Press.

Rathje, A. 2000. "'Princesses' in Etruria and Latium Vetus?" In *Ancient Italy in its Mediterranean Setting. Studies in honour of Ellen Macnamara*, eds D. Ridgway, *et al.*, 294–300. London: Accordia Specialist Studies on the Mediterranean 4.

Redhouse, D.I. and Stoddart, S. 2011. "Mapping Etruscan state formation." In *State Formation in Italy and Greece. Questioning the neoevolutionist paradigm*, eds N. Terrenato and D.C. Haggis, 162–78. Oxford: Oxbow.

Renfrew C. and Cherry J.F., eds, 1986. *Peer Polity Interaction and Socio-political Change*. Cambridge: Cambridge University Press.

Renfrew C. and Level, E.V. 1979. "Predicting polities from Centers." In *Transformations: Mathematical approaches to culture change*, eds C. Renfrew and K.L. Cooke, 145–67. New York: Academic Press.

Riva, C. 2004. "Keeping up with the Etruscans? Picene élites in Central Italy during the Orientalising period." *Accordia Research Papers* 9: 69–91.

Riva, C. 2010a. *The Urbanisation of Etruria. Funerary practices and social change, 700–600 BC*. Cambridge: Cambridge University Press.

Riva, C. 2010b. "Trading settlements and the materiality of wine consumption in the North Tyrrhenian Sea region." In *Material Connections in the Ancient Mediterranean: Mobility, materiality and identity*, eds P. van Dommelen and A.B. Knapp, 210–32. London/New York: Routledge.

Rix, H. 1991. *Etruskische Texte. Editio minor*, 2 vols. Tübingen: G. Narr. Heidelberg: C. Winter.

Rix, H. 2002. *Sabellische Texte: die Texte des Oskischen, Umbrischen und Südpikenischen*.

Roth, R. and Keller, J., eds, 2007. *Roman by Integration: Dimensions of group identity in material culture and text*. Portsmouth, RI: *Journal of Roman Archaeology* Suppl. 66.

Rowlands, M., Larsen, M., and Kristiansen, K., eds, 1987. *Centre and Periphery in the Ancient World*. Cambridge/ New York: Cambridge University Press.

Ruby, P., ed. 1999. *Les princes de la protohistoire et l'émergence de l'État*. Rome: Centre Jean Bérard/ Ecole française.

Rutter, N.K., ed. 2001. *Historia Numorum, Italy*. London: British Museum Press.

Salmon, E.T. 1967. *Samnium and the Samnites*. Cambridge: Cambridge University Press.

Säström, M. 1940. *A Study in the Coinage of the Mamertines*. Lund: C.W.K. Gleerup.

Scheid, J. 2003. *An Introduction to Roman Religion*. Edinburgh: Edinburgh University Press.

Schultz, C. and Harvey, P., eds, 2006. *Religion in Republican Italy*. Cambridge: Cambridge University Press.

Scopacasa, R. 2010. "Beyond the warlike Samnites: rethinking grave goods, gender relations and social practice in ancient Samnium (Italy)." In *TRAC 09: Proceedings of the Nineteenth Theoretical Roman Archaeology Conference*, 120–31. Oxford: Oxbow.

Scopacasa, R. 2015. *Ancient Samnium: Settlement, culture and identity between history and archaeology.* Oxford: Oxford University Press.

Serrati, J. 2006. "Neptune's altars: the treaties between Rome and Carthage (509–226 B.C.)." *Classical Quarterly* 56: 113–34.

Shennan, S. 1994. *Archaeological Approaches to Cultural Identity.* London: Routledge.

Sherwin-White, A.N. 1973, 2nd edn. *The Roman Citizenship.* Oxford: Clarendon Press.

Sisani, S. 2001. *Tuta Ikuvina: Sviluppo e ideologia della forma urbana a Gubbio.* Rome: Quasar.

Smith, C.J. 2007a. *The Roman Clan: The Gens from ancient ideology to modern anthropology.* Cambridge: Cambridge University Press.

Smith, C.J. 2007b. "The hinterland of Rome: Latium and the Latins." In *Ancient Italy, Regions without boundaries*, eds G. Bradley, E. Isayev, and C. Riva, 161–78. Exeter: University of Exeter Press.

Spivey, N. 1991. "The power of women in Etruscan society." *Accordia Research Papers* 2: 55–68.

Stek, T.D. 2009. *Cult Places and Cultural Change in Republican Italy: A contextual approach to religious aspects of rural society after the Roman conquest.* Amsterdam: Amsterdam University Press.

Tagliamonte, G. 1994. *I figli di Marte: mobilità, mercenari e mercenariato italici in Magna Grecia e Sicilia.* Rome: «L'Erma» di Bretschneider.

Terrenato, N. and Haggis, D.C., eds, 2011. *State Formation in Italy and Greece. Questioning the neoevolutionist paradigm.* Oxford: Oxbow.

Thiel, J.H. 1954. *A History of Roman Sea-power Before the Second Punic War.* Amsterdam: North-Holland Publishing Company.

Torelli, M. 1988. "Le popolazioni dell'Italia antica: società e forme del potere." In *Storia di Roma, I. Roma in Italia.* Turin: Giulio Einaudi.

Torelli, M. 1999. *Tota Italia. Essays in the cultural formation of Roman Italy.* Oxford: Clarendon Press.

Turfa, J.M. and Steinmayer, A.G. Jr. 2002. "Interpreting early Etruscan structures: the question of Murlo." *Papers of the British School at Rome* 70:1–28.

Untermann, J. 2000. *Wörterbuch des Oskisch-Umbrischen.* Heidelberg: C. Winter.

Vetter, E. 1953. *Handbuch der italischen Dialekte.* Heidelberg: C. Winter.

Wallace-Hadrill, A. 2008. *Rome's Cultural Revolution.* Cambridge: Cambridge University Press.

Weiss, M.L. 2010. *Language and Ritual in Sabellic Italy: The ritual complex of the third and the fourth tabulae Iguvinae.* Leiden and Boston: Brill.

Whitehouse, R. 1992. *Underground Religion: Cult and culture in prehistoric Italy.* London: Accordia Research Centre.

Whitehouse, R. D. and Wilkins, J. B. 1989. "Greeks and natives in south-east Italy: approaches to the archaeological evidence." In *Centre and Periphery: Comparative studies in archaeology*, ed. T.C. Champion, 102–26. London/ New York: Routledge.

Wiseman, T.P. 2008. *Unwritten Rome.* Exeter: University of Exeter Press.

PART I

The Impact of Rome – Unification and Integration

CHAPTER 2

Rome's Encroachment on Italy

Rafael Scopacasa

2.1 Introduction

Rome's encroachment on Italy is often seen as the process by which a unique city-state conquered the entire peninsula in a surprisingly short period of time. Yet in many ways the Roman expansion was an Italian phenomenon, in the sense that Italian communities and institutions had a decisive impact on the development of Roman hegemony from the outset. The Roman drive towards expansion can to some extent be understood as a product of the harsh interstate environment of Archaic Italy, where constant warfare encouraged aggressive competition (Eckstein, 2006). The city's expansion was possible because Italian communities supplied the necessary manpower and resources, fought the wars, and participated in colonization schemes of various kinds (Cornell, 1989; Bradley and Wilson, 2006). The means by which Rome maintained its dominance with the cooperation of Italian aristocracies owed much to earlier forms of elite collaboration from the Archaic period (Gabba, 1989), and helped to preserve the social structure of many Italian communities (Terrenato, 2007). It was not inevitable that Rome should emerge as the sole hegemonic power. In the fourth and early third centuries the Romans encroached on Italy almost as much as Italians encroached on Rome and on each other. It was only after the Hannibalic war (202 BC) that Rome became the political hub of the peninsula, but even then we have evidence that many Italian states behaved as independent partners rather than dependents.

For much of the twentieth century, the Roman expansion in Italy was seen as a steady process of unification, not just in a political sense but socio-cultural as well (e.g. Sherwin-White, 1973: 159). This view can be traced back to nineteenth-century Germany, and particularly to the work of Theodor Mommsen. His idea that Italian communities almost inevitably converged under Roman leadership was probably influenced by the atmosphere of German national unification in his own day, and the modern expectations of nation building under the guidance of a dominant state, in this case Prussia (Mouritsen, 2006).

Yet on a deeper level, this teleological view of Roman encroachment reflects the surviving historical narratives from antiquity, which were the chief sources available to Mommsen. The ancient historical accounts portray the Roman "conquest" of Italy as the first stage in the city's inevitable rise to world domination. Whilst such narratives offer an invaluable basis for

A Companion to Roman Italy, First Edition. Edited by Alison E. Cooley.
© 2016 John Wiley & Sons, Ltd. Published 2016 by John Wiley & Sons, Ltd.

understanding how Rome extended its territory and power, they also pose serious challenges. With the exception of Polybius, most of the surviving texts were written from the mid-first century BC onwards, at least 200 years after the events that they describe. These authors wrote about the mid-Republican past in view of their own political agendas and anxieties as upper-class Romans of the late Republic and Principate (Dench, 2005: 152ff; Kraus and Woodman, 1997). Although individuals such as Livy were eager to understand how Roman hegemony had come about, they were mostly unconcerned with social and administrative transformations. They offer vivid accounts of battles and wars, but only faint sketches of the political settlements between Rome and Italian communities.

On the other hand, a growing body of epigraphic, numismatic, and archaeological sources – from survey data to ceramics and architecture – offer a rich evidence base that is contemporaneous with the process of Roman encroachment. This material allows us to explore the social and cultural transformations that Italian communities experienced, ultimately supporting alternative histories of Republican Italy. Yet the fragmentary nature of the archaeological and epigraphic record also makes for very challenging problems of interpretation, as we shall see below.

This chapter discusses the role of Italian communities in Rome's rise as a hegemonic power between the fifth and early second centuries BC, and how this process transformed Italy as a result. I begin by sketching a narrative of events that mark the extension of Roman territory and power in Italy, from the founding of the Republic (509 BC) to the start of the first Punic war (264 BC) – seeking, whenever possible, to reconstruct the Italian perspective on these events. The second part of the chapter discusses the social and political impact of Roman dominance between the late fourth and early second centuries. I emphasize the current shift towards a new narrative of Roman hegemony in third-century Italy, where colonization, extensions of citizenship, and alliances are being approached not simply as instruments of Roman oppression, but also as complex and changing phenomena in which Italians as well as Romans played a key role. Whilst colonization surely helped to consolidate Roman territorial expansion at the expense of Italian communities, the colonies themselves were autonomous communities with permeable borders, which included large numbers of Italians – both locals and migrants (Bradley and Wilson, 2006; Coles, 2009). Colonies and the extension of citizenship promoted new patterns of integration and mobility across the peninsula through trade, intermarriage, and army service, which affected Rome as well as Italy (Roselaar, 2012). Growing knowledge of such mobility allows us to rethink the link between Roman hegemony and the cultural changes that we see in the material and epigraphic record of Italy in the fourth–second centuries, which is discussed towards the end of this chapter.

2.2   The Early Years (Circa 509–390 BC)

Italy in the late sixth century was home to a variety of political communities which gravitated around a number of regionally dominant powers. To the south, the poleis of Magna Graecia had been flourishing since the eighth century (Lomas, 1993). Further inland, the situation differed broadly between Tyrrhenian and Adriatic zones. The Adriatic half of the peninsula was home to Oscan- and Umbrian-speaking communities that were just beginning to undergo unique state formation processes (Bradley, 2000). These were highly flexible polities which by the mid-fifth century were able to act independently as well as collectively as large ethnic leagues, the most powerful of which were the Samnites and the Lucanians further west (Salmon, 1967; Isayev, 2007; Scopacasa, 2015a). A rather different situation existed on the Tyrrhenian seaboard between Etruria and Campania, where the early development of exceptionally large and resourceful city-states made for a fragmented political landscape where interstate rivalry was high (Scullard, 1967: 235).

Rome was among the larger of these Tyrrhenian city-states. The city had been emerging since the late seventh century, which is when we start to see archaeological evidence of political organization in the form of monumental public buildings and spaces (Ammerman, 1990; Smith, 1996). Roman elites were integrated with the aristocracies of neighboring cities through guest-friendship relations (Ampolo, 1976–1977). The ivory *tessera hospitalis* from the Forum Boarium probably linked a Roman noble man to an Etruscan counterpart, for example (Pallotino, 1979). On a more general level, the funerary evidence reveals that Tyrrhenian elites partook of a shared culture of martial prowess and status display, which is also visible in the Esquiline necropolis in Rome (Colonna, 1977).

It was against this backdrop of aristocratic connectivity that rivalry and competition developed between the Tyrrhenian city-states (Sherwin-White, 1980: 179). Rome had been exposed to Etruscan warfare for most of the sixth century, and the Tarquin kings of Rome may originally have been Etruscan warlords (Cornell, 1995: 151–72). In Latium, communities attempted to alleviate warfare by forming interstate leagues that were centered on shared sanctuaries. The Alban mount, for example, housed a common cult where representatives from various Latin cities attempted to resolve their differences (Dionysius of Halicarnassus, *Roman Antiquities*: 4.49). We do not know how closely Rome was involved in these leagues, but the historical tradition maintains that the last Roman kings adopted an aggressive foreign policy towards many Latin cities (Livy: 1.38.4; Cornell, 1989: 248). In the final years of the sixth century we hear of a league of Latin cities headed by Tusculum, which confronted Rome and was defeated – at the battle of Lake Regillus according to tradition (Livy: 2.19).

The outcome of Rome's victory was the so-called Cassian treaty of 493 BC, which marked the beginning of Roman ascendancy in Latium (Dionysius of Halicarnassus, *Roman Antiquities*: 6.95.1–3). The treaty established mutual military assistance between Rome and the league of Latin cities, against the surrounding hill communities of the Sabines, Aequi, and Volscians (Cornell, 1989). An allied army is mentioned, and Rome is likely to have played an important part in organizing it. The treaty also made provisions for the sharing of spoils, and colonization was one of the means by which Rome and the Latin league shared conquered land (Salmon, 1969: 40–41). Among the colonies that are said to have been founded in the fifth century are Ardea, Norba, and Signia (see Figure 2.1). We should not be too ready to see these settlements as the outcome of organized state-led schemes. Considering that government systems in fifth-century Rome and Latium were still relatively underdeveloped, these early "colonies" were probably informal ventures led by military commanders, both Roman and Latin, who distributed conquered land to their clients (Bradley, 2006: 162–69).

In addition to the Cassian treaty, Rome's ruling aristocracies strengthened ties with the leaders of Latin cities through the sharing of reciprocal rights to intermarry (Livy: 4.1) and to conduct legally binding transactions (Dionysius of Halicarnassus, *Roman Antiquities*: 6.95.2). The effects of this policy can be seen in the clause of the Twelve Tables (circa 450 BC) which forbade intermarriage between patricians and plebeians in Rome (Drummond, 1989).

As Rome's position in Latium was consolidated, struggles with the Etruscan cities became more frequent. Rome's major competitor in the fifth century BC was Veii, its closest Etruscan neighbor. Initially Veii appears to have had the advantage, and in the 470s BC it conquered Fidenae, which lay halfway between itself and Rome. Yet towards the end of the century Rome managed to take Fidenae (426 BC) and ultimately Veii itself in 396 BC (Livy: 5.30.8; Cornell, 1989: 311ff.). This was a major turning-point in Rome's relationship with its neighbors, since the treatment that Veii received after the conquest already foreshadows some of the practices that were to characterize Roman encroachment over the next two centuries. The entire territory of Veii was confiscated, which made the Roman territory (*ager Romanus*) twice as big as it had been in 509 BC (Diodorus Siculus: 14.102.4). After the Gallic sack of Rome in 390 BC the people of Veii were given Roman citizenship.

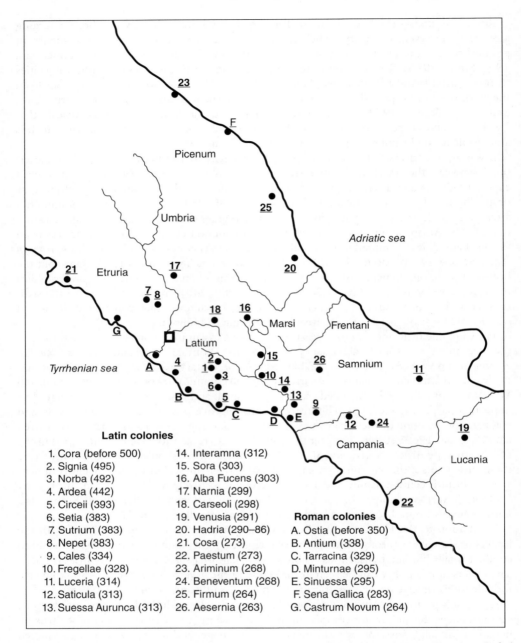

Latin colonies

1. Cora (before 500)
2. Signia (495)
3. Norba (492)
4. Ardea (442)
5. Circeii (393)
6. Setia (383)
7. Sutrium (383)
8. Nepet (383)
9. Cales (334)
10. Fregellae (328)
11. Luceria (314)
12. Saticula (313)
13. Suessa Aurunca (313)
14. Interamna (312)
15. Sora (303)
16. Alba Fucens (303)
17. Narnia (299)
18. Carseoli (298)
19. Venusia (291)
20. Hadria (290–86)
21. Cosa (273)
22. Paestum (273)
23. Ariminum (268)
24. Beneventum (268)
25. Firmum (264)
26. Aesernia (263)

Roman colonies
A. Ostia (before 350)
B. Antium (338)
C. Tarracina (329)
D. Minturnae (295)
E. Sinuessa (295)
F. Sena Gallica (283)
G. Castrum Novum (264)

Figure 2.1   Roman and Latin colonies in central/southern Italy down to 263 BC. Drawing: Rafael Scopacasa, adapted from Cornell, 1989.

The causes of early Roman belligerence and expansionism have long been a major focus of debate. One group of scholars (Harris, 1979; Raaflaub, 1996; Oakley, 1993; Cornell, 1989) sees the drive towards expansion as the result of a highly militarized *ethos* that was exceptional to Rome, where war was necessary for the normal functioning of society more than in any other Italian state. They argue that Roman nobles needed wars to gain status and access to public office. After the internal political struggles of the fifth century, distinction in war became a crucial means by which the new plebeian aristocracy could legitimize itself before patricians and people (Harris, 1979: 28). The Roman state also looked to war as a means to reduce social tension, such as by distributing conquered land to the poor.

A different approach sees Roman bellicosity as a product of the political context of early Italy. With the aid of realist political theory, Eckstein (2006) argues that early Italy was an anarchic and highly militarized interstate environment, where, in the absence of international law, individual states had to adopt an aggressive foreign policy to survive. Rome was not the only highly belligerent state in Tyrrhenian Italy, but one among several that competed with each other, in an environment where self-protection often meant aggressive expansionism. According to Eckstein, what was truly special about Rome was its ability to incorporate former enemies (see later in this chapter). Both Eckstein and the proponents of "Roman exceptionalism" emphasize important aspects of Roman foreign policy. It may help to maintain a more balanced outlook that takes proper account of the exceptional aspects of Roman bellicosity, without losing sight of what this behavior owed to the broader Italian context in which it developed.

2.3   Italy Encounters Rome (Circa 390–264 BC)

The integration of Veii after 390 BC expanded the sphere of Roman military activity north of the Tiber, and there soon followed serious engagements with major Etruscan cities such as Tarquinii, Volsinii, and Falerii in the 370s and 360s BC. By the 350s BC all of these cities had agreed to forty-year truces with Rome (Livy: 5.16.2–6; 5.30.4–6). At the same time we hear of renewed fighting in Latium, particularly with the cities of Tibur and Praeneste (Livy: 7.19.1; Diodorus Siculus: 16.45.8). In south Latium there were also confrontations with Satricum and Velitrae (Livy: 6.16.5). From 362 BC, a string of victories ended with Rome conquering the Pomptine marshes in southern Latium, where Roman citizens were settled and two new voting tribes established, the Pomptina and the Publilia (Livy: 7.5.11; Cornell, 1989: 320). Within a few years, Rome's hegemonic ambitions in Latium were blatant. The second treaty between Rome and Carthage (348 BC) stipulated that the Carthaginians were allowed to sack those Latin cities "that were not obedient to Rome," provided they handed them over afterwards (Polybius: 3.24).

Shortly before the treaty with Carthage, in 354 BC Rome made an alliance with the Samnites, who by that point were emerging as a powerful ethnic league of polities that controlled a huge swathe of central and south Italy (Salmon, 1967; Scopacasa, 2015a; on the treaty see Livy: 7.19.4; Diodorus Siculus: 16.45.8). It is significant that this treaty came about only a decade before Rome became involved in Campania, the rich and fertile region south of Latium. Both Rome and the Samnites were developing interests in this extremely prosperous area of Italy, and the Romano-Samnite treaty can be seen as an attempt to negotiate spheres of influence (Salmon, 1967; Cornell, 1989: 360).

Eventually war broke out in 343 BC, and Livy's account captures some of the competitive atmosphere that sparked it. According to Livy, the Samnites attacked a neighboring people called the Sidicini who lay between themselves and Campania. The Sidicini sought protection from Capua, one of the chief Campanian cities. The Samnites then defeated the Capuan army on two occasions, at which point Capua appealed to Rome for assistance (Livy: 7.29–31). Stephen Oakley has argued that Livy is here summarizing what was actually a very complex dispute between various polities over Campania's resources (Oakley, 1997–2005: II. 285). There is surely pro-Roman bias in the way that Livy emphasizes how the Capuan ambassadors begged Rome for help. But this does not mean that the Capuan appeal – or the various similar ones said to have been made by other Italian communities in subsequent years – did not actually happen. Rather, the Romans most likely took advantage of the interstate rivalries in Italy as a means of justifying their interference and extending their power (Fronda, 2010: 20–21). After three poorly recorded battles the Samnites were driven out of Capua in 341 BC (Livy: 8.1.7–2.3), but this was just the beginning of a series of confrontations that would unfold over the next five decades.

It was also in 341 BC that the Latin league declared war on Rome. Livy (8.4) implies that the Latins revolted because they were being treated as subjects rather than allies, which is consistent with the above-mentioned indications of Roman hegemonic ambitions in Latium. It is difficult to reconstruct the details of the Latin war, but we know that Capua and other Campanian cities joined in at some point on the side of the Latins. This shows how quickly alliances could be made and broken in this volatile environment.

The war ended with the defeat of the Latin league in 338 BC (Livy: 8.13.8). Scholars agree that it was at this juncture that Rome began to put together the policies which were to become the basis of its subsequent encroachment on the peninsula (Sherwin-White, 1973). To begin with, the Latin league was dissolved, which meant that Latin communities now had to deal with Rome on an individual basis. Some of the Latin cities were fully incorporated as Roman citizens and made into *municipia*, which were newly devised administrative units (Bispham, 2007). According to Livy (8.14) the cities that received the full citizenship in 338 BC included Lanuvium, Aricium, Nomentanum, and Pedum, their territory becoming *ager Romanus*. Other Latin communities such as Tibur and Praeneste remained independent but found themselves individually bound to Rome by bilateral treaties of alliance, which put them under the obligation to provide military assistance to Rome, and prevented them from having any dealings amongst themselves (Cornell, 2000: 213). As a result, from 338 BC the Roman army as a rule included contingents of allies who fought alongside citizen troops.

Another major change after 338 BC was that communities outside Latium and south Etruria found themselves drawn into the sphere of Roman dominance. Capua and the other Campanian cities that sided with the Latins (Suessula and Cumae), as well as the Volscian towns of Fundi and Formiae, became bound to Rome by a set of agreements which our sources elusively call the *civitas sine suffragio* ("citizenship without the vote": Livy: 8.14.10–11). This status was later extended to the Latin community of Acerrae in 332 BC and to Privernum in 329 BC (Sherwin-White, 197: 213). There is still debate as to what this status entailed (see later in this chapter), but scholars agree that it included the right to trade and intermarry with Romans, as well as duties such as service in the Roman army. It used to be thought that the granting of *civitas sine suffragio* meant that the community's territory officially became part of the *ager Romanus*, and whilst this does not mean that previous inhabitants were dispossessed or lost their autonomy, some of the land was allotted to settlers. We can trace this process in view of the new voting tribes that were created in 318 BC (Oufentina and Falernia), which included the Roman citizens who settled around Capua, Fundi, and Formiae (Taylor, 1960). Although this system was innovative, it owed much to earlier forms of elite cooperation from the Archaic period (Gabba, 1989). The rights to intermarry and trade will have been crucial in forging links with the elites of incorporated communities (see later in this chapter).

With the Latin league dissolved, Rome had greater control over the founding of colonies. Our sources maintain that there were two main types of colonization at this stage: the allotment of plots to individual settlers ("viritane" allotment) and the foundation of entire colonial settlements, which are classed as either "Latin" or "Roman." "Latin" colonies were autonomous communities with their own magistrates and armies. The designation "Latin" was juridical rather than ethnic – it meant that these colonies had rights and duties that had previously been granted to communities in Latium since the fifth century, such as the right to intermarry and conduct legally binding transactions with Roman citizens. "Roman" colonies, on the other hand, are described as smaller settlements of Roman citizens only (Salmon, 1969). Yet Livy occasionally refers to Latin colonies as "Roman" (27.9.7), which suggests that these clear-cut distinctions simplify what was probably a more fluid reality (Bispham, 2006).

After 338 BC the location of new colonies indicates that Rome was attempting to use them as strategic outposts, in addition to their traditional role as alleviators of land hunger (Patterson, 2006). The first Latin colony founded after 338 BC was Cales (334 BC), just northwest of Capua, which suggests it was created with a view to protecting Rome's influence in Campania against Samnite encroachment. By 327 BC, Samnite and Roman ambassadors were vying for influence over Naples, one of the most powerful Greek cities in Campania (Dionysius of Halicarnassus, *Roman Antiquities*: 15.5–8). Eventually the Samnites succeeded in winning over the Neapolitan elites, which suggests that their "Hellenic credentials" outstripped those of the Romans (Dench, 1995: 63). The situation was already delicate, since in the previous year Rome had founded another Latin colony at Fregellae (328 BC) on the eastern side of the Liris river, which the Samnites considered their sphere of influence (Livy: 8.22.1–2). Yet the Samnites were also encroaching on Roman territory, according to the Roman accusations that they were attempting to win over Fundi and Formiae, which had only just received partial Roman citizenship (Livy: 8.23; Dionysius of Halicarnassus, *Roman Antiquities*: 15.8).

The second "Samnite war" broke out in 326 BC, and in 321 the Samnites managed to trap the entire Roman army in a mountain pass, forcing them to surrender (Livy: 9.5–6). Yet five years later Rome ignored the peace treaty and launched a new offensive. After marching across the Apennine mountains and down the Adriatic coast they seized the Apulian city of Luceria, which was a Samnite ally, and founded a Latin colony there in 314 BC (Diodorus Siculus: 19.72.8). In 313–12 BC, another three Latin colonies (Saticula, Suessa, Interamna) were planted in such a way as to surround the Samnite heartland from Campania. All of these colonies probably aided in launching the devastating campaigns into Samnium that soon followed (Livy: 9.44.14).

In addition to colonies, road building helped in the consolidation of Roman dominance (Laurence, 1999). In 312 BC the construction of the *via Appia* began, directly linking Rome and Capua. This was the first major road in Italy, and its construction was almost certainly carried out by Roman citizens with the help of the Campanian cities under Roman influence. An issue of silver didrachms which display the legend *romano* circulated in Campania when the *via Appia* was being built. These coins may have been Roman pay for the Campanians who helped to build the road (Crawford, 1985: 28). Not only did the *via Appia* serve a strategic purpose of communication with Campania, it was also an assertion of hegemonic Roman leadership, and its construction offered new scope for integration between Romans and Campanians (Laurence, 1999: 15).

The Samnites' position grew weaker until they finally settled for another treaty of alliance in 304 BC. They were joined by several other peoples of central Italy (Frentani, Marsi, Marrucini, Vestini) who had resisted until that point, but were persuaded to form alliances with Rome in view of the near annihilation of their neighbors the Aequi (Livy: 9.45.18).

Before the Samnite war was over, fighting with the Etruscan cities resumed in 311 BC. An attack by Tarquinii and Volsinii on Roman territory prompted a Roman counter-offensive into the Ciminian hills, which ended with the formation of thirty-year truces (Livy: 9.32–5; Diodorus Siculus: 20.35.5). At the same time, alliances were made with Umbrian communities close to Etruria, first Camerinum in 310 and later Iguvium in 295 BC (see Bradley, 2000: 301, who argues that there were more treaties which went unrecorded). In the meantime Rome tightened her grip on central Italy by founding another string of Latin colonies at Sora (303 BC), Alba Fucens (303 BC), Narnia (299 BC), and Carseoli (298 BC). These colonies probably disrupted joint military action between the central Italian peoples and the Samnites further south.

It did not take long for war to break out once again. From 298 BC the Samnites led diplomatic missions with the purpose of forming a multi-ethnic coalition against Rome. By 296 BC they had attracted Etruscan and Umbrian cities as well as Gallic forces, which together confronted the Roman armies near the Umbrian town of Sentinum in 295 BC, in what was probably the largest battle ever fought in peninsular Italy until that date. Although the anti-Roman forces were formidable, Rome's alliance policy allowed it to muster up a huge amount of manpower for the occasion.

The Roman victory at Sentinum gave new impetus to its encroachment. After the Samnites were defeated in 293 BC, much of their land adjacent to Campania was confiscated and made into *ager Romanus*. In the following decades, two Latin colonies were founded well within Samnite territory in Beneventum (268 BC) and Aesernia (263 BC), which will have helped to divide the polities that formed the Samnite ethnic league (Salmon, 1967). Massive land confiscations also took place further north in central Italy, after the defeat of the Sabines and Praetutii in 290 BC (Dio Cassius: fr.37.1/ Zonaras: 8.2; [Aurelius Victor] *On Famous Men*: 33.1–3). The *ager Romanus* now stretched all the way to the Adriatic coast, where the Latin colony of Hadria was founded in 286. Rome had effectively driven a wedge across the whole peninsula. The whole area would later be traversed by the *via Flaminia* (circa 220 BC), which linked Rome to the Latin colony of Ariminum (founded 268 BC; Livy: Book 20 Summary/ *Periocha*). The *via Flaminia* is likely to have created what Ray Laurence (1999: 23) calls a "Rome-centred geography" in central Italy, where the Latin colonies and allied communities were linked amongst themselves and to Rome.

In the south, Rome planted another Latin colony at Venusia in 291 BC. Alliances were probably formed in the succeeding decades with communities in Lucania and the western Greek cities including Tarentum, which had attempted to contain the advance of Rome by calling on help from Pyrrhus of Epirus, who was defeated in 272 BC. (For a more detailed account, see Chapter 13 by Lomas in this volume.) The only securely attested treaty between Rome and a western Greek city is that of Heraclea in 278 BC (Cicero, *For Archias*: 6). In Bruttium (modern Calabria) the Sila forest was confiscated for its timber (Dionysius of Halicarnassus, *Roman Antiquities*: 20.15). In 273 BC, the fertile stretch of coastal land around the Gulf of Salerno was made into *ager Romanus*, and the colony of Paestum was established on the site of Poseidonia.

2.4   The Impact of Roman Encroachment: Italy in the Third and Early Second Centuries BC

It is extremely difficult to gauge the amount of land in Italy that Rome controlled as a result of its expansion (Roselaar, 2010: 31–33). However, as Rome entered its first war with a major overseas power in 264 BC, its territory most likely amounted to about 20% of the Italian peninsula (see Figure 2.2). The *ager Romanus* probably grew from 5525 km^2 with a population of 347 300 in 338 BC, to an estimated 26 850 km^2 with a population of around 900 000 at the start of the first Punic war (Brunt, 1971: 59). In addition, the various Latin colonies founded by Rome since 334 BC may have occupied up to 7000 km^2, and together housed up to 70 000 men and their families (Cornell, 1989: 405). Italian communities that were not made into colonies or turned into full or partial Roman citizens were bound to Rome as allies – some of them after considerable fighting and resistance, such as the Samnites.

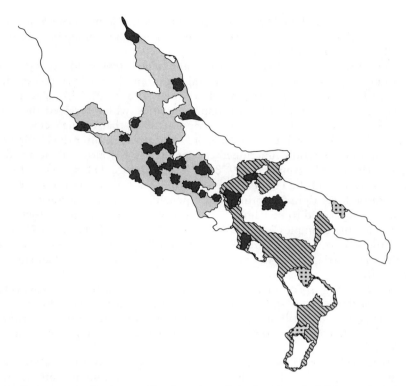

Figure 2.2 Roman expansion in central and southern Italy. Drawing: Rafael Scopacasa, adapted from Cornell, 1989.
■ Latin colonies until 263 BC; □ *ager Romanus* until 263 BC; ▦ Latin colonies founded after 263 BC; ◪ additions to *ager Romanus* after 263 BC

Roman dominance in the third century was mostly about controlling Italian manpower (Broadhead, 2008). Generally speaking, the various political agreements between Rome and the Italians can be seen as different means to that end, since the one thing Italians had in common was the obligation to provide troops for Rome. Yet the impact of Roman dominance on Italian communities varied considerably, and in many cases it was less drastic than we would expect. Because Rome relied on the cooperation of Italian aristocracies, local social structures were often preserved. Our understanding of this complex interplay between continuity and change has improved over the past few decades, as a result of new approaches to written and material evidence that focus on the agency of Italians within the new geopolitical context.

2.4.1 Between second-class citizens and allies with benefits: extensions of citizenship

The diverse effects of Roman encroachment start to become evident once we take a closer look at those communities which are said to have received the "citizenship without the vote." Scholars agree that this status entailed the right to intermarry and conduct legally binding transactions with Romans (Humbert, 1978; Cornell, 1989). But upon closer inspection, the expression *civitas sine suffragio* can be seen to cover a range of communities whose status in relation to Rome varied greatly (Mouritsen, 2007).

On one level, the condition described as *civitas sine suffragio* could entail the reciprocal exchange of political rights between Rome and autonomous Italian states, similar to the agreements of *isopoliteia* in the Greek world (Gruen, 1984: 70). This appears to be the case for Capua, one of the wealthiest Campanian cities, which received the *civitas sine suffragio* in 338 BC (Livy: 8.14). Official inscriptions show that Capua's chief magistrates (Oscan *meddiss tuvtiks*) remained in possession of their powers after the change of status, and that local administration functioned independently for most of the third century (Frederiksen, 1984: 241; Humbert, 1978: 370–71). Before 211 BC, when the city was punished for defecting in the Hannibalic war (218–02 BC), there are no references to the elimination of political rights or other severe penalties. On the contrary, the exchange of intermarriage rights led to new links between Roman and Capuan aristocrats. Among the most remarkable examples is the case of the Capuan noble Pacuvius Calavius, who married a daughter of Appius Claudius Pulcher (*cos.* 212 BC: Livy: 23.4.7) and gave his own daughter in marriage to a Marcus Livius, possibly Marcus Livius Salinator, *cos.* 219 (Livy 23.2.5–6).

At the other end of the spectrum, we are told that the Hernican town of Anagnia was given the *civitas sine suffragio* as punishment for rebelling against Rome in 307–06. In this case the new status involved a wholesale stripping of the community's autonomy – its citizens were banned from holding councils, and magistrates were only allowed to perform religious tasks (Livy: 9.43.24).

The fact that the historical record lumps such different cases as Anagnia and Capua into a single category probably reflects the concerns of late-Republican authors, who constructed a schematic account of what will have been fluid political settlements (Mouritsen, 2007). The fact that Livy occasionally refers to the Capuans as allies (*socii*) (Livy: 23.10.1) is more than mere inconsistency: it hints at the fluidity and overlap that probably existed between notions of "partial citizens" and "allies" in the fourth and third centuries. It might have been because of Capua's exceptional wealth and influence that Rome decided to create closer bonds with its elites. Yet even the integration brought about by intermarriage did not prevent Capua from defecting to the Carthaginians in the Hannibalic war. Indeed, Pacuvius Calavius, who was linked to Roman consuls by marriage, was chief magistrate when the city went over to Hannibal after the Roman defeat at Cannae in 216 BC. Integration with Rome did not eliminate the hegemonic ambitions of the Capuan elites, nor did it diminish their discontent at having to raise troops for Rome (Livy: 23.6.3; Fronda, 2010: 119–20).

The *civitas sine suffragio* used to be seen as an intermediary stage in the enfranchisement of Italians (Humbert, 1978). Yet the only secure evidence of *cives sine suffragio* receiving full Roman citizenship concerns the towns of Fundi, Formiae, and Arpinum in 188 BC (Livy: 38.36.7–8; Mouritsen, 2007: 144). A similar development apparently occurred a few decades earlier with regard to the Sabines in central Italy, whose land was made into *ager Romanus* sometime after 290 BC. Any Sabines who were not killed or driven away probably received some form of partial citizenship (Brunt, 1969: 121). They or their descendants will have been fully enfranchized in 241 BC, with the creation of the voting tribes Quirina and Velina (Livy: *Per*.19; Afzelius, 1942). However, it is difficult to generalize. A close reading of Livy suggests that the Romans themselves were uncertain as to when and how the change of status could be done, indicating that there was no set procedure (Mouritsen, 2007: 144–45).

2.4.2 Allied communities: subject states or independent partners?

Although the *cives sine suffragio* did not constitute a homogeneous group, many of them stood apart from other Italian communities who were bound to Rome by a different set of agreements. As allies (*socii*), the majority of Italians remained nominally independent, but were bound by treaty to raise troops for Rome from their own communities, pay these troops (Polybius: 6.21.5), and follow Roman foreign policy (Harris, 1971; Bispham, 2007: 35). A glance at Figure 2.2 reveals that allies were chiefly located in Etruria and Umbria, and further south in Lucania, Apulia, and Magna Graecia. The situation in the central section of the peninsula was more complex because of the land confiscations of the early third century, but large areas in Samnium and along the Adriatic coast were controlled by allied communities. Latin colonies were technically also allies (Livy often calls them "allies of the Latin name") but their status was special as they were allowed to trade and intermarry with Roman citizens (see later in this chapter).

The availability of allied manpower was crucial for Rome's success. At the battle of Sentinum in 295 BC the allied contingents already outnumbered the Roman citizen legions (Livy: 10.26.4), and on the eve of the Hannibalic war (218 BC) they outnumbered the Romans by three to two (Brunt, 1971: 44–60; Cornell, 1989). When Scipio was organizing his African expedition in 205 BC, which secured Rome's victory in the war, he obtained the money and materials from Etruscan cities, and the manpower from allies in Umbria and the central Apennines (Livy: 28.45.14–21).

One reason why Italians complied with the Roman demands was that they profited from their association with Rome. They received shares of war spoils, and as veteran soldiers they were included in land assignments (see later in this chapter). Particularly important was the fact that Rome supported the aristocracies of allied communities in exchange for their manpower and resources (Cornell, 1989: 387). We hear of many instances where Romans will have protected the interests of local aristocracies by suppressing popular revolts, as appears to have been the case at Arretium in 302 BC (Livy: 10.3.5), in Lucania in 296 BC (Livy: 10.18.8), and at Volsinii in 264 BC (Zonaras: 8.7.4–8). Personal relationships between Roman and Italian aristocrats were formed during the third century, of which we hear only incidentally. Fabius Maximus Rullianus, four times consul between 322 and 297 BC, had a brother who was educated in Caere at the home of guest-friends, which made him fluent in Etruscan (Livy: 9.36.2–3). Ti. Sempronius Gracchus (*cos.* 215, 213 BC) was the guest-friend of a Lucanian noble called Flavus (Livy: 25.16.5). A similar relationship linked Titus Manlius Torquatus (*cos.* 235, 224 BC) and C. Staiodius, an aristocrat of the Marsi in central Italy, as can be inferred from a bronze *tessera hospitalis* with both men's names inscribed along with the Latin word *hospes* (*CIL* 1² 1764; see Fronda, 2010: 306). Among the non-elites, service in the Roman army will have been a key context where Italians could interact closely and constantly with Roman soldiers under a common purpose (Ilari, 1974). However, allies served in separate "ethnic" units and under their own commanders, which might also have contributed to the Italians' sense of their own ethnicity (Keppie, 1984; Bradley, 2000: 199–200). At the battle of Gereonium in 217 BC, for example, the Samnites formed a separate contingent under the command of a Numerius Decimus from Bovianum (Livy: 22.24), and two squadrons of Samnite horsemen are later noted at Pydna in 168 BC (Livy: 44.40).

Despite the convergence of interests among Romans and Italians, there was some discrepancy in the way that each side perceived its relationship with the other. On the one hand, the Roman view of Italy as a coherent unit that was under its guardianship may have already been in place by the early third century. The historian Philinus refers to a treaty between Rome and Carthage from before 264 BC, where Italy is described as a Roman domain. Polybius (3.26.2–4) doubted the historicity of this treaty, but it may have been the renewal of an earlier treaty from 306 BC which Livy (9.43.26) records (Serrati, 2006: 120–29; Fronda, 2010: 24). The Italians themselves, however, appear to have seen things differently. Polybius implies that at the battle of Telamon in 225 BC against the Gauls, the Italian allies were fighting alongside Rome not because of subservience but out of a shared fear of the Gauls, and were ultimately moved by their own interests (Polybius: 2.23.11–13; Fronda, 2010: 28).

We should certainly not overstress the cohesiveness of the Roman alliance network in the third century. A large number of Italian communities that had been Roman allies since the late fourth century lost no time defecting in the middle of the Hannibalic war, after the Carthaginian victory at Cannae in 216 BC. With Rome severely crippled, the Italian states chose their own allies and enemies according to earlier patterns of interstate rivalry which predated the Roman expansion. Fronda (2010) demonstrates that certain groups of cities in Campania, Apulia, Lucania, and Magna Graecia tended to fight on the same side before becoming Roman allies, and carried on doing so after Cannae, when Rome could not control their foreign policy. Defections after Cannae were most frequent in southern Italy, which included some of Rome's most powerful allies such as Capua and the Apulian cities. Had it not been for the loyalty of most communities in Etruria, Umbria, and the central Apennines, Hannibal would probably have won. Clearly the decades of Roman alliance did not make Italian states any less capable of deciding on their own foreign policy to their advantage, or to the advantage of their ruling elites. In this context, the above-mentioned cases of personal aristocratic friendship did not necessarily guarantee a state's loyalty to Rome. The Mopsii family of Compsa in Samnium remained faithful to Rome, even though most of their fellow citizens went over to Hannibal (Livy: 23.1.1–3; Isayev, 2013). The Lucanian Flavus, on the other hand, appears to have betrayed Sempronius Gracchus to the Carthaginians (Livy: 25.16.6).

All of this is generally consistent with the picture that we get from the archaeological evidence, which is one of communities developing as politically autonomous entities throughout Italy. In the countryside, archaeological survey shows that small farms multiply on an unprecedented scale in the fourth and third centuries (Samnium: Lloyd, 1995; north Etruria: Terrenato, 1998; Messapia: Burgers, 1998; but see Bradley, 2000: 229–34 for different developments in Umbria). Whilst scholars are still discussing the significance of this pattern, it appears that rural communities experienced a general increase in prosperity (Terrenato, 2007). Much of the surplus generated will have been appropriated by local elites, who in turn financed the monumentalization that we see in major settlements and sanctuaries during this period. From the late fourth century, the material record of Italy shows an increasing amount of wealth being diverted away from private spheres of ostentation, such as burials, and onto more public spaces and structures. Large nucleated settlements emerge more or less concurrently in Samnium (e.g. Monte Vairano: De Benedittis, 1991; Scopacasa, 2015a), Lucania (e.g. Roccagloriosa: Isayev 2007) and Umbria (e.g. Vettona, Ameria, and Ocriculum: Bradley, 2000: 163–71). Many of these sites display clear signs of urban development, such as large public buildings and temples, street grids, elite housing, and fortifications. In regions such as Etruria, where large urban centers were already present since the Archaic period, many centers also continue to thrive, as the case of Perusia shows (Bradley, 2000: 166). Inscriptions from these sites reveal the development of administrative hierarchies where power was shared by yearly elected magistrates, while the spread of coinage signals the emergence of centralized authority capable of managing communal resources (Bradley, 2000: 178–83; Isayev, 2007: ch.1; Scopacasa, 2015a). Even though the types of state organization varied between regions, there is an overall trend towards centralization and complexity of political organization.

The political definition of communities can also be traced in view of the development of monumental sanctuaries, which were key venues for the negotiation of political membership in the ancient world. Sanctuaries were located either inside the major settlements, or in rural settings where people converged on a region-wide level, such as the major sanctuary at Pietrabbondante which played a role in the ethnic union of polities in Samnium (La Regina, 1976). Recent topographical approaches show that many sanctuaries probably functioned as boundary markers or as common ground between neighboring polities on a local level (Stek, 2009).

All these trends can be seen as the continuation of long-term state formation processes which stretch back to the Archaic period (Bradley, 2000, who focuses on Umbria). The socio-political development of Italian communities was not brought to a halt by the encounter with Rome in the mid-fourth century, but rather provided the context for growing interaction with Rome. It was by relying on the social and administrative structures of burgeoning Italian states that Rome managed to obtain the cooperation of local aristocracies and the resources that it needed (Bradley, 2000: 126). On the other hand, Roman expansion brought about new levels of political interaction that primarily involved the Italian elites, who used their new position to secure advantages and special treatment for themselves and their communities. One exceptionally well-documented example is that of Volaterrae in Etruria, where local aristocracies resorted to their Roman contacts with the objective of limiting the impact of colonial allotments on their land (Terrenato 1998). This is consistent with the results of archaeological survey in the territory of Volaterrae, which reveal the continuity of farmsteads and rural sites after the city's alliance with Rome in the third century. The survival of local patterns of landholding may reflect the preservation of Volaterrae's social structure.

2.4.3 Colonization, mobility, and integration

Late-Republican and Imperial authors regarded the colonies of the fourth–third centuries BC as key instruments of Roman expansion. Cicero famously called them "bulwarks of empire" (*On the Agrarian Law* 2.73), and Aulus Gellius (16.13.9) described them as miniature replicas of Rome. Based on such views, modern scholars primarily regarded mid-Republican colonies as instruments that secured the Roman state's hold on conquered territory (e.g. Salmon, 1969: 14).

Recently, there has been growing awareness that the literary sources offer heavily Rome-centered accounts of colonization in Italy (Bradley, 2006; Coles, 2009). The Roman state did have an important role in the founding of colonies, and many colonies probably did function as military outposts. But the idea that colonization was a strategically planned process through which Rome "duplicated" itself throughout the peninsula is difficult to maintain for the period before the second century BC (Bispham, 2006: 74). It is true that many colonies emulated certain aspects of Roman urbanism, the most famous example being the construction of colonial *capitolia* which supposedly referred back to the Capitol in Rome. However, archaeology shows that this trend only really develops after 200 BC, when newfound Roman confidence after the Hannibalic war redefined the city's relationship with the colonies and with Italy in general. Cosa, for example, was founded in 273 BC in the territory of the Etruscan city of Vulci, but public buildings of "Roman" inspiration start to emerge only a century later (Fentress, 2000; cf. Fentress and Perkins, ch.19 this vol.).

Mid-Republican colonies were far from being miniature replicas of Rome, and were much more than strategic Roman outposts. By putting the historical record in perspective with the archaeological and epigraphic sources, we can appreciate the diversity of colonial encounters, and the agency of Italians in the development of colonies as autonomous communities.

The many-sided character of colonization is evident in the different policies that were adopted towards previous occupants. In some cases they appear to have been excluded, as for example at Cosa, where archaeological survey shows a decrease in the number of rural settlements in the colony's territory during the third century BC (Fentress, 2000), although such a pattern could also reflect changes in land use. In several instances, however, we have positive evidence that local populations were integrated (Bispham, 2006: 91). A Latin inscription from Aesernia (Samnium) was set up by a group who called themselves the "Samnite residents (*incolae*)" (*CIL* 1² 3201; Terzani, 1991). Whether they were descendants of the original inhabitants or migrants from surrounding areas, these Samnites were clearly part of the colony, even if their status as *incolae* meant that they had different rights and obligations from the landed *coloni*. Whereas legal texts from Late Antiquity describe *incolae* as either previous inhabitants of areas made into colonies who were allowed to remain, or as people from outlying areas who settled in colonies (*Digest*: 50.16.239.2; *Justinian Codex*: 10.40.7), it is unclear to what extent such definitions apply to mid-Republican Italy. The continued presence of previous occupants is also plausible at Beneventum, which was founded on the site of a major Samnite settlement (Torelli, 2002). Although the archaeological record at Beneventum is fragmentary, there are no signs of great disruption following the establishment of the colony. Rather, the site's previous layout appears to have been largely respected. The Roman walls, for example, were constructed in such a way as to incorporate the *arx* of the pre-colonial town, which had been the focus of terracing and building works in the fourth century (see Figure 2.3). In addition, the epigraphy of Beneventum reveals Oscan family names among the colonial magistrates (e.g. Afinii, Fufii, Munatii, Ofelii, Paccii, Vibii; see Torelli, 2002: 77), which suggests that local aristocracies were integrated into the colonial administration (see Bradley, 2006, for further evidence).

Extensive participation of Italians in colonial schemes stimulated mobility across the peninsula. In 197 BC, 1000 families were sent to reinforce the Latin colony at Cosa. Livy (33.24.8–9) points out that these new colonists were especially chosen from communities that had not defected from Rome during the Hannibalic war. This means that the settlers will have included veterans from Etruria, Umbria, Samnium, and the central Apennines, where defections were few. Large numbers of people from central and southern Italy are likely to have participated in the great wave of colonization of the Po valley in the early second century. Inscribed boundary markers from Pisaurum (184 BC) suggest that most of the colonists came from west-central Italy (Harvey, 2006: 119–26). Italians were also entering colonies independently of official Roman initiative. Movements of this kind are probably what made the colonists in Narnia (Umbria) complain to the senate in 199 BC that people "of a different status" (*non sui generis*) were entering the colony and passing themselves off as settlers (Livy: 32.2.6). Lack of evidence makes quantification difficult, but certain passages hint at the very large scale of these migratory fluxes. In 177 BC, 4000 Samnite and Paelignian families moved to the colony at Fregellae (Livy: 41.8.8). Neither Rome nor the Samnite states seem to have been prepared for the consequences of such mobility, and in that same year the senate passed a law limiting migration (Livy: 41.8.11–12; Broadhead, 2008; Isayev, in press).

In view of the evidence that colonies included previous inhabitants and settlers from various parts of Italy, scholars have focused on how activities such as cult and the construction of public venues aided in the integration of the diverse social and ethnic groups that made up the colonies, and also how the topographical placement of buildings and monuments helped to articulate the colonies' claims to nearby routes and resources. By examining the construction of sacred space at Fregellae, Coles (2009, 167–68) demonstrates that the placement of extra-urban sanctuaries next to the *via Latina* suggests an effort to define community cohesion and

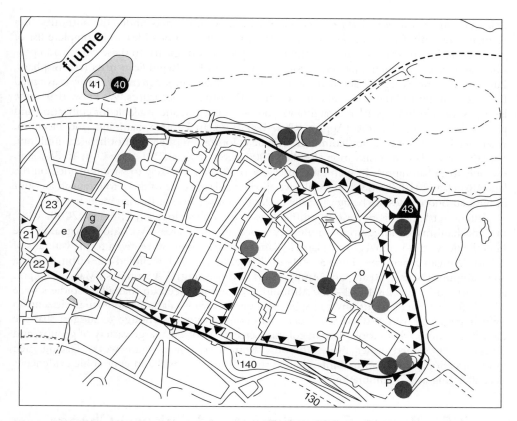

Figure 2.3 Eastern sector of Beneventum, showing Roman wall surrounding pre-colonial *arx*, pre-colonial find spots, and colonial find spots. Drawing: Rafael Scopacasa, adapted from Giampaola, 2000. ▬ Roman wall; ▲ Pre-colonial *arx*; ● pre-colonial find spot; ● colonial find spot

boundaries. Similarly, the incorporation of deities that were widespread in Italy (e.g. Hercules) afforded a common ground for the negotiation of identities in colonial encounters (Bispham, 2006, 113–22; Coles, 2009, 163). Yet integration was not a universal phenomenon, given that there were instances where colonists and locals lived alongside each other as separate communities in what can be called "dual settlement" situations (see Pelgrom, 2012: 180–87, who discusses the cases of Poseidonia/Paestum, Thurii/Copia, Vibo Valentia, Croton, and Tarentum). Some colonies do stand out for their eagerness to advertise their affiliation with Rome. Beneventum and Ariminum are the only Latin colonies where the chief magistrate had the title of consul (*CIL* 9.1633, 9.1547). This may have been related to the fact that these two colonies were positioned at the outskirts of the *ager Romanus*. The colonists may have sought to counterbalance their marginal position by emphasizing their Roman-ness (Bispham, 2006, 91).

Integration also happened in those areas of Italy where plots of land were assigned to individual settlers through the process known as "viritane allotment". We know that this form of colonization was common in the parts of central Italy that were confiscated by Rome in the first half of the third century BC (see Figure 2.2), and which were made into administrative units that our sources call *praefecturae*. Technically, these were districts under the authority of a Roman magistrate (*praefectus iure dicundo*). Festus (p.262 L.) provides an incomplete list of *praefecturae* in Umbria, Sabinum, Samnium, Latium, and Campania; to these we can add possible cases based on epigraphy and passing references in late Republican texts (see Bispham, 2007). Our sources are usually silent on the amount of land in *praefecturae* that was assigned to settlers, and very little is said about the fate of the original occupants. We know that some land was not allotted to settlers straightaway, but was instead made available for cultivation and pasture in exchange for tolls (Appian, *Civil War.* 1.7). In Umbria, Samnium and Picenum, where fertile farmland was less common, viritane colonization often did not happen until long after the initial date of confiscation (Bradley, 2000: 139; Roselaar, 2010; see Livy: 40.38 for an example from Samnium). In such cases, previous occupants are likely to have remained on the land (Roselaar 2010, 80–83). This will have allowed at least some of them to retain an amount of local autonomy, despite being officially under the jurisdiction of Roman magistrates.

Viritane settlement is notoriously difficult to trace archaeologically (Bradley, 2000: 138), but mechanisms of integration surely developed in these areas. We know that after the Hannibalic war, individual plots of land in Samnium and Apulia were given to the veterans of Scipio's African expedition (Livy: 31.4.1–2). These, we are told, included allies from Umbria and Sabinum (Nursia, Reate, and Amiternum) and the central Apennines (Marsi, Paeligni, and Marrucini: Livy: 28.45.11–12). Although we cannot be certain that allied soldiers were eligible for viritane distributions, the Sabines in Scipio's army will have had Roman citizenship by that stage and were probably included. This example alone is enough to suggest that the daily interactions which took place in colonial settings involved a large variety of groups, and cannot be subsumed under a dichotomous "Roman vs. Italian" framework. Tracing such multi-directional socio-cultural interchange through the material and epigraphic evidence is as challenging as it is stimulating.

2.5   Roman Encroachment and Cultural Change

The Roman expansion brought about new social relationships and connections throughout Italy which stimulated cultural dynamism and change – whether through elite intermarriage and guest-friendship, colonial interactions between Romans, Latins and other Italians, or allied contingents from various parts of Italy fighting together in the Roman army (Roselaar, 2012). Yet it is important to remember that there already was substantial cultural interchange in Italy before Roman encroachment. Material culture and inscriptions reveal patterns of connectivity stretching back to the Iron Age (circa 1000 BC), with regions such as Campania, Etruria, and Magna Graecia acting as major nodes of socio-cultural networks that extended to Samnium, Umbria, Latium, and Lucania (Tagliamonte, 1996; Bradley, 2000; Herring, 2007; Isayev, 2007; Scopacasa, 2015a; see also Isayev, ch. 1 this vol.). These earlier patterns had a bearing on the cultural development of Italy in the fourth and third centuries BC.

In Umbria, for example, the growth of Roman political influence is paralleled by an increase in imports from Latium and the Faliscan area (Bradley, 2000: 201). These mainly consist of black-gloss pottery which may have been produced in or around Rome, such as the black-gloss wares with stamped palmettes (*petites estampilles*: Morel, 1969: 113–14) which become ubiquitous throughout Italy in this period. However, these new connections did not eliminate the traditional cultural links between Umbrian communities and Etruria. Umbrian funerary urns and *stelai* continue to show strong Etruscan influence as late as the first century BC (Bradley, 2000: 202–03). A very similar phenomenon occurs in Samnium (Scopacasa, 2015a), where the dissemination of black-gloss wares (including possibly Roman-made *petites estampilles*) adds to, rather than precludes, long-standing connections with central and south Italy.

Italy has figured prominently in debates about the link between Roman hegemony and cultural change (e.g. Webster and Cooper, 1996; Mattingly, 1997, 2004, 2011; Terrenato, 1998; van Dommelen, 2001; Keay and Terrenato, 2001; Roth, 2007). Nicola Terrenato's study of the Etruscan city of Volaterrae (1998) pioneered approaches to the diversity of cultural responses to Roman dominance, thus redefining the traditional concept of Romanization. As a result, earlier attempts to trace the spread of Roman culture in the material record of Italy have given way to more sophisticated approaches, which take into account the two-way nature of cultural contact, the diversity of social agents involved (Romans, Latins, Italian allies from various regions), the fact that Roman identity itself changes, and the complex issue of cultural resistance to Roman dominance. The spread of the Latin alphabet and language has equally been subject to re-evaluation. Rather than a progressive switch from Italian languages to Latin, what we have is a multilingual scenario where individuals were able to resort to Oscan, Umbrian, Greek, Latin, and other languages depending on the context (see also Bispham, ch. 4 and Lomas ch. 11 this vol.).

As Rome expanded, it took part in what can be characterized as "global" cultural trends in which other Italian communities also participated on their own account. One context where we can see this clearly is cult and worship. The spread of anatomical terracotta figurines is one of the most striking trends in the material record of central Italy in the fourth and third centuries BC. Before then, the local votive assemblages consisted mainly of bronze figurines, pottery vessels, jewelry, and weapons (Comella and Mele, 2005). In contrast, the new terracotta figurines depict men, women, and child worshippers, either in full body or only the head. A large number of them have been labeled "anatomical votives" as they represent limbs and organs that were in need of healing, or had been healed. Among the most commonly depicted body parts are feet, hands, arms, legs, genitals, and uteruses (Comella, 1981).

It used to be consensual that these types of votive artefact originated in Tyrrhenian Italy, where they appear to occur most frequently. The earliest known pieces come from the vicinity of Rome – Lavinium and Veii – and can be dated to the fifth century BC (Comella and Mele, 2005). Outside Latium and Etruria, terracotta anatomical votives tend to be more frequent in Latin colonies, a good example being Luceria in Apulia where over 500 have been recovered (D'Ercole, 1990). Because these artefacts seem to spread into central Italy along with the Roman expansion and colonization, many scholars regarded them not only as a direct reflection of the Roman conquest, but also as instruments of Roman domination on a cultural level (Coarelli, 2000: 200; de Cazanove, 2001: 199).

However, our knowledge of the geographical distribution of the anatomical terracottas is currently changing as a result of more systematic excavations in central and Adriatic Italy, an area which was long marginalized in favor of the Tyrrhenian zone. Anatomical terracotta votives have been found in the central Apennines at Iuvanum, Rapino, San Buono (Fonte San Nicola), and Vacri (Porcareccia), as well as sporadically at Archi, Chieti, Fresagrandinaria, Guilmi, Pollutri, San Salvo, and Villalfonsina (Morelli, 1997; for their distribution in Umbria see Bradley, 2000). Paestum and Luceria are the two most southerly sites where such objects have thus far been attested (Comella and Mele, 2005). Consequently, previous assumptions that the anatomical figurines spread from Tyrrhenian to Adriatic Italy are being challenged – especially since it now seems that in some cases these artefacts precede the colonial foundations by several decades. Anatomical terracotta votives appear to have been already present at Carseoli since the mid-fourth century BC, at least fifty years before the foundation of the Latin colony in 298 BC (Gentili, 2005). Similar cases can be made for the Latin colonies at Paestum (273 BC) and Salerno (194 BC).

Rather than seeking to identify one-way influences from Rome and Latium into central Italy, it is more profitable to focus on the contextual analysis of the terracotta votives, and what they tell us about broader patterns in cultural practice that sweep through the peninsula.

In this sense, what is unique about the anatomical votives is the emphasis that they place on the person of the worshipper rather than the deity. They can be seen as a direct expression of the worshipper's personal health concerns (Glinister, 2006; Scopacasa 2015b). What we appear to be witnessing is a growing need among worshippers to assert themselves and their personal needs before the deity. Such a redefinition of attitudes to worship and the divine was a supra-regional phenomenon in which communities in Rome and throughout Italy actively participated. It is surely possible that the social networks and connectivity which emerged in association with Roman encroachment helped to create channels through which the new religious *koine* could travel faster and longer, but Rome was by no means the matrix from which cultural change spread (Bradley, 2000: 202–03). It helps to recall that the earliest known anatomical votives come from Corinth, which suggests that their spread in Italy is partly the result of long-term interaction with the Greek world (Glinister, 2006: 17–26 notes the differences between Italian and Greek anatomical figurines; see also Schultz, ch.3 this vol., for the impact of Greek culture on Italy in the second century BC.)

2.6   Conclusion

The process by which Rome encroached on Italy involved a number of ad hoc arrangements which proved successful in the long run. It is crucial to distinguish between the complex interstate relations of the fourth and third centuries BC, and retrospective thinking about these relations by Roman authors of the late Republic, whose main concern was to include Italy in a grand narrative of how Rome had been predestined for world supremacy.

After the Hannibalic war, Rome established itself as a world power. This affected the city's relationship with Italy, and particularly with the Italian aristocracies (Badian, 1958: 11–12; Wiseman, 1971, 34ff.; Fronda, 2010: 323). It is not coincidental that Roman interference in the affairs of Italian states appears to increase during the second century. In some cases such interference probably interested Italian communities, such as the suppression of slave revolts in Latium in 198 and in Etruria in 196 BC (Livy: 32.26.4–18; 33.36.1–3). But in other instances, allied states will have regarded Roman interference as an infringement on their sovereignty, such as the suppression of the Bacchanalia in 186 BC (Livy: 39.8–19). The degree to which Rome and Italians were on a convergence course in the second century BC, and how the Gracchan reforms added to this complicated scenario, are some of the key issues discussed by Bispham, in chapter 4 of this volume.

In the end, it was not just Rome's expansion that impacted on Italy, but also Italy that impacted on Rome. The integration processes of the fourth and third centuries BC both enabled and shaped Rome's transformation into an Empire. Rome's interaction with Italian peoples had long-lasting effects on its culture, politics, and society. This is clear in Roman literature and historical writing. Late-Republican authors drew on Italy as a source of models with which Roman identity was defined (Dench, 1995; 2005). On the one hand, the Sabines incorporated the stereotype of pious and austere worthiness, and their early integration into the Roman citizen body made it possible for the Roman aristocracy to use them as a "moral resource" (Dench, 1995: 85–94). Sabine elites actively contributed to the construction of this stereotype, from which they derived political benefits as newly incorporated citizens in the third and second centuries BC (Farney, 2007). At the other end of the spectrum, the Samnites represented the stereotype of warlike and decadent barbarians, an image that had a key role in Rome's self-legitimising ideologies during the Imperial period (Dench, 1995; Scopacasa, 2007). This is one sense in which the Italian peoples lived on long after Italy became Roman.

FURTHER READING

On Archaic Latium and Rome see C.J. Smith 1996. Cornell 1989, Oakley 1993, Raaflaub 1996, and Eckstein 2006 offer comprehensive narratives of the political and military aspects of Roman expansion in Italy, though from different theoretical perspectives: whilst Oakley, Cornell, and Raaflaub tend to favor the thesis of "Roman exceptionalism," Eckstein emphasizes the similarities between Roman and Italian bellicosity. Ilari 1974 and Keppie 1984 discuss Italians in the Roman army; Roselaar 2010 focuses on land-based issues, and Broadhead 2008 and Isayev 2013 discuss mobility. Earlier studies on the extension of Roman citizenship (Humbert, 1978; Sherwin-White, 1973) must be put in perspective with recent work on the complexity of this phenomenon (Bispham, 2007; Mouritsen, 2007). The volume edited by Bradley and Wilson 2006 challenges many preconceptions about colonization in Republican Italy, and has stimulated innovative approaches to colonial landscapes (Coles, 2009; Pelgrom, 2012). There are a number of recent studies on socio-political development and cultural identities in Italy in the last four centuries BC (Bradley, 2000; Isayev, 2007; Bradley, Isayev and Riva, 2007; Scopacasa, 2015a). Fronda 2010 analyzes the foreign policy of Italian states during the Hannibalic war. The cultural impact of Roman hegemony on Italy has been widely discussed (e.g. Terrenato, 1998; Keay and Terrenato, 2001; Roth, 2007). The edited volume by Roselaar 2012 is representative of current approaches to integration and socio-cultural change in the Republican period, as is van Dommelen and Terrenato 2007, which is not restricted to Italy. Stek 2009 provides a fresh discussion of cult places and cultural change, whilst Glinister 2006 questions the idea of religious Romanization by focusing on votive offerings. On the writing of the history of Republican Italy since the nineteenth century, see Mouritsen 2006.

REFERENCES

Afzelius, A. 1942. *Die römische Eroberung Italiens (340–264 v. Chr.)*. Copenhagen: *Acta Jutlandica* 14.

Ammerman, A. 1990. "On the origins of the Forum Romanum." *American Journal of Archaeology* 94: 627–45.

Ampolo, C. 1976–1977. "Demarato. Osservazioni sulla mobilità sociale arcaica." *Dialoghi di Archeologia* 9–10: 333–45.

Badian, E. 1958. *Foreign Clientelae, 264–70 BC*. Oxford: Clarendon Press.

Bispham, E.H. 2006. "*Coloniam deducere*. How Roman was Roman colonization during the Middle Republic?" In *Greek and Roman Colonization. Origins, ideologies and interactions*, eds G.J. Bradley and J.-P. Wilson, 73–160. Swansea: Classical Press of Wales.

Bispham, E.H. 2007. *From Asculum to Actium: the municipalization of Italy from the Social War to Augustus*. Oxford: Oxford University Press.

Bradley, G. 2000. *Ancient Umbria. State, culture and identity in central Italy from the Iron Age to the Augustan era*. Oxford: Oxford University Press.

Bradley, G. 2006. "Colonization and identity in Republican Italy." In *Greek and Roman Colonization. Origins, ideologies and interactions*, eds G. Bradley and J.-P. Wilson, 161–87. Swansea: Classical Press of Wales.

Bradley, G., Isayev, E. and Riva, C., eds. 2007. *Ancient Italy: Regions without boundaries* Exeter: University of Exeter Press.

Bradley, G. and Wilson, J.-P., eds. 2006. *Greek and Roman Colonization. Origins, ideologies and interactions*. Swansea: Classical Press of Wales.

Broadhead, W. 2008. "Migration and hegemony: fixity and mobility across the 2nd century." In *People, Land, and Politics. Demographic developments and the transformation of Roman Italy, 300 BC–AD 14*, eds L. De Ligt and S. Northwood, 451–70. Leiden: Brill.

Brunt, P.A. 1969. "The enfranchisement of the Sabines." In *Hommages à M. Renard*. Vol. 2, ed. J. Bibauw, 121–29. Brussels: Latomus.

Brunt, P.A. 1971. *Italian Manpower, 225 BC–AD 14*. Oxford: Clarendon Press.

Burgers, G.-J.L.M. 1998. *Constructing Messapian Landscapes: Settlement dynamics, social organization and culture contact in the margins of Graeco-Roman Italy*. Amsterdam: Gieben.

Cazanove, O. de. 2001. "Itinéraires et étapes de l'avancée romaine entre Samnium, Daunie, Lucanie et Etrurie."In *Le censeur et les Samnites. Sur Tite-Live, livre IX*, eds D. Briquel and J.P. Thuillier, 147–92. Paris : Études de littérature ancienne 11.

Coarelli, F. 2000. "Il Lucus Pisaurensis e la romanizzazione dell'ager Gallicus." In *The Roman Middle Republic. Politics, religion, and historiography, c. 400–133 B.C.*, ed. C. Bruun, 195–205. Rome: Institutum Romanum Finlandiae/ Acta Instituti Romani Finlandiae 23.

Coles, A.J. 2009. *Not effigies parvae populi Romani. Gods, agency and landscape in mid-republican colonization*. Unpublished PhD thesis. University of Pennsylvania.

Colonna, G. 1977. "Un aspetto oscuro del Lazio antico. Le tombe del VI–V sec. a.C." *Parola del Passato* 32: 131–65.

Comella, A. 1981. "Tipologia e diffusione dei complessi votivi in Italia in epoca medio- e tardo-reppublicana." *Mélanges de l'Ecole Française de Rome, Antiquité* 93.2: 717–803.

Comella, A. and Mele, S., eds. 2005. *Depositi votivi e culti dell'Italia antica dall'età arcaica a quella tardo-repubblicana*. Bari: Bibliotheca archaeologica 16/ Edipuglia.

Cornell, T.J. 1989. "Rome and Latium to 390 BC;" "The recovery of Rome;" "The conquest of Italy." In *The Cambridge Ancient History*. Vol. 7.2. *The Rise of Rome to 220 BC*, 2nd edn, eds F.W. Walbank *et al.*, 243–419. Cambridge: Cambridge University Press.

Cornell, T.J. 1995. *The Beginnings of Rome: Italy and Rome from the Bronze Age to the Punic Wars (c. 1000–264 BC)*. London: Routledge.

Cornell, T.J. 2000. "The city of Rome in the middle Republic (400–100 BC)." In *Ancient Rome. The Archaeology of the Eternal City*, eds J. Coulston and H. Dodge, 42–60. Oxford: Oxford University School of Archaeology.

Crawford, M.H. 1985. *Coinage and Money under the Roman Republic: Italy and the Mediterranean economy*. London: Methuen.

De Benedittis, G., 1991. "L'abitato di Monte Vairano." In *Samnium. Archeologia del Molise*, eds S. Capini and A. Di Niro, 127–30. Rome: Quasar.

Dench, E. 1995. *From Barbarians to New Men. Greek, Roman and modern perceptions of peoples from the central Apennines*. Oxford: Clarendon Press.

Dench, E. 2005. *Romulus' Asylum. Roman identities from the age of Alexander to the age of Hadrian*. Oxford: Oxford University Press.

D'Ercole, M.C. 1990. *La stipe votiva del Belvedere a Lucera. Corpus delle stipi votive in Italia*. Vol. 3. Rome: «L'Erma» di Bretschneider.

Dommelen, P.A.R. van. 2001. "Cultural imaginings. Punic tradition and local identity in Roman Republican Sardinia." In *Italy and the West. Comparative issues in Romanization*, eds S. Keay and N. Terrenato, 68–84. Oxford: Oxbow.

Dommelen, P.A.R. van and Terrenato, N., eds. 2007. *Articulating Local Cultures. Power and identity under the expanding Roman Republic*. Portsmouth, RI: *Journal of Roman Archaeology* Suppl. 63.

Drummond, A. 1989. "Rome in the fifth century I: the social and economic framework." In *The Cambridge Ancient History*. Vol. 7.2. *The Rise of Rome to 220 BC*, 2nd edn, eds F.W. Walbank *et al.*, 113–71. Cambridge: Cambridge University Press.

Eckstein, A.M. 2006. *Mediterranean Anarchy, Interstate War, and the Rise of Rome*. Berkeley: University of California Press.

Farney, G. 2007. *Ethnic Identity and Aristocratic Competition in Republican Rome*. Cambridge: Cambridge University Press.

Fentress, E. 2000. "Frank Brown, Cosa, and the idea of a Roman city." In *Romanization and the City. Creations, transformations and failures*, ed. E. Fentress, 9–24. Portsmouth, RI: *Journal of Roman Archaeology* Suppl.38.

Frederiksen, M. 1984. *Campania*, ed. N. Purcell. London: British School at Rome.

Fronda, M. 2010. *Between Rome and Carthage. Southern Italy during the Second Punic War*. Cambridge: Cambridge University Press.

Gabba, E. 1989. "Rome and Italy in the second century BC." In *The Cambridge Ancient History*. Vol. 8. *Rome and the Mediterranean to 133 B.C.*, 2nd edn, eds A.E. Astin, et al., 197–243. Cambridge: Cambridge University Press.

Gentili, M.D. 2005. "Riflessioni sul fenomeno storico dei depositi votivi di tipo etrusco-laziale-campano." In *Depositi votivi e culti dell'Italia antica dall'età arcaica a quella tardo-repubblicana*, eds A.M. Comella and S. Mele, 367–78. Bari: Bibliotheca archaeologica 16.

Giampaola, D. 2000. "Benevento. Dal centro indigena alla colonia romana." In *Studi sull'Italia dei Sanniti*, 36–46. Rome: Electa.

Glinister, F. 2006. "Reconsidering 'religious Romanization'." In *Religion in Republican Italy*, eds C.E. Schultz and P.B. Harvey, 10–33. Cambridge: Cambridge University Press.

Gruen, E. S. 1984. *The Hellenistic World and the Coming of Rome*. Berkeley/ London: University of California Press.

Harris, W.V. 1971. *Rome in Etruria and Umbria*. Oxford: Clarendon Press.

Harris, W.V. 1979. *War and Imperialism in Republican Rome, 327–70 BC*. Oxford/ New York: Clarendon Press/ Oxford University Press.

Harvey, P.B. 2006. "Religion and memory at Pisaurum." In *Religion in Republican Italy*, eds C.E. Schultz and P.B. Harvey, 117–36. Cambridge: Cambridge University Press.

Herring, E. 2007. "Daunians, Peucetians and Messapians? Societies and settlements in southeast Italy." In *Ancient Italy: Regions without boundaries*, eds G. Bradley, E. Isayev, and C. Riva, 268–94. Exeter: University of Exeter Press.

Humbert, M. 1978. Municipium et civitas sine suffragio: *l'organisation de la conquête jusqu'à la guerre sociale*. Rome: Ecole française de Rome.

Ilari, V. 1974. *Gli italici nelle strutture militari romane*. Milan: Giuffrè.

Isayev, E. 2007. *Inside Ancient Lucania: Dialogues in history and archaeology*. London: Institute of Classical Studies.

Isayev, E. 2013. "Italian perspectives in the period of Gracchan land reforms and the Social War." In A. Gardner, E. Herring, and K. Lomas eds, *Creating Ethnicities and Identities in the Roman World*. Bulletin of the Institute of Classical Studies, Suppl. 120. London, 9–32.

Isayev, E. in press. *Migration Mobility and Place in Ancient Italy*. Cambridge: Cambridge Universtty Press.

Keay, S. and Terrenato, N., eds. 2001. *Italy and the West. Comparative issues in Romanization*. Oxford: Oxbow.

Keppie, L.J.F. 1984. *The Making of the Roman Army, from Republic to Empire*. London: Batsford.

Kraus, C.S. and A.J. Woodman. 1997. *Latin Historians*. Oxford: Oxford University Press for the Classical Association.

La Regina, A. 1976. "Il Sannio." In *Hellenismus in Mittelitalien*, ed. P. Zanker, 219–44. Göttingen: Vandenhoeck und Ruprecht.

Laurence, R. 1999. *The Roads of Roman Italy. Mobility and social change*. London: Routledge.

Lloyd, J.A. 1995. "Pentri, Frentani and the beginnings of urbanisation (500–80 BC)." In *A Mediterranean Valley: Landscape archaeology and Annales history in the Biferno valley*, ed. G. Barker, 181–212. London: Leicester University Press.

Lomas, K. 1993. *Rome and the Western Greeks, 350 BC–AD 200. Conquest and acculturation in south Italy*. London: Routledge.

Mattingly, D.J. 1997. "Dialogues of power and experience in the Roman empire." In *Dialogues in Roman Imperialism. Power, discourse, and discrepant experience in the Roman empire*, ed. D. J. Mattingly, 7–24. Portsmouth, RI: *Journal of Roman Archaeology* Suppl. 23.

Mattingly, D.J. 2004. "Being Roman: expressing identity in a provincial setting." *Journal of Roman Archaeology* 17: 5–25.

Mattingly, D.J. 2011. *Imperialism, Power and Identity. Experiencing the Roman empire*. Princeton: Princeton University Press.

Morel, J.P. 1969. "L'atelier des petites estampilles." *Mélanges de l'Ecole Française de Rome, Antiquité* 81: 1–59.

Morelli, C. 1997. "Dalla devozione popolare alla 'follia terapeutica': le terrecotte votive." In *I luoghi degli dei: sacro e natura nell'Abruzzo antico*, eds A. Campanelli and A. Faustoferri, 89–98. Chieti: Carsa Edizioni.

Mouritsen, H. 2006. "Hindsight and historiography. Writing the history of pre-Roman Italy." In *Herrschaft ohne integration? Rom und Italien in der republikanischer zeit*, eds H.M. Jehne and R. Pfeilschifter, 23–37. Frankfurt: Verlag Antike.

Mouritsen, H. 2007. "The *civitas sine suffragio*: ancient concepts and modern ideology." *Historia* 56.2: 141–58.

Oakley, S.P. 1993. "The Roman conquest of Italy." In *War and Society in the Roman World*, eds J. Rich and G. Shipley, 9–37. London: Routledge.

Oakley, S.P. 1997–2005. *A Commentary on Livy, Books VI–X* (4 vols). Oxford: Clarendon Press.

Pallottino, M. 1979. "The origins of Rome." In *Italy before the Romans: the Iron Age, Orientalizing, and Etruscan periods*, eds D. Ridgway and F.R. Ridgway, 197–222. London: Academic Press.

Patterson, J.R. 2006. "Colonisation and historiography: the Roman Republic." In *Greek and Roman Colonization. Origins, ideologies and interactions*, eds G. Bradley and J-P. Wilson, 189–218. Swansea: Classical Press of Wales.

Pelgrom, J. 2012. *Colonial Landscapes. Demography, settlement organization and impact of colonies founded by Rome (4th–2nd centuries BC)*. Unpublished PhD thesis. University of Leiden.

Raaflaub, K. 1996. "Born to be wolves? Origins of Roman Imperialism." In *Transitions to Empire: Essays in Greco-Roman History, 360–146 B.C., in honor of E. Badian*, eds R.W. Wallace and W.V. Harris, 271–314. Norman, OK/ London: University of Oklahoma Press.

Roselaar, S.T. 2010. *Public Land in the Roman Republic. A social and economic history of ager publicus in Italy, 396–89 BC*. Oxford: Oxford University Press.

Roselaar, S.T., ed. 2012. *Processes of Integration and Identity Formation in the Roman Republic*. Leiden: Brill.

Roth, R. 2007. *Styling Romanisation. Pottery and society in central Italy*. Cambridge: Cambridge University Press.

Salmon, E.T. 1967. *Samnium and the Samnites*. Cambridge: Cambridge University Press.

Salmon, E.T. 1969. *Roman Colonization under the Republic*. London: Thames & Hudson.

Scopacasa, R. 2007. *Essere Sannita. Rappresentazioni di un popolo italico nelle fonti letterarie e storiografiche antiche*. Campobasso: Istituto Regionale per gli Studi Storici del Molise "V. Cuoco".

Scopacasa, R. 2015a. *Ancient Samnium: Settlement, culture and identity between history and archaeology*. Oxford: Oxford University Press.

Scopacasa, R. 2015b. "Moulding cultural change: a contextual approach to anatomical votive terracottas in Central Italy, fourth-second centuries BC." *Papers of the British School at Rome* 83: 1–27.

Scullard, H.H. 1967. *The Etruscan Cities and Rome*. London: Thames & Hudson.

Serrati, J. 2006. "Neptune's altars: the treaties between Rome and Carthage (509–226 B.C.)." *Classical Quarterly* 56: 113–34.

Sherwin-White, A.N. 1973, 2nd edn. *The Roman Citizenship*. Oxford: Clarendon Press.

Sherwin-White, A.N. 1980. "Rome the aggressor?" *Journal of Roman Studies* 70: 177–81.

Smith, C.J. 1996. *Early Rome and Latium: Economy and society c. 1000–500 BC*. Oxford: Clarendon Press.

Stek, T.D. 2009. *Cult Places and Cultural Change in Republican Italy: A contextual approach to religious aspects of rural society after the Roman conquest*. Amsterdam: Amsterdam University Press.

Tagliamonte, G. 1996. *I Sanniti. Caudini, Irpini, Pentri, Carricini, Frentani*. Milan: Longanesi.

Taylor, L.R. 1960. *The Voting Districts of the Roman Republic*. Rome: American Academy in Rome.

Terrenato, N. 1998. "*Tam firmum municipium*: The Romanization of Volaterrae and its cultural implications." *Journal of Roman Studies* 88: 94–114.

Terrenato, N. 2007. "The clans and the peasants. Reflections on social structure and change in Hellenistic central Italy." In *Articulating Local Cultures. Power and identity under the expanding Roman Republic*, eds P. van Dommelen and N. Terrenato, 13–22. Portsmouth, RI: *Journal of Roman Archaeology* Suppl. 63.

Terzani, C. 1991. "La colonia latina di Aesernia." In *Samnium. Archeologia del Molise*, eds S. Capini and A. Di Niro, 111–12. Rome: Quasar.

Torelli, M. 2002. *Benevento romana*. Rome: «L'Erma» di Bretschneider.

Webster, J. and N. Cooper, eds. 1996. *Roman Imperialism: Post-colonial perspectives*. Leicester: University of Leicester.

Wiseman, T.P. 1971. *New Men in the Roman Senate*. London: Oxford University Press.

CHAPTER 3

Italy and the Greek East, Second Century BC

Celia E. Schultz

3.1 Introduction

The second century BC is bracketed by two important Roman military victories. The first, over Hannibal and the Carthaginians near the city of Zama in what is now Tunisia in the year 202 BC, established Rome as the predominant power in the Mediterranean and greatly expanded its sphere of influence. The second, over the Cimbri at Vercellae (mod. Vercelli) in northeast Italy in 101 BC, stopped the encroachment of Germanic tribes on Roman territory. The ramifications of these events on life in Italy were largely political and military, with limited impact on the cultural development of the Romans themselves. In contrast, Rome's increasing political and military entanglement in the Greek East during the century between these two victories was to have a substantial impact on nearly every aspect of life in the Italian peninsula and contributed, in ways that are still subject to debate, to the political crisis suffered by the Roman state in the 130s and 120s BC that crystallized in the tribunates of Tiberius Sempronius Gracchus (133 BC) and his younger brother Gaius (123–122 BC).

The subject of the present chapter is the second century as an extended moment in the history of Roman, and more broadly Italian, interaction with Greeks and Greek culture. Our period is unevenly documented: the first half is relatively well documented because Livy's account is extant through the events of 167 BC; Polybius's, though fragmentary, survives in large pieces and can be supplemented by passages scattered throughout other authors. The first book of Appian's *Civil Wars* provides our only detailed description of the important agricultural changes that took place in our period. More details can be gleaned from Plutarch's biographies of prominent men of the period. Unfortunately, much of the literature produced in the second century BC by the Greeks and the Romans is lost or is preserved only in fragments. The major exceptions to this rule are, of course, Polybius's history and Cato's *On Agriculture*. After a sketch of Roman interaction with the Greeks in the third and second centuries BC, we shall turn to a consideration of some of the major ramifications of that engagement (See Figure 3.1).

A Companion to Roman Italy, First Edition. Edited by Alison E. Cooley.
© 2016 John Wiley & Sons, Ltd. Published 2016 by John Wiley & Sons, Ltd.

Figure 3.1   Map of Italy and the Greek East. Drawing: Christopher Ratté.

3.2   Romans and Greeks to 205 BC

First, it will bear pointing out that the Romans were never entirely free from the influence of, or interaction with, Greeks. Greek ways of life were introduced to the Romans and their Italic and Etruscan neighbors not directly from mainland Greece itself, but rather by those Greeks who had settled in colonies in south Italy and Sicily as early as the mid-eighth century BC. At that time, Rome was just one among many small, unimportant Latin villages. The cultural and social impact of the Greek colonists on the native populations was significant: there is ample archaeological evidence, in the form of imported Greek pottery and votives in Etruscan and Italic settlements, to suggest extensive interaction among the upper social strata of the various ethnic groups (Cornell, 1995: 86–97). Numa Pompilius, the second king of Rome, was supposed to have been associated with the philosopher Pythagoras, who had settled in south Italy in the latter half of the sixth century BC. Later writers pointed out the chronological impossibility (Dionysius of Halicarnassus, *Roman Antiquities*: 2.59.1–2; Cicero, *On the Republic*: 2.28.1–9.2; Livy: 1.18.1–4). In the late fourth and third centuries BC, we start to find consuls with Greek *cognomina*.

Greek culture penetrated to the very core of Roman society. For example, Romans embraced the story of the Trojan leader Aeneas as the founder of their people if not their city, thus linking the origins of Rome to the Trojan War. This is first preserved for us in a fragment of the Greek writer Alcimus who wrote in the later fourth century BC (Festus, *On the Meaning of Words*: 326, 328L; Gruen, 1992: 15–16). Another prime example of early Hellenization is the Sibylline Books, prophetic texts of central importance to the Romans' relationship with their gods. Tradition said that the Books had come to Rome in the sixth century BC and that they contained the utterances of the Sibyl, a priestess who was inspired to prophecy by the Greek god Apollo (Dionysius of Halicarnassus, *Roman Antiquities* 4.62.1–6) and who had lived at Cumae, the first Greek settlement on the Italian mainland (Parke and McGing, 1988: 71–99, 190–215).

Because the Books purported to be direct communications from the god himself through his priestess, they were unusual at Rome. In general the Romans preferred technical divination, such as augury or extispicy, which allowed the testing of interpretations against a received body of knowledge. The Greeks were always more comfortable with natural divination, such as inspired prophecy and dreams. The Greekness of the Books is further underscored by the fact that they were written in Greek hexameters (the only extant prophecy from the Books is preserved in Phlegon, *On Marvels*: 10). Consulted in times of crisis, the Books often sent the Romans to seek resolution to their problems in the Greek world through, for example, the importation of a Greek god, such as Aesculapius from Epidaurus in 291 BC, Venus Erycina from Eryx in Sicily in 217, and Cybele from Pergamon in 204 BC.

The Romans were aware of the wider Greek world long before their first sustained military engagement in the region. They made dedications at Delphi in 394 BC (in honor of their victory over Veii – Livy: 5.28.1–5, Valerius Maximus: 1.1. ext. 4) and again in 222 BC (for victory over the Gauls – Plutarch, *Life of Marcellus*: 8.6 with 30.4) and maintained diplomatic relations with Greeks on the east coast of the Adriatic, particularly with Alexander I of Epirus in the later fourth century (Justinus, *Epitome*: 12.2.1–15). This political engagement seems to have followed after commercial interaction: Italian traders were already frequent visitors to the region. Eventually, diplomacy was not enough. Rome's first military foray across the Adriatic was in response to piracy against Italian traders, primarily from the Latin colony of Brundisium but also probably from some of Rome's Italiote Greek allies (that is, allied Greek communities in Italy), by the Illyrians in 229 BC (Polybius: 2.1–12; Appian, *Illyrian Wars*: 7–8; Dio Cassius: 12, fr. 49 = Zonaras: 8.19). Commercial interests might also have been behind Rhodes' diplomatic efforts toward Rome in 305 BC (Polybius: 30.5.6–8, though see Walbank, 1957–79: 3.423–25).

Roman activity east of the Adriatic in this period was intermittent: most Roman experience with Greeks came from the Italiote cities in the south of Italy. Friendly relations between Rome and her Greek neighbors are implied by events like the receipt of grain from Cumae and other Greek cities during famines in the sixth and fifth centuries BC (Dionysius of Halicarnassus, *Roman Antiquities*: 12.1.9) and the importation of Venus from Eryx in Sicily (see earlier). Cooperation gave way, however, to armed conflict as Roman power expanded throughout the peninsula in the third century BC (a good summary of this period can be found in Lomas, 1993: 39–84) and encroached on the Greek sphere of influence in south Italy. The growing tension came to a head in 280 BC with the opening of the hostilities between Rome and Tarentum, the most powerful of the Italiote cities.

By 275 BC, the Romans had defeated the Tarentines and Pyrrhus, the King of Epirus, who had been brought in by Tarentum to fight on its behalf. The victory confirmed Rome's position as the dominant power in Italy and established it as a rival to the other Mediterranean powers, the great Hellenistic states (Ptolemaic Egypt, the Seleucid Empire, and Antigonid Macedonia), Greek cities, and, most importantly, Carthage. Overtures of friendship soon followed from Ptolemy II Philadelphus of Egypt, and an embassy was sent to Rome by the city of Apollonia on the eastern Adriatic coast, though its exact purpose is unknown (Livy: Books 14 and 15 Summary/*Periocha*; Valerius Maximus: 6.6.5). Less friendly were interactions between the Romans and the Carthaginians. Rome began the first of three wars against Carthage a mere eleven years after defeating Pyrrhus. When Carthage finally fell to the Romans in 241 BC, so, too, did many Greek cities of Sicily. A Roman alliance with Hiero, king of Syracuse, effectively brought about Roman control of the whole island.

At the end of the First Carthaginian War, the Romans continued to focus their attention westward. As regards the Greeks in the East, Rome continued its earlier policy of limited engagement on an ad hoc basis aimed at protecting its own interests on the eastern coast of the Adriatic. The Romans made no effort to engage with those further east, nor were they interested in establishing a permanent presence in the Balkan Peninsula. Rome conducted a brief war in 219 BC against the Illyrians, whose expansionist activities had threatened Roman shipping interests. Immediately thereafter, Rome's attention was diverted for several years by the Second Carthaginian War (218–202 BC).

By 215 BC, however, the senate again was compelled to involve itself on the other side of the Adriatic. By chance, Roman ships had intercepted a Macedonian vessel carrying several high-ranking Carthaginians and a draft of a treaty that established an alliance between Hannibal and Philip of Macedon (Livy: 23.38.1–7; Polybius: 7.9.1–17). The initial response was rather measured – a strengthening of the Roman fleet off the coast of Apulia – but a year later, when Philip attacked several Greek towns friendly to Rome, it was now clear that some more vigorous action was required. Since Rome was already engaged with Carthage in Spain, Sicily, and Italy, they sought a Greek ally to take on the brunt of the war with Philip. The Aetolian league answered the call. When, after some initial allied success, the First Macedonian War reached a stalemate and ultimately petered out in 205 BC, the Romans had already turned their attention away from Greece to focus on Italy and North Africa. Yet the stage was set for expanded Roman engagement and long-term entanglement with the Greeks beyond the Adriatic.

3.3   Romans and Greeks in the Second Century BC

The conclusion of the First Macedonian War left Rome with many friends and allies in the East. Over the course of the second century, as power shifted among the Hellenistic kingdoms, Macedonia and Syria each tried to expand its influence in the region as Egypt's power declined. Many Greek polities sought protection in alliance with Rome. Time and again, Rome responded, simultaneously protecting the interests of its friends and expanding its own sphere of influence. Rome's motivation and the nature of Roman dominance in the East have been the subject of vigorous debate of late.

Until the 1970s, the prevailing interpretation of the relationship between Rome and the weaker powers over which she exerted some form of control was that it was, in essence, defensive imperialism: Roman hegemony arose as an unintended consequence of engagement in a series of conflicts for more limited aims. There was no overarching Roman drive for domination. An important and influential critique of this view was then advanced by a school of historians, the most significant of whom is W.V. Harris. In a series of publications (esp. Harris, 1979), Harris emphasizes certain aspects of Roman culture and the undeniable economic advantages in the acquisition of empire as part of his argument that Roman actions in the third and second centuries BC were essentially aggressive, part of a deliberate move toward empire.

Harris's interpretation has been widely, but not universally, accepted. Two of the most forceful correctives have come from Gruen (1984) and Eckstein (2008). Although their approaches are very different – Gruen offers a close and critical reading of the sources, the traditional method of the modern study of ancient history, and Eckstein borrows a theoretical framework (Realism) from the study of modern international relations – both strive to set Rome's behavior into the wider Mediterranean context, emphasizing the "pull" of Greek interests rather than the "push" of Roman desire. This school of thought does not deny that Rome was a heavily militaristic society nor that it was interested in arranging things to its own advantage, but it also sees Rome as just one of many powers operating in the East, none of them with a grand plan for domination.

Further Roman engagement in the East came almost immediately after the conclusion of the First Macedonian War in 205 BC. The Romans had failed to curtail the expansionist aims of Philip, Macedonia's king, and by late 201 BC, Rhodes and Pergamum sent ambassadors to

Rome seeking aid against Philip's activities in Greece and Asia Minor (Livy: 31.2.1–2). Roman troops were in Greece early the next year, and the Second Macedonian War, which would run until 196 BC, was under way. The Romans' objective seems to have been to protect their allies and to check any potential rivals to Roman influence in the region. At the end of the war, a greatly weakened Philip maintained control in Macedonia, and the Roman general T. Quinctius Flamininus, who had brought the war to a conclusion, announced the freedom of all Greeks in Europe and Asia (the wording was critical; Polybius: 18.44.2) with great fanfare at the Isthmian Games. The Greek audience received the news with such enthusiasm that, Plutarch tells us, their loud cheering caused birds to drop dead out of the sky (*Life of Flamininus*: 10.3–6).

This second engagement with Philip, in fact, established a pattern that was to be repeated in the succeeding decades: Greek allies raised complaints about an expanding eastern power; Rome responded; the offending party was left weakened but otherwise intact; Roman interests were protected and expanded; and then the Romans went home, leaving the area in the control of Rome's friends. The pattern was repeated just a few years later in Rome's war with King Antiochus III of Syria, who had taken advantage of Philip's preoccupation with the Romans to move into Asia Minor and even across the Hellespont into Europe. With the declaration of freedom of the Greeks in Greece and Asia in 196 BC, the Romans sent a message to Antiochus that, as far as they were concerned, the region was within their sphere of influence. Thus when Pergamum and Rhodes again complained of encroachment on their territory, Rome responded. As a result of the Syrian War (192–188 BC), the Romans had removed Antiochus from Europe and Asia Minor, leaving him greatly weakened, but still in control of much of his Asiatic empire.

Rome's handling of Philip and Antiochus was rather restrained. This ended, however, with the Third Macedonian War (171–168 BC), a conflict so long in coming that Livy claims it was planned by Philip but carried out by his son, Perseus (Livy: 42.11.1–9). Perseus ascended the throne upon Philip's death in 180 BC. Over the course of the 170s BC, Perseus successfully positioned Macedonia as an alternative to Rome for Greek states seeking a more powerful ally. He also reinforced his ties to other Hellenistic kings with dynastic marriages: his own marriage to a daughter of Seleucus of Syria and his sister's to Prusias of Bithynia. Roman irritation grew until Eumenes of Pergamum came to Rome in 172 BC to lodge complaints against Perseus. Reaction was swift and, this time, the resolution was permanent. After their victory at Pydna in 168 BC, the Romans broke Macedonia into four independent republics. Perseus and his family were taken to Rome as captives. His Greek allies were also punished. The kingdom of Illyria was dismantled. The Achaeans, whose allegiance to the Romans had been insufficiently on display, were required to turn over a thousand hostages whose loyalties were suspect. Worse was in store for the Aetolians, whose relationship with Rome had deteriorated since 205 BC: more than 500 leading men were killed and others exiled. In Epirus, Roman soldiers were permitted to sack 70 towns that had gone over to Perseus, and 150 000 people were sold into slavery (Polybius: 30.15.1).

The political configuration of the Balkan Peninsula was much changed after 168 BC, but the restructuring was not yet finished. The end of Greek independence and the nearly complete integration of the Greeks into the Roman world came 20 years later when Rome stepped into a conflict between Sparta and the Achaean League. The events leading up to the Achaean War of 146 BC and the motivations of all parties involved are difficult to reconstruct and interpret (Gruen, 1976), but the ramifications of the victory brought about by L. Mummius, which included the razing of the Achaeans' capital of Corinth and the establishment of Macedonia as a Roman province, are clear. The interconnectedness of East and West was permanent; the Greeks were no longer truly independent; Rome's direct control of part of the East was firmly established and poised to grow.

3.4.1   The impact on Italy: political and demographic

The military successes of the second century sparked a cultural and political transformation of Roman and Italian society remarkable for the speed at which it occurred and for the comprehensiveness of its scope. Both pace and scope are due to the ease with which people and commerce moved between East and West.

At an official level, there were of course soldiers and generals from Italy now moving about in the East. There was also a far greater number of senators, many of whom may not have had prior direct experience with Greeks outside Italy, now traveling to Greece and Asia Minor as part of official delegations and fact-finding missions. Even those senators who stayed in Rome had more first-hand experience with Greeks as a great many delegations, and even a few Greek kings, came to petition the senate. Also in the city for a more extended period were numerous aristocratic Greek hostages, including the children of some of the Greek kings and the thousand Achaeans who resided in Rome from 167 to 150 BC. Among them was the historian Polybius, who developed long-lasting friendships with Scipio Aemilianus and other high-ranking Romans. The Roman elite also interacted with the numerous Greek intellectuals and artists (including sculptors, painters, and architects) who came to meet the demand for refinement and luxury in Rome (see section 3.4.2 of this chapter).

Commercial traffic flowed not just into Italy but out from it as well. Epigraphic and literary evidence makes clear that far greater numbers of Roman citizens and traders from elsewhere in Italy, especially from Campania and further south, were active throughout the East than there had been previously (Wilson, 1966: 94–126; Lomas: ch.13 this vol.). The best attested community is that of the *Italikoi* (so identified regardless of what citizenship they actually held back home in Italy) on the island of Delos, one of the major commercial hubs in the eastern Mediterranean. Ample epigraphic documentation has allowed scholars to identify these *negotiatores* as a mix of Romans and other Italians, including Oscans and Italiote Greeks. Many came from locally prominent families, and most were engaged in banking or in Delos's primary industry, the slave trade (Hatzfeld, 1912; Strabo, *Geography*. 14.5.2; Lomas: ch.13, this vol.).

It was common practice in ancient warfare, including among the Romans, to sell into slavery captured and conquered enemy combatants and many civilians as well. Plutarch (*Life of Flamininus*: 13.4–6) and Livy (37.60.3–7) report the repatriation of thousands of Roman and allied men who had been captured by Hannibal and sold as slaves in Greece. Given the Romans' long string of military victories, however, they were far more often the purchasers than the purchased. The wars fought in the East between 201 and 167 BC are said by our sources to have added 300 000 slaves to the market – a number that does not include those taken in the conflicts in northern Italy and Spain in the same period (Scheidel, 2011: 294). Italy benefited economically both from the profits of the sale of captives, and from the relatively low cost of slave labor.

The traditional interpretation of the impact of the influx of people and wealth from the East on Italy has remained, until recently, largely unchallenged. A vigorous debate about the nature of life in second-century Italy has been sparked, however, by the application of new archaeological techniques and of statistical modeling borrowed from the social sciences, both of which have produced results that seem to contradict the portrait painted by the ancient sources. No new consensus has yet arisen. It will, therefore, be worthwhile to review the standard position, taken over almost wholesale from the ancient literature, and some of the critiques of it.

The orthodox position follows a tidy narrative. As the Romans took control of more land in peninsular Italy in the fourth and third centuries BC, the numbers of small farms increased. The demands of nearly 120 years of almost uninterrupted military conflict on several fronts (especially during the Second Carthaginian War), however, resulted in a significant depletion of the freeborn Roman and Italian population to work those farms. As a result, many were abandoned by the early second century BC. At the same time, victories overseas resulted in a tremendous influx of wealth to Italy in the form of indemnities, booty, and commercial profits. Most of that wealth ended up in the hands of a relatively small portion of the population, some of whom used it to buy out small farms and convert them into large, slave-run industrial plantations called *latifundia* (on the term, see White, 1967). The *latifundia* grew luxury crops or supported massive herds of animals that grazed on huge swaths of *ager publicus* taken over from their former allies by the Romans in the aftermath of the Hannibalic War. It has been thought that this new type of farm was perhaps imported from Carthage, Greece, the south of Italy, or Etruria. Families displaced from their homesteads flocked to urban centers, especially Rome, swelling the number of unlanded poor. Because there was a property requirement for military service, not enough men were available to serve in the army. The result was an unstable situation of insufficiently manned legions, large numbers of minimally supervised slaves, unruly crowds of impoverished citizens in the city, and growing anger among the allies at the loss of their land and at Rome's imperious behavior. All of this served as the backdrop to the political crisis and the Gracchan land reform efforts of the late 130s and 120s BC. The tensions that those reforms could not alleviate boiled over in the late 90s BC in the Social War (see Bispham: ch.4, this vol.).

With some variation in detail, this is the scenario described by Appian (*Civil Wars*: 1.7.1) and Plutarch (*Life of Tiberius Gracchus*: 8.1–9.5), both of whom wrote in the second century AD. Their accounts draw support from Livy, who records instances where established colonies requested from the Roman senate that their populations be replenished, as in the cases of Venusia (31.49.6), Narnia (32.2.7), Cosa (33.24.8–9), and Cremona and Placentia (37.46.9–11), and where allies had difficulty meeting the quota of soldiers they were obligated to supply (e.g., Livy: 41.8.6–12). Livy and others also preserve population counts that buttress the idea that the Roman citizen population declined dramatically after the Hannibalic War, such as a drop from 214 000 adult male citizens in 204 BC (Livy: 29.37.5–6) to 143 704 in 194 BC (Livy: 35.9.2). Increases in subsequent censuses can be attributed in large part to the extension of citizenship to other groups in Italy. Scattered references in several authors indicate a steady decline in the property qualification for service in the army, suggesting there were not enough small landholders to fill the legions (Gabba, 1976: 1–19). A rare piece of contemporary evidence, Cato's *On Agriculture*, describes the proper management of slave-run farms that produced cash-crops for market (see Pollard: ch.17, this vol.). There is also some literary evidence for large-scale transhumant pastoralism, that is, the movement of herds of animals from warmer lowland pastures in the winter to cooler pastures at higher elevations in the summer. The growing slave population, left largely unsupervised, is thought to have been the root cause of the three large slave revolts and several smaller uprisings that occurred between 136 and 71 BC (Bradley, 1989: 18–20).

The two critical elements that form the lynchpin of this elegant reconstruction – the expansion of industrial farming driven by slave labor and the dwindling numbers of small landholders – have been called into question in recent decades. We shall take up each of these in turn. The most unreliable evidence is precisely that which appears the most author-itative at first glance (Brunt, 1971: 15–120): the census figures preserved mostly by Livy, with important supplements from Polybius and a handful of other authors (a complete list is found in Toynbee 1965: 1.438–40). At the most basic level, numbers are prone to corruption in the manuscript tradition: it is entirely possible that the numbers we have are not the numbers our authors wrote. Even if these numbers are accurate, we are not certain what they represent. Just *iuniores*, that is those of military age (17–45)? Or does the number include all adult males? Only those who were *sui iuris*, free from the authority of their fathers (*patria potestas*)?

Only those who were *assidui*, meaning they met the minimum property qualification for military service? Do the numbers include soldiers serving abroad at the time of the census? Do they include both adult men and adult women? Perhaps children, too? An additional complication for historians arises from the straightforward difficulty of conducting a census in a society without street addresses and a population that had disincentive to register because of conscription and taxation, for example. We cannot tell how accurate any given census number might be. The likelihood that any is accurate is very low, as is the likelihood that they are all inaccurate to the same degree. No real consensus exists concerning the answers to these basic questions of inclusion and accuracy (see the various, sometimes conflicting, approaches in de Ligt and Northwood, 2008).

The answer to the question of who was counted in the census is critical since it affects how scholars have estimated the size of the Roman population and, by extension, the population of Italy during the Republic. The total population numbers will necessarily include many unregistered individuals, who are estimated at a certain percentage of those who were counted officially, the proportion depending on what class(es) of individuals are thought to be represented in the census numbers. A few scholars (most notably Lo Cascio, 1994; Lo Cascio and Malanima, 2005) subscribe to a "high count" of about 10 million in mainland Italy over the second century with rapid growth to twice that number in the high Empire. In this scenario, mid-Republican Italy had a rather well-populated countryside, larger urban centers, and a lower rate of militarization, that is, the percentage of the adult male population serving in the legions. A more popular and more persuasive scenario, however, is the "low count" of somewhere in the neighborhood of 5 million people in the second century and a moderate growth rate (Brunt, 1971: 121–30). This means that the ancient Italian countryside was sparsely populated and urban centers were on the smaller side. Another ramification of a smaller population is that the rate of militarization must have been higher. The advantages of each of the two schools of thought are compared in Scheidel (2008: 17–70).

Another sector of the population certainly not included in the census numbers is the slave population. The sources are unanimous that slavery in Italy expanded during the second century as a direct result of Roman activities in the East, yet none provides any notion of the real scope of the issue. Scholars have tried to get around this by estimating the slave population at approximately one-third of the total population, a figure extrapolated from the percentage of slaves in nineteenth-century United States and Brazil (e.g., Bradley, 1994: 12; 2011: 244). A stronger approach is taken by Scheidel (2005), who attempts a quantitative reconstruction through an estimation of the number of slaves likely to have been in Italy (given the needs of urban elites and agricultural producers) and an estimation of the rate of attrition of the slave population already in Italy, which in turn points to the rate at which the slave population was replenished by imports from abroad. He concludes that Italy's slave population was significantly smaller than is usually thought: 600 000 by the late Republic rather than somewhere between two and three million. But even this is a "highly tenuous conjecture" (Scheidel, 2011: 289).

Scheidel's reconstruction differs from the orthodox position in another respect: he concludes that the slave population in Italy was concentrated in urban centers rather than in agricultural areas. This contradicts what the ancient sources say (e.g., Appian, *Civil Wars*. 1.7), but is in line with recent archaeological work that poses a significant challenge to the idea that the slave mode of agricultural production was widespread in this period. Growing interest in the excavation of sites away from the major ancient metropoleis of west-central Italy has combined with the introduction of systematic regional survey (a technique that aims to get a sense of human activity of an entire region by surface reconnaissance of material evidence, well described in Alcock, 2007) to produce a very different picture of rural Italy. First, small farms appear throughout a much wider swath of Italy and at an earlier period than previously thought, suggesting that the expansion is not tied directly or exclusively to the spread of Roman influence in Italy during the fourth and third centuries BC. Second, the small farms seem neither to have declined in number nor to have fallen into disuse over the course of the second century BC, but rather remained a vibrant part of the rural landscape. Also interesting is what all this recent archaeological work has *not* found: great numbers of large villa estates. While earlier excavations of the 1960s and 1970s did find a few villas along the coast of Campania and southern Etruria, similar farms have been scarce elsewhere. Furthermore, villas that have been found date largely to the first century BC, after the Gracchan crisis (Terrenato, 2007).

It is too soon to say what we should make of the apparent disconnect between the literary evidence that forms the basis for the orthodox narrative of the second century BC and the recent revelations of demography and archaeology. Because these findings are so new, their verification is not very far advanced. At the very least, a re-evaluation of the literary sources is in order. Indeed, Cato's *On Agriculture* in particular has been subject to re-readings that treat it as an exercise in aristocratic self-fashioning (Reay, 2005; 2012; Terrenato, 2012) rather than as a straightforward manual on how to run a farm. The narratives of Appian and Plutarch remain, however, difficult to explain away. One thing is clear: once the dust settles, a fresh new synthesis of the impact of Rome's rise to power on life in the Italian peninsula will need to be written.

3.4.2   *The impact on Italy: cultural*

As Roman hegemony in the East expanded, money, art, and people flowed westward into Rome at an unprecedented pace. Whereas the political and social repercussions of this influx are highly controversial, we are on firmer territory with the impact this wave of Greeks and Greekness had on the cultural life of Roman Italy. As has been mentioned earlier, Roman and Italian elites had used their wealth to acquire Greek luxury goods from a very early point in their history: the passion for all things Greek is not new in the second century BC. What is new, again, is the scale on which Greek ideas and products were brought into Italy and the extent to which they permeated all aspects of the culture already established.

Our sources pinpoint the beginning of the Romans' passion for Greek art to the triumph of M. Claudius Marcellus over Syracuse in 211 BC (Livy: 25.40.1–2; Plutarch, *Life of Marcellus*: 21.1–5). In addition to the traditional sale of captives into slavery, Marcellus brought back to Rome statues and paintings from the conquered city. Two years later, Q. Fabius Maximus Cunctator brought back statues and paintings from Tarentum, although he preferred to leave the statues of the gods in their destroyed city (Livy: 27.16.7–8; Pliny the Elder, *Natural History*: 34.40). Flamininus and the other Roman generals who were active in Greece in the decades following also brought home works of art for display in their triumphs (a full catalog can be found in Pollitt, 1978). Notable among them is M. Fulvius Nobilior, the conqueror of Ambracia in 189 BC, who brought back from Greece marble and bronze statues. His decision to leave behind the terracotta statues, even though some were by the famed sculptor Zeuxis, suggests that he had not yet become a real connoisseur of fine art (Pliny the Elder, *Natural History*: 35.66; cf. Livy: 34.4.4).

Some artworks disappeared into private collections, but many were set up in temples and other public spaces, often on bases that proclaimed the occasion of a piece's arrival in Italy and the name of the general responsible. Fabius Maximus dedicated a colossal Herakles from Tarentum on the Capitoline in Rome (Plutarch, *Life of Fabius Maximus*: 22.6). After his triumph over the Macedonians in 168 BC, L. Aemilius Paullus dedicated a statue of Athena by Pheidias in a shrine of Fortuna Huiusce Diei ("Fortune of this Day") on the Palatine (Pliny the Elder, *Natural History*: 34.54). In 148 BC, Q. Metellus dedicated in his new porticus-temple complex, the *Porticus Metelli* (*LTUR*: 4.130–2), the Granicus Monument, a group of 25 bronze statues of Alexander and the Companions that Metellus had taken from Macedonia. In the course of the second century, "Rome became a museum of Greek art" (Pollitt, 1978: 157) as many of the most important and famous works of art were transferred there. Yet it was not just the capital city that took in Greece's treasures. L. Mummius, conqueror of Corinth in 146 BC, kept none of the artwork he pillaged for himself ([Aurelius Victor] *On Famous Men*: 60.3), but adorned Rome and many other towns throughout Italy as well, as is attested by several statue bases such as these:

> L. *Mummius* | *cos. ded*(*it*) N(*ursinis*) (*CIL* 1² 628; from Nursia)
> "L. Mummius, the consul, gave this to the citizens of Nursia"

> L. *Mummius* | *cos.* P(*opulo*) P(*armensi*) (*CIL* 1² 629; from Parma)
> "L. Mummius, the consul, gave this to the people of Parma"

Not just moveable Hellenistic art, but also new forms of urban grandeur came to Italy. Rome was now a powerful capital city, and over the course of the second century BC it came to look like one. Most significant among the spate of building projects is the reconfiguration of the Roman Forum, which was in desperate need of revitalization after fires in 213 and 210 BC (Livy: 24.47.15–16; 26.27.1–4). Among the additions and improvements to the area were three *basilicae*, buildings of a relatively new type (only one earlier basilica, also in the Forum, is attested in Rome): the *Basilica Porcia* of 184 BC; the *Fulvia et Aemilia* of 179 BC, which replaced the only, older basilica already in the Forum; and the *Sempronia* of 169 BC (Richardson, 1991: 392–402). Although their exact model is subject to some debate (Welch, 2003), their name, derived from the Greek feminine adjective meaning "royal," implies that it lay in some sort of monumental structure associated with Hellenistic kings. These new buildings helped to change the Forum from an Italic central square surrounded by houses of the wealthy to something more like (but not identical to) a Greek public space surrounded by colonnades, giving it a dignity and monumentality that it did not have before. A famous example of this new kind of Greek-inspired adornment found outside Rome comes from Praeneste, where an elegant mosaic depicting the Nile river and the temples, peoples, plants, and animals found along its banks (all labeled in Greek) was on display in the building that housed the city's treasury, right off the Praenestine Forum (Meyboom, 1995).

Throughout Italy, new, more impressive, more elaborate temples began to appear. We have already mentioned the Granicus monument, imported from Macedonia and set up in Rome in 147 BC by Q. Caecilius Metellus Macedonicus in his new *Porticus Metelli*. The *porticus* itself surrounded two temples, those of Juno Regina and Jupiter Stator (Velleius Paterculus: 1.11.3–5; Vitruvius, *On architecture*: 3.2.5). Metellus rebuilt the latter temple completely in marble, a first at Rome. Both the material and the architect for the project, Hermodorus of Salamis, were Greek imports. Other marble temples soon followed, including the round temple of Hercules Olivarius in the *Forum Boarium*, the oldest marble temple standing in Rome today. These new structures differed from traditional Roman temples in their material and decoration: they were "purely and simply Greek temples transplanted to the banks of the Tiber" (Morel, 1989: 508). Indeed, Strabo refers to the temple of Venus Erycina dedicated in Rome in 181 BC as a copy of her temple in Sicily (*Geography*: 6.2.6). Statues of the gods became Hellenized, too: Greek marble came to replace the traditional materials of wood, terracotta, and bronze in cult statues throughout the city (Pliny the Elder, *Natural History*: 34.34).

Other cities also monumentalized their local cults on a grand scale as expressions of their own wealth, status, and community pride (Wallace-Hadrill, 2008: 73–143). A selective list includes sanctuaries at Fregellae, Tibur, and Tarracina in Latium close to Rome, but also

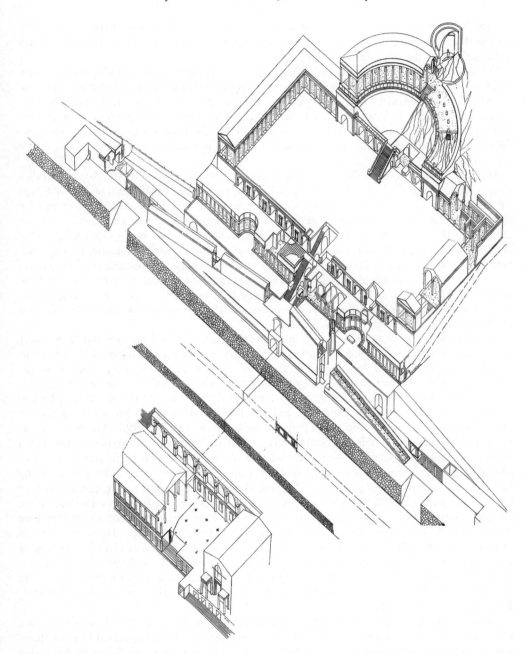

Figure 3.2 Sanctuary of Fortuna Primigenia, Praeneste. Redrawn by Christopher Ratté from F. Fasolo and G. Gullini, *Il Santuario di Fortuna Primigenia a Palestrina* (Istituto di archeologia, Università di Roma: Rome, 1953): vol. 2, plate 3.

further afield at Sulmo in Paelignian territory in east-central Italy and Macchia di Rossano in Lucania. The most impressive of these is the sanctuary of Fortuna Primigenia, built into a steep hillside at Praeneste (see Figure 3.2). The complex's multiple terraces are connected by staircases and ramps that imply the ritual movement of people and animals. The theatre-temple that crowns the hilltop offers a commanding view of the valley below. There is nothing at Rome to rival the grandeur of the place.

No area of life in the Italian peninsula was affected more than intellectual life, but here, too, this was not entirely new in the second century. Some form of Greek education was available by the early third century. The earliest record of Romans speaking Greek is an awkward address by the ambassador L. Postumius Megellus to a jeering audience of Tarentines in 282 BC (Dionysius of Halicarnassus, *Roman Antiquities*: 19.5.1–5). Things improved over time, and bilingual senatorial Romans with a strong foundation in Greek literature were not rare a century later.

The high value placed on Greek literature, philosophy, and science by the Romans finds a clear articulation in the story of L. Aemilius Paullus, the victor of Pydna in 168 BC, who kept for himself nothing of the tremendous wealth he brought back from Macedonia except for the royal library. Paullus instructed his sons, who already had the best Greek education he could give them, to take whatever volumes they wanted for themselves (Plutarch, *Life of Aemilius Paullus*: 28.10–11). They had accompanied him on campaign against Perseus and, before returning home, he had taken them on a tour of the major historical and religious sites of Greece. Paullus's son Scipio Aemilianus, who became close friends with Polybius and the philosopher Panaetius, would be viewed by later generations as the most outstanding man of his day, not just because of his military and political skills, but because of his intelligence and erudition (Velleius Paterculus: 1.12.3).

After Pydna, there were many Greek intellectuals at Rome: Polybius mentions how many he encountered there (31.24.6–7). But Greek writers, philosophers, and artists had been in Italy long before 168 BC. For some, like Polybius who was in Rome as a political hostage, their presence was a direct result of the political situation. Many came in a diplomatic capacity. Among them was the ambassador sent by Antiochus III to deal with the Romans at Delphi in 196 and at Rome in 193 BC, the poet and scholar Hegesianax, who had written a history of Troy that appears to have been flattering to the Romans (Farrow, 1992). Other diplomats took the opportunity to deliver popular lectures in Greek on scholarly topics, suggesting a Roman audience with a sophisticated knowledge of Greek and Greek literature. Crates of Mallos, the Stoic grammarian and literary critic, came to Rome in the second quarter of the second century, probably as part of the Pergamene delegation to assist with negotiations after the battle of Pydna in 168 BC. While taking a tour of the Forum, he broke his leg (Suetonius, *On Grammarians*: 2). To pass the time as he convalesced, he gave lectures on Greek literature that sparked an interest in textual criticism among his Roman audience. The major schools of Hellenistic philosophy were introduced by an embassy from Athens in 155 BC consisting of Carneades, head of the New Academy, Critolaus the Peripatetic, and the Stoic Diogenes of Babylon. Carneades's lectures for and against justice made a particular impression on the Romans, enthralling some and scandalizing others (Cicero, *On Oratory*: 2.155–6; Plutarch, *Life of Cato the Elder*: 22.2–5).

Greek-speaking writers had already started to come to Rome in the third century BC, though not always as willing immigrants. Livius Andronicus, whose impact on Roman litera-ture is nothing greater than giving it a start, was brought as a captive to Rome by M. Livius Salinator, victor in the war with Tarentum that ended in 272 BC. He was eventually freed and made his living as a *grammaticus*, offering instruction in Greek and Latin to aristocratic young Romans. Andronicus also wrote plays in Latin. These clearly had Hellenic models, but they were not direct translations of earlier Greek works. The performance of one such play at the *Ludi Romani* in 240 BC is generally identified as the birth of Latin literature.

Roman drama, both comedy and tragedy, maintained a close relationship to its Greek models (even when the subjects were purely Roman) while developing its own distinctive aesthetic. Theatrical works at Rome reached their height in the second century BC with the plays of other Greek-speaking transplants to Rome (Ennius, Pacuvius, Accius, Plautus, and Terence). Andronicus was also responsible for bringing epic poetry into Latin with his translation of Homer's *Odyssey*, rendered into Italic Saturnians. This same meter was also used by Naevius, another immigrant from Greek-speaking Italy (this time from Campania), in his *Bellum Poenicum*, an original epic account of the First Carthaginian War, in which Naevius had served on the Roman side.

Andronicus and Naevius created works that blended Greek and Roman traditions into something new, and Ennius brought this new literature to a higher level. As a member of a Calabrian contingent in the Roman army in 204 BC, Ennius came to the attention of M. Porcius Cato, then serving as quaestor under Scipio Africanus. Cato brought Ennius with him back to Rome, where the poet enjoyed the patronage of M. Fulvius Nobilior (the same fellow who left Zeuxis's terracotta statues untouched) and the friendship of Scipio Africanus and his family (Nepos, *Cato*: 1.4; Cicero, *Tusculan Disputations*: 1.3). Ennius spoke Oscan, Greek and Latin (Aulus Gellius, *Attic Nights*: 17.17.1), and proudly proclaimed his Roman citizenship (Skutsch, 1985: 525; Cicero, *For Archias*: 22). The range of his written works was prodigious: in addition to tragedies and comedies for the stage, Ennius wrote philosophical works and learned poetry in the Hellenistic tradition (e.g., the *Hedyphagetica*, a didactic poem on gastronomy, perhaps a reflection of the Romans' new-found appreciation of cooking as an art: see Bober, 1999: 169–84).

The work that established Ennius as Rome's national poet was his *Annales*, an epic account of Rome's history from Aeneas down to the author's own day. The extant fragments of the work are collected in Skutsch (1985). Ennius's poem was groundbreaking in several respects. First, Ennius eschewed the Saturnian meter of Andronicus and Naevius in favor of dactylic hexameters, the meter of Greek epic and prophecy. This demonstrated Ennius's artistry in adapting the language and the meter to each other: Ennius developed rules on word placement, the handling of vowels and the caesura, and established the proper style and diction for the epic form at Rome. Second, Ennius wedded a native Italic aesthetic to the Greek form, including the heavy use of alliteration, homoioteleuton, and paranomasia, all of which are common in archaic Latin but are rare in the refined Greek poetry of the Hellenistic period. Third, the *Annales* covered new ground in its subject, scope, and structure. It was an epic account of the whole sweep of a nation's history, not just the city's foundation and mythical past nor a single event. Ennius arranged his work in a year-by-year structure adapted from the oldest Roman archive of the *annales maximi* (see later in this chapter). Finally, Ennius presented a history of Rome that exemplified the *virtus* of the Roman elite, with success in war, wisdom and restraint in peace, and excellence in speaking, all in pursuit of the greater glory of the Roman state. Ennius presented the Romans to themselves at their best, linking his contemporaries to their noble ancestors. The *Annales* remained the quintessential school text until Virgil's *Aeneid* replaced it more than a century later.

Although Latin poetry found an eager audience in the Roman ruling class, the writing of it was left, for the most part, to those of foreign birth and lower social status. The prose genres of oratory, history, and to a lesser extent didactic works, however, were sufficiently dignified to be a proper pastime for senators and generals. The earliest Roman prose work appeared after the Hannibalic War: this was a history by the senator Q. Fabius Pictor, who had served as the Roman envoy sent to consult the oracle at Delphi in the aftermath of the military disasters of 216 BC. He wrote in Greek, probably so that he might better counter the Greek history of Philinus that took a decidedly pro-Carthaginian stance (Polybius: 1.14.1–15.13). Of course, most of Fabius's fellow senators would have been able to read his work as well.

It may have been written in Greek, but the structure of Fabius's work was thoroughly Roman. The history took its name (*Annales*) and basic arrangement of events, as did the great poetic work of his contemporary Ennius, from the *annales maximi*, bare bones records of events like eclipses, famines, and floods (Cicero, *On Oratory*. 2.51–54; Cornell, 1995: 13–16) maintained by the *pontifex maximus* and posted on boards outside the *Regia*, his home in the Forum. Annalistic histories, the dominant form of history at Rome from Fabius onward, are arranged on a year-by-year basis, presenting first domestic and then foreign affairs. The shift from one year to the next is punctuated by notices of election results, prodigy reports, and significant deaths, a mechanism that gives shape to an otherwise unwieldy large subject yet interrupts the narrative in an awkward fashion.

Several of Fabius's contemporaries–L. Cincius Alimentus, C. Acilius, and A. Postumius Albinus–all of senatorial status, followed him in writing annalistic histories in Greek. The latter apologized in his preface for his imperfect Greek, and was mocked for it by Cato (Aulus Gellius, *Attic Nights*. 11.8.1–5), whose hostility toward excessive Greek-style refinement and pretension among his countrymen will be discussed later in this chapter (section 3.5). Cato himself asserted the suitability of Latin to prose writing, starting a tradition of Latin prose histories with his *Origines*, a work in seven books that departed from the annalistic format. The first three books dealt with the origins of Rome and other Italic cities, whereas the remaining books covered relatively recent history from the First Carthaginian War down to at least 152 BC. Cato's innovation was partly successful: history at Rome was written thereafter in Latin, but *annales* remained the dominant form, reaching its apogee with Livy's *Ab Urbe Condita*. There was a flowering of experimentation with contemporary history, monographs of more narrow scope, and political autobiography around the time of the Gracchan crisis, as competing interests sought to establish the definitive account of the great schism in Roman Republican politics.

3.5   Resistance

The Roman enthusiasm for all things Greek was widespread, but it was not universal nor was it as uncomplicated as it has sometimes seemed. Modern scholars no longer perceive the Roman senate of the second century BC as divided between two parties, with a philhellenic group centered around the family of the Scipiones and their friends (the so-called Scipionic circle) and the opposition, headed by Cato, that strived to limit Greek influence in Rome and took a hard line regarding Rome's treatment of states in the East. In place of this schematic view, historians now favor a model that includes varying, sometimes conflicting, degrees of acceptance and intolerance at play among the Romans as, over time, they negotiated their new relationship to the most prestigious culture in the Mediterranean.

A good example of the intricacies of Roman attitudes is the reception of philosophy, an intellectual pursuit not native to Italy. There is no question that Greek philosophy found an enthusiastic audience in Rome, but it is also clear that there were limits to what the Romans could accept or absorb. At least twice, in either 173 or 154 and certainly in 161 BC, the senate decreed the expulsion of philosophers and rhetoricians from Rome (Athenaeus: 12.547a; Aulus Gellius, *Attic Nights*: 15.11.1; Suetonius, *Grammarians*: 25). Yet, only six years after the latter event, the Athenians accurately surmised that an embassy of three philosophers – prominent representatives of the Academic, Stoic, and Peripatetic schools – would be an effective diplomatic tool (section 3.4.2 of this chapter). Similar issues are raised by the two main foci for modern discussion of resistance to the Hellenization of Roman life – the crackdown on the cult of Bacchus in 186 BC and the career of M. Porcius Cato (consul 195, censor 184 BC). Neither now seems a straightforward example of Roman hostility to Greek culture. Where, for a long time, there was just black and white, there are now many, many shades of gray.

Despite being one of the better-documented events in the second century, the crisis of 186 BC remains a mystery. According to our main source, Livy's account in Book 39 (8.1–19.7), accusations of criminal activity under the cover of rites of the Hellenized cult of Bacchus (Dionysus, assimilated to Italic Liber Pater and Etruscan Fufluns) were brought to Rome's attention by the consul of the year, Sp. Postumius Albinus, who received his information from two people with direct experience of the cult, the equestrian Aebutius and his lover, the freedwoman Hispala Faecenia.

The senate's reaction to the news was swift and violent: legions were mobilized and 7000 people were punished; more were put to death than were jailed. This seems out of proportion to the crimes of which the cult members were accused (illicit sex, forgery of documents, corruption of the youth, perjury, and murder). In its scope, speed, and aggression, the reaction to Dionysiac rites far exceeds all other instances of senatorial curtailment of religious activity, such as the confiscation of religious writings and the ban on foreign-type sacrifices enforced in 213 BC and the expulsion of Chaldean astrologers and Jews in 139 BC. Even the imperial persecution of Christians does not match it.

It is difficult to know what to make of all this. Livy's story is not unimpeachable. Although on the whole coherent, it is also heavily colored by the author's hostility to his subject, contains significant inconsistencies in its details (North, 1979), and has strong structural similarities to stage productions, suggesting the narrative has been arranged for dramatic effect (Wiseman, 1998: 43–48). The extant paraphrase of the senate's actual decree on the matter, the so-called *senatus consultum de Bacchanalibus*, preserved in an inscription found at Tirolo in Bruttium (*CIL* 1² 581, the most thorough study of which remains Tierney, 1947), does not resolve many of the questions raised by Livy's account. It confirms much of what the historian says about the senate's actions, but it gives no indication of what moved the senate to act. Myriad explanations for the crackdown have been proposed, including the cult's undeniable Greekness (Gruen, 1990: 72–73). Yet if one puts Livy aside entirely and looks only at the *senatus consultum*, which is preoccupied with restricting the participation of citizen and allied men in the cult, it would seem that the senate's major concern was of a political nature (Schultz. 2006: 89–92; see also North, 1979).

Much is uncertain, but one thing is clear. The worship of Bacchus may have been objectionable for many reasons, but novelty was not one of them. This is suggested by Livy's own narrative (e.g. 39.13.14 and 14.4) and proved by ample evidence external to Livy that the cult had been widespread in Italy for centuries before the crackdown. There is archaeological evidence for its popularity among the upper classes in Etruria and Campania as early as the sixth century BC (Pailler, 1976; Colonna, 1991). The comedies of Plautus, who died in 184 BC, make clear that his Roman audience was well enough acquainted with the cult that the playwright could make jokes about it. Thus it seems unlikely that the cult's Greekness was the core of the problem in 186 BC. The answer to the question of what sparked the crisis will have to be sought elsewhere.

In the tradition that has come down to us, the loudest, most consistent criticism of the Greeks and Greek culture comes from M. Porcius Cato, whose political career spanned more than 60 years and touched on most of the important events of the second century. What remains of Cato's own works (the *De Agricultura* and fragments of his *Origines*, speeches, and minor works) is consistent with the characterization of him by later authors, as a vigorous defender of the traditional Roman values of frugality, moral uprightness, and sacrifice for the greater good. He was also a fierce critic of those who embraced Hellenic luxury. The danger of decadence brought about by Rome's new wealth is a consistent theme in the fragments of Cato's speeches. Livy gives him a lively speech defending the *lex Oppia* from repeal in 195 BC, at one point linking the need for the sumptuary law to Rome's eastward expansion (34.4.1–4). Cato may also have sponsored a law that aimed at curbing the predations of provincial governors (Gruen, 1992: 54, but see also Richardson, 1986: 168–69 and Crawford, 1996: 331–40). He disparaged the verbosity and insincerity of Greek oratory, railed against Greek medicine and its practitioners, called Socrates a raging babbler, and referred to Greeks as "a most vile and ignorant race" (Pliny the Elder, *Natural History*: 29.13–14 and Plutarch, *Life of Cato the Elder*: 23.1–3). The list goes on.

Yet for all this, Cato was acquainted with Greek culture (Astin, 1978: 157–81). Plutarch records a boast of Cato's that he chose to address the Athenians in Latin in 191 BC even though he could have easily done so in Greek (*Life of Cato the Elder*: 12.4). This was, of course, an assertion of Roman superiority, but Cato here reveals that by his 40s he was fluent in the language he claimed to despise. What survives of his work demonstrates knowledge of Greek history, and it has been noted that a fragment of the preface to his *Origines* (Peter, *HRR*: 1² fr. 2) imitates the opening of Xenophon's *Symposium*. Several sources report that, in his later years, Cato devoted some of his time to Greek literature (e.g., Nepos, *Cato*: 3.2; Plutarch, *Life of Cato the Elder*: 2.4), but he may well have started earlier.

3.6 Conclusion

The picture of Roman Italy in the second century BC is, at present, much less clear than it was fifty years ago. Scholars are bringing together new evidence and new methods of interpretation as they reconsider the motivation for, and ramifications of, Rome's involvement in the Greek East from almost every conceivable angle. There is no doubt about the speed and scope of the Hellenization of Roman society that took place in this period, but the narrative of how that process played out is undergoing significant revision. It is too soon, and the questions are too unsettled, for a comprehensive synthesis to establish the new story of what happened to Rome after it became entangled in the internal affairs of the Greeks, but perhaps that day is not far off.

FURTHER READING

The bibliography for each of the topics covered here is enormous, and what follows is highly selective. To begin, the reader is well advised to explore other publications by the authors cited, especially Eckstein 1987 and 2006, Scheidel 2001 and 2004, and Astin 1967. Champion 2004 collects the main ancient sources and several important smaller modern studies of Roman imperialism; see also Sherwin-White 1984, Rosenstein 1990 and 2004. Arguments for and against the use of field surveys to refine demographic arguments are laid out in the contributions by Jongman, Fentress, and Mattingly in Bowman and Wilson 2009. For the development of Latin literature, numerous histories are available including Conte 1994, and Kenney and Clausen 1982. On historiography in particular, see Marincola 1997, Kraus and Woodman 1997, and Mellor 1999. The foundational collections of fragments of ancient historiography remain Peter's *HRR* and Jacoby's *FGrH*, but see now also Chassignet 1996–2004 and Beck and Walter 2001–04. Rawson 1985 provides a thorough survey of intellectual life in the Republic; see also the articles collected in Rawson 1991.

REFERENCES

Alcock, S. 2007. "(4a) The essential countryside: the Greek world." In *Classical Archaeology*, eds S. Alcock and R. Osborne, 120–38. Oxford: Blackwell.

Astin, A.E. 1967. *Scipio Aemilianus*. Oxford: Clarendon Press.

Astin, A.E. 1978. *Cato the Censor*. Oxford: Clarendon Press.

Beck, H. and Walter, U. 2001–04. *Die frühen römischen Historiker.* 2 vols. Darmstadt: Wissenschaftliche Buchgesellschaft.

Bober, P.P. 1999. *Art, Cuisine, and Culture: ancient and medieval gastronomy.* Chicago, IL/ London: University of Chicago Press.

Bowman, A.K. and Wilson, A. eds. 2009. *Quantifying the Roman Economy: methods and problems.* Oxford: Oxford University Press.

Bradley, K.R. 1989. *Slavery and Rebellion in the Roman World.* Bloomington, IN: Indiana University Press.

Bradley, K.R. 1994. *Slavery and Society at Rome.* Cambridge: Cambridge University Press.

Bradley, K.R. 2011. "Slavery in the Roman Republic." In *The Cambridge World History of Slavery.* Vol. I: *The Ancient Mediterranean World,* eds K. Bradley and P. Cartledge, 241–64. Cambridge: Cambridge University Press.

Brunt, P.A. 1971. *Italian Manpower, 225 BC–AD 14.* Oxford: Clarendon Press.

Champion, C.B. 2004. *Roman Imperialism: readings and sources.* Oxford: Blackwell.

Chassignet, M. ed. 1996–2004. *L'annalistique romaine.* 3 vols. Paris : Les Belles Lettres.

Colonna, G. 1991. "Riflessioni sul dionisismo in Etruria." In *Dionysos, mito e mistero: atti del convegno internazionale, Comacchio 3–5 Novembre 1989,* ed. F. Berti, 117–55. Ferrara: Liberty House.

Conte, G.B. 1994. *Latin Literature: a history* (trans. J.B. Solodow). Baltimore, MD/London: Johns Hopkins University Press.

Cornell, T.J. 1995. *The Beginnings of Rome: Italy and Rome from the Bronze Age to the Punic Wars (c. 1000–264 BC).* London: Routledge.

Crawford, M. H. ed. 1996. *Roman Statutes.* 2 vols. London: Institute of Classical Studies/BICS Supplement 64.

Eckstein, A.M. 1987. *Senate and General: individual decision-making and Roman foreign relations, 264–194 B.C.* Berkeley/London: University of California Press.

Eckstein, A.M. 2006. *Mediterranean Anarchy, Interstate War, and the Rise of Rome.* Berkeley: University of California Press.

Eckstein, A.M. 2008. *Rome Enters the Greek East: from anarchy to hierarchy in the Hellenistic Mediterranean, 230–170 B.C.* Oxford: Blackwell.

Farrow, J.G. 1992. "Aeneas and Rome: pseudepigrapha and politics." *Classical Journal* 87: 339–59.

Gabba, E. 1976. *Republican Rome, the Army and the Allies* (trans. P.J. Cuff). Oxford: Blackwell.

Gruen, E.S. 1976. "The origins of the Achaean War." *Journal of Hellenic Studies* 96: 46–69.

Gruen, E.S. 1984. *The Hellenistic World and the Coming of Rome.* Berkeley/London: University of California Press.

Gruen, E.S. 1990. *Studies in Greek Culture and Roman Policy.* Berkeley/London: University of California Press.

Gruen, E.S. 1992. *Culture and National Identity in Republican Rome.* Ithaca: Cornell University Press.

Harris, W.V. 1979. *War and Imperialism in Republican Rome, 327–70 BC.* Oxford/New York: Clarendon Press/Oxford University Press.

Hatzfeld, M.J. 1912. "Les italiens résidant à Délos mentionnés dans les inscriptions de l'île." *Bulletin de correspondance hellénique* 36: 5–218.

Kenney, E.J. and Clausen, W.V. eds. 1982. *The Cambridge History of Classical Literature.* Vol. 2: *Latin Literature.* Cambridge: Cambridge University Press.

Kraus, C.S. and A.J. Woodman. 1997. *Latin Historians.* Oxford: Oxford University Press for the Classical Association.

Ligt, L. de and Northwood, S. 2008. *People, Land and Politics: demographic developments and the transformation of Roman Italy.* Leiden: Brill.

Lo Cascio, E. 1994. "The size of the Roman population: Beloch and the meaning of the Augustan census figures." *Journal of Roman Studies* 84: 23–40.

Lo Cascio, E. and Malanima, P. 2005. "Cycles and stability. Italian population before the demographic transition (225 B.C.–A.D. 1900)." *Rivista di Storia Economica* 21: 197–232.

Lomas, K. 1993. *Rome and the Western Greeks, 350 BC–AD 200. Conquest and acculturation in south Italy.* London: Routledge.

Marincola, J.M. 1997. *Authority and Tradition in Ancient Historiography*. Cambridge: Cambridge University Press.

Mellor, R. 1999. *The Roman Historians*. London: Routledge.

Meyboom, P.G.P. 1995. *The Nile Mosaic of Palestrina. Early evidence of Egyptian religion in Italy*. Brill: Leiden.

Morel, J-P. 1989. "The transformation of Italy, 200–133 B.C. The evidence of archaeology." In *The Cambridge Ancient History*. Vol. 8: *Rome and the Mediterranean to 133 B.C.* (2nd edn), eds A.E. Astin *et al.*, 477–516. Cambridge: Cambridge University Press.

North, J.A. 1979. "Religious toleration in Republican Rome." *Proceedings of the Cambridge Philological Society* 25: 85–103.

Pailler, J.-M. 1976. "'*Raptos a Diis Homines Dici...*' (Tite-Live, XXXIX, 13): les Bacchanales et la possession par les nymphes." In *L'Italie préromaine et la Rome républicaine: mélanges offerts à Jacques Heurgon*, Vol. 2, 731–42. Rome: École française de Rome/ Collection de l'École française de Rome 27.

Parke, H.W. and McGing, B.C. 1988. *Sibyls and Sibylline Prophecy in Classical Antiquity*. London: Routledge.

Pollitt, J.J. 1978. "The impact of Greek art on Rome." *Transactions of the American Philological Association* 108: 155–74.

Rawson, E. 1985. *Intellectual Life in the Late Roman Republic*. Baltimore, MY: Johns Hopkins University Press.

Rawson, E. 1991. *Roman Culture and Society*. Oxford: Clarendon Press.

Reay, B. 2005. "Agriculture, writing, and Cato's aristocratic self-fashioning." *Classical Antiquity* 24: 331–61.

Reay, B. 2012. "Cato's *De Agri Cultura* and the spectacle of expertise." In *Roman Republican Villas: architecture, context, and ideology*, eds J.A. Becker and N. Terrenato, 61–68. Ann Arbor: University of Michigan Press.

Richardson, J.S. 1986. Hispaniae: *Spain and the development of Roman Imperialism, 218–82 BC*. Cambridge University Press.

Richardson, L., Jr 1991. "Urban development in ancient Rome and the impact of empire." In *City States in Classical Antiquity and Medieval Italy*, eds A. Molho, K. Raaflaub, and J. Emlen, 381–402. Ann Arbor: University of Michigan Press.

Rosenstein, N. S. 1990. Imperatores Victi: *military defeat and aristocratic competition in the Middle and Late Republic*. Berkeley/Oxford: University of California Press.

Rosenstein, N. S. 2004. *Rome at War: farms, families and death in the Middle Republic*. Chapel Hill/ London: University of North Carolina Press.

Scheidel, W. 2001. *Debating Roman Demography*. Leiden: Brill/Mnemosyne Suppl. 211.

Scheidel, W. 2004. "Human mobility in Roman Italy, I: The free population." *Journal of Roman Studies* 94: 1–26.

Scheidel, W. 2005. "Human mobility in Roman Italy, II: The slave population." *Journal of Roman Studies* 95: 64–79.

Scheidel, W. 2008. "Roman population size: the logic of the debate." In *People, Land and Politics: demographic developments and the transformation of Roman Italy*, eds L. de Ligt and S. Northwood, 17–70. Leiden: Brill.

Scheidel, W. 2011. "The Roman slave supply." In *The Cambridge World History of Slavery*. Vol. I: *The Ancient Mediterranean World*, eds K. Bradley and P. Cartledge, 287–310. Cambridge: Cambridge University Press.

Schultz, C.E. 2006. *Women's Religious Activity in the Roman Republic*. Chapel Hill, NC/ London: University of North Carolina Press.

Sherwin-White, A.N. 1984. *Roman Foreign Policy in the East 168 B.C. to A.D. 1*. London: Duckworth.

Skutsch, O. 1985. *The Annals of Q. Ennius*. Oxford: Oxford University Press.

Terrenato, N. 2007. "(4b) The essential countryside: the Roman world." In *Classical Archaeology*, eds S. Alcock and R. Osborne, 139–61. Oxford: Blackwell.

Terrenato, N. 2012. "The enigma of 'Catonian' villas: the *De Agricultura* in the context of the second-century BC Italian architecture." In *Roman Republican Villas: architecture, context, and ideology*, eds J.A. Becker and N. Terrenato, 69–93. Ann Arbor: University of Michigan Press.

Tierney, J.J. 1947. "The *Senatus Consultum de Bacchanalibus*." *Proceedings of the Royal Irish Academy* 51: 89–117.

Toynbee, A. 1965. *Hannibal's Legacy: the Hannibalic War's effects on Roman life.* 2 vols. London: Oxford University Press.

Walbank, F.W. 1957–79. *A Historical Commentary on Polybius.* 3 vols. Oxford: Clarendon Press.

Wallace-Hadrill, A. 2008. *Rome's Cultural Revolution.* Cambridge: Cambridge University Press.

Welch, K. 2003. "A new view of the origins of the Basilica: the Atrium Regium, Graecostasis, and Roman diplomacy." *Journal of Roman Archaeology* 16: 5–34.

White, K.D. 1967. "*Latifundia.*" *Bulletin of Institute of Classical Studies* 14: 62–79.

Wilson, A.J.N. 1966. *Emigration from Italy in the Republican Age of Rome.* Manchester: Manchester University Press.

Wiseman, T.P. 1998. *Roman Drama and Roman History.* Exeter: University of Exeter Press.

CHAPTER 4

The Social War[1]

Edward Bispham

4.1 Introduction

In late 91 or early 90 BC a Roman *praetor* Q. Servilius, on duty in central Italy, was informed that the allied city of Asculum, one of the chief places of the Picentes, was exchanging hostages with another community. Such exchanges were normally a prelude to war, to keep all participants "honest" if the going got difficult. Italian communities were not supposed to engage in war with anyone independently of Rome, whose hegemony guaranteed and demanded stability in Italy. Servilius now hurried to Asculum, where a festival was in full flow, which he interrupted with a flood of dire threats unless they desisted from the exchange. But the people of Asculum were in no mood to be bullied: the *praetor* and his legate, Fonteius, were lynched, and every last Roman in Asculum was hunted down and killed, and their goods plundered (Appian, *Civil* Wars: 1.38.171–74; Diodorus Siculus: 37.12.2; Cicero, *In Defence of Fonteius*: 41, 48). Appian's narrative then continues immediately with the outbreak of what became known as the "war of the allies" (the Social War; also known as the "Marsic" or "Italian" war), when most of Rome's allies in central and southern Italy rose up against her; the causal link between Servilius and the war is made explicit by Velleius Paterculus (2.15.1), and in the *Summary* of Livy Book 72. It was for this epochal conflict, as Servilius had intuited, that hostages were being exchanged. As Florus put it, "the people which arbitrated between kings and peoples, was unable now to govern itself, to the point where Rome, the conqueror of Asia and Europe was attacked from Corfinium" (2.6.7).

Another incident, also from Diodorus's 37th book, thus contemporary with the Servilius debacle, and often conflated with it, also involved Picentes at a *panēguris* or festival (although not necessarily at Asculum). A mixed Roman and Picentine audience had gathered to see a comic performance; tensions were running high between the different groups in the audience. It seems that the theatre, often a focal point for the expression of consensus or discontent, where political comment could be read into lines of dialog and even the gesture of an actor, now became an incendiary point in the political and social fabric of the city. Apparently on the day in question the Romans in the audience had lynched a comic actor who had allowed his dominant mode to be grief (or perhaps indignation), instead of making them laugh. Now, in revenge, the locals were preparing to kill the "buffoon" Saunio, whose popularity with the

A Companion to Roman Italy, First Edition. Edited by Alison E. Cooley.
© 2016 John Wiley & Sons, Ltd. Published 2016 by John Wiley & Sons, Ltd.

Roman contingent they found intolerable, despite his uncanny ability to make the whole audience laugh without even opening his mouth. Saunio picked up on the crackling hostility in the theatre, and instantly realized that he now needed, literally, the performance of his life. He deployed all his good humor and charm to slake the bitter thirst for revenge which threatened him; but, crucially, he was able to identify, and identify with, the underlying sense of grievance. "For I am no Roman, but just like you, subject to the rods [i.e. the *fasces* of Roman magistrates] I wander around Italy …" (Diodorus Siculus: 37.12).

The Social War itself was one of the bloodiest and most intense conflicts seen in Italy, even though its duration was relatively brief (less than four years): Velleius claims that the dead alone numbered more than 300 000 (2.15.3). While the Romans had begun, as we shall see, to register the increasing discontent of the allies, and to gather information and put in place measures against armed insurrection, the very fact of this conflict was, in psychological terms, deeply shocking. The Romans were being attacked by their closest allies, men who inhabited the same favored corner of the world, men who had shed their blood with the Romans, and indeed done much of the "heavy lifting" required to build the empire of the Roman people. They were, above all, men related to the Romans, both generally in terms of claims of consanguineity, expressed through myths of origin, and specifically, in terms of intermarriage between Roman and allied elites (Diodorus Siculus: 37.15.2). The natural order of things under Roman hegemony was built on a common conception of Italy as *terra Italia* (the land of Italy), on the triptych of Romans, the Latin name, and the allies; and on agreements based on sworn treaties between Roman and each allied state. For those same men to murder Romans in broad daylight during a festival of the gods was not simply intrinsically disturbing, but a rupture in the natural order. No wonder that the simple fact of the Asculum slaughter is included as a prodigy in Julius Obsequens' list for 91 BC, beside great balls of fire, bleeding bread, rains of stones, and sweating statues. As in the case of any prodigy, the question must be asked: why is this happening?

4.2   Italian Grievances and Aspirations

Divine displeasure in antiquity is not ours to ascertain in the early twenty-first century, although we would be wrong to discount the force of such interpretations at the time; as for the displeasure of the mortals who rebelled against Rome, we are at least in a position to make some informed guesses. It is also important to note that different sources, from a range of dates and viewpoints, inevitably yield different perspectives. No single reason could be advanced for the war even at the time, and in a large area like Italy, it would be foolish to expect uniformity of attitudes or motivations. Many of the urbanized city-states of the Tyrrhenian coast were slow to join in, had to be coerced into revolt, or did not rebel at all; rather, the areas of upland Italy, where a state-formation had taken a different route, with more dispersed settlement patterns, were the drivers of the revolt. Of the Latins only a single colony, Venusia, rebeled (one of the most distant from Rome, and surrounded by rebels) – clearly the unhappiness of Saunio was not shared by all his fellow Latins. This raises an important question: how far did elites and masses in Italy aspire to or resent similar things on the eve of war? Not very much, one suspects, and yet evidently the leaders, or some leaders in communities, were able to gain ideological traction on their citizens, or at least those liable for military service, and ensure that they were willing to vote for war and to serve, in massive numbers; indeed, as on the Roman side, recruitment must have stretched beyond the traditional *assiduus* catchments.

I said "some leaders" above, since there are a few interesting cases which clearly show that elites were split (as they had often been at the time of the Hannibalic War – indeed, the leading families were always divided by a common political culture) between pro- and anti-Roman stances, between loyalty and secession. The best-known case is that of Minatius Magius, member of a leading family from Aeclanum, a principal settlement of the Hirpini situated close to the *via Appia*. The city had joined the rebellion at the outset (Appian, *Civil Wars*: 1.51.222), but Magius raised a legion of loyalists (from among the Hirpini, not necessarily from Aeclanum itself), and fought alongside the Roman commanders Didius and Sulla as they reduced the rebel cities of Campania to subjection (Velleius Paterculus: 2 6.2–3, with Bispham, 2011). So even within an ethnic group, a state or a town, we cannot assume that either elites or the mass of the population would have the same grievances, or be motivated to act in uniform ways. Under such circumstances the search for a single answer to why the Social War happened is doomed to failure.

Nevertheless, there are some historiographical caveats which affect the overall shape of the debate, to which Henrik Mouritsen (1998) drew attention in a very important study: they concern ancient and modern perceptions about the Roman citizenship, widely acknowledged until the end of the twentieth century as the rebels' goal. Roman citizenship had been used before the Social War, as it was during and after it, as a reward for signal service to Rome (Cicero, *In Defence of Balbus*: 46; Valerius Maximus: 5.2.8; Plutarch, *Life of Marius* 28 (Marius and Camertine cohorts at Vercellae, 101 BC); *ILLRP* 515 (Cn. Pompeius Strabo at Asculum, 89 BC)). After the war, from the late Republic into the Principate, the disparity between Roman and other statuses in terms of power and privilege grew still further, and with it a reluctance to grant the citizenship without good cause, and then only to grant it to loyal friends and servants as a favor (cf. Appian's use of the word *charis*, "favor", in the context of the enfranchisement proposal of Fulvius Flaccus in 125 BC (see later in this chapter), *Civil Wars*: 1.21.86). This created a widespread perception that citizenship was highly desirable, and must have been desired by the Italian allies on the eve of the war. Such a viewpoint is visible in late Republican texts, but strongly colors the later narrative of Appian, for whom it was impossible that the Italians should *not* have wanted the citizenship. It does not follow that we should consider all later texts (and almost all the relevant texts *are* later than the war) suspect when they allege a desire for Roman citizenship as a motivation for the Social War; but it is very important not to *assume* that it was a widely shared or dominant motivation for the war.

Many scholars have, however, made just this assumption. As Mouritsen showed brilliantly, the cognate idea that the political unification of Italy through the citizenship (and concomitant cultural unification) was not only desirable but inevitable, is an artefact of nineteenth-century nationalism. Historians like Theodor Mommsen, writing in an age when the nation-states of Germany and Italy were being forged (in the Italian case partly through war) from a number of smaller polities, saw in the Social War a paradigm for contemporary political journeys. Conversely, the desirable teleology of the political unification of a number of small, contiguous and culturally similar polities into a larger whole, capable of imperial ambitions, was read back from European experience into the interpretation of the longer-term historical development of Italy, in which the Social War was seen as crucial. Many accounts of Italian history up to the principate of Augustus (e.g. Salmon, 1982) are unconsciously teleological in just this sense, seeing the march of history as inevitably tending towards political and then cultural unification.

The dominant mode of analysis prior to Mouritsen's revisionist thesis was essentially an elaboration of the viewpoint of Appian. Appian's *Civil Wars* forms part of his larger project surveying all the conflicts in Roman history up to the conclusion of the Civil Wars; he counts the Social War as a civil war. Appian's whole narrative structure implicates the Social War in one particular approach to late Republican history, focusing on civil conflict and internecine bloodshed. In other words Appian is – like all historians – constructing, not just telling, history. In particular, he is concerned to unify and see as part of a wider pattern the various internal political struggles which culminated in political violence on the one hand, and the Social War on the other. This is something which he makes explicit himself when he comes to discuss the Social War: "I have included it in this history, because it began out of the civil strife (*stasis*) in Rome, and led to another much worse *stasis*" (*Civil Wars*: 1.34.151). The latter is certainly true; the former is debatable.

There are three Italian "threads" in Appian's account. One is the support for Ti. Gracchus's agrarian laws of those whom both Appian and Plutarch call *Italiōtai* (*Civil Wars*: 1.7.30; cf. Plutarch, *Life of Gaius Gracchus*: 5.1). These were laws which, Appian says, were designed to benefit them: when the *lex Sempronia agraria* was passed, Tiberius was "escorted to his house by the multitude as the founder not of a single city, nor of one race, but of all the peoples (*ethnē*) which are in Italy" (*Civil Wars*: 1.13.56, cf. Plutarch, *Life of Tiberius Gracchus*: 9. 4–5, an excerpt from a speech in support of his *lex agraria*). But there are problems here: it is not clear that Appian always knows what he means by *Italiōtai*. The word often means "Greeks living in southern Italy," but this is not the sense in Appian; rather, he could be understood as referring to either "Italian allies" or "those (Romans or others) living in rural Italy" (similar to the usage of Polybius: 2.31.7 and elsewhere). In fact, it is not clear that, at the time at which he wrote, in which all inhabitants of Italy had the citizenship, he was always conscious of a difference between these two alternatives. More worryingly, despite the undoubted fact that Tiberius's rhetoric concerned the *Italikon genos* ("Italian race", e.g. *Civil Wars*: 1.9.35), there is no evidence that he actually benefited Italian allies by his land reforms (*pace* Richardson, 1980), still less – and this is the eccentric claim of Velleius (2.2.2) – that he proposed to enfranchise any Italians. Rather, there is good reason to suspect that Tiberius's rhetoric contrasted the "Italian race" not with Romans, but with the "race of slaves" in Italy. The essential dichotomy, intended to gain traction with voters both rich and poor, was that between free and slave; further elaboration of this rhetoric, to suggest that Tiberius intended to enfranchise the Italians, was the work not of Tiberius himself, but the *biblion* (book) which his brother wrote about him after his death (Plutarch, *Life of Tiberius Gracchus*: 8.7), which seems to have served as a means to legitimate some controversial additions to his brother's political legacy which Gaius intended.

The second Italian thread can be summarized (from a Roman perspective) as "votes for land." The Gracchan land-distribution program had become snarled up in a judicial process partly driven by allied complaints, and it was felt that the offer of citizenship would unblock things, with allied elites likely to withdraw their objections in exchange for the greater benefit now offered (Appian, *Civil Wars*: 1.21.86–87 – "they preferred the citizenship to lands"). This line of argument then continues with the allies growing frustrated at "votes for land" being put on the table first by Gracchus and his associates and then by Livius Drusus, only for the deal to be removed by conservatives; in the end they went to war for what they had been offered and then denied. To be fair to Appian, this equation is only explicitly made in connection with the proposal of the consul (and Gracchan triumvir for redistributing land) Fulvius Flaccus in 125 BC (and the idea was initially, according to Appian, put forward by unnamed others); but it is often assumed that Gaius Gracchus was impelled by the same motivation.

Yet the two proposals seem to be different. Flaccus (in a bill about which we really know very little) seems to have proposed citizenship (we are not told for whom, although the word "Italiae" ("to Italy") is normally restored into the text), and for those who did not want citizenship, *prouocatio*, or the right of appeal to the people against arbitrary treatment by Roman magistrates. It is unclear if this alternative was to be offered to individuals or (as the citizenship was later offered) to whole communities. Gaius Gracchus, on the other hand offered Roman citizenship to the Latins (Appian, *Civil Wars*: 1.23.99; Plutarch, *Life of Gaius Gracchus*: 8.3, 9.3), and to the other allies "suffrage" (Appian, *Civil Wars*: 1.23.99; Plutarch, *Life of Gaius Gracchus*: 5.1; Velleius Paterculus: 2.6.2 may garble the same idea). It is not clear what this means, but the common assumption that it refers to a grant of Latin status (*ius Latii*) to non-Latin allies, while not impossible, has little to commend it. If both Flaccus and Gracchus were really motivated by a desire to sugar the pill of the removal of *ager publicus* for redistribution to the Roman poor, it is striking that they seem to have gone about it in different ways and addressed different constituencies.

Finally we may note that the "votes for land" solution is one sometimes offered to try to thread together the bewildering range of proposals made by Livius Drusus in his tribunate in 91 BC. Drusus's chief preoccupation is often thought to have been the controversial matter of the composition of juries in the standing criminal courts: senators vs equestrians. Rather like the old woman in the children's story who cannot get her pig to jump over a stile, Drusus has, on this view, to set up a complex chain of favorable preconditions to achieve his primary aim: the people have to be seduced with the promise of colonies and an agrarian law (Drusus here borrowing a tactic from his father, the opponent of C. Gracchus); to get more *ager publicus* freed up for colonists, Italians have to be pushed off the land, and thus need the sweetener of the citizenship. I note simply that this (although it is a recasting of Appian's own reasoning: the Roman people to be bought off from opposing enfranchisement by an agrarian law, 1.35.156) reads rather a lot into what the sources say. Furthermore, if Mouritsen is right (cf. Aurelius Victor, *On Famous Men*: 66), Drusus was only intending to give citizenship to the Latins, which further problematizes this line of explanation. Nevertheless, viewed from an Italian point of view, there is a lot to be said for the thesis that the Gracchi, in pursuit of *ager publicus* for their resettlement programs, were forced to remove Italians from public land which they had been legitimately occupying, often for considerable periods (Cicero, *On the Republic*: 1.31; 3.41; Roselaar, 2010: 71–84). This specific discontent can also be subsumed within the next alleged motivation for the war.

The final Italian "thread" in Appian is political, and it is the most persuasive line of explanation he suggests. Put simply it concerns the wish of the Italians, encouraged by Roman political leaders, to be partners with the Romans, not subjects. In Appian's text this idea first surfaces with his second mention of the legislation of Fulvius Flaccus, which is re-introduced to provide context for the tribunate of Drusus and the Social War. Here there is none of the standard imperial discourse of citizenship as a favor, but rather the claim that Flaccus was the first to bring "right into the open" the ambitions of the Italians to be "partners in rule, rather than subjects" (*Civil Wars*: 1.34.152; a related word for partnership – *koinōnia* – recurs at Plutarch, *Life of Gaius Gracchus*: 8.3, where Gracchus "summons the Latins to partnership in political rights"). This antinomy between equality and subjection recurs in other contexts in Appian: it is why the senate resist Flaccus's bill in the first place (1.21.87, being reluctant to make "subjects" into men with equal political rights, *isopolitai*); in the unhappiness of the Italians after the deaths of Flaccus and Gracchus (1.34.154); and in the motivation for Drusus to bring forward a citizenship bill (1.35.135).

That it was primarily equality in the political sphere that was at stake (or at least of interest to Appian's source(s)) is suggested by the emphasis on voting and on political rights throughout the accounts of what Flaccus and C. Gracchus were trying to do. Fulvius Flaccus's alternative of citizenship or *prouocatio* (in Valerius Maximus) shows not only, as has often been noted, that there were Italians who were thought not to want the citizenship as well as Italians who were believed to want it, but also that both groups were seeking (or thought to be seeking) to buttress their political rights against interference and maltreatment, even if some were not prepared to surrender their own citizenship in the process. Again, Gracchus was offering *isopsēphia*, equal voting rights, to the Latins, according to Plutarch (*Life of Gaius Gracchus*: 9.3; and to all the Italians: 5.1), and voting rights to the non-Latins according to Appian. That fundamental political rights were at issue is suggested also by one of the counterproposals made (but never carried through) by Livius Drusus to wean support away from

Gaius Gracchus: Latins were no longer to be liable to being beaten with rods on military service (Plutarch, *Life of Gaius Gracchus*: 9.3). It was clear to all sides that the Latins were after an improvement in their status, and this was the minimum that the conservative majority was willing to concede.

Appian, Plutarch, and Valerius Maximus give us information which, with no undue effort or over-reading, can be combined to suggest that there was a fundamental interest in equality, above all equality of political rights, but also equality of political power. Flaccus and Gracchus were thus seeking to redress a situation in which, whether they wanted the citizenship or not, Latins and Italians had come to see themselves as subjects (this is essentially the thesis of Pobjoy, 2000). This perception is, pleasingly, one which emerges from other sources too, bringing us back to the anti-Roman *pogrom* in Asculum with which we began. We have already noted Saunio's complaint about being subject to the *fasces* – not a concern with the symbols of power, but the real threat of being thrashed with them. Diodorus's allusion to the anger of Servilius at Asculum is also revealing: like Appian he has Servilius make threats, but says that he "treated them disgracefully as if they were slaves" (37.12.2). Diodorus is an important source because, although his work survives at this point only in late excerpts, he is in fact one of our earliest sources on the Social War (writing in the 30s BC). The contrast here is one between slavery and freedom, a starker version of the antinomy in Appian and Plutarch between subjection and partnership in power, but not incompatible with it. Indeed, "freedom" may be what the Italian grievances can be boiled down to, ultimately, and what had most traction on the masses, those who did the fighting in the war. Freedom *from*, from subjection and unfair treatment, was more important to them than the hypothetical possibility of exercising the vote (freedom *to*), which will on the other hand have mattered to the Italian elites. Freedom was unquestionably what the war was about: as Sherwin-White (1973) noted some forty years ago, Strabo and others talk about "revolt" (*apostasis*, 5.4.2; Appian, *Civil Wars*: 1.38.169 uses the same word), and, as we shall see, the war took the form of a *breakaway* from Roman control, and from the Roman Empire (Sherwin's idea has been more fully developed by Mouritsen, 1998 and Pobjoy, 2000, the latter drawing attention to the hitherto undervalued and contemporary evidence provided by rebel coinage). And it is perhaps not surprising that Velleius makes the Samnite leader Pontius Telesinus at the battle of the Colline Gate in 82 BC – in language which suggests that for the Samnites this conflict is an extension of the Social War – stir his troops against the "Roman wolves" in their lair with an appeal to "Italian freedom" (*libertas Italica*; see Bispham, 2011 on this passage).

That "freedom" was at the root of what Romans thought the allies' concerns were chimes well with the general concerns of the *popularis* ideology within which Flaccus and Gracchus worked, the political strengths of which Livius Drusus tried to tap into. The rights of *prouocatio*, the freedom of citizens from execution or arbitrary punishment by magistrates, and the right to exercise a meaningful political sovereignty through their votes, were at the heart of the Gracchan program, and of other *popularis* reformers in their wake. It is unsurprising that we find many of these same concerns surfacing in the measures which they tried to pass in favor of the allies. Gaius Gracchus himself drew attention to recent shocking incidents of cruel and overbearing treatment by Romans, magistrates and their entourages, against Italian allies, in a speech made "on the laws which have been proposed" (Aulus Gellius, *Attic Nights*: 10. 3. 3; see Bispham, 2007: 156–60 on this passage). Indeed, although some (Galsterer, 1976; Mouritsen, 1998) have made serious arguments to the contrary, it does seem that the second century BC had seen an increasing amount of Roman interference in allied affairs, and instances of deception and harsh treatment, which if they do not amount to a pattern of systemic abuses, nevertheless reveal a stark asymmetry in how the Romans saw their relationship with other Italians (for a full discussion see Bispham, 2007: ch. 3). That over the same period Romans began to behave in increasingly unaccountable and domineering ways to subjects elsewhere in the Mediterranean, especially at Carthage and in Greece – where the Achaeans, who had a favorable treaty with Rome, ended up crushed in a humiliating war in 146 BC – strongly suggests that signs of deterioration in Roman treatment of those under her hegemony should be taken seriously. What Gracchus complained of was not the fact of Roman abuse of power, but its intensification, in that Italians, and members of Italian elites at that, had been physically abused, and one had taken his own life in fear of Roman reprisals. We come back to the blood spilt in the Picentine theatre in 91 BC, and Saunio's close escape.

4.3   Which Italians?

I have generally talked in terms of what Roman politicians thought the Italians wanted; but the evidence just discussed for the increasing high-handedness of *some* Roman aristocrats shows that this was over-cautious. The Italian concerns, and the consequent attempts in some quarters about mitigating them, were real enough. One might add other concerns which possession of the citizenship might address. More than half a century ago, Emilio Gabba argued that the Social War was driven by the aspirations of the Italian commercial classes, who sought the citizenship in order to gain access to the economic advantages which Roman *publicani* enjoyed in the empire; the position was restated more recently in his chapter on the Social War (Gabba, 1994). Although typically clever in approaching the problem from a new angle, this thesis has not found wide acceptance: the allied cities of southern Campania, which had substantial commercial interests in the Greek East, were not leaders of the revolt; indeed, some had to be compelled to join in. Yet the interests of allied businessmen cannot have been extraneous to the Social War, and Gabba rightly focused attention on the economic angle of the conflict. Commercial ambitions also underlined problems of status dissonance for Italians: in the provinces it seems that Rome's subjects made no distinction between Italians and Romans, for both represented the hegemonic power in their eyes. Italians must have been increasingly sensitive to the contrast between, say, the Greek East, where they were treated as members of the "master race", and Italy, where they were increasingly at risk of arbitrary abuse, and treated not as second-class citizens, but, as we have seen, as if they were subjects or even slaves.

In the generation before the Social War there were backlashes against the exploitation of imperial opportunities in Asia (the revolt of Aristonikos), and in Sicily (the slave revolts, especially the second, for the first seems more associated with Sicilian Greek mistreatment of slaves). Most signally, in Numidia, where the Senate was reluctant to send an army to frustrate the ambitions of Jugurtha, the incumbent king Adherbal found his last line of defence provided by those whom Sallust calls *togati* (toga-wearers) and *Italici*, Italian businessmen, and perhaps some Romans as well, although this is not made explicit. When Jugurtha took Cirta, Adherbal's capital, which had been defended by the *Italici*, he killed those whom he came across under arms (Sallust, *Jugurtha*: 21, 26).

The uncertainty as to whether *Italici* includes Romans or not in this case is worth pausing over. There were probably no Romans killed in Cirta, as the sources would have made more of it had this been the case. But *Italici* as a group recur in a variety of contexts in the Mediterranean: on Delos above all, but also in Egypt, Africa, Sicily, Argos, and Korinth (*ILLRP* 320, Sicily; 343, Alexandria (where the restoration of Marius as honorand is fantasy); 359–60, 362, 369, Delos; 370, Aegium; 374, 376, Argos; 380, Agrigentum). It is important to understand that *Italici* is an identity which is never defined in opposition to *Romani*; where it is defined, at least on Delos, it is in opposition to *Graeci*; indeed, the Agrigentum text is clearly a post-Social War inscription, thus from a period when all Italians south of the Po were Romans. In other words, it looks as if this is a constructed ethnic, which can (but need not always) embrace both Italians and Romans, and connotes a superior status with respect to indigenes. In the Polla inscription (*ILLRP* 454), the (unknown) magistrate from the Gracchan era commemorates not only his road-building activities, but also that when he was *praetor* in Sicily (almost certainly during the First Servile War) he rounded up 917 runaway slaves belonging to *Italici*, and returned them. The calculus of Roman abuses towards Italians needs to take account of the fact that there were areas in which Romans and Italians co-identified in the face of provincial populations; that they interacted in honoring Roman magistrates (on a very Hellenistic model); and received *beneficia* from them. This means that no simple picture of exploitation by Romans of Italians will be adequate, but also underscores what was said above about status dissonance. There was no space to continue to be an *Italicus* when one returned to Italy from overseas. That said, to return to motives for the Social War, it is entirely comprehensible that episodes like that at Cirta should engender in allied *negotiatores* a wish to be able to influence Roman policy in the provinces, as members of the first voting-class in the centuriate assembly. That Italian businessmen would have more rights, and more security, as Roman citizens, is a natural assumption, for all that the Asiatic Vespers of 88 BC proved it to be unfounded. Any account of motivations for rebellion cannot separate out political and economic motives.

4.4 Attitudes to the Citizenship

Yet it has been argued that the Italians did not *want* the citizenship anyway, and that sources which claim that they did are deceived by the filter of imperial attitudes through which they necessarily looked back to different times. On this view, far from being subject to Roman interference, or seduced by the superiority of Roman culture, the allies were accorded a large measure of autonomy within Roman Italy, and did not feel that they were in any sense on a trajectory of cultural or political convergence with Rome. Furthermore, the fact that the Social War was without question a revolt *from* Rome is incompatible with the idea of a demand for citizenship, indeed diametrically opposed to it (these are, in crude summary, the views of Mouritsen, 1998, a study which deserves serious attention by every student of this subject).

These points all merit a reflection. As to the problem of changing preconceptions about the citizenship, it is well made – but it is also important not to throw the baby out with the bath water. Here we need to confront the problem of motivations versus rhetoric. This is one of the biggest problems in any historical analysis: what people thought and desired is always to some degree refracted by the arguments put forward to achieve those aims. There is a danger that what we have in our sources is to some degree *how the issues were couched* rather than a straightforward reflection of what Romans or Italians, or subsets of Romans or Italians, wanted. I have already observed that *libertas* is not only desirable in itself (worth fighting for, as Brunt, 1988 stressed), but that it has ideological purchase: it can be used to argue for war and to rouse the troops. What are we to make of another theme, which appears as early as Ti. Gracchus, but recurs right up to the outbreak of the war: that Latins/Italians *deserved* the citizenship? This claim comes in two overlapping forms. The first is that the Italians (or just the Latins) as relatives of the Romans deserved better treatment, indeed, equal treatment. According to Appian, Tiberius referred to the Italians as *sungenes*, kinsmen, of the Romans (*Civil Wars*: 1.9.35). This is probably a claim which derives from the political propaganda of Gaius Gracchus, and his massaging of his brother's legacy (see earlier in this chapter; so, too, the idea of Tiberius as a "founder" of all the peoples of Italy). Gaius himself made the argument, according to Appian, that it was disgraceful that the Senate should refuse to give their "kinsmen" the Latins "all the privileges the Romans possessed," i.e. the citizenship (*Civil Wars*: 1.23.99). Velleius (a privileged commentator as we have seen, descended from a protagonist in the war) calls the rebels "men of the same race and blood" (2.15.2). He joins to this the other variation on the idea that the Italians *deserved* the citizenship: that they had fought, indeed shouldered most of the burden, to build the Roman Empire in the first place (cf. Diodorus Siculus: 37.22).

Now, such statements are often dismissed on the grounds that they simply reflect an early imperial inability to imagine a world other than that in which every right-thinking foreigner would want the citizenship. But they do not fit clearly into this kind of discourse: it is hard to imagine, let us say, Seleukos of Rhosos, enfranchised by Octavian in the thirties BC, or the leading citizens of Volubilis, enfranchised by the emperor Claudius, or even the Transpadani given the citizenship by Caesar in 49 BC, as being able to justify their claim (if they ever dared to make a claim) for the citizenship in terms of *just deserts*. This is as unlikely as an appeal to *sungeneia*, kinship. In other words, for the Italian allies, and for them only, the claim that their contribution to the making of the *imperium Romanum* should be rewarded by the Roman citizenship makes perfect sense; nor is it the kind of thing that an early imperial writer would be likely to make up, since it could no longer logically appear in the discourse surrounding grants of citizenship, which had been reduced to favor recognizing loyalty.

When in Diodorus a Cretan mercenary commander is offered the citizenship by a consul for betraying some of the rebels (37.18), he laughs, calling it a "fine-sounding trifle" – Cretans want to be paid, not given empty titles. Of course, this is meant to show us what we might have suspected anyway, that Cretans are a bad lot. But their mercenary attitude is also highlighted in the story because it in turn throws into relief the fact that others (those who have proper, non-Cretan value systems) *do* want the citizenship, and indeed will pay with their blood "for this trifle which you fight about." The story has its own internal logic, but it cannot have made sense either to Diodorus's source, or to Diodorus, unless Italians really were prepared to fight for the citizenship. Here there is again a disjunction between the dominant imperial way of seeing the citizenship (a reward for services), and an argument about citizenship which operates at a completely different level, which is about ideology not material gain. Again, it is very hard to see this sort of claim being made of any early imperial enfranchisement, just as it is hard to see why it should make sense to any early imperial writer that the citizenship could be extorted from Rome by force. In the end it is highly problematic to sweep up this and other testimonies, which require a widespread Italian desire for the citizenship in order to make sense, into a dustbin marked "early imperial focalization"; some of them belong here, but others work better as reflecting contemporary aspirations of the generation prior to the Social War.

The second important objection to the traditional narrative of desire for citizenship is that the Italians were entirely indifferent to Roman culture and society, and were on a parallel, not a converging, track. This argument seems to me to misconstrue the problem, and to be trapped in the same teleological paradigm from which it seeks to escape. Romans and Latins and allies were part of a wider Hellenistic *koinē*, and their cultural worlds were already enmeshed, and in dialog with each other, whether they liked it or not, and had been for a long time before Ti. Gracchus came along (Wallace-Hadrill, 2008 for cultural "dialog" in Italy). In reality, the idea of a separate Italian Hellenistic identity is as unlikely as that of a "pure" Roman religion, unsullied by foreign imports. Modes of burial, artistic styles, fine tableware, elite behaviors, political structures: all these show the increasing cultural interpenetration of Italian polities, whether or not we want to call it Romanization or Hellenization, or neither of these things (although we are certainly not witnessing a deletion of indigenous cultures in favor of Roman ones). And whether the intensity of the cultural dialog remains static, or is increasing, or occupying more areas, it has nothing to do with citizenship.

There is a remarkable contemporary testimony which bears on the problem of how Italians felt about Rome. In 2008, Filippo Coarelli published a fragmentary inscription on a statue base from Falacrinae in the Sabina (Coarelli, Kay, and Patterson 2008: 52–55). The inscription records the dedication of a statue to an unknown individual after a conflict, as a consequence of a vow. The spellings and the letter-forms indicate a date in the fifty or so years between circa 125 and 75 BC. The text refers to *Italia* in the first line of face A, and to the liberation of *Italia* in the second line of face B. Coarelli related the inscription to the Social War. He offered an ingenious series of supplements to complete the text, whereby it would commemorate the impious attack by Italy on Rome and the courage of the Romans in defense of the "single fatherland", as well as the rout of the enemy, the "liberation" of Italy and the great booty gained, ending in the outstanding conduct of the honorand and his vow.

It seems odd, however, that Italy should be the villain in face A, and then freed in face B, and that moreover having been freed, "increased booty" should be evoked. Logic is too strained by this reconstruction, typically ingenious as it is. Something simpler may work, however. If we take the Cimbric Wars as the context, we may have *Italia* being attacked in face A by wicked people who despise the gods; have them repulsed by the Romans' courage; and thus Italy freed, and the celebration of the acquisition of Celtic booty in the process. In this context the phrase *unica patria* ("single fatherland") becomes extremely important. Scholars have long argued that the Cimbric threat and the career of Marius, intimately bound up with it, must have been important in shaping a pan-Italian consciousness of shared advantage and vulnerability, in short a collective identity which included Romans and allies (Brunt, 1988). It has been argued that the Pyrrhic War had worked in a similar way; and Polybius (2.23.12) wrote that the Celtic invasion of 225 BC made Italians conscious of being threatened by a common danger to the extent that they forgot to ask whether they were Rome's allies, or the instruments of her hegemony. It seems to me that with this new text we have a strong argument that there was indeed a consciousness of Italy as a common fatherland for all, either as a result of, or even prior to, the Cimbric Wars. If so, it would be powerful evidence that there was ideological convergence in Italy, or at least that it was possible. Let it be said, also, that such convergence was clearly a work in progress, and the Social War was to show its fragility.

Finally, how can citizenship be compatible with war, or even revolt? How can one realistically, as the Cretan mercenary commander imagined, fight a bitter war, hoping to end up obtaining the citizenship of your enemies? It seems certain that the Social War is best understood as a revolt from Rome. But again the dichotomy between desire for the citizenship and desire for independence is a false one. Citizenship was sought, initially not by all, but by some, and then by increasing numbers, because it would bring the equal rights and freedom which, I have suggested earlier in this chapter, were at the heart of what Italians now sought. Initially, there was a feeling that some Italians were not prepared to sacrifice their own citizenship, and would settle for *prouocatio*. Indeed, when it came to it, faced with the offer of citizenship in 90 BC, there was considerable debate within Greek *poleis* of Neapolis and Herakleia; as *socii nauales* they may have had rather advantageous treaties anyway, and fears for their enhanced cultural distinctiveness as Greek foundations were weighed against the benefits of citizenship. In the end neither refused the offer. As we have seen, Fulvius Flaccus offered *prouocatio* as an alternative to citizenship, and the same alternative recurs in the *lex repetundarum* of 123 BC (Crawford, 1996: I, 1, lines 72–79), where successful prosecutors under the statute may obtain the Roman citizenship, or if they do not desire citizenship, *prouocatio* and immunity from military service (*uacatio militiae*) and from compulsory labor. It would be most peculiar (although not utterly impossible) if the *lex repetundarum* went to all the trouble of making available rewards which no one wanted. Indeed, the *lex Servilia* (of the very end of the second century BC) restricted the reward of citizenship in such cases to Latins, and it has been argued that for this reason Cicero calls it "most harsh" (Cicero, *In Defence of Balbus*: 54).

Although our sources are deplorably scrappy for the generation before the Social War, *prouocatio* seems to have dropped out of the debate by the time of the War. Instead, Italian aspirations could only be met by the citizenship, and it was this which Drusus the younger offered (whether to Latins only or to all Italians). And it seems that at the census of 97 BC large numbers of well-to-do Italians decided to take advantage of the nature of the census (simply turning up and making a declaration to the censors of name, wealth, tribe, and domicile) in order to pass themselves off as Roman citizens. This seems to be the implication of the fact that in 95 BC the consuls established by the *lex Licinia Mucia* a *quaestio* (a special court) to hear cases of fraudulent acquisition of the citizenship, with the aim of returning suppositious Roman citizens to their proper juridical statuses. We know most about the law from Asconius (p.67–8C), who goes on to say that when the allies' "very great desire for the Roman citizenship" was frustrated by the rulings of the *quaestio*, this proved to be "much the greatest cause of the Italian War." It is not implausible either to imagine that the 10 000 men who accompanied the Marsian leader Poppaedius Silo to Rome with swords under their tunics (Diodorus Siculus: 37.13) out of fear of the *euthunai* (investigations) were those who feared for their status under the terms of this law. Of course, we might dismiss Asconius's vision as distorted by imperial-tinted spectacles; but the fact is that he was a careful (though not infallible) researcher, and his words should not be lightly set aside. His comment is elicited to explain Cicero's comment that while the *lex Licinia Mucia* was the brain-child of two very eminent and wise statesmen, it was still "useless and dangerous" to the Roman state (*In Defence of Cornelius*, Asconius: p.67C). Asconius could have simply inferred on the basis of Cicero's text that the *lex Licinia Mucia* was a cause of the Social War; but he clearly knows about the context of the law, more than we could glean from other surviving references in Cicero, and the fact that he assigns this as the *greatest* cause of the War implies that he knew there were others, but had reason to make this the most significant one. This does not look like guesswork.

Asconius's evidence is important because it illustrates nicely that citizenship and revolt are not mutually exclusive alternatives, but that they are points along a spectrum. Citizenship was sought; when it was repeatedly denied, usurped, and then revoked, it became clear that this avenue to the benefits sought was closed off as far as Romans are concerned. In that case, the only way to obtain freedom and equality was to seek independence from Rome, and that could only be done through war. As Mouritsen (1998) has shown, the preparations for war began before Drusus's tribunate in 91 BC, with the Romans becoming aware, dully, of trouble stirring in the late nineties. In the meantime the allies' "below the radar" approach allowed them to wait and see what would happen with Drusus's attempt to extend the franchise.

Yet this was more than revolt, it was an attempt to establish a new order. The depth of Italian preparation for the war comes across clearly in the "substantial *agora* and *bouleuterion*" built at Corfinium, which was renamed Italica, and was to be the central place of a new *Italian* polity (Diodorus Siculus: 37.2.4f.); there was to be a representative council, and magistrates, to run the war. The rebel coinage also points in the same direction, with the name of the *imperator* (or in Oscan *embratur*) in the exergue beneath a variety of scenes, including oath-swearing, but above all the Roman wolf being gored (or worse) by the Italian bull (*vitelliu* in Oscan meant bull, but was also cognate with the name of *Italia*; see Pobjoy, 2000).

4.5   The War

The motives for war are complicated, and much disputed, hence the emphasis earlier in this chapter on them. By contrast, poor though our sources are, the course of much of the war itself is relatively uncomplicated. It is worth stressing that the conflict was a supreme effort on both sides. Republican Rome never minted more silver *denarii* than during the conflict, and nothing, in a way, is more eloquent about the scale of the challenge than this unprecedented monetary intervention (Howgego, 1995). The money, like the rebel silver *denarii*, was for paying troops; it is a striking feature of the war that, beside the heroism and desperation of both Italians and Romans, there are a remarkable number of non-Italians who appear as protagonists, from the Cretan mercenary named above (paid in those Roman *denarii*) to the Cilician pirate Agamemnon, freed from captivity by the Italians, and becoming an irregular in their service.

There were two theaters, a northern and a southern; in addition there was an abortive attempt at revolt in both Etruria and Umbria, which seems to have been quickly and brutally repressed. The rebels had the best of the first year of war, with the consul Rutilius Lupus falling in the field. Yet they were unable to subdue either the whole of Campania in the southern theater, or to break out from their positions in the northern theater, centered on Asculum. In 89 BC the Romans began to roll back the Italian advance, bringing to bear superior reserves of manpower and money; in December Asculum fell after a long siege, and by 88 BC the Italians were pinned back into a number of small enclaves, notably Nola in southern Campania. By this point Roman interest had become introverted again, with internal struggles over the fate of the new citizens being hopelessly entwined with the ambitions of Marius and Sulla to have the command against Mithridates in the East (the rebels had at one point hoped that the king would come to their aid). The army besieging Nola seems to have temporarily abandoned its post to march on Rome in support of Sulla's claim to the command. In fact, the Social War was never properly finished off, and the Samnites and Lucanians were left to a de facto independence, having suffered no definitive defeat, until Sulla's return from the East in 83 BC.

By this time they, like all Italians, had the citizenship. It seems that at the end of 90 BC the Romans feared further defections, not only those which were already manifesting themselves in Etruria and Umbria, but others among "neighboring peoples" – which may in fact refer to the culturally related Latins, whose loyalty had been crucial to Rome's survival hitherto – and offered the citizenship via the *lex Iulia* to those who had either remained loyal or laid down their arms quickly (Appian, *Civil Wars*: 1.49.211–15). This, perhaps more than any military loss, as Appian said, took the wind out of the rebels' sails. Those who had remained loyal felt they had been rewarded, and those whose commitment to the rebellion was less than copper-bottomed now wavered. In consequence, the rebels became polarized in 89 BC between the die-hard separatists (mainly the Samnites and Lucanians) and those likely to give in if military reverses continued. As 89 and 88 BC wore on, the numbers of those who had surrendered piled up, and they were enfranchised, en masse in 88 BC by one or more laws; other laws, such as the *lex Calpurnia* (recognizing gallantry) and the *lex Papiria Plautia*, coped with other ancillary categories of new citizen (the scope of the latter cannot be shown to have been anything more than a law to deal with those who were honorary citizens of allied cities, and wished to gain Roman citizenship now that the granting city had been enfranchised).

The enfranchisement of Italy was paradoxical, but necessary. The Romans conceded under pressure that which, had it been given in good time, would have obviated the need for revolt. Not to concede it would simply have meant a repeat of the Social War down the line, no matter how decisive any Roman victory – and the sequel quickly showed that internal dissent in Rome meant that the Italians could not be left disgruntled, but in fact were courted by many of the competing factions. The enfranchisement was also profound, as it entailed the most drastic changes seen in Italy for centuries, and created the tableau against which the Civil Wars played out and the Principate was created. These changes are the subject of the next chapter.

ENDNOTE

1 In formulating the views expressed, I owe a lot to discussions with Jonathan Prag, Mark Pobjoy, and Young-chae Kim; I am grateful to Lisa Bligh and Alison Cooley for reading and commenting on the text.

FURTHER READING

The course of the war itself is clearly set out in Keaveney 1987, who provides a rather conventional survey of the causes. Both Salmon 1982 and Brunt 1988 offer versions of what one might call the "orthodox" or "teleological" view of the causes of the war, linked into a discourse of natural cultural convergence. This view was challenged by Mouritsen 1998, building on Sherwin-White 1973, and in turn elaborated by Pobjoy 2000, all stressing the war as rebellion, rather than a war for citizenship. Mouritsen's arguments are clever and deserve to be treated with respect, but I have tried to show why there is still room for the sort of arguments advanced by Brunt; see Bispham 2007 for an attempt to justify the traditional view of Italian mistreatment of allies in the second century, against the revisionist views of Galsterer 1976 and Mouritsen. For Italian traders in the Mediterranean, Hatzfeld 1919 remains fundamental; for commercial interests in the conflict, see Gabba 1976: 70–130, reprised in Gabba 1994. The ideas about cultural change and cultural dialog drawn on above are indebted to Wallace-Hadrill 2008. For the Falacrinae inscription see Coarelli, Kay, and Patterson 2008; on the literary sources see Mouritsen 1998, a sustained critique of Appian, with considerable discussion of other sources; on Velleius, see Bispham 2011. Bispham 2007 discusses the enfranchisement laws during the Social War; and on the *lex Licinia Mucia* see Tweedie 2012.

REFERENCES

Bispham, E.H. 2007. *From Asculum to Actium: The municipalization of Italy from the Social War to Augustus.* Oxford: Oxford University Press.
Bispham, E.H. 2011. "Time for Italy in Velleius Paterculus." In *Velleius Paterculus. Making History*, ed. E. Cowan, 17–58. Swansea: Classical Press of Wales.
Brunt, P.A. 1988. "Italian aims at the time of the Social War." In *The Fall of the Roman Republic and Related Essays*, 93–143. Oxford: Clarendon Press.
Coarelli, F., Kay, S., and Patterson, H. 2008. "Investigations at Falacrinae, the Birthplace of Vespasian." *Papers of the British School at Rome* 76: 47–73.
Crawford, M.H., ed. 1996. *Roman Statutes.* 2 vols. London: Institute of Classical Studies/BICS Suppl. 64.
Gabba, E. 1976. *Republican Rome, the Army and the Allies.* (Trans. P.J. Cuff) Oxford:Blackwell.
Gabba, E. 1994. "Rome and Italy: The Social War." in *The Cambridge Ancient History*, Vol. 9, *The Last Age of the Roman Republic, 146–43 B.C.*, 2nd edn, eds J.A. Crook, A. Linott, and E. Rawson, 104–28. Cambridge: Cambridge University Press.
Galsterer, H. 1976. *Herrschaft und Verwaltung im republikanischen Italien.* Munich: Beck.
Hatzfeld, M.J. 1919. *Les trafiquants italiens dans l'orient hellénique.* Paris: De Boccard.
Howgego, C. 1995. *Ancient History from Coins.* London/New York: Routledge.
Keaveney, A. 1987. *Rome and the Unification of Italy.* London: Croom Helm.
Mouritsen, H. 1998. *Italian Unification. A study in ancient and modern historiography.* London: BICS Suppl. 70.
Pobjoy, M.P. 2000. "The first *Italia*." In *The Emergence of State Identities in Italy in the First Millennium BC*, eds E. Herring and K. Lomas, 187–211. London: Accordia specialist studies on Italy 8.
Richardson, J.S. 1980. "The ownership of Italian land: Tiberius Gracchus and the Italians." *Journal of Roman Studies* 70: 1–11.

Roselaar, S.T. 2010. *Public Land in the Roman Republic. A social and economic history of ager publicus in Italy, 396–89 BC.* Oxford: Oxford University Press.

Salmon, E.T. 1982. *The Making of Roman Italy.* London: Thames and Hudson.

Sherwin-White, A.N. 1973, 2nd edn. *The Roman Citizenship.* Oxford: Clarendon Press.

Tweedie, F.C. 2012. "The *Lex Licinia Mucia* and the *Bellum Italicum*." In *Processes of Integration and Identity Formation in the Roman Republic*, ed. S.T. Roselaar, 123–39. Leiden: Brill.

Wallace-Hadrill, A. 2008. *Rome's Cultural Revolution.* Cambridge: Cambridge University Press.

CHAPTER 5

The Civil Wars and the Triumvirate

Edward Bispham

5.1 Rome and Italy: Ideological Imbrication?

Romano-centric writers saw the Social War as arising out of the dysfunction of Roman politics in the late second and early first centuries BC. As Florus had put it, "the people which arbitrated between kings and peoples, *was unable now to govern itself*, to the point where Rome … was attacked from Corfinium" (2.6.7, cf. Appian, *Civil Wars*: 1.34.151). In chapter 4 we saw that the Social War had deeper systemic roots, many of which were embedded in fundamental concerns about equality of rights and political freedom, both of which had degenerated perceptibly across the second century BC, and were seen to be further under threat as the Gracchan resettlement program had removed the access of many allies, especially elites, to Roman *ager publicus* in order to redistribute it to landless Romans. Nevertheless, if these concerns had not been catalysed by the reforming legislative programs of *popularis* tribunes and their associates, they might have taken longer to find expression, and found it in a different form. There is thus some truth in the view noted at the beginning of this paragraph of Florus and Appian that the Social War was a product of internal political tensions, even if citizenship was not, as it was not for Livius Drusus, *per se* a primary part of the political agenda, or even on offer to all Italians.

Barely was the Social War underway when the backlash began within Rome: the tribune Q. Varius Hybrida passed a bill establishing a *quaestio* (standing court) whose ostensible purpose was to bring to trial those who had incited the allies to rebel. There was a lot of hostile propaganda flying around, much of it at the expense of the recently deceased Livius Drusus, of which the "oath of Drusus" is only the most signal example. This, as "preserved" in Diodorus, purports to be the form of words used to swear to support at all costs Drusus (and fellow oath-takers), having the same friends and enemies, and to consider him the "greatest benefactor" if the citizenship is obtained (Diodorus Siculus: 37.11). The oath is obviously a fake. Yet taken beside the story of the friendship between Poppaedius Silo, the Marsic rebel leader, and Drusus (Valerius Maximus: 3.1.2; Plutarch, *Life of Cato the Younger*: 2.1–4, where the young Cato refuses to support their claim for the citizenship despite being hung upside down out of a window of Drusus's house by Poppaedius), it is suggestive about perceptions of Drusus, even shortly after his death, as too friendly with prominent rebels, whom he was

A Companion to Roman Italy, First Edition. Edited by Alison E. Cooley.
© 2016 John Wiley & Sons, Ltd. Published 2016 by John Wiley & Sons, Ltd.

thought to have pushed into war by encouraging them to hope for the citizenship. The story also expresses acute fears about the possibility of constructing a substantial *clientela* built out of new citizen votes, and independent of existing political culture and ingrained loyalties. In fact the Varian *quaestio* looks suspiciously like a piece of political opportunism. It certainly chimed with the mood of public anger at the outbreak of the revolt, and was the only court allowed to continue in session during the war (Cicero, *Brutus*, 304f.; Asconius, *On the Pro Cornelio*, p.73C). Yet the sources associate it with an attempt by the *equites* to strike back at the nobility (which had tried to take the courts back from them), and to increase its unpopularity by blaming it for the war. Those exiled on conviction (until Varius was hoist by his own petard and convicted as well) were friends of Drusus (Asconius, *On the Pro Scauro*: p.22C; Valerius Maximus; 8.6.4; Appian, *Civil Wars*: 1.37.165–9, naming the prominent victims; Badian, 1969 provides a thorough analysis).

Already before the war ended, Italian ambitions and their political and social manifestations had been once again overtaken by, and enmeshed in, the introspective web of Roman domestic politics. In this respect the continuity between the pre- and post-Social War situations is striking. The enfranchisement laws seem to have done little beyond offer the citizenship, either to individuals, or, as in the case of the *lex Iulia*, to peoples, *populi*, which they were free either to adopt (a process called *fundus fieri*) or reject; there were a few cases of hesitation, but none of rejection. But for a people to take up the citizenship, to complete *fundus fieri*, was in itself insufficient to complete the enfranchisement process, above all for those who had desired the active rights and privileges of the citizenship.

For example, all citizens had to be assigned a *classis* and a century (voting-group) within that *classis*, in order to participate in the *comitia centuriata*, and elect consuls, praetors and censors, or vote on declarations of peace or war (in as far as these now came before these *comitia*). This assignation could not happen until there was a census; there was one in 86/85 BC, which registered 463 000 adult male citizens (Jerome, *Chronicle from Abraham*: 173.4). This represents an increase of almost 70 000 since the last completed census in 115/14 BC, or about 17% on the last total. Such a population growth is implausible even over thirty-odd years: populations simply do not grow that fast. Moreover, the Social War, and the mass killing of Romans in the east by Mithridates of Pontus in 88 BC (not to mention other military setbacks around the empire) had meant substantial falls in the citizen population (and the overall allied demographic trend will have been similarly depressed). The increase must then represent a modest enrollment of new citizens by the censors of 86/85 BC, which not only made good recent losses to the Roman population, but increased the overall total (some scholars have sought to emend Jerome's figure to 963 000, but while this is possible textually, it assumes mass registration in what were, as we shall see, very unsettled times; furthermore the figure of 910 000 for the census of 70/69 would actually represent a fall in recorded population, which seems unlikely). We may thus assume that less than a quarter of new citizens had been able to register themselves at the 86/85 BC census.

New citizens also needed a tribe, which corresponded to their geographical origin, and was their voting unit in the *comitia tributa* and *concilium plebis*, as well as determining the groups through which the levy was organized; it was also a part of a Roman's formal nomenclature. Either via the enfranchisement laws, or through subsequent enabling legislation, new tribes were quickly created, apparently in pairs, to which the new citizens were assigned, to a total of eight (Sisenna: *FRHist* 26 fragment 38, fragment 17P; Velleius Paterculus: 2.20; whatever the word *dekateuontes* means in Appian (*Civil Wars*: 1.49.214) – and it is probably "organizing" or something similar – it does not refer to ten tribes). We also learn from Appian (*Civil Wars*: 1.49.214f.) that these tribes voted last, rather than, as with the 35 tribes (the geographically based voting groups established by the Romans over time until 241 BC), according to an order determined by lot; he adds that on account of this, their votes were "often useless." "Often" is a strange qualification to introduce here; the important thing, which must have come clearly out of Appian's sources, is that the Italians were alienated by being made into, literally, second-class citizens. There is no need for Appian to add "often", no need to nuance the bottom line; and it is certainly not the sort of detail which someone who did not fully understand voting procedures in the late Republic would invent as a piece of colorful detail. The inevitable conclusion seems to be that, even while the war was going on, there were *comitia* at which new citizens did vote, and of these there were a few instances where the vote of the 35 tribes was so clearly split down the middle that the votes of at least some of the extra eight tribes were needed to achieve an absolute majority. We would dearly love to know what these votes were on. But the main point is that the Italians quickly chafed under this form of political restraint.

The association of popular reformers with (before the Social War) Italians and (after the war) the new citizens is far from being an inflexible rule, but does represent a real ideological axis, which sometimes had political consequences. In another piece of political opportunism one of the tribunes of 88 BC, P. Sulpicius, espoused the cause of the new citizens, and brought a bill advocating their distribution through the 35 existing tribes. This seems to have been linked primarily to his alliance with Marius, who was now agitating for the command against Mithridates; large numbers of newly re-registered Italians could then be expected to support a vote to transfer the command from Sulla to Marius. Marius had been associated with the ambitions of "new men" two decades earlier when he first rose to the consulship, and with the broad *popularis* movement aroused by the corruption and incompetence of the nobility. Now, seeking to resurrect his career, the old man again dallied with populist methods, but his espousal of popular sovereignty was aimed above all at consolidating his own power. Neither he, nor Sulpicius, nor Cinna and Carbo, with whom he later allied and who continued to hold power as "Marians" until the return of Sulla from the east in 83 BC, can be classed as serious *popularis* ideologues. They realized that there was a large – and growing – pool of discontented new citizens whose *libertas* was infringed by their registration within the new tribes; and that, if redistributed, their votes could be called upon, using the principle of popular sovereignty to get their way, that is, overturn inconvenient earlier votes or senatorial dispositions.

The new citizens were not unaware that they were pawns in a wider game, and it seems that their support for any of the contending parties in the Civil War which succeeded the Social War (87–82 BC) was lukewarm at best. The Samnites and Lucanians, although conceded the citizenship in 87 BC despite not having been definitively defeated, seem to have maintained an effective independence during the "tyranny of Cinna," and to have intervened as autonomous players against Sulla late in the Civil War, at the battle of the Colline Gate (82 BC). There were thus competing discourses of *libertas* in Italy in these troubled years. Across the traditional tension between senatorial *libertas* and popular freedoms which had dominated Roman politics for half a century before the Social War ran other potential fault lines: the desire of some new citizens for a *libertas* which recognized their integration into the *res publica* on the one hand and the unreconstructed desire of (many) Samnites and Lucanians for freedom *from* Rome on the other.

In the end, however, popular ideas of *libertas* seem to have had more traction on Italian attitudes in general than other formulations. Sulla had his supporters in Italy, both committed followers and nasty opportunists like Statius Oppianicus at Larinum (Cicero, *In Defence of Cluentius*); but in general he was perceived as hostile to Italian interests, and in some cases rightly so. The Marians had at least made concessions. Again, popular agitation in the 70s BC embraced not only the restoration of *libertas* through the revival of tribunician powers (the tribunate was a legitimate aspiration from Italian elites who would struggle to attain the higher curule magistracies), but also reform of the courts (greater equestrian representation on juries would entail greater Italian participation). There was also a desire for a census (Cicero, *Against Caecilius*: 8), and much of this must have been driven by new citizens who had not yet been registered by the censors, and therefore were not yet able to enjoy fully the benefits of Roman citizenship. Thus the aspirations of the new citizens were broadly aligned with those who, from commitment or convenience, carried the banner of popular reform in the 70s and 60s BC, above all the circle of Pompeius (some of whose supporters, such as Lollius Palicanus and Petreius were probably drawn from among his Picentine, thus Italian, clients).

That these populist trends were to some degree present within Italian politics before the Social War is clear from the remarkable episode in Arpinum in the late second century BC, where the leading families were locked in a struggle over the introduction of the secret ballot (Cicero, *On the Laws*: 3.36) – the same episode shows, incidentally, that not all statutes passed in the *comitia* at Rome applied automatically in a municipal context. A growing Italian interest in popular politics may be implied too by attestations of magistracies called "tribunes of the *plebs*" in Italian towns like Teanum Sidicinum in the later second century BC (Crawford, ed. 2011, Teanum Sidicinum: 2). Finally, that the Social War, and the integration of the Italians into the Roman state, with all its attendant problems, coincided to a large degree with popular rather than conservative political trends is suggested by Pliny's anecdote that there were two fig trees before the temple of Quirinus in Rome, one patrician and the other plebeian (*Natural History*: 15.120–21). For a long time the patrician tree flourished and the plebeian one struggled, but *after the Social War* their positions were reversed. That said, Italian elites were not radicalized by the experience of the Social and Civil Wars, and remained conservative land-owning "bourgeoisies" after these conflicts as they had before it. Their mobilization by Pompeius and Sestius in 57 BC to bring back Cicero from exile shows that Italian attitudes could be harnessed against, as well as by, Roman populist positions. Popular politics appealed to many in that both the *populares* and the Italians shared a dislike of the exclusiveness of the oligarchic nobility and its reluctance to make concessions. Popular politics was, above all, a means to an end for many Italians.

5.2 Out of the Frying Pan into the Fire

The conclusion of the Social War had brought the citizenship to the Italians, but as we have seen, it did not bring the full suite of citizen rights, and did not bring at once the *libertas* which had been so important an aspiration in the run-up to the Social War (see Bispham, ch. 4, this vol.). More immediately, the Social War did not bring an end to conflict within the peninsula. Sulpicius's attempt to redistribute the new citizens and transfer the Mithridatic command sparked Sulla's unprecedented march on Rome in 88 BC, as his army abandoned the siege of Nola (one of the few remaining centers of Italian resistance) to vindicate their general's rights to command and their own to Pontic booty. Sulpicius, Marius, and ten others were declared public enemies; Marius avoided the fate of Sulpicius and most of the others by making a dramatic escape to Africa, which included breaking out of temporary confinement in the coastal colony of Minturnae. When Sulla, having taken Rome and retained his command by force, went east to claim his prize, Marius returned from Africa, and like Bonnie Prince Charlie in 1745 in Scotland, raised the standard of revolt at Telamon in Etruria. He had substantial support in the region, and brought this to the aid of one of the consuls of 87 BC, Cornelius Cinna, who had withdrawn from Rome in the face of optimate opposition to his plan to revive Sulpicius's proposals and then attempted to raise troops in the cities of Latium. Together, Marius and Cinna forced their way into Rome, and executed dozens of their opponents. The ensuing three years are commonly referred to as the "tyranny of Cinna" (*dominatio Cinnae*), even though Cinna himself was killed in 85 BC, leaving his henchman

Carbo as sole consul. Cinna successfully re-introduced the tribal bill of Sulpicius, and other measures concerning the organization of Italy were begun during this period. Yet neither the Cinna faction, nor the Roman Senate as a whole, nor even the returning Sulla seem to have gained serious traction on Italian loyalties in this period; as we have seen, large parts of the south of the peninsula enjoyed a de facto independence. The Samnites and Lucanians did join the Civil War which re-ignited on Sulla's return, but it is significant that they brought their full might to bear only at the critical juncture at which Rome was about to fall to Sulla, rather than to oppose his return. That is to say, they had no love for the Marian faction, and probably regarded Sulla as the worst of a bad lot.

The feeling was reciprocated. After his victory Sulla took a terrible vengeance on those who had opposed him (as he had threatened he would). Towns which had supported Marius (or failed to support Sulla) had colonies of his veterans imposed on them (some 80 000 men were settled across Italy; Brunt, 1987), or were (illegally) stripped of their citizenship and relegated to something like Latin status (we know this happened to Volaterrae and Arretium in Etruria, but there may have been other communities so punished). Further veterans were settled on some of the estates confiscated from those whom Sulla had declared enemies of the state (the "proscribed"), who could be killed with impunity and whose property was forfeit. Some, like Sex. Roscius of Ameria were killed for their land by greedy relatives, and then had their names inserted *post eventum* on the proscription lists to legitimize the act. And Sulla took a fairly genocidal interest in the Samnites in particular, declaring that Italy would never be safe as long as there were any Samnites of distinction left alive (a riposte to the rallying cry of Pontius Telesinus at the Colline Gate (see Bispham, ch. 4, this vol.)).

The devastation caused by the Social War in the center and south of the peninsula had been profound, but it was only exacerbated by the fighting of the next few years, and the bloody repression perpetrated by Sulla. Institutional, religious and social dislocation compounded loss of life and destruction of livelihood. The underwhelming character of settlement in parts of central Apennine Italy between 80 and 30 BC represented a retrograde step given trends of monumentalization in the generation before the Social War. It is in part attributable to the impact of Sullan measures, especially in Samnium, where the socio-economic basis on which communal wealth and private euergetism depended died with the dictator's persecution of Samnite elites. Major centers like the fortified settlement of Monte Vairano, which had been taking on an increasingly monumental character in preceding generations, now quickly declined into oblivion. It used to be thought that the great rural sanctuaries, the pinnacle of the central Italic settlement hierarchy, were systematically dismantled by Sulla. Certainly some were abandoned, but what we witness at Pietrabbondante, for example, is steady decline rather than sudden decapitation. Other rural sanctuaries in the former rebel heartland, like that at Castel di Ieri, appear to display no break in continuity. In other cases, as at S. Giovanni in Galdo, we cannot yet say whether intense imperial frequentation of the sanctuary can be characterized as revival or continuity (Stek, 2009: 79–106). We are thus dealing with a more articulated series of changes than used to be thought, where the relationship of sanctuaries to local municipal centers (if any) may be one important factor, political loyalties of the local elites another.

These loyalties, or simple ugly opportunism, played a major factor in developments: Italian elites were agents of upheaval as well as its victims (and the same is true of those who fought in the various conflicts on either side). Cicero's *In Defence of Cluentius* is a striking example of the sort of thing that might happen. The whole speech has a complex back-story: in 66 BC Cicero defended Cluentius, a member of the elite of Larinum in the lower Biferno valley, on a charge of murder, but in 74 BC he had spoken for the other side (Statius Oppianicus, father of the prosecutor in 66) against Cluentius. Every claim in this speech (probably the one referred to by Quintilian when he talks about Cicero boasting of having thrown dust in the eyes of the jury, 2.21) needs to be considered with the utmost circumspection, even Cicero's suggestion that what orators say in court cases does not represent their own personal views (*In Defence of Cluentius* 139). Nevertheless, if the statements made were not inherently plausible, and did not chime with the sort of thing known to the jurors by hearsay or direct experience, Cicero would have been laughed out of court.

Leaving aside the garish light cast on intermarriage (and inter-murder) by elite families, we may take two examples. The first is the claim that an aristocrat from Larinum, A. Aurius, had gone missing after the Social War; eventually, but no thanks to Oppianicus, who tried to hush it up, it was discovered that he had been captured with the other rebel fighters in Asculum Picenum when it fell to Pompeius Strabo in the winter of 89 BC. From prisoner of war it was a small step to enslavement, and he ended up in the *ergastulum* (slave barracks) of the senator Q. Sergius (a relative of Catilina?) in the *ager Gallicus*, a little to the north of Asculum, where he seems to have languished for most of the rest of the decade before his relatives finally tracked him down (*In Defence of Cluentius*. 21–4). If a member of a local aristocracy could be made to vanish, to reappear a decade or so later as the slave of a Roman senator, one shudders to think of the fate of others with less social clout. The lawlessness of the times, and unscrupulousness of the Roman victors in the war, emerge clearly. Similarly in our second episode, Cicero relates that when Oppianicus heard of Sulla's victory at the Colline Gate, he assembled a brute squad, stormed into Larinum, deposed the sitting magistrates, and declared that he and his cronies had been appointed in their place by Sulla (*In Defence of Cluentius*. 25). We are meant to see Oppianicus as someone who acted outside the law, hoping that when the dust settled Sulla would not displace a man who claimed to be his partisan (and probably was: Larinum made a dedication to Sulla as its patron at this time, as an inscription reveals: *CIL* 1^2.2951b). Whether or not that is true, whether Oppianicus was acting on instructions or simply exploiting the turmoil caused by the civil war, it is entirely plausible that up and down Italy local elites ventilated their atavistic jealousies, and used the (latest) breakdown of law and order to settle scores and advance the position of their own lineage or faction; that Sulla in turn exploited this process where it left his partisans in power is equally certain.

Elsewhere, tens of thousands of Italians were dispossessed by Sulla's veterans, and into parts of Italy as diverse as Pompeii in Campania and Faesulae in Etruria came Romans, with their language, law, and customs. Relations between the new settlers and the dispossessed were predictably tense, and boiled over in Faesulae as early as 78 BC, when the rogue consul Lepidus tried to capitalize on their support to bring about a counter-revolution in Rome (Sallust, *Histories* 1. 57 (McGushin); Granius Licinianus, 36. 36–7C). Others, especially Etruscans, lived with uncertainty of legal status and title to land; this situation persisted into the sixties (Cicero, *In Defence of Caecina*). Indeed, the whole complex of psychological, institutional, religious, social and economic trauma provoked by Sulla's consolidation of his power after 82 BC was productive of unrest and disturbance down to the end of the sixties. This is most clearly seen in the Catilinarian "conspiracy."

Whatever Catiline's aims in terms of Roman power-politics (and they are probably not what Cicero at least would have us believe), it was evidently plausible that someone aiming at revolution would seek to capitalize on widespread discontent in Italy, especially in the countryside (Sallust, *Catilinarian Conspiracy*. 24, 27, 28.4, 30), but not only there: it was evidently plausible that the continuing disputes of colonists and indigenes at Pompeii could be claimed to be part of the conspiracy (Cicero, *In Defence of Sulla*: 62, refutes such an accusation, but not the essential plausibility of the idea). Here, as throughout Italy, the credit-crunch associated with the renewal of the Mithridatic War in the 70s BC and the loss of Rome's wealthy Asiatic provinces had generated considerable economic hardship and indebtedness; but the problem was more acute in Italy given that it followed a decade of war on Italian soil, and in many areas the depredations of the Spartacan revolt too (Stewart, 1995). And indeed, in the end, Catiline made his last stand with a ragtag army composed of failed

Sullan veterans (although we should strongly resist the moralizing tendency in the literary sources which sees Sullan farmers *generally* as ne'er-do-wells who squandered the favorable situation in which Sulla left them) and the victims of Sullan dispossession. The harsh agrarian and economic conditions of the 70s and 60s BC compounded the political and military upheaval of the 90s and 80s. Much of the Italian countryside was lawless and miserable; the support Catiline found was a symptom of a wider problem, not a cause of decline. This can be seen in the mission of C. Octavius, the father of the future emperor Augustus, who was ordered to deal with disorder in the *ager Thurinus* in the instep of the Italian "boot" on the way to his province of Macedonia (Suetonius, *Life of Deified Augustus:* 3.1); this disorder was characterized as the fag-end of the Spartacan and Catilinarian bands, but they were just the flotsam and jetsam left by the crisis of the previous generation, and need have no relation to either movement.

5.3   Practical Developments

It would, however, be wrong to suggest that the generations following the Social War were exclusively characterized by crisis and contraction. Nor would it be correct to suggest that no measures were taken by the senate which had a positive impact on Italy, although we can hardly speak of reforming zeal, either. As we have noted, the symbiosis between new citizens and *populares* was a utilitarian one as much as an ideological one and, for that reason if no other, fitful in its manifestations.

As we have seen, full redistribution of the new citizens through the thirty-five tribes was achieved by Cinna in 87 BC. Lily Ross Taylor argued that this was intended to support Marian power, with new citizens being assigned to the tribes of leading figures in the Marian circle (Taylor, 1960); but even if we had enough evidence to demonstrate that this was the case (and we do not know to which tribes most of the protagonists belonged), it is not clear that this would be a rational way in which to attempt a long-term gerrymander. In any case, Sulla did not seek, on his return to Italy in 83 BC, to overturn the new disposition, which cannot thus have contained a clear structural bias in favor of the Marians. What is clear is that many of the Social War rebels, especially the upland peoples of central and southern Italy, were "confined" to single tribal blocks: for instance the Pentrian Samnites were largely registered in the *tribus Galeria*; in this way the voting power of these populous regions was concentrated rather than being diffused across the *populus Romanus*. On the assumption that there were issues on which Samnite elites, for example, might want to vote in unison in the *comitia tributa* or *concilium plebis*, their concentration in a single tribe made their impact potentially nugatory. It does seem that neighboring communities might well feel that they had enough in common, at least in elections, to vote for local candidates; Cicero's *In Defence of Plancius* is interesting on the effects of neighborhood (*uicinitas*); that there were issues which bound neighbors together, and that these were more potent than issues which divided them, is less clear, but the possibility should not be dismissed out of hand. Of course, neighborhood and ethnic solidarity are not the same thing. On the other hand, voting in a single tribe did allow for greater coordination of the votes of such former Italic peoples, and make it easier for those who wished to buy votes to obtain the support of such a tribe in a targeted way. The tribal distribution thus carried potential advantages and disadvantages, but it did integrate the new citizens into the body politic in a way which did not require registration at the census to become valid.

Even after the census of 70/69 BC, and the huge leap in the number of Roman citizens registered as a result, it remains likely that those registered with the censors were a minority of the new citizens. Thus the failure of successive censors to conclude a census fully must have been a source of frustration to those Italians who had not registered yet. This may have been more galling, if the census had already been reformed to allow decentralized registration, with local magistrates collecting the data according to the prescribed formula used in Rome, and transmitting this information to Rome within 60 days of a census being announced. Such a system is attested in an inscription on bronze from Heraclea (*tabula Heracleensis*; Crawford, 1996b: no. 24) which is almost certainly of Caesarian date, but collects together a range of material some of which is earlier. In other words, the decentralized census could already have been operating by 70/69 BC, for example (and is indeed known in the exceptional case of the punishment of the recalcitrant Latin colonies in 205 BC). Thus a means for registration, which obviated the potential difficulties of getting from e.g. the south of Italy to Rome and making a declaration in front of the censors, and thus over time could have maximized Italian registration and the extension of full civic rights, was possibly thwarted by the squabbles of the Roman censors themselves.

What had formerly been autonomous sovereign communities had now become communities of Roman citizens, *municipia*, subordinated to the will and needs of the *populus Romanus* as a whole. This transition, both symbolically and practically, was not an easy one to manage, and the question of what could remain, and what should change, in communities often at least as old as Rome was far from trivial. The overall process of managing change and achieving a balance between standardization and common rules on the one hand, and the needs of local identities on the other, is what scholars call municipalization. Magisterial structures showed an important change from outward variety (Oscan **meddíss**; Etruscan *zilath*; Umbrian **uhtur**) to a uniform structure of four magistrates (the quattuorvirate), at some point divided into a higher and a lower pair. These local differences were submerged within what was a Roman institutional framework, which may have helped the elaboration of new kinds of local identity; it also marked off the new citizen communities from the pre-Social War *municipia*, where much greater institutional variety persisted. On the other hand, each community had, or aspired to have, a *lex* or charter, which gave the detail of the rules by which it operated. The *lex* replaced the pre-War *foedus* or treaty, which had elaborated the areas in which each community was obligated to Rome, and the privileges which it retained. In the new *lex* (we have a part of the *lex* of Tarentum in southern Italy; large parts of the Caesarian colony of Urso in Spain; and the *tabula Heracleensis* may be the raw material for an abortive *lex*; Crawford, 1996b: nos 15, 24, 25) institutional structures were spelled out, and rules governing areas such as communal *sacra* (religious rites), eligibility for office and elections, eligibility for membership of the local senate (*ordo*), and management of public money, not least for the holding of games, were elaborated. It seems likely that it was here that local privileges and traditions might be enshrined. The Roman People had a say in this, since it passed enabling legislation which allowed the *lex* to be drafted and given to the community in question (the process of *leges dare*); the *pontifices*, according to Festus, also took an interest in local cults, deciding which ones were to be retained, under the title of *municipalia sacra* ("municipal cults").

This process of municipalization was long drawn out and uneven. Some elements, like the introduction of *quattuoruiri*, depended simply on legislation at Rome; the statute in question, like that ordering tribal redistribution (and, we presume, laying down the principles on which it took place), is probably Cinnan, as Oppianicus found *quattuoruiri* in office, whom he replaced, when he mounted his coup at Larinum. But the process of granting *leges* required both local initiative and probably sponsorship within the Roman elite in order both to draw up the content and secure approval in Rome. Thus communities will have acquired *leges*, and stabilized both their engagement with Roman practices and with their new identities, at different speeds; the *tabula Heracleensis* implies either that Heracleia had no *lex* in the Caesarian period, or had one which it found inadequate (its public records were destroyed in the Social War – Cicero, *In Defence of Archias*: 8), and institutional dysfunction may have been chronic by Caesar's time). Caesar himself passed a general *lex municipalis*, as did Augustus after him, both of which probably aimed to bring some normalization to what had hitherto been a bundle of poorly coordinated actions happening in different places at different speeds, although Caesar's law was probably less ambitious, and more in the way of tidying up, than has sometimes been assumed. At the same time, from the Caesarian and triumviral period onwards, older *municipia* within Italy took advantage of the increasing coordination of legislation and reform concerning Italy to upgrade their institutions; other communities now sought and attained municipal status. Such cases account for some but not all of the instances of duoviral *municipia* in Italy; in other cases the prestige of colonies – which also had *duouiri* – may have been an important factor.

Colonization is a *Leitmotiv* of this period; it accompanied periods of intense stress, especially the Sullan settlement and the discharge of triumviral veterans after Philippi; it is no coincidence that Sulla's dictatorship and the Triumvirate both witnessed the use of proscription (on Sullan colonization: Santangelo, 2007; on Caesarian and Triumviral colonization: Keppie, 1983). Colonies now more than ever before were associated with, and drew prestige from, the military strongmen who founded them; it may be in the first century BC that much of the mythological paradigm and ritual process which we associate with colonization, and colonial association (effective, if not intended) with the spread of Roman language and culture, assume a coherent and systematic form. Colonization could be associated with revival as much as with repression: thus Caesar's colonization of Capua recreated a great Italian city (a trope he was to try to repeat at Corinth and Carthage as dictator); and in Samnium the Caesarian colony at Bovianum doubtless did much to boost the flagging urban culture there. Colonization enhanced an already marked (if unquantifiable) Italian mobility, and with it contributed to the mixing up of populations and cultures within the peninsula, and thus the decline of local distinctiveness in areas such as language and burial customs (see Lomas, ch. 11; Hope and Graham, ch. 9, this vol.). One thing which colonization could not do any more than municipalization, was bring about detailed and universal knowledge and adoption of Roman civil law. How this happened is frustratingly difficult to know. A section of an inscribed Caesarian bronze law from Gallia Cisalpina, sometimes called the *lex Roscia* (Crawford, 1996b: no. 28) details how certain cases should be formulated *in iure* (in court), but does not seem to indicate the basic rules from which actions themselves might spring; the text also refers to the "re-hearing at Rome" (*reuocatio Romae*) of cases where the sum at stake was greater than a particular minimum – in other words, in Cisalpine Gaul at least, there were limits to local autonomy within the municipal system.

5.4   Political Involvement

The volume of Ciceronian evidence gives the impression that the 50s BC were different in Italy from the preceding decades. In large part this may reflect the fact that for the 50s (and to an extent for the later 60s) we simply have a great deal more evidence about Italy and Italians than for the earlier period. The evidence we have suggests considerable interaction between Italian communities and Rome on the political level, and socially between their leading men. This took a number of forms. Italian communities could seek to adopt patrons who would represent their interests in Rome as well as assisting in local difficulties, and ideally engaging in benefactions; they could entice major political figures in Rome, whether local sons or not, to hold magistracies or priesthoods within the community; and as corporate entities they could make their views known on political issues and individual statesmen through testimonials in court cases and the transmission of their senate's or people's decrees to the senate. There is every sign that many communities were active in this area, and that

Roman advocates and politicians in turn were able to mobilize them to further their objectives: the recall of Cicero is only the most famous example, but a large and well-orchestrated Italian turnout could be decisive in any of the assemblies. Italians also now had the opportunities to be recognized as members of the equestrian order and the money-making societies of the *publicani*; and to seek election to the senate via the quaestorship (Nicolet, 1966/1974; Wiseman, 1971 are still indispensable). Indeed, the accession to the senate of "new men" from municipal or colonial backgrounds was one of the most important trends of this period. Like all the processes listed above, it is not new in the last decade or so of the Republic – far from it. In terms of making municipal resolutions known to Rome, we may note the deputation from Ameria which came to Sulla to protest at the treatment of the younger Sex. Roscius, but was fobbed off by his freedman Chrysogonus (*In Defence of Sextus Roscius*: 25); as for the phenomenon of *nouitas*, it is as old as the Republic itself. But it is hard to resist the impression that as the Republic unraveled and as the stakes grew higher, so there was a loosely correlated increase in the frequency and intensity of interaction between center and periphery in Italy. By the time of the Caesarian dictatorship, let alone the Triumvirate, these trends, especially in the appearance of senatorial "new men" from parts of Italy which had never produced a senator, becomes palpable, and is in turn part of the renewal of the Roman governing class which Syme referred to as "the triumph of Italy over Rome" (Syme, 1939: 453–54): the names of key triumviral players such as Ventidius, Salvidienus Rufus, Vipsanius Agrippa and even "Octavian" himself, are important here.

If involvement increased, the number of real issues at stake declined correspondingly. By the late 50s BC Italians were faced, as individuals and communities, with the starkest of choices: if, and when, civil war came, would they declare for Caesar or Pompeius? Pompeius's illness and recovery in 50 BC generated a surge of formal interaction, with Italian communities queuing up to express thanks for the great man's recovery. But this case also reveals the limits of such formal expressions of communal opinion as evidence. Pompeius himself was, or allowed himself to be, deceived: he boasted that he could now raise troops against Caesar in Italy simply by stamping his foot. But when Caesar crossed the Rubicon with a single legion, the towns of Picenum, Pompeius's fief, which had provided three legions to the young adventurer when he declared for Sulla in 83 BC, now opened their doors to his enemy without a murmur, whatever the benefactions Pompeius or his lieutenants had bestowed on them (Caesar, *Civil War*: 1.14). As Cicero contemptuously put it, Italian elites only cared for "their fields, their little villas, their small savings" (*Letters to Atticus*: 8. 13. 2). If Sallust was well able to see the dire legacy which Sulla's settlement had left Italy in the late 60s BC, Pompeius proved spectacularly unable to see it in the late 50s, when it became widely feared (and was not denied) that he intended to introduce proscriptions if victorious. No wonder Italy failed to support him; perhaps in any case he had long decided to emulate Sulla in other respects, to abandon Italy to his enemies, and rely on the wealth of the east and client kings to mount an irresistible invasion, the kind he had himself eschewed in 62 BC.

Pompeius's withdrawal and Italy's quiet capitulation to Caesar meant that the Civil War of 49 to 45 BC, although begun with the crossing of the Rubicon, largely passed Italy by. The exceptions were the increase in the number of Italians – Caesar's partisans – who now entered an enlarged senate; the repercussions of a revolt against debt, which cost the life of the brilliant but mercurial Caelius Rufus; and most importantly of all, one of Caesar's first measures, the enfranchisement of Cisalpine Gaul, a crucial reserve of wealth and manpower, which Caesar had already been exploiting as its governor since 58 BC, and whence, despite the legal impropriety, he had recruited a legion, the V Alaudae, or Larks. Despite doggerel circulating at Rome about Asterix-like figures turning up in Rome, clad in trousers and asking the way to the senate house, the enfranchisement laid the foundations for a major change in the sociology of the upper classes in the early empire.

The Triumvirate was another matter. War returned to Italy, as Caesar's veterans were courted by those who sought to redeem his political legacy and underwrite their own power. Local communities and Caesarian veterans both played their parts in the struggles which culminated in two battles at Mutina in 43 BC. M. Antonius was chased out of Italy by the coalition between the republicans and Caesar's heir, "Octavian" (as he is commonly known in modern parlance); but the deaths of both consuls left too tempting a power vacuum for the fragile coalition to survive intact, and by the end of the year Octavian, Antonius and M. Lepidus, Caesar's nominal deputy during the dictatorship, were on an island in the river Reno near Bononia, agreeing what was in effect a three-man *junta*, with a term of office of five years, and the stated aim of putting the commonwealth in order (*rei publicae restituendae causa*). The reality was somewhat different: enemies and wealthy neutrals alike were purged in a new proscription to provide money and remove opposition at home; both were necessary in order to make possible the campaign against Brutus and Cassius which culminated at Philippi in 42 BC.

After the victory, the 18 wealthiest cities of Italy were selected by the triumvirs as the rewards for their veterans, and became colonies. Caesar had been unwilling as dictator to settle colonies where locals would be forcibly displaced, but the triumvirs showed no such scruples. Once again, dispossession and rootlessness were the dominant characteristics of the day in Italy. But whereas no one dared to oppose Sulla, Octavian had to reckon with two colleagues and their supporters. L. Antonius, the triumvir's brother, and Fulvia, his brother's forceful wife, catalyzed resistance to the confiscations to produce armed insurrection in Italy while M. Antonius was away settling the east; the result is known as the Perusine War. It was the last armed conflict in Italy until the Year of the Four Emperors, but not, as is sometimes asserted, the last round of the conflict between Rome and Italy which had begun with the Social War: that is to misunderstand both conflicts. The conflict, which did not spread outside eastern Etruria, ended with a protracted siege of Perusia, which culminated in unnecessary bloodshed (although we should not believe all the gruesome stories told of Octavian's behavior) and the burning down of the city.

Octavian, or Imperator Caesar as he became in 38 BC, may have learnt some lessons from his unpopularity and the outcome of the war. In the normalization of his control of Italy which began following his victory over Sextus Pompeius at Naulochos in 36 BC (which allowed him to portray himself as the defender of the peninsula against pirates, cf. *Res Gestae*: 25.1), the peninsula began to assume a central ideological role, becoming not the site of triumviral predation, but the *patria* which he would undertake to defend against foreign threats. As such, it was the "political community" which demanded that he lead it against Antonius and Cleopatra in the Actian war (*Res Gestae*: 25.2); and Virgil's *Aeneid* duly has him leading the Italians into battle (*Aeneid*: 8. 678–81). The elevation of Italy and its myths and traditions into a central place in Augustan ideology helped legitimize the Principate, and is every bit as remarkable and important as its corollary, the renewal of the governing class from Italian stock (see Cooley, ch. 6, this vol.).

5.5   *Tota Italia*

How unified was Italy during this period? We have already seen (Bispham, ch. 4, this vol.) that Italy could be spoken of as a "common fatherland" even before the Social War, even if it took another 50 years for a Roman to elaborate a theoretical basis for the relationship of the community of birth (local origin) to the community of citizenship (Rome) – Cicero, *On the Laws*: 2.5. But local diversity remained strong in this period as well, and tensions could be read in many forms of discourse. Thus the *denarius* of 70 BC with Roma and Italia shaking hands (Figure 5.1) on the reverse illustrates a gesture of reconciliation but reminds the viewer

Figure 5.1 *Denarius* of 70 BC with Roma and Italia shaking hands. Courtesy of Prof. C. Howgego & the Trustees of the Ashmolean Museum.

of the need for reconciliation; Roma's foot on the globe reminds us that there is an unequal power dynamic at play, just as there was before the Social War, a dynamic which indeed caused the war. Perhaps the crucial determinant was the passing of the generation which had fought the Social War. From about 50 BC we see the rapid eclipse of Oscan and Umbrian, and indeed all the surviving Italian non-Latin languages except for Greek and Etruscan; Etruscan now becomes increasingly rare in monoglossial contexts, appearing more and more in bilingual inscriptions, or simply giving way to Latin (see also ch. 11, this vol.). Homogenization of burial customs becomes more apparent, although local peculiarities never vanish entirely. The vast wave of public building which characterized many of the towns of the peninsula (Gabba, 1994) saw the further spread and absorption of architecture and building techniques, as well as a surge in an ever more uniform epigraphic habit. The transition from Black Gloss to Italian Terra Sigillata as the primary fineware used in the peninsula meant a massive reduction in the range of styles in circulation, a standardization which is only partly explicable by a decrease in the number of production centers. Cicero refers in the *In Defence of Cluentius* to a wedding conducted "according to the style of the Larinates" (probably a big reception is involved) at which Cluentius is "implausibly" supposed to have attempted murder despite the throng of guests (166). But there are no corresponding later survivals of local practices. In Cisalpina the Gallic inhabitants whom Caesar would shortly enfranchise were already being transformed in the Roman imagination, de-Celticized and renamed as Transpadani, suitably unthreatening. And changes too can be observed in the way in which groups of Italian traders overseas referred to themselves. The name "Italici" is used of both non-Romans and Romans (see ch. 4, this vol.) both before and after the Social War (a classic example of a constructed identity); but about the time of the Caesarian dictatorship the members of such groupings begin to abandon the name Italici, and to refer to themselves as "the Roman citizens who do business in X" (*ILLRP* 387: Panhormus; 408: Cos; 433: Mytilene). We may be sceptical of *tota Italia* as a convenient fiction, whether elaborated by Cicero in 63 BC or Octavian in 32 BC. But the generation who lived through the very last years of the Republic, the dictatorship of Julius Caesar, and the Triumvirate – those of them who *did* live through all of these tumultuous events – were also living through enormous changes in *mentalités* and cultural practices. Italy became what it had never been before; it would never be the same again.

FURTHER READING

Many of the topics discussed here are considered in Bispham 2007, where further reading can be found. For colonization, see Keppie 1983; also Brunt 1987 on settlement, and a remarkable range of other matters relevant to this chapter. Rural settlement and identity are ably dissected in Stek 2009. An excellent study of the transition of an Italian region from allied to Roman status, with sensitive assessment of a range of evidence as well as models for its comprehension, is Bradley 2000 on Umbria; cultural dialogue and cultural change are the subject of stimulating exploration in Wallace-Hadrill 2008. A magisterial survey of Italy in this period in Crawford 1996a.

REFERENCES

Badian, E. 1969. "*Quaestiones Varianae.*" *Historia* 18: 447–91.

Bispham, E.H. 2007. *From Asculum to Actium: the municipalization of Italy from the Social War to Augustus.* Oxford: Oxford University Press.

Bradley, G. 2000. *Ancient Umbria. State, culture and identity in Central Italy from the Iron Age to the Augustan era.* Oxford: Oxford University Press.

Brunt, P.A. 1987 (rev'd edn). *Italian Manpower, 225 B.C.–A.D. 14.* Oxford: Clarendon Press.

Crawford, M.H. 1996a. "Italy and Rome from Sulla to Augustus." in *The Cambridge Ancient History*, Vol. 10. *The Augustan Empire 43 BC–AD 69*, 2nd edn, eds A.K. Bowman, E. Champlin, A. Lintott, 414–33. Cambridge: Cambridge University Press.

Crawford, M.H., ed. 1996b. *Roman Statutes.* 2 vols. London: Institute of Classical Studies/BICS Suppl. 64.

Crawford, M.H., ed. 2011. Imagines Italicae. *A corpus of Italic Inscriptions.* London: BICS Suppl. 110.

Gabba, E. 1994. "Urbanizzazione e rinovamenti urbanistici nell'Italia centro-meridionale del I sec. a.C." In *Italia romana*, ed. E. Gabba, 63–103. Como: Edizioni New Press.

Keppie, L.J.F. 1983. *Colonisation and Veteran Settlement in Italy, 47–14 B.C.* London: British School at Rome.

Nicolet, C. 1966/1974. *L'Ordre équestre à l'époque républicaine (313–43 av. J.-C.).* 2 vols. Paris: E. De Boccard

Santangelo, F. 2007. *Sulla, The Elites and the Empire. A study of Roman policies in Italy and the Greek East.* Leiden: Brill.

Stek, T.D. 2009. *Cult Places and Cultural Change in Republican Italy: A contextual approach to religious aspects of rural society after the Roman conquest.* Amsterdam: Amsterdam University Press.

Stewart, R. 1995. "Catiline and the crisis of 63–60 B.C.: the Italian perspective." *Latomus* 54: 62–78.

Syme, R. 1939. *The Roman Revolution.* Oxford: Oxford University Press.

Taylor, L.R. 1960. *The Voting Districts of the Roman Republic.* Rome: American Academy in Rome.

Wallace-Hadrill, A. 2008. *Rome's Cultural Revolution.* Cambridge: Cambridge University Press.

Wiseman, T.P. 1971. *New Men in the Roman Senate.* London: Oxford University Press.

CHAPTER 6

Coming to Terms with Dynastic Power, 30 BC–AD 69

Alison E. Cooley

6.1   *Tota Italia*

"The whole of Italy of its own accord swore an oath of allegiance to me and demanded me as its commander for the war in which I conquered at Actium" (*iuravit in mea verba tota Italia sponte sua et me bel[li] quo vici ad Actium ducem depoposcit*). In this way, the ideal of "the whole of Italy" (*tota Italia*) was invoked by Augustus as he looked back at the end of his life on his achievement in rallying support in Italy on the eve of his showdown with Antony some decades earlier (*Res Gestae*: 25.2, with Cooley, 2009 ad loc.). Nebulous though this claim is, it shows the importance of Italy to Augustus's self-representation. Just as earlier in the third century it was Pyrrhus's invasion of Italy that had encouraged Rome to promote the idea of *terra Italia* as a means of rallying support against the foreign king (Bispham, 2007a: 55–56, 64), so Augustus re-enacted a similar scenario in order to muster support against Antony and Cleopatra.

Indeed, it was largely thanks to the actions of Augustus himself that *tota Italia* had, by the end of his lifetime, become well defined. The concept of *Italia* as a political entity was still relatively new (Bispham, 2007a: ch.1): it was Augustus who regularized and defined the peninsula by dividing it up into 11 regions (Pliny the Elder, *Natural History*: 3.46), four of which were located in Cisalpine Gaul (Figure 6.1). In doing so, Augustus did not simply formalize existing arrangements, but divided the peninsula up in new ways, cutting across existing ethnic and cultural boundaries, despite using, for most of his regions, names which evoked ethnic affiliations (Crawford, 1996a: 431; Bispham, 2007b: 46–51). The most striking innovation was that the area between the Apennines and the Alps to the north of the river Po – long a source of suspicion because of its Gallic flavor (Williams, 2001: 127–37) – became properly integrated into Italy for the first time. The avoidance of ethnic names for two of the regions in this area – Aemilia and Transpadana – effectively neutralized their problematic Gallic character (Bispham, 2007b: 48). At the same time, the arrangement of the regions itself was centered upon Rome and its road system (Laurence, 1999: 162–65, 172–75). This achievement should not be underestimated: in post-antique times, it was not until 1861 that the Italian peninsula was once again reunified to any significant degree. As we shall see, the reshaping of Italy was not just a superficial administrative reform, but was part of profound

A Companion to Roman Italy, First Edition. Edited by Alison E. Cooley.
© 2016 John Wiley & Sons, Ltd. Published 2016 by John Wiley & Sons, Ltd.

Venetia et Histria

XI

X

Transpadana

Liguria   Aemilia

IX   VIII

Umbria

VI

VII

Etruria   V

Picenum

Samnium

Apulia et
Calabria

I   IV

II

Latium &
Campania

III

Lucania
et Brutii

Sicilia

Figure 6.1   Schematic map of Italy's regions under Augustus. Drawing: A.E. Cooley.

changes in the culture and society of Italy that contributed fundamentally to the success of the Augustan regime. Of course, it also made possible the ultimate accolade for Augustus, hailed as father of the fatherland (*pater patriae*) in 2 BC (*Res Gestae*: 35.1).

As the young Caesar, Augustus had focused on his allegiance to Rome and Italy early on, by fulfilling Julius Caesar's legacy to the urban plebs (Appian, *Civil Wars*: 3.21–23), by constructing his grandiose Mausoleum on the banks of the river Tiber as a monumental riposte to Antony's desire for burial at Alexandria (Kraft, 1967), and by recruiting to his cause the veteran soldiers of Italy who had earlier served under his great-uncle (Cicero, *Letters to Atticus*: 16.8). Nor was Italy of importance only in the early stages of his career: elsewhere in the *Res Gestae* he also emphasized how people had flocked to Rome from the whole of Italy in order to elect him as supreme pontiff (*pontifex maximus*) in 12 BC: "After several years, on the eventual death of the man who had taken the opportunity of civil unrest to appropriate it, I did accept this priesthood; from the whole of Italy a crowd, such as it is said had never before this time been at Rome, flooded together for my election" (*qu]od sacerdotium aliquot[⸢⸣] post annos, eo mor[t]uo d[emum qui civilis tu]m[ultus] occasione occupaverat, cuncta ex Italia [ad comitia mea] confluen[te mu]ltitudine, quanta Romae nun[q]uam [fertur ante i]d temp[us fuisse], recep[i]* – *Res Gestae*: 10.2). He also realized the importance of linking the capital to the rest of the peninsula by building highways (Patterson 2003: 93–94), and in his *Res Gestae* (20.5) he recorded in some detail his repair of the *via Flaminia*, the main arterial route up towards the Adriatic heading north-east from Rome. This road was commemorated by an arch at Ariminum (modern Rimini), constructed in 27 BC to celebrate Augustus's restoration of the *via Flaminia*. Its dedicatory inscription refers to his restoration of "the rest of the most frequented roads in Italy on his initiative and at his expense" (*ILS* 84), in this way treating this one highway as representative of a more extensive road-building program throughout Italy. Coinage issued in 17 BC commemorated Augustus "because the roads have been repaired" (*quod viae mun(itae) sunt*) (*RIC* I² (Augustus) 142). Augustus was said, however, to have encouraged other triumphal generals to restore roads with the booty from their conquests (Suetonius, *Life of Augustus*: 30.1), and so did not pay for the whole project himself: for instance, the *via Latina* was repaired by C. Calvisius Sabinus and M. Valerius Messalla Corvinus (*CIL* 10.6895–6901, *AE* (1969/70) 89; Tibullus: 1.7.57-62 – chronology disputed by Knox, 2005).

Having lived through decades of civil war and the disruption caused by veteran colonization (Keppie, 1983: 101–04, 127–32), Augustus's contemporaries were keenly conscious of the desirability of achieving a peaceful coexistence between the inhabitants of Italy's towns and countryside and those of the capital at Rome. This theme is explored by some of the most influential voices of the period, among them Virgil, Propertius, Horace, and Livy, all of whom came from outside Rome. Strictly speaking, Virgil was not even born an Italian, since his home town of Mantua was part of Transpadane Gaul until 42 BC (cf. ch. 14.5, this vol.). His poetry repeatedly touches upon the relationship between Rome and Italy (Ando, 2002), from the stark picture in the *Eclogues* (1 and 9) of the impact of the triumviral confiscations upon the Po valley to the exploration of "national identity" in the *Aeneid* (Toll, 1991). The catalog of Turnus's forces (*Aeneid*: 7.64–1817), for example, is both an expected part of epic paraphernalia and a vivid foreshadowing of the peninsula's unification under Rome (Williams, 1961). A resolution to the problem of how to mediate between the demands of Italians and proto-Romans comes only in Jupiter's final speech, in which he promises Juno that the Italians will retain their own traditions and not simply be engulfed, as might be expected for the defeated party (*Aeneid*: 12.833–40). By the end of the epic, we find that Rome will be founded as a hybrid, accommodating but not swallowing up the peoples of Italy. This is perhaps a reflection both of contemporary aspirations (Toll, 1997; Reed, 2007) as well as of an ongoing debate about the cultural relationship between Rome and Italy (Habinek, 1998: 88–102).

Nor was it only writers who came to prominence at Rome. By 30 BC, many of the old senatorial families of Rome had been severely depleted during the civil wars, through fighting and proscription alike (Syme, 1939: 61–62, 196–201). They were replaced by "new men" from the municipalities of Italy, supporters of the young Caesar (Syme, 1939: 349–68; Wiseman, 1971: 9–12, 183 for a chronological index of new men), continuing a trend set earlier by Julius Caesar (Syme, 1939: 78–96, 490–508). A sea-change among those in charge of Rome was evident straightaway after Antony's defeat: although best known as a literary patron, Maecenas – wealthy equestrian and descendant of Etruscan kings (Horace, *Odes*: 1.1) – enjoyed an anomalous position during this period as in effect equestrian commander of Rome and Italy in the absence of the young Caesar (Tacitus, *Annals*: 6.11). His was not just a nominal position: his suppression of the "conspiracy" of young Lepidus was reminiscent of the arbitrary wielding of power during the triumvirate (Velleius Paterculus: 2.88.1–3). On his return to Rome in 29 BC, one of Octavian's first acts was to revise the membership of the Senate (*Res Gestae*: 8.2; Dio Cassius: 52.42.1), arbitrarily naming himself as its *princeps* (the title traditionally given to the "leader of the house") (*Res Gestae*: 7.2). He then proceeded to conduct further reviews of the Senate's membership in 18 and 11 BC (*Res Gestae*: 8.2; Cooley, 2009, ad loc.). Many of the new senators were from Italian towns, and some of these went on to achieve the consulship (Wiseman, 1971: 177–78, 203), such as the two brothers

A. Caecina Severus (*cos.* 1 BC, *PIR*² II 106) and C. Silius A. Caecina Largus (*cos.* AD 13) from Volaterrae. Local communities might express pride at now being represented at the heart of government: Q. Varius Geminus was honored by the Superaequani because "he first of all Paelignians was appointed senator" (*is primus omnium Paelign(orum) senator / factus est* – *ILS* 932). To a large extent, Augustus's power-base was founded upon the loyalty of such newly created senators (Galsterer, 1990: 16–17), and the mutual dependency of the regime and its new servants led to a fundamental shift in attitude towards Italian notables. Gradually, the kind of prejudice towards Italian "new men" that Cicero had met with a generation earlier, as the "Romulus from Arpinum" (Pseudo-Sallust, *Invective against Cicero*: 7.1), was transferred onto provincials who aspired to membership of the Senate, as revealed by Claudius's speech on the admission of Gauls to the Senate in AD 48 (*ILS* 212).

The rise of the Italian local elite at Rome had an impact not only upon the political landscape of the capital, but also upon the physical landscape of their home towns. New senators like Varius Geminus functioned as civic patrons representing local interests at Rome and acting as benefactors in their towns. The Caecinae of Volaterrae are an excellent example of the dual spheres of influence now open to the local elite of Italy. They played a crucial role in defending the interests of their town at Rome and also paid for a grand new theater back home, as shown by its monumental inscription and brickstamps: "Aulus Caecina Severus, son of Aulus, consul; Gaius Caecina Larg[us] son of Aulus, [c]onsul" (Terrenato, 1998: 107–09; *AE* (1994) 610 + (1998) 440). This trend began in the decade or so preceding Actium, but it became a particular feature of Italian towns from the Augustan era. Indeed, the way in which Augustus and members of his family came to monopolize the sponsorship of public buildings at Rome incidentally encouraged senators to turn elsewhere in order to construct their monuments (Eck, 1984: esp. 141–42). Some of these building projects emphasized the sense of connection and loyalty between the towns of Italy and the capital of Rome. The theater built by the Caecinae, for example, was decorated with portrait statues of Augustus, Livia, and Tiberius (Fuchs, 1987: 100; Pizzigati, 1993: 59–61 (photographs), 65–67; Sear, 2006: 170).

In the case of theater construction, the impact of Augustan ideology went further still, given that both new and existing theaters reflected the regulation of society imposed by the *lex Iulia theatralis*, whose detailed instructions regarding where different social groups were permitted to sit in the theater had an impact upon the design of the buildings themselves (Rawson, 1987; Small: 1987, 91–93; Zanker, 1988a: 147–53). In this way, the decision to sponsor the building of a theater might act as a statement of support for the Augustan regime (Bejor, 1979: 128–31; Cooley, 1999), as well as providing a venue where people could express their respect towards the imperial family: statues honoring the imperial family set up in theaters were complemented by the sacrifices and acclamations performed for their benefit, and indeed the shows themselves often occurred within the context of festivals honoring the emperor (Bejor, 1979: 134–37; Fishwick, 1991: 574–76).

Another major social change was the new prominence and importance attributed to the equestrian order by Augustus at Rome (Nicolet, 1984: 96–107). Under Augustus we find a new category of *tribunus militum a populo* ("military tribune by popular demand") among leading equestrians of Italy (Nicolet, 1967). This was a short-lived honorific title known only under Augustus and found only in Italy, whose function is rather obscure, but which was clearly a mark of distinction for its holders, who were apparently promoted on the recommendation of their local towns. Some of them played a conspicuous role in promoting imperial ideology in their home towns. At Pompeii, for example, Holconius Rufus was civic patron, priest of Augustus, *duovir* five times, as well as military tribune by popular demand (*CIL* 10.830 = Cooley and Cooley, 2014: F93): his pride in this last title is evident in his statue representing him in military guise, complete with tunic, breastplate, and cloak (Cooley and Cooley, 2014: F93, Plate 6.1). His loyalty towards Augustus emerges from his paying for modifications to the fabric of the town's theater in order to promote greater social differentiation among the audience (*CIL* 10.833-34 = *ILS* 5638 = Cooley and Cooley, 2014: D54) in accordance with the *lex Iulia theatralis*. He also set up a statue of Augustus there, of which only the inscribed base survives from the area of the stage (*CIL* 10.842 = Cooley and Cooley, 2014: D59). Some of the emperor's most loyal supporters were to be found in the towns of Italy, therefore, whether known by name and literary output, like Tiberius's loyal encomiast Velleius Paterculus, or whether anonymous, but to be inferred from the material culture left behind, such as the two silver cups among the treasure excavated from a rustic villa at Boscoreale near Pompeii, which depict scenes of Augustus as world ruler and Tiberius celebrating a triumph (Kuttner, 1995). The villa's owner is unknown, but it is hard not to assume that the choice of imagery on his silverware reflected a sense of loyalty to the Julio-Claudians. The desire to be associated with Rome and its rulers was not just a feature of senators or equestrians but spread throughout society (Zanker, 1988b; 1988a: 265–95).

By the first century AD, therefore, the relationship between Rome and Italy had become a harmonious partnership (Patterson, 2003: 96–98): Italy was regarded as a privileged extension of Rome and Latium, smiled upon by the gods and to be clearly distinguished from the mere provinces that were subject to Rome's rule. An early reflection of this new symbiosis between Rome and Italy can be found in Vitruvius: "Although therefore these matters have been settled in this way by nature in the world and all nations are different because of their unrestrained compounds, yet the Roman people occupies territory across the expanse of the whole world and in the middle of the world's area. For the peoples who are most temperate in both respects – both for their bodies and the vital intelligence that is a match for bravery are in Italy… In this way, a divine intelligence placed the city of the Roman people in an excellent and temperate area, so that it might acquire the right to rule over the whole world" (*cum ergo haec ita sint ab natura rerum in mundo conlocata et omnes nationes inmoderatis mixtionibus disparatae, vero inter spatium totius orbis terrarum regionisque medio mundi populus Romanus possidet fines. namque temperatissimae ad utramque partem et corporum membris animorumque vigoribus pro fortitudine sunt in Italia gentes. …ita divina mens civitatem populi Romani egregiam temperatamque regionem conlocavit, uti orbis terrarum imperii potiretur.*) (Vitruvius, *On Architecture*: 6.1.10–11). Rome and Italy were regarded as complementary components of a single unit – a far remove from the conflicts of the early first century BC – as emerges from two senatorial decrees of AD 47 and 56 found at Herculaneum, which show how the townscapes of Italy and the cityscape of Rome itself were now both equally the object of imperial concern to protect them against unscrupulous property-developers (*ILS* 6043 = Cooley and Cooley, 2014: F132a/b). The emperor's desire to demonstrate concern not only for the city of Rome, but for Italy in general foreshadows the ideology of the later alimentary schemes (Woolf, 1990), particularly as commemorated visually on the arch of Trajan at Beneventum (Rotili, 1972: tav. LIV) (see Cooley, ch.7 this vol.).

Imperial power was also now on occasion wielded from the regions of Italy outside Rome, given that power now lay with the figure of the emperor: at whatever imperial residence the emperor chose to reside, whether at Capri, Baiae, or Antium, that was where petitioners had to track him down. Tacitus (*Annals*: 4.74) describes vividly the crowding of petitioners upon the shoreline opposite Capri, in their hope of approaching Tiberius during his seclusion on the island which posed such serious problems for the functioning of government. Similarly, Philo (*Embassy to Gaius*: 185) describes how in its attempt to secure a meeting with the emperor, the embassy from Alexandria followed Gaius from Rome to Campania as he moved between his properties: "We had come to the Bay of Naples from Rome, following Gaius to Puteoli as he switched between his many country estates. He had gone down to the seaside and was spending time in his luxurious villas." Rome was no longer the sole location of decision-making and power.

Although the phrase *tota Italia* was used by Augustus as primarily a political device, the diverse cultures of the peninsula also became more homogeneous during the first half of the first century AD (Crawford, 1996a; however, for a discussion emphasizing continuing diversity, see Horsfall, 2001). One element that underlay this emerging homogeneity was the common adoption and adaptation of Trojan mythology by families in different parts of Italy (Torelli, 1999: 174–80). Another element that contributed to the decline of local distinctiveness was the large scale of veteran colonization in Italy, with many thousands of veterans being transplanted into new areas of Italy during the period down to 14 BC when land-grants were generally replaced by cash gratuities (Scheidel, 2004: 11–12, 22–24; Patterson, 2008: 488; cf. Wallace-Hadrill, 2008: 439). The homogeneity that did emerge, therefore, was not just some independent cultural development (what might once have been called "Romanization"), but reflected the fundamental changes in politics and society that gradually established themselves after Augustus emerged victorious over Antony, in short what has been dubbed a "cultural revolution" (Wallace-Hadrill, 2008: 36, ch.8). As the next section will explore, the new social and political structures that gradually emerged at Rome had far-reaching impact upon material culture in Italy. This entailed nothing less than the reshaping of Italy, via the emergence of a distinctive visual language (Zanker, 1988a: 167–238; Galinsky, 1996: 342–46; for similar patterns in the provinces, see Woolf, 1995; Keay 2001: 131, 133).

6.2   *Domus Augusta* and *Familia Caesaris*

Augustus, then, built up a special relationship with the rest of Italy, but this did not remain entirely his prerogative: crucially for the success of his regime, it encompassed a dynastic element, embracing other members of the imperial family as well. Nor was the relationship developed on his side alone. Augustus and his family acted as a common focal point for expressions of loyalty on the part of diverse communities in Italy (Bispham, 2007a: 444). The emergence of dynastic power at Rome that was marked by Augustus's promotion of his adopted sons Gaius and Lucius as his successors (Aulus Gellius, *Attic* Nights: 15.7.3) was acknowledged by Italian towns eager to recognize the centrality of the imperial family to Roman society as a whole. Towns in Italy co-opted members of the imperial family as their civic patrons or as honorary local magistrates. Alongside Augustus himself, Agrippa, Marcellus, Tiberius, Gaius and Lucius Caesars, Agrippa Postumus, and Germanicus are all found named as town patrons in inscriptions. Lucius Caesar, for example, was patron of Pisa (*ILS* 139), Cosa (*AE* (1977) 249), Alba Fucens (*CIL* 9.3914), Aesis (*CIL* 11.6200), and Praeneste (*CIL* 14.2910). This is a feature of the Augustan and early Tiberian eras; it is unclear why towns thereafter ceased to appoint emperors or members of the imperial family as patrons (Cogitore, 1992: 826–28). Other ways of maintaining links with the imperial family also emerged, however: Gaius Caligula was twice nominated as *duovir* at Pompeii – the first time in AD 34, when he was still merely Tiberius's heir (*CIL* 10.901–02 = Cooley and Cooley, 2014: F138), and then again in AD 40–41 when emperor (*CIL* 10.904). This position was purely honorific: the real work of the magistracy was instead carried out by a prefect (*praefectus*) appointed from the local elite as substitute for the imperial post-holder. This practice continued until the time of Commodus (Menella, 1988).

Members of the imperial family also acted as benefactors towards the towns of Italy, funding the construction of public buildings, such as the theatre at Ostia built by Agrippa (*CIL* 14.82; Cooley, 1999). This heralded an important shift in the sponsorship of public buildings, moving away from the expectation that such sponsorship was the responsibility of local magistrates towards it being associated with the private generosity of individuals

(Alföldy, 1997). One possibility is that such benefactions reflected patterns in imperial landowning, and that towns may have benefited from imperial estates in their territories (Coarelli, 2000; on imperial estates see also section 6.3 in this chapter). It is also likely that towns themselves approached the emperor and his family with requests for financial help in erecting public buildings (Patterson, 2003: 92). Veteran colonies in particular appear to have attracted imperial sponsorship (Patterson, 2003: 90; Keppie, 1983: 114–16). Although no new veteran settlements were established within Italy after 14 BC, some small pockets of veteran colonists were still added to existing communities, such as Saepinum (Keppie, 1983: 9). The town's walls, gateways, and towers were paid for by Tiberius in AD 4–5, before he became emperor, as attested by an inscription on each of the gates. This would have involved major financial outlay. One possibility is that this building activity is linked to imperial interest in the transhumance route through the town (Coarelli, 2000: 143), but the fact that Tiberius included his already deceased brother Drusus as co-dedicator suggests that the case is not so straightforward. The gateways were decorated with statues of barbarians, recalling their recent conquest of Dalmatia, perhaps even with the aid of veteran soldiers now settled in the town (Patterson, 2006: 99, 126; *ILS* 147). This probably reflects the care with which Augustus cultivated a sense of personal allegiance towards himself in the legions; the ideology of imperial concern for veterans was manifested in other actions too, such as Augustus's establishment of the military treasury (*aerarium militare*) through his personal investment in order to fund retirement pay for veteran legionaries (*Res Gestae*: 17.2).

By the time of Augustus's death, the concept of the imperial family as the Augustan household (*domus Augusta*) was firmly established at Rome, commemorated in both monuments and literature, by statues set up by the consul Norbanus Flaccus at the *Circus Flaminius* (*Tabula Siarensis* = Crawford, 1996b, no. 37a ll.10; Flory, 1996) and in the poetry of Ovid (Millar, 1993). In the absence of any sons, this concept was a crucial one for Augustus in mapping out a possible hereditary succession by replacing the narrower concept of the *gens* with a family that could include both Julians and Claudians. In fact, the lack of males related by blood to Augustus himself brought women into new prominence, as they made possible the ties of adoption and marriage alliances by which a sequence of heirs was put in place (Corbier, 1995; 2001). For example, the simultaneous adoption of Tiberius by Augustus and of Germanicus by Tiberius was designed to ensure that future emperors would be direct descendants of Augustus himself, since Germanicus enjoyed a fruitful marriage to Agrippina, Augustus's granddaughter. As a result, women gradually occupied an increasingly prominent place in the public perception of the imperial family, as new ideas about what constituted correct female behavior emerged: imperial women emerged as patrons, property-owners, and builders, and at the same time (and in some cases even earlier) elite women in the towns of Italy also began to play new roles in public life (Milnor, 2005; Cooley, 2013). This in turn led to the new practice of setting up public statues to honor women (Flory, 1993; Hemelrijk, 2005).

Dynastic statue groups were a typical feature of many public buildings in Italy during the time of Claudius (Cogitore, 1992). Some of these, such as the Claudian group at Caere which included deified Augustus, Tiberius as Jupiter, Drusus the Elder, Livia, Agrippina, Britannicus, and Claudius as Jupiter, were probably associated with temples for emperor-worship (Fuchs, Liverani, Santoro, 1989: 8, 53–88, 97–102; Cogitore, 1992: 840–43 for inv. 9952 as Agrippina rather than Messalina), but other groups were prominently displayed in other types of public space, such as the basilica at Velleia (Saletti, 1968). These were not always set up by the town itself; individuals might choose to pay for statues of the imperial family. At Herculaneum, L. Mammius Maximus set up statues honoring *divus* Augustus (*AE* (1979) 172), Tiberius (*AE* (1979) 173), *diva* Augusta (*ILS* 123), Germanicus (*ILS* 177),

Agrippina the Younger as wife of Claudius (*CIL* 10.1418), Antonia Augusta as mother of Claudius (*ILS* 150), Nero as Caesar and son of Claudius (*AE* (1979) 175), and Octavia (*AE* (2009) 225; Cooley and Cooley, 2014: F124–F131). Although no inscription for Claudius himself has yet been found, he must have been the focal point of the group. This pattern is no coincidence: these statues of Julio-Claudians, past and present, boosted Claudius's own legitimacy as ruler (Cogitore, 1992: 847–52). In the case of Mammius Maximus, this statue-cycle represented an appropriate investment and lavish expression of loyalty for an *Augustalis* in the town (*CIL* 10.1452 = *ILS* 6352; Cooley and Cooley, 2014: D68a/b, with Plate 4.6), and was perhaps dedicated at the time of Nero's adoption in AD 50 (Cogitore, 1992: 824). Such monuments consolidated the idea of the Julio-Claudian dynasty as a recognisable unit, with Germanicus and Agrippina the Elder acting as the glue binding the two families. Similar tactics were subsequently used in consolidating the Flavian and later dynasties. In this way, statues of the men, women, and even children who belonged to the imperial family became a common sight in town centers, in *fora*, theaters, and temples, and even in private residences. These portraits of the imperial family were strikingly uniform in style, making a contribution of their own to the process of cultural homogenization outlined earlier in this chapter (Terrenato, 2001: 58).

Statues were not the only way in which the imperial family's presence became felt. Already under Augustus, some towns included buildings in their *fora* for cult directed towards and for the benefit of the imperial family: Pisae (*ILS* 139, by AD 2), Ferentinum (*CIL* 11.7431, probably AD 12), Firmum Picenum (*AE* (1975) 354, possibly Augustan in date) and Beneventum (*ILS* 109, by 15 BC) all had an *Augusteum* or *Caesareum*, whilst the forum at Fanum Fortunae contained a temple of Augustus (Vitruvius, *On Architecture*: 5.1.7). The statement in Dio Cassius (51.20.6–8) that Augustus received no cult in Italy during his life-time is demonstrably misleading, even though it has in the past been influential (Gradel, 2002: 73–91). In the case of the new forum at Puteoli that was laid out under Augustus, local families paid for various public buildings which took their titles not just from those families, but also from the imperial family (Demma, 2007: 170–73; Camodeca, 1979: 20–23): we find references to the Hordionian Altar of Augustus (*ara Augusti Hordioniana*: *TPSulp* 1–9, 16–17, 40), the Sextian Portico of Augustus (*porticus Augusti Sextiana*: *TPSulp* 83–86, 88, 90–92), the Suettian *Chalcidicum* of Augustus (*chalcidicum Augusti Suettianum*: *AE* (1974) 256, AD 113), the Suettian Altar of Augustus (*ara Augusti Suettiana*: *TPSulp* 18), and the Annian Basilica of Augustus (*basilica Augusti Anniana*: *CIL* 10.1782–83, 1786, 2nd century AD). At least some of these names continued to be used for many decades, appearing still in inscriptions from the late second century AD. The emperor's name also began to be included in commemorative building-inscriptions, even if he had not been directly involved in financing or initiating the work. The amphitheater at Luceria, for example, displayed two copies of a monumental dedicatory inscription: "Marcus Vecilius Campus, son of Marcus, grandson of Lucius, prefect of engineers, military tribune, joint chief magistrate with judicial powers, priest, saw to the construction of the amphitheater on his private land and the enclosure wall surrounding it at his own expense in honor of Imperator Caesar Augustus and of the colony of Luceria" (*AE* (1938) 110). As a result, the imperial presence became pervasive within the urban monumental landscape in the towns of Italy, and it spread out into the countryside too in the form of the milestones that bore Augustus's titulature (Alföldy, 1991: 299–302).

As well as having an impact upon the monumental appearance of towns, the imperial family became increasingly prominent in urban ceremonial life as well. These aspects are less obvious in the archaeological record, but we can gain glimpses of the vows, sacrifices, and games that were often focused upon successive emperors and their families, as well as of the impact of the journeys and visits made by the emperor and his entourage around the peninsula, both alive and dead (cf. Benoist, 2005, for a study focusing on ceremonial in the city of Rome). At Pompeii, for example, an individual fulfilled his vow for the welfare of Gaius Caligula by setting up a dedication to Jupiter (*CIL* 10.796 = Cooley and Cooley, 2014: E11), whilst gladiatorial combat at nearby Nuceria was provided by a *flamen augustalis* in honor of the *numen Augusti* ("divine spirit of Augustus") (*CIL* 4.3882). Even after the ban on gladiatorial combat at Pompeii, a show of hunting and athletics was advertised on behalf of the welfare of Nero (*CIL* 4.7989a, c = Cooley and Cooley, 2014: D44), whilst the *Augustales* of Puteoli put on games in the amphitheater in honor of Nero and Agrippina, along with Jupiter Best and Greatest and the *genius* of the colony (*CIL* 10.1574). Performances in theaters and amphitheaters were good opportunities for towns to display their loyalty to the imperial family through acclamations.

Finally, imperial funeral corteges might travel for many miles through Italy. Augustus's funeral procession journeyed from Nola in Campania, with his body being borne in state back to Rome. This procession and the arrangements for his funeral were carefully calculated to reflect the newly reinforced hierarchy of Augustan society, and gave an important role not just to the aristocracy of Rome, but also to the municipal elite: "Town councillors of municipalities and of colonies carried his body from Nola as far as Bovillae, at night on account of the time of year, when in the meanwhile it was laid to rest in the basilica of some town or in the greatest of the sacred buildings. From Bovillae the equestrian order took it up, and carried it to the city and placed it in the vestibule of his house" (*corpus decuriones municipiorum et coloniarum a Nola Bovillas usque deportarunt, noctibus propter anni tempus, cum interdiu in basilica cuiusque oppidi vel in aedium sacrarum maxima reponeretur. a Bovillis equester ordo suscepit, urbique intulit atque in vestibulo domus conlocavit*, Suetonius, *Life of Augustus*: 100). Other funeral processions, like Agrippina's return with Germanicus's ashes from Brundisium to Rome, were less carefully controlled, offering the populace an opportunity to demonstrate their sentiments (Tacitus, *Annals*: 3.1–2).

At the same time as the imperial family was becoming prominent throughout Italy, members of the local elite adopted new strategies to associate themselves with the imperial court as a source of prestige for themselves. In this way, the local elite was not sidelined by the imperial family, unlike the senatorial aristocracy at Rome. Some of their strategies – such as the naming of the buildings in the forum at Puteoli – have already been noted. At Pompeii, the public priestess Eumachia funded a lavish public building that dominated one side of the forum, and dedicated it to Augustan Concord in her own name and that of her son (*CIL* 10.810, 811 = Cooley and Cooley, 2014: E56). This appears to have been designed to recall similar imperial actions at Rome, where in 7 BC Augustus dedicated the *porticus Liviae* ("portico of Livia") in the names of Livia and her son Tiberius, to which Livia then added a few months later a shrine to Augustan Concord (Richardson, 1978). At the same time, however, Eumachia's decision to dedicate to Augustan Concord, and to add alongside this a dedication to Augustan Pietas as well, demonstrates that she was not simply slavishly copying what Livia had already done at Rome. Instead, she emerges as an active agent in disseminating and further developing ideas only slowly emerging at Rome (Cooley, 2013: 31–36). Emperor-worship and other cults associated with the imperial family were also a source of prestige: inscriptions on the bases of statues set up to honor two major local benefactors of Pompeii, Holconius Rufus and Holconius Celer, consistently referred to their posts as priests of Augustus as well as to their local magistracies (*CIL* 10.830, 837, 840, 943–48 = Cooley and Cooley, 2014: F93, D56, D58). Temples to Augustan deities sprang up rapidly around the peninsula. At Rome, the altar of *Pax Augusta* ("August(an) Peace") dedicated in 9 BC is the first surviving example of such a cult, but all kinds of "Augustan" deities quickly spread in Italy (Cooley, 2006: 246–52), with the temple of Augustan Fortune at Pompeii, for example, being established by AD 3 (*CIL* 10.820, 824 = Cooley and Cooley, 2014: E44, E47). This contributed to the process of homogenization described earlier in this chapter (section 6.1), with even local deities – Belenus, Eia, Ika, Melosocus, and Tria in northern Italy, for example – becoming Augustan (Gregori, 2009), and helped to reinforce a sense of loyalty and connection between the towns of Italy and Rome.

The other major change brought about by the new political structures at Rome was the emergence of the *familia Caesaris* ("Caesar's household"), the slaves and freedmen/women who belonged to the imperial household (Weaver, 1972: esp. 5–8). Many of these – among them, gardeners, litter-bearers, doorkeepers, chefs, tasters, doctors, wet-nurses – performed the duties to be expected in any elite household, looking after the personal needs of their masters and overseeing domestic matters. Secretaries and financial agents were also an unexceptional part of an upper-class household, but what is extraordinary in the case of the *familia Caesaris* is the way in which members of the imperial household increasingly came to serve as a tool for administering public concerns, "a private household with a central role in public life" (Wallace-Hadrill 1996: 287). In itself, this was not entirely without precedent: magistrates had long been used to employ their own staff in fulfillment of public duty. What was new was the degree to which there was now a lack of clarity in defining what belonged to the emperor, and what belonged to the state (Rathbone, 1996: 320–22). In 28 BC, Augustus transferred the administration of the state treasury from the two urban quaestors (*quaestores urbani*), relatively junior magistrates who were answerable to the consuls (Corbier, 1974: 633) to two relatively senior magistrates, ex-praetors who were to serve as prefects of the treasury (*praefecti aerarii*) (Corbier, 1974: 637–39). In this way, Augustus shifted the administration onto relatively senior magistrates, and this change in administrative structure allowed Augustus rather than the Senate to influence which individuals were appointed to supervise the treasury (Speidel, 2000: 127). Crucially, the treasury's regular staff consisted of imperial freedmen and slaves. As a result, Augustus effectively had control over the issuing of accounts and over access to detailed financial information; knowledge about state finances became effectively the monopoly of the emperor himself, via his freedmen agents. The importance of this is clearly revealed at the very end of Suetonius's biography of Augustus, where he reports that one of Augustus's last acts was to supply the names of freedmen from whom financial information necessary for the smooth running of the empire could be sought (Suetonius, *Life of Augustus*: 101.4). In this way, the transferral of imperial slaves and freedmen to his heir was a crucial component in the smooth transition of the first succession from Augustus to Tiberius.

Under Claudius, the power wielded by his freedmen became notorious, as they exploited to the full the potential to act as intermediaries in securing imperial favor by controlling access to the emperor. It is no coincidence that freedmen were given titles according to their role in controlling different routes of communication, with freedmen in charge of letters (*ab epistulis*), petitions (*a libellis*), embassies (*a legationibus*), and legal hearings (*a cognitionibus*) (Wallace-Hadrill, 1996: 297). Although literary sources tend to dwell in particular upon their colorful role at the court in Rome, epigraphic sources show clearly that imperial freedmen were also active in Italy and the provinces. The running of Claudius's new harbor at Ostia, for example, was charged to the imperial freedman procurator Claudius Optatus (*ILS* 1533). That their importance far exceeded their humble social status as freedmen was recognized by other parties: Gaius Julius Gelos, freedman of deified Augustus, was honored with exemptions from local taxes for himself and his children, as well as receiving an "honorific seat of his own among the *Augustales* at all the games in our *municipium*, and to take part in all public feasts among the town councillors" by decree of the town council of Veii in AD 26, because he "has at all times not only helped the *municipium* of Veii with his advice and goodwill, but also wanted it to be celebrated because of his investment" (*ILS* 6579). As we shall see in the next section, imperial financial interests had far-reaching impact upon Italy, and these interests were chiefly under the management of staff from the imperial household.

6.3   The Economic Impact of Dynastic Power

As a direct result of the political and military upheavals of the triumviral period, the emperor, members of his family, and close friends began to amass vast tracts of property in the provinces. The conquest of foreign foes and fellow-Romans alike led to property changing hands. In Egypt, for example, estates came into the possession of Livia, Antonia the Younger, Germanicus, and Maecenas (Crawford, 1976: 39–43; Rowlandson, 1996: 55–56; Parassoglou, 1978), whilst much of Sicily was taken over by imperial estates, with Agrippa also assuming ownership of lands on the island following his defeat of Sextus Pompeius (Wilson, 1996: 437). These conquests had continuing impact upon the ownership of lands under the later Julio-Claudians too: powerful imperial freedmen, such as Doryphorus, Pallas, and possibly Narcissus, all owned property in Egypt. Pallas may even have acquired land whilst still a slave of Antonia the Younger, or immediately after his manumission, and his name is associated in 11 different districts with a variety of property types, including grain-land, garden-land, and pastures (Crawford, 1976: 39, 41; Parassoglou, 1978: 22–24, 77, 80, 81).

Inheritance also extended imperial property-ownership, as it became standard practice to name the emperor in wills: Augustus declared that he had acquired 1400 million sesterces from legacies in his last 20 years alone, but had spent almost all of it for the benefit of the state (Suetonius, *Life of Augustus*: 101, cf. 66.4; contrasting with the abuses of legacies of Gaius and Nero – Suetonius, *Life of Caligula*: 38; *Life of Nero*: 32). Inscriptions relating to financial administrators (procurators) which record how they served different members of the imperial family also show how estates were gradually amassed, as Tiberius inherited from Augustus and Livia (Julia Augusta), Caligula from Tiberius, and so on. Gaius Herennius Capito, procurator of Julia Augusta, Tiberius Caesar Augustus, and of Gaius Caesar Augustus Germanicus, set up a silver bust of Tiberius at Teate Marrucinorum in Samnium (*AE* (1941) 105). Having served in the army, Herennius Capito had become manager of imperial estates in Jamnia in Judaea, which had been bequeathed to Julia Augusta by Salome, sister of Herod the Great (Josephus, *Jewish Antiquities*: 18.158). The career of Nero's praetorian prefect Afranius Burrus also illustrates how imperial estates might accumulate, since he was procurator of Julia Augusta, Tiberius Caesar, and deified Claudius (*ILS* 1321). Although the name of Gaius was omitted in this list, this omission probably reflected the desire not to mention the assassinated emperor rather than reflecting a break in Burrus's career.

Despite Tacitus's assertion (*Annals*: 4.6) that under Tiberius, imperial lands in Italy were few and far between (*rari per Italiam Caesaris agri*), this simply reflects a contrast with his contemporary world, when the emperor had become the biggest landowner in Italy (Camodeca, 2007: 158). In fact, already under the Julio-Claudians, imperial landownership extended the length and breadth of Italy (Pupillo, 2007). In addition to the momentum created by inheritance from emperor to emperor within the Julio-Claudian dynasty, the wives of emperors contributed to this accumulation of property in their own right, as they inherited from their fathers or former husbands. An estate of Messalina in the *ager Tusculanus*, to the north of modern Frascati, was probably inherited from her grandfather M. Valerius Messalla Corvinus (consul, 31 BC), whilst Agrippina the Younger appears to have inherited a villa at Frascati from her second husband C. Passienus Crispus (Granino Cecere, 2010: 114, 120). It seems likely that the portfolio of imperial lands was also enhanced in a more sinister way too, as a result of confiscating property from individuals convicted of treasonous plotting. This probably happened in the case of Ser. Asinius Celer, executed by Claudius in AD 47

(Segenni, 2007: 131) and C. Calpurnius Piso, convicted of conspiracy by Nero in AD 65 (Camodeca, 2007: 152). These imperial possessions must have made an impact upon the regions of Italy because of the resulting imperial visits and the permanent presence of imperial slaves and freedmen involved in the estate management. Such freedmen might subsequently become integrated into the life of nearby towns, as illustrated by the case of C. Iulius Gelos (see section 6.2 in this chapter) (Zaccaria, 2007: 66–67). Landownership is also another aspect of the impact of the emergence of the *familia Caesaris* (section 6.2 in this chapter), with imperial freedmen becoming significant landowners themselves certainly by the time of Claudius. The fabulously wealthy Pallas, for example, owned brickworks known as the *Praetorium Pallantianum* in the Sabine area (Phlegon, *FGrH* IIB 257, IV p.1188; Patterson, 2004: 68). These were later confiscated by Nero (Segenni, 2007: 128).

The impact of imperial ownership of lands upon the towns of Italy in whose vicinity they lay was not always positive (Patterson, 2004: 68). Valuable resources were drained from the regions of Italy for the benefit of the emperor. Not only did members of the imperial family own agricultural land, but they also exploited the natural resources of their properties outside Rome, such as clay-pits to produce bricks and tiles (e.g. the tile- and iron-works at Vagnari in Apulia: Small, Volterra, and Hancock, 2003). Emperors came to own large quantities of land in the Tiber valley, and by the second century AD many of the brickworks there were under imperial control. Augustus's actions in improving the Tiber channel in Rome itself and beyond the city for as far as 20 miles strongly suggest imperial interest in communications through the valley for economic reasons well before the second century, however (Patterson, 2004: 68; Pseudo-Isidore, *Chronicle* (Vidal, 1961: 21)). Other types of precious resources and sources of prestige which might be based in towns of Italy were also owned by Julio-Claudian emperors, as illustrated by the large troupe of several thousand gladiators based at Capua. Probably inherited from Julius Caesar, they remained under imperial control, becoming known as the *Neroniani* (Jacobelli, 2003: 19). Although other troupes existed outside the capital, such as the *familia gladiatoria* of N. Festius Ampliatus, known to have performed at Pompeii (Jacobelli, 2003: 45; *CIL* 4.1183–84), the *Neroniani* enjoyed especial kudos (Sabbatini Tumolesi, 1988: 131; *CIL* 4.1421, 2508, 10237–38 = Cooley and Cooley, 2014: D38, D37, D31–32).

The unique power and resources of the emperor also on occasion brought about major changes to the economy and landscape of Italy. The emperor could now accomplish changes to the landscape on a previously unheard-of scale, whether in the form of Caligula's bridge of boats at Baiae (Suetonius, *Life of Caligula*: 19), Claudius's draining of the Fucine lake and construction of the harbor at Ostia (Suetonius, *Life of Claudius*: 20.1), or Nero's plan for a canal from Lake Avernus to Ostia (Suetonius, *Life of Nero*: 31.3; Tacitus, *Annals*:15.42). To hostile eyes, such projects might appear as the result of hubris on a par with Xerxes' bridging of the Hellespont. Literary sources wishing to mock the emperor and his freedmen represented such projects as pretty much an irrational impulse, but it is also possible to see them in a more positive light (Griffin, 1984: 107–08). Claudius's draining of the Fucine Lake and construction of a harbor at Ostia, along with measures to encourage ship-owners (Suetonius, *Life of Claudius*: 18–19), were in fact part of a rational plan to increase the security of the capital's basic food supplies, and this aim is clear from the design of coins issued in AD 41–43 on the theme of *Ceres Augusta* (Letta, 1994: 203; *RIC* I² 119, 127 no.94, 129 no.110). The emperor could now embark upon construction projects that were more ambitious than ever before (and, significantly, foreshadowed only by Julius Caesar: Suetonius, *Life of Iulius*: 44; Plutarch, *Life of Caesar*: 58), but their negative portrayal in literature plays down their economic potential. They were perhaps rather the harbingers of later projects, such as Trajan's cutting of the *via Appia Nova* at Terracina or Domitian's *via Domitiana* (eulogized by Statius, *Silvae*: 4.3), road-building projects designed to shorten journeys between Rome and Brundisium and Puteoli respectively. Nevertheless, the idea of such projects being designed as a display of power was not without some foundation. Claudius's staging of a sea-battle on the Fucine Lake just before its draining (mocked by Suetonius, *Life of Claudius*: 21, 32) shows his desire to make a spectacle out of what might otherwise have seemed a rather unexciting piece of engineering, as described by Tacitus (*Annals*: 12.56.1): "At this time, once the mountain-side had been cut through, between the Fucine Lake and the River Liris he displayed a sea-battle on the lake itself, so that the splendour of the project might be viewed by more people" (*sub idem tempus inter lacum Fucinum amnemque Lirim perrupto monte, quo magnificentia operis a pluribus viseretur, lacu in ipso navale proelium adornatur*). The physical landscape of Italy too, therefore, was now potentially subject to the whim of one powerful individual, who might choose to subordinate Italy's natural landscape to the interests of Rome.

6.4   The End of the Dynasty

By the time of the last of the Julio-Claudians, therefore, the change in political regime at Rome had impinged not only upon Italy's political landscape, but also upon its religious and economic character, and even upon its physical landscape. It had changed the ways in which buildings were constructed, and even the ways in which local elites represented themselves. Inscribed monuments in particular had also become newly prominent in towns and along the major roads that crossed the peninsula (Alföldy, 1991). The downfall of Nero, and the subsequent civil wars known as the "Year of the Four Emperors," however, brought military action to the peninsula itself for the first time for many decades, and Rome's political problems had a devastating impact upon northern Italy in particular. Once again, seismic shocks produced by political tremors at Rome extended across the rest of Italy, and fate of the capital and Italy were closely intertwined.

On a mundane front, for example, the rapid succession of emperors (and hence, consuls) at Rome produced confusion among the population of Italy as they tried to keep abreast of the latest developments at Rome in dating legal documents. At Herculaneum, the consular dating of a set of three tablets reflects the potential for confusion. Where usually a consular date is found on such tablets, we read *Act. Herculani / VII K. Febr. / Imp. [[Galba]] Othone Caesare [Aug. cos. (?)]* – "Transacted at Herculaneum on 26th January, when Imperator ~~Galba~~ Otho Caesar [Augustus was consul(?)]." In this way, the writer has first written Galba's name, but has then struck it through, before altering it to Otho. This document happens to date from a moment of particular confusion: after Galba and his fellow consul T. Vinius had been killed on 15 January, no consul was then in office for 11 days until Otho and his brother were then elected to consulships on 26 January. Given that this tablet dates from that very day, the writer at Herculaneum did not yet know that this was the case, but has made an educated guess at what he thinks the situation is likely to be. The tablets merely concern judgment of a property dispute, the issue being whether Cominius Primus has legally removed the 306 wooden stakes that separated off his estate from his neighbor's, in order to challenge the current position of the boundary between them, illustrating the way in which political confusion at Rome could impinge upon the everyday concerns of ordinary individuals (Camodeca, 1994: esp. 137, 143 = *AE* (1994) 416 = Cooley and Cooley, 2014: G30). Politics at Rome also created more serious problems for the local elite of towns of Italy. In choosing to support Vitellius, for example, it appears that the local elite families of Capua then adversely affected their chances of promotion under the Flavians (Patterson, 2006: 194).

The introduction of troops on active duty into Italy was in response to the uprising led by C. Iulius Vindex in Gaul from March of AD 68 (Chilver, 1979: 11–12): the 14th Legion Gemina was sent to the Po Valley, along with its Batavian auxiliaries, commanded by P. Petronius Turpilianus (Wiedemann, 1996: 259). Before these troops were mobilised against him,

Vindex was defeated in battle at Vesontio by the Rhine legions, but the Batavians were later to claim that they had seized Italy from Nero (Tacitus, *Histories*. 2.27): even though these civil wars were to reveal, as Tacitus claimed (*Histories*. 1.4), the secret that an emperor could be chosen outside Rome, Italy – and Rome itself, of course – still remained the end-goal for claimants to the empire. Consequently, northern Italy became a battleground between the forces of Otho and Vitellius (Tacitus, *Histories*. 2.11–13, 17–45) and then between Vitellians and Flavians (Tacitus, *Histories*. 3.6–42, 50–63). Tacitus highlighted the fate of two cities in particular, Placentia, whose amphitheater was burnt down (*Histories*. 2.21), and Cremona, which was besieged over four days, eventually being entirely destroyed apart from the temple of Mefitis outside the town walls (*Histories*. 3.19–35).

The strikingly slow pace of Tacitus's narrative of the civil wars in the opening books of his *Histories*, with the year AD 69 being covered over three whole books, leaving the remaining nine books to cover the following 27 years down to the assassination of Domitian, illustrates how critical he considered these events to have been for the fate of Rome and Italy (Ash, 2009: 88–90). One of the themes of Tacitus's account is the way in which Italy became treated as foreign foe by the opposing armies (*Histories*. 2.12; cf. 2.87), and, conversely, how the Vitellians in particular acted the part of invading barbarians (Ash, 1999: 37–51): "It did not seem that Italy was being approached, nor the places and homes of their fatherland: as if foreign shores and enemy cities they set fire, pillaged, and seized, all the more appallingly because nothing anywhere had been prepared against fears of this kind" (*non Italia adiri nec loca sedesque patriae videbantur: tamquam externa litora et urbes hostium urere, vastare, rapere eo atrocius quod nihil usquam provisum adversum metus* (Tacitus, *Histories*. 2.12). The civil wars left behind a trail of destruction, not just as a result of the fighting, but as a consequence of plundering by the victorious Vitellians (*Histories*. 2.56, 87–88) in both town and country-side (even allowing for the influence in this of anti-Vitellian propaganda): how the Flavians went about soothing the wounds left in Italy (for the rebuilding of Cremona, Tacitus, *Histories*. 3.34) will be left to the next chapter.

FURTHER READING

Fundamental changes in the society and culture of Italy under Augustus are discussed by Eck 1984 and Nicolet 1984, whilst Alföldy 1991 explores in some detail how these changes can be mapped through inscriptions of the period; Zanker 1988a and Galinsky 1996 remain fundamental to our understanding of its visual language. The prosopographical studies of Syme 1939 and Wiseman 1971 illuminate how Italian local elites came to prominence at Rome under Augustus. Torelli 1999 focuses upon the emergence of an "Italian" identity via detailed study of archaeological material, whilst Habinek 1998 offers a literary study on a similar theme. The development of the concept of the *domus Augusta* has been explored in several articles by Corbier, of which 1995 is accessible in English. On the fundamental change wrought by the emergence of the imperial court, see Wallace-Hadrill 1996. Imperial property-ownership in Italy is explored region by region by chapters in Pupillo, ed., 2007. Tacitus's *Histories* remain the most vivid account of Italy's tribulations during the civil wars, with interesting discussion in Ash 1999.

REFERENCES

Alföldy, G. 1991. "Augustus und die Inschriften: Tradition und Innovation. " *Gymnasium* 98: 289–324.
Alföldy, G. 1997."Euergetismus und Epigraphik in der augusteischen Zeit." In *Actes du Xe congrès international d'épigraphie grecque et latine*, eds M. Christol and O. Masson, 293–304. Paris: Publications De La Sorbonne.

Ando, C. 2002. "Vergil's Italy: ethnography and politics in first-century Rome." In *Clio and the Poets. Augustan poetry and the traditions of ancient historiography*, eds D.S. Levene and D.P. Nelis, 123–42. Leiden: Brill.

Ash, R. 1999. *Ordering Anarchy. Armies and leaders in Tacitus' Histories*. London: Duckworth.

Ash, R. 2009. "Fission and fusion: shifting Roman identities in the *Histories*." In *The Cambridge Companion to Tacitus*, ed. A.J. Woodman, 85–99. Cambridge: Cambridge University Press.

Bejor, G. 1979. "L'edificio teatrale nell'urbanizzazione augustea." *Athenaeum* 57: 126–38.

Benoist, S. 2005. *Rome, le prince et la Cité*. Paris: Presses Universitaires de France.

Bispham, E.H. 2007a. *From Asculum to Actium: the municipalization of Italy from the Social War to Augustus*. Oxford: Oxford University Press.

Bispham, E.H. 2007b. "Pliny the Elder's Italy." In Vita vigilia est. *Essays in honour of Barbara Levick*, eds E. Bispham, G. Rowe, with E. Matthews, 41–67. London: *BICS Suppl.* 100.

Camodeca, G. 1979. "La *gens Annia* puteolana in età giulio-claudia: potere politico e interessi commerciali." *Puteoli* 3: 17–34.

Camodeca, G. 1994. "Riedizione del trittico ercolanese *TH 77* + 78 + 80 + 53 + 92 del 26 gennaio 69." *Cronache ercolanesi* 24: 137–46.

Camodeca, G. 2007. "Sulle proprietà imperiali in Campania." In *Le proprietà imperiali nell'Italia romana. Economia, produzione, amministrazione*, ed. D. Pupillo, 143–67. Florence: Quaderni degli Annali dell'Università di Ferrara: Le Lettere.

Chilver, G.E.F. 1979. *A Historical Commentary on Tacitus' Histories I and II*. Oxford: Clarendon Press.

Coarelli, F. 2000. "Alcune ipotesi sull'evergetismo imperiale in Italia." In *Les élites municipales de l'Italie péninsulaire de la mort de César à la mort de Domitien*, ed. M. Cébeillac-Gervasoni, 137–48. Rome: Coll.EFR 271.

Cogitore, I. 1992. "Séries de dédicaces italiennes à la dynastie julio-claudienne." *Mélanges de l'Ecole Française de Rome, Antiquité* 104.2: 817–70.

Cooley, A.E. 1999. "A new date for Agrippa's theatre at Ostia." *Papers of the British School at Rome* 67: 173–82.

Cooley, A.E. 2006. "Beyond Rome and Latium: Roman religion in the age of Augustus." In *Religion in Republican Italy*, eds C. Schultz and P.B. Harvey Jr, 228–52. Cambridge: *Yale Classical Studies* 33, Cambridge University Press.

Cooley, A.E. 2009. *Res Gestae divi Augusti*. Cambridge: Cambridge University Press.

Cooley, A.E. 2013. "Women beyond Rome: trend-setters or dedicated followers of fashion?" In *Women and the Roman City in the Latin West*, eds E. Hemelrijk and G. Woolf, 23–46. Leiden: Brill.

Cooley, A.E. and Cooley, M.G.L. 2014. *Pompeii and Herculaneum. A sourcebook*. London and New York: Routledge.

Corbier, M. 1974. *L'Aerarium Saturni et l'Aerarium Militare. Administration et prosopographie sénatoriale*. Rome: Coll.EFR no.24.

Corbier, M. 1995. "Male power and legitimacy through women: the *domus Augusta* under the Julio-Claudians." In *Women in Antiquity. New assessments*, eds R. Hawley and B. Levick, 178–93. London and New York: Routledge.

Corbier, M. 2001. "*Maiestas domus Augustae*." In *Varia Epigraphica. Atti del Colloquio Internazionale di Epigrafia*, eds G. Angeli Bertinelli and A. Donati, 155–99. Faenza: Fratelli Lega Editori.

Crawford, D.J. 1976. "Imperial estates." In *Studies in Roman Property*, ed. M.I. Finley, 35–70. Cambridge: Cambridge University Press.

Crawford, M.H. 1996a. "Italy and Rome from Sulla to Augustus." In *The Cambridge Ancient History*, Vol. 10. *The Augustan Empire 43 BC–AD 69*, 2nd edn, eds A.K. Bowman, E. Champlin, and A. Lintott, 414–33. Cambridge: Cambridge University Press.

Crawford, M. H., ed. 1996b. *Roman Statutes*. 2 vols. London: Institute of Classical Studies/ *BICS Suppl.* 64.

Demma, F. 2007. *Monumenti pubblici di Puteoli. Per un'archeologia dell'architettura*. Rome: Monografie della Rivista «Archeologia Classica»: «L'Erma» di Bretschneider.

Eck, W. 1984. "Senatorial self-representation: developments in the Augustan period." In *Caesar Augustus. Seven aspects*, eds F. Millar and E. Segal, 129–67. Oxford: Clarendon Press.

Fishwick, D. 1991. *The Imperial Cult in the Latin West. Studies in the ruler cult of the western provinces of the Roman Empire* II, 1. Leiden: Brill.

Flory, M.B. 1993. "Livia and the history of public honorific statues for women in Rome." *Transactions of the American Philological Association* 123: 287–308.

Flory, M.B. 1996. "Dynastic ideology, the *domus Augusta*, and imperial women: a lost statuary group in the Circus Flaminius." *Transactions of the American Philological Association* 126: 287–306.

Fuchs, M. 1987. *Untersuchungen zur Ausstattung römischer Theater in Italien und den Westprovinzen des Imperium Romanum*. Mainz am Rhein: Philipp von Zabern.

Fuchs, M., Liverani, P., and Santoro, P. 1989. *Il teatro e il ciclo statuario giulio-claudio. Caere – 2*. Rome: Consiglio Nazionale delle Ricerche.

Galinsky, K. 1996. *Augustan Culture: an interpretive introduction*. Princeton, NJ: Princeton University Press.

Galsterer, H. 1990. "A man, a book, and a method: Sir Ronald Syme's *Roman Revolution* after fifty years." In *Between Republic and Empire. Interpretations of Augustus and his Principate*, eds K.A. Raaflaub and M. Toher, 1–20. Berkeley and Los Angeles: University of California Press.

Gradel, I. 2002. *Emperor Worship and Roman Religion*. Oxford: Clarendon Press.

Granino Cecere, M.G. 2010. "Proprietà di *Augustae* a Roma e nel *Latium vetus*." In Augustae. *Machtbewusste Frauen am römischen Kaiserhof?*, ed. A. Kolb, 111–27. Berlin: Akademie Verlag GmbH.

Gregori, G.L. 2009. "Il culto delle divinità Auguste in Italia: un'indagine preliminare." In *Dediche sacre nel mondo greco-romano. Diffusione, funzione, tipologie*, eds J. Bodel and M. Kajava, 307–30. Rome: Acta Instituti Romani Finlandiae 35.

Griffin, M.T. 1984. *Nero. The end of a dynasty*. London: Batsford.

Habinek, T.N. 1998. *The Politics of Latin Literature. Writing, identity, and empire in Ancient Rome*. Princeton, NJ: Princeton University Press.

Hemelrijk, E.A. 2005. "Octavian and the introduction of public statues for women in Rome." *Athenaeum* 93: 309–17.

Horsfall, N. 2001. "The unity of Roman Italy: anomalies in context." *Scripta Classica Israelica* 20: 39–50.

Jacobelli, L. 2003. *Gladiators at Pompeii*. Rome: «L'Erma» di Bretschneider.

Keay, S. 2001. "Romanization and the Hispaniae." In *Italy and the West. Comparative issues in Romanization*, eds S. Keay and N. Terranato, 117–44. Oxford: Oxbow.

Keppie, L.J.F. 1983. *Colonisation and Veteran Settlement in Italy, 14–47 B.C.* London: British School at Rome.

Knox, P.E. 2005. "Milestones in the career of Tibullus." *Classical Quarterly* 55.1: 204–16.

Kraft, K. 1967. "Der Sinn des Mausoleums des Augustus." *Historia* 16: 189–206.

Kuttner, A.L. 1995. *Dynasty and Empire in the Age of Augustus*. Berkeley: University of California Press.

Laurence, R. 1999. *The Roads of Roman Italy. Mobility and social change*. London: Routledge.

Letta, C. 1994. "Rileggendo le fonti antiche sul Fucino." In *Sulle rive della memoria. Il lago Fucino e il suo Emissario*, ed. E. Burri and A. Campanelli, 202–13. Pescara: CARSA edizioni.

Mennella, G. 1988. "Sui prefetti degli imperatori e dei cesari nelle città dell'Italia e delle province." *Epigraphica* 50: 65–85.

Millar, F. 1993. "Ovid and the *Domus Augusta*: Rome seen from Tomoi." *Journal of Roman Studies* 83: 1–17.

Milnor, K. 2005. *Domesticity and the Age of Augustus. Inventing private life*. Oxford: Oxford University Press.

Nicolet, C. 1967. "Tribuni militum a populo." *Mélanges de l'École française de Rome, Antiquité* 79: 29–76.

Nicolet, C. 1984. "Augustus, government, and the propertied classes." In *Caesar Augustus. Seven aspects*, eds F. Millar and E. Segal, 89–128. Oxford: Clarendon Press.

Parassoglou, G.M. 1978. *Imperial Estates in Roman Egypt*. Amsterdam: Hakkert.

Patterson, J.R. 2003. "The emperor and the cities of Italy." In *"Bread and Circuses." Euergetism and municipal patronage in Roman Italy*, eds K. Lomas and T. Cornell, 89–104. London and New York: Routledge.

Patterson, J.R. 2004. "City, territory and metropolis: the case of the Tiber Valley." In *Bridging the Tiber. Approaches to regional archaeology in the Middle Tiber Valley*, ed. H. Patterson, 61–73. London: Archaeological Monograph of the British School at Rome, 13.

Patterson, J.R. 2006. *Landscapes and Cities. Rural settlement and civic transformation in early imperial Italy.* Oxford: Oxford University Press.

Patterson, J.R. 2008. "Modelling the urban history of the Tiber Valley in the imperial period." In *Mercator placidissimus. The Tiber Valley in Antiquity*, eds H. Patterson and F. Coarelli, 487–98. Rome: Quasar: Quaderni di Eutopia 8.

Pizzigati, A. 1993. "La decorazione architettonica del teatro di Volterra: analisi preliminari." In *Il teatro romano di Volterra*, ed. G. Cateni, 55–76. Florence: Octavo.

Pupillo, D., ed. 2007. *Le proprietà imperiali nell'Italia romana. Economia, produzione, amministrazione.* Florence: Quaderni degli Annali dell'Università di Ferrara: Le Lettere.

Rathbone, D.W. 1996. "The imperial finances." In *The Cambridge Ancient History*, Vol. 10. *The Augustan Empire 43 BC–AD 69*, 2nd edn, eds A.K. Bowman, E. Champlin, and A. Lintott, 309–23. Cambridge: Cambridge University Press.

Rawson, E. 1987. "*Discrimina ordinum*: the *lex Julia theatralis*." *Papers of the British School at Rome* 55: 83–114.

Reed, J.D. 2007. *Virgil's Gaze: Nation and poetry in the Aeneid.* Princeton, NJ: Princeton University Press.

Richardson, L., Jr 1978. "Concordia and Concordia Augusta: Rome and Pompeii." *Parola del Passato* 33: 260–71.

Rotili, M. 1972. *L'arco di Traiano a Benevento.* Rome: Istituto Poligrafico dello Stato.

Rowlandson, J. 1996. *Landowners and Tenants in Roman Egypt. The social relations of agriculture in the Oxyrhynchite nome.* Oxford: Clarendon Press.

Sabbatini Tumolesi, P. 1988. *Epigrafia anfiteatrale dell'Occidente Romano* I: *Roma* Rome: Quasar: Vetera 2.

Saletti, C. 1968. *Il ciclo statuario della basilica di Velleia.* Milan: Casa Editrice Ceschina.

Scheidel, W. 2004. "Human mobility in Roman Italy, I: The free population." *Journal of Roman Studies* 94: 1–26.

Sear, F. 2006. *Roman Theatres. An architectural study.* Oxford: Oxford University Press.

Segenni, S. 2007. "Considerazioni sulla proprietà imperiale nella *Regio IV* (*Sabina et Samnium*)." In *Le proprietà imperiali nell'Italia romana. Economia, produzione, amministrazione*, ed. D. Pupillo, 125–41. Florence: Quaderni degli Annali dell'Università di Ferrara: Le Lettere.

Small, A., Volterra, V., and Hancock, R.G.V. 2003. "New evidence from tile-stamps for imperial properties near Gravina, and the topography of imperial estates in SE Italy." *Journal of Roman Archaeology* 16: 179–99.

Small, D.B. 1987. "Social correlations to the Greek cavea in the Roman period." In *Roman Architecture in the Greek World*, eds S. Macready and F.H. Thompson, 85–93. London: Society of Antiquaries Occasional Papers 10.

Speidel, M.A. 2000. "Geld und Macht. Die Neuordnung des staatlichen Finanzwesens unter Augustus." In *La Révolution Romaine après Ronald Syme. Bilans et Perspectives*, ed. A. Giovannini, 113–66. Geneva: Fondation Hardt.

Syme. R. 1939. *The Roman Revolution.* Oxford: Oxford University Press.

Terrenato, N. 1998. "*Tam firmum municipium*: The Romanization of Volaterrae and its cultural implications." *Journal of Roman Studies* 88: 94–114.

Terrenato, N. 2001. "A tale of three cities: the Romanization of northern coastal Etruria." In *Italy and the West. Comparative issues in Romanization*, eds S. Keay and N. Terranato, 54–67. Oxford: Oxbow.

Toll, K. 1991. "The *Aeneid* as an epic of national identity: *Italiam laeto socii clamore salutant*." *Helios* 18.1: 3–14.

Toll, K. 1997. "Making Roman-ness and the *Aeneid*." *Classical Antiquity* 16.1: 34–56.

Torelli, M. 1999. Tota Italia. *Essays in the Cultural Formation of Roman Italy.* Oxford: Clarendon Press.

Vidal, A.B. 1961. *Crónica Seudo Isidoriana.* Valencia: Textos Medievales 5.

Wallace-Hadrill, A. 1996 "The imperial court." In *The Cambridge Ancient History*, Vol. 10. *The Augustan Empire 43 BC–AD 69*, 2nd edn, eds A.K. Bowman, E. Champlin, A. Lintott, 283–308. Cambridge: Cambridge University Press.

Wallace-Hadrill, A. 2008. *Rome's Cultural Revolution*. Cambridge: Cambridge University Press.

Weaver, P.R.C. 1972. Familia Caesaris: *a social study of the emperor's freedmen and slaves* London and New York: Cambridge University Press.

Wiedemann, T.E.J. 1996. "From Nero to Vespasian." In *The Cambridge Ancient History*, Vol. 10. *The Augustan Empire 43 BC–AD 69*, 2nd edn, eds A.K. Bowman, E. Champlin, and A. Lintott, 256–82. Cambridge: Cambridge University Press.

Williams, J.H.C. 2001. *Beyond the Rubicon. Romans and Gauls in Republican Italy*. Oxford: Oxford University Press.

Williams, R.D. 1961. "The function and structure of Virgil's catalogue in Aeneid 7." *Classical Quarterly* 11.2:146–53.

Wilson, R.J.A. 1996. "Sicily, Sardinia and Corsica." In *The Cambridge Ancient History*, Vol. 10. *The Augustan Empire 43 BC–AD 69*, 2nd edn, eds A.K. Bowman, E. Champlin, and A. Lintott, 434–48. Cambridge: Cambridge University Press.

Wiseman, T.P. 1971. *New Men in the Roman Senate*. London: Oxford University Press.

Woolf, G. 1990. "Food, poverty and patronage: the significance of the epigraphy of the Roman alimentary schemes in early imperial Italy." *Papers of the British School at Rome* 58: 197–228.

Woolf, G. 1995. "The formation of Roman provincial cultures." In *Integration in the Early Roman West*, eds J. Metzler *et al.*, 9–18. Luxembourg: Dossiers d'Archéologie du Musée National d'Histoire et d'Art IV.

Zaccaria, C. 2007. "Proprietà imperiali nel territorio Aquileiese. Revisione dei documenti e problemi." In *Le proprietà imperiali nell'Italia romana. Economia, produzione, amministrazione*, ed. D. Pupillo, 65–91. Florence: Quaderni degli Annali dell'Università di Ferrara: Le Lettere.

Zanker, P. 1988a. *The Power of Images in the Age of Augustus*, trans. A. Shapiro. Ann Arbor: The University of Michigan Press.

Zanker, P. 1988b. "Bilderzwang: Augustan political symbolism in the private sphere." In *Image and Mystery in the Roman World*, eds J. Huskinson, M. Beard, and J. Reynolds, 1–21. Gloucester: Alan Sutton Publishing.

CHAPTER 7

Italy during the High Empire, from the Flavians to Diocletian

Alison E. Cooley

7.1 Rebuilding After Civil Wars

One of the most shocking episodes in the "Year of the Four Emperors" was the burning down of the Capitol at Rome during the confrontation between Vitellians and Flavians. As Tacitus described it (*Histories*: 3.72), "this crime, the most appalling and foul since the city's foundation, struck the state of the Roman people" (*id facinus post conditam urbem luctuosissimum foedissimumque rei publicae populi Romani accidit*). It was all the more shocking because the Capitol was regarded as a pledge of Rome's imperial rule (*pignus imperii*), and Tacitus lamented that the temple which had withstood enemy attack in the past should now be burned down by the Romans themselves amid civil conflict. The speed with which the rebuilding of the Capitoline temple was set in motion just months later (Tacitus, *Histories*: 4.53), and Vespasian's instructions to re-inscribe and re-erect 3000 senatorial decrees, treaties, and records of privileges whose bronze had melted down in the conflagration (Suetonius, *Life of Vespasian*: 8.5) indicate the importance of being seen to restore normality at the center of the empire. Rome was not, though, the only city to have suffered. In northern Italy, the clashes between Vitellians and Flavians in the area around Bedriacum (modern Cremona) had caused similar devastation (Tacitus, *Histories*: 3.33–34), resulting in the almost complete destruction of the town.

Consequently, one of the prominent themes espoused by the new Flavian regime was the claim to be restoring normality to Rome and Italy, putting to rights the disruptions caused by the tumultuous civil wars. As shown by the "law on Vespasian's official powers" (*lex de imperio Vespasiani*: Crawford, 1996: vol. 1, no. 39; Griffin, 2000: 11–13), Vespasian was officially represented as succeeding the "good" Julio-Claudians – Augustus, Tiberius, and Claudius – and this was reinforced by Vespasian quickly changing his titulature to drop his own family name '"Flavius" and his praenomen Titus in favor of names with an imperial pedigree. Consequently, he was transformed from T. Flavius Vespasianus into Imperator Caesar Vespasianus Augustus. One of the keys to the success of the new regime was Vespasian's ability to promise a smooth transition of imperial power via a dynastic succession. The fact that Vespasian already had not just one successor lined up – Titus, who had already proven his mettle in Judaea – but, Domitian too, an heir and a spare, was promoted upon coins

A Companion to Roman Italy, First Edition. Edited by Alison E. Cooley.
© 2016 John Wiley & Sons, Ltd. Published 2016 by John Wiley & Sons, Ltd.

issued by the state mint in AD 70 (*RIC* II.1 (2008) nos 5, 15–16). This theme was picked up in towns of Italy, where dynastic statue groups of the Flavians reminiscent of their Julio-Claudian predecessors were put in place (Cogitore, 1992). As with the Julio-Claudians, imperial women were a prominent part of this public profile. At Herculaneum, for example, life-sized bronze statues of Flavia Domitilla, Titus, Domitia Longina, and Julia daughter of Titus (and presumably Vespasian and Domitian, although no traces of these survive), were set up in the so-called basilica alongside an earlier group set up under Claudius consisting of deified Augustus, deified Julia Augusta, Antonia Minor, Claudius, Agrippina Minor, Nero or Britannicus (Najbjerg, 2002, 147–48).

Even more pressing, though, was the need to restock the treasury (Griffin, 2000, 26–32; Levick, 1999, ch.7). Vespasian implemented a range of financial reforms, including reducing the amount of silver in the coinage and increasing his revenue from taxation, and was proactive in sending out his agents into Italy and the provinces in order to ensure income streams. His agent Suedius Clemens, for example, was prominent in the last decade of Pompeii's existence, recovering public lands from usurpation by private individuals and ensuring the efficacy of his judgments by setting up inscribed markers outside at least four of the town's gates (Cooley and Cooley, 2014: F148). Similar concern for reclaiming public land is also apparent in Narbonensis and North Africa (*AE* (1936) 28): the inscriptions emphasized that such action was being carried out in Vespasian's name: *ex auctoritate Vespasiani*. People may have grumbled that Vespasian was so mean that he had even imposed a tax on the urine collected by fullers (Suetonius, *Vespasian*: 23.2–3), but financial security was essential to the stability of Flavian rule.

7.2   Italy and the Emperors

One of the main changes experienced by Italy during the period discussed in this chapter is that its privileged place at the heart of empire was gradually eroded so that by the time of Diocletian's administrative reforms (see section 7.5 of this chapter) Italy was treated on an equal footing with other provinces. The shift towards the provincialization of Italy was very gradual, and several measures illustrate the persistence of the concept that Italy was special. Ever since the Caesarian period, the origins of senators had become increasingly diverse, as individuals first from Spain and southern Gaul, then from northern Gaul (Gallia Comata) under Claudius, and later notably those who had supported Vespasian's rise to power in the Greek East, had been promoted to senatorial rank. By the time of Hadrian, cities of the Greek East were strongly represented, with members of their elite being not only appointed to the senate but also achieving the highest rank of consul (Levick, 1999: ch.11, esp. 173–74; Eck, 2000: esp. 219). Ti. Julius Celsus Polemaeanus of Sardis (who had supported Vespasian's acclamation as military tribune in Alexandria) was consul in AD 92 and he was followed a few years later in 109 by C. Julius Antiochus Epiphanes Philopappus, grandson of the last king of Commagene before it became a province. Both men paraded their Roman status upon monuments – on the library of Celsus in Ephesus and tomb of Philopappus on the Hill of the Muses in Athens (Smith, 1998). In response to this increased diversity in the senate's membership, Trajan required provincials to invest a third of their money in Italian land in order to qualify for membership of the senate (Pliny the Younger, *Letters*: 6.19; Eck, 2000: 223).

At the same time, Vespasian's Sabine origins (underlined by the name of his elder brother Sabinus) were used to underpin a positive representation of the new emperor, since the traditional association of Sabinum with old-fashioned Roman morality, simple living, and toughness resulting from hard work (often alluded to by Horace in talking of his "Sabine villa," for example in *Odes*: 1.20, 2.18, 3.1) was used to emphasize that Vespasian was not going to indulge in the decadent behavior of the likes of Nero. Indeed, Tacitus *Annals*: 3.55 described him as "being himself of ancient behavior and lifestyle" (*antiquo ipse cultu victuque*; Dench, 1995). This idea that Vespasian, as a product of Sabinum, must essentially share its fundamentally decent character, was arguably supported by his new style of portraiture, which moved away from the pattern established by Augustus and followed by other Julio-Claudians of a heroic, non-ageing profile towards a more "realistic" style that showed him as a balding emperor with furrows in his brow.

With the accession of Trajan in AD 98, Rome became subject, for the first time, to rule by a non-Italian emperor, since Trajan's family came from Italica in southern Spain. As a result, it seems that Trajan almost over-compensated for his non-Italian origins by making absolutely clear how very highly he prioritized the interests of Rome and Italy, showing his concern for the welfare of Italy and Italians through a number of measures. Although his construction of the artificial hexagonal harbor at Portus and his development of harbor facilities there seem at first sight primarily for the benefit of the capital (Meiggs, 1973, 58–62), the development of Portus was not an isolated phenomenon, but should be seen in the context of harbor facilities developed elsewhere in Italy, at Terracina, Centumcellae, Ancona, and possibly Brundisium (Keay, 2008: 11). The transformation of Portus must have had an impact upon Italy and the Mediterranean more widely rather than just upon Rome itself (cf. Keay, 2008: 19).

Another major feat of engineering undertaken by Trajan was the construction of the *via Traiana* in 109, a shorter alternative to the *via Appia* leading south-east from Rome between Beneventum and Brundisium (Ashby and Gardner, 1916; on imperial road building in general, see Patterson, 2003: 93–96). Dozens of milestones have been found from along the route specifying that Trajan had paid for the road to be constructed at his own expense (*CIL* 9.5999–6000, 6003–04, 6008–09, 6013, 6015–17, 6021–25, 6029–37, 6040–42, 6044–47, 6049–6054; *AE* (1981) 245; *AE* (1987) 293a, 295–96, 298; *AE* (2009) 255; *SupIt*-23-B, 1): "Imperator Caesar, son of deified Nerva, Nerva Trajan Augustus Germanicus Dacicus, chief pontiff, in his 13th year of tribunician power, hailed victorious commander six times, consul five times, father of the fatherland, constructed the road from Beneventum to Brundisium at his own expense": *Imp(erator) Caesar / divi Nervae f(ilius) / Nerva Traianus / Aug(ustus) Germ(anicus) Dacic(us) / pont(ifex) max(imus) tr(ibunicia) pot(estate) / XIII imp(erator) VI co(n)s(ul) V / p(ater) p(atriae) / viam a Benevento / Brundisium pecun(ia) / sua fecit.* This last unusual detail, that he funded the road-building personally, shows how much he wanted to advertise his personal investment (literally) in the road. The prominence given to his title *pater patriae*, which stands out on a line of its own in the inscriptions, may also have been intended to remind viewers of his role as guardian of Italy. The road's construction was also commemorated on coins, depicting the road itself as a reclining person-ified figure holding a wheel (reminding viewers that the road was good enough for wheeled vehicles to pass along it), and honoring Trajan as "best leader" (*optimus princeps*) (*RIC* 2 nos 266, 636–41). In addition to this new stretch of road, Trajan also created a short-cut for the *via Appia* at Terracina on its course nearer Rome, a striking feat of engineering that involved cutting through the headland for a depth of 36 m (120 Roman feet) of rock, to save travellers from having to climb up and over at this stretch of coast. The depth of the cutting was monumentalized in a series of numerals cut into the cliff-face at 10-foot intervals (Figure 7.1), and an arch was built at the base of the cutting (Potter, 1987: 138).

The potential enthusiasm of Italian communities for road improvements which enabled travel across the Italian peninsula to occur more speedily and commodiously is nicely illus-trated by responses to Domitian's new road linking Rome with Puteoli from Sinuessa, the *via Domitiana*, constructed in AD 95. The poet Statius composed a poem (*Silvae* 4.3) eulogizing the road's solid construction and new level of comfort for its travelers: "Here once the traveler carried along sluggishly on his single axle would totter on a pendulous cross, and the spiteful

Figure 7.1   100-foot marker on the cliff-face at Terracina. Photograph: A.E. Cooley.

earth would suck up his wheels, and the Latin people in the middle of their fields would shud-
der at the evils of their voyage; nor were there any swift journeys, but the clinging tracks
would delay the impeded journey, whilst the exhausted quadruped would crawl along beneath
the high yoke complaining of its excessive burden. But now a journey that used to waste a
complete day is accomplished in scarcely two hours." (*hic quondam piger axe vectus uno /
nutabat cruce pendula viator / sorbebatque rotas maligna tellus, / et plebs in mediis Latina
campis / horrebat mala navigationis; / nec cursus agiles, sed impeditum / tardabant iter orbitae
tenaces, / dum pondus nimium querens sub alta / repit languida quadrupes statera. / at nunc
quae solidum diem terebat, / horarum via facta vix duarum.* (*Silvae,* 4.3.27–37, ed. Coleman,
1988)). Statius's over-inflated language is even echoed by the dedicatory inscription of an
arch erected in honor of Domitian in 95–96 by the town of Puteoli. Although its inscription
was later erased, its text can still be deciphered, and illustrates that the rather flowery language of court poetry was equally espoused by this Italian community, which adopts the
conceit that the road's construction has effectively moved Rome closer to hand: "To
Imperator Caesar Domitian Augustus Germanicus, son of the deified Vespasian, chief priest,
in his 15th year of tribunician power, hailed victorious commander 22 times, consul 17 times,
perpetual censor, father of the fatherland. The Flavian Augustan Puteolan colony through the
indulgence of the greatest and divine leader moved closer to his City": *Imp. Caesari/ divi
Vespasiani f. / Domitiano Aug/ German. pont. max./ trib. potest. xv imp. xxii/ cos xvii cens
perpet p p / colonia Flavia Aug / Puteolana / indulgentia maximi / divinique principis/ urbi
eius admota* (Flower, 2001). The town's subsequent embarrassment at its enthusiasm for an
emperor who ended up assassinated and condemned is clear from the decision to erase the
whole text (not just the emperor's name as was more usual practice).

Aside from such feats of engineering, Trajan also demonstrated his commitment to the
population of Italy by encouraging the development of alimentary schemes, or *alimenta*
(Woolf, 1990). In brief, such schemes encouraged Italian landowners to accept large

endowments of cash in exchange for returning annual contributions in perpetuity to funds devoted to the support of children in the local towns. The establishment of such schemes could be commemorated in style by impressive inscriptions upon bronze tablets, displayed in public places. A good example from Veleia (*CIL* 11.1147 = *ILS* 6675), a large bronze tablet 1.38 m by 2.86 m, lists in seven columns the 49 estates being pledged to produce enough revenue to support 264 boys and 36 girls (Criniti, 2006). Such inscriptions served to advertise the landowners' commitment to supporting local children and also to ensure that they adhered to the terms of the schemes. Some of the schemes were put in place by agents of the emperor, such as T. Pomponius Bassus at Ferentinum (*CIL* 6.1492 = *ILS* 6106), who was consequently appointed as a patron of the town, whilst the heading to the Veleia tablet describes its scheme as being put in place "through the indulgence of our best and greatest leader, Emperor Trajan" (*ex indulgentia optimi maximique principis Imp(eratoris) Caes(aris) Nervae / Traiani Aug(usti) Germanici Dacici*). Coins in gold, silver, and base metal were minted to celebrate the emperor's concern for the population of Italy (*RIC* II, Trajan nos 93, 230, 243, 459, 460–62, 604–05), depicting images of Trajan, children, and *Annona* or *Abundantia* holding a cornucopia and ears of corn, along with the texts "Senate and People of Rome to the best of leaders/alimentary schemes of Italy" (*S.P.Q.R.OPTIMO PRINCIPI/ALIM ITAL*).

The alimentary schemes were continued under the Antonines and Severans, with girls being singled out for support by Antoninus Pius, who established the "Faustinian girls" (*puellae Faustinianae*) in memory of his wife the elder Faustina (*RIC* III Antoninus Pius nos 397–99) and Marcus Aurelius who endowed the "new Faustinian girls" (*novae puellae Faustinianae*) in honor of his wife, the younger Faustina. The fact that the setting up of such schemes became an expected part of the emperor's role is reflected in the suggestion in the Augustan History (*Life of Severus Alexander*. 57.7) that under the next imperial dynasty too, recipients of another scheme were associated with Julia Mammaea by Severus Alexander. It is not entirely clear whether the Italian landowners would have welcomed this imperial intervention requiring them to mortgage their lands, even if they did receive public recognition for their "generosity." Pliny the Younger (*Letters*. 7.18) at any rate represents himself as having set up such a scheme enthusiastically for the upkeep of the children of his hometown, Comum, but his enthusiasm seems largely to stem from his distrust of the local authorities not to mismanage funds entrusted to them. As he observes to his addressee Caninius Rufus, "You might pay the capital sum to the public authorities: but there must be a fear of its vanishing into thin air. You might donate the lands: with the consequence that, as public lands, they are neglected. In the end I can come up with nothing more beneficial than what I myself have done." *numeres rei publicae summam*. *verendum est ne dilabatur*. *des agros*. *ut publici neglegentur*. *equidem nihil commodius invenio, quam quod ipse feci*. (*Letters*. 7.18.1–2). The attitude of the Italian landowners is, though, perhaps beside the point: the key aim was for the emperor to be able to project an image of active concern for sustaining the population of Italy.

That Trajan's message of commitment to Italy communicated itself successfully can be illustrated by the way in which the Roman senate and people likewise publicized his Italian credentials in the design of the arch dedicated to him in AD 114 at Beneventum (Hannestad, 1988: 177–86). This arch is unusual as a triumphal arch dedicated by the senate and people of Rome outside the capital, and may have been intended to form part of an extended triumphal processional route from his point of disembarkation at Brundisium to Rome following his expected triumphs in the East (note that this time, he is celebrated as *fortissimus princeps* – *CIL* 9.5998) (Ashby and Gardner, 1916: 117), from which, however, he was destined not to return alive. The scenes on this arch depict a balanced picture of imperial concerns. Scenes on the north-west side of the arch facing the direction of Rome, illustrated his building of the harbor at Portus and ceremonies in his honor held at Rome. Scenes on the arch's south-east side, facing towards Brundisium and beyond, however, represented Trajan's activities in the provinces and in Italy. One of the two reliefs flanking the passageway through the arch includes a scene that may be interpreted as alluding to his care for the children of Italian towns as evidenced by his new alimentary schemes. The scene shows the handing-out of money (or perhaps corn) to children, watched over by the emperor himself. The scene depicts some of the children informally, riding on their fathers' shoulders, but the presence of four city-goddesses should remind us that even in the midst of a very life-like image, we are not looking at a "real" historical moment, but at an ideologically charged composition. Even though Trajan was in fact absent from Italy for much of his reign, on campaign in Dacia and Parthia, Italy remained at the forefront of imperial ideology.

Alongside demonstrating his commitment to Italy, Trajan also seems to have been aware of potential problems in municipal administration, especially in terms of towns' financial commitments. The towns of Italy were in charge of managing their own finances, deriving income from rent and local taxes, and benefiting from the fees paid by annual office-holders as well as from the same individuals' voluntary generosity. Nevertheless, in ways similar to the cities of Bithynia-Pontus being investigated at the same period by Pliny the Younger for financial mismanagement (illustrated in book 10 of his *Letters*), the towns of Italy also seem to have caused concern for over-committing themselves to programmes of expenditure. An innovation that starts right at the end of the first century was the appointment of high-ranking individuals to act as *curator rei publicae*, whose task was to oversee towns' finances, and to stop them from overspending. These *curatores* were imperial appointments, as explicitly stated in relation to at least 13 of them (Jacques, 1984: 259–67), and potentially limited towns' autonomy (Jacques 1983 and 1984). We are largely reliant upon inscriptions to trace the spread and activities of such appointees in Italian towns, which means that in many cases we only know that a certain individual served as a *curator* (because this is listed among his posts on a statue base), rather than knowing much about what such officials actually did.

The limited epigraphic evidence we do have for their actions, however, illustrates how a town now might seek permission from the *curator* to undertake specific building projects. In AD 113, for example, the *curator* Curiatius Cosanus wrote a letter to the town council of Caere approving the proposal of Ulpius Vesbinus (perhaps not coincidentally a freedman of the emperor Trajan) to build a meeting place for the *Augustales* of the town at his own expense on public land ("under the portico of the *basilica Sulpiciana*") (*CIL* 11.3614 = *ILS* 5918a; with Jacques, 1983: 254–59). In this case, although Vesbinus promised to meet the expenses of the building project, consent was needed for the building to be erected on a plot of public space. This at any rate is the implication of the reply from Cosanus in which he observed that this particular space seemed fit for this purpose, because it was currently not being used and because it was otherwise impossible to raise any revenue from it (*qui locus rei p. in usu non est nec ullo reditu esse potest*). This specific example gives the impression of friendly cooperation between town council and *curator*: having already agreed in principle to the proposal, the town councillors decided to invite their *curator* to comment on it too ("it was unanimously agreed to send a letter about this matter to Curiatius Cosanus, the *curator*"/ *placuitq. universis Curiatio Cosano curatori, ob eam rem epistulam mitti*), and he validated their decision. That this was important is reflected in the decision to inscribe a detailed account of the decision-making process, publishing extracts from the town's daily record book, thanks to which we know about this particular example. Given the tendency of epigraphic evidence usually to commemorate positive outcomes, it is difficult to know how restraining an influence such *curatores* were in reality: we hear from inscriptions of the instances where the *curator* has granted permission rather than refused it. Similarly, the act of appointing a *curator* might be presented as the result of imperial *indulgentia*

(*CIL* 10.453 = *InscrIt*-03-01.1), but again it is difficult to judge the reality behind the rhetoric. It is undeniable, however, that appointing *curatores* was a new phenomenon from the end of the first century, and the fact that they continued to be appointed throughout the period under discussion here shows that they were regarded as a success in their missions.

7.3   The Impact of Women on the Landscapes of Italy

The continuing visibility of imperial women in statues set up in the towns of Italy has already been noted. During the second and third centuries, however, women from the municipal elite also grew in prominence within the public life of their towns (Hemelrijk and Woolf, 2013), not necessarily as individuals, but often within the context of their families. One of the distinctive new mechanisms allowing elite women to play a role in public life and to derive prestige from this, which became embedded in Italian municipal life during this period, was the holding of posts as imperial priestess (*flaminicae*) tending to the cult of deified empresses, the *divae* (Hemelrijk, 2006; Raepsaet-Charlier, 2008). Although such posts originated during the Julio-Claudian era with the deification of Caligula's sister Drusilla (cf. *CIL* 5.7345 for a *flaminica divae Drusillae* in the Cottian Alps), they appear to have become more common as more imperial women during the second and third centuries – Plotina, Marciana, Matidia, Sabina, Faustina the Elder, Faustina the Younger, Julia Domna, Julia Maesa, Paulina – were elevated to the status of *diva* after their deaths. Although, as Hemelrijk, 2006, has explored, the exact relationship between the holding of an imperial priesthood and acting as a public benefactor is unclear, such women donated a range of public buildings, such as a temple of Juno Regina at Larinum (*AE* 1997, 343), and possibly an aqueduct at Albingaunum (*AE* 1975, 403) and Vibo (*CIL* 10.54). They might receive honors such as a statue or public funeral in recognition of their status within the town.

The profile of such imperial priestesses fits into a pattern of women becoming increasingly visible in public life more generally. Although they remained excluded from holding municipal magistracies, a few women of high rank even became patrons of cities during the second and third centuries (Hemelrijk, 2004). Such women were expected to wield influence informally in the interests of the city and to make financial contributions to the physical fabric and civic life of the city, but only women of exceptional wealth and status, with close connections to the court and administration at Rome, were in a position to do this. In addition, a handful of women were celebrated as "mothers" (*matres*) of colonies or municipalities (Cenerini, 2013), a status that has so far been found only in Italian towns during the second century.

The distinction between *patrona* and *mater* is found at a lower level of society too. Far from being excluded from playing some part in civic life, some women of lower status, including freedwomen, were named as "mothers" (*matres*) of professional associations (*collegia*) (Hemelrijk, 2008). The title of *mater* was awarded to women of relatively humble social background (the "sub-elites" discussed by Perry, ch. 25, this vol.), who themselves belonged to the association in question and were of the same social class as the majority of its members. Freedwomen therefore could be recognized as *matres* by associations of which they were members. So far as we can tell, such women were not subsequently honored more widely in public, though; the context for their recognition remained internal to the association. In addition, associations might appoint women as their patrons, but these women tended to be both higher in status (equestrian or senatorial in rank) and not otherwise to belong to the association in question. This is a feature of towns in central Italy. By having two types of honorific title for women, the associations could allow women of both higher and lower rank, especially freedwomen, to be honored, whilst maintaining the traditional pattern of social hierarchy. Admittedly, men still dominated civic life as magistrates and public benefactors, but during the period from the Flavians onwards, a greater variety of routes became available to women by which they might become involved in municipal life. Some individual women accumulated public profiles by several of these routes at once, as is illustrated by the case of Cantia Saturnina, who was honored by the town council at Ariminium (modern Rimini) as "mother of the colony" (*mater coloniae*), and also priestess of deified Plotina (*flaminica sacerdos divae Plotinae*) not just at Ariminum but at Forum Sempronii (modern Fossombrone) too (*CIL* 11.407).

Imperial women themselves could also make significant impact upon local Italian communities. A particularly curious example is that of Domitia Longina (Levick, 2002), who had been awarded the title Augusta, and who survived her husband Domitian by several decades, until at least AD 129. She was regarded as implicated in his assassination plot on some accounts, such as that of Suetonius, *Life of Domitian*: 14.1. Although the wife of an assassinated emperor, Domitia Longina did not have to rely solely on her role as imperial consort for prestige, since her father, Domitius Corbulo, had been a famous general in the time of Nero. Consequently, after Domitian's assassination and erasure from the historical record, Domitia Longina continued to be honored as daughter of Corbulo rather than as emperor's wife. Her memory was even still honored publicly in 140 at Gabii in Latium, perhaps her place of birth. On 23 April 140, the local town council approved the setting up a temple "in honor of the memory of the house of Domitia Augusta daughter of Gnaeus Domitius Corbulo" [*in honorem memoriae domus Domitiae Augustae Cn(aei) Domiti Corbulonis fil(iae)*] (*CIL* 14. 2795 = *ILS* 272; Chausson, 2003). This curious choice of words shows how she was still regarded both as Domitia Augusta and as Corbulo's daughter, even though it seems that it is because of her kinship to Corbulo rather than in virtue of her imperial connections that she was being honored in this particular case. By comparison, an epitaph set up at Peltuinum to one of Domitia Longina's slaves, Phoebus, by his sister, a family freedwoman named Domitia Athenais, mentions a *collegium* of the "hero" Corbulo and his wife Longina (*ILS* 9158: *ex collegio heroi Corbulonis et Longinae*, with Chausson, 2003: 113). At Gabii, the temple construction and its decoration had been funded by Domitius Polycarpus and Domitia Europe, a husband and wife whose names indicate that they had been freed by Domitia Longina. In addition to the temple, the revenue generated from interest accruing from a donation was to fund a distribution to town councillors and *seviri Augustales* annually on the anniversary of Domitia's birthday. The bronze tablet recording the town council's decree has not survived, but the fact that the surviving inscription is upon a lintel 3.50 m wide (Chausson, 2003: 103) indicates that the temple was indeed built.

The impact of Domitia Longina upon Gabii – the building of a temple to honor her memory and the annual distributions on her birthday – should perhaps best be seen in the context of private honors funded by her freedman and freedwoman. Nevertheless, the fact that their donation was approved by the town council, and that the decree concerning the matter was to be engraved upon a bronze tablet, indicate that the matter was regarded at Gabii as of more than mere private significance. A clear-cut example of an imperial woman acting as public benefactor is to be found, though, in the Campanian town of Suessa Aurunca. Matidia the Younger (circa 85 – circa 162) had impeccable imperial connections (Bruun, 2010). Although she may have been deliberately marginalized under Hadrian, she came to the fore in various towns of Campania under his successor, Antoninus Pius, being honored at Minturnae and Sinuessa, as well as at Suessa and is likely to have owned significant estates in the region (Cascella, 2012). Unlike Domitia Longina and other imperial women, Matidia's prestige was not derived from a role as imperial wife. Inscriptions set up in her honor instead put the spotlight upon her place within the wider network of the imperial family, honoring her as daughter of *diva* Matidia Augusta (the elder), granddaughter of *diva* Marciana (Trajan's sister), sister of *diva* Sabina, and aunt of Antoninus Pius (even though this was only via adoption). For example, the people of Suessa honored her as follows: "To Matidia daughter of Augusta, granddaughter of Diva Marciana Augusta, sister of Diva Sabina Augusta, aunt of Imperator Antoninus Augustus Pius, father of the fatherland" (*Matidiae/ Aug(ustae) fil(iae) Divae/ Marcianae Aug(ustae)/nepti Divae Sabinae/ Aug(ustae) sorori / Imp(eratoris) Antonini/ Aug(usti) Pii p(atris) p(atriae) materterae/ Suessani (posuerunt)*) (*CIL* 10.4745). From fragmentary epigraphic evidence it seems likely that Matidia funded the reconstruction of the town's theater, perhaps jointly with Antoninus Pius (Cascella, 2012). Its *scaenae frons* included statues of members of the imperial family, past and present, including Trajan, Hadrian, Plotina, Matidia the Elder, Sabina, and Faustina the Elder, as well as a striking over-life-sized (height: 2.40m.) image of Matidia the Younger herself in the guise of a nymph, with flowing robes and revealing gown, not at all in the style of a modest imperial matron (Bruun, 2010: 225; Valeri and Zevi, 2004). She may also have paid for a library (a *Bibliotheca Matidiana* is known in AD 193, *CIL* 10.4760), and, most extraordinary of all, her name appears in the nominative case (i.e., as road-builder) on a milestone for road-building in the territory nearby (*AE* (1991) 492). Although it seems that Matidia had a special relationship with Suessa Aurunca, reflected in the seven inscriptions naming her from the town, and may well have owned a large villa there, she was honored with inscribed monuments at nine other locations elsewhere in Italy and the provinces (Bruun, 2010: 216). Even though she was never herself awarded with the title Augusta, she appears to have been particularly prominent in the reign of Antoninus Pius, who, in turn, of course, stood to benefit considerably from being associated with an individual with such impeccable dynastic roots (Cascella and Ruggi D'Aragona, 2012).

7.4   Patterns in City Life

New patterns in city life may also be observed during this period, many of which have been traced in detail by Patterson (2006). Whereas the Augustan and Julio-Claudian eras can be characterized as continuing a trend set in the mid-first century BC of cities becoming equipped with an impressive array of public buildings, by the second century such investment in new public buildings seems to diminish. Instead, benefactors appear to have favored non-monumental forms of benefaction, such as the distribution of cash and food to a city's citizen population (or to certain defined favored sections of it, such as town councillors and *Augustales*), free supplies of olive oil for use in the public baths, or the provision of feasts (Patterson, 2006: ch.2). This reassessment of shifting interests among the municipal elites offers an alternative explanation for the apparent declining numbers of public buildings being constructed to the hypothesis that local elites were becoming disenchanted with undertaking magistracies and associated costs, and moves away from an image of decline in Italian urban life.

This is not to claim, however, that no new public buildings were constructed; as Patterson has pointed out, instead, the range of buildings contracted, with public baths, amphitheatres, and market-buildings being newly prioritized compared with other types of public buildings, such as theaters (on which see Cooley, ch.6, this vol.). Of course there may be a practical element in such choices: after all, once a town had a theater it did not really need to keep adding new ones alongside it. To some extent too, this pattern may reflect once again the impact of Rome upon Italy's towns: there was a definite trend to imitate closely the new Flavian amphitheater (or Colosseum) in towns like Puteoli and Capua. Likewise, the new dominance of imperial baths at Rome, with the baths of Titus and Trajan, may have paved the way for a more adventurous and luxurious style of baths to be constructed beyond the capital too (Patterson, 2006: 125–69).

Alongside this shift in public benefaction away from providing funding for new public buildings towards the funding of social activities, this period also sees evidence for concern that towns did not overstretch themselves in their financial undertakings, as discussed in section 7.2 of this chapter in relation to the appointment of high-ranking *curatores rei publicae*. Hadrian went a step further, appointing four officials to oversee jurisdiction in Italy's four judicial districts (Appian, *Civil War*: 1.38), but it appears that this was an unpopular move, cancelled by Antoninus Pius. The impetus to bring Italy under more direct control, though, seems to have gathered momentum, since Marcus Aurelius then appointed officials known as *iuridici* (*ILS* 1118–19), whilst the third century heralded the appointment of individuals to oversee the administration of Italy, such as C. Octavius Suetrius Sabinus, "appointed to put right Italy's state of affairs" (*electus ad corrigendum statum Italiae, ILS* 1159) under Caracalla, or Pomponius Bassus, "reformer of the whole of Italy" (*corrector totius Italiae*) in around 268–9 (*CIL* 6.3836; Purcell, 2000: 425; Lo Cascio, 2005: 165–69). Such appointments have sometimes been viewed as foreshadowing the later process of provincialization under Diocletian (on which see section 7.5 in this chapter), but should not necessarily be interpreted as showing imperial interest in improving administrative efficiency in Italy, as Purcell (2000: 425) points out: "the changes in the government and the personnel of government, which steadily eroded the institutional differences between Italy and the provinces, were concerned with power politics in the senatorial and equestrian circles much more than with practical administrative goals."

7.5   Administration of Italy

Although centrally appointed officials like the *curatores* might intervene in the affairs of Italian towns, ideologically there remained for much of the third century a sense that Italy was a special case. This was reflected in awards of Italian right (*ius Italicum*) to favored communities in the provinces (like Julia Domna's home town of Emesa in Syria or Lepcis Magna, home town of Septimius Severus), a legal fiction whereby an area in a province was treated as if it were instead part of Italy. This meant that such provincial communities could enjoy the taxation benefits traditionally enjoyed by Italy, namely exemption from having to pay land tax (*tributum soli*) (Lo Cascio, 2005, 165–66). Some aspects of military recruitment to the legions also reflected the centrality of the population of Italy to the welfare of the empire as a whole. A significant proportion of the officer corps of legions and auxiliaries consisted of the municipal elite of Italian towns well into the later third century (Traverso, 2006; e.g. L. Petronius Taurus Volusianus: *CIL* 11.1836 = *ILS* 1332, Arretium). At the same time, however, one major change was evident in the pattern of recruiting praetorian soldiers. Whereas the recruitment of legionary soldiers from within Italy had begun to decline during the first century, the same had not been true in the case of the praetorians who had, since the time of Augustus, enjoyed preferential terms of service, with a higher level of salary and shorter term on active duty. As a result, it seems that a large proportion of praetorians remained Italian-born. This changed with Septimius Severus, however, who executed many praetorians for their role in the assassination of the previous emperor Pertinax, and for the first time non-Italians became prominent within the praetorian ranks (Dio Cassius: 74 (75) 1.1, 2.4-6; Patterson, 2003: 100). Another important change made in relation to the army in Italy by Severus included permanently increasing the garrison of the peninsula by basing the legio II Parthica at Albanum.

    In 293, the character of imperial power and administration was fundamentally transformed by the establishment of the tetrarchy, whereby the empire was ruled jointly by two Augusti and two Caesars. From this date, the empire was divided geographically so that Maximian and Constantius Chlorus ruled the west, Diocletian and Galerius the east. Diocletian also introduced a new era for the peninsula, in overhauling the division of the Roman Empire into provinces, in response to pressing financial concerns, and subsumed Italy into being just another province, making its population subject to land tax for the first time. A new system of administration was implemented, subdividing the provinces into smaller entities than before, more than doubling the number of administrative units (Lo Cascio, 2005: 179–81). Italy was subdivided into regions, which were governed by *correctores*, and Italy itself became a diocese (one of 12 extensive territorial districts) during the first reorganization of circa 313. Although most dioceses were governed by a single *vicarius*, an equestrian official answerable to a praetorian prefect, Italy fell under the jurisdiction of two *vicarii*. It is significant, though, that the decision to entitle the districts of Italy as *regiones* and their governors as *correctores* appears to reflect a deliberate effort to mask the reality by avoiding the standard terminology of *praeses* and *provincia*. In fact, it was only during the Ostrogothic period that the term *provincia* was first used of the Italian regions.

FURTHER READING

Excellent surveys of the changing relationship of Italy and Rome can be found in chapters in the *Cambridge Ancient History* volumes 11 and 12 by Purcell 2000 and Lo Cascio 2005. A series of thought-provoking articles on the role of elite women within public life by Hemelrijk is complemented by the volume edited by Hemelrijk and Woolf 2013 and the recent monograph by Hemelrijk 2015, and by a volume focusing upon imperial women edited by Kolb 2010. Patterson's monograph (2006) is fundamental in offering an alternative to the traditional assumption of "decline" within Italian towns during the second and third centuries, tracing instead a change in patterns of urban activity.

REFERENCES

Ashby, T. and Gardner R. 1916. "The via Traiana." *Papers of the British School at Rome* 8:104–71.
Bruun, C. 2010. "Matidia die Jüngere – Gesellschaftlicher Einfluss und dynastische Rolle." In Augustae. *Machtbewusste Frauen am römischen Kaiserhof?*, ed. A. Kolb, 211–33. Berlin: Akademie Verlag.
Cascella, S. 2012. "Il periodo Antonino: Matidia Minore e Suessa." In *Memorie Suessane di Matidia. Suessa: Città e territorio dagli Aurunci all'età romana*, eds S. Cascella and M.G. Ruggi D'Aragona, 57–59. Oxford: BAR International Series 2445.
Cascella, S. and Ruggi D'Aragona, M.G. 2012. *Memorie Suessane di Matidia. Suessa: Città eterritorio dagli Aurunci all'età romana*. Oxford: BAR International Series 2445.
Cenerini, F. 2013. "The role of women as municipal *matres*." In *Women and the Roman City in the Latin West*, eds E. Hemelrijk and G. Woolf, 9–22. Leiden: Brill.
Chausson F. 2003. "Domitia Longina: reconsidération d'un destin impérial." *Journal des savants*, 101–29.
Cogitore, I. 1992. "Séries de dédicaces italiennes à la dynastie julio-claudienne." *Mélanges de l'Ecole Française de Rome, Antiquité* 104.2: 817–70.
Coleman, K.M. 1988. *Statius Silvae IV*. Oxford: Clarendon Press.
Cooley, A.E. and Cooley, M.G.L. 2014. *Pompeii and Herculaneum. A Sourcebook*. London and New York: Routledge.
Crawford, M. H., ed. 1996. *Roman Statutes*. 2 vols. London: Institute of Classical Studies, *BICS Suppl.* 64.
Criniti, N., ed. 2006. Res publica Veleiatium. *Veleia, tra passato e futuro*. Parma: MUP.
Dench, E. 1995. *From Barbarians to New Men. Greek, Roman and Modern Perceptions of Peoples from the Central Apennines*. Oxford: Clarendon Press.
Eck, W. 2000. "Emperor, senate and magistrates." In *The Cambridge Ancient History* vol. 11, 2nd edn, *The High Empire AD 70–192*, eds A.K. Bowman, P. Garnsey, and D. Rathbone, 214–37. Cambridge: Cambridge University Press.

Flower, H.I. 2001. "A tale of two monuments: Domitian, Trajan and some praetorians at Puteoli (*AE* 1973, 137)." *American Journal of Archaeology* 105.4: 625–48.

Griffin, M.T. 2000. "The Flavians." In *The Cambridge Ancient History vol. 11, 2nd edn, The High Empire AD 70–192*, eds A.K. Bowman, P. Garnsey, and D. Rathbone, 1–83. Cambridge: Cambridge University Press.

Hannestad, N. 1988. *Roman Art and Imperial Policy.* Aarhus: Aarhus University Press.

Hemelrijk, E.A. 2004. "City patronesses in the Roman empire". *Historia* 53.2: 209–45.

Hemelrijk, E.A. 2006. "Priestesses of the imperial cult in the Latin West: benefactions and public honour." *L'Antiquité classique* 75: 85–117.

Hemelrijk, E.A. 2008. "Patronesses and 'Mothers' of Roman *collegia*." *Classical Antiquity* 27.1: 115–62.

Hemelrijk, E.A. 2015. *Hidden Lives, Public Personae. Women and Civic Life in the Roman West.* Oxford: Oxford University Press.

Hemelrijk, E.A. and Woolf, G., eds. 2013. *Women and the Roman City in the Latin West.* Leiden: Brill.

Jacques, F. 1983. *Les curateurs des cités dans l'occident romain de Trajan à Gallien.* Paris: Nouvelles Editions Latines.

Jacques, F. 1984. *Le privilège de liberté: politique impériale et autonomie municipale dans les cités de l'occident romain (161–244)* Rome: Collection de l'Ecole française de Rome 76.

Keay, S. 2008. "Portus and the Alexandrian grain trade revisited." *Bollettino di Archeologia Online*: 11–22.

Kolb, A., ed. 2010. Augustae. *Machtbewusste Frauen am römischen Kaiserhof?* Berlin: Akademie Verlag GmbH.

Levick, B. 1999. *Vespasian.* London: Routledge.

Levick, B. 2002. "Corbulo's daughter." *Greece and Rome* 49.2: 199–211.

Lo Cascio, E. 2005. "The emperor and his administration." In *Cambridge Ancient History* vol. 12. *The Crisis of Empire, AD 193–337*, eds A. Bowman, A. Cameron, and P. Garnsey, 131–83. Cambridge: Cambridge University Press.

Meiggs, R. 1973. (2nd edn). *Roman Ostia.* Oxford: Clarendon Press.

Najbjerg, T. 2002. "The so-called Basilica in Herculaneum." In *Pompeian Brothels, Pompeii's Ancient History, Mirrors and Mysteries, Art and Nature at Oplontis, and the Herculaneum "Basilica,"* 123–65. Portsmouth, RI: *Journal of Roman Archaeology* Suppl. 47.

Patterson, J.R. 2003. "The emperor and the cities of Italy." In *"Bread and Circuses": Euergetism and Municipal Patronage in Roman Italy*, eds K. Lomas and T. Cornell, 89–104. London and New York: Routledge.

Patterson, J.R. 2006. *Landscapes and Cities. Rural Settlement and Civic Transformation in Early Imperial Italy.* Oxford: Oxford University Press.

Potter, T.W. 1987. *Roman Italy.* London: British Museum Press.

Purcell, N. 2000. "Rome and Italy." In *The Cambridge Ancient History* vol. 11, 2nd edn, *The High Empire AD 70–192*, eds A.K. Bowman, P. Garnsey, and D. Rathbone, 405–43. Cambridge: Cambridge University Press.

Raepsaet-Charlier, M.T. 2008. "L'activité évergétique des femmes clarissimes sous le haut-empire." In *Epigrafia 2006. Atti della XIVe rencontre sur l'épigraphie in onore di Silvio Panciera* vol. 3, 1029–45. Tituli 9, Quasar: Rome.

Smith, R.R.R. 1998. "Cultural choice and political identity in honorific portrait statues in the Greek east in the second century AD." *Journal of Roman Studies* 68: 56–93.

Traverso, M. 2006. *Esercito romano e società italica in età imperiale. 1. I documenti epigrafici.* Rome: Bretschneider.

Valeri, C., Zevi, F. 2004. "La statua di Matidia Minore e il teatro di Sessa Aurunca." In *Adriano: le memorie al femminile*, ed. A.M. Reggiani, 128–33. Milan: Electa.

Woolf, G. 1990. "Food, poverty and patronage: the significance of the epigraphy of the Roman alimentary schemes in early imperial Italy." *Papers of the British School at Rome* 58: 197–228.

CHAPTER 8

Late Roman and Late Antique Italy: from Constantine to Justinian

Neil Christie

8.1   Introduction

In AD 533, Cassiodorus, as Master of Offices, composed for the Ostrogothic king Athalaric a letter addressed to the City Prefect of Rome, one Salventius, *vir illustris*, stating (*Variae*: 9.16):

> I have sent to the blessed Pope decrees that surpass the former in their brilliance, in order that worldly and corrupt ambition may be removed from the honor of the Holy Church. I wish you to bring this without any delay to the notice of the Senate and Roman people, so that a measure which I desire to be carefully observed by everyone may be fixed in the hearts of all. Indeed, to impress this princely benefit on both present and future ages, I order my command and the Senate's resolution alike to be fittingly engraved on marble tablets, and placed in the atrium of the church of the blessed Apostle Peter as a public testimony. For the place is worthy to hold both my glorious gift, and the praiseworthy decree of the noble Senate.

This letter implies continuity in the heart of the old Eternal City – of Senate, Roman people, text, display, law (and corruption!) – through into the sixth century, if with a statement of a new authority, namely the Church with its focus of the basilica of St Peter's. But this was a much different Rome and Italy: Ostrogothic not Roman; one no longer head of a Western Roman Empire; Rome as a papal seat and with Ravenna as the royal capital; and with Goths as the soldiery, and dukes and counts as state civil-military officials in the main towns. Other letters from Cassiodorus point to other changes: while villas and vineyards are still recorded, Italy more widely had a militarized landscape, dominated by fortified urban centers, in which monuments of the past played a reduced role. This chapter charts the key historical events of the late Roman to early Byzantine period and explores some of the impacts of these on the peninsula, assessing levels of change and of continuity in settlement, society, and economy. It also addresses the question of unity: how far was northern Italy the same as Apenninic or southern Italy across AD 300–550 and how different were the capitals from other urban centers?

8.2   Constantine and a New Order

Constantine's takeover of Rome in AD 311, deposing Maxentius (whose hastily concealed imperial insignia of scepter, spears and banners were rediscovered in 2007 on the Palatine slopes – Panella, 2008), was the latest in a long line of strong arm usurpations stretching back to the earlier third century. Unlike his predecessors, Constantine celebrated this civil war triumph in full, his victory arch beside the Colosseum depicting the overthrow of tyranny, with sieges of Italian towns part of the repertoire of symbolic images (a slightly earlier, Tetrarchic arch includes commemoration of the defeat of the British usurper Allectus – Coarelli 1999, 26–27, 31–32; see Figure 8.1). Other emperors would follow suit in displaying in Rome and in provincial capitals such "home victories" on arches or columns (Ammianus Marcellinus, 21.16.15 on such works by Constantius II in the 350s; see Mayer, 2006). Constantine's rule was brutal and firm like Diocletian's, but his target was to oversee the whole Empire – even if shortly initiating an alternative Rome in the East at old Byzantion, the new Constantinople. Imperial building activity was duly promoted in Rome and Milan as a sign of continuity and renewal, but this was designed also to overshadow notable works of the deposed Maxentius (Coarelli, 1999 for Rome; Rinaldi Tufi, 2005 for wider programmes).

Figure 8.1   Rome, Arch of Constantine, south face, left side passage: view of the re-used and reworked Hadrianic-period roundel sculptures set over a Constantinian frieze depicting a siege by Constantine's troops of a fortified city in Italy, either Susa or Verona. A winged victory on the left flies in to help deliver the city's capture. Photograph: N. Christie.

Baths and basilicas saw construction and there was renewal of services like aqueducts and roads, but it is difficult to gauge how extensive such works were outside the larger Italian cities: despite restoration of the state after the third-century crisis, the old order of willing private euergetism in the urban sphere appears badly eroded beyond some of the wealthier central Italian regions, and the picture for the fourth century is of urban projects of limited scope and now generally overseen by governors (*correctores*) or magistrates such as the *cura-tores*. Many "traditional" components of the urban fabric such as theaters, amphitheaters, temples, and even baths, appear frequently to have suffered neglect and were no longer seen as priorities – except when individual governors and occasional private patrons chose to revive them (Ward-Perkins, 1984: ch. 2). In some cases, however, needs had changed: at Rimini, the amphitheater was incorporated into the modified late third-century city wall – matching new militarized urban configurations in Gaul, such as at Tours, where the amphitheater became both defensive bulwark and monumental south gate and presumably saw conversion into stores or housing; and the theater at Turin and the suburban public baths at Albenga were both redundant by the early fourth century, subsequently being exploited as quarries for materials and then replaced by later fourth-century churches (Rimini: Gelichi, 1994; Turin: Pejrani Baricco, 1998; Albenga: Massabò, 2003).

8.2.1   The growth of the urban church

Traditional euergetism must surely have faltered in the wake of Constantine's acceptance of Christianity as a tolerated and even state-promoted religion from AD 312 (Cameron, 2006). Laws against pagan worship, or more specifically against sacrifice, were not immediate and indeed remain elusive until the mid-fourth century (Lee, 2000: 80–110), but the start of substantial, imperial-funded building campaigns for Christian basilicas at Rome, Ostia, and Milan in Italy, and in capitals such as Trier and Arles in the West were loud enough statements of intent (Rinaldi Tufi, 2005; Henig, 2006). In the case of Rome, the major new complexes of St John the Lateran and St Peter's respectively blotted out a palace and barracks of Maxentian creation, and canceled out an ancient necropolis and compromised a major pagan sanctuary on the *Vaticanum*, that of Transtiberian Magna Mater or Cybele – although dedi-cations from the latter show a re-opening in circa AD 350 and usage into the 380s, reflecting a potentially "awkward" co-existence of elite pagan and Christian spaces in the Vatican zone (Liverani 2003. More widely on Rome's Christianization, see Curran, 2000). Much has been made of possible "pagan resistance" and opposition from elites in the capitals of Rome and Milan, but most scholars now prefer to recognize a progressive waning of old cults and related priesthoods, retained by some of the older senatorial aristocracy, whose ancestors were intimately tied to these ancient cults. Being a pagan and holding a set of priesthoods did not prevent high office-holding: the City Prefect of AD 365, Lampadius and his sons were thus devotees of Cybele at the *Vaticanum* and in Ostia; other City and Annona Prefects had strong pagan leanings, and keenly pursued the provision of games at Rome in the second half of the fourth century. Yet members of the same families could be Christian and pagan–Christian marriages were not uncommon (Liverani, 2003: 73–74). In Rome and Milan, ancient traditions and cultic heritage lingered but were probably not as vocal as some contemporary and later Christian commentators claimed.

Beyond the metropoleis, however, we are far less aware of pagan urban survivals – the pic-ture is variable according to the archaeology and was presumably dependent on the depth of elite presence and the vitality of resident bishops. Indeed, one key factor to note is the delayed creation of bishoprics in various parts of Italy – matching to some degree the patchy legislation against old cult centers. Indeed, the 248 documented Italian urban dioceses predating the seventh century are a chronological patchwork: in central Italy, to the north of Rome, for example, the earliest bishops are documented at Pisa, Siena, Florence, and Chiusi in AD 313; while Arezzo, Lucca, Spoleto, and Gubbio follow in the mid-fourth century, it is another century or more before bishoprics like Luni and Volterra are attested. In the north-west, episcopal seats at Lodi, Pavia, Novara, and Genoa date from AD 381, and at Turin by 398; others belong to the fifth century, such as Tortona and Albenga. For south-east Italy, many larger towns like Lecce, Otranto, and Taranto show episcopal development later in the fourth century; and for Sicily only with the Church Council here in the mid-360s can we claim an established diocesan organization (Testini, Cantino Wataghin, and Pani Ermini, 1989; Campione and Nuzzo, 1999: 17–21, 25ff; Sami, 2010). Potentially those earliest bishoprics reflect where pre-Constantinian Christian presences were most active and later ones coincide with where pagan aristocrats retained some greater hold or else where a lack of any early Christian community (or martyrs) delayed Church colonization. Sicily, often seen as a strong senatorial base, is an odd mix, since martyrial shrines of the first half of the fourth century are known in seats like Catania and Agrigento and yet episcopal building works cluster around AD 400 (Bonacasa Carra, 2004). Indeed, archaeological input is crucial in mapping the phases and modes of "Christianization" of Italian towns, otherwise undocumented by text bar through occasional epitaphs (e.g. see papers in Marcenaro, 2003b; Pani Ermini, 2000 for Rome). Excavations are also vital in revealing how churches often overlie elite houses or *domus*, although it is problematic to determine whether these signify early house-churches, *domus* donated to churches, or decayed secular space colonized by the Church (Luni: Lusuardi Siena, 2003; Rome: Guidobaldi, 1999).

The approximate rule of thumb is that episcopal churches with associated baptistery mark a first intramural insertion; otherwise, extramural or periurban cemeteries and martyrs' tombs provided early foci of Christian veneration. In larger cities, episcopal palaces were established as points of reception and debate (effectively variations of late Roman secular elite *domus* and villas) and denote how, from the fifth century in particular, bishops and clergy increasingly gained urban administrative roles (best studied is Milan: Lusuardi Siena, 1997 and papers in *La città e la sua memoria*; Rome: papers in Pani Ermini, 2000; Marano, 2010). From circa AD 400, with paganism fully banned by law, church building in town and country increased substantially and the urban Christian imprint became far more prominent, with cathedrals often taking central locations. The splendour of the mosaic-encrusted baptistery at Albenga of the mid-fifth century (Sciarretta, 1966; Marcenaro, 2003a) would by then have formed a major contrast with the ruinous and part robbed classical urban fabric (see Figure 8.2). Impetus now came also from high elites, nearly all converted by the first decades of the fifth century and with patronage of churches and monasteries taken as indicators of their "accommodation" within the Church. Key documented figures include Paulinus of Nola in Campania, whose secular wealth and influence as governor enabled him to found a major cult center to St Felix in circa 400, and whose learning and contacts helped in the promotion of the cult (through poems, visits by bishops and aristocrats, accumulation of relics, and using skilled artists in decorating church and attached male and female monasteries). Elected bishop of Nola, Paulinus oversaw the town's efforts to counter capture by Alaric's Visigoths; refugees from Alaric's siege of Rome in AD 410 sheltered at his shrine of St Felix (Trout, 1999).

Intriguing is the epigraphic evidence for Campania, likewise viewed as a senatorial "stronghold." Here the quantity and range of inscriptions suggest vocal Christian communities well established only from the mid-fifth century when church building also accelerates; interestingly we can observe a persistence even on epitaphs of some of the old symbols of secular aristocratic authority – i.e. rank and office – since labels such as *vir spectabilis* or *illustris* endure fully into the mid-sixth century (Lambert, 2008).

Figure 8.2 View of the exterior of the fifth-century baptistery at Albenga in western Liguria, north-west Italy; the windows and interior identify notable later eighth-century restorations here. Photograph: N. Christie.

8.2.2   Rural Christianization

That bishops were central to the Christianization of the landscape is reflected in the words and actions of figures such as Ambrose of Milan, Vigilius of Trento, and Maximus of Turin for the 370s–400s – matching the well-known deeds of St Martin of Tours in Gaul. References to postings of imperial constitutions against pagan cults, requiring farmers and their landlords to abandon their old religions, plus likely armed interventions – such as in retaliations against the apparent murder of three clerics who had been sent to convert peasants (alleged Saturn-worshippers) in the Val di Non in the mountains near the city of Trento (Lizzi, 1990) – suggest quite forceful state-backed evangelization efforts. As Caseau (2004) has flagged, however, many rural temples were "private" establishments, set up by landowners on their estates or to serve villages; their legal status was such that they might not be considered "sacred" (in state eyes) and so might not be directly hit by bans on worship at "public" temples and sanctuaries. Missionary work might thus have mainly been aimed at converting landowners. A problem lies of course in the dominance of Christian-based textual sources, whether sermons or hagiographies, meaning uncertainty on the real depth or nature of these residual and persistent rural pagans – indeed, when in circa AD 600 Pope Gregory complains about pagan rituals among landowners and peasants on Church lands in Sicily and Sardinia, is this anything more than individual and age-old traditions and private superstitions? Bishops, monks, and saints needed some proper foes and emphasizing resistance was vital to highlight the prowess of the converters. In other cases though, the conversions were progressive affairs: thus some of the early fifth-century poems by Paulinus of Nola reveal how 'rude peasants' happily frequented the shrine of St Felix, if often at night and with drink and food, although Paulinus hoped that the images, relics, and sanctity of the site (plus the painted words, though he admits these rustics are illiterate) would impact on their souls.

Archaeology should provide an important guide to tracing the ends (brutal or gradual) or persistences of rural cults, although often the material evidence for this can be ephemeral – occasional worship at an otherwise 'closed' cult site may be near invisible or undatable. Thus, for example, in the Alpine Trentino, excavations since the late 1960s at Monte San Martino (near Riva at the north end of lake Garda) have uncovered a sanctuary with open central space with two presumed main altars flanked by cult buildings for storing votive offerings and lesser altars; 'native' deities seem to have held center stage (the *Matres*, and some unknown divinities), though statuettes to more 'standard' Roman gods like Minerva, suggest varied cults saw worship here. Pottery and coin evidence show frequentation to the end of the fourth century, but with a structural peak in circa AD 200. While there is no clear destruction deposit, it is striking that much material from the shrine area was reused in the medieval church located just 200 m downslope; sculptural finds here suggest an early medieval phase, with a fifth- or sixth-century origin also possible (Ciurletti, 2007). Indeed, it is more through insertions of baptismal churches in the landscape that we might chart Christian starts and pagan ends across Italy, although securing fine chronologies to the foundation of many rural churches is not easy: for the modern territories of Friuli, Liguria, and Apulia, fifth- and sixth-century dates are generally clear (based on ceramic evidence or on architectural typologies), with re-elaboration and new foundations in the early medieval period (Friuli: Sannazaro, 2001; Liguria: Marcenaro, 2003b; Apulia: Volpe, 2001: 237–49). For Friuli some parish churches appear on hilltops or spurs linked to a modified, more militarized late Roman rural landscape and may signify the Church playing a role in reorganizing communities in this epoch. Similarly, we might note how for AD 443 pope Leo's letter to the bishop of Lilibeo (Marsala) on Sicily refers to a church "in the high mountains and thick woods" in the small settlement called 'Meltinas,' whose baptismal font miraculously filled and emptied of its own accord on the night of Easter when the few locals came to be baptized (Fiocchi Nicolai and Gelichi, 2001: 305–06).

8.3   Emperors, Invaders and Italy, AD 340–490

Conflict, resistance, and victory were not the preserve of the Church in fourth-century Italy. What the sources – documentary, far less archaeological – report are ongoing bouts of succession and power struggles played out in the northern provinces, in the Alpine zones, and in Rome itself. When Constantine left the Empire to his sons Constantine, Constantius, and Constans, purges against rivals duly occurred, but divisions soon set in: Constantine II was killed when invading Constans' territory in Italy in AD 340; a coup led by Magnentius in Rome saw Constans' end in 350 (Hunt, 1998: 10–22). Frontier troubles from the 350s especially distracted many of the emperors (and usurpers) and it appears a rare occurrence that the emperor spent time in Milan or managed to visit Rome – as Constantius did in AD 357 to celebrate the 20th anniversary of his accession (Ammianus Marcellinus: 16.10). Conflict between Western and Eastern courts later played a part in the disastrous failure by the Eastern emperor to wait for Gratian to assist in Roman military action at Adrianople against the huge numbers of Goths being resettled from over the Danube in the late 370s. While Theodosius restored some stability, internal wars again flared in the West to debilitate and fragment its armed forces: the British usurper Magnus Maximus campaigned against Gratian in 383 (Gratian was then murdered by his troops at Cologne) and against Valentinian II in the Alps and in north-east Italy before being defeated by Theodosius's Roman and Gothic army in AD 388. Italy saw further disruption in 392–94 when Theodosius fought the usurper Eugenius and his Frankish general Arbogast, eventually triumphing beside the river Isonzo in the Julian Alps (Zosimus, 4: 35–58; Eunapius, *Breviarum*: 9: 60).

Subsequent independent Visigothic action in the later 390s impacted heavily on the Balkans and then Italy. The key protagonists were the Roman generalissimo Stilicho and the Visigothic king Alaric, with Alaric's efforts focused on gaining recognition, territory, and imperial military command. Their armies clashed on a couple of occasions, notably at Pollenzo in north Italy in AD 402, and Stilicho was forced, without Eastern aid, to bolster his army by thinning out northern frontier forces, and by recruiting Huns. Italy faced also invasion from Goths under Radagaisus, whose plundering in the north was halted in late AD 405 with defeat near Florence, after which 30 000 of his men were drafted and others sold off as slaves, apparently glutting the market at Rome. But when Stilicho was executed in AD 408, Alaric exploited the power void by moving on Rome and besieging it, blockading its ports. Many elites had already fled east or south; many slaves now deserted; and famine and pestilence then hit the remaining inhabitants, who temporarily paid off Alaric. During a second blockade in AD 409, he forced acceptance by the Senate of a puppet emperor, Attalus, but eventually, on 24 August AD 410, a more brutal approach saw Alaric's troops breach the city. His followers freely ransacked the city's public and private buildings – some related archaeology is known in destructions and abandonments of *domus* on hills such as the Caelian and Aventine – and much treasure and many captives were taken when the Visigoths withdrew, moving south and then north-west. Poets like Rutilius Namatianus and inscriptions such as that erected by Constantius in Albenga chart something of their movement and disruption onward to lands formally allocated by the emperor Honorius in southern Gaul (Lançon, 2000: 35–42; Christie, 2006: 28–30).

In the 430s Rome lost Africa to the Vandals (Humphries, 2000). Their inheritance of the Roman *annona* fleet and its personnel swiftly enabled them to attack within the central and western Mediterranean and by the 460s they controlled the islands of Malta, Sardinia, Corsica, the Balearics, and, crucially, Sicily. These Vandal conquests effectively blockaded Rome and broke the fragile economic imperial unity of the western Mediterranean (De Souza, 1999: 231–38). Vandal raids consistently hit southern and western coastal Italy, forcing emergency defensive responses here (urban circuits, garrisons, or rural evacuations); their impact is attested in the Roman law codes, responding to provincials' failures to pay taxes or requesting locals to be vigilant, and even to bear arms if needed, to help save the state (Christie and Rushworth, 1988; key edicts: *Theodosian Code, Valentinian Novels*: 1.2 and 9.1). Events culminated in the targeting of Rome itself, succumbing rapidly to king Geiseric's forces in AD 455. Priscus reported how Rome was already in disorder after the assassination of Valentinian III, with open conflict for replacements, and one Petronius Maximus prevailing "through his distribution of money" and taking Valentinian's widow, Eudoxia, as his wife, only to be killed amid the confusion of the arrival of the Vandals. While the vandalism inflicted in their two weeks of occupation sounds greater than that of AD 410 (Rome's churches also suffered, despite appeals by the pope), archaeologically the damage seems harder to trace, perhaps signifying an emphasis on amassing moneys, metals, and slaves as opposed to the burning down of buildings.

Papal entreaties had worked better on Attila in AD 452 when the Hunnic overlord led a substantial confederate army into north Italy, sacking Aquileia, occupying Milan, holding other cities to ransom, and meeting little military opposition from the debilitated troops of the general Aetius; the latter apparently recommended that the emperor Valentinian III flee and establish a new capital in Gaul. But pope Leo met Attila near Milan on the banks of the Mincio river and successfully secured Italy's deliverance (*Book of Pontiffs*: Life of Leo I) – perhaps assisted by a major financial incentive and by the fact that Attila's army was suffering from disease and was ready to withdraw anyway.

Subsequent events in Italy saw a mix of external threats, internal conflict and power-brokering, to be set alongside the progressive and final fragmentation of Rome's western provinces. The picture is confusing and confused, and the human and material repercussions are still not well understood. Power now lay firmly in the hands of military generalissimos, many of German birth, if long in Roman arms (Innes, 2007: 112–15). Notable is Ricimer, an Arian Christian, son of a Sueve, related to the Visigothic king Wallia, and with links to the Burgundian court, whose 15-year period of domination included the deposition of emperor Avitus and the elevation of Majorian, the latter's execution in AD 461, election next of senator Libius Severus, agreement with the Eastern emperor Leo I to select Anthemius as successor in AD 465 (in return for help in a major but failed expedition against the Vandals), civil war in Italy, continued Vandal raids, followed by a lasting treaty with the Vandals who forced acceptance of their king Geiseric's nomination as emperor of another senator, Anicius Olybrius – brother-in-law to Geiseric's son. Ricimer eventually died in AD 472, to be replaced as military supremo by the Burgundian prince Gundobad, who briefly installed his own emperor Glycerius before returning to Burgundian territory to stake his claim for the throne there – implying that the Burgundian throne meant far more than control of Italy.

Next on the throne in Ravenna was Julius Nepos, elected by his army in Dalmatia, but he was removed by the Italian general Orestes who made his own son, Romulus, emperor; within a year he too was gone, unable to meet the troops' excessive demands. Orestes also departed quickly when a lesser commander, Odoacer, perhaps of Scirian descent, murdered him and retired Romulus to a fine villa at the promontory of Pizzofalcone near Naples in September AD 476. Odoacer chose not to employ a puppet emperor and so forced Romulus to send envoys to the emperor Zeno in Constantinople, to propose that Odoacer be recognized as a patrician and legal overseer of Italy (Innes, 2007: 121–23). As with the rulers since established in Visigothic Spain, Vandal Africa, and Burgundia, Odoacer maintained much of the residual Roman administration, issued laws, and promoted urban and Church upkeep; he stabilized his frontiers, although this did include formal withdrawal from Noricum, still nominally under Italian rule, and ceding a final chunk of Gaul to the Visigoths. Italy had therefore shrunk down into an independent territory, no longer fighting to control distant provinces, but set within more manageable confines, able, perhaps, to start to restore some of its battered population and economy.

8.4   Changed Landscapes

The events rapidly outlined in preceding sections of this chapter reflect a peninsula that suffered significant political, military, and economic damage across the fourth and, particularly, fifth centuries. When Odoacer took over and for the subsequent Ostrogothic rule, towns remained points of secular and religious administration, coinage still circulated, ceramics continued to be produced, and animals still bred and traded. Losses had built up, however, and in this section are considered some of the physical and structural changes that can be recognized in both town and countryside. Were towns mere defensive shells, were fortresses prominent, and to what degree were fields emptied of farmers?

8.4.1   *Militarized townscapes*

First we need to note the shift in imperial seat, away from Milan, adopted as capital by the Tetrarchs, to Ravenna, selected under Stilicho and Honorius in part for its coastal location, in touch with the Adriatic fleet, and for its natural marshy defensive support (Gillett, 2001).

Figure 8.3   Internal view of the main gate and circuit of the citadel or *castrum* of Susa, of circa AD 300. Photograph: N. Christie.

What is striking here is the massive redevelopment of an earlier *colonia*, expanding over eastern periurban spaces and exploiting materials (*spolia*) from demolished *domus* and public units. A wall circuit built largely *ex novo* enclosed palace and churches, plus circus; but there was almost no pagan inheritance here and Ravenna stands out for the survival of an array of fifth- and sixth-century church architecture and art, signifying that moneys, labor, and skills continued to be present in late Roman Italy, if increasingly restricted to this new and the older capitals, since both Milan and Rome remained important architectural arenas for the Church (Ravenna: Augenti, 2003, 2006a; Cirelli, 2008; Deliyannis, 2010. Rome: *Storia di Roma III*; Ensoli and La Rocca, 2000; Harris, 1999; Pani Ermini, 2000; Augenti, 2003). Excavations at Ravenna's port of Classe – itself walled and designated a city – have revealed high levels of trade across the fifth and sixth centuries reaching the capital, although not many of these commodities (including oil, wine, amphorae, and lamps from North Africa and the eastern Mediterranean, as well as some Italian products) penetrated far beyond the city to lesser urban and rural markets (Cirelli, 2008: 130–40). The same appears true for Rome, although the archaeology of Portus and Ostia reveals changing fortunes and roles: Ostia for the fourth century was more of an aristocratic retreat, perhaps for elites connected to the port trades, and Portus from the early fifth shows a shrinkage in space to a fortified core and a reduction in warehousing, the indications being that the blockades of AD 408–410 and like events prompted the authorities to ensure more rapid transshipment of grain and goods to Rome via canals and up the Tiber, rather than relying on longer-term stockpiling outside the city (Coccia, 1996; Keay *et al.*, 2005: 291–95; Augenti, 2010: 39–43, noting episcopal survival at Portus into the ninth century). Although seriously affected by the sieges and military events, Rome's population remained enormous – if greatly shrunken from the early imperial high – with estimates between a quarter to half a million still for the mid-fifth century. Ravenna, by contrast, may have attained a mere 10 000–15 000 (with as many people at Classe), although letters of the sixth century indicate healthy concern also here with ensuring the supply of grain and oil for the population (Deliyannis, 2010: 116).

Defensive considerations were high in the selection and delineating of Ravenna. Investment in urban defense had surfaced in significant fashion from the later third century in response to both internal warfare and barbarian intrusions over the frontiers. The larger Italian centers were among the first to redefine themselves in the later Empire (Dey, 2011: 111–31): Verona under Gallienus, Rome under Aurelian, and Milan under the Tetrarchs experienced major physical transformations, with high walls, restricted gates, and wide ditches, all requiring disruption to internal and external spaces, and marking – very evident in the case of Verona – a first phase of creation and reuse of *spolia* from demolished public and private structures. In part structural sacrifices came through necessity – namely the route chosen for the circuit walls – but they responded also to the noted drop of euergetism, with older temples, shrines, even entertainment venues closed and redundant. We cannot be certain how far there was competition for towns to (re-)wall themselves, to what degree it was a state requirement, whether priorities were made as to which towns (if any) received state aid, and whether individual town councils drew up proposed wall courses, since virtually no written testimony survives related to walls and barely any epigraphic commemorations of such works. One might argue against panic measures following Rome's early fortification; rather, we might suggest that the Tetrarchs instigated an ordered program of urban defense work and that with the dispersal of sizeable external and internal threats in the fourth century, work progressed at variable paces. Either way, walls became part of the required late Roman urban fabric (Christie, 2006: ch. 4).

Nonetheless, the fifth-century traumas must have accelerated works and repairs in various urban centers: Naples saw refortification to counter Vandal assault; Rome's walls were heightened under Honorius in the early fifth century; a new militarized bishop's seat arose at Grado in partial replacement of Aquileia (often hit by invading forces) at the head of the Adriatic; and citadels can be recognized at sites like Susa in the north-west Alps (see Figure 8.3). The south of Italy, as well as the islands, despite the documented Vandal raids, in general appear to have been sluggish in terms of urban fortification: in the 530s Cassiodorus (*Variae*: 12, 15) highlights the main city of Bruttium, Squillace, as still unwalled. This indicates a cushioning of the south from many of the politico-military dramas of the third to fifth centuries. Against this view are signs of the failing and loss of a number of southern Italian towns; however, this may be far less due to insecurity than to changed economic directions (e.g. the state obtaining greater landholding shares to ensure supplies) and with administrative roles concentrated in fewer urban seats (such as Canosa, Lucera, Siponto) (Volpe, 2001). Even close to Rome urban losses are registered, not through warfare or through natural disasters, but through failures to retain a population: artificial market creations like Forum Novum and Falerii Novi in South Etruria dribble to a small episcopal center and to a largely empty walled shell respectively in the fourth to fifth centuries (Patterson, 2004: chs 15, 16).

The Church populated most late Roman and late antique towns and provided a glue to their populations. Arguably, urban archaeology has tended to concentrate on the built ecclesiastical spaces, since basilicas, baptisteries, church furniture, and cemeteries form strongly tangible guides to urban fortunes. Foundations of churches, repairs, rebuildings, and burial insertions may offer windows onto a community's economic health. But these do not directly inform on demographics and ordinary living conditions, and more recent archaeologies have done much to explore the fate of the large private *domus* (these often seeing partitioning or even loss across the fourth century except in the capitals (Brogiolo, 1994)), breakdowns in public architectural display such as theaters, amphitheaters, and *fora*, ailing amenities such as piped water supply and bathing, changing attitudes to space (evidenced by rubbish disposal patterns or intrusions of burials within the walled space), and material culture (supplies of goods, local industries, use of coin). Despite the often substantial problems in exploring sites which have seen continuous urban use, results from major excavations in centers like Rome (e.g. at the Crypta Balbi and the Fori Imperiali), Milan, Brescia, Verona, Naples, and Otranto have done much to chart changing townscapes across the late Roman period and into the early Middle Ages, identifying diverse trajectories in terms of public and private spaces, of reuse or robbing of structures, of organization of civic spaces like markets, of technological change (notably using wood alongside *spolia*), as well as of health and diet (though still too few burial populations have been subjected to modern analysis). Most scholars accept the appearance of much-altered urban innards, with the qualities and technologies of display much reduced (churches and palaces being the few structures of monumental and permanent character, with mosaic production increasingly limited to these), but there is debate as to how these centers were organized, how old or ruinous spaces were controlled and regarded, how Church control worked, how far military presences existed, and how supply systems functioned (Urban archaeologies and debates: see especially papers in Augenti, 2006b, plus Brogiolo, 1994. Rome: Arena *et al.*, 2001; Meneghini and Santangeli Valenzani, 2007; Milan: Caporusso, 1991; Brescia: Brogiolo, 1999; Verona: La Rocca Hudson, 1986; Naples: Arthur, 2002; Otranto: Michaelides and Wilkinson, 1992. Much work is active to review older excavations, finds, and archive data to gather fuller urban histories from Roman into medieval times – for example, Dall'Aglio and Di Cocco, 2004 for Pesaro; Cirelli, 2008 for Ravenna; Scampoli, 2010 for Florence). We perhaps expect too much from late antique towns, given the highs of the classical period; instead we should view them as increasingly functional, but set within the confines of now decayed display, and readily exploiting the old fabric.

Part of this functional image appeared already from the early fourth century in some northern Italian towns which were selected as the locations of the state's arms and cloth factories (*fabricae*). These were designed to equip Italy's mobile army and to supply Danubian units (James, 1988). As recognized elsewhere in the northern provinces, these city factories produced specific goods: arrows at Concordia (duly often named Concordia Sagittaria), shields and arms/armor (Verona), armor (Mantua), shields (Cremona), bows (Pavia), and swords (Lucca). Most probably these were Tetrarchic establishments, but in some instances developed from earlier industries (as suggested for Concordia, where an inscription mentions a second-century *decuria armamentaria*). The (branded) workers were ex-soldiers or the equivalent of soldiers; undoubtedly military units were posted as guards at these industrialized towns (Croce Da Villa and Di Filippo Balestrazzi, 2001). Soldiers are otherwise attested in larger towns from the early fifth century, although it is unclear whether these were temporary garrisons (in response, for example, to Alaric's incursions), detachments of the mobile armies billeted in towns when not on active service, or fixed militia. An army presence on one level may have given townspeople reassurance, though laws equally refer to issues of soldiery harassing townsfolk and overstepping billeting rights. Notable is Ennodius's description of the Gothic troops of Theoderic winter-quartered at Pavia in AD 489: "You would have seen the city teeming with vast throngs of troops, and huge *domus* cut up into the narrowest of huts. You would have seen even the largest buildings disappear from their foundations, nor was the ground itself sufficient to take such a dense mass of people…" (*Monumenta Germaniae Historica, Auctores Antiquissimi, VII*: p.98, 15).

8.4.2   Militarized landscapes

For the fifth century overall there are signs of a more militarized Italian landscape: heavily fortified towns in the Alpine regions and subalpine zones, reinforced by forts and watchtowers on the main and subsidiary roads and valleys, with potential networks of forts and defended upland villages created, as suggested for Friuli in the north-east. There were also forts created on islands and around the northern lakes, and fleets installed: the former luxurious villa (perhaps of the first-century BC poet Catullus) on the promontory at Sirmione at the south end of lake Garda may have been transformed into a garrison base, while the promontory itself was girded by a circuit wall. The forts all denote an inward-creeping militarization, responding to failures of the more distant Danubian frontiers and also of Alpine installations of the fourth century. The latter were concentrated in the north-eastern Julian Alps, guarding the weaker link in the mountain chain, and are termed *Claustra Alpium Iuliarum*; these comprised road forts, barriers, and towers, and were probably instigated under Constantine as a means of controlling traffic into Italy. The fortifications saw usage more during civil war conflicts, however, and may well have been disbanded by Theodosius at the end of the century. *Claustra, clusae* or *clusurae* are documented elsewhere in the Alps and even Apennines and may signify additional 'blockings' or watch systems, although almost none have been securely identified or dated archaeologically (often due to substantial medieval reuse or destruction later) (Christie, 2006, 324–48). Of relevance here are finds of items of military dress (so far around 70 artefacts, chiefly fixed-plate, chip-carved belt buckles, or with punched or perforated decoration), deriving often from burials, from 30 locations in the northern Adige valley in central northern Italy: one main example is the Pomarolo necropolis

Figure 8.4 Colossal (5 m high) bronze imperial statue at Barletta in south-eastern Italy, argued to represent Valentinian I (AD 364–375). Photograph: N. Christie.

at Servis, set on a high isolated terrace, where the finds suggest a military station, perhaps comprising Germanic federates, observing a strategic Alpine routeway. Intriguingly, the perforated buckles recovered here have roots in British and northern Gallic contexts, and the fixed-plate and chip-carved items may signify Upper Danube and Rhenish soldiery. Potentially, therefore, these are material traces of troops withdrawn from Britain, Gaul, and Germany under Stilicho in the early fifth century and stationed across Alpine Italy in a reactive policy of military entrenchment (Cavada, 2002).

8.4.3   Roads

As well as defending routeways, the late Roman state and military authorities targeted the maintenance of the road system, with emphasis placed on the major highways on the coastal bands and those leading from the Po plain to the main Alpine pass routes. Tetrarchic and later emphasis on the mobility of troops and the supply of goods to these, plus, of course, the need for (more) rapid communication via the *cursus publicus*, is reflected in numerous fourth-century milestones indicating road repair and state attention (Basso, 1986). Texts also refer to bridge repair, as on the *via Flaminia* outside Pesaro in AD 378–9 (*CIL* 11.6328 – noting a bridge 'ruined by age' but revitalized for the *cursus publicus*; Dall'Aglio and Di Cocco, 2004: 76–77). Milestones (these to be interpreted less as markers of distance and more as honorific 'flags' set up by emperors, governors, or local elites) are likewise prominent in the 370s–380s under Gratian and Valentinian in the Alps, Venetia province, and in Apenninic zones – finds in Le Marche, for instance, reflect the need to maintain west–east communications and to ensure supplies of wood, charcoal, and sheep from upland zones to the urban and military centers; attention also went on protecting imperial *saltus* – extensive woodland and pasture, as documented for the late fourth century in Picenum and around the Monti Sibillini (Campagnoli and Giorgi, 2004: 182–84, 190–94). Equally valuable were the southern Italian road networks, since the provinces of Apulia, Calabria, and Bruttium gained increasing prominence for grain, wine and oil production, and sheep- and pig-raising and transhumance to serve the Italian capitals. Road itineraries such as the *Tabula Peutingeriana* (originating circa AD 350), milestones, and excavations point to renewal and even extensions to main highways such as the Appian and Trajanic Ways, with new rest-stations or *mutationes* created, and agricultural townships (*vici*) developing on or near these; many of the coastal and riverine ports also show good survival, with archaeology starting to show better their engagement in serving Italy with wider Mediterranean trade flows into the sixth century (Volpe, 2001: 59–83 on communications; 257–310 on agricultural and animal output. Arthur, 2004: 105–09 on south Italian *vici*).

Road maintenance was no doubt problematic. In AD 399, at a time when rapid movement of troops and supplies was vital, the emperors Arcadius and Honorius at Milan posted this edict (*Theodosian Code*: 15.3.4): "It was formerly established that the patrimonies of Illustrious dignitaries should be considered exempt from the construction and repair of roads. But on account of the immense ruin of the highways, it is Our will that all persons, with helpful devotion, shall eagerly desire to hasten to the repair of the public roads." References to brigands in mountains and on highways start to resurface in this period. Rutilius Namatianus (*On his Home-coming*: Book 1, lines 39–42), heading in AD 416 from Rome to Gaul, had to "travel by water because roads can flood or be littered by slides and falling rocks; Tuscany and the Aurelian Highway have already fallen to the Goths. It is best to trust the sea because the rivers are not bridged and the land has become wild again." A century later, Cassiodorus (*Variae*: 12.18) sought repairs to the *via Flaminia*, by then "furrowed by the action of torrents… and rough woods choke the sides of the highway."

With a broken economy and weakened urbanism, funds to service roads and bridges were badly curtailed. The lack of fifth-century milestones is very noticeable.

8.4.4   *Rural change*

These roads of course traversed the rural landscape, which remained crucial for feeding both towns and armies. How far had settlement and exploitation changed or decayed since the 'third-century crisis'? Scholars have moved away from older images of blanket loss and decay of farms and farmers in the face of military conflicts and economic upheavals, recognizing firstly that most of the warfare was intermittent and did not target rural communities; secondly that general urban continuity implies rural persistence; thirdly that references in laws to *agri deserti* in zones like Campania and Samnium relate more to marginal and not core agricultural lands; and finally that earlier landscape archaeology projects struggled to recognize and date non-fineware ceramics of late Roman to early medieval date, leading to claims of major rural depopulation. Some middle- and low-ranking Roman towns did fail, particularly in upland zones, but also in areas where large *vici* and estate villages appear, as in Apulia and perhaps Sicily. Such *vici* – related conceivably initially to private estates, plus state lands, then later to Church properties – themselves are indicators of a busy enough landscape, with roles in storage, redistribution, marketing, and industrial processing (of agricultural goods and of livestock). Here, perhaps, a working landscape, geared to serving the power centers of Rome and Ravenna, canceled out the older hierarchy of settlement and society based on towns.

Villas in the north of Italy particularly show a flourish of fourth-century activity in line with sequences in the Danubian regions, as well as other western provinces (see Christie, 2004; Sfameni, 2004). Reception and dining rooms, mosaic and statuary displays, and possible mausolea are attested for sites like Varignano in Liguria and Desenzano at Lake Garda, and denote heightened elite rural structural investment, perhaps to be set alongside accumulation of larger landed estates. A well-known Sicilian example, rich in mosaic floors, whose imagery shows an owner linked to trade in wild animals from Africa, is Piazza Armerina; for south Italy, an equally stunning complex lies at Faragola in Apulia (Volpe, De Felice, and Turchiano 2005). Italy so far lacks comparanda for the militarized early fourth-century imperial and high elite complexes like Galerius's fortified 'villa' at Gamzigrad in the Balkans, and evidence for defensive works on Italian villas in the fifth century is also minimal. Currently, too few data exist to show how long-lived the luxury villas were: fifth- and sixth-century activity often appears ephemeral and might comprise basic repairs or disuse of rooms and related rubbish-dumping, plus the insertion of burials in and around the sites. In other instances we might trace churches as part of the fifth-century plan (e.g. San Giusto), sometimes as part of the villa complex, or sometimes as an independent unit amidst largely abandoned villa space (e.g. Monte Gelato and San Vincenzo) (Brogiolo, 1996). Problematic is determining ownership, whether the same families but with diminished economic scope, estate tenants moving in, monks establishing a base, or Church officials having been donated the property. As in the towns, so we can also observe recycling and robbing of materials in late- and post-villa phases, for lime, brick, stone, glass, and metals (Volpe, De Felice, and Turchiano, 2005: 284–85 on early medieval metal-workshops over the decayed Faragola villa).

Italy is well served by landscape archaeology/field survey projects, with a long emphasis on the central Italian belt (South Etruria survey, Ager Cosanus, Tuscania, Pescara valley), but with projects pushing northwards, for example, into the territory of Siena and various Padane sectors, and south into ancient Lucania and Apulia (e.g. Celone and Basentello valleys) (Christie, 2006: 412–28; Volpe and Turchiano, 2005. One case study for the Veronese: Saggioro, 2004). Briefly, it can be claimed that central and northern Italian trends are broadly comparable, often with a sizeable dip in settlement numbers in the third century AD, but with most larger units persisting. Despite some diminution in numbers into the fifth century, the picture is fairly stable, but the quality and depth of activity on most sites, especially the larger ones, decline from the fifth. By the sixth century, numbers and scale are further reduced, timber usage becomes more dominant, and 'luxury' features such as baths and mosaics are lost. The Gothic and Lombard Wars of the 530s and 570s mark a further downward spiral in open farm sites, but growing data point to the emergence of villages, often in elevated settings, and perhaps showing a communal response to rural insecurity (this may, as noted above, have been happening in the Alpine, and most probably in northern Apenninic zones, from a much earlier date) (Francovich and Hodges, 2003, offer an excellent synthesis). For the south, work in ancient Apulia especially is revealing heightened rural activity from the fourth century and enduring into the sixth, with some high quality elite and Church estates, plus *vici*, responding to state food needs. Here too, however, the later sixth century sees a substantial drop in sites and activity. But archaeologists generally now stress the persistence (if limited material visibility) of land use and farmers. After all, towns, even if themselves reduced, continued to be centers of clerical and often military authority, and required feeding. Monasteries figure more prominently from the sixth century and are also land-based; papal records, such as Gregory the Great's letters, document sizeable Church estates with workers, slaves, tenants, and pagans in the south, in Sicily, and in Sardinia (most, no doubt, direct inheritances from state and elite ownership (Mazza, 2005); and papyri from Ravenna point to soldiers as landowners.

   A final element to note alongside the archaeology are textual references to depopulation and faltering productivity across late Roman Italy which testify to state anxieties: imperial edicts mention failures in meeting tax payments, problems in food supply, and desertion of peasants and slaves. There are documented settlements of defeated and other barbarian groups, often near larger urban nuclei, to help regenerate the land or boost efficiency. Thus in the north, the late fourth-century *Notitia Dignitatum* registers the presence of *praefecti* overseeing Sarmatian units (*gentiles*), settled in the 330s near seats such as Oderzo, Cremona, Turin, Ivrea, and Pollenzo; Ammianus Marcellinus (31.9) records Alemannic prisoners being given 'fertile cantons' along the Po in the 370s, and Goths and Taifali defeated in Thrace in AD 377 were based on lands around Modena, Reggio, and Parma; and place-name evidence may designate fifth-century colonies of Bulgars, Alans, Goths, and Burgundians (Cracco Ruggini, 1984: 25–26, 31–32). Potentially Italy was a constantly changing mix of cultures and groups in the late Roman period, reflecting a multinational military.

8.5   From Ostrogoths to Lombards

In AD 493 the Ostrogoths under Theoderic displaced Odoacer to establish a new kingdom in Italy. Theoderic's long rule and his forging of alliances and economic ties with other western powers, combined with comfortable contacts with Constantinople, fostered a healthy regeneration. Traded goods at Classe comprise materials from across the Mediterranean, including the East; Theoderic also obtained architects, mosaicists, and marbles from the Eastern Empire to help embellish his capital of Ravenna, where, as observed, a stunning heritage of art and architecture survives in complexes such as Sant'Apollinare Nuovo, Sant'Apollinare in Classe, and the royal palace (Deliyannis, 2010; Augenti, 2002). The Gothic heartland lay in the north of Italy, and other urban seats such as Verona and Como witnessed structural renewals (including to the city walls), while rural palaces such as Monte Barro and Galeata signify elite villa emulation. Rome too saw funds to help renew a city now investing mainly in churches and pilgrim venues, but it is disputed whether many other towns benefited much from Ostrogothic patronage – more probably security and economic stability were their main gains (see papers in *Teodorico il Grande*, plus sections in Ward-Perkins 1984). The south of Italy, meanwhile, largely outside of direct Gothic settlement, remained prosperous and agriculturally productive, as recorded in letters by Cassiodorus, but documented also through excavation and survey work.

The stability promoted by Theoderic and his immediate successors was progressively eroded by changing and deteriorating relationships with the Eastern Roman/Byzantine emperor. The figure of Justinian (AD 527–565) looms large in the final chapter of a 'late classical' Italy: from the early 530s, as detailed by Procopius' *History of the Wars* narratives, Justinian instigated campaigns against Vandal Africa, Gothic Italy, and Visigothic Spain to renew Roman rule in the central and western Mediterranean. Despite compact army numbers, rapid gains in the south of Italy – this featuring few Gothic garrisons, despite its economic worth – raised expectations of swift conquest, but stiff resistance came in the northern territories. Although Ravenna fairly soon became Byzantine, in reality the years AD 538–550 saw fluctuating fortunes, manifested most in the protracted series of sieges and counter-sieges of Rome, with Procopius at one stage claiming a mere 500 persons remained in a disease-ridden, battered, and despoiled city. Patterns of raids, sieges, occasional pitched battles, crop failures, plague, plus incursions by Franks in the north, and major distractions further afield in the Balkans and against Persia, saw a dramatic deterioration of town and country across much of the peninsula. It is easy to overplay the military devastation card, just as it is to ignore the possible impact of the so-called Justinianic plague, but many scholars would see the Italy that emerged at the close of Byzantine-Gothic hostilities (only fully terminated in the early 560s) as in serious decay: few elites and little money remained, the economy was fractured, the landscape compromised. New enemies in the shape of the Lombards, invading from the north-east in AD 568, then prompted another thirty or so years of disruption as the incomers carved up territories (a kingdom, but comprising often rival duchies) in the north, in the center (lands progressively taken in Tuscany and in Abruzzo), and south (centered on the duchy of Benevento). While divisions had always been a feature of Italy, the redesigned Byzantine-Lombard Italy of circa AD 600 engendered a series of political, economic, and even religious divisions (Brown, 1984; Zanini, 1998). Even if pope Gregory the Great at that time could discourse with fellow bishops in Sicily and Sardinia, many of these bishops can be seen to be semi-independent, and also struggling to maintain cohesion – Gregory himself used the Church to help pay troops, repair defences and aqueducts, organize grain supplies, and to oversee transfers of threatened people in the countryside to military havens. In the 300 years since Constantine Rome and Italy had become much changed beasts, but the basic needs of governance, food and security conditioned many aspects of continuity. But whereas in AD 500, a 'Roman' Italy still existed via the Senate, the high aristocracy and their landowning, in coinage, in games and in mind, quite how 'Roman' the Italians on 'Byzantine' soil felt a century later cannot be answered – perhaps only in religion, law, learning and language and then only in the capitals might this *Romanitas* still be recognized.

FURTHER READING

Italy benefits from a rich tradition of national and regional conferences and related proceedings relevant to the Roman to medieval periods, such as the *Congresso Nazionale di Archeologia Cristiana; Antichità Altoadriatiche* (with themes embracing northern Italy and extending east); the *Corso di Cultura sull'Arte Ravennate e Bizantina*; the *Settimana di Studio del Centro Italiano di Studi sull'Alto Medioevo*; and seminars held in north Italy on key themes of late antique-early medieval transition (e.g. Brogiolo, 1994 and 1996; Brogiolo and Cantino Wataghin, 1998; Augenti 2006b). For southern Italy the conference series published as *Mediterraneo tardoantico e medievale. Scavi e ricerche* has become essential, as have monographs in the University of Bari's *Scavi e ricerche* series. As well as regional journals, the principal source is *Archeologia Medievale*, along with the *Papers of the British School at Rome*. Important are volumes in the *Biblioteca di Archeologia Medievale* series (e.g. Francovich and Noyé, 1994; Augenti, 2006b; Cirelli, 2008), but other regional works include *Studi e scavi* from Bologna University (e.g. Farioli Campanati *et al.*, 2009). Some major exhibition catalogs contain detailed and authoritative articles; notable titles include *Milano. Capitale dell'Impero Romano* (= Sena Chiesa, 1990), *Christiana Loca* (= Pani Ermini, 2000), *Aurea Roma* (= Ensoli and La Rocca, 2000), and *Costantino il Grande* (= Donati and Gentili, 2005). For surveys of Italy in the late Roman period, see *Storia di Roma III*, plus Christie 2006 as the most current overview, supplemented by many city-based studies such as Giardina 1986, Harris 1999, Augenti 2006a, Deliyannis 2010, and Arthur 2002; Ward-Perkins 1984 remains invaluable for urban changes in the center and north of Italy. Historical overviews include Wickham 1981, Brown 1984, La Rocca 2002, and shorter, focused analyses in the *Cambridge Ancient History* vols XII, XIII, and XIV.

REFERENCES

Arena, M.S., Delogu, P., Paroli, L., Ricci, M., Sagui, L., and Venditelli, L., eds. 2001. *Roma dall'antichità al medioevo. Archeologia e storia nel Museo Nazionale Romano Crypta Balbi*. Milan: Electa.

Arthur, P. 2002. *Naples. From Roman town to city-state*. London: Archaeological Monographs of the British School at Rome 12.

Arthur, P. 2004. "From *vicus* to village: Italian landscapes, AD 400–1000." In *Landscapes of Change: rural evolutions in Late Antiquity and the Early Middle Ages*, ed. N. Christie, 103–33. Aldershot: Ashgate.

Augenti, A., ed. 2002. *Palatia. Palazzi imperiali tra Ravenna e Bisanzio*. Ravenna: Biblioteca Classense.

Augenti, A. 2003. "Le sedi del potere a Roma tra tarda antichità e alto medioevo: archeologia e topografia." In Domus et splendida palatia. *Residenze papali e cardinalizie a Roma fra XII e XV secolo*, ed. A. Monciatti, 1–16. Pisa: Edizioni della Normale.

Augenti, A. 2006a. "Ravenna e Classe: archeologia di due città tra la tarda antichità e l'alto medioevo." In *Le città italiane tra la tarda antichità e l'alto medioevo*, ed. A. Augenti, 185–217. Florence: Biblioteca di Archeologia Medievale, 20/ All'Insegna del Giglio.

Augenti, A., ed. 2006b. *Le città italiane tra la tarda antichità e l'alto medioevo*. Florence: Biblioteca di Archeologia Medievale, 20/ All'Insegna del Giglio.

Augenti, A. 2010. *Città e porti dall'antichità al medioevo*. Rome: Carocci editore.

Basso, P. 1986. "I miliari della Venetia romana." *Archeologia Veneta* 9: 11–228.

Bonacasa Carra, R.M. 2004. "I modelli di Roma cristiana in area siciliana: aspetti e problematiche." In *Roma e la Liguria Maritima: secoli IV–X. La capitale cristiana e una regione di confine*, ed. M. Marcenaro, 51–62. Genoa-Bordighera: Istituto internazionale di studi liguri.

Brogiolo, G.P., ed. 1994. *Edilizia residenziale tra V e VIII secolo*. Mantua: Documenti di Archeologia 4/ Società Archeologica Padana.

Brogiolo, G.P., ed. 1996. *La fine delle ville romane: trasformazioni nelle campagne tra tarda antichità e alto medioevo*. Mantua: Documenti di Archeologia, 11/ Padus.

Brogiolo, G.P., ed. 1999. *S. Giulia di Brescia. Gli scavi dal 1980 al 1992. Reperti preromani, romani e alto medievali*. Florence: All'Insegna del Giglio.

Brogiolo, G.P. and Wataghin Cantino, G. 1998. *Sepolture tra IV e VIII secolo*. Mantua: Società archeologica padana.

Brown, T.S. 1984. *Gentlemen and Officers. Imperial administration and aristocratic power in Byzantine Italy, AD 554–800*. London: British School at Rome.

Cameron, A. 2006. "Constantine and Christianity." In *Constantine the Great. York's Roman emperor*, eds E. Hartley, *et al.*, 96–103. London and New York: York Museums Trust/Lund Humphries.

Campagnoli, P. and Giorgi, E. 2004. "Viabilità e uso del suolo tra età romana e altomedievale nell'area dei Monti Sibillini e dei Monti della Laga." In *L'Appennino in età romana e nel primo medioevo. Viabilità e popolamento nelle Marche e nell'Italia centro-settentrionale*, eds M. Destro and E. Giorgi, 173–200. Bologna: Studi e scavi, nuova serie 6/ Ante Quem.

Campione, A. and Nuzzo, D. 1999. *La Daunia alle origini cristiane*. Bari: Scavi e ricerche 10/ Edipuglia.

Caporusso, D., ed. 1991. *Scavi MM3. Ricerche di archeologia urbana a Milano durante la costruzione della linea 3 della Metropolitana, 1982–1990*, 5 vols. Milan: Ministero per i Beni Culturali e Ambientali/Soprintendenza Archeologica della Lombardia: Edizioni ET.

Caseau, B. 2004. "The fate of rural temples in Late Antiquity and the Christianisation of the country-side." In *Recent Research on the Late Antique Countryside*, eds W. Bowden, L. Lavan, and C. Machado, 105–144. Leiden and Boston: Late Antique Archaeology 2/ Brill.

Cavada, E. 2002. "*Militaria* tardoantichi (fine IV–V secolo) dalla valle dell'Adige e dalle aree limitrofe. L'informazione archeologica." In Miles Romanus *dal Po al Danubio nel Tardoantico*, ed. M. Buora, 139–62. Pordenone: Lucaprint.

Christie, N., ed. 2004. *Landscapes of Change: rural evolutions in Late Antiquity and the Early Middle Ages*. Aldershot: Ashgate.

Christie, N. 2006. *From Constantine to Charlemagne: an archaeology of Italy, AD 300–800*. Aldershot: Ashgate.

Christie, N. and Rushworth, A. 1988. "Urban fortification and defensive strategy in fifth- and sixth-century Italy: the case of Terracina." *Journal of Roman Archaeology* 1: 73–88.

Cirelli, E. 2008. *Ravenna: archeologia di una città*. Florence: All'Insegna del Giglio.

Ciurletti, E., ed. 2007. *Fra il Garda e le Alpi di Ledro. Monte S. Martino. Il luogo di culto (Ricerche e scavi 1969–1979)*. Trento: Soprintendenza per i Beni Archeologici.

Coarelli, F. 1999. "L'edilizia pubblica a Roma in età tetrarchica." In *The Transformations of Vrbs Roma in Late Antiquity*, ed. W.V. Harris, 23–33. Ann Arbor: Journal of Roman Archaeology Suppl. 33.

Coccia, S. 1996. "Il *Portus Romae* alla fine dell'antichità nel quadro del sistema di approvvigionamento della città di Roma." In *"Roman Ostia" Revisited. Archaeological and historical papers in memory of Russell Meiggs*, eds A. Gallina Zevi and A. Claridge, 293–307. Rome: British School at Rome.

Cracco Ruggini, L. 1984. "I barbari in Italia nei secoli dell'impero." In *Magistra Barbaritas. I barbari in Italia*, 3–51. Milan: Libri Scheiwiller/ Credito Italiano.

Croce Da Villa, P. and Di Filippo Balestrazzi, E., eds. 2001. *Concordia. Tremila anni di storia*. Rubano: Esedra.

Curran, J. 2000. *Pagan City and Christian Capital. Rome in the fourth century*. Oxford: Clarendon Press.

Dall'Aglio, P.L. and Di Cocco, I., eds. 2004. *Pesaro romana: archeologia e urbanistica*. Bologna: Studi e scavi, nuova serie 4/ Ante Quem.

Deliyannis, D.M. 2010. *Ravenna in Late Antiquity*. Cambridge: Cambridge University Press.

De Souza, P. 1999. *Piracy in the Graeco-Roman World*. Cambridge: Cambridge University Press.

Dey, H.W. 2011. *The Aurelian Wall and the Refashioning of Imperial Rome, AD 271–855*. Cambridge: Cambridge University Press.

Donati, A. and Gentili, G., eds. 2005. *Costantino il Grande*. Milan: Silvano.

Ensoli, S. and La Rocca, E., eds. 2000. *Aurea Roma. Dalla città pagana alla città cristiana*. Rome: «L'Erma» di Bretschneider.

Farioli Campanati, R., Rizzardi, C., Porta, P., Augenti, A., and Baldini Lippolis, I., eds. 2009. *Ideologia e cultura artistica tra Adriatico e Mediterraneo orientale (IV–X secolo). Il ruolo dell'autorità ecclesiastica alla luce di nuovi scavi e ricerche*. Bologna: Studi e scavi, nuova serie 19/ Ante Quem.

Fiocchi Nicolai, V. and Gelichi, S. 2001. "Battisteri e chiese rurali (IV–VII secolo)." In *L'edificio battesimale in Italia: Aspetti e problemi*, ed. D.Gandolfi, 303–84. Bordighera: Istituto internazionale di studi liguri.

Francovich, R. and Hodges, R. 2003. *Villa to Village. The transformation of the Roman countryside in Italy, c. 400–1000*. London: Duckworth.

Francovich, R. and Noyé, G., eds. 1994. *La storia dell'alto medioevo italiano (VI–X secolo) alla luce dell'archeologia*. Florence: Biblioteca di Archeologia Medievale 11/ All'Insegna del Giglio.

Gelichi, S. 1994. "L'edilizia residenziale in Romagna tra V e VIII secolo." In *Edilizia residenziale tra V e VIII secolo*, ed. G.P. Brogiolo, 157–67. Mantua: Documenti di archeologia 4/ Società archeologica padana.

Giardina, A., ed. 1986. *Società romana e impero tardoantico Vol. II: Roma: politica, economia, paesaggio urbano*. Rome-Bari: Laterza.

Gillett, A. 2001. "Rome, Ravenna and the last western emperors." *Papers of the British School at Rome* 69: 131–67.

Guidobaldi, F. 1999. "Le *domus* tardoantiche di Roma come 'sensori' delle trasformazioni culturali e sociali." In *The Transformations of Vrbs Roma in Late Antiquity*, ed. W.V. Harris, 53–68. Ann Arbor: Journal of Roman Archaeology Suppl. 33.

Harris, W.V., ed. 1999. *The Transformations of Vrbs Roma in Late Antiquity*. Ann Arbor: Journal of Roman Archaeology Suppl. 33.

Henig, M. 2006. "Religious diversity in Constantine's Empire." In *Constantine the Great. York's Roman emperor*, eds E. Hartley, *et al.*, 85–95. London and New York: York Museums Trust/Lund Humphries.

Humphries, M. 2000. "Italy, AD 425–605." In *The Cambridge Ancient History*. Vol. 14. *Late Antiquity: Empire and Successors, A.D. 425–600*, eds A. Cameron, B. Ward-Perkins, and M. Whitby, 525–51. Cambridge: Cambridge University Press.

Hunt, D. 1998. "The successors of Constantine." In *The Cambridge Ancient History*. Vol. 13. *The Late Empire, A.D. 337–425*, eds A. Cameron and P. Garnsey, 1–43. Cambridge: Cambridge University Press.

Innes, M. 2007. *Introduction to Early Medieval Western Europe, 300–900. The sword, the plough and the book*. Abingdon and New York: Routledge.

James, S. 1988. "The *fabricae*: state arms factories of the later Roman Empire." In *Military Equipment and the Identity of Roman Soldiers*, ed. J.C. Coulston, 257–332. Oxford: BAR, International Series 394.

Keay, S., Millett, M., Paroli, L., and Strutt, K. 2005. *Portus. An Archaeological Survey of the Port of Imperial Rome*. London: Archaeological Monographs of the British School at Rome 15.

La città e la sua memoria. Milano e la tradizione di sant'Ambrogio. 1997. Milan: Electa.

Lambert, C. 2008. *Studi di epigrafia tardoantica e medievale in Campania. Volume I. Secoli IV–VII*. Florence: Medioevo Scavato III/ All'Insegna del Giglio.

Lançon, B. 2000. *Rome in Late Antiquity. Everyday Life and Urban Change, AD 312–609*. Edinburgh: Edinburgh University Press.

La Rocca, C., ed. 2002. *Italy in the Early Middle Ages*. Oxford: Oxford University Press.

La Rocca Hudson, C. 1986. "'Dark Ages' a Verona. Edilizia privata, area aperte e strutture pubbliche in una città dell'Italia settentrionale." *Archeologia Medievale* 13: 31–78.

Lee, A.D. 2000. *Pagans and Christians in Late Antiquity. A sourcebook*. London and New York: Routledge.

Liverani, P. 2003. "Vaticano pagano, vaticano cristiano." In *Roma e la Liguria Maritima: secoli IV–X. La capitale cristiana e una regione di confine*, ed. M. Marcenaro, 73–78. Genoa-Bordighera: Istituto internazionale di studi liguri.

Lizzi, P. 1990. "Ambrose's contemporaries and the Christianization of northern Italy." *Journal of Roman Studies* 80: 156–73.

Lusuardi Siena, S. 1997. "Il complesso episcopale. Il gruppo cattedrale." In *La città e la sua memoria. Milano e la tradizione di sant'Ambrogio*, 36–39. Milan: Electa.

Lusuardi Siena, S. 2003. "Gli scavi nella cattedrale di Luni nel quadro della topografia cittadina tra tarda antichità e medioevo." In *Roma e la Liguria Maritima: secoli IV–X. La capitale cristiana e una regione di confine*, ed. M. Marcenaro, 195–202. Genoa-Bordighera: Istituto internazionale di studi liguri.

Marano, Y.A. 2010. "L'edilizia cristiana in Italia settentrionale nel V secolo: la testimonianza dei complessi episcopali." In *Le trasformazioni del V secolo. L'Italia, i barbari e l'Occidente romano*, eds P. Delogu and S. Gasparri, 285–341. Turnhout: Brepols.

Marcenaro, M. 2003. "La diocesi di Albenga e il suo centro episcopale." In *Roma e la Liguria Maritima: secoli IV–X. La capitale cristiana e una regione di confine*, ed. M. Marcenaro, 177–88. Genoa-Bordighera: Istituto internazionale di studi liguri.

Marcenaro, M., ed. 2003. *Roma e la Liguria Maritima: secoli IV–X. La capitale cristiana e una regione di confine*. Genoa-Bordighera: Istituto internazionale di studi liguri.

Massabò, B. 2003. "Dalle terme romane ad un insediamento cristiano: gli scavi di San Clemente ad Albenga." In *Roma e la Liguria Maritima: secoli IV–X. La capitale cristiana e una regione di confine*, ed. M. Marcenaro, 189–94. Genoa-Bordighera: Istituto internazionale di studi liguri.

Mayer, E. 2006. "Civil war and public dissent: the state monuments of the decentralised Roman Empire." In *Social and Political Life in Late Antiquity*, eds W. Bowden, A. Gutteridge, and C. Machado, 141–55. Leiden: Late antique archaeology 3/ Brill.

Mazza, R. 2005. "Tra Oriente e Occidente: la gestione del *patrimonium Petri* in Italia Meridionale." In *Paesaggi e insediamenti rurali in Italia meridionale fra tardoantico e altomedioevo*, eds. G. Volpe and M. Turchiano, 703–13. Bari: Edipuglia.

Meneghini, R. and Santangeli Valenzani, R. 2007. *I Fori Imperiali. Gli scavi del Comune di Roma (1991–2007)*. Rome: Viviani Editore.

Michaelides, D. and Wilkinson, D., eds. 1992. *Excavations at Otranto*. Vol. I. *The excavation*. Galatina: Università di Lecce. Dipartimento di Scienze dell'Antichità, Settore Storico-Archeologico, Collana del Dipartimento, 5/ Congedo Editore.

Panella, C. 2008. "Imperial insignia from the Palatine Hill." In *Rome and the Barbarians. The birth of a new world*, ed. J.-J. Aillagon, 86–91. Milan: Palazzo Grassi/Skira Editore.

Pani Ermini, L., ed. 2000. *Christiana Loca. Lo spazio cristiano nella Roma del primo millennio*. Rome: Fratelli Palombi Editori.

Patterson, H., ed. 2004. *Bridging the Tiber. Approaches to regional archaeology in the Middle Tiber Valley*. London: Archaeological Monographs of the British School at Rome, 13.

Pejrani Baricco, L. 1998. "La basilica del Salvatore e la cattedrale di Torino: considerazioni su uno scavo in corso." In *Archeologia in Piemonte*. Vol. III. *Il Medioevo*, eds L. Mercando and E. Micheletto, 133–51. Turin: Soprintendenza Archeologica del Piemonte.

Rinaldi Tufi, S. 2005. "La grande architettura fra Diocleziano e Costantino a Roma e nel mondo romano." In *Costantino il Grande. La civiltà antica al bivio tra Occidente e Oriente*, eds A. Donati and G. Gentili, 92–105. Milan: Silvana Editoriale.

Saggioro, F. 2004. "Late antique settlement on the plain of Verona." In *Recent Research on the Late Antique Countryside*, eds W. Bowden, L. Lavan, and C. Machado, 505–34. Leiden and Boston: Late Antique Archaeology 2/ Brill.

Sami, D. 2010. "Changing beliefs: the transition from pagan to Christian town in late antique Sicily." In *Debating Urbanism. Within and beyond the walls, A.D. 300–700*, eds D. Sami and G. Speed, 213–37. Leicester: Leicester Archaeology Monograph 17.

Sannazaro, M. 2001. "Insediamenti rurali ed *ecclesiae baptismales* in Friuli: il contributo della ricerca archeologica." In *Paolo Diacono e il Friuli altomedievale (secc. VI–X)*, 253–80. Spoleto: CISAM.

Scampoli, E. 2010. *Firenze, archeologia di una città (secoli I a.C –XIII d.C.)*. Florence: Firenze University Press.

Sciarretta, V. 1966. *Il Battistero di Albenga*. Ravenna: Quaderni di Antichità Ravennati, Cristiane e Bizantine, n.7/ Edizioni di A. Longo.

Sena Chiesa, Gemma, 1990. *Milano capitale dell'impero romano, 286–402 d.C.* Milan: Silvana.

Sfameni, C. 2004. "Residential villas in late antique Italy: continuity and change." In *Recent Research on the Late Antique Countryside*, eds W. Bowden, L. Lavan, and C. Machado, 335–75. Leiden and Boston: Late Antique Archaeology 2/ Brill.

Storia di Roma III: L'età tardoantica. I: Crisi e trasformazioni. 1993. Turin: Giulio Einaudi.

Teodorico il Grande e i Goti in Italia. 1995. Ravenna: CISAM.

Testini, P., Cantino Wataghin, G., and Pani Ermini, L. 1989. "La cattedrale in Italia." In *Actes du XIe congres international d'archéologie chrétienne*, 5–229.

Trout, D. 1999. *Paulinus of Nola: life, letters, and poems.* Berkeley, Los Angeles and London: University of California Press.

Volpe, G. 2001. *Contadini, pastori e mercanti nell'Apulia tardoantica.* Bari: Munera 6/ Edipuglia.

Volpe, G., De Felice, G. and Turchiano, M. 2005. "Faragola (Ascoli Satriano). Una residenza aristocratica e un 'villaggio' altomedievale nella Valle del Carapelle: primi dati." In *Paesaggi e insediamenti rurali in Italia meridionale fra tardoantico e altomedioevo,* eds. G. Volpe and M. Turchiano, 265–97. Bari: Edipuglia.

Volpe, G. and Turchiano, M., eds. 2005. *Paesaggi e insediamenti rurali in Italia meridionale fra tardoantico e altomedioevo.* Bari: Edipuglia.

Ward-Perkins, B. 1984. *From Classical Antiquity to the Middle Ages. Urban public building in northern and central Italy, A.D. 300–850.* Oxford: Clarendon Press.

Wickham, C. 1981. *Early Medieval Italy. Central power and local society, 400–1000.* London: Longman.

Zanini, E. 1998. *Le Italie bizantine.Territorio, insediamenti ed economia nella provincia bizantina d'Italia (VI–VIII secolo).* Bari: Edipuglia.

PART II

Local and Regional Diversity

2.1 Cultural Diversity

CHAPTER 9

Funerary Practices

Emma-Jayne Graham and Valerie M. Hope

9.1   Introduction

The way in which the people of Roman Italy were treated in death mattered. It mattered in terms of their security in the afterlife and how they continued to be remembered by the living; it mattered to grieving families; subsequently, it matters to those wishing to understand the complexities of the communities to which they belonged. Funerary practice has always had a role to play within studies of Roman Italy, but as a continually evolving area of research it has received increased attention in recent years. In particular, studies have begun to move away from reconstructing afterlife beliefs and the typology of monuments, to focus upon what funerary practices and commemorative activities reveal about social hierarchy, the construction of individual or group identity, and memory. Involving historians, archaeologists, epigraphists, classicists, and physical anthropologists, funerary studies is a particularly vibrant avenue of research, drawing upon an extensive range of often contradictory material. The sheer range of this evidence makes it possible to examine Roman death from a multiplicity of complementary angles.

How this evidence and these approaches relate to the Italian peninsula can be problematic. Some of the fundamental insights – funerary processions depicted in relief carvings (see Figure 9.1), inscriptions listing the regulations imposed upon undertakers – come from Italian towns. In contrast, the majority of written sources describe the activities of the elite community at Rome over the course of several centuries. As a result, there is often inconsistency within perceptions of funerary practice: the merging of Roman, Italian, and even Empire-wide evidence can produce a composite picture of customs and traditions. Simultaneously, certain practices or material expressions come to be defined as "Roman" and viewed as a distinctive template against which to gauge regional behavior. It is impossible to disentangle in full the relationship between Rome and Italy and the flow and counterflow of influences. However, our intention here is to examine funerary evidence from across the peninsula in order to explore conformity, diversity and individuality and, ultimately, the extent to which Rome may have acted as a model or dominant influence on the funerals of these Italian communities. Funerary activities were constantly evolving, but the broadest range of evidence in terms of excavated cemeteries and especially of epitaphs and monuments, is provided by the late Republic and early Empire on which this chapter focuses.

A Companion to Roman Italy, First Edition. Edited by Alison E. Cooley.
© 2016 John Wiley & Sons, Ltd. Published 2016 by John Wiley & Sons, Ltd.

Figure 9.1 Funerary relief from Amiternum showing a funerary procession. Drawing: J. Willmott. From M. Carroll, 2011b. "'The mourning was very good.' Liberation and liberality in Roman funerary commemoration." In *Memory and Mourning. Studies on Roman Death*, eds V.M. Hope and J. Huskinson, Oxford, Oxbow, 126–49, Fig. 8.1.

9.2   A "Roman" Way of Death?

What did a typical "Roman" funeral entail? Attempting to reconstruct an archetypal or standard funeral is misguided, in large part because it is impossible to determine which elements were considered relevant at different times, in different places by people of different social or economic position (Hope, 2009; Noy, 2011). Laws stipulated that the dead be buried outside the city walls and cremation pyres maintain a safe distance (Cicero, *On the Laws*: 2.23.58), but little legislation directed the nature of the funeral. Sumptuary laws seem to have been largely ignored by the Imperial period, even if traditionalists continued to frown upon excessive display, leaving families free to interpret the funeral in a way that suited their needs, beliefs, or resources.

Perhaps unsurprisingly the majority of evidence for funerals reflects elite practice at Rome, although significant elements of any account are also derived from Italian evidence: a relief from Amiternum (Aquila) depicting the funerary procession of a freedman (see Figure 9.1), regulations regarding public undertakers at Puteoli (AAVV, 2004; Hinard and Dumont, 2003; Bodel, 2004), and the writings of authors who were born outside Rome such as Pliny the Elder (from Comum). These go some way to balancing an emphasis on Rome, but for the majority of Italian towns there are no accounts of funerals, nor are there recorded eulogies or descriptions of post-funeral activities. In some cases evidence for funerary activities in Italian towns survives in the form of epitaphs, which might refer to aspects of ritual such as arrangements for the *Parentalia* festival, or who was granted access to a tomb. These allow for ease of comparison between regions, and can signal variations in the influence of Rome and the spread of Latin. Nonetheless, most are short, recording only the names of deceased and commemorator – they were designed to promote memory and identity, not to provide a full record of funerary practice. Most have also become isolated from the grave or monument with which they were originally associated, divorcing them from the cemetery context itself and potentially obfuscating their more complex role in funerary practice (see later in this chapter). For this reason it is essential not to underplay archaeological evidence. Cemeteries in the earlier days of excavation may have been the poor relation of urban monuments and structures, but this is no longer the case and new excavations have made it possible to explore mortuary environments more thoroughly. Despite these caveats, one of the most exciting aspects of studying funerary practice is the

sheer scale of evidence, with thousands upon thousands of individual graves, each representing a person and the acts of other people.

Drawing together piecemeal evidence spanning multiple centuries risks producing a
composite picture that might bear only passing resemblance to real funerals. Nevertheless, it
is possible to highlight types of activity that might have been performed. Most contemporary
descriptions of death speak as if the dying person spends his last moments lying ill in his own
home, although this was undoubtedly not the case for everyone. Tradition dictated that the
closest relative catch the last breath (Statius, *Silvae*: 5.1, 155–98) before the lifeless body was
placed on the floor in order to check that the individual was indeed dead, whilst they were
called on loudly by name (*depositio*: Artemidorus: 1.13; Ovid, *Letters from Pontus*: 2.245;
Servius, *On the Aeneid* : 2, 395; Corbeill, 2004; Šterbenc Erker, 2011; *conclamatio*: Lucian
On Mourning: 11). The women of the family or, increasingly during the Imperial period,
funerary professionals (Bodel 2000, 2004), were charged with washing, anointing and
dressing the deceased before the body was placed in the *atrium* of the house to lie in state
(*collocare*: Lucian *On Mourning*: 11–15; Virgil, *Aeneid*: 4.683, 9.486–89; Graham, 2011b;
Mustakallio, 2005; Šterbenc Erker, 2011). Other household preparations were made –
cypress fixed to the door warned those susceptible to spiritual pollution of the presence of a
corpse, lamps might be lit and incense burned, and a coin placed in the mouth of the deceased
(Pliny the Elder, *Natural History*: 16.60.139; Lindsay, 2000).

When the period of lying-in-state ended, the body might be moved through the streets of
the town to the extramural cemetery. In some instances, such as that illustrated by the
Amiternum relief (see Figure 9.1) or described by Polybius (6.53–4), this might entail an
elaborate procession (*pompa*), with horn, trumpet, and flute players, mourners (familial and
hired), people wearing the masks of illustrious ancestors (*imagines*), torch-bearers and crowds
of onlookers (Flower, 1996; Bodel, 1999). This was an opportunity for display, enabling
mourning families to make public statements about their identity and social position (Pliny
the Elder, *Natural History*: 7.139–40). The procession might pause in the forum for a eulogy –
an honor accorded only to significant members of the community (Polybius: 6.53–54).
Eulogies were probably given in the cemetery for those denied the honor of an official
pronouncement, as suggested by epigraphic records of speeches given in honor of women
(*Laudatio Turiae*: CIL 6.1527, 31670).

From this point forwards, activities depended upon whether the deceased was to be
cremated or inhumed. In instances of cremation, the body was placed on a pyre scented with
perfumes and spices, perhaps surrounded by personal belongings or offerings from mourners
(Martial: 11.54; Persius: 6; Pliny the Elder, *Natural History*: 12.41.83; Pliny the Younger,
Letters: 4.2.3–4). The pyre could burn for many hours and the final embers might be extin-
guished with wine, the remains (sometimes only a sample) being collected and deposited in
a family tomb or buried in the ground (Statius, *Silvae*: 2.6, 84–93; Virgil, *Aeneid*: 6.226–28).
Once the remains were covered with earth and a pig had perhaps been sacrificed (*porca
praesentenea*: Cicero, *On the Laws*: 2.22.55–57), mourners engaged in a funerary meal before
dispersing (*silicernium*: Festus: 377L). They might reconvene nine days later for the *cena
novemdialis*, another meal shared with the dead (Petronius, *Satyricon*: 65), and a final purification ceremony (*suffitio*) (Varro, *On the Latin Language*: 5.23; Graham, 2011a; Lindsay,
2000). The end of the funeral, however, did not mark the end of the relationship between the
living and the dead. There were a number of ongoing commemorative activities – the erection
of a funerary monument, further meals during the festivals of the *Parentalia* and *Feralia*
(13–21 February; Ovid, *Fasti*: 2. 533–42) or on the anniversary of the death, and the making
of offerings in the form of libations or flowers.

These activities do not necessarily reflect the reality of an individual funeral – each element
could be changed or manipulated according to the resources and needs of the mourners, and

specific customs seem to have gone in and out of fashion. Searching for the "typical Roman funeral" is therefore a thankless task, but recurring features can be found. The extent to which these varied across space and time forms the focus of this chapter.

9.3   Inhumation and Cremation

Romans themselves believed that inhumation was the traditional rite of their ancestors during the Monarchy and the early Republic, as it had been in some areas of pre-Roman Italy (Cicero, *On the Laws*: 2.56; Pliny the Elder, *Natural History*: 7.187). Evidence for both inhumation and cremation during the eighth–sixth centuries BC recovered from the Roman Forum (Toynbee, 1971: 39), and the Twelve Tables, which make no distinction between the two rites (Cicero, *On the Laws*: 2.58), suggest that they coexisted for much of early Roman history. Throughout the mid–late Republic cremation appears to have been the more favored form of disposal at Rome, even if in some areas of the Italian peninsula variability continued. In northern and eastern Italy, for example, Ortalli (2001) reports a process of homogenization during the course of the late Republic, with cremation adopted as part of the colonization process, but notes the occasional persistence of inhumation even within these areas – perhaps, he argues, a consequence of Italic rather than purely Latin colonists introducing their own traditions (Ortalli, 2001: 225). Even at Rome, inhumation never completely ceased, most famously used by the Cornelii family until the time of Sulla (Cicero, *On the Laws*: 2.56). Nevertheless, by the Julio-Claudian period cremation was largely dominant, and early regional differences and exceptional circumstances notwithstanding, the practice could be described by Tacitus (*Annals*: 16.6) as the "*Romanus mos*" ("Roman custom") for both Rome and the peninsula.

At some point during the late first century AD cremation began to be abandoned in favor of inhumation. The circumstances surrounding this change remain poorly understood. The widespread re-emergence of inhumation is usually assigned to the late first and early second century AD, although, as noted earlier in this chapter, a closer look reveals that it never completely disappeared, hinting that the change might not have been as dramatic as later scholarship has sometimes assumed. Indeed, Vismara (1992) observed that at Rome the change of rite was not particularly momentous, with contemporary literature displaying a rather ambivalent attitude. Rather than focusing on inhumation, the writings of authors such as Cicero (*Tusculan Disputations*: 1.45.108) draw attention to the foreign nature of practices such as embalming and other strange customs. Lucretius (3: 870–93), writing in the first century BC, comments that "For if it is really an evil after death to be mauled by the jaws of animals, I cannot see why it is not painful to roast in the hot flames of a funeral pyre, or to lie embalmed in honey, stifled and stiff with cold, on top of an icy rock, or to be crushed under a heavy weight of earth." Here inhumation is simply one among many possible forms of disposal and evokes neither overt disapproval nor censure. Inhumation seems not to have been considered strange, unusual or even particularly worthy of comment unless it was coupled with something out of the ordinary, as it was in the case of Poppaea who, in AD 66, "was not cremated in the Roman fashion, but in the tradition of foreign courts was embalmed by stuffing with spices" (Tacitus, *Annals*: 16.6). The same seems to be true of other areas of Italy. Even in places where cremation had been readily adopted by the early Imperial period, there is some evidence for the continued use of both rites, sometimes by members of the same family (Ortalli, 2001; see also examples at Fiano Romano – Bianchi *et al.*, 2004).

Explanations for the re-adoption of inhumation have been sought from a number of perspectives, and the reasons behind it (rather than its consequences) have tended to remain the focus of study. Traditional explanations fall largely into three, not entirely separate, categories: religious motivations, elite competition, and eastern influence. A number of Empire-wide cults stressed bodily integrity as a necessity for achieving peace in the afterlife. Amongst these were Christian and Jewish beliefs, as well as the so-called "mystery" cults (Mithras, Isis, Orphism), and Pythagoreanism. These rejected cremation, at least in theory. Nevertheless, underlying changes in religious belief have been largely rejected on the grounds that traditional rites continued (Nock, 1932). In truth, none of these cults possessed the requisite level of influence to bring about such a widespread change, certainly not across the wider peninsula (Toynbee, 1971: 40; Morris, 1992).

Morris (1992: 68–69) has argued for "diffusion from the Greek East to the Latin West," since inhumation had always remained prevalent in the eastern Mediterranean. A general rise in philhellenism during the course of the Empire may have contributed to making inhumation increasingly popular. Ortalli (2001) also suggests that the location and cosmopolitan nature of cities like Ravenna – centers with strong eastern trade contacts and, in this instance, the presence of the imperial fleet – might explain the uneven adoption outside Rome and Latium. Eastern practices may have offered the elite of Italian towns a new means by which to express their identity. Nevertheless, Morris (1992: 68) notes that although the initial stimulus for inhumation may have lain with a fashion for Hellenism, its use by the elite and imperial family transformed it into something Roman: having lost its original overt eastern associations, it spread as a *Roman* practice.

The elite also feature at the heart of Nock's (1932) proposal that inhumation was linked to changes in fashion, particularly the desire for ostentatious sarcophagi, the production of which became increasingly widespread from the second century AD. However, J.M.C. Toynbee (1971: 40) argued that these expensively carved coffins are unlikely to have brought about such a widespread and lasting change in burial practice. Other changes in tomb architecture and the design of commemorative monuments were not associated with major changes in the treatment of the body. What is more, it seems unlikely that the extensive sarcophagus industry began before inhumation became popular enough to support the production and large-scale import of such expensive objects (Elsner and Huskinson, 2010).

In addition to these commonly cited explanations, J.M.C. Toynbee (1971: 41) suggested that "inhumation could be felt to be a gentler and more respectful way of laying to rest the mortal frame," pointing towards another factor which might have influenced the choice of rite – changing attitudes towards, and treatment of, the corpse. New work is beginning to draw attention to evidence from cemetery sites across Italy which points towards increased concern with the integrity and protection of the dead body. This is indicated not only by the use of tile or stone pillows and the concealment of the corpse with shrouds and coffins, but is also reflected in contemporary textual sources in the form of an ever-more sentimentalized image of the dead (Graham, 2015; Hope, 2011). These theories, which promote a more nuanced "embodied" approach, may yet offer new perspectives on this complex, multifaceted process.

In contrast to the steady uptake of cremation, inhumation was adopted more sporadically across the peninsula, in some areas not reaching the ascendancy until the early third century AD. Cremation was used exclusively in a necropolis at Salò (Brescia) from the late-first to mid-third century AD (Massa, 2001), and in the years leading up to 200 AD cremation accounted for 89% of burials at Sarsina (Ortalli, 2001: 226). The two rites often coexisted for a considerable period of time. Contemporary cremation and inhumation graves of the second century AD have been found at Fralana (Malafede, Ostia), where the grave typologies and restricted range of grave goods associated with both remain similar and consistent, suggesting that differences in rite were not related to economic status or access to resources (Pellegrino, Falzone, and Olivanti, 1999; Falzone, Olivanti, and Pellegrino, 2001). Inhumation is also found alongside cremation in the necropolis of Isola Sacra (Baldassarre *et al.*, 1996; Taglietti,

2001), and a *bustum* burial (in situ cremation) of an adult female at Fiano Romano, to the north east of Rome, was found to contain the inhumed remains of a 13–14- year-old boy (Bianchi *et al.*, 2004: 257). Further north, cremation burials continued alongside the increasingly more dominant rite of inhumation at sites such as Gubbio (Umbria) where at least one can be dated to the mid-third century, and another not earlier than AD 176 (Cipollone, 2002: 26–29). Sites such as this might suggest that cremation continued to be used in order to make statements about the status or identity of particular individuals or groups: de Filippis (2001: 55) suggests that four *busta sepulchra* on the Boccone d'Aste estate to the north of Rome point towards greater financial commitment and a clear desire to differentiate these individuals. At some sites, the nature of cremation burials begins to alter, if not disappear, during the course of the second century AD. At Classe in the north-east of Italy the tradition of secondary cremations in urns is replaced with primary *busta* burials (Maioli, Ortalli, and Montevecchi, 2008).

Ortalli (2001: 226) accounts for this diversity in terms of local context, arguing that major cities were more open to cultural influences (especially from the East) than "conservative" rural areas, drawing attention to a lead coffin from the first century AD at Ravenna, and a mid-third-century cremation at the rural site of Casalecchio di Reno near Bologna. The cultural and political context may be significant. The uptake of cremation was closely connected with the adoption of other aspects of Roman cultural identity, and played an important role in expressions of that identity. Without this context of cultural change and its incentives, there may have been less immediate need to turn towards inhumation than there had been to adopt specifically Roman forms of cremation burial in earlier centuries. By the end of the first century AD it was no longer necessary to express "Romanitas"– such an identity was now a given.

9.4   Rituals and Graves

During the last two centuries, thousands upon thousands of graves, containing individual or multiple cremation and inhumation burials, from both urban and rural environments have been excavated. Some graves were marked with monumental or commemorative structures (see later in this chapter), whilst many more remained unmarked. Graves, however humble or unremarkable in terms of construction, define cemetery areas and in many cases demonstrate that burial took place alongside and around concentrations of mausolea. At Pian di Bezzo (Sarsina), for example, the full extent of the burial ground is revealed only by the non-monumental graves (Ortalli, 1987), and at Isola Sacra (Portus) over 600 modest graves occupied the spaces between house-tombs (Angelucci *et al.*, 1990; Baldassarre *et al.*, 1996; Taglietti, 2001). Graves are instrumental for reconstructing rituals performed before, during, and after burial, revealing which rites were being performed when and by whom, hinting at which elements were considered the most important and, significantly, indicating how these concerns changed over time.

Graves take a number of forms, the simplest being a pit into which could be placed the cremated remains – sometimes, but not necessarily, within a ceramic or glass urn, bag or box – or the intact body, sometimes wrapped in a shroud, in a coffin, terracotta sarcophagus, or on a bier. In some instances the body would be cremated directly over the grave-pit, with the remains of the body and pyre collapsing into it before being covered with soil (*busta sepulchra*), although sometimes these are found to contain very few burnt remains (Bel, Blaizot, and Duday, 2008). Ortalli (2001: 228) has noted that, in northern parts of Italy at least, indirect cremation burials placed into a pit were often mixed with the residue of the pyre, whereas burial in an urn appears to have involved more careful selection of bone.

With the greater popularity of inhumation, grave typologies became more complex, making use of a variety of different materials to construct subterranean or above-ground covers for the grave. Amongst these are numerous examples of *alla cappuccina* burials: two rows of (reused) tiles or stone slabs forming a gabled roof, the joints sealed with smaller vessels, tiles, or bricks (see Figure 9.2). Well-preserved examples are known from sites in and around Rome such as the *Via Triumphalis* (Vatican), Isola Sacra, and Pianabella and Acilia (Ostia), but also much further afield at Sarsina and Ravenna (Emilia-Romagna), Gubbio (Umbria), Alba (Piedmont), Vagnari (Puglia), and in fact appear at most Imperial period cemeteries. In other cases, tiles or stones might be laid flat over the grave, or the body might be covered with broken amphorae or brick. Some of the graves in these cemeteries were also furnished with a tile or tufa "pillow" for the head of the deceased (de Filippis, 2001, 58; Prowse and Small, 2008), a feature repeated at sites elsewhere, including via dei Poggi necropolis at Ravenna where wooden pillows have been recovered (Leoni, Maioli, and Montevecchi, 2008). Infants are sometimes found deposited inside complete *amphorae* (Carroll, 2011a; 2012). Graves such as these have been excavated across the length and breadth of Italy and although they appear to conform to certain structural norms, this is perhaps more closely related to the dimensions of the human body and the availability of inexpensive, reusable materials than adherence to cultural expectations.

In terms of the items found within graves, there is a need to distinguish between those that were personal possessions of the deceased, perhaps worn when the corpse was incinerated or buried, and those that represent offerings from mourners. Amongst those of the first

Figure 9.2 Cappuccina burial F216, Vagnari. Reproduced with permission: Tracy Prowse and Alastair Small.

category, tools, dress accessories, jewelry, and the dolls and toys found with the remains of children are most common, such as the miniature set of kitchen utensils buried with a young girl in the necropolis of the *via Collatina* near Rome (Buccellato *et al.*, 2008: 30; Carroll, 2011a; 2012). In cases of cremation burial it is necessary to differentiate still further between objects that might be burnt, broken or contorted by the pyre and those that were placed directly into the grave. Ceramic or glass vessels and cups are found frequently both inside and outside the grave, some presumably having been used in post-burial commemorative rituals (Ortalli, 2001: 230).

The type of object found in graves is rather standardized. The most common include low denomination coins, most frequently an *as*, which might be placed in the mouth, in the hand or in the vicinity of the head. These coins have traditionally been interpreted as payment for passage across the Styx, although they may represent a more general superstition concerning good fortune and new status (Ceci, 2001: 91). Coins are found in cremation and inhumation graves, but their absence from many suggests that they were not an essential part of funerary ritual and their inclusion was determined by those responsible for burial. Of 52 burials excavated at Nave, 30 contained coins (Passi Pitcher, 2001), with only four recovered from seventeen graves at Fiano Romano (Bianchi *et al.*, 2004). This variability can be found throughout the range of ritual activities associated with the grave – indeed, there appear to have been very few, if any, practices that were considered essential, rendering even assemblages from the same cemetery very different. Other common objects include lamps (to light the way of the dead or a remnant of funerals conducted at night?), small ceramic jugs, glass balsamaria (were these empty when deposited or did they still hold scented oils and perfumes?), and increasingly during the Imperial period, iron nails. Nails might be placed deliberately in the grave, sometimes inserted into a small jug, and are found in instances of both cremation and inhumation. These may also have had a magical function, perhaps thought to "fix" the dead in the grave (Ceci, 2001: 90). These general categories hold sway across Italy with little difference in patterns of deposition. The objects themselves tend to reflect local wares, such as the wide-mouthed *olpai* found in graves at Nave – a typical product of Brescia found rarely elsewhere (Passi Pitcher, 2001).

The occasional recovery of organic items, or fixtures such as metal hinges or worked bone decoration, suggest that other perishable items were deposited too. A rare instance of a laurel branch placed on the base of a grave, beneath a wooden coffin, in the Via dei Poggi necropolis at Ravenna (Leoni *et al.*, 2008) provides evidence for the deposition of plants with particular symbolism, and study of plant residues associated with a funerary enclosure of the Nucerian Gate necropolis at Pompeii has revealed the presence of, amongst other things, chickpea, peas, lentil, naked wheat, dressed barley, millet, figs, berries, grapes, olives, dates, pomegranates, peaches, apples, walnuts, and both pine and cypress cones (Zech-Matterne, 2008; Matterne and Derreumaux, 2008). Some of these were no doubt deposited deliberately as symbolic items associated with death (notably pine cones and pomegranates), but also as food intended to accompany the dead on their final journey. Food played an important role in funerary ritual in general, with offerings made to the dead and meals consumed by the living as part of the funeral and later commemorative activities. Amphorae with cut bases were inserted into the grave in order to serve as libation conduits, and other reused vessels could serve the same purpose (Isola Sacra: Angelucci *et al.*, 1990; Sarsina and Rimini: Ortalli, 2001). At Rimini, holes were made in the brick cover of graves in order to insert lead pipes (Ortalli 2001: 230), and at Gubbio cremation urns were fitted with carefully sealed lead lids and pipes (Cipollone, 2002). Other facilities associated with commemorative meals include dining couches (*biclinia*) such as those found at Isola Sacra and small masonry tables known as *mensae* (Graham, 2005; Baldassarre *et al.*, 1996). A *mensa* associated with a group of second-century AD cremation graves on the *via Flaminia* at Rimini was found with the remains of cooked animal bones on the top (Ortalli, 2001: 231) and a cremation burial at Salò included a skillet containing the remains of a food offering (Massa, 2001: 266).

Animal remains seem to have sometimes served a ritual function. At Voghenza (Ferrara) the remains of horses and cows were found on the covers of cremation and inhumation graves and a large number of dogs were recovered from one mausoleum in the *via Collatina* necropolis in the Roman suburb (Buccellato, Catalano, and Musco, 2008: 85). Cattle remains may be related to funerary feasts, but horse was rarely consumed in Roman Italy and is not connected with any known ritual. Horses possibly represented a symbol of status or wealth, whilst dogs may have been viewed as guardians of the tomb or faithful companions of the deceased. Pigs, on the other hand, are closely linked with funerals as reported in the ancient sources and fragmentary and entire pig skeletons can perhaps be associated with the comments of Cicero (*On the Laws*: 2.22.57): "… places of burial do not really become graves until the rites are performed and the pig is killed." Pigs have been found alongside the dead at sites such as Collelongo near L'Aquila (Abruzzo) and in the via Basiliano area of the *via Collatina* necropolis (Buccellato, Catalano, and Musco, 2008: 87). However, once again pig remains do not appear in all cemeteries, let alone all graves within a single burial ground. This might be a consequence of economic circumstances (meat was expensive) or perhaps simply a matter of personal preference. The rite may have been performed in a purely symbolic manner – pork eaten as part of the funerary feast but not placed in the grave. Symbolic libations appear to have occurred at sites in the Cispadana region where the base of a number of amphorae libation tubes remained intact, meaning that anything poured into them would not actually reach the deceased (Ortalli, 2001: 232).

The same customs, styles, and practices can be detected in all areas of the peninsula but there is a distinct lack of consistency even within individual cemeteries. Each community can be seen to be conforming to certain cultural norms, but beneath the surface there runs a far higher degree of variability, perhaps related to the availability of materials and the socio-economic status of the mourners. Attempts have been made to use items deposited in graves to ascribe status (i.e. wealth) and gender identities to the deceased (for recent examples, see Massa, 2001 and Passi Pitcher, 2001). Unfortunately, inconsistencies in terms of the frequency with which certain items were deposited means that it is not possible to identify anything other than rather general patterns – jewelry tends to accompany female rather than male remains, for instance. Expression of particular identities in the form of grave furnishings was probably far more complex and context-specific than this data is capable of revealing, and reducing these to male/female, rich/poor or young/old dichotomies masks the nuances of personal, social, and cultural identities.

9.5 Monuments

Many graves in a Roman cemetery, whether of cremated or inhumed remains, probably remained unmarked in any permanent form. An earth mound, a tile, amphora, a wooden plank or even plants may have indicated a place of burial, or the site of a burial may simply have been known by family and associates. Such graves must have often faded from view, remembered individually for a relatively short space of time, even if collectively such graves retained potency as an anonymous presence. Ideas of permanency were rooted in stone and a range of stone monuments visually characterized many periurban cemeteries, including the few well-preserved examples such as at the *via Appia* (Rome), Isola Sacra (Portus), Pompeii, Sarsina, and Aquileia. It may have been a common comment among the great poets and writers that actually such stone monuments did not last forever, or indeed for very long at all: "funerary monuments too have their allotted fate" (Juvenal, *Satire*: 10.146; compare, for example, Seneca, *Consolation to Polybius*: 18.2), but many people, even if still a minority, did seek to set up stone markers and monuments, and sought to remember through and be remembered by them. What remains of these monuments now line the walls and cloisters of many an Italian museum: slabs and blocks of stone, inscribed, sculpted, or architecturally moulded, disconnected from the cemetery and graves that they once marked or contained.

Research on stone funerary monuments has traditionally been organized by typologies and decorative themes, and the material readily lends itself to this approach. The monuments fall into broad categories based on shape and function, such as stelae, altars, cinerary urns, and sarcophagi, all of which could range greatly in terms of quality of execution, size, and extent of decor (for example, stelae: Mansuelli, 1967; Mercado and Paci, 1995). In addition, more substantial structures could take the form of towers, temples, houses, and walled enclosures (Toynbee, 1971; von Hesberg, 1992). The subjects of sculptural decor – floral and architectural designs, portraiture, mythological themes, representations of tools and objects, dining scenes and work scenes – can also be readily categorized (for example: Zimmer, 1982; Franzoni, 1987; Scarpellini, 1987; Pflug, 1989; Tocchetti Pollin, 1990). The grouping of the material in this way often identifies shared features across the Italian peninsula, that the cemeteries of the Roman era had a common vocabulary of design, decoration and symbols. This may have been broadly the case, but there were regional and chronological variations.

To take a specific example: walled funerary enclosures were common throughout Italy and elsewhere in the Empire, and although performing the same basic purpose could vary in detail (Cresci Marrone and Tirelli, 2005). At Pompeii, for example, we find high walled enclosures, some with central altars raised on high bases, often doubling as a burial chamber for cremated remains (Kockel, 1983; see Figure 9.3). In northern Italy, at sites such as Aquileia, the walls are lower, and central memorials are altar-like but often with distinctive pyramidal shaped tops, while the cremated remains were placed directly into the body of the altar or into the ground of the surrounding enclosure (Brusin, 1941; Toynbee, 1971, 79–82; Reusser, 1987; see Figure 9.4). Equally some decorative motifs could be more favored in some regions than in others, representing local preferences, but also the repertoire of local sculptors and workshops. In Ravenna, for example, stelae could be decorated with rows of portrait busts, placed in several registers (Mansuelli, 1967); in the region of Piemonte the image of the she-wolf suckling the twins was a favored symbol on a number of stelae (Mercado and Paci, 1995). This is not to say that these designs were unparalleled elsewhere, but their clustering in certain areas suggests both conformity in the adoption of "Roman" funerary forms, and simultaneously localized individualizing in the choice of details.

There was often a dialog between cultural forms and varied influences. The municipal elite of Italy may have been particularly influenced by the monuments of Rome, especially during the late Republic and early Empire (see below). In fact, with the advent of the first emperor, who dominated the cityscape of Rome, the hometowns and villa estates of many a senator may have gained a fresh appeal for the construction of a lasting memorial (Bodel, 1997: 18). For example circular tombs, perhaps inspired by Augustus's mausoleum (in turn itself probably drawing on Etruscan influences) created a run of imitations in Italy, at Tusculum, Tivoli, Pozzuoli, Naples, Regio Emilia, Polla, Pompeii, and Pietrabbondante, among others (Toynbee, 1971: 143–63; von Hesberg, 1992: 113–34; Schwarz, 2002). Elite emulation and colonization may have sown the seeds of a level of homogeneity in Italian funerary art and architecture, but in some regions at least there were pre-existing cultures of commemoration which were revived or adapted to the Roman trends. Some areas did maintain or develop striking types of monument. In the Campanian towns of Pompeii, Nola, Stabiae, Surrentum,

Figure 9.3 The Herculaneum Gate Necropolis, Pompeii. Photograph: Valerie Hope.

Figure 9.4 The Via Annia Necropolis, Aquileia. Photograph: Valerie Hope.

and Nocera distinctive so-called *columellae* were used to mark cremated remains. These stone markers were shaped into the form of faceless human head and upper torsos, often with associated libation pipes leading directly to the remains (Cooley, 2012: 54–62). In the Cispadana region of northern Italy, natural stones, uncut and unsculpted, but often inscribed, were used as markers (Häussler, 1998: 37–38; Carroll, 2006: 96). In the Veneto, circular grave altars were used as markers, perhaps originally influenced by Greek prototypes, and these persisted into the Roman period (Ghedini, 1984). In urban settlements the major influences were also mediated by the origins and experiences of a range of visitors and incomers. The impact of military funerary designs, so prevalent on the Rhine frontier, can be felt in northern Italian towns, to which some old soldiers returned or retired (Hope, 2001: 46). In Verona, for example, the veteran standard-bearer Lucius Sertorius Firmus was pictured in military garb, holding the legionary eagle (C. Franzoni, 1987: n.30; *CIL* 5.3375), a design echoed at military forts in Germany and Britain. Coastal links and trade routes affected styles and workshops elsewhere; similarities between memorials in northern Italy, from towns such as Aquileia, and neighboring provinces such as Noricum and Dalmatia have been identified, suggesting both the exporting and importing of modes of commemoration (Picottini, 1976; Verzár Bass 1985).

Chronology is also key to understanding the level of use of stone, and monuments in general, in Italian cemeteries. The best preserved examples of working cemeteries such as at Pompeii (see Figure 9.3) or the Isola Sacra, which cement the image of "the street of tombs," had their heyday in the first and second centuries AD. It was during the late Republic and early Empire that stone monuments came more widely into use. In many parts of Italy prior to this date the marking of graves by stone, at least outside elite circles, may have been rare. A new wave of commemoration, perhaps initially fueled by emulation of Rome's elite and then local elites, and also in some areas perhaps by shifting of display away from Rome (see above) created an upsurge in the creation of inscribed funerary monuments. Subsequently there were shifts in the nature of the monuments, with a greater emphasis on what have been viewed as more communal and inward looking tombs from the late first and early second centuries AD (von Hesberg and Zanker, 1987; von Hesberg, 1992), prefiguring the shift to inhumation (see above). This was followed by a general decline in levels of monumental and stone tombs and markers (see below also for the "epigraphic habit").

It is difficult to explain these changes, and the vagaries and individuality of local patterns are also not always well documented. What was happening in one town or region may not have been simply mirrored in another region. What has been more fully investigated in recent years is the role that funerary monuments played in social dialogs about status, identity, and the right or need to be remembered. At certain periods, and in certain contexts, funerary monuments appealed more to some social groups than to others, and this could impact on the desirability of some forms and designs. Freed slaves have been a particular focus for recent studies, which have explored the role of the cemetery, and its monuments, as a potent communicative medium to alleviate some aspects of status dissonance and also to construct individual identity (Zanker, 1975; Kleiner, 1977; Kockel, 1983; Mouritsen, 2004, 2005; Hackworth Petersen, 2006). Freed slaves could be successful, and become wealthy and well-respected, but always lived in the shadow of servitude and the legal and social handicaps this entailed. Funerary monuments allowed these ex-slaves to celebrate their freedom, successes, and families in the face of these stigmas and to mark their integration into Roman society. Portraits of freed slaves may have rarely been seen in a town's forum, but could be widespread in a town's cemetery. This is not to say that the issues and needs of one or certain social groups always dominated the landscape of the Roman cemetery, but monuments did have a role in social dialogs, and as these dialogs changed, the nature of and need for certain types of monument may have shifted also.

Discussions about stone monuments, organized cemeteries, and social groups, such as freed slaves, inevitably have an urban bias. Some striking funerary monuments were located in the Italian countryside; rural and periurban villas could be a favored spot for commemorative monuments, promoting a real or illusory sense of family continuity: there was an "inherent emotional appeal of securing burial on a family estate" (Bodel, 1997: 22). Such rural tombs could impose themselves onto the landscape, dominating sight-lines and claiming territory. Villas also may have had more modest cemeteries for the wider *familia*; for example, a villa at San Martino in Pensilis, in Apulia, had an area set aside for burials, and several modest stelae commemorating slaves have been found (Ceglia, 2008). But it is worth remembering that many such rural cemeteries were not monumentalized; for the poor, both urban and rural, decent burial, in a semi-permanently marked grave may have often sufficed (Graham, 2006).

9.6   Epitaphs

Epigraphy provides an access point into Roman and Italian society that is, arguably, bigger and better than any other written source. The sheer volume of inscriptions is staggering (Saller and Shaw, 1984: 124; Bodel, 2001: 8), and the majority of these inscriptions are epitaphs. The use of epigraphy has often been regarded as the ultimate symbol of Romanization (Häussler, 1998, 2002; Adams, 2003; Lomas, 2004). The content of inscriptions, especially epitaphs, reflects the wide adoption and penetration of Roman ways through use of the Latin language, names, and social, political, and familial structures. In addition, epitaphs from different regions often shared conventions and abbreviations. Sometimes it can be difficult to tell one epitaph from another from across the peninsula.

This veneer of epigraphic conformity and standardization, as powerful as it is, can at times mislead. In areas that had a pre-existing inscribing culture, pre-Roman forms persisted into the first century AD and sometimes beyond. In Naples, for example, Greek epitaphs and tombstone designs were not rapidly abandoned (Lomas, 2004). Epigraphy can suggest "complex cultural interactions" (Benelli, 1994, 2001); and it has been noted that beneath the apparent stereotypic surface "there are never two identical epigraphic assemblages. Local identities and issues are still visible in Latin epigraphy" (Häussler, 2002: 71). There were also other, chronological, inconsistencies. In the 1980s, building on the work of Mrozek, MacMullen identified what he called the "epigraphic habit", a culture of inscribing which was far from uniform (Mrozek, 1973, 1988; MacMullen, 1982). In particular, MacMullen noted how this "epigraphic habit" rose in popularity (during the first and second centuries AD) and then peaked and rapidly fell (during the third century AD). Put simply, the sheer numbers of inscriptions (many of which were epitaphs), that were inscribed and displayed were not constant across the Roman period. This was an Empire-wide trend, but the wave of increase followed by decrease can and did vary for different sites, although the nuances for individual Italian settlements have rarely been plotted, especially since the accurate dating of the inscriptions can be fraught with difficulty. However, it does seem that the act of inscribing in Latin, and setting up certain types of monument (see earlier in this chapter), went in and out of fashion. Attempts to explain the "epigraphic habit" have emphasized regional variations and patterns, and have sought explanations in terms of status display, social mobility, geographic mobility, elite emulation, and patronage networks (Meyer, 1990; Woolf, 1996; Häussler, 1998). There may be no simple all-encompassing explanation which suits all sites equally, and it is certainly the case that finding factors for the uptake of inscribing is often easier than accounting for its decline. Most inscriptions were epitaphs, and if the "epigraphic habit" faltered and ultimately failed, this suggests not just changes in epigraphy, but also wider changes in how people were buried and commemorated.

There is a great temptation with epitaphs to extract information and place it all together to create numerous tables and graphs. *En masse* epitaphs become ripe for number crunching and statistical analysis, which can provide many valid and important insights into Roman society (for example, Saller and Shaw, 1984). But this approach is not without difficulties. The debunking of figures and statistics on life expectancy drawn from epitaphs is a well-known cautionary tale. Scholars have long sought to understand Roman age structures in order to gain fundamental insights into the expectations and experiences of Roman society; age structure impacts on factors such as family continuity and economic stability which shape the roles of individuals and thus society overall. It might be thought that the thousands upon thousands of ages stated on epitaphs could be used to generate some workable statistics. We could, for example, add up all the ages and divide by the total to obtain a mean average age at death. However, age statements have inherent characteristics. Many of the recorded ages were far from precise, since inscribed ages often ended in the Latin numerals V or X, suggesting that ages were rounded up or down, or may simply have been guessed at. Nor do the recorded ages span the breadth of the population: babies and infants were rarely commemorated and more males than females were generally recorded. Detailed studies suggest that ages were most often given for boys and adolescents, for soldiers and sometimes the elderly. Epigraphic age statements characterized certain groups and are thus limited in what they now disclose about Roman demography (Hopkins, 1966, 1987; Duncan-Jones, 1977, 1990; Parkin, 1992; Frier, 2000; Revell, 2005).

Not everyone participated equally in the commemorative culture epitomized by the "epigraphic habit." Nor should we assume that all Italian epitaphs had the same function, content or significance. Some formulae, for example, were geographically confined. Expressions such as HMHNS (*hoc monumentum heredem non sequitur* – "this monument does not go to the heir") and *libertis libertabusque posterisque eorum* ("for the freedmen and freedwomen and their descendants") are common in Rome and its environs, but less frequent (though far from unknown) in the rest of Italy; inclusion of statements of age at death and recorded age ranges can vary by region (Häussler, 1998: 36–38; McWilliam, 2001: 79–81; Revell, 2005); and in northern Italy more people can be named together in an epitaph than in southern regions of Italy (Gallivan and Wilkins, 1997; Hope, 2001: 68). There were clear regional variations in Italian commemorative practices, but accounting for the differences is not always straightforward. Some variations, for example a tendency toward recording the elderly in some communities, may reflect regional pre-Roman cultural traditions (Revell, 2005), but in other cases it is less easy to isolate social, practical and idealizing factors. For example, do the more limited references to slaves and freed slaves indicate that there were fewer slaves in some parts of Italy compared with Rome; or that these slaves and ex-slaves were valued differently; or that they were buried and commemorated differently?

How an epitaph functioned, and thus its content, could be related to its monumental role and visibility. A titular epitaph on an altar tomb or enclosure marker might say different things and name different people from an inscription placed at an internal niche or on a cinerary urn. Some of the larger communal structures found at Rome, such as *columbaria* are not duplicated elsewhere; nor were house-tombs (with walls lined with numerous urns) very widespread. Some regional differences in epitaph content, thus may be accounted for by differences in the roles and placement of the monuments onto which the epitaphs were inscribed. Rome may have provided many funerary models to be adopted and adapted, but the resulting tombs and epitaphs were often similar but not identical, being subject to localized traditions, expectations, and needs. In compiling statistics from epitaphs, and then making comparisons, it is perhaps best to remember that Latin epitaphs were not just texts, but part of commemorative practices, part of physical monuments and part of death ritual. An epitaph was both verbal and non-verbal, both text and object.

9.7   Bones and Bodies

Recent anthropological and osteological studies of cemetery populations have begun to demonstrate the immense wealth of information that can be gleaned from skeletal evidence (see individual studies on particular issues of health and diet at certain sites: Isola Sacra: FitzGerald *et al.*, 2006; Ravenna and Rimini: Facchini, Rastelli, and Brasili, 2004; Urbino: Paine *et al.*, 2009; Vallerano: Cucina *et al.*, 2006). Amongst these, studies of several thousand individuals excavated from a number of imperial period sites in the suburb of Rome have emphasized the importance of funerary archaeology for understanding wider demographic, cultural, occupational, and lifestyle issues (Catalano, Minozzi, and Pantano, 2001; Catalano *et al.*, 2006). For example, both sexes were almost equally represented across these cemeteries, although in some cases it was observed that men were more likely to receive monumental burials, and women were associated with a higher frequency of grave goods (Catalano *et al.*, 2006). Most individuals died between the ages of 20 and 40 years, with those over 40 being more restricted and those over 50 rarer still. Infant mortality was slightly elevated but comparable with sites across Italy, with almost a third of the remains studied belonging to individuals who had not reached maturity (Catalano, Minozzi, and Pantano, 2001: 137). Infant mortality and the funerary treatment of the very young is currently very underresearched, but recent work points towards a far higher degree of concern for the burial of babies and young children than has been assumed (Carroll, 2011a). This data is being used to refine understandings of Italian mortality and the life course previously based on epigraphic evidence (see earlier in this chapter; Scheidel, 2010). Importantly, it is beginning to shed light on the reasons for these patterns of mortality, with studies revealing the nuances of living conditions and poor levels of health amongst both urban and rural communities, particularly a world of traumatic injury, infectious disease, and strenuous occupational activity (Graham, 2013).

Palaeopathology also offers intriguing insights into perceptions of the human body. An unusual collection of burials from the *via Collatina* may not be typical but points towards particular attention to the burial of individuals who suffered from particularly debilitating conditions (Buccellato, Catalano, and Musco, 2008; Graham, 2013). Of the four individuals recovered from a mausoleum, three were found to exhibit evidence for severe disability and abnormal appearance. A male, aged about 30, had survived at least two major head injuries which had caused acute deformations to his face, along with trauma to the vertebrae and muscles (Buccellato, Catalano, Musco, 2008: 68–69). Another young male may have had an abnormal appearance as a result of congenital chondrodysplasia and arthritis (Buccellato, Catalano, Musco, 2008: 71). The only female was older (aged 45–55) and suffered from ankylosing spondylitis causing fusion and curvature of the spine and the development of a distinct "S-shaped" posture and upturned face (Buccellato, Catalano, Musco 2008, 72). Their burial in a (reused) mausoleum cannot be entirely coincidental. All three suffered from circumstances which altered their appearance, particularly their facial features, although they do not appear to have undergone social stigmatization in life. Indeed, both males display evidence of participation in heavy occupational activities, and to reach a comparatively mature age the woman must have been capable of supporting herself or have been supported by others.

In general, and in a pattern repeated across Italy, anthropological work is revealing a population engaged in strenuous occupational activities, living difficult lives and suffering from repeated episodes of stress related to nutritional deficiencies or disease. These episodes were, however, survivable and although conditions of life and health were relatively low, they were not critical (Catalano, Minozzi, and Pantano, 2001: 137).

9.8   Conclusions

This chapter has provided only a glimpse into the wealth of information, interpretations and significance of funerary practices in Roman Italy. Regional studies of patterns of inhumation and cremation, the use of certain grave goods, and the style of monuments are often lacking and clearly there is much scope for such work. Not only would this have the potential to provide a more nuanced picture of burial and commemorative practices across the peninsula, but also to shed light on the continual development of these practices themselves and their underlying motivations. Looking at burial rites, graves, epitaphs, and monuments separately is perhaps inevitable given the sheer volume of available evidence, but looking at these aspects together allows us to see parallel changes in, for example, epitaph production, burial rite, and styles of monument, which surely must be related. Too often explanations are sought for phenomena, such as the "epigraphic habit," without relating these to wider contexts, including the context of the rituals of death.

The emphasis here has been on examining the relationship between Rome and the communities of the rest of the peninsula, which has been shown to be complex and not entirely straightforward. In many respects this makes clear that certain innovations and fashions may have been initiated by the elite of the capital, or at least have been understood to be "Roman" in nature, but that these were adopted with varying levels of enthusiasm and with local modification across the regions of Italy. The use of stone monuments, Latin epitaphs, and cremation were adopted during the colonization process of the last few centuries of the Republic, and were caught up as active components of the social negotiations of the period, but even these were often adapted to suit the needs, circumstances, and preferences of local communities. From the first century AD onwards, we witness increasing variation, even if this was tied consistently to certain cultural norms and traditions. Once the peninsula had been fully subsumed by Rome it became less essential to respond to the fashions of the capital so quickly, unless it was deemed relevant to the specific needs of a community, and more specifically those of the elite. For this reason, apparently major shifts in practice such as the adoption of inhumation occurred at different, sometimes surprisingly slow, rates. Where styles of monument were adopted quickly, this was usually done in the context of elite competition and self-expression. Across Italy, then, it is possible to find numerous examples of variations on a common theme, but nowhere is there evidence for anything that bucked the trend in the extreme. In many ways this reveals that in the sphere of death, burial, and commemoration, the influence of Rome was important for introducing overarching ideas, forms, and practices, and that the initial unification of practice, working through the ambitions of the elite, was restricted in terms of the individual expression of these within a local or regional context. This pattern continued into the later Empire with even the introduction of Christianity failing to result in a sea change of practice. The way in which the Christian corpse was treated and commemorated remained much the same – inhumation and the use of traditional grave goods continued and epitaphs were still produced, albeit with more overtly Christian content (Carroll, 2006). Although their form and expression remained constant the meanings behind ritual practices undoubtedly altered in accordance with a new system of belief, but these are details that we unfortunately often cannot access. Only later (during the fourth and fifth century AD) was burial relocated to a new setting connected with saints and holy sites, often within the boundaries of cities. Funerary practices, in many ways, are susceptible to manipulation for the simple reason that they are focused upon intensely personal experience and the needs of different people within diverse contexts. In first-century AD Italy, cremating the deceased and erecting a stone memorial was a "Roman" way of dealing with the process of the funeral, in conformity with general cultural expectations, but the manner of that cremation, the items placed with the remains of the dead, the information presented on the monument and its design, and the rites performed at the graveside were choices made on a much smaller, often a very personal, scale.

FURTHER READING

There are no books which provide an overview of Italian funerary customs in the Roman period. Studies of funerary monuments, funerary portraiture, and epigraphy also tend to be regionally based, and excavation reports for graves and cemeteries are usually site-based with little direct comparison between sites, and often only published within regional Italian journals with limited circulation. Works are beginning to emerge which range across the peninsula for monument typologies (e.g. Schwarz, 2002) and there are several edited volumes that bring together material (particularly monumental) from diverse Italian locations aiding comparisons (e.g. von Hesberg and Zanker, 1987; Heinzelmann, 2001; Cresci Marrone and Tirelli, 2005). General overviews of Roman death ritual, which provide essential background include: Toynbee, 1971; von Hesberg, 1992; Morris, 1992; Hope, 2007 and 2009; but these do tend to focus on customs in Rome or on monument typologies. The importance of Italian evidence, for understanding Roman practices overall, is highlighted by recent work on undertakers (Bodel, 2000 and 2004). Recent work at Pompeii (van Andringa *et al.*, 2008; Lepetz and van Andringa, 2011) and Isola Sacra (Prowse *et al.*, 2004; Taglietti, 2001) has begun to demonstrate how an integrated approach (monuments, skeletal remains, botanical residues) can provide groundbreaking insights. The latter approaches are dependent upon the circumstances of excavation, and the recent construction of new road and rail links in the suburbs of Rome has offered notable opportunities to put an integrated approach into practice (Buccellato, Catalano, and Musco, 2008; and Buccellato *et al.*, 2008; Catalano *et al.*, 2006). This is, however, a methodology that is also being adopted across the peninsula, with attention increasingly being paid to the relationship between the treatment of the body in the ground and grave typology, as well as anthropological and botanical data (Duday and Demangeot, 2008; Leoni, Maioli, and Montevecchi, 2008; Lepetz and van Andringa, 2008; Ortalli, 2008; Prowse and Small, 2008).

REFERENCES

AAVV. 2004. *Libitina e dintorni. Libitina e i luci sepolcrali. Le leges libitinariae campane.* Iura sepulcrorum: *vecchie e nuove iscrizioni.* Rome: Quasar.

Adams, J.N. 2003. "Romanitas and the Latin language." *Classical Quarterly* 53.1: 184–205.

Andringa, W. van, Lepetz, S., Duday, H., Gailliot, A., Joey, D., Lind, T., Malagoli, C., Matterne, V., Derreumaux, M., Tuffreau-Libre, M., Creissen, T., and de Larminat, S. 2008. "I riti e la morte a Pompei: nuove ricerche archeologiche nella necropolis di Porta Nocera." In *Nuove ricerche archeologiche nell'area vesuviana (scavi 2003–2006)*, eds P.G. Guzzo and M.P. Guidobaldi, 377–87. Rome: «L'Erma» di Bretschneider.

Angelucci, S., Baldassarre, I., Bragantini, I., Lauro, M. G., Mannucci, V., Mazzoleni, A., Morselli, C., and Taglietti, F. 1990. "Sepolture e riti nella necropolis dell'Isola Sacra." *Bollettino di Archeologia* 5–6: 49–113.

Baldassarre, I., Bragantini, I., Morselli, C., and Taglietti, F. 1996. *Necropoli di Porto. Isola Sacra.* Rome: Istituto Poligrafico e Zecca Dello Stato/ Libreria dello Stato.

Bel, V., Blaizot, F., and Duday, H. 2008. "Bûchers en fosses et tombes bûcher." In *Pour une archéologie du rite: nouvelles perspectives de l'archéologie funéraire*, ed. J. Scheid, 233–47. Rome: École Française de Rome.

Benelli, E. 1994. *Le iscrizioni bilingui etrusco-latine*. Florence: Istituto nazionale di studi etruschi ed italici.

Benelli, E. 2001. "The Romanisation of Italy through the epigraphic record." in *Italy and the West: Comparative Issues in Romanization*, eds S. Keay and N. Terrenato, 7–16. Oxford: Oxbow.

Bianchi, F., Felici, F., Fontana, S., and Stanco, E.A. 2004. "Fiano Romano: un'area funeraria della prima età imperiale in località Palombaro." *Bullettino della Commissione archeologica Comunale di Roma:* 223–66.

Bodel, J. 1997. "Monumental villas and villa monuments." *Journal of Roman Archaeology* 10: 5–35.

Bodel, J. 1999. "Death on display: looking at Roman funerals." In *The Art of Ancient Spectacle*, eds B. Bergmann and C. Kondoleon, 258–81. Washington DC: National Gallery of Art/ Studies in the History of Art 56.

Bodel, J. 2000. "Dealing with the dead: undertakers, executioners and potter's fields in ancient Rome." In *Death and Disease in the Ancient City*, eds V.M. Hope and E. Marshall, 104–27. London: Routledge.

Bodel, J., ed. 2001. *Epigraphic Evidence: Ancient History from Inscriptions*. London and New York: Routledge.

Bodel, J. 2004. "The organization of the funerary trade at Puteoli and Cumae." In *Libitina e dintorni, AAVV*, 147–72. Rome: Quasar.

Brusin, G. 1941. *Nuovi monumenti sepolcrali di Aquileia*. Venice: Le Tre Venezie.

Buccellato, A., Catalano, P., and Musco, S. 2008. "Alcuni aspetti rituali evidenziati nel corso dello scavo della necropolis Collatina (Roma)." In *Pour une archéologie du rite: nouvelles perspectives de l'archéologie funéraire*, ed. J. Scheid, 59–88. Rome: École Française de Rome.

Buccellato, A., Musco, S., Catalano, P., Caldarini, C., Pantano, W., Torri, C., and Zabotti, F. 2008. "La nécropole de Collatina", in *Rome et ses morts*, eds P. Catalano, J. Scheid, and S. Verger, 22–31. Dijon: *Les dossiers d'archéologie 330*/Editions Faton.

Carroll, M. 2006. *Spirits of the Dead. Roman Funerary Commemoration in Western Europe*. Oxford: Oxford University Press.

Carroll, M. 2011a. "Infant death and burial in Roman Italy." *Journal of Roman Archaeology* 24: 99–120.

Carroll, M. 2011b. "'The mourning was very good.' Liberation and liberality in Roman funerary commemoration." In *Memory and Mourning. Studies on Roman Death*, eds V.M. Hope and J. Huskinson, 126–49. Oxford: Oxbow.

Carroll, M. 2012. "'No part in earthly things.' The death, burial and commemoration of newborn children and infants in Roman Italy." In *Families in the Roman and Late Antique World*, eds L. Larsson Lovén and M. Harlow, 41–63. London: Continuum Press.

Catalano, P., Amicucci, G., Renassi, V., Caldarini, C., Caprara, M., Carboni, L., Colonnelli, G., De Angelis, F., Di Giannantonio, S., Minozzi, S., Pantano, W., and Porreca, F. 2006. "Gli insiemi funerari d'epoca imperiale: l'indagine antropologica di campo." In *Roma. Memorie dal sottosuolo. Ritrovamenti archeologici, 1980/2006*, ed. M.A. Tomei, 560–66. Rome: Electa.

Catalano, P. Minozzi, S., and Pantano, W. 2001. "Le necropoli romane di età imperiale: un contributo all'interpretazione del popolamento e della qualità della vita nell'antica Roma." In *Urbanizzazione delle campagne nell'Italia antica*, eds L. Quilici and S. Quilici Gigli, 127–37. Rome: *Atlante tematico di topografia antica* 10/ «L'Erma» di Bretschneider.

Ceci, F. 2001. "L'interpretazione di monete e chiodi in contesti funerari: esempi dal suburbia romano." In *Römischer Bestattungsbrauch und Beigabensitten in Rom, Norditalien und den Nordwestprovinzen von der späten Republik bis in die Kaiserzeit*, eds M. Heinzelmann, J. Ortalli, P. Fasold, and M. Witteyer, 87–97. Rome: Deutches Archäologisches Institut Rom.

Ceglia, V. 2008. "San Martino in Pensilis, CampoBasso, Malise, Italy: the villa of Contrada Mattanelle." in *Archaeology and Landscape in Central Italy: Papers in Memory of John A. Lloyd*, eds G. Lock and A. Faustoferri, 191–204. Oxford: Oxford School of Archaeology Monograph 69.

Cipollone, M. 2002. "Gubbio (Perugia). Necropoli in loc. Vittorina. Campagne di scavo 1980 – 1982 (1)." *Notizie degli Scavi* (Series 9) 11–12: 5–371.

Cooley, A.E. 2012. *The Cambridge Manual of Latin Epigraphy*. Cambridge: Cambridge University Press.

Corbeill, A. 2004. *Nature Embodied: Gesture in Ancient Rome*. Princeton: Princeton University Press.

Cresci Marrone, G. and Tirelli, M. 2005. "Terminavit sepulcrum": *i recinti funerari nelle necropoli di Altino*. Rome: Quasar.

Cucina, A., Vargili, R., Mancinelli, D., Ricci, R., Santandrea, E., Catalano, P., and Coppa, A. 2006. "The Necropolis of Vallerano (Rome, 2nd–3rd Century AD): an anthropological perspective on the ancient Romans in the *suburbium*." *International Journal of Osteoarchaeology* 16: 104–17.

Duday, H. and Demangeot, C. 2008. "La tombe 77 de la nécropole romaine de Classe à Ravenne." In *Pour une archéologie du rite: nouvelles perspectives de l'archéologie funéraire*, ed. J. Scheid, 197–210. Rome: École Française de Rome.

Duncan-Jones, R. 1977. "Age-rounding, illiteracy and social differentiation." *Chiron* 7: 333–53.

Duncan-Jones, R. 1990. *Structure and Scale in the Roman Economy*. Cambridge: Cambridge University Press.

Elsner, J. and Huskinson, J., eds. 2010. *Life, Death and Representation. Some New Work on Roman Sarcophagi*. Berlin: De Gruyter.

Facchini, F., Rastelli, E., and Brasili, P. 2004. "Cribra orbitalia and cibra cranii in Roman skeletal remains from the Ravenna area and Rimini (I–IV Century AD)." *International Journal of Osteoarchaeology* 14: 126–36.

Falzone, S., Olivanti, P., and Pellegrino, A. 2001. "La necropolis di Fralana (Acilia)." In *Römischer Bestattungsbrauch und Beigabensitten in Rom, Norditalien und den Nordwestprovinzen von der späten Republik bis in die Kaiserzeit*, eds M. Heinzelmann, J. Ortalli, P. Fasold, and M. Witteyer, 127–38. Rome: Deutches Archäologisches Institut Rom.

Filippis, M. de 2001. "Ricerche in sepolcreti suburbani tra Salaria et Nomentana." In *Römischer Bestattungsbrauch und Beigabensitten in Rom, Norditalien und den Nordwestprovinzen von der späten Republik bis in die Kaiserzeit*, eds M. Heinzelmann, J. Ortalli, P. Fasold, and M. Witteyer, 55–61. Rome: Deutches Archäologisches Institut Rom.

Fitzgerald, C., Saunders, S., Bondioli, L., and Macchiarelli, R. 2006. "Health of infants in an Imperial Roman skeletal sample: perspective from dental microstructure." *American Journal of Physical Anthropology* 130: 179–89.

Flower, H.I. 1996. *Ancestor Masks and Aristocratic Power in Roman Culture*. Oxford: Clarendon Press.

Franzoni C. 1987. Habitus atque habitudo militis. *Monumenti funerari di militari nella Cisalpina Romana*. Rome: «L'Erma» di Bretschneider.

Frier, B. 2000. "Demography." In *The Cambridge Ancient History*, vol. 11, 2nd edn, *The High Empire AD 70–192*, eds A.K. Bowman, P. Garnsey, D. Rathbone, 787–816. Cambridge: Cambridge University Press.

Gallivan, P. and Wilkins, P. 1997. "Familial structures in Roman Italy: a regional approach." In *The Roman Family in Italy. Status, Sentiment and Space*, eds B. Rawson and P. Weaver, 239–80. Oxford: Clarendon Press.

Ghedini, F. 1984. "La romanizzazione attraverso il monumento funerario." In *Misurare la terra: centurazione e coloni nel mondo romano. Il caso Veneto*, 52–71. Modena: Edizioni Panini.

Graham, E-J. 2005. "The Quick and the Dead in the extra-urban landscape: the Roman cemetery at Ostia/Portus as a lived environment." In *TRAC 2004. Proceedings of the Fourteenth Annual Theoretical Roman Archaeology Conference. Durham 2004*, eds J. Bruhn, B. Croxford and D. Grigoropoulos, 133–43. Oxford: Oxbow.

Graham, E-J. 2006. *Death, Disposal and the Destitute: The Burial of the Urban Poor in Italy in the Late Roman Republic and Early Empire*. Oxford: BAR International Series 1565/ Archaeopress.

Graham, E-J. 2011a. "From fragments to ancestors: re-defining *os resectum* and its role in rituals of purification and commemoration in Republican Rome." In *Living through the Dead: Burial and Commemoration in the Classical World*, eds M. Carroll and J. Rempel, 91–109. Oxford: Oxbow.

Graham, E-J. 2011b. "Memory and materiality: re-embodying the Roman funeral." In *Memory and Mourning: Studies on Roman Death*, eds V. M. Hope and J. Huskinson, 21–39. Oxford: Oxbow.

Graham, E-J. 2013. "Disparate lives or disparate deaths? Post-mortem treatment of the body and the articulation of difference." In *Disabilities in Roman antiquity. Disparate bodies* 'a capite ad calcem', eds C. Laes C. Goodey and M.L. Rose, 249–74. Leiden: Brill.

Graham, E-J. 2015. "Corporeal concerns: the role of the body in the transformation of Roman mortuary practices." In *Death Embodied: Archaeological Approaches to the Treatment of the Corpse*, eds Z.L. Devlin and E-J. Graham, 41–62. Oxford: Oxbow.

Hackworth Petersen, L. 2006. *The Freedman in Roman Art and Art History*. Cambridge and New York: Cambridge University Press.

Häussler, R. 1998. "Resta, viator, et lege: thoughts on the epigraphic habit." *Papers from the Institute of Archaeology* 9: 31–56.

Häussler, R. 2002. "Writing Latin – from resistance to assimilation: language, society and culture in N. Gaul and S. France." In *Becoming Roman, Writing Latin?: Literacy and Epigraphy in the Roman West*, ed. A.E. Cooley, 61–76. Portsmouth RI: *Journal of Roman Archaeology* Suppl. 48.

Heinzelmann M. 2001. "Les nécropoles d'Ostie: topographie, développement, architecture, structure sociale." In *Ostia, Port et porte de la Rome antique*, ed. J.-P. Descoeudres, 373–84. Geneva: Georg.

Hesberg, H. von. 1992. *Römische Grabbauten*. Darmstadt: Wissenschaftliche Buchgesellschaft.

Hesberg, H. von and Zanker, P. 1987. *Römische Gräberstrassen: Selbstdarstellung, Status, Standard.* Munich: C.H. Beck.

Hinard, F. and Dumont, J.C., eds. 2003. Libitina. *Pompes funèbres et supplices en Campanie à l'époque d'Auguste. Édition, traduction et commentaire de la* Lex Libitina Puteolana. Paris: De Boccard.

Hope, V.M. 2001. *Constructing Identity: the Roman Funerary Monuments of Aquileia, Mainz and Nimes*. Oxford: BAR, International Series 960.

Hope, V.M. 2007. *Death in Ancient Rome. A Sourcebook*. London: Routledge.

Hope, V.M. 2009. *Roman Death: Dying and the Dead in Ancient Rome*. London and New York: Continuum.

Hope, V.M. 2011. "Livia's tears: the presentation of Roman grief." In *In Memoriam: Commemoration, Communal Memory and Gender Values in the Ancient Greco-Roman World*, ed. H. Whittaker, 91–125. Newcastle-upon-Tyne: Cambridge Scholars Press.

Hopkins, K. 1966. "On the probable age structure of the Roman population." *Population Studies* 20: 245–64.

Hopkins, K. 1987. "Graveyards for historians." In *La mort, les morts et l'au-delà dans le monde romain*, ed. F. Hinard, 113–26. Caen: University of Caen Press.

Kleiner, D.E.E. 1977. *Roman Group Portraiture: the Funerary Reliefs of the Late Republic and Early Empire*. New York: Garland.

Kockel, V. 1983. *Die Grabbauten vor dem Herkulaner Tor in Pompeji*. Mainz: Zabern.

Leoni, C., Maioli, M.G., and Montevecchi, G. 2008. "Scavi in aree umide. Le necropolis di Classe, Ravenna." In *Pour une archéologie du rite: nouvelles perspectives de l'archéologie funéraire*, ed. J. Scheid, 89–104. Rome: École Française de Rome.

Lepetz, S. and Andringa, W. van. 2008. "Archéologie du ritual." In *Pour une archéologie du rite: nouvelles perspectives de l'archéologie funéraire*, ed. J. Scheid, 105–26. Rome: École Française de Rome.

Lepetz, S. and Andringa, W. van. 2011. "Publius Vesonius Phileros vivos monumentum fecit: Investigations in a sector of the Porta Nocera cemetery in Roman Pompeii." In *Living through the Dead: Burial and Commemoration in the Classical World*, eds M. Carroll and J. Rempel, 110–33. Oxford: Oxbow.

Lindsay, H. 2000. "Death-pollution and funerals in the city of Rome." In *Death and Disease in the Ancient City*, eds V. M. Hope and E. Marshall, 152–73. London: Routledge.

Lomas, K. 2004. "Funerary epigraphy and the impact of Rome in Italy", in *Roman Rule and Civic Life: Local and Regional Perspectives. Impact of Empire*, vol. 4, eds L. de Ligt, E.A. Hemelrijk, and H. W. Singor, 179–98. Amsterdam: J.C. Gieben.

MacMullen, R. 1982. "The epigraphic habit in the Roman empire." *American Journal of Philology* 103: 234–46.

Maioli, M. G., Ortalli, J., and Montevecchi, G. 2008. "La nécropole du port militaire de Classe." In *Rome et ses morts. Les dossiers d'archéologie 330*, eds P. Catalano, J. Scheid, and S. Verger, 74–81. Dijon: Editions Faton.

Mansuelli, G.A. 1967. *Le stele romane del territorio Ravennate e del basso Po*. Ravenna: Longo.

Massa, S. 2001. "Il sepolcreto del Lugone (Salò): elementi di rituali e struttura sociale." In *Römischer Bestattungsbrauch und Beigabensitten in Rom, Norditalien und den Nordwestprovinzen von der späten Republik bis in die Kaiserzeit*, eds M. Heinzelmann, J. Ortalli, P. Fasold, and M. Witteyer, 263–69. Rome: Deutches Archäologisches Institut Rom.

Matterne, V. and Derreumaux, M. 2008. "A Franco-Italian investigation of funerary rituals in the Roman World: 'Les rites et la mort à Pompéi.' The plant part: a preliminary report." *Vegetation History and Archaeobotany* 17.1: 105–12.

McWilliam, J. 2001. "Children among the dead: the influence of urban life on the commemoration of children on tombstone inscriptions." In *Childhood, Class and Kin in the Roman World*, ed. S. Dixon, 74–98. London and New York: Routledge.

Mercado, L. and Paci, G. 1995. *Stele romane in Piemonte*. Rome: «L'Erma» di Bretschneider.

Meyer, E. 1990. "Explaining the epigraphic habit in the Roman empire: the evidence of epitaphs." *Journal of Roman Studies* 80: 74–96.

Morris, I. 1992. *Death Ritual and Social Structure in Classical Antiquity*. Cambridge: Cambridge University Press.

Mouritsen, H. 2004. "Freedmen and freeborn in the necropolis of Imperial Ostia." *Zeitschrift für Papyrologie und Epigraphik* 150: 281–304.

Mouritsen, H. 2005. "Freedmen and decurions: epitaphs and social history in Imperial Italy." *Journal of Roman Studies* 95: 38–63.

Mrozek, S. 1973. "A propos de la répartition chronologique des inscriptions latines dans le haut-empire." *Epigraphica* 35: 113–18.

Mrozek, S. 1988. "A propos de la répartition chronologique des inscriptions latines dans le haut-empire." *Epigraphica* 50: 61–64.

Mustakallio, K. 2005. "Roman funerals: identity, gender and participation." In *Hoping for Continuity: Childhood, Education and Death in Antiquity and the Middle Ages*, eds K. Mustakallio, J. Hanska, H.-L. Sainio and V. Vuolanto, 179–90. Rome: Acta Instituti Romani Finlandiae, vol. 33.

Nock, A.D. 1932. "Cremation and burial in the Roman Empire." *Harvard Theological Review* 25.4: 321–59.

Noy, D. 2011. "'Goodbye Livia': dying in the Roman home." In *Memory and Mourning: Studies on Roman Death*, eds V.M. Hope and J. Huskinson, 1–20. Oxford: Oxbow.

Ortalli, J. 1987. "La via dei sepolcri di Sarsina. Aspetti funzionali, formali e sociali." In *Römische Gräberstraßen. Selbstdarstellung – Status – Standard*, eds H. von Hesberg and P. Zanker, 155–84. Munich: Bayerische Akademie der Wissenschaften.

Ortalli, J. 2001. "Il funerario della Cispadana romana. Rappresentazione e interiorità." In *Römischer Bestattungsbrauch und Beigabensitten in Rom, Norditalien und den Nordwestprovinzen von der späten Republik bis in die Kaiserzeit*, eds M. Heinzelmann, J. Ortalli, P. Fasold, and M. Witteyer, 215–41. Rome: Deutches Archäologisches Institut Rom.

Ortalli, J. 2008. "Scavo stratigrafico e contesti sepolcrali. " In *Pour une archéologie du rite: nouvelles perspectives de l'archéologie funéraire*, ed. J. Scheid, 137–59. Rome: École Française de Rome.

Paine, R.R., Vargiu, R., Signoretti, C., and Coppa, A. 2009. "A health assessment for Imperial Roman burials recovered from the necropolis of San Donato and Bivio CH, Urbino, Italy." *Journal of Anthropological Sciences* 87: 193–210.

Parkin, T. 1992. *Demography and Roman Society*. Baltimore and London: Johns Hopkins University Press.

Passi Pitcher, L. 2001. "Riti funerari particolari: negazione della vita e congedo. Il caso della necropoli di Nave." In *Römischer Bestattungsbrauch und Beigabensitten in Rom, Norditalien und den Nordwestprovinzen von der späten Republik bis in die Kaiserzeit*, eds M. Heinzelmann, J. Ortalli, P. Fasold, and M. Witteyer, 257–62. Rome: Deutches Archäologisches Institut Rom.

Pellegrino, A., Falzone, S., and Olivanti, P. 1999. "L'insediamento rustico di Fralana (Acilia)." In *Dalle Necropoli di Ostia. Riti e Usi Funerari*, ed. A. Pellegrino, 26–40. Rome: Soprintendenza Archeologica di Ostia.

Pflug, H. 1989. *Römische Porträtstelen in Oberitalien. Untersuchungen zur Chronologie, Typologie und Ikonographie*. Mainz: Zabern.

Piccottini, G. 1976. "L'influenza di Aquileia sull'arte sepolcrale del Norico mediterraneo." *Antichità Altoadriatiche* 9: 141–151.

Prowse T., Schwarcz H., Saunders S., Bondioli L., and Macchiarelli R. 2004. "Isotopic paleodiet studies of skeletons from the Imperial Roman cemetery of Isola Sacra, Rome, Italy." *Journal of Archaeological Science* 31.3: 259–72.

Prowse, T. and Small, A. 2008. "Excavations in the Roman cemetery at Vagnari, 2008. Preliminary report." *Journal of Fasti Online*. http://www.fastionline.org/docs/FOLDER-it-2009-131.pdf. Accessed August 3, 2015.

Reusser, C. 1987. "Gräberstrassen in Aquileia." In *Römische Gräberstrassen: Selbstdarstellung, Status, Standard*, eds H. von Hesberg. and P. Zanker, 239–49. Munich: C.H. Beck.

Revell, L. 2005. "The Roman life course: a view from the inscriptions." *European Journal of Archaeology* 8: 43–63.

Saller, R. and Shaw, B. 1984. "Tombstones and Roman family relations in the Principate: civilians, soldiers and slaves." *Journal of Roman Studies* 74: 124–56.

Scarpellini, D. 1987. *Stele romane con* imagines clipeatae *in Italia*. Rome: «L'Erma» di Bretschneider.

Scheidel, W. 2010. "Physical wellbeing in the Roman world." *Princeton/Stanford Working Papers in Classics*. http://www.princeton.edu/~pswpc/pdfs/scheidel/091001.pdf. Accessed August 3, 2015.

Schwarz, M. 2002. Tumulat Italia tellus. *Gestaltung, Chronologie und Bedeutung der römischen Rundgräber in Italien*. Leidforf: Internationale Archäologie 72.

Šterbenc Erker, D. 2011. "Gender and Roman funeral ritual." In *Memory and Mourning: Studies on Roman Death*, eds V.M. Hope and J. Huskinson, 40–60. Oxford: Oxbow.

Taglietti, F. 2001. "Ancora su incinerazione e inhumazione: la necropolis dell'Isola Sacra." In *Römischer Bestattungsbrauch und Beigabensitten in Rom, Norditalien und den Nordwestprovinzen von der späten Republik bis in die Kaiserzeit*, eds M. Heinzelmann, J. Ortalli, P. Fasold, and M. Witteyer, 149–58. Rome: Deutches Archäologisches Institut Rom.

Tocchetti Pollin, U. 1990. *Stele funerarie romane con ritratti dai municipia di Mediolanum e Comum*. Milan: Comune di Milano, Civiche raccolte archeologiche.

Toynbee, J.M.C. 1971. *Death and Burial in the Roman World*. London: Thames & Hudson.

Verzár Bass, M. 1985. "Rapporti tra l'alto adriatico e la dalmazia: a proposito di alcuni tipi di monumenti funerari." *Antichità Altoadriatiche* 26.1: 183–208.

Vismara, C. 1992. "L'apport des textes antiques." In *Incinérations et inhumations dans l'Occident romain aux trois premiers siècles de notre ère, 107–47*. Paris/ Toulouse: Ministère de la culture et de la communication / Association pour la Promotion du Patrimoine Archéologique et Historique en Midi-Pyrénées.

Woolf, G. 1996. "Monumental writing and the expansion of Roman society in the early Empire." *Journal of Roman Studies* 86: 22–39.

Zanker, P. 1975. "Grabreliefs römischer Freigelassener." *Jahrbuch des Deutschen Archäologischen Instituts* 90: 267–315.

Zech-Matterne, V. 2008. "Les végétaux dans les funérailles. L'exemple de la nécrople de Porta Nocera à Pompéi." In *Rome et ses morts. Les dossiers d'archéologie 330*, eds P. Catalano, J. Scheid, and S. Verger, 66–67. Dijon: Editions Faton.

Zimmer, G. 1982. *Römische Berufsdarstellungen*. Berlin: Mann.

CHAPTER 10

Diversity in Architecture and Urbanism

Margaret L. Laird

10.1 Introduction

The material culture of any society is inherently diverse. A chapter addressing the physical remains of Roman Italy might survey, for instance, a variety of building types (such as amphitheaters, temples, or houses), various artworks (sculpted portraits, wall painting, or mosaic), and even quotidian objects (vessels, lamps, jewelry). These artifacts vary greatly in scale and are made from different fabrics: stone, clay, wood, metals, pigments, and gemstones. Even a single category of object that seems coherent at first glance is intrinsically diverse: bath buildings, for instance, differ in plan from one town or region to another, or may be constructed from different materials worked in distinctive techniques. Or mythological stories can be depicted in a variety of artistic styles or through certain iconographies (conventional ways of depicting a particular subject). Finally, material culture can diverge across cultures, geography, and time.

Because of these variables, this chapter cannot hope to provide a comprehensive survey of the art and architecture produced in Italy. Rather, it will focus primarily on civic and sacred architecture and city planning to understand the cultures of the Italian peninsula during key periods of social change, first as Latins, Etruscans, and Greeks overlapped in the Archaic period (late seventh to fifth century BC); then as Rome expanded beyond Italy to the eastern Mediterranean in the Late Republic; and finally as a common "Roman" material culture united the peninsula in the Principate. The chapter examines how, in the earlier period, architecture reflects the cultural diversity of the peninsula, marks indigenous responses to Roman encroachment, and demonstrates acceptance of, and resistance to, Roman culture. It explores how, in the later periods, a common architectural language that appears monolithic nevertheless allows for local and regional diversity that can parallel or overlap traditional cultural patterns.

Before turning to these questions, it is worth understanding the importance of material culture as evidence as well as some of its inherent difficulties. While many ancient objects and buildings were (and remain) aesthetically pleasing, they were not created as "art for art's sake." Rather, artists, architects, and craftsmen catered to the needs and tastes of buyers who might be more or less involved in the planning and execution of particular commissions

A Companion to Roman Italy, First Edition. Edited by Alison E. Cooley.
© 2016 John Wiley & Sons, Ltd. Published 2016 by John Wiley & Sons, Ltd.

(Stewart, 2008: 10–38). The forms that objects and buildings took resulted from a series of deliberate choices that were consistent with (or broke from) traditional patterns and conformed to notions of how that particular object or building should be used (Izzet, 2007: 25–27). At the same time, objects and buildings shaped the expectations of their users. Buildings, for instance, provided stages in which to enact patterned social practices and thus perpetuated and reinforced them. As civic groups and individuals performed specific activities in and around buildings, the structures could play a role in developing community identities (Bourdieu, 1977; Giddens, 1979, 1984; Yaeger and Canuto, 2000: 9). In opening a window onto these various facets of ancient life, material culture complements other forms of evidence, such as literary or epigraphic texts.

Despite its importance for understanding ancient life, scholars must be aware of several difficulties inherent to material culture. The objects and buildings that survive from antiquity are only a slim fraction of what was originally produced. Nor have archaeologists discovered all that remains. Durable (and more costly) materials tend to survive the best, skewing the evidence towards objects made for a society's elite. We also must consider the way in which things are discovered and recorded, because objects in and of themselves cannot "speak." Prior to the late nineteenth century, excavators frequently showed little concern for the contexts in which artifacts were found. Without this information, it is difficult to pinpoint when an object was made and how it might have been used. Modern archaeologists aim for more careful documentation by, for instance, carefully recording stratigraphic data (the relationship of archaeological layers to one another), or noting how objects and built features relate within a stratum, or collecting faunal or plant remains. Even with these advances, the interpretation of archaeological material is not always straightforward. Objects may be found far from their original places of use, destruction phases may compromise a site, or excavation and recording techniques may vary. Most importantly, a scholar's particular research questions, methodological approaches, or biases inevitably influence what gets excavated, what gets studied, and how it is interpreted.

A brief discussion of the changing ways in which the material record has been interpreted around the topic of "Romanization" illustrates this last point. Romanization, a modern and much-debated term, describes the spread of Roman culture in Italy and throughout the empire. While the settlement patterns and urban architecture of the Italian peninsula varied widely throughout the Republican period, by the early first century AD most Italian towns included a standard repertoire of spaces and buildings that replicated those found at Rome (such as fora, basilicas, and theaters) (see Figure 10.1). Buyers commissioned works of art and used objects whose formal styles recalled those of the capital. To scholars in the late nineteenth and early twentieth centuries, this shift from diversity to homogeneity suggested that conquered Italian communities adopted Roman material culture because Roman prod-ucts and practices were superior to indigenous products and practices (for the early historiog-raphy of Romanization, see Hingley, 2005: 14–48).

As theoretical models shifted in the 1960s, scholars recognized the biases inherent in this top-down model: it implies that culture flowed from the conqueror to the conquered and denies local populations agency in the changes found in the archaeological record. The earliest of these scholars focused on the archaeology of Romanizing cultures, such as the Britons and the Gauls, and particularly explored the role that local elites played in negotiating Roman culture (e.g. Millett, 1990; Woolf, 1998). These studies understood Roman buildings and objects as part of a broader cultural array that also included Roman behaviors, rituals, and the Latin language (see Lomas, ch.11, this vol.). The wealthiest classes could adopt elements of this palette and use it to express their participation in the empire and, equally as important, their status and position within their local communities (Woolf, 1998).

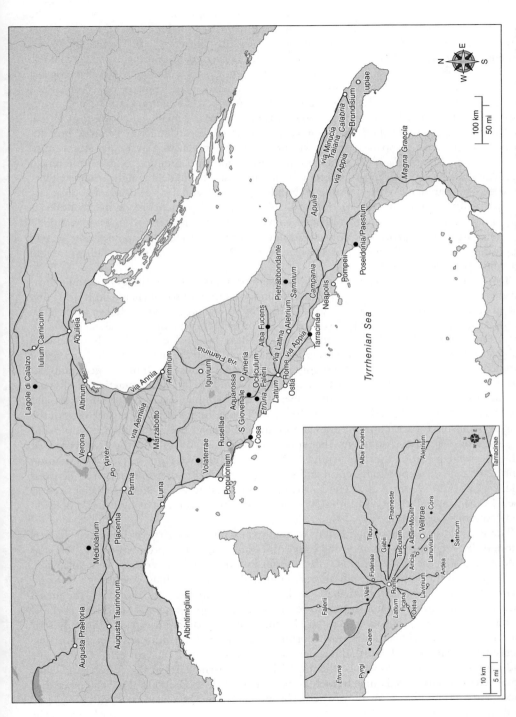

Figure 10.1 Map of ancient Italy labeling the towns, regions, and other features discussed in this chapter. Adapted from a map generated with Antiquity À-la-carte, Ancient World Mapping Center (awmc.unc.edu).

More recently, scholars have noted that these readings artificially limit what a building or object can mean: while a Samnite buyer might have considered *terra sigillata* pottery to be valuable (and worth purchasing), we cannot guarantee that she appreciated this ware for its Roman-ness or even that she used it in an identifiably "Roman" way (Roth, 2007). To broaden our understanding of the processes of cultural change beyond the urban elite and to examine Romanization from the bottom up, some scholars have studied the archaeology of single towns and their territories (essays in van Dommelen and Terrenato, eds, 2007; Roth and Keller, 2007; Keay and Terrenato, 2001). This approach has demonstrated that communities reacted differently and unpredictably to Rome's encroachment, mirroring the cultural and material diversity of the Italian peninsula and the regions of the empire more broadly. Other scholars have compared material culture to language, drawing particular attention to the notion of "bilingualism." According to this model, individuals understood the differences between indigenous and Roman objects and buildings, and could deliberately "code-switch," or select the "language" (be it an object, building, or even visual style) deemed appropriate to a particular circumstance (Wallace-Hadrill, 2008). These approaches recognize that objects might have multiple meanings that depend on place and time. Importantly, these new models demonstrate that the process of Romanization was not monolithic and should not be seen in opposition to cultural diversity. Indeed, elements of Roman and indigenous cultures could and did exist simultaneously.

This chapter relies on this new research, focusing on a series of case studies to examine how diversity in the built environment informs our understanding of social change in Italy. It first surveys the formal differences in architecture made by several groups on the Italian peninsula – Etruscans, Greeks, and the Italic Romans – within the context of the Hellenic *koine*, or common culture, of the Archaic and early Republican periods. It examines how material culture responds to the needs of particular cultures and how the material record can reveal moments of cultural change and exchange. In addition, it considers how the geography of the Italian peninsula influenced settlement patterns and architectural practice. Following Rome's expansion through the Mediterranean in the Republic, exposure to Greek art and architecture influenced developments in the city of Rome. At the same time, the towns of the Italian peninsula took on a more unified appearance. Roman policies of road building and colonization were direct strategies that spread Roman ways of life and the architecture in which to stage it throughout the peninsula. Yet colonies also were products of the common culture of the late Republican period and showed some degree of adaptability (cf. Fentress and Perkins, ch. 19, this vol.). The towns of Rome's Italian allies likewise participated in "self-Romanization" that was motivated by local aspirations as much as by Rome's political and economic hegemony.

The second part of this chapter begins with a brief examination of the architectural changes wrought by Augustus in Rome in the early Principate. Augustus's program of building and renewal signaled the city's status as a Mediterranean capital with the *princeps* as its sole ruler. As elements of the Augustan program were emulated throughout Italy, a cohesive "Roman" architectural style emerged, particularly in the civic architecture commissioned by the urban elite. Such outward standardization, however, belies continued regional and local diversity. Just as cities and peoples had negotiated Hellenic culture in different ways, so they adjusted canonical Roman architectural forms to promote groups and individuals within a particular local context. Moreover, beneath this apparent homogeneity, traditional patterns of settlement and land use survived throughout the imperial period, particularly in the countryside. This simple chapter outline veils an extremely complex narrative. It is important to remember that social and cultural change in Italy, whether it was motivated by encounters with Greeks or Romans, or was an independent development on a regional or local scale, never happened in just one way or at just one moment.

10.2 Cultural Diversity in Early Italy

The archaeological diversity of the Italian peninsula, particularly before the Principate, reflects the variety of ethnic groups who shared it (see Figure 11.1). Italic peoples, each speaking different languages (Latin, Oscan, Umbrian, Venetic, and Messapic), lived alongside non-Italic Etruscans, Greeks, and Celts (cf. Lomas, ch. 11, this vol). While each group was distinguished by its own language and customs, as contact between these various groups intensified from the Archaic period onward, significant overlaps emerged particularly in their material culture (Cornell, 1995: 164). The architecture produced by three of these groups – the Greeks of Magna Graecia, the Etruscans in Etruria, and the Latins in the city of Rome – reveals both cultural particularity and areas of intersection.

10.2.1 Greek colonies and their architecture

Greek colonization began in southern Italy and Sicily in the eighth century BC (Lomas, 1993; Cerchiai, Jannelli, and Longo, 2004). Settlers from towns in Greece and Asia Minor established independent communities, whose inhabitants in turn established new centers. At their head was an *oikist*, a founder responsible for establishing the city's plan and its fortification walls, assigning houses and farmland, and establishing public and sacred space (Homer, *Odyssey*: 6.7–11; Wilson, 2006: 36–38, 43–48). The plans of these settlements and their architecture provided spaces suited to typically Greek political and religious activities. Most Greek colonies had orthogonal city plans with streets intersecting at right angles to create regular city blocks. In many of these settlements, a sizeable proportion of the city was given over to public space. At Neapolis (modern Naples), the agora (the political and commercial center) occupied nearly one third of the town (Greco, 2002: 214–15; Cerchiai, Jannelli, and Longo, 2004: 59). The center of Poseidonia (later, renamed Paestum) was the site of an open agora bounded to the north and south by large sanctuaries (see Figure 10.2). As at Poseidonia, many agoras were bounded by streets, making them easy to reach from a city's gates (Sewell, 2010: 22–23). These central spaces were the site of key civic and ritual buildings. A covered theater, an open theater, a temple, and civic monuments surrounded the agora at Neapolis. At Poseidonia, an *ekklesiasterion*, a circular, stepped assembly place where citizen males could gather for political meetings, stood on the east (Greco and Theodorescu, 1983b, 34–49). Similar structures have been found in Athens and, in the Greek west, at Metapontium and at the Sicilian settlement of Agrigentum (Agrigento) (Mertens, 1982; Fiorentini, 1990). On the north-western edge of Poseidonia's agora stood a low, rectangular structure covered with a pitched roof and buried under an earthen tumulus (Greco and Theodorescu 1983b, 25–33, 74–79; Sestieri, 1955; see Figure 10.3). Objects discovered within it – five iron swords, eight bronze vessels containing wine and honey, and an Attic Black Figure amphora depicting the apotheosis of Herakles – suggest that the structure functioned as a heröon, or a hero shrine dedicated to an *oikist*. Founders of other Greek colonies were venerated as heroes probably beginning in the late sixth century (Wilson, 2006, 44–48). Literary and archaeological evidence has located a similar shrine in the agora in the colony of Cyrene in North Africa (Pindar, *Pythian Ode*: 5; Büsing, 1978: 71–73). At Poseidonia, the absence of human remains in the shrine suggests that the structure served not as a cult site for that colony's founder, but as a cenotaph for the founder of Sybaris, Poseidonia's mother city that was destroyed in 510 BC (Zancani-Montuoro, 1954). If this is the case, the heröon provided a built reminder of the colonists' passage from Greece to Sybaris and then to Poseidonia. In the fourth century, a long stoa, or colonnaded hall, was constructed across the center of the agora, dividing the square into commercial and political/religious zones.

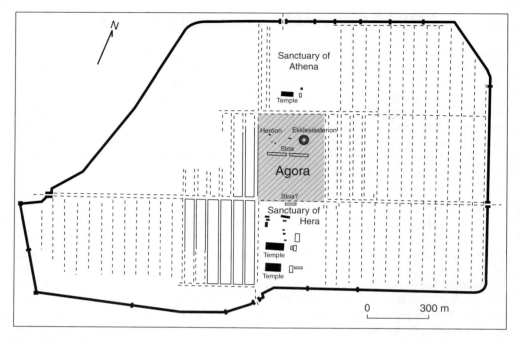

Figure 10.2 Plan of the Greek colony of Poseidonia. (The agora is shaded grey) Adapted from Gros and Torelli, 2010: Fig. 88, and Cerchiai, Jannelli, and Longo, 2004: 62.

Figure 10.3 The heröon in the agora of Poseidonia (circa 520–510 BC) surrounded by the Roman enclosure wall (circa 273 BC). Album/Art Resource.

The architecture and design of the sanctuaries to the north and south of Poseidonia's agora likewise followed Greek cultural norms. The two urban precincts contain three large temples

Figure 10.4 Poseidonia, the temple of Athena in the northern sanctuary, built late sixth century BC. Photograph: M. Laird, with the kind permission of the Soprintendenza per i Beni Archeologici di Salerno.

and an assortment of smaller shrines, altars, and other structures (see Figure 10.4). The temples' primary function was to house the cult statue of the deity to which they were dedicated; sacrifices and other religious rituals took place at altars in front of their eastern ends. The temples, constructed from local limestone, follow Greek architectural principles. All sit on low platforms (a stylobate and stereobate) that step up on all four sides. The structures are fully peripteral, with a single row of columns surrounding the *cella* on all sides. Their superstructures make use of the Doric order, a construction style recognizable by its fluted columns, pillow-shaped capitals, and the row of alternating triglyphs and metopes that run along the entablature below the roof. Wooden structures in the Doric order originated in mainland Greece; by the early sixth century, public buildings (primarily temples) were being constructed in stone using this style. Taken together, Poseidonia's urban plan and buildings met the needs of a particularly Greek community, providing spaces for Greek political and religious practices, a shrine commemorating the colonists' Greek origins, and buildings whose architecture explicitly linked the town to Greek and other Italiote communities.

10.3   The Etruscans

By about 700 BC, a distinctly Etruscan society had emerged in Etruria, the fertile and mineral-rich region to the north of Rome. The Etruscans had their own economic, social, and political systems, as well as a unique language that was unrelated to the other ancient Indo-European languages spoken on the Italian peninsula (Barker and Rasmussen, 1998; Lambrechts, 1959; Bonfante and Bonfante, 2002; Bonfante, 1990; cf. Lomas, ch. 11, this vol.). The Etruscans coalesced as a series of independent cities that controlled sizeable territories that might include dependent settlements and port installations on the coast (Gros and Torelli, 2010). In the sixth and fifth centuries BC, Etruscan influence spread northwards and southwards into the Po Valley and Campania, and to Rome itself (Torelli, 1981; Frederiksen, 1979; essays in Cristofani, ed., 1990). The size of Etruscan towns and the wealth of aristocratic burials indicate that elites exploited the area's natural wealth, which they traded with the Greeks to the south; in particular, metals were exchanged for Greek pottery. These commercial interactions had cultural implications. For instance, Etruscans adopted both the Greek alphabet to write their language and the deities and myths of the Greek pantheon, although they rendered the names of the gods in their own native language and developed Etruscan iconographies to depict the myths.

Ancient (non-Etruscan) authors cite the importance of ritual to Etruscan city foundation. Priests took auspices and analyzed bird flight, lightning, and animal entrails to determine the location and founding date of new settlements (Plutarch, *Life of Romulus*: 11.1; Varro, *On the Latin Language*: 5, 143). Although the accounts of these Roman writers may reflect their desires to root Roman traditions of their day in (then) ancient Etruscan practices, divinatory aids, such as a bronze model of a liver found in Placentia (Piacenza), demonstrate the Etruscans' close association between different deities, the heavens, and augural practice and their implications for terrestrial apportioning.

The plans of the earliest Etruscan towns appear haphazard in comparison with the regular Greek colonies (Izzet, 2007: 165–207). The earliest Iron Age settlements at Acquarossa, San Giovenale, and Marzabotto consisted of round or oval huts scattered (apparently) randomly (Östenberg, 1975; Berggren and Berggren, 1981; Bentz and Reusser, 2008). Gradually, buildings and settlements became more regularized. By the fifth century, Etruscan town plans had become orthogonal, akin to the grids of the Greek colonies to the south. This shift is most clearly seen in the Etruscan colony at Marzabotto founded around 500 BC in the Po Valley (Izzet, 2007: 171; Bentz and Reusser, 2008; see Figure 10.5). There, a wide street and narrower secondary roads run rigidly north to south. They are bisected by three broad streets to create long, narrow city blocks. The houses, built on rectangular plans, take their orientation from this framework. On the terraced hill overlooking the north-west section of town stood two temples, two podia to support altars, a well and, perhaps, an *auguraculum*, the site from which a priest would take the auspices (described in Bentz and Reusser, 2008: 58–62, with bibliography). A second large temple, dedicated to the god Tinia, the Etruscan equivalent to Jupiter, has been identified in the northern section of town. No civic structures have been conclusively excavated in the town itself. Perhaps they were located in the south-west sector, which has been eroded by the flow of the Reno river (Gros and Torelli, 2010: 50). Or perhaps areas within Marzabotto that intentionally were left empty functioned as public space (Izzet, 2007: 179–81, comparing similar lacunae at Veii (Veio) recognized as public space by Colonna, 1986: 426). Archaeological and literary evidence suggests, at any rate, that areas analogous to *fora* or agoras were included in some Etruscan towns (Broise and Jolivet, 2004; Livy: 7.19). Marzabotto also provides evidence for zoning, or at least the commercial specialization of certain areas within the town: a communal kiln for firing pottery and bricks was located in the northern sector, a foundry for metalworking in the south. The towns of Caere (Cerveteri) and Populonia also segregated industrial production in discrete districts (Izzet 2007: 173).

The architecture of Etruscan religious sanctuaries underwent a similar transformation in the sixth century BC. Etruria's earliest ritual sites focused on natural features of the landscape (groves, springs, lakes) and lacked any associated architecture (Edlund, 1987). Although these sites continued in use, they were joined in the late sixth century by sanctuaries whose buildings included a temple, altar(s), subsidiary structures, and votive deposits. These ensembles were enclosed by walls and located at a key site within the city or on a significant boundary (for example, the borders of a town's territory) (Colonna, 1985: 23–27). Various cultural changes may underlie this development. The formalized sanctuaries may respond to the complexifying social (and urban) situation (Colonna, 1986); they may have provided venues where developing Etruscan communities could compete with each other and project a particular identity (Rendeli, 1990); they may have assisted in defining the

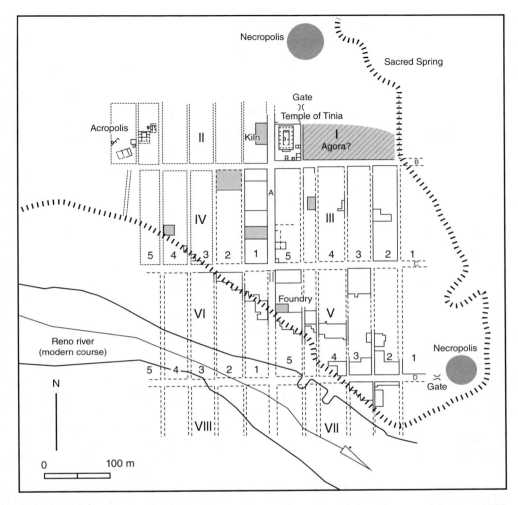

Figure 10.5 Plan of the Etruscan colony at Marzabotto. Adapted from Bentz and Reusser, 2008: abb. 12.

boundaries of a town's territory (Zifferero, 1995); or, they may reflect a growing desire to fix ritual in a new, spatially defined manner (Izzet, 2007).

In these precincts, the Etruscans built distinctive temples whose architecture and decoration differs from the Greek temples in Magna Graecia (Izzet, 2007: 130–41; Boëthius, 1978: 35–64; Vitruvius, *On Architecture*: 4.7; see Figure 10.6). Etruscans placed their temples on tall podia ornamented with convex and concave moldings that accentuated the structure of the buildings. A single stairway at the front of the temple led up to a porch with (generally) three *cellae* (for three individual cult statues) arranged behind. The form of the temple's columns also differed from the Greek Doric order (or any other Greek order): the unfluted shafts stood on a low base and were capped by a narrower and simpler Tuscan capital. They stood in a single or double row aligned with the chamber walls, rather than enclosing the *cella*, as did the columns of Greek peripteral temples. These features gave the building a single axis and an imposing frontality.

The decoration of Etruscan temples also differed from Greek cult buildings. Molded and painted terracotta slabs were affixed to the temple where the *cella* walls met the pitched roof,

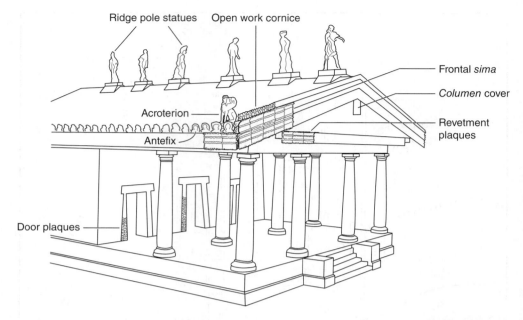

Figure 10.6 An Etruscan temple and its decorative system. Adapted from Izzet, 2007: fig. 4.3.

along the outside edge of the roof itself, and around the *cella* doors (Boëthius, 1978: 59–63; Colonna, 2006: 147–64). These brightly colored panels created bands of rhythmically repeating pattern, in contrast to the more figural (and narrative) metopes or friezes found on Greek temples. Antefixes, often molded to resemble the heads of gorgons, satyrs, and other apotropaic creatures, terminated the tiles covering the terracotta roof. Additional terracotta statues might adorn the ridgepole of the roof or the center of the pediment beneath the front gable.

In aggregate, these details distinguish the typical "Tuscan" temple from Greek varieties, although it is important to recognize significant overlaps: the presence of *cellae*, columns, *acroteria* and antefixes, as well as the primary function of the temple building, to house the cult statue (Wallace-Hadrill, 2008: 151; Coarelli, 1996: 18–20). Nonetheless, the overall impact of the Etruscan temple suggests that it met different, culturally specific needs. The repeating patterns of the terracotta plaques and their placement at significant boundaries (eaves, doors) suggest a desire to demarcate clearly the edges between the temple space and the ritual zone in front of it (Izzet, 2007: 130–41). Furthermore, these buildings' insistent frontality and axiality may have responded to (and facilitated) the directionality of Etruscan rituals of divination and augury (Coarelli, 1996: 20).

10.4 Early Latium and Rome: Between Etruria and Greece

A specifically Latin material culture, called Villanovan for its type-site, emerged in the tenth century BC in Rome and in surrounding communities like Praeneste (Palestrina) and Gabii (C. Smith 2000; Cornell, 1995: ch. 2). By the eighth century BC, settlements of round, thatched-roof huts appear in Latium. At Fidenae, north of Rome, archaeologists discovered holes cut into the bedrock that supported vertical posts (Holloway, 1994: 51–52; Bietti Sestieri, de Grossi Mazzorin, and De Santis, 1990). The spaces between were filled with clay (although at other sites builders used wattle and daub). Thin poles acted as rafters to support a sloped roof. A single door was protected by a small, covered porch. Similar remains of a slightly earlier date have been found on the southern Palatine in Rome, at Lavinium (Pratica di Mare), Satricum (Le Ferriere) and, perhaps, at Gabii (the former three sites summarized with bibliography by Holloway 1994, ch. 4; for Gabii, see Mogetta and Becker, 2014: 176). Urns buried with Latin elites help reconstruct the appearance of these simple structures.

Paralleling developments in Etruria, the eighth and seventh centuries BC saw an increase in prosperity, population, and urbanization throughout Latium. These developments are documented earliest in Rome where, by the late eighth century, a fortification wall and gate bounded the settlement on the Palatine hill. The first paving of the Forum dates shortly thereafter (Carafa, 2000). As Rome began to expand its control in the region through the seventh and sixth centuries BC, other Latin towns like Ficana, Fidenae, Praeneste, and Cora (Cori), responded by fortifying their communities and solidifying their urban plans (Fischer-Hansen, 1981; Quilici Gigli, 1990: 155–56; Gatti, 2011; Palombi, 2001). At the same time, Latin communities began to monumentalize their intramural and extramural sanctuaries. Beginning in the mid-sixth century, 13 large altars were constructed in the sanctuary outside Lavinium, south of Rome (Castagnoli, 1974; Holloway 1994, ch. 10). Carved out of blocks of local volcanic *tufo*, their design is characteristically Latin: a U-shaped base with a rounded torus molding topped by a flat slab for offerings. In Roman myth, Lavinium was founded by Aeneas and was the home of the *Penates*, household gods brought from Troy, which were worshiped throughout Latium. The 13 altars were the locus for shared rituals by members of the so-called Latin League, a grouping of towns unified first loosely by cultural affinities and shared rights, later formally by their alliance

Figure 10.7 A Villanovan miniature hut urn from the Iron Age cemetery at Osteria dell'Osa, eighth century BC. Drawing: M. Laird after Bietti Sestieri, 1992: fig. 4.6.

against Rome's hegemony in the region (differentiated nicely by Cornell, 1989). The slight variations between the altars' dates of construction and decoration suggest that each was used by a separate community. Shared ritual celebrations at Lavinium and at other pan-Latin sanctuaries on the Alban Mount and at Tusculum, Aricia (Ariccia), and even at Rome, recognized and reinforced the continuities between Latin peoples. In addition, sanctuaries near the coast became important trade emporia. Later, in the fifth century BC, they became meeting places for a politicized Latin League and sites of resistance against Rome (Cornell, 1989: 264–74).

By the end of the sixth century, monumental temples analogous to those found in Greek and Etruscan towns dignified other Latin centers such as Rome, Lanuvium (Lanuvio), and Ardea. At Satricum, near Latium's border with Campania, several phases of temple construction demonstrate the ways in which Latins navigated Etruscan and Greek architectural styles. Around 540–530 BC, Satricum's inhabitants constructed a shrine dedicated to Mater Matuta on the settlement's acropolis, long a sacred area (Holloway, 1994: 142–55; de Waele, 1997). A covered, rectangular building known by scholars as the *oikos* (Greek for "house," used here to describe a sacred building) stood in front of, and perpendicular to, a second structure, called the *sacellum* (shrine). As with Rome's Sant'Omobono temple, one of these buildings (probably the *sacellum*) was richly decorated with architectural terracottas. The roof is called by scholars the "Etrusco-Ionian roof" or "Roof 2" (Winter, 2009: 398–400, 558–59; Knoop, 1987: 13–71). Antefixes in the shape of female heads and a frieze of horsemen adorned the roof and pediment. Statues representing deities of Greek origin – Herakles accompanied by his divine champion, Athena – probably stood on the ridgepole (see Figure 10.8). The terracotta plaques resemble examples from the Etruscan town of Caere, suggesting they were imported, whilst the sculptural group closely parallels similar statues that adorned temples at Veii, Rome, and, perhaps, Caere and Pyrgi (Lulof, 1997: 88–90).

Figure 10.8   The roof system of the Etrusco-Ionian roof (Roof 2) from Satricum, circa 540 BC. Lulof, 1997: fig. 1, by permission of the author.

The precise nature of Etruscan influence in the region is controversial. Literary evidence indicates that the Romans themselves viewed key rituals and religious practices, such as augury, divinization, and the triumph, as Etruscan in origin (for Etruscan origins of the triumph, see, e.g., Versnel, 1970, questioned by Beard, 2007). Livy describes two of Rome's final three kings as Etruscan immigrants, leading scholars to postulate direct Etruscan control of the city at the end of the Regal period (Livy: 1.34, 1.46; Cristofani, 1990). Other scholars view Etruscan influence as the effect of close ties between Latian elites and the Etrurian nobles who may have lived among them (Cornell, 1995: esp. ch. 6).

Archaeological and textual evidence, however, clearly demonstrates that Etruscan crafts-men and their wares had infiltrated Latium in the sixth century. Literary accounts place Etruscan artisans and workmen in Rome (Livy: 1.56.1; Pliny the Elder, *Natural History*: 35.157). Stamped terracotta plaques made around 530 BC to decorate several buildings in Rome (among them the *Regia*, the temple at S. Omobono, and temples on the Palatine and Capitoline hills) appear to have been made in the same mold as examples found in the Etruscan town of Velitrae (Velletri). Both may have been created in the Etruscan town of Veii (Winter, 2009: ch. 5 and 555–56). The links between Etruscan and archaic Latin temple architecture and decoration suggests that patrons favored "a few highly skilled artists whose work was distributed by others or by themselves throughout the region" (Smith, 2000: 28, speaking of Rome but applicable to Latium more broadly). At Satricum, although the deities depicted were Greek and the visual style and, perhaps, workmanship was Etruscan, the statues must have borne local symbolism; Patricia Lulof (1997) postulates that they might have likened Satricum's leaders to the man-turned-god, Herakles.

Latium did not look solely to Etruria, however. Bronze and clay statuettes and vessels, some inspired by Greek models, others actual imports, are included in votive deposits at many Latin sites beginning in the eighth century (overviews of this material in Sommella Mura, 1990 for Rome; Gilotta, 1990 and Coen, 1990 for Lavinium; Zaccagni, 1990 for Gabii). If ethnic Greeks did not leave these gifts, they provide evidence that Latins were directly trading with Magna Graecia or indirectly acquiring Greek objects via the Etruscans. By the early fifth century, literary testimony indicates the presence of Greek painters and sculptors working in Rome itself (Pliny the Elder, *Natural History*: 35.154; Coarelli, 1996: 34–37). Indeed, many scholars have identified Rome as the node through which Greek architectural and sculptural styles filtered into Latium and beyond, presuming that as Italy became more Hellenized it also became more "Roman" (e.g., Zevi, 1990: 151; Salmon, 1982: 100, cited and challenged by Wallace-Hadrill, 2008: 98). While Rome in the sixth and fifth centuries was the most powerful city in the region (and growing), it was not nec-essarily a cultural clearinghouse. To a certain degree, this characterization reflects the emphasis on urban excavation at Rome (as opposed to the exploration of extra-urban necropoleis and sanctuaries of Latium's sites). But it is also rooted in an assumption that Rome, which came to dominate the Mediterranean by the end of the Republic, must have led in all things in all periods.

We find an important counter example on the acropolis at Satricum. In the late sixth and early fifth centuries the *oikos* and *sacellum* were replaced twice: first by a pseudo-peripteral temple, then by a fully peripteral temple that owes much to Greek architectural styles (de Waele, 1997 for the construction dates and bibliography). The latest temple (built circa 510) was richly dec-orated with sculptures. In fabric and placement they followed Etrusco-Italic conventions but their subject matter and sculptural style were fully Greek. Antefixes depicted a variety of figures drawn from Greek mythology. Plaques in the pediment depicted an amazonomachy, whilst six near-life-size groups located on the ridge of the roof represented a battle between Greek gods and giants. This is the only monumental example of such a theme found in Italy in this period. These terracottas represent an early example of a sophisticated new decorative system and their exquisite workmanship suggests that they may have been the product of a provincial

Greek atelier (Lulof, 2010; 1997: 94–101). Did the style originate in Rome, or, as Lulof (2010) intimates, could it have arisen in an Etruscan (or, I wonder, Latian) center? Although the evidence is elusive (and contested), it is important to note that the Temple to Iuppiter Optimus Maximus, dedicated on Rome's Capitoline Hill in 509 BC, resolutely hewed to an Etrusco-Italic plan and elevation and featured sculptures that may have been imported from Veii (Stamper, 2005: 6–33; Winter, 2009: 556; Pliny the Elder, *Natural History*: 35, 157–59).

10.5   Geographical Diversity

Thus far, this chapter has concentrated on how architecture can express cultural individuality, concentrating on three discrete groups (Etruscans, Greeks, and Latins) all living on the western side of the Italian peninsula. In many ways, the cultural overlaps of these three peoples were furthered by the geography of the region. Along the coast, the Tyrrhenian Sea and its coastal lowlands facilitated transportation and communication, while the favorable climate and rolling, fertile landscape encouraged agriculture and population growth (Torelli, 1995: 3–7) (see Figure 10.1). This, in turn, led to economic expansion that promoted the early development of urbanized towns and vigorous trade and exchange of ideas.

In contrast, the mountainous spine of central Italy and the foothills of the Apennines restricted agricultural production to valley floors. Animal husbandry was more common in these areas and communication was limited. Different settlement patterns characterize these areas in the pre-Roman period (Torelli, 1995: 9–12). In inland Samnium, for instance, where settlements consisted of smaller villages, elites focused their resources on monumentalizing large, extra-urban sanctuary complexes. By the second century BC, the largest of these, at Pietrabbondante, included two large temples and a theater, all reflecting Hellenistic architectural influences (La Regina, 1976; Patterson, 1991). In Umbria, the small villages and hilltop forts of the Bronze and Iron Ages had evolved into closely spaced nucleated settlements, as at Amelia (Ameria). Although these towns were contained within fortification walls (perhaps inspired by the nearby towns of Etruria and Roman colonies such as Cosa), their civic centers remained relatively undeveloped (Bradley, 2000: 29–102).

While the Romans considered the size and sophistication of cities to be one index of "civilization," we should not conclude that Umbrians and Samnites were "less civilized" or that these peoples lacked an "urban mentality." Andrew Wallace-Hadrill postulates that the Samnites consciously rejected the highly urbanized Roman model perhaps as a means of expressing Samnite ethnic identity (Wallace-Hadrill, 2008: 104–05). Guy Bradley argues that the lack of urban embellishment in Umbrian towns is a marker of a culturally specific state system that had begun developing in the Iron Age. And, while Umbrians may not have prized large-scale urban projects prior to the second century BC, this does not mean that they were oblivious to the significance of urban spaces. The Iguvine Tables, religious texts inscribed in the Umbrian language found in the town of Iguvium (Gubbio), prescribe that specific rituals must be conducted in specific parts of the town, such as the forum and the gates. Here, the built environment and ritual interdepend and combine to express a collective community identity (Bradley, 2000: 42–83).

10.6   Republican Italy: Rome, Colonies and Allied Towns

Beginning in the fourth century, Rome expanded into Italy, Magna Graecia, and Sicily before finally conquering Greece and the eastern Mediterranean by the end of the Republican period. This period of growth saw new patterns of architecture and urbanism emerge both in Rome and throughout Italy. This section briefly surveys some of the important changes in Rome before turning to examine developments on the peninsula in more detail.

10.6.1   Rome "Hellenizes"

As Greek works of art arrived in Rome as spoils of war and as Romans saw at first hand the monumental cities of the Hellenistic east, Roman art and architecture assumed a more Hellenized appearance as Romans appropriated Greek forms and practices. For instance, conquering generals adopted the Hellenistic practice of dedicating temples to gods who had brought them victory on the battlefield. Built with the spoils of their campaigns, many of these votive temples stood along the triumphal route in Rome (Ziółkowski, 1992). Gradually, these buildings began to incorporate Greek elements, first by using blocks spoliated from already existing Greek buildings, then by importing new structures made of Greek marble designed by Greek architects (Livy: 42.3; Cornell, 2000: 48). One of the latest of these votive buildings, a round temple dedicated perhaps to Hercules Victor in the *Forum Boarium*, provides an example of the degree to which Hellenic architecture permeated. Constructed from Pentelic (Greek) marble, the fully peripteral temple sits on a Greek-style stylobate and uses the Corinthian order. These temples, and a new type of building, the basilica, brought Hellenistic urban sensibilities to the the heart of Roman political, civic, and religious life. In plan, basilicas derive from Greek models. Initially these long, covered, colonnaded halls may have provided impressive spaces in which to receive and entertain foreign embassies. Later they primarily accommodated commerce and legal proceedings (Welch, 2003). Their columned fronts gave the Forum a regular border reminiscent of Greek agoras and temple precincts surrounded by colonnaded stoas.

Scholars of an earlier generation tended to view the absorption of Greek forms as evidence that the Romans lacked creativity. But the Romans did not unthinkingly copy Greek art and architecture. Rather, they carefully selected particular elements for their capacity to express power and prestige at a time of increasing competition at home and abroad (Cornell, 2000: 57 n. 39, citing Weinstock, 1957). As Rome's authority in the Mediterranean grew, its leaders recognized the need to project a more impressive urban image that conveyed the city's international status. The opulent marble architecture of the Hellenistic kings set the standard (Favro, 1996: 55–78). As rivalries between Rome's elites intensified, architecture became a tool for competitive display. Victory temples were named for their triumphant dedicators and permanently commemorated their success. Likewise, basilicas, though built with public money, bore the family names of the censors who were responsible for their construction – Porcia, Fulvia/Aemilia, and Sempronia. It is important to note, as well, that many architectural forms, such as the basilica, and triumphal arches (which also were first built in the early second century BC), were distinctly Roman inventions that combined indigenous and Greek forms (Welch, 2003; De Maria, 1988; Kleiner, 1985). Indeed, Roman art and architecture might accurately be categorized as Etrusco-Hellenic. At any rate, Rome's indebtedness to these cultures has troubled modern scholars more than it did the Romans, who saw their art and architecture as the "modern practice of ancient art," the extension (and perfection) of Greek and Etruscan traditions (Marvin, 2008: 179).

One of the most important sites for playing out the competition of the later Republic was in the Forum, which, more than a mere civic center, had become a repository for collective identity (see Figure 10.9). Its architecture reflected the political system of the Republic and indexed the city's history in built form (Favro, 1988: 17–18). The *curia* (meeting hall for the

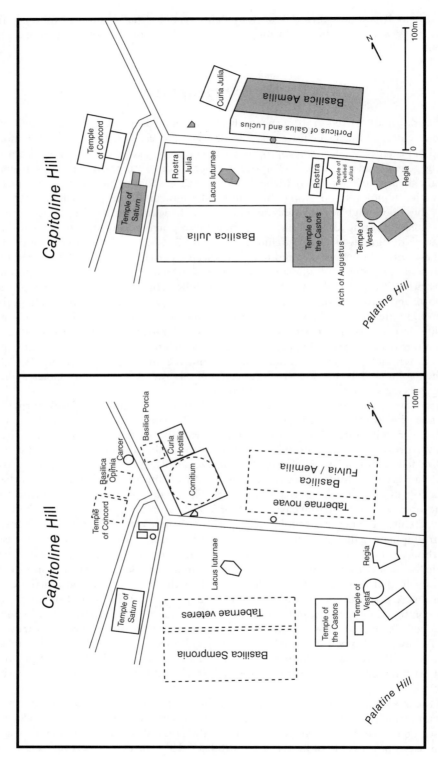

Figure 10.9 The Roman Forum circa 100 BC (left) and circa AD 10 (right). Buildings indicated with a dashed line are conjectural. Buildings shown in grey are Republican structures that survived into the Augustan period. Plan: M. Laird.

senate), the *comitium* (a circular site for popular assembly) and the *rostra* (speaker's platform) dominated the north-west end of the square. Temples around the Forum, like that dedicated to the gods Castor and Pollux to celebrate their aid in the battle at Lake Regillus in 496 BC, celebrated key Roman victories. Artistic commissions, such as the sculpted frieze in the *Basilica Aemilia* (*Paulli*), related stories of the city's early (mytho-) history. Above the Forum on the Capitoline hill stood the imposing temple dedicated to Iuppiter Optimus Maximus, Juno, and Minerva, the three primary deities of the Roman state. Because of these multiple layers of meaning, the forum became a prestigious location in which to dedicate victory monuments and honorific statues of individual Romans. These commemorated a man's heroism and merit and served as vehicles of political promotion (Pliny the Elder, *Natural History*: 34.30; Stewart, 2003: 86–91, 129–30; Lahusen, 1983).

10.6.2 *Republican Italy: direct and indirect Romanization*

The same period saw changes throughout Italy. By the early Principate, a recognizably Roman material culture emerged from the many disparate cultural and geographical styles and practices. This transition resulted both from deliberate policies on the part of Rome and from less intentional processes of acculturation. Following Wallace-Hadrill, it is helpful to divide these transformations into direct and indirect forms of Romanization (Wallace-Hadrill, 2008: 78–143). As Rome moved to integrate parts of Italy into the Roman state, construction became a deliberate tool. Land confiscation and redistribution reorganized rural space and divided the countryside with physical features like roads, walls, or boundary markers (Gargola, 1995: esp. ch. 4). Roads and colonies, which will be more fully explored in the following section, literally built Roman political and social practices onto the landscape. Simultaneously, this infrastructure facilitated the indirect acculturation of the surrounding allied towns. Although Rome's policy of governing by alliance prior to 90 BC left many indigenous communities locally autonomous, nonetheless the architecture and urban design of these towns changed as communities integrated Roman and Hellenic urban forms with traditional building techniques to project local identities.

10.6.3 *Roads and colonies*

Coincident with expansion, the Romans constructed a network of roads that emanated from the capital and spread throughout the peninsula and beyond (see Figure 10.1). Their surfaces were paved with compacted gravel or, in high traffic areas, hard stone surfaces (van Tilberg, 2007). Many of these thoroughfares bore the name of the censors who conceived and financed them, and, like urban building projects, functioned as a commemorative monument (Kissel, 2002; Laurence, 1999). The symbolic value of these highways should not be underestimated. Some, like the *via Appia*, projected straight from the capital, imposing order on the ground. Others, like the *via Aemilia*, crossed difficult terrain, signalling Rome's technological command over the countryside (Purcell, 1990; Laurence, 1999; Witcher, 1998; Zanker, 2000).

On a more strategic level, roads allowed troops and materials to move quickly from place to place. They gave the inhabitants of the towns along their routes greater access to the capital, while sidelining those in communities they bypassed. This marginalization could be intentional: the *via Appia*, for instance, constructed in the late fourth century BC to connect

Rome with allied towns in Campania, was routed to avoid the hostile inland communities along the pre-existing *via Latina*. But elsewhere, the outcomes were inadvertent: indigenous Messapian centers along the southern stretch of the *via Appia* and the *via Minucia Traiana*, for instance, survived longer (and even flourished), in contrast to those on less traveled roads (Laurence, 1999; Yntema, 2006: 106; Burgers, 1998). Roads also facilitated the spread of Roman-style goods and practices. Prior to the construction of the *via Annia*, the inhabitants of the Venetic town of Altinum (Altino) had buried their dead in two extramural necropoleis to the north and the west of the city. After the Roman road was routed through the center of town, a third necropolis was developed along the sides of the thoroughfare. Although this cemetery did not replace the traditional burial sites, it provided an alternative that was explicitly associated with the Roman road. Perhaps tellingly, the tombs in this necropolis were constructed in a new, Roman style (Gambacurta, 1999). Altinans who chose to erect tombs in the *via Annia* necropolis may have done so to project their participation in a changed cultural community (*pace* Zanker, 2000: 31).

Colonies were another component of "direct" Romanization. These settlements were founded by Rome at strategic sites, often along consular roads, to control the surrounding territory. Many first functioned as garrisons or as provisioning points and were visible reminders of Rome's military presence. Some colonies were founded *ex novo*. Cosa, founded in 273 BC in the territory of the conquered Etruscan city of Veii, was sited high on a hill overlooking the Mediterranean, from which it could control the Etruscan ports and the activities of the growing Carthaginian fleet (Brown, 1980) (cf. Fentress and Perkins, ch. 19, this vol.). Other colonies were inserted into pre-existing indigenous settlements. At Poseidonia, the Roman forum replaced the Greco-Lucanian agora (Pedley, 1990: 11–28; Torelli, 1999: 46–49, 65–88). Likewise, the colony of Brundisium (Brindisi) in Apulia probably replaced a walled town belonging to the indigenous Calabri (Yntema, 2006: 95). Still other colonies were founded on the sites of Roman military camps, as at Luna (Luni) and Albintimiglium in Liguria (Gambaro, 1999).

Colonies expressed continuities with Rome through cultural practices. Many colonists were Roman citizens or Latins, who might join or be joined by remnants of indigenous peoples (as at Paestum and Falerii Novi, respectively) or who moved to the colony to enjoy its social and economic benefits (as at Brundisium) (Yntema, 2006). Although these communities were usually self-governing, they were subject to Roman law. Colonists brought traditional Roman or Italic cults and their rituals with them. The urban environments of colonies reinforced these connections. Consular roads ran through the center of many colonies, linking them physically and conceptually to the capital (Laurence, 1999; Zanker, 2000). Furthermore, colonies were endowed with an array of identifiably Roman buildings and spaces that accommodated Roman institutions (Sewell, 2010).

This is dramatically illustrated at Poseidonia, which, after its absorption by the Lucanians who renamed it Paestum, became a Roman colony in 273 BC (see Figure 10.10). Following the colonists' arrival, several important buildings of the Greco-Lucanian town were decommissioned, including the *ekklesiasterion* and, significantly, the heröon. The southern corner of the agora and the northern edge of the sanctuary of Hera were transformed into a Roman-style forum whose buildings fulfilled primarily economic and political needs (Torelli, 1988; 1999; Greco and Theodorescu, 1983a; Pedley, 1990: 114–23). In sharp contrast to the Greco-Lucanian agora, the colonial forum was smaller, rectangular, and oriented east to west. As at the colonies of Cosa and Alba Fucens, rows of shops, built to a standard plan, bounded the public square. On the north side, a rectangular complex combined a *comitium* with an adjoining *curia*. Similar structures, which provided space for Roman political processes, appear in other early colonies such as Cosa, Alba Longa, and Fregellae. Each adapts the orientation and form of the *comitium* and *curia* found in the Forum at Rome.

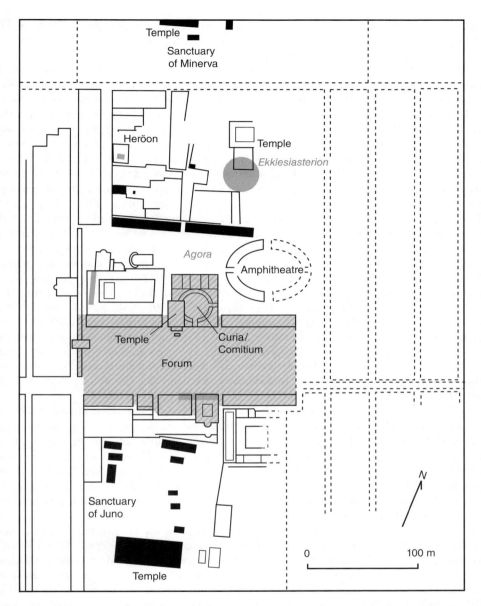

Figure 10.10 Paestum, plan of the forum and surrounding areas after 273 BC. Destroyed Greek buildings are shown in grey. Greek buildings which were reused are shown in black. Adapted from Sewell, 2010: fig. 13, and Greco and Theodorescu, 1983a: fig. 3.

Paestum's forum may include another reminder of Rome's topography. To the east of the *curia/comitium*, a small, rectangular structure may have served as a jail (*carcer*) or, perhaps, a treasury (*aerarium*). Still other buildings recalling the architecture of the capital were added in later periods. Along the northern flank an Italic podium temple was built into the *curia/comitium* with, perhaps, a structure on which to display texts of laws. Several rows of pits used in some way for voting were dug into the forum itself (Sewell, 2010: 44–47, 58–80 for the debate about the function of the pits; Torelli, 1999: 48). Along the southern edge a basilica and *macellum* (meat market) were constructed.

Colonies like Paestum, however, were not mere *simulacra* of the capital; Roman urban planners did not simply replicate Rome in miniature (*pace* Aulus Gellius, *Attic Nights*: 16.13.8–9 and Brown, 1980; *contra*, see Fentress, 2000). We see differences on many levels: Paestum's regular grid contrasts with Rome's organic, winding streets. Unlike the Roman Forum, Paestum's central space had no temples at its foundation, and notably lacked a *Capitolium*. Moreover, several of Paestum's most "typically Roman" features – notably, the *comitium/curia* and the enigmatic pits – diverge in plan and construction technique from their prototypes in Rome and from versions found in other colonies (Sewell, 2010: 67–81). It is clear, too, that colonies were free to adopt and adapt cults that particularly resonated in their community (Beard, North, and Price, 1998: 331–34; Stek, 2009: 21–28). At Paestum, the colonists rededicated the large sanctuaries to the north and south to Roman versions of their original deities: Minerva (to whom were added Jupiter and Liber) in the north, and Juno and Apollo Medicus in the south. Uniquely Roman gods were worshiped at the new Italic temples and shrines in and around the forum: *Bona Mens* (Good Mind) in the temple built into the *comitium*, *Fortuna Virilis/Venus Verticordia* in a sacred precinct and pool behind the north-western row of shops; and the town's *Lares*, or protective spirits, in a shrine on the western side (Torelli, 1999: 52–79; 1988: 52–81). Finally, it is important to note that the changes wrought by the colonists at Paestum (and elsewhere) unfolded over several generations (Crawford, 2006). Only in the second half of the second century BC was a basilica added to the forum (Torelli, 1999: 83–85). Over time, this "urban furniture" illustrated and staged Rome's distinctive political and ritual aspects, creating an urban image, or mental impression, of a distinctly Roman place (Laurence, 1999: 11–26, 148–61; Zanker, 2000).

While colonies projected a Roman identity, they were also, in part, products of the late Republican Hellenistic *koine*. Details of siting, plan, and the design of individual buildings suggest that Roman urban planners integrated elements of Greek city design, whether they hired Greek architects or consulted Greek architectural manuals. Settlements like Cosa and Alba Fucens were sited to exploit the strategic advantage of the terrain. Streets were laid out according to an orthogonal (Hippodamian) plan, with *fora* located at the intersection of the main streets leading from the gates. Even certain fortification designs find their origins in Greek practices (Sewell, 2010).

Recent analysis has even suggested that colony design could be adapted to incorporate certain indigenous (non-Roman) features. Falerii Novi, constructed to replace Falerii Veteres after the defeat of the Faliscans in 241 BC, was planned as an orthogonal grid whose principal east–west street runs parallel to a stream to the south. A temple, perhaps a *Capitolium*, occupies a rise to the west (see Figure 10.11). These features, plus details such as the division of the *insulae* (city blocks), adhere to standard colonial design. Several irregular features, however, may deliberately replicate or recall key attributes of the town that it replaced. The fortification walls of Falerii Novi were monumentalized by intentionally quarrying away the cliff on which they sat, perhaps to resemble the topography of the site of Falerii Veteres and the dramatic approach it created. The D-shaped circuit of the walls likewise may echo (not copy) the shape of the destroyed town and incorporate a group of religious sanctuaries, while a series of terraces in the south-east sector of the city may emulate the terracing of a Faliscan sanctuary at Falerii Veteres (Millett, 2007). Although this evidence is equivocal, it complicates our understanding of the Roman planned town as an explicit expression of Roman identity. In Falerii Novi, did the Romans purposely "recreat[e] aspects of the traditional cultural identity, even of a defeated people"? (Millett, 2007: 73).

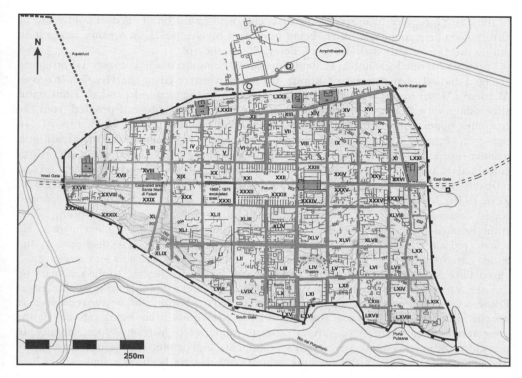

Figure 10.11 Plan of Falerii Novi. Millett 2007: fig. 3, by permission of the author and *Journal of Roman Archaeology.*

10.6.4 Allied towns and self-Romanization

Roman colonies shared the peninsula with communities of Italic *socii* and non-allied towns. Although the allied communities had certain obligations to Rome (for instance, they had to provide troops to the army), their social and political structures remained intact. Moreover, there is no evidence for systematic intervention in the planning or architecture of the towns themselves, even after the *Lex Iulia* of 90 BC and the *Lex Plautia Papiria* of 89 BC granted citizenship broadly (cf. Bispham, ch. 4, this volume). Rather, local identities remained strong throughout the peninsula and the material effects of Roman hegemony varied greatly from region to region or even from town to town. This situation created a patchwork that Nicola Terrenato characterizes as a "bricolage," meaning that "each community combined Roman and local elements on an *ad hoc* basis, depending on their particular situation and their reactions to Roman culture" (Terrenato, 1998a: 25).

Some communities embraced Roman architectural forms, particularly in the later Republican period. Urbanization was particularly intense in Latium and Campania, less so in other regions, like Samnium, where efforts continued to concentrate on rural sanctuaries (Patterson, 1991: 151). Inscriptions and literary testimonia provide evidence for the underwriters of civic works. Communities might use public funds (for example, to construct the Forum Baths at Pompeii) (Castrén, 1975: 87–88). Some Roman magistrates commissioned and paid for works, primarily to solidify ties of clientship in regions or towns of particular interest to them (Patterson, 1991; Bandelli, 1999: 291). More frequently, the underwriters of these projects were members of the local elite who might be obliged to contribute by virtue of holding municipal office, being motivated by civic pride, or seeking recognition during their life or after their death (cf. Berry, ch. 15, this vol.).

The works of one local noble, L. Betilienus Varus, demonstrates how these civic programs engaged and adapted patterns of Roman urbanism. Varus lived in the Hernican town of Aletrium (Alatri) in the second century BC. Aletrium had gained independent Latin status after siding with Rome during a rebellion in 362 BC and its elite had profited from the economic opportunities brought by Roman expansion (Wallace-Hadrill, 2008: 116–21). In the second century, the town's monumental fortification walls, constructed in the traditional manner using polygonal "Cyclopean" masonry, were renovated. Subsequently, Varus embarked on an extensive urban commission that is described on an honorific inscription that probably stood in the town's forum (*CIL* 10. 5807=*CIL* 1².1529 = *ILS* 5348 = *ILLRP* 528; Zevi, 1976). Varus's works touched nearly all of the town's public and religious spaces and added canonically Roman elements of urban furniture. In and around the forum, Varus commissioned a sundial and seating, plastered the basilica, and built a meat market. He engineered an aqueduct to bring water up into the town, laid pipes to distribute it, and added cisterns at the town's bath and near one of the gates. He built a field for exercising and paved all of Aletrium's streets. Finally, he constructed a portico leading to the sanctuary on the *arx*. Varus seems to have been aware of architectural and technological developments at Rome, where basilicas had recently been constructed on the Forum and pressurized aqueduct systems, like those of the *aqua Marcia* and the *aqua Tepula*, were being refined. At the same time, certain features of Varus's program emphasized Aletrium's local identity. In particular, the portico to the *arx* created a monumental entry to the town's most sacred spot. The contemporary style of this building, whose remains have been excavated, would have contrasted deliberately with the Cyclopean masonry of the citadel's retaining walls, the new validating the traditional.

At Aletrium and at other towns throughout Italy, projects of urban renewal layered Graeco-Roman structures onto the pre-existing urban fabric. In some ways, the expansion of Rome and, particularly, the process of municipalization following the Social War, necessitated new architectural forms that suited shifting political and social patterns (Crawford, 1996: 424). A desire to construct administrative spaces in emulation of actual Roman architecture and practices, however, should not be seen as the only factor motivating these changes. By prioritizing political, social, religious, and cultural institutions in the city center, traditional power structures coalesced in a process akin to "crystallization" (Morley, 2008: 129). Thus cities became sites for competition, and urbanization a means of control. Urbanization, then, was not motivated by a specific desire to be Roman, but rather to express power relations in a Roman way. Just as elites at Rome adopted a Graeco-Roman architecture to express their position, elites throughout Italy used their commissions to signal their participation in this common culture (Wallace-Hadrill, 2008: 100–01).

10.6.5   Survival of traditional spaces

While the urbanistic boom changed the faces of many communities in Latium and Campania, there were areas of continuity, particularly in regards to indigenous cult sites and cult practices. For instance, bronze *simpula* (ladels) continued to be dedicated in the sanctuary at Lagole di Calalzo in the Veneto into the imperial period, although the god to whom they were given was now the Roman Apollo, rather than the Venetic deity, *Trumusijatei*. The Roman divinity had been assimilated to (or had replaced) the native (Adam, 2000: 53–54).

Figure 10.12   Praeneste, view of the Sanctuary of Fortuna Primigenia. Late first century BC. Scala/Art Resource, NY.

Some traditional cult sites not only survived but were expanded. In the late second century BC, the sanctuary of Fortuna Primigenia at Praeneste was monumentalized (Fasolo and Gullini, 1953: 441–48; Coarelli, 1989; Wallace-Hadrill, 2008: 111–16; cf. Schultz, ch. 3, this vol.; see Figure 10.12). The sanctuary was extended across a series of axially oriented terraces cut into a steep hillside overlooking the town. Colonnaded ramps and passages orchestrated a worshiper's passage upwards to a circular *tholos* at the apex. The scenographic design and use of Greek architectural elements ties the sanctuary at Praeneste (and similar projects in other Latin towns like Gabii and Tibur (Tivoli)) to developments in the Hellenistic east. However, the concrete faced with *opus incertum* used to realize the complex was a recent Latin-Campanian invention, a new building technique exploited by the sanctuary's designers (Hanson, 1959; Torelli, 1995). At the same time, the expansion of the sanctuary made a positive statement of Praenestine identity, in pointed opposition to the situation at Rome. The construction was financed by a group of local elites, whose collaborative efforts directly contrasted with the competitive building by individuals at Rome. Moreover, the sanctuary surpassed contemporary structures in Rome in both design and scale. Praeneste was only one of many communities in Latium and throughout Italy to monumentalize local cult sites in this period, indicating the power of these sites to express "local religiosity and local pride" (Wallace-Hadrill, 2008: 115).

Not all traditional sanctuaries survived, however. At about the same time as the Praenestines were elaborating their sanctuary, many traditional cult sites in the Salento region of Apulia were abandoned. These sanctuaries had played an important role in promoting tribal cohesion in the pre-Roman period. As social structures shifted, their traditional functions were no longer necessary (Yntema, 2006). The traditional rural sanctuaries in central Italy, such as Pietrabbondante in Samnium, also had been religious, political and social centers for the pre-Roman tribes (Stek, 2009, ch. 3). Following the Social War, activity at these sites declined for a variety of reasons (ransacking, suppression, a shift towards urbanization, the impact of Roman presence) (Stek, 2009).

10.7   Rome in the Principate

The processes of urbanization and the development of a distinctly Roman visual and architectural language that intensified during the late Republic culminated in the early first century AD under Augustus. To understand this shift, it is necessary to return to Rome. By the second century BC, Rome was the undisputed capital of the Hellenistic Mediterranean (Smith, 2002: 89). The city's plan, amenities, and monuments, however, did not reflect its status as a world capital (Haselberger, 2007: 40–69; Favro, 1996). Rome's streets radiated in an organic tangle from the Forum; an agglomeration of small victory temples, basilicas, and civic structures were arranged haphazardly along the triumphal route and the *Forum Romanum*. Until the middle of the first century BC, Rome even lacked baths and permanent stone theaters and amphitheaters common in Hellenized Italic cities like Pompeii and Puteoli (Wallace-Hadrill, 2008: 99–100). This contrast exposed Rome to derision by its rivals (Livy: 40.5; Favro, 1996: 42).

Competition through monument building intensified in the first century BC, reflecting the disintegration of Rome's republican system (Favro, 1996: 55–78). Generals like Sulla, Pompey, and Caesar rebuilt some of the city's most salient structures: the temple of Jupiter on the Capitoline Hill, the *Curia*, and the *Basilica Sempronia*, which Julius Caesar replaced with the *Basilica Julia*, named for his family (Dio Cassius 44.5; Favro, 1996: 63). Most dramatically, Caesar began work on a new forum immediately to the north of the *Forum Romanum*. The marble porticoes on each side of the precinct created a forecourt for a temple dedicated to Venus in her role as the mythological founder of the Julian family. Although the complex ostensibly was constructed to accommodate business and legal proceedings that had expanded beyond the capacity of the *Forum Romanum*, Caesar's new forum evoked the architectural projects of the Hellenistic kings and justified a single man's position as the head of the state.

Like his political successors, Augustus used architecture and art to express his role as political leader. Although Augustus relied on the traditional built language of power, the message it expressed had changed dramatically (Zanker, 1988). Augustus's programmatic interventions, relying on Hellenic architectural forms realized in glistening native Luna marble, formalized an urban image of the city as center of the empire overseen by the *princeps* (Favro, 1996). Works included the restoration of key sacred and civic structures and the construction of new urban spaces, such as the Forum of Augustus, a third civic space in the city. Like Sulla and Julius Caesar, Augustus paid particular attention to the *Forum Romanum* (Favro, 1996: 196–201; Zanker, 1988: 79–82) (see Figure 10.9). A new basilica and a portico reoriented the central Forum, creating a strong east–west axis contained within a series of colonnaded facades (Stambaugh, 1988: 59–62). Access points were reduced and sited to choreograph a visitor's experience of the space: the ensemble of gleaming, new buildings united by style and imagery no longer celebrated the prominent families of the Republic but the new order brought by Augustus and his family. The changes also marginalized significant buildings of the Republic. The *Curia Julia*, tucked behind the *Basilica Aemilia* (*Paulli*), no longer extended into the center of the square, and the Temple of Vesta and the *Regia* were now hidden behind the tall podium of a temple dedicated to deified Julius Caesar (Favro, 1996: 198–99). Augustus's comprehensive overhaul set the agenda for subsequent emperors, for whom building projects became a means to legitimize their rules (see, for example, Darwall-Smith, 1996 [Flavians]; Boatwright, 1987 [Hadrian]; Holloway, 2004 [Constantine]; and the essays in Ewald and Noreña, eds, 2010).

10.8   Urban Change in Augustan Italy

Around 7 BC, Augustus reorganized the Italian peninsula into 11 regions, codifying the juridical reality brought by the *lex Julia* and the *lex Roscia* (Pliny, *Natural History*: 3.46; Gros and Torelli, 2010: 243) (see Figure 6.1). Augustus's policy of renewal in Rome was extended throughout Italy and included the revitalization of traditional urban centers (as at Veii and Caere), the foundation of colonies (as at Augusta Taurinorum (Turin) and Augusta Praetoria (Aosta)) and the conferring of colonial status on favored towns. This imperial interest in the welfare of Italy combined with developments in art and architecture in the capital created a wave of building activity. The results were more monumental and included a more consistent ensemble of public buildings than seen in the Republic (Gros and Torelli, 2010: 247). Whereas urban embellishment in the late Republic had concentrated in certain regions, under Augustus and the Julio-Claudian emperors it expanded across the entire Italian peninsula, tending to be especially vigorous in Augustan or triumviral colonies and in administrative centers (Patterson, 1991: 151–52). Even in highly urbanized areas, like Campania and Magna Graecia, where there were few structures still to add, elites repaired existing structures or added Roman-style leisure buildings like baths and amphitheaters (Lomas, 1993: 168; Zanker, 2000).

These building programs orchestrated an arriving visitor's visual experience and introduced the city as "Roman" through a compounding series of canonical structures and monuments (Laurence, 1999; Dyson, 1992). The narrative began outside, where honorific arches were constructed before the city gates. Some, like that at Ariminum (Rimini), were built by the Roman Senate to commemorate Augustus's repair of the *via Flaminia* (De Maria 1988; see Figure 10.13). City walls and gates, too, were the focus of attention. At Saepinum (Sepino), the imperial family underwrote the construction of a fortification wall whose gates bore images of captured barbarians (Zanker, 2000: 32). At the Augustan colony of Verona, magistrates commissioned architecturally complex marble gates to cover the late-Republican brick and limestone portals to the city (Mangani *et al.*, 1993: 172–75; Laurence, 1999: 43–45).

Once past these gates, the main road generally led directly to the forum. Many of these central civic spaces were expanded and codified in the early Principate. Improvements at Iulium Carnicum (Zuglio), which became a *municipium* or colony in the Augustan period, include the enlargement of the square and the construction of a temple and a basilica. The latter structure was one of 15 basilicas that were constructed in Italy during the Julio-Claudian period; a number of basilicas appended small rooms in which to display imperial statues, a sign of growing emperor worship (Gros and Torelli, 2010: 249; Nünnerich-Asmus, 1994). At Tarracina (Terracina), a member of the local elite paved the forum and added a temple dedicated to Roma and Augustus (during his lifetime) (Coppola, 1984; *CIL* 10.6305; Coarelli, 1993: 314–19). At about the same time, Tarracina's Etrusco-Italic *Capitolium* was faced with marble relief panels whose garlands recall those of the Altar of Augustan Peace

Figure 10.13 Arch commemorating Augustus's repair of the *via Flaminia*, outside Ariminum, circa 27 BC. Alinari / Art Resource, NY.

(*Ara Pacis Augustae*) in Rome (Coarelli, 1993: 314). In Tarracina, we can see the various ways in which developments in the capital were expressed on a local level. The style and imagery of the *Capitolium* reliefs show a receptivity to the visual forms of the *pax Romana*, while the temple of Roma and Augustus, an expression of imperial cult, emulates the form, siting, and rhetoric of the temple to deified Julius Caesar in the *Forum Romanum* (Hänlein-Schäffer, 1985). Following Augustus's death and deification, imperial cult temples became increasingly common features of civic *fora* (found, for instance, at Ostia and Pompeii). Buildings for entertainment and leisure, such as theaters, amphitheaters and baths, were also important elements of civic ensembles (Zanker, 2000: 37). Theaters dating to the Augustan or Julio- Claudian period were constructed in towns as diverse as Ostia, Parma, and Lupiae (Lecce) (Cooley, 1999; Catarsi, 2007; D'Andria, 1999).

The canonical forms assumed by building types and, to some extent, their standardized locations within towns helped to define communities visually as participants in the system of empire. At the same time, these structures were sites where local and imperial power overlapped. Building programs, even those that paralleled developments at Rome, were still a potent way for a town's elites to express their authority on a local level. *Fora* provided buildings for municipal government and sites for tax collection. Basilicas included tribunals for local magistrates alongside shrines for emperor worship. Imperial portraits shared space with honorific images of local notables. Seating in theaters and amphitheaters, which was segregated according to social status, physically reiterated a town's internal organization. As spectators observed where they fitted into a community, they might also find themselves confronted with statues of emperors and their family members who occupied the niches in the scenery building (Hingley, 2005: 81; Gros and Torelli, 2010: 249; Parker, 1999; Fuchs, 1987; see Figure 10.14).

The preceding description characterizes the urban and architectural development of the early Principate as a monolithic, one-size-fits all movement that created identical communities. Indeed, a great degree of outward standardization is undeniable. Perhaps its roots may be found in a new sense of pan-Italian identity or result from demographic shifts occasioned by settling veterans following the civil wars (Crawford, 1996: 431–33). It is important, however, to recognize that there was no centrally mandated programme and that the system was flexible enough to permit diversity, particularly on a local level. Individuals and groups could adapt standard urban and architectural forms to meet the needs of their particular communities. Two examples demonstrate this malleability.

An inscription from Caere dating to the early second century AD records how a certain Vesbinus, freedman of Trajan, petitioned the town council for space in a corner of the *Basilica Sulpiciana* in order to build a meeting place for the town's *Augustales* (*CIL* 11.3614 = *ILS* 5918a). Before granting this request, the decurions wrote to the regional official (the *curator rei publicae*) for final approval. In their letter, the council described how the meeting hall would embellish an unused spot in the basilica and enhance the town's status. The magistrate agreed and the council voted to assign the space to Vesbinus, whose hall was dedicated on 1 August, AD 114. Vesbinus's project, which redefined the use of public civic space, was seen as a positive initiative that would, perhaps, spur other similar projects. Locating the *Augustales* within the

Figure 10.14 Portraits of the imperial household at Caere, first century AD. From left to right: Deified Augustus, Deified Livia, Tiberius in the guise of Jupiter. © Vanni Archive/Art Resource, NY.

basilica affirmed their integration into the social fabric of the town. Additionally, it gave them a place where, through meetings, they could assert their status as a discrete community.

The visual language of the imperial cult, too, could be adapted to suit local needs. Family galleries of imperial statues commissioned by individuals or groups were a unifying feature of many towns. These reflected current ideological trends, particularly dynastic succession (Rose, 1997; Boschung, 2002). At Ocriculum (Otricoli), for instance, a group of statues assembled between the late Tiberian and Claudian period included a heroically nude statue of deified Augustus, two togate youths (probably Gaius and Lucius or Britannicus and Nero), draped portraits of Livia and Drusilla, and an over-life-size bust of Claudius (Dareggi, 1982). Local elites were also honored with family galleries that celebrated their civic positions. At Rusellae (Roselle), six marble statues of members of the Bassus family were found in an apsidal brick building on the northern side of the forum. Togate portraits of Bassus and his grandfather stood in niches opposite Bassus's father, Maximus and, probably, Bassus's wife. The image of Bassus's son, Valerianus, occupied the back apse, and a portrait of his daughter, Priscilla, stood slightly to the side. The statue of Valerianus is particularly interesting (see Figure 10.15). The

Figure 10.15 Marble portrait of Valerianus, from the Basilica of the Bassus family at Rusellae. Late first century AD. With the kind permission of the Soprintendenza per i Beni Archeologici della Toscana.

youth's pose – seated and nude save for a mantel around his lap – is derived from the cult statue of Jupiter Capitolinus. The sculptural type was also used to depict emperors (compare the statue of Tiberius as Jupiter from the theater at Caere, Figure 10.14). The family grouping, which closely paralleled imperial portrait cycles, expressed the same message: "the imperial dynasty governed Rome, just as the family of Valerianus did at Roselle, though on a smaller scale" (Liverani, 1994: 170).

10.8.1 Survival of indigenous culture

Terrenato's archaeological survey of the Etrucan town of Volaterrae (Etruscan Velathri, now Volterra) and its territory reveals how a veneer of common urban forms can exist over (and obscure, at least from our eyes) the survival of traditional ways (Terrenato 1998b). By the late first century BC, Volaterrae appeared highly Romanized: Latin predominated on funerary inscriptions, Roman magistrates ran the town, and Latin cults existed alongside their Etruscan counterparts. Under Augustus, the town received colonial status, and a theatre and *porticus post scaenam* were constructed by the Caecina family, members of the traditional Etruscan aristocracy. Outwardly, the situation at Volaterrae appears to parallel that in other communities like Rusellae and Aletrium, where local elites were instrumental in spreading Roman practices and the buildings to accommodate them. Looking beyond the city and its public architecture, however, there is evidence for continuity, particularly among the indigenous elites, the same group credited as "Romanizers." Elaborately carved alabaster cinerary urns, a typical feature of wealthy Etruscan burials in the pre-Roman period, continued to be used into the Principate. Archaeological survey of the territory of Volaterrae has revealed extremely stable settlement patterns: the same sites were occupied into the Late Roman period, with the same types of farmsteads producing the same crops. Terrenato argues that this stability may demonstrate the persistence of "rural areas where Etruscan traditional social order was still the norm in late Roman times" that reflects "widespread [Etruscan] perceptions of how the landscape should be organized, underpinned by deep religious beliefs" (Terrenato, 1998b: 112).

10.9 Conclusion

Terrenato's finds in the countryside surrounding Volaterrae raise several interrelated points relating to the particular nature of material evidence. The first is that, to a great degree, the recognizably Roman architectural forms and styles that united the Italian peninsula from the late Republic into Late Antiquity are deeply enmeshed in patterns of urbanism. Typically Roman buildings, like amphitheaters or temples, or typical monuments, like arches, even typical behaviors, like civic benefaction, were found almost exclusively in ancient towns. Yet towns have garnered a disproportionate amount of archaeological attention. The second point has to do with the nature of the evidence itself. At most sites, urban or rural, a basilica or a *Capitolium* are much easier to uncover and identify than a farmstead or a makeshift shrine: such evanescent remains demand sophisticated and sensitive excavation techniques. As a consequence of these two issues it becomes difficult – but not impossible – to recognize patterns of continued cultural diversity in the imperial period. We are on much firmer footing, however, in earlier periods. The material record demonstrates that Greeks, Latins, Etruscans, Samnites, Hirpini, Gauls, Romans, and others created built environments that suited their particular needs. But they did not create these spaces in a vacuum. Even the earliest archae-ological evidence demonstrates cultural interchange and negotiation between native and foreign forms.

In examining these interchanges and negotiations, this chapter has focused particularly on periods of cultural tension or change, first as Rome expanded into Latium, then beyond the Italian peninsula, and finally as the empire transitioned from a Republic into the Principate. It has, however, largely ignored the architecture of Late Antiquity, a period of profound social, cultural, and religious transformation (these are addressed by Christie, ch. 8, this vol.). This omission is not accidental. By Late Antiquity, the definition of "diversity" used in this chapter (meaning "the cultural, religious, and political differences between various groups, tribes or ethnicities") no longer applies. By the second century AD, patrons across Italy used a consistent "Roman" architecture to express power relation-ships, suggesting (outwardly) that they shared a common culture – they had "become Roman." This held true into Late Antiquity, when even Gothic emperors portrayed themselves as Roman nobles and commissioned Roman-style buildings. Built forms no longer distinguished cultural groups and their practices but the practices of different communities within Roman society. The most obvious example is found in the new community of Christians. Bishops became benefactors but focused their energies on their congregations (rather than on their towns, as elites did during the empire). The congre-gation gathered inside a basilica, a secular Roman building whose proportions and axiality were well suited to the requirements of Christian ritual. Now a sacred space, the basilica's walls circumscribed the Christian community in both life and death. Distinctly Roman patterns of architecture became the raw materials for a new diversity contained by Roman culture itself.

FURTHER READING

The most comprehensive study of Roman urbanism is that of Gros and Torelli 2010. Vitruvius's work, *On architecture*, provides a first-century AD Roman view of their architecture. Modern accounts of the development of Etruscan and early Roman and imperial architecture are those of Boëthius 1978 and Ward-Perkins 1992, respectively. Chapters in the *Cambridge Ancient History* volumes VII.2, VIII, X, and XI provide helpful overviews of the archaeology of the various periods considered in this essay. Among the many works covering diversity, Romanization and its theoretical problems, especially thought – provoking are those of Woolf 1998 and Wallace-Hadrill 2008 (the latter with a thorough bibliography). A number of volumes of the *Journal of Roman Archaeology Supplementary Series* also take the issue as their subjects (e.g. Fentress, ed. 2000; van Dommelen and Terrenato, eds. 2007; Sewell 2010). Izzet 2007 emphasizes the role of cultural identity in the production of Etruscan architecture and civic space. Much of the archaeology of early Italy and Etruria is published in Italian. For syntheses in English, see Cornell 1995; Holloway 1994. Essays in Cristofani, ed. 1990 are also important. The excavations at Poseidonia/Paestum are published in a series by that name (e.g. Greco and Theodorescu 1983b). Pedley 1990 summarizes the findings in English. The typology and chronology of Italian architectural terracottas up to 510 BC are exhaustively examined by Winter 2009. A volume on later examples is in preparation by an international team. Until its publications, see the published proceedings of the *Deliciae Fictiles* conferences. The issue of Hellenization in the republican period is addressed in the proceedings of the conference *Hellenismus in Mittelitalien* (e.g. Zevi 1976). On the Romans' complicated relationship to Greek art, architecture, and culture (and the historiography of the problem), see Marvin 2008. Zanker 1988 is still essential for material culture's central role in the age of Augustus. Favro 1996 focuses on the architecture of Rome in the same period. Studies on the material culture of the regions examined in this chapter include those of Gambaro 1999 (Liguria); Cresci Marrone and Tirelli, eds. 1999 (the Veneto); Terrenato 1998b (Etruria); Bradley 2000 (Umbria). Italy's many archaeological sites are presented by region in the *Guide archeologiche Laterza* (e.g. Greco 2002; Coarelli 1993;

Mangani *et al.* 1993). An invaluable starting point for research on specific sites is Zenon DAI (http://opac.dainst.org/), an online database of archaeological publications catalogued by the Deutsches Archäologisches Institut.

REFERENCES

Adam, A.-M. 2000. "Survivances Vénètes et Celtiques et Romanisation des cultes dans le nord-est de l'Italie." In *Les cultes polythéistes dans l'Adriatique romaine*, eds C. Delplace and F. Tassaux, 53–64. Bordeaux: Ausonius.

Bandelli, G. 1999. "Roma e la *Venetia* orientale dalla guerra gallica (225–222 a.C.) alla guerra sociale (91–87 a.C.)." In *Vigilia di romanizzazione. Altino e il Veneto orientale tra II e I sec a.C. Atti del Convegno, Venezia, S. Sebastiano, 2–3 dicembre 1997*, eds G. Cresci Marrone and M. Tirelli, 285–301. Studi e Ricerche sulla Gallia Cisalpina, 11. Rome: Quasar.

Barker, G. and T. Rasmussen. 1998. *The Etruscans.* Oxford: Blackwell.

Beard, M. 2007. *The Roman Triumph.* Cambridge, MA: Belknap Press.

Beard, M., North, J., and Price, S. 1998. *Religions of Rome.* Vol. 1. *A History.* Cambridge: Cambridge University Press.

Bentz, M. and C. Reusser. 2008. *Marzabotto: Planstadt der Etrusker.* Mainz am Rhein: Philipp von Zabern.

Berggren, E. and K. Berggren. 1981. *San Giovenale: Excavations in Area B, 1957–1960.* Stockholm: P. Åströms / Skrifter utgivna av Svenska institutet i Rom 4.26: II, 2.

Bietti Sestieri, A. M., Grossi Mazzorin J. de, and De Santis, A. 1990. "Fidenae: La struttura dell'età del ferro." *Archeologia Laziale* 10: 115–120.

Boatwright, M.T. 1987. *Hadrian and the City of Rome.* Princeton, NJ: Princeton University Press.

Boëthius, A. 1978. *Etruscan and Early Roman Architecture.* Revised by R. Ling and T. Rasmussen. Harmondsworth: Penguin Books.

Bonfante G. and Bonfante L. 2002. (rev. edn). *The Etruscan Language. An introduction.* Manchester: Manchester University Press.

Bonfante, L. 1990. *Reading the Past: Etruscan.* London: British Museum.

Boschung, D. 2002. Gens Augusta. *Untersuchungen zu Aufstellung, Wirkung und Bedeutung der Statuengruppen des julisch-claudischen Kaiserhauses.* Mainz am Rhein: Philipp von Zabern.

Bourdieu, P. 1977. *Outline of a Theory of Practice.* Cambridge: Cambridge University Press.

Bradley, G. 2000. *Ancient Umbria. State, culture and identity in Central Italy from the Iron Age to the Augustan Era.* Oxford: Oxford University Press.

Broise, H. and Jolivet, V. 2004. "Un habitat fortifié étrusque d'époque hellénistique: le cas de Musarna." In *Des Ibères aux Vénètes*, eds S. Agusta-Boularot and X. Lafon, 31–37. Rome: École française de Rome.

Brown, F.E. 1980. *Cosa: the making of a Roman town.* Ann Arbor: University of Michigan Press.

Burgers, G.-J.L.M. 1998. *Constructing Messapian Landscapes: settlement dynamics, social organization and culture contact in the margins of Graeco-Roman Italy.* Amsterdam: Gieben.

Büsing, H. 1978. "Battos." In *Thiasos: sieben archäologische Arbeiten*, ed. T. Lorenz, 51–79. Amsterdam: Castrum Peregrini Presse.

Carafa, P. 2000. "I contesti archeologici dell'età Romulea e della prima età regia." In *Roma: Romolo, Remo e la fondazione della città*, eds A. Carandini and R. Cappelli, 68–73. Milan: Electa.

Castagnoli, F., ed. 1974. *Lavinium II: Le tredici are.* Rome: De Luca.

Castrén, P. 1975. Ordo Populusque Pompeianus. *Polity and Society in Roman Pompeii.* Rome: Bardi.

Catarsi, M. 2007. "Parma e Fidenza: due città a confronto." In *Forme e tempi dell'urbanizzazione nella Cisalpina (II secolo a.C.-I secolo d.C.)*, ed. L.B. Taborelli, 97–101. Florence: All'Insegna dell Giglio.

Cerchiai, L., Jannelli, L., and Longo, F. 2004. *The Greek Cities of Magna Graecia and Sicily.* Los Angeles: Paul Getty Museum.

Coarelli, F. 1989. "Il santuario della Fortuna Primigenia: struttura architettonica e funzionicultuali." In *Urbanistica ed architettura dell'antica Praeneste. Atti del convegno di studi archeologici, Palestrina 16–17 aprile 1988*, 115–35. Palestrina: Comune di Palestrina.

Coarelli, F. 1993. *Lazio*. (3rd edn). Rome and Bari: Laterza.

Coarelli, F. 1996. Revixit Ars: *Arte e ideologia a Roma. Dai modelli ellenistici alla tradizione repubblicana*. Rome: Quasar.

Coen, Alessandra. 1990. "Ceramica d'importazione greca." In *La Grande Roma dei Tarqini*, ed. M. Cristofani, 188–190. Rome: «L'Erma» di Bretschneider.

Colonna, G., ed. 1985. *Santuari d'Etruria*. Milan: Electa.

Colonna, G. 1986. "Urbanistica e architettura." In *Rasenna: storia e civiltà degli Etruschi*, ed. G. Pugliese Carratelli, 371–530. Milan: Libri Scheiwiller.

Colonna, G. 2006. "Sacred Architecture." In *The Religion of the Etruscans*, eds N.T. de Grummond and E. Simon, 132–168. Austin, TX: University of Austin Press.

Cooley, A.E. 1999. "A new date for Agrippa's theatre at Ostia." *Papers of the British School at Rome* 67: 173–82.

Coppola, M.R. 1984. "Il foro emiliano di Terracina: rilievo, analisi technica, vicende storiche del monumento." *Mélanges de l'Ecole Française de Rome, Antiquité* 96: 325–77.

Cornell, T.J. 1989. "Rome and Latium to 390 BC"; "The recovery of Rome"; "The conquest of Italy." In *The Cambridge Ancient History*. Vol. 7.2. *The rise of Rome to 220 BC*, 2nd edn, eds F.W. Walbank *et al.*, 243–419. Cambridge: Cambridge University Press.

Cornell, T.J. 1995. *The beginnings of Rome: Italy and Rome from the Bronze Age to the Punic Wars (c. 1000–264 BC)*. London: Routledge.

Cornell, T.J. 2000. "The city of Rome in the middle Republic (400–100 BC)." In *Ancien Rome. The archaeology of the eternal city*, eds J. Coulston and H. Dodge, 42–60. Oxford: Oxford University School of Archaeology.

Crawford, M.H. 1996. "Italy and Rome from Sulla to Augustus." in *The Cambridge Ancient History*, Vol. 10. *The Augustan Empire 43 BC – AD 69*, 2nd edn, eds A.K. Bowman, E. Champlin, and A. Lintott, 414–33. Cambridge: Cambridge University Press.

Crawford, M.H. 2006. "From Poseidonia to Paestum via the Lucanians." In *Greek and Roman Colonization: origins, ideologies and interactions*. eds G. Bradley and J.-P. Wilson, 59–72. Swansea: Classical Press of Wales.

Cresci Marrone, G. and Tirelli, M., eds. 1999. *Vigilia di romanizzazione. Altino e il Veneto orientale tra II e I sec a.C. Atti del Convegno, Venezia, S. Sebastiano, 2–3 dicembre 1997*. Studi e Ricerche sulla Gallia Cisalpina, 11. Rome: Quasar.

Cristofani, M., ed. 1990. *La grande Roma dei Tarquini. Roma, Palazzo delle Esposizioni, 12 giugno–30 settembre 1990*. Rome: «L'Erma» di Bretschneider.

D'Andria, F., ed. 1999. *Lecce romana e il suo teatro*. Galatina and Lecce: M. Congedo.

Dareggi, G. 1982. "Il ciclo statuario della 'Basilica' di Otricoli: la fase giulio-claudia." *Bollettino d'Arte* 14: 1–36.

Darwall-Smith, R.H. 1996. *Emperors and Architecture: a study of Flavian Rome*. Brussels: Latomus.

De Maria, S. 1988. *Gli archi onorari di Roma e dell'Italia romana*, Rome: «L'Erma» di Bretschneider.

Dommelen, P.A.R. van and Terrenato, N., eds. 2007. *Articulating local cultures. Power and identity under the expanding Roman Republic*. Portsmouth, RI: *Journal of Roman Archaeology* Suppl. 63.

Dyson, S.L. 1992. *Community and Society in Roman Italy*. Baltimore: Johns Hopkins University Press.

Edlund, I.E.M. 1987. *The Gods and the Place: Location and function of sanctuaries in the countryside of Etruria and Magna Graecia (700–400 BC)*. Stockholm, Göteborg: Paul Åströms: Skrifter utgivna av Svenska institutet i Rom 4.43.

Ewald, B.C. and Noreña, C.F. eds. 2010. *The Emperor and Rome: Space, representation, and ritual. Yale Classical Studies 35*. Cambridge and New York: Cambridge University Press.

Fasolo, F. and Gullini, G. 1953. *Il santuario della Fortuna Primigenia a Palestrina*. Rome: Istituto di archeologia, Universitá di Roma.

Favro, D. 1988. "The Roman Forum and Roman Memory." *Places* 5.1: 17–24.

Favro, D. 1996. *The Urban Image of Augustan Rome*. Cambridge: Cambridge University Press.

Fentress, E. 2000. "Frank Brown, Cosa, and the idea of a Roman city." In *Romanization and the City. Creations, transformations and failures*. ed. E. Fentress, 9–24. Portsmouth, RI: *Journal of Roman Archaeology* Suppl. 38.

Fiorentini, G., ed. 1990. *Gli edifici pubblici di Agrigento antica.* Agrigento: Museo Archeologico Regionale.

Fischer-Hansen, T. 1981. "Fortificazioni nel Lazio e a Ficana nell'età del ferro." In *Ficana: una pietra miliare sulla strada per Roma. Mostra itinerante degli scavi italo nordici a Ficana (Acilia), 1975–1980,* 59–65. Rome: Viella.

Frederiksen, M. 1979. "The Etruscans in Campania." In *Italy Before the Romans,* ed. D. Ridgway and F. Ridgway, 277–311. London: Academic Press.

Fuchs, M. 1987. *Untersuchungen zur Ausstattung römischer Theater in Italien und den Westprovinzen des Imperium Romanum.* Mainz am Rhein: Philipp von Zabern.

Gambacurta, G. 1999. "Acqua, città e luoghi di culto nel Veneto preromano." *Ocnus* 7: 179–186.

Gambaro, L. 1999. *La Liguria costiera tra II e I secolo a.C. Una lettura archeologica della romanizzazione.* Mantova: Documenti di Archeologia, 18/ Società Archeologica Padana S.R.L.

Gargola, D.J. 1995. *Land, Laws, and Gods: magistrates and ceremony in the regulation of public lands in Republican Rome.* Chapel Hill and London: University of North Carolina Press.

Gatti, S. 2011. "Le mura poligonali di Praeneste." *Atlante tematico di topografia antica (ATTA)* 21: 139–159.

Giddens, A. 1979. *Central Problems in Social Theory: action, structure and contradiction in human evolution.* Berkeley: University of California Press.

Giddens, A. 1984. *The Constitution of Society: outline of a theory of structuration.* Berkeley: University of California Press.

Gilotta, F. 1990. "Bronzetti a figura umana." In *La Grande Roma dei Tarqini,* ed. M. Cristofani, 187–188. Rome: «L'Erma» di Bretschneider.

Greco, E. 2002. *Archeologia della Magna Grecia.* 5th edn. Rome and Bari: Laterza.

Greco, E. and Theodorescu, D. 1983a. "Continuité et discontinuité dans l'utilisation d'un espace publique: l'exemple de Poseidonia-Paestum." In *Architecture et société de l'archaïsme grec à la fin de la République romaine. Actes du Colloque international organisé par le Centre national de la recherche scientifique et l'École française de Rome (Rome 2–4 décembre 1980),* 93–104. Rome: École française de Rome.

Greco, E. and Theodorescu, D. 1983b. *Poseidonia-Paestum II: L'Agora.* Rome: École française de Rome.

Gros, P. and Torelli. M. 2010. (2nd edn). *Storia dell'urbanistica: il mondo romano.* Rome: Laterza.

Hänlein-Schäfer, H. 1985. Veneratio Augusti: *Eine Studie zu den Tempeln der ersten römischen Kaisers.* Rome: G. Bretschneider.

Hanson, J.A. 1959. *Roman Theater Temples.* Princeton, NJ: Princeton University Press.

Haselberger, L. 2007. Urbem adornare: *die Stadt Rom und ihre Gestaltumwandlung unter Augustus/ Rome's Urban Metamorphosis under Augustus.* Portsmouth, RI: *Journal of Roman Archaeology* Suppl.64.

Hingley, R. 2005. *Globalizing Roman Culture: unity, diversity and empire.* Abingdon and New York: Routledge.

Holloway, R.R. 1994. *The Archaeology of Early Rome and Latium.* London and New York: Routledge.

Holloway, R.R. 2004. *Constantine and Rome.* New Haven and London: Yale University Press.

Izzet, V. 2007. *The Archaeology of Etruscan Society.* Cambridge: Cambridge University Press.

Keay, S. and Terrenato, N., eds. 2001. *Italy and the West. Comparative issues in Romanization.* Oxford: Oxbow.

Kissel, T. 2002. "Road-building as a *munus publicum.*" In *The Roman Army and the Economy,* ed. P. Erdkamp, 127–60. Amsterdam: Gieben.

Kleiner, F. 1985. *The Arch of Nero in Rome. A study of the Roman honorary arch before and under Nero.* Rome: «L'Erma» di Bretschneider.

Knoop, R.R. 1987. Antefixa Satricana: *Sixth century architectural terracottas from the Sanctuary of Mater Matuta at Satricum (Le Ferriere).* Assen and Maastricht: van Gorcom.

Lahusen, G. 1983. *Untersuchungen zur Ehrenstatue in Rom: literarische und epigraphische Zeugnisse.* Rome: G. Bretschneider.

Lambrechts, R. 1959. *Essai sur les magistratures des républiques étrusques.* Rome: L'Institut Historique Belge de Rome.

La Regina, A. 1976. "Il Sannio." In *Hellenismus in Mittelitalien*, ed. P. Zanker, 219–44. Göttingen: Vandenhoeck und Ruprecht.

Laurence, R. 1999. *The Roads of Roman Italy. Mobility and social change*. London: Routledge.

Liverani, P. 1994. "Il ciclo di ritratti dell'edificio absidato di Bassus a Roselle: iconografia imperiale e glorificazione familiare." *Mitteilungen des Deutschen Archäologischen Instituts, Römische Abteilung* 101: 162–73.

Lomas, K. 1993. *Rome and the Western Greeks, 350 BC–AD 200. Conquest and acculturation in south Italy*. London: Routledge.

Lulof, P.S. 1997. "Myths from Greece. The representation of power on the roofs of Satricum." *Mededelingen van het Nederlands Instituut te Rome* 56: 85–114.

Lulof, P.S. 2010. "The Late Archaic Miracle: roof decoration in central Italy between 510 and 450 BC." In Deliciae Fictiles *IV. Architectural Terracottas in Ancient Italy. Images of Gods, Monsters and Heroes. Proceedings of the International Conference held in Rome (Museo Nazionale Etrusco di Villa Giulia, Royal Netherlands Institute) and Syracuse (Museo Archeologico Regionale 'Paolo Orsi') October 21–25, 2009*, eds P. Lulof and C. Rescigno, 23–31. Oxford: Oxbow.

Mangani, E. *et al.* 1993. *Emilia Venezie*. (3rd edn). Rome and Bari: Laterza.

Marvin, M. 2008. *The Language of the Muses: The dialogue between Roman and Greek sculpture*. Los Angeles: Getty Publications.

Mertens, D. 1982. "Metaponto: Il teatro-ekklesiasterion." *Bollettino d'arte* ser. 6, 16: 1–18.

Millett, M. 1990. *The Romanization of Britain: an essay in archaeological interpretation*. Cambridge: Cambridge University Press.

Millett, M. 2007. "Urban topography and social identity in the Tiber Valley." In *Roman by Integration: dimensions of group identity in material culture and text*, eds R. Roth and J. Keller, 71–82. Portsmouth RI: *Journal of Roman Archaeology* Suppl. 69.

Mogetta, M. and Becker, J.A. 2014. "Archaeological research at Gabii, Italy: the Gabii project excavations, 2009–2011." *American Journal of Archaeology* 118: 171–81.

Morley, N. 2008. "Urbanisation and development in Italy in the Late Republic." In *People, Land, and Politics: demographic developments and the transformation of Roman Italy 300 BC–AD 14*, eds L. de Ligt and S. Northwood, 121–37. Leiden and Boston: Brill.

Nünnerich-Asmus, A. 1994. *Basilika und Portikus. Die Architektur der Säulenhallen als Ausdruck gewandelter Urbanität in später Republik und früher Kaiserzeit*. Cologne: Böhlau.

Östenberg, C.E. 1975. *Case etrusche di Aquarossa*. Rome: Multigrafica.

Palombi, D. 2001. "Intorno alla mura di Cori." In *Fortificazioni antiche in Italia. Età repubblicana*, eds L. Quilici and S. Quilici Gigli, 91–102. *Atlante Tematico di Topografia Romana*, 9. Rome: «L'Erma» di Bretschneider.

Parker, H.N. 1999. "The Observed of all Observers: spectacle, applause, and cultural poetics in the Roman theater audience." In *The Art of Ancient Spectacle*, eds B. Bergmann and C. Kondoleon, 163–79. Studies in the History of Art, 56. Washington, DC: National Gallery of Art.

Patterson, J.R. 1991. "Settlement, city and elite in Samnium and Lycia." In *City and Country in the Ancient World*, eds J.Rich and A.Wallace-Hadrill, 147–68. London: Routledge.

Pedley, J.G. 1990. *Paestum: Greeks and Romans in southern Italy*. London: Thames & Hudson.

Purcell, N. 1990. "The creation of provincial landscape: the Roman impact on Cisalpine Gaul." In *The Early Roman Empire in the West*, eds T. Blagg and M. Millett, 6–29. Oxford: Oxbow.

Quilici Gigli, S. 1990. "Fidenae." In *La Grande Roma dei Tarqini*, ed. M. Cristofani, 155–56. Rome: «L'Erma» di Bretschneider.

Rendeli, M. 1990. "Materie prime, tecniche e tipi edilizi." In *La Grande Roma dei Tarqini*, ed. M. Cristofani, 138–39. Rome: «L'Erma» di Bretschneider.

Rose, C.B. 1997. *Dynastic Commemoration and Imperial Portraiture in the Julio-Claudian Period*. Cambridge: Cambridge University Press.

Roth, R. 2007. "Introduction: Roman culture between homogeneity and integration." In *Roman by Integration: dimensions of group identity in material culture and text*, eds R. Roth and J. Keller, 7–10. Portsmouth, RI: *Journal of Roman Archaeology* Suppl. 66.

Roth, R. and Keller, J., eds. 2007. *Roman by Integration: dimensions of group identity in material culture and text*. Portsmouth, RI: *Journal of Roman Archaeology* Suppl. 66.

Salmon, E.T. 1982. *The Making of Roman Italy*. London: Thames and Hudson.

Sestieri, P.C. 1955. "Il sacello-heroon poseidoniate." *Bollettino d'arte* 40: 53–64.

Sewell, J. 2010. *The Formation of Roman Urbanism, 338–200 B.C.: Between contemporary foreign influence and Roman tradition*. Portsmouth, RI: *Journal of Roman Archaeology* Suppl. 79.

Smith, C.J. 2000. "Early and Archaic Rome." In *Ancient Rome: The archaeology of the Eternal City*, eds J. Coulston and H. Dodge, 16–41. Oxford: Oxford University School of Archaeology.

Smith, R.R.R. 2002. "Use of images: visual history and ancient history." In *Classics in Progress: essays on Ancient Greece and Rome*, ed. T.P. Wiseman, 59–102. Oxford and New York: The British Academy.

Sommella Mura, A. 1990. "Il tempio arcaico e la sua decorazione." In *La Grande Roma dei Tarqini*, ed. M. Cristofani, 115–30. Rome: «L'Erma» di Bretschneider.

Stambaugh, J.E. 1988. *The Ancient Roman City*. Baltimore: Johns Hopkins University Press.

Stamper, J.W. 2005. *The Architecture of Roman Temples: The Republic to the Middle Empire*. Cambridge: Cambridge University Press.

Stek, T.D. 2009. *Cult Places and Cultural Change in Republican Italy: a contextual approach to religious aspects of rural society after the Roman conquest*. Amsterdam: Amsterdam University Press.

Stewart, P. 2003. *Statues in Roman Society: representation and response*. Oxford and New York: Oxford University Press.

Stewart, P. 2008. *The Social History of Roman Art*. Cambridge: Cambridge University Press.

Terrenato, N. 1998a. "The Romanization of Italy: Global Acculturation or Cultural *Bricolage*?" In *TRAC 97: Proceedings of the Seventh Annual Theoretica Roman Archaeology Conference. Nottingham 1997*, eds C. Forcey, J. Hawthorne and R. Witcher, 20–27. Oxford: Oxbow Books.

Terrenato, N. 1998b. "*Tam firmum municipium*: The Romanization of Volaterrae and its cultural implications." *Journal of Roman Studies* 88: 94–114.

Tilberg, C. van. 2007. *Traffic and Congestion in the Roman Empire*. London and New York: Routledge.

Torelli, M. 1981. *Storia degli Etruschi*. Rome and Bari: Laterza.

Torelli, M. 1988. "Le popolazioni dell'Italia antica: società e forme del potere." In *Storia di Roma. I. Roma in Italia*. Turin: Giulio Einaudi.

Torelli, M. 1995. *Studies in the Romanization of Roman Italy*, ed. and trans. by H. Fracchia and M. Gualtieri. Edmonton, Alberta: University of Alberta Press.

Torelli, M. 1999. Tota Italia. *Essays in the Cultural Formation of Roman Italy*. Oxford: Clarendon Press.

Versnel, H.S. 1970. Triumphus: *An Inquiry into the Origin, Development and Meaning of the Roman Triumph*. Leiden: Brill.

Waele, J.A.K.E. de. 1997. "Cronologia ed architettura dei templi della Mater Matuta di Satricum." *Mededelingen van het Nederlands Instituut te Rome* 56: 69–84.

Wallace-Hadrill, A. 2008. *Rome's Cultural Revolution*. Cambridge: Cambridge University Press.

Ward-Perkins, J.B. 1992. *Roman Imperial Architecture*. New Haven: Yale University Press.

Weinstock, S. 1957. "Victor and Invictus." *Harvard Theological Review* 50: 211–47.

Welch, K. 2003. "A new view of the origins of the Basilica: the Atrium Regium, Graecostasis, and Roman diplomacy." *Journal of Roman Archaeology* 16: 5–34.

Wilson, J.-P. 2006. "'Ideologies' of Greek colonization." In *Greek and Roman Colonization: origins, ideologies and interactions*, eds G. Bradley and J.-P. Wilson, 25–57. Swansea: Classical Press of Wales.

Winter, N.A. 2009. *Symbols of Wealth and Power. Architectural terracotta decoration in Etruria and Central Italy, 640–510 B.C.* Rome: Memoirs of the American Academy in Rome Supplementary Series, 9.

Witcher, R. 1998. "Roman roads: phenomenological perspectives on roads in the landscape." In *TRAC 97: Proceedings of the Seventh Annual Theoretical Roman Archaeology Conference*, eds C. Forcey, H. John and R. Witcher, 60–70. Oxford: Oxbow.

Woolf, G. 1998. *Becoming Roman. The origins of provincial civilization in Gaul*. Cambridge: Cambridge University Press.

Yaeger, J. and M. A. Canuto. 2000. "Introducing an Archaeology of Communities." In *The Archaeology of Communities. A New World perspective*. eds M.A. Canuto and J. Yaeger, 1–15. London and New York: Routledge.

Yntema, D.G. 2006. "The birth of Roman Southern Italy: a case study." *Bulletin Antieke Beschaving* 81: 91–133.

Zaccagni, P. 1990. "Bronzetti votivi." In *La Grande Roma dei Tarqini*, ed. M. Cristofani, 160–63. Rome: «L'Erma» di Bretschneider.

Zancani-Montuoro, P. 1954. "Il Poseidon di Poseidonia." *Archivio storico per la Calabria e la Lucania* 23: 165–85.

Zanker, P. 1988. *The Power of Images in the Age of Augustus*, trans. A. Shapiro. Ann Arbor: The University of Michigan Press.

Zanker, P. 2000. "The city as symbol: Rome and the creation of an urban image." In *Romanisation and the City*, ed. E. Fentress, 25–41. Portsmouth, RI: *Journal of Roman Archaeology* Suppl. 38.

Zenon DAI. Deutsches Archäologisches Institut. http://opac.dainst.org/. Accessed 9/7/2011.

Zevi, F. 1976. "Alatri. " In *Hellenismus in Mittelitalien*, ed. P. Zanker, 84–96. Göttingen: Vandenhoeck and Ruprecht.

Zevi, F. 1990. "Il Lazio." In *La Grande Roma dei Tarquini*, ed. M. Cristofani, 149–51. Rome: «L'Erma» di Bretschneider.

Zifferero, A. 1995. "Economia, divinità e frontiera: sul ruolo di alcuni santuari di confine in Etruria meridionale." *Ostraka* 4: 333–50.

Ziółkowski, A. 1992. *The Temples of mid-Republican Rome and Their Historical and Topographical Context*. Rome: «L'Erma» di Bretschneider.

CHAPTER 11

Language and Literacy in Roman Italy

Kathryn Lomas

11.1 Introduction

Language is frequently accorded a privileged status in the formation and maintenance of cultural identities. Latin, in particular, came to be regarded as an important indicator of Roman culture. It was one of a number of cultural practices, the adoption of which were regarded as signs of the process sometimes termed "Romanization," as defined in a somewhat ideologically charged text, by Tacitus, in which he describes the encouragement of Roman culture in Britain. In this, he lists adoption of Latin, along with Roman dress, forms of worship, and public and private buildings, as an essential attribute of Roman culture (Tacitus, *Agricola*: 21). Adoption of Latin was, therefore, a symbol of integration with Rome and adoption of Roman culture, as well as an important tool for promoting communication throughout Italy and the empire. Italy was a multilingual region containing a number of different ethnic groups, each with its own language, and Latin came to serve as an important globalizing influence, allowing communication between people from all areas of Italy and beyond (Hingley, 2005). However, the third/second-century BC poet Ennius, who came from Rudiae in the Messapic area of Italy famously described himself as having *tria corda* ("three hearts," or possibly "three tongues") – Greek, Roman, and Oscan (Aulus Gellius, *Attic Nights*: 17.17.1). Latin co-existed with, rather than replaced, other Italian languages for quite some time after the conquest of Italy, and was not established as the universal dominant language until the late first century BC.

Many different factors influenced the ability or willingness of particular groups of people to adopt and use Latin, including social status, gender, or occupation. The context of a social interaction may also influence choice of language, with Latin preferred for some forms of interaction and different languages for others (Leiwo, 1996: 121–27; Adams, 2003a; 558–59; Häussler, 2002; Häussler and Pearce, 2007: 222–24; Wallace-Hadrill, 2008: 93–96). Latin may have become the language of officialdom and public life, for instance, while other languages may have been used in less formal situations. In a region such as ancient Italy, where many languages were in contact, bilingualism may have been the norm rather than the

A Companion to Roman Italy, First Edition. Edited by Alison E. Cooley.

exception. This chapter will explore the various factors which may have promoted the spread of Latin, and will consider the motivations for its adoption by the rest of Italy.

Two problems immediately present themselves. One is the difficulty of making inferences about language in general when our evidence is confined to written language. An examination of language change or bilingualism conducted according to the accepted linguistic methodologies requires evidence covering different types of linguistic interaction, both written and spoken. Typically, these examine the choice of language in a range of formal and informal situations, such as public business, religious ritual, schooling, interaction within families or with friends, and between people of varying statuses and relationships, such as interaction with officials, employers, employees, parents, children, friends, or acquaintances (Dorian, 1999). For Roman Italy, of course, such a comprehensive examination is impossible as our evidence is much more limited. Some ancient authors comment on linguistic matters, giving us a little information about languages and their use and development, but this adds up to a relatively small amount of evidence, and mostly concerns the use of languages in the public domain (Dubuisson, 1982). Our evidence is also biased towards the use of language amongst those of high social status. It is much more difficult to recover evidence of language choice and language use in informal interactions and more private contexts.

We cannot know much with any degree of certainty about the languages actually spoken, particularly in multilingual contexts, or about the relation between written and spoken language. It is entirely possible that some languages which disappear from the written record in the first century BC continued to be spoken long after they had ceased to be used in formal written documents of the type which survive. Equally, as Bradley observes in the context of Umbria, local notables may have commissioned inscriptions in Latin because they were prestigious, even if they spoke little Latin personally (Bradley, 2000: 203). We must remain aware, therefore, that there may be whole substrata of linguistic behavior which we cannot recover.

This emphasis on written language also means that it is impossible to study the spread of Latin in Italy without also studying the phenomenon of literacy. Given that most of our evidence for the non-Latin languages of Italy comes from inscriptions, we must also take into account the nature of epigraphic evidence. Inscriptions are, by their very nature, not just texts but also material objects, in many cases designed for display and preservation. What they say cannot be examined in isolation from the visual impact of the inscription and how it was supposed to be displayed (Corbier, 2006). Roman inscriptions were often very different in appearance from those in other languages, using a different alphabet and different epigraphic formulae and phrases. An inscription did not just signal its Roman character by its use of Latin but also by many other aspects of its appearance, by the type of inscription it was, and how and where it was intended to be displayed (MacMullen, 1982; Woolf, 1996; Corbier, 2006). Changes in epigraphic conventions, in the types of inscriptions set up, and who the intended audience may have been may all give an insight into the processes of Romanization. This chapter will discuss not only the spread of Latin in Italy and the demise of other languages, but also the changing nature of written language as a symbol of Roman culture.

11.2   Languages in Pre-Roman Italy

Italy was a multilingual region from a very early date. Our earliest evidence dates to the eighth century BC in the case of Etruria and Latium, and from the seventh/sixth centuries for many other regions. A full review of the philological evidence for the languages of Italy is outside the scope of this chapter, but it may be useful to summarize the main linguistic groups (Figure 11.1). (For a fuller discussion, see Penney, 1988; Clackson and Horrocks, 2011: 37–76). Although it may seem perverse to begin a discussion of Roman language and literacy with a description of non-Roman practices, Italy was so linguistically and culturally diverse that it is important to understand the pre-Roman situation in order to grasp fully the impact of Rome.

Etruscan, with over 13 000 surviving inscriptions, is one of the better-documented non-Latin languages. It was written and spoken not only in Etruria itself, but also in other areas of Etruscan influence and settlement such as Campania, Emilia-Romagna, the Po valley, and north-west Italy (Agostiniani, 2000; Bonfante and Bonfante, 2002: 49–63). Raetic, which is found in the area north of Verona, is similar and may be related to Etruscan: sources describe the Raeti as descendants of Etruscan migrants (Livy: 5.33.11; Pliny, *Natural History*: 3.133; Justin, *Epitome of Pompeius Trogus*: 20.5; cf. Morandi, 1999: 35–44). Etruscan is also the most controversial of the Italian languages, as it is very different from most others and may

Figure 11.1 The principal non-Latin languages of Italy. Drawing: K. Lomas.

not be of indo-european origin, a factor which touches on the problematic issue of Etruscan origins (Barker and Rasmussen, 1998: 43–84; Briquel, 2000). Whatever its origins, however, it was undeniably distinctive and also enjoyed some prestige as an elite language.

Most other languages of Italy, in contrast, belong to the indo-european linguistic family, and many are recognizably of the same linguistic family. Oscan, for instance, looks very different to Latin, but is philologically close – a roughly similar relationship to that between the Irish/Gaelic and Welsh/Cornish/Breton subgroups of Celtic languages (Clackson and Horrocks, 2011: 48–73). The most immediate neighbors of the Etruscans – the Umbrians, Faliscans, Sabines, and Praenestines – all used languages which were related to each other and to Latin, while the Picenes of the Adriatic coast had a language which seems to be related to Oscan. Most of our knowledge of the languages of southern Italy derives from the period after the Oscan migrations of the fifth century, although there is a small number of earlier inscriptions, including some in Etruscan (Lazzarini and Poccett, 2001; Rix, 1991). From this point onwards, much of central and southern Italy adopted Oscan (sometimes also called Sabellian) as the major language. Greek was dominant in some of the coastal areas, and survived alongside Oscan in some areas of Greek settlement which had been overrun by Oscans, such as Paestum and Cumae (Kaimio, 1979; Lomas, 1993: 172–85; Adams, 2003b: 143–55). The other major language spoken in southern Italy was Messapic, the language of southeast Italy. Finally, to complete this brief survey, there are two major languages in northern Italy: Venetic, which has some similarities to Latin, although also some important differences (Prosdocimi, 1990; Marinetti,1999), was spoken in an area corresponding to the modern Veneto; and a group of languages variously referred to as Lepontic, Ligurian, and Gallo-Lepontic, all of which seem to be forms of ancient Celtic, and are found in Liguria, Lombardy, Piedmont, and parts of southern Switzerland (Lejeune, 1971; Solinas, 1994).

Although linguistic maps of Italy look neatly regionalized, and books frequently associate specific languages with particular ethnic groups, linguistic and cultural boundaries were probably much more fluid than this suggests. Polybius, for instance, comments that the Veneti and the Celts shared many cultural attributes and were difficult to distinguish but for the fact that they spoke different languages (Polybius: 2.15–17). Elsewhere, however, the same language may have been shared by groups which came to perceive themselves as ethnically different. Oscan was a language shared between the Samnites, Campanians, Lucanians, and Bruttians, who regarded themselves as politically and ethnically separate from each other. Greek and Oscan and Etruscan coexisted in parts of Campania, for instance, and in parts of Puglia – principally around Teanum Apulum – the population used both Oscan and Messapic (Sanpaolo Antonacci, 2001). The relationship between language and identity in pre-Roman Italy is, therefore, much more complex than it is in some other areas of the ancient Mediterranean. Whereas for the Greeks, language was a strong marker of cultural identity (Herodotus: 5.22, 8.144.2; Harrison, 2002: 11–12; Hall, 2002: 111–17), in Italy it was much more ambiguous, and linguistic plurality and contact between language groups may have been the norm even before the Roman conquest.

This raises other important questions, such as the mutual intelligibility of these languages, the extent to which languages overlapped, and the relationship between language and ethnicity. The fact that ancient authors, particularly those such as Polybius and Cato who were writing shortly after the conquest of Italy, commented on linguistic differences suggests that Italic languages were distinctively and not mutually comprehensible. There were, however, significant areas of language contact and overlap, which suggests that awareness of (and competency in) multiple languages may not have been unusual, particularly for people living on cultural and political boundaries, or amongst members of elite groups who may have interacted across such boundaries regularly. As Adams (2003b: 1) notes, bilingualism was the norm in the ancient world.

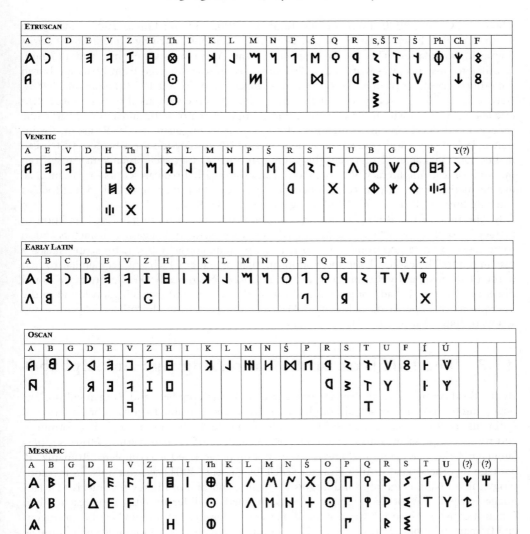

Figure 11.2 A selection of Italian alphabets: Etruscan, Venetic Early Latin, Oscan, Messapic. Prepared using Alphabetum font © Juan-José Marcos.

The same diversity is also evident when we consider literacy and its implications. The earliest inscription in Italy, dating to circa 775 BC and found in a tomb at Osteria dell'Osa near Rome, appears to be written in Greek (Ridgway, 1996). Further eighth-century Greek inscriptions, including the famous Nestor cup, were found on Ischia and at other sites of early Greek settlement (Cordano, 1984). By the seventh century, literacy was well established in Etruria, although our evidence is confined mainly to inscriptions naming the owner or giver of grave goods (Stoddart and Whitley, 1988; Bagnasco Gianni, 1996). By the sixth century, literacy had spread from areas of Greek and Etruscan settlement to most areas of Italy (Figure 11.2). The scripts used fall into two main groups. In central and northern Italy, they were based on the Etruscan alphabet, which was itself derived from Phoenician and early Greek scripts

(Bagnasco Gianni, 2000; Bonfante and Bonfante, 2002, 52–57; Lomas 2007), and in the south, they were based on Greek scripts. These two traditions of writing sometimes cut across linguistic boundaries. The Oscan language in the Apennines, Campania, and northern Lucania, for instance, was written in a distinctive Oscan script derived from Etruscan, but in a modified Greek script in areas south of this (Lejeune, 1970 and 1972; Lazzeroni, 1983). Italy was, therefore, a region of many scripts, although some were used to write more than one language. Even within these broad groups, scripts were not static and show considerable variation and development. Sometimes, this is driven by linguistic needs. Etruscan, for instance, lacked the vowel <o>, so those languages which developed scripts based on Etruscan had to add a character to represent this sound. In other cases, developments may arise from methods of teaching literacy. Venetic, Picene, and some early Etruscan scripts for instance, all use distinctive forms of punctuation between syllables which may be linked to methods of teaching literacy (Prosdocimi, 1990; Langslow, 2007: 86–91).

By the time of the Roman conquest, therefore, Italy had a well-established tradition of literacy in local scripts which had developed their own distinctive regional characters and in some cases had diverged from their "parent" script quite considerably. Latin script is itself a case in point. The earliest Latin inscriptions used an alphabet which was very similar to that of the Etruscans, but by the third century BC, it looked recognizably like the letters we would discern as Roman. It had not yet reached the level of clarity and formalization found in the inscriptions of imperial date, but it looked very different from the other Etruscan-based scripts of Italy (Wallace, 1989).

11.3   The Diffusion of the Latin Language and Alphabet

By the third century BC, the Roman conquest of Italy was complete and Roman culture was beginning to make an impact, although local cultures also remained strong. The adoption of Latin, and of Romanized epigraphic habits – Roman types of inscription, alphabet, formulae, and ways of expressing things – were important markers of Roman culture. However, new language, script, and epigraphic practices were not simply adopted as a complete "Romanized" package by other Italians. An important article by Benelli (2001) sets out a useful methodology for studying epigraphic and linguistic change, and one of his key findings is that language, scripts, and other epigraphic forms changed at different rates from each other. Linguistic "Romanization" was not just a matter of adopting Latin, but also of a more general Roman epigraphic culture, such as Romanization of names, adoption of Roman formulae and abbreviations, and use of the Roman alphabet (see Table 11.1).

The chronology of the disappearance of non-Roman languages and the spread of Latin varied considerably between regions. In Umbria, the local language remained in use throughout the second century, despite a high degree of Roman settlement and colonization in the area (Livy: 10.10.5, Summary/ *Periocha:* 15 and 20, 27.9; Velleius Paterculus: 1.14.7–8; Bradley, 2000: 128–39, 203–04). However, there are signs of increasing use of Latin and of the erosion of other aspects of Umbrian culture such as the local script. For instance, second-century BC inscriptions on a sundial found at Bevagna and a boundary stone from Assisi, both set up by local notables (Poccetti, 1979, no. 4), were inscribed in Umbrian, but the Bevagna sundial used Umbrian script and the Assisi *cippus* used the Roman alphabet. The famous Iguvine Tables, a long ritual inscription from Iguvium, were written in Umbrian language but switched from Umbrian to Latin script halfway through (Table V.b; Prosdocimi, 1984: 192–93; Bradley, 2000: 12–13, 76–78, 206). The earliest Latin inscriptions are found mainly in areas of Roman colonization, such as Narnia, Spoletium, and Ariminum, but by the early/ mid second century, Latin inscriptions are also found in Umbrian settlements such as Ameria,

Table 11.1 Changes to language, script and personal names at Chuisi, Perugia and Arezzo (after Benelli, 1994).

	Writing/language	Personal names	Onomastic forms	Epigraphic forms
Pre-100 BC	Predominantly Etruscan language Predominantly Etruscan script Small number of Latin inscriptions	Predominantly Etruscan names; some Roman or Romanized names	Predominantly Etruscan forms (name + filiation + matronymic)	Mainly Etruscan
Early first century BC	Predominantly Etruscan language Predominantly Etruscan script Small number of Latin inscriptions	Some individuals have both Roman and Etruscan name	Roman and Etruscan forms coexist, even within same families	Latin and Etruscan coexist, sometimes in same tomb
Late first century BC	Increasing numbers of Latin inscriptions Etruscan confined to limited areas	Use of Roman names increasing; Etruscan names confined mainly to Etruscan inscriptions	Greater use of Roman name-forms (*tria nomina*) Etruscan forms confined to limited areas	Roman formulae increasing, but some Etruscan forms persist, even in Roman(ized) texts
Early first century AD	Predominantly Latin	Names mainly Romanized	Name-forms mainly Romanized	Epigraphic forms mainly Romanized

and by circa 80 BC, the Umbrian language has largely disappeared from the written record (Bradley, 2000: 207–10). A similar pattern is found in northern Italy, where local languages such as Venetic and Lepontic, and the associated local alphabets, seem to die out by the early first century BC.

Etruria, in contrast, presents a rather different picture. Etruscan remained in widespread use throughout the second century BC but by the mid-first century BC Latin script was widely used, and the Etruscan language was less frequently used and concentrated into smaller geographical areas (Kaimio, 1975; Benelli, 2001). During the second and early first centuries BC, however, there were many bilingual inscriptions. The bilingual epitaph of Lucius Cafatius, probably from Pisaurum and dating to the mid-first century BC (*CIL* $1^2.2127$; Benelli, 1994: 13–15) gives prominence to the Latin inscription listing his Roman name and titles, which is inscribed in large monumental Roman capitals but it also includes the same information in Etruscan language and script, placed underneath and in much smaller letters. Another example, an epitaph on an urn shaped like a temple, from Perugia and dating circa 10–1 BC (*CIL* $1^2.2037$; Benelli 1994: 18–20) has an inscription in Latin script and language on the front of the urn (*P. Volumnius A.f. Violens Cafatia natus;* "Publius Volumnius Violens, son of Aulus, and of Cafatia"), whereas the Etruscan translation (*pup velimna au cahatial*) is placed on the top of the urn in a position where it would be much less visible. In Etruria, therefore, there seems to have been a long period of linguistic coexistence between Latin and Etruscan. Etruscan script fell into disuse in the mid-first century BC and the language eventually disappeared from the epigraphic record in circa AD 15–20 (Rix, 1991: Ar 1.8; Benelli, 1994: 15–16). The emperor Claudius was said to have been a keen scholar of Etruscan culture and learning, but by that time Etruscan seems to have been a dead language, studied mainly by people with an interest in Etruscan religious knowledge (Suetonius, *Life of Claudius*: 42).

Further south, we find an equally mixed pattern. Messapic disappeared as a written language relatively early, certainly by the middle of the first century BC and possibly as early as the late second century (de Simone and Marchesini, 2002: 6–11). Both language and alphabet disappeared fairly abruptly, and almost no bilingual inscriptions have been found here, so it is impossible to chart the process of transition with any certainty. Greek, on the other hand, persisted in some areas of Campania and southern Italy until the second/third centuries AD (Lomas, 1993: 174–85; Leiwo, 1994). Relatively few traces of Greek are found in the Greek cities of the south coast of Italy, but there are significant numbers of Greek inscriptions found at Rhegium, Velia, and Naples, some of which date to the early- and mid- empire (see Lomas, ch.12, this vol., on Naples). Ancient sources also make reference to the continuation of Greek culture and language in some areas (Strabo, *Geography*: 5.4.7, 6.1.2, 6.3.4).

The processes by which Oscan language and epigraphy disappeared are complex. By the middle of the second century BC, it was not uncommon for inscriptions – including those recording acts of state – to be written in Roman script and an increasing number of inscriptions were also written in the Latin language. Where the Oscan language continued to be used, there is evidence of the increasing influence of external influence in epigraphic practices. For example, second-century BC inscriptions from the sanctuaries at Pietrabbondante and Rossano di Vaglio were written in Oscan language and also, for the most part, in Oscan scripts, but used dedicatory formulae almost indistinguishable from those found on contemporary Roman inscriptions, despite the fact that they were set up by local dignitaries (cf. Poccetti, 1979: nos 14–16, 167; Lejeune, 1975).

A similar pattern is found at Pompeii. Second-century BC dedicatory inscriptions recording building by civic magistrates have survived, written in Oscan language and north Oscan script, but their content is very similar to that of contemporary Latin inscriptions elsewhere, suggesting a convergence between Roman and non-Roman epigraphic habits (Vetter, 1953: nos 8–20; Cooley, 2002a; see Figure 11.3). Both Oscan language and script disappear from the monumental epigraphic record after the foundation of a Roman colony at Pompeii in circa 80 BC but

Figure 11.3   Pompeii: Latin inscription commemorating the donation of a new *mensa ponderaria* (official standard of weights and measures) by the city's magistrates. Late first century BC (*CIL* 10.793). Photograph: L.H. Davies, by kind permission of the Soprintendenza Speciale per i beni Archeologici di Napoli e Pompei.

Oscan dipinti and graffiti, some of them in Oscan script, are found in contexts which may post-date the founding of the colony, suggesting that the two languages and scripts may have coexisted for a time.

Perhaps the most complex example is the *Tabula Bantina*, a bronze tablet from Bantia in Lucania which was reused, having a Latin inscription on one side and an Oscan one, written in Roman script, on the other. There is some argument over the relative dating of the inscriptions, and of the identification of the Latin inscription, but it seems fairly certain that the Oscan text is the later of the two (Crawford, 1996: 193–208, 271–92). This dates to the period immediately before the Social War, probably circa 100–90 BC, and records part of the constitution of the community, laying down regulations for the conduct of magistrates and the local town council. At one level, the use of Oscan as the official language of record at Bantia in the years before the Social War suggests that the Oscan language – but not necessarily Oscan script – was a powerful symbol of local identity and anti-Roman feeling (however, cf. Dench, 1995: 214, for an alternative view of language in the Social War), but the format and content of the document are very close to that of Latin municipal or colonial charters of the late second and first centuries BC, implying that even when official documents were written in the local language, their form was closely based on Roman models.

To sum up, there seems to be a consistent pattern of the disappearance of non-Roman alphabets and scripts in the later second century BC, a period in which we find an increasing number of inscriptions in non-Latin languages written in the Roman alphabet. This is followed by the disappearance of most Italian languages during the first century BC. The date at which this happened varies between regions, and there are two notable exceptions – Etruscan and Greek – which persist for longer, for reasons which will be discussed further later in this chapter, but by the end of the first century BC, Latin was established as the almost universal written language of Italy.

11.4   Literacy: The Uses of Writing in Ancient Italy

As well as having its own language, each region of Italy developed its own culture of literacy between the seventh and fourth centuries BC. Most early inscriptions are of a broadly ritual or funerary nature, although different areas of Italy developed their own epigraphic cultures. In Etruria, for instance, most early inscriptions are gift inscriptions or marks of ownership inscribed on items such as pottery or metal vessels, mirrors and other personal items, often found as grave goods (Stoddart and Whitley, 1988; Bagnasco Gianni, 1996). Later, epitaphs and other inscriptions on walls of tombs became popular, and more inscriptions of a legal or administrative nature are found (for a selection of inscriptions, see Bonfante and Bonfante, 2002). In the Veneto, a large number of inscriptions are found on votive offerings, whereas in Celtic areas most inscriptions are on grave goods, and in Puglia a high proportion are epitaphs incised into the fabric of a tomb (Pellegrini and Prosdocimi, 1967; Piana Agostinetti, 2004; Lomas, 2015). Both Rome and the Oscan-speaking areas, in contrast, have a higher proportion of inscriptions set up by the state, or relating to public business and administration (Crawford, 2011). At the time of the Roman conquest, therefore, literacy was well established throughout Italy, but there were significant differences in what sort of inscriptions were being set up, and what they looked like, as well as in the languages and scripts in use.

Writing was not just confined to epigraphy. Cornell (1991) has argued that at Rome and in Etruria written records and accounts were kept on perishable media such as wax tablets or papyrus scrolls, from an early date. The Romans believed that their main records of state, the *Annales Maximi*, were already established before the Gallic sack of 390 BC and the Twelve Tables, Rome's first systematic law-code was written down in 451–50 BC (Livy: 3.33–40, 6.1).

The proportion of people who were literate was, however, limited. Harris's influential study estimates that even as late as 100 BC, circa 5% or less of the male population, and an even smaller proportion of the female population, would have been literate (Harris, 1989: 323–33). Furthermore, literacy is likely to have been restricted to specific social groups. Writing implements deposited as grave goods in aristocratic tombs (e.g. a seventh-century ivory tablet from Marsiliana d'Albegna in Etruria (Rix, 1991: ET AV 9.1)) or as votive offerings in sanctuaries (e.g. the bronze votive tablets from Este in the Veneto (Marinetti, 1990: 95–142)) suggest that literacy was seen as a prestigious accomplishment and was associated with elite status. However, there is also evidence for the use of scribes to keep written records from an early date (Cornell, 1991: 25–27), and the signatures of craftsmen inscribed on items such as pottery or tiles suggests that literacy was also associated with craft production.

From the third century onwards there are a number of changes which point to both an increase in literacy and to a change in its nature. Although this was not entirely due to the influence of Rome, it may also have some connection with the impact of Rome on public life and culture. The overall number of inscriptions rose throughout all areas of Italy from this date, and increased dramatically again from the middle of the first century BC. Whilst there is always a danger that numbers of inscriptions reflect patterns of survival rather than reality, these increases are too consistent to be explained away by this, and there is other evidence that literacy was becoming more widespread and that the uses of literacy were changing.

Harris suggests that literacy rates may have risen to circa 20–30% in some areas of the Roman world during the empire (Harris, 1989: 323–33), with female literacy rates significantly lower, although these figures can only ever be a very rough estimate. The growing complexity of civic bureaucracy, private business dealings, and patterns of property ownership, as discussed below, may also have prompted a greater need for written records and therefore literacy. There is also more evidence for formal education from this date. Previously, most teaching seems to have taken place within the household (Harris, 1989: 159–60), but in the mid-third century a freedman, Carvilius, established the first school at Rome (Plutarch, *Moralia*: 278e; Harris, 1989: 158–59).

The greater complexity of state organization meant that there was an ever-increasing emphasis on the keeping of written records and archives, both in Rome and in other areas of Italy. Municipal laws and charters were inscribed for preservation or public display, and religious documents were often recorded and placed on display, as were boundary stones and other documents relating to property. After 90 BC, all Italians were subject to the Roman census, and even before this date, Italian states needed to supply Rome with manpower figures for military purposes (Polybius: 2.24–5; Brunt, 1971: 56–60). The survival of archives belonging to Caecilius Iucundus at Pompeii and two merchants from Puteoli demonstrates that private business records were kept (Andreau, 1974; Camodeca, 1999). Further archives of tablets were found in three adjacent houses at Herculaneum, recording legal cases in which the inhabitants were involved (selection in Cooley and Cooley, 2014: G1–13, H102–115). These provide striking evidence of the keeping of written records by ordinary families.

Beyond the confines of the social and economic elite, there is evidence that many craftsmen and tradesmen possessed a limited form of literacy. Signatures on manufactured objects, such as the pots signed by slaves working in a pottery at Cales in Campania (*ILLRP* 1215), and the graffiti found on many buildings at Pompeii and Herculaneum (Franklin, 1991), demonstrate that literacy levels beyond the elite were increasing by the second/first centuries BC. These examples, however, do not necessarily imply fluent literacy, and the boast by Hermeros the freedman (Petronius, *Satyricon*: 58.7) that he "knew stone letters" suggests that he could make out the words on monumental inscriptions but implies that he was not fluently literate. This raises an important point. Even for people with only a limited grasp of literacy, the presence of significant quantities of written Latin and of Roman types of inscription in the urban environment could be a powerful indicator of being ruled by Rome even for those who were only marginally literate.

We should be wary of identifying literacy as a primarily Roman cultural trait, if only because it gives a false impression that Roman culture was somehow inherently more advanced than those of the rest of Italy. In the early period of its history, Rome was certainly no more literate than any other part of Italy, and probably less so than some Etruscan cities. Nevertheless, there are some interesting connections between literacy and Romanization. The increasing need for written records which grew out of the social, economic, and cultural changes of the second century BC may have promoted the increase in the use of writing and the number of people who needed to learn to read and write. It may also have helped to promote the spread of Latin as the language of public life and official records. From the second century BC onwards, monumental inscriptions became an increasingly prominent feature of the Italian urban landscape. As well as recording civic matters such as laws and decrees, they became an important way of displaying status, recording the lives, achievements, and munificence of members of the elite. Roman styles of inscription, written in Latin and couched in Romanized language, were prestigious objects, and became a symbol of new urban and Roman identities. It is perhaps not surprising that epigraphic change was a significant element of the cultural changes following the Roman conquest. The adoption of writing in many areas of Italy has been linked with the emergence of new – or better-defined – cultural and ethnic identities in the seventh/sixth centuries BC, and early inscriptions are often clustered on boundaries (Marchesini, 1999; Cristofani, 1999; Lomas, 2007). The changes in epigraphic habit from the first century BC onwards, with new forms of inscriptions and more of them, and use of a different language and alphabet, are very much in the same tradition of using public forms of writing as a way of displaying new cultural identities.

11.5 Language, Literacy and Cultural Identities

The diffusion of Latin throughout Italy, to the point where it displaced other languages, was promoted by a number of different factors. Large-scale political change such as foundation of a colony or a grant of Roman citizenship (and in particular, the political and legal integration of Italy after 89 BC) undoubtedly provided a strong impetus for the adoption of Latin at state level, as the official language of public business in a community. The spread of Latin as a day-to-day language was, however, a more complex and diverse process. Demographic changes, such as the foundation of a colony or allocations of land to groups of people from other areas of Italy played a part in forcing different linguistic groups into contact, and may have encouraged the use of Latin as a *lingua franca*, a common language to allow different groups of inhabitants to communicate. This may have been the case, for instance, when a group of Ligurians were settled in Samnium in 180 BC (Livy: 40.38). A more extreme example may be found on Delos, where a substantial community of traders from all parts of Italy gathered and needed to communicate, although in this case Greek may also have served as a common language (Hatzfeld, 1912; Adams, 2003b: 642–82). The increased level of population mobility in the second century, with migration from countryside to towns, and from the peripheries of Italy to Rome, as well as between Italy and other parts of the empire, may all have helped to promote the value and importance of shared languages.

A further large-scale phenomenon which may have promoted the use of Latin was military service. Before 90 BC, all adult male Italians of military age were liable for military service if Rome decided to call on their community to provide troops. Men from Roman colonies or from cities with *civitas sine suffragio* would have served in the Roman army and therefore needed to acquire enough Latin to communicate. Others served in their own local units under their own officers, but since Roman armies were composed of units from many different areas of Italy, anyone who spent time on active service is likely to have needed to acquire Latin. Officers, in particular, would have needed to be able to communicate with their Roman counterparts. Since Italians were conscripted in large numbers, and for increasingly long terms of service, in the second century BC, the pool of people who were proficient in Latin is likely to have grown significantly.

So far, many of the aspects discussed, such as use of Latin in public business, trade, or military service, have been areas of activity restricted to men. This raises some interesting questions about whether language-change is a gendered process, and if so, how this affects women. It also raises the question of whether choice of language for use in a given situation is influenced by whether the situation is a public or a private one. The prevalence of male-dominated activities associated with the acquisition and use of Latin would naturally seem to suggest that women, who by definition did not serve in the army or take part in public life, may have had less opportunity to learn Latin and less need to do so. A modern parallel could be found in the language choices of Asian women in British society, whose culture may discourage female activity outside the home, and who may lack the opportunity to learn English or have less need to do so. One could, therefore, speculate that women were more likely to retain and use non-Latin languages for longer than men, and be slower to adopt Latin. Women can, however, make a very active contribution to the choice of language within a community, particularly in areas of demographic movement, colonization, or contact between different groups. Where people from different linguistic and ethnic groups have intermarried, as is often the case where a large group of male settlers arrives in an area, women play an important role in transmitting both sets of language and culture to the next generation. Studies of colonization – both Greek and Roman – have highlighted the important role of women in mixed communities in maintaining linguistic and cultural traditions within families (Hodos, 1999; Glinister, 2009).

The choice of whether to use Latin or a local language may also be dependent on context. Latin rapidly became established from the late second century BC as the language of public discourse, and as the preferred language for large public inscriptions which were intended to provide a visual display of Roman power as well as to convey information. Less formal inscriptions, intended for less public contexts, sometimes showed different choices having been made. For example, the epigraphy of north-west Italy shows some interesting trends. A large and roughly shaped stone block found near Briona, dating to the second century BC and clearly a public inscription set up by a magistrate, is inscribed in the local Celtic language and alphabet. Another example of similar date from Vercelli is bilingual, with both Lepontic and Latin language and script (Lejeune, 1988: 26–37; Häussler, 2002: 64–65; see Figure 11.4). By the late first century BC, Latin language and the Roman alphabet had supplanted Lepontic for the majority of public and monumental inscriptions. However, a cemetery from Oleggio in Piedmont, a small rural community, has produced a series of 15 Lepontic graffiti dating from the second century BC to the first century AD, and consisting of short inscriptions – mainly personal names – on fragments of pottery vessels (Gambari, 1989: 195–97; Häussler and Pearce, 2007: 221–24). These are likely to have been domestic objects or personal possessions, and they suggest that both the Celtic language and writing in the local Celtic script continued in private use long after they had been abandoned for high-status uses and public contexts.

The level of bilingualism (or perhaps more properly, multilingualism) in ancient Italy is likely to have been quite high, especially amongst the elite. Livy mentions that the brother of Fabius Rullianus, consul in 322 BC, was educated at Caere and knew "Etruscan letters" – and presumably also the Etruscan language (Livy: 9.36.3). The importance of Etruscan knowledge and tradition for some aspects of Roman religion, especially haruspicy, may also have preserved some knowledge of Etruscan and given the language a prestigious status. Ennius, as noted

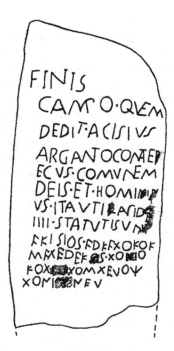

Figure 11.4 Vercelli: Bilingual inscription in Lepontic and Latin. Early first century BC. After Häussler, 2002.

above, famously spoke three languages – the two elite languages of southern Italy, Greek and Latin, and his own native Oscan. How far this persisted after the Social War is, however, a matter of conjecture. The non-Latin language of Italy may well have continued to be spoken for some time after they disappeared from the epigraphic record, but the increasing dominance of Latin in public life is likely to have increased pressure to become competent in this, and to have relegated other languages to use in less formal contexts.

There is, however, one notable exception to the dominance of Latin. Greek had always been spoken in some areas of southern Italy, and, by the second century BC, it may have been widely spoken by the Oscan population, especially amongst the elite. Many of the Italians known to have been involved in trade with the eastern Mediterranean were from southern Italy and they would have required Greek in order to function in the main trading centers such as Delos (Adams, 2003b: 9–14). By the first century BC, an ability to speak and read Greek well was established as a mark of elite culture for many Romans and Italians (Adams, 2003b: 9–14; Wallace-Hadrill, 2008: 17–35). Despite the ambivalent attitude of some Romans, acquiring Greek became part of an elite Roman education, and some knowledge of Greek culture was a valued social accomplishment. The continued use of Greek was, therefore, less of a stigma than – say – Oscan, and some of the Greek communities seem to have actively promoted their Greek language and identity as a mark of cultural status (Strabo, *Geography*: 5.4.7, 6.1.3; Lomas, chs 12–13, this vol.). What we see emerging is a situation in which Latin had become dominant in public life, but coexisted with Greek as a language of prestige, and as a *lingua franca* which enabled communication with people from the eastern part of the empire, while the other languages of Italy gradually faded from view.

There has been some debate about whether Rome actively pursued a policy of imposing or officially encouraging the use of Latin, but in most cases this seems unlikely (Dubuisson, 1982;

Adams, 2003b: 113, 289; Wallace-Hadrill, 2008: 82–85). There is some evidence that Roman magistrates sometimes insisted on using Latin in their dealings with people from elsewhere in the empire, and in particular in their dealings with Greek-speaking areas (Cicero, *On Moral Ends*: 1.9 and 5.89, *Tusculan Disputations*: 5.108, *Brutus*: 131, *On the Consular Provinces*: 15, *Against Verres* 2.4.147; Valerius Maximus: 2.2.2–3; Dubuisson, 1982. On Romans and the Greek language more generally, see Kaimio, 1979). However, there is no evidence of anything similar from Italy. Latin seems to have been adopted for official business in both Roman and Latin colonies from the point of foundation (Crawford, 2011), and is found in inscriptions recording acts of magistrates, or dedications to important cults from colonies.

In other cases, however, adoption of Latin even for the formal business of civic administration seems to have been the decision of individual communities. Cumae, for instance, successfully petitioned the senate in 188 BC to be permitted to use Latin as the official language of the city (Livy: 40.42.13). This did not mean that Oscan was abandoned as a language in daily use, but it did mean that all the public business of the city was to be conducted in Latin. It is notable that this was done on the initiative of Cumae itself, rather than because of any pressure from Rome. It is also an interesting case because Cumae had the status of *civitas sine suffragio* and had therefore held a limited form of Roman citizenship since 338 BC (Livy: 8.14). The implication – borne out by epigraphic evidence from other places with the same status – is that even communities with a form of citizenship were not required to adopt Latin. There may have been an assumption on the part of Rome that Latin would be fairly rapidly adopted for official business in communities which had gained full Roman citizenship – something which is implied by the appearance of municipal laws and charters written in Latin in the period shortly after the Social War (for instance the *Lex Tarentina*, Table of Heraklea and municipal law from Este, collected in Crawford, 1996; on the dissemination and publication of such laws and charters in Italy, see Crawford, 1996: 25–31) – but there seems to have been no direct compulsion. It would have been surprising if the legal, political and administrative integration of Italy which took place during the first century BC had not provided a strong impetus for the adoption of Latin for official business, but this does not seem to have been the result of direct Roman action.

All of these factors give some insight into why Latin became prevalent in Italy, but offer us less information about why other languages fell into disuse, and why some did so more quickly than others. The answer to this may lie in social status and the competitive nature of ancient Italian societies. By the second century, Latin had acquired growing cultural prestige as an elite *lingua franca* (Homeyer, 1957: 427–33, 437–40; Dubuisson, 1982; Woolf, 1998: 77–105). It was also closely linked to Roman citizenship, since citizens were expected to have some competence in Latin, and this may also have enhanced its prestige. For the social and political elites of Italy, Latin was an important tool as it enabled them to network with their Roman counterparts. Writing in Latin, and particularly large-scale epigraphic writing, came to be perceived as appropriate and effective as a means of elite status display. Italian societies – particularly at the elite level – were characterized by constant competition between leading men in a community for power, and for status and dominance within the peer-group. There was a consequent pressure to demonstrate their pre-eminence and social status in a wide variety of ways, and to advertise their achievements and generosity towards the community. At a regional level, there were also similar levels of competition between cities and communities for regional dominance. The growing pre-eminence of Roman culture means that by the end of the second century BC, indigenous languages, scripts, and epigraphic habits were no longer the best medium for elite status display. Symbols of Roman culture such as Latin script, Latin language, and Romanized idiom and epigraphic forms were adopted as the symbolic language in which members of the elite sought to establish their status vis-à-vis each other. As a result, there was a strong impetus for the adoption of Roman epigraphic practices and for Roman habits to be absorbed into indigenous traditions. The same process encouraged a more general Romanization of the types of inscriptions which were set up. By the end of the first century BC, there is a trend away from pre-Roman inscribing cultures and towards the type of large-scale inscriptions on public monuments which are characteristic of the late Republic and early Empire.

However, the pattern of adoption of Latin ways, whether in script, language, or general epigraphic culture, was a complex one, and the motives for choosing one language, or form of cultural representation, over another in any given situation can be difficult to pin down. A recent study of Roman culture (Wallace-Hadrill, 2008) has argued that code-switching between different languages or forms of cultural behavior was not always a deliberate and conscious process. The decision about which language to use might arise naturally out of a particular context – Latin for dealing with a Roman magistrate, Greek for conversing with learned friends, another language for speaking to family or to one's slaves – and be an automatic or subconscious, rather than deliberate, choice. Similarly, adoption of particular cultural attributes may not always be the result of a desire to accept or reject Roman ways – or conversely, local ones – but may arise naturally from the emergence of an increasingly hybrid Roman/Italic/Greek culture. Nevertheless, this is not a straightforward matter. Although the distinctions between Roman and non-Roman aspects of the culture of Roman Italy may have become blurred by the early Empire, the cultural choices may have been starker during the period immediately after the conquest of Italy. The processes of language change in Italy were not directly dictated by Rome, but they were undoubtedly tied to issues of Roman power, culture and citizenship.

FURTHER READING

The bibliography on literacy in the ancient world is now substantial, although little of it focuses specifically on Roman Italy. Harris's influential, although somewhat controversial, book (Harris 1989) is a good starting point, and there are a number of collections of essays – especially Beard *et al.* 1991; Cooley, ed. 2002b; Lomas, Whitehouse, and Wilkins 2007; Baird and Taylor 2011 – which cover various aspects of literacy in the ancient Mediterranean. Wallace-Hadrill 2008 provides an excellent discussion on the spread of Latin and its significance, as does Hingley 2005, while Adams 2003b is a mine of information about bilingualism and language change. Lomas 2008 provides an overview of the disappearance of non-Roman scripts and Woolf 1996 discusses the Romanization of the epigraphic habit. Finally, a major new edition of inscriptions from Italy (Crawford, ed. 2011), collects the evidence for many of the non-Latin languages, with the exception of Etruscan.

REFERENCES

Adams, J.N. 2003a. "Romanitas and the Latin language." *Classical Quarterly* 53.1: 184–205.
Adams, J.N. 2003b. *Bilingualism and the Latin language.* Cambridge: Cambridge University Press.
Agostiniani, L. 2000. "The language." In *The Etruscans*, ed. M. Torelli, 485–99. London: Thames and Hudson.
Andreau, J. 1974. *Les affaires de Monsieur Jucundus.* Rome: École française de Rome.
Bagnasco Gianni, G. 1996. *Oggetti iscritti di epoca orientalizzante in Etruria.* Florence: Olschki.
Bagnasco Gianni, G. 2000. *L'etrusco dalla A alla 8: l'acquisizione della scrittura da parte degli Etruschi.* Milan: Cooperativa Universitaria, Editrice Milanese.
Baird, J. and Taylor, C. 2011. *Ancient graffiti in context.* London: Routledge.
Barker, G. and T. Rasmussen. 1998. *The Etruscans.* Oxford: Blackwell.
Beard M., *et al.*, 1991. *Literacy in the Roman World.* Portsmouth, RI: *Journal of Roman Archaeology* Suppl. 3.

Benelli, E. 1994. *Le iscrizioni bilingui etrusco-latine*. Florence: Istituto nazionale di studi etruschi ed italici.

Benelli, E. 2001. "The Romanisation of Italy through the epigraphic record." In *Italy and the West: Comparative Issues in Romanization*, eds S. Keay and N. Terrenato, 7–16. Oxford: Oxbow.

Bonfante G. and Bonfante L. 2002, rev. ed. *The Etruscan Language. An Introduction*. Manchester: Manchester University Press.

Bradley, G. 2000. *Ancient Umbria. State, Culture and Identity in Central Italy from the Iron Age to the Augustan Era*. Oxford: Oxford University Press.

Briquel, D. 2000. "The origins of the Etruscans: a controversy handed down from antiquity." In *The Etruscans*, ed. M. Torelli, 43–51. London: Thames and Hudson.

Brunt, P.A. 1971. *Italian Manpower, 225 BC–AD 14*. Oxford: Clarendon Press.

Camodeca, G. 1999. Tabulae pompeianae Sulpiciorum (TPSulp.): *edizione critica dell'archivio puteolano dei Sulpicii*. 2 vols. Rome: Vetera 12/Quasar.

Clackson, J. and Horrocks, G. 2011. A Blackwell *History of the Latin Language*. Oxford: Blackwell.

Cooley, A.E. 2002a. "The survival of Oscan in Roman Pompeii." In *Becoming Roman, Writing Latin? Literacy and Epigraphy in the Roman West*, ed. A.E. Cooley, 77–86. Portsmouth, RI: *Journal of Roman Archaeology* Suppl. 48.

Cooley, A.E., ed. 2002b. *Becoming Roman, writing Latin? Literacy and epigraphy in the Roman West*. Portsmouth, RI: *Journal of Roman Archaeology* Suppl. 48.

Cooley, A.E. and Cooley, M.G.L. 2014. *Pompeii and Herculaneum. A Sourcebook*. London and New York: Routledge.

Corbier, M. 2006. *Donner à voir, donner à lire. Mémoire et communication dans la Rome ancienne*. Paris: CNRS.

Cordano, F. 1984. "L'uso della scrittura in Italia meridionale e Sicilia nei secoli VIII e VII a.C." *Opus*, 3 (2): 281–309.

Cornell, T.J. 1991. "The tyranny of the evidence: a discussion of the possible uses of literacy in Etruria and Latium in the archaic age." In *Literacy in the Roman World*, 7–34. Portsmouth, RI: *Journal of Roman Archaeology* Suppl. 3.

Crawford, M. H., ed. 1996. *Roman Statutes*. 2 vols. London: Institute of Classical Studies/BICS *Supplement* 64.

Crawford, M.H., ed. 2011. Imagines Italicae: *A Corpus of Italic Inscriptions*. London: *BICS Supplement* 110.

Cristofani, M. 1999. "Litterazione e processi di autoidentificazione etnica fra le genti dell'Italia arcaica." In *La colonisation greque en Méditerranée occidentale*, 345–60. Rome: École Française de Rome.

Dench, E. 1995. *From Barbarians to New Men. Greek, Roman and Modern Perceptions of Peoples from the Central Apennines*. Oxford: Clarendon Press.

Dorian, N.C. 1999. "Linguistic and ethnographic fieldwork." In *Handbook of Language and Ethnic Identity*, ed. J. Fishman, 25–41. New York and Oxford: Oxford University Press.

Dubuisson, M. 1982. "Y-a-t-il un politique linguistique romaine?" Ktema 7: 187–210.

Franklin, J.L., Jr. 1991. "Literacy and the parietal inscriptions of Pompeii." In *Literacy in the Roman World*: 77–98. Ann Arbor: *Journal of Roman Archaeology* Suppl. 3.

Gambari, F.M. 1989. "L'iscrizione vascolare della T.53 di Oleggio-Loreto." In *Il Ticino. Strutture, storia e società nel territorio tra Oleggio e Lonate-Pozzolo*, ed. G. Amoretti, 195–97. Turin: Nicolini.

Glinister, F. 2009. "Burning boats and building bridges: Women and cult in Roman colonisation." In *Gender Identities in Italy in the 1ˢᵗ Millennium BC*, eds E. Herring and K. Lomas, 117–26. Oxford: Archaeopress.

Hall, J.M. 2002. *Hellenicity: Between Ethnicity and Culture*. Chicago and London: Chicago University Press.

Harris, W.V. 1989. Ancient Literacy. Cambridge, Mass.: Harvard University Press.

Harrison, T. 2002. "Introduction." In *Greeks and Barbarians*, ed. T. Harrison, 1–14. Edinburgh: Edinburgh University Press.

Hatzfeld, M.J. 1912. "Les italiens résidant à Délos mentionnés dans les inscriptions de l'île." *Bulletin de correspondance hellénique* 36: 5–218.

Häussler, R. 2002. "Writing Latin – from resistance to assimilation: language, society and culture in N. Gaul and S. France." In *Becoming Roman, Writing Latin?: Literacy and Epigraphy in the Roman West*, ed. A.E. Cooley, 61–76. Portsmouth RI: *Journal of Roman Archaeology* Suppl. 48.

Häussler, R. and Pearce, J. 2007. "Literacy and Empire." In *Literacy and State Societies in the Ancient Mediterranean*, eds K. Lomas, J. Wilkins and R. Whitehouse, 219–36. London: Accordia Research Institute.

Hingley, R. 2005. *Globalizing Roman Culture: Unity, Diversity and Empire*. Abingdon and New York: Routledge.

Hodos, T. 1999. "Intermarriage in the Western Greek colonies." *Oxford Journal of Archaeology*, 18: 61–78.

Homeyer, H. 1957. "Some observations on bilingualism and language shift in Italy from the sixth to the third century BC." *Word* 13: 415–34.

Kaimio, J. 1975. "The ousting of Etruscan by Latin in Etruria." In *Studies in the Romanization of Etruria*, ed. P. Bruun, 85–245. Rome and Helsinki: Institutum Romanum Findlandiae.

Kaimio, J. 1979. *The Romans and the Greek Language*. Helsinki: Societas Scientarum Fennica.

Langslow, D. 2007. "Alphabets, spelling and punctuation in pre-Roman Italy." In *Literacy and the State in the Ancient Mediterranean*, eds K. Lomas, R. Whitehouse, J.B. Wilkins, 81–94. London: Accordia Research Institute.

Lazzarini, M.L. and Poccetti, P. 2001. *L'Iscrizione paleoitalica da Tortora*. Naples: Loffredo Editore.

Lazzeroni, R. 1983. "Contatti di lingue e di culture nell'Italia antica. Modelli egemoni e modelli subordinate nelle iscrizioni osche in grafie greche." *Annali dell'Istituto universitario orientali di Napoli (Ling)* 5: 171–82.

Leiwo, M. 1994. Neapolitana: *a study of population and language in Graeco-Roman Naples*. Helsinki: Societas Scientarum Fennica

Leiwo, M. 1996. "Language attitudes and patriotism." *Arctos* 30: 121–37.

Lejeune, M. 1970. "Phonologie osque et graphie grecque. I." *Revue des Études Anciennes* 72: 271–316.

Lejeune, M. 1971. *Lepontica*. Paris: Les Belles Lettres.

Lejeune, M. 1972. "Phonologie osque et graphie grecque. II." *Revue des Études Anciennes* 74: 5–13

Lejeune, M. 1975. "Inscriptions de Rossano di Vaglio." *Rendiconti di Lincei* ser. 8, 30: 319–39.

Lejeune, M. 1988. *Recueil des inscriptions gauloises* I. *Textes gallo-étrusques.textes gallo-latins sur pierre*. Paris: CNRS.

Lomas, K. 1993. *Rome and the Western Greeks, 350 BC–AD 200. Conquest and Acculturation in South Italy*. London: Routledge.

Lomas, K. 2007. "Writing boundaries: Literacy and state identities in the ancient Veneto." In *Literacy and the State in the Ancient Mediterranean*, eds K. Lomas, R. Whitehouse, J. Wilkins, 149–70. London, Accordia Research Institute.

Lomas, K. 2008. "Script obsolescence, writing and power in pre-Roman and early Roman Italy." In *The Disappearance of Writing Systems: Perspectives on Literacy and Communication*, eds J. Baines, D.J. Bennet, 109–138. London, Equinox.

Lomas, K. 2015. "Hidden writing: epitaphs within tombs in early Italy." In *L'écriture et l'espace de la mort. Épigraphie et nécropoles à l'époque pré-romaine*, ed. M.-L. Haack. Pari/Rome: École française de Rome. http://books.openedition.org/efr/2704. Accessed March 4, 2015.

Lomas, K., Whitehouse, R.D. and Wilkins, J.B., eds. 2007. *Literacy and the state in the ancient Mediterranean*. London: Accordia Research Institute.

MacMullen, R. 1982. "The epigraphic habit in the Roman empire." *American Journal of Philology* 103: 234–46.

Marchesini, S. 1999. "Confini e frontiera nella Grecità d'occidente: la situazione alfabetica." In *Confini e frontiera nella Grecità d'occidente. Atti di XXVII° convegno di studi sulla Magna Grecia*, 173–212. Taranto: Istituto per la Storia e l'Archeologia della Magna Grecia.

Marinetti, A. 1990. "Le tavolette alfabetiche de Este." In *Alfabetari e insegnamento della scrittura in Etruria e nell'Italia antica*. eds M. Pandolfini and A.L. Prosdocimi, 95–142. Florence: L.S. Olschki.

Marinetti, A. 1999. "Venetico 1976–1996. Acquisizioni e prospettive." In *Protostoria e storia del "Venetorum Angulus": Atti del XX Convegno di studi etruschi ed italici*, ed. O. Paoletti, 413–23. Pisa: Istituti editoriali e poligrafici internazionali.

Morandi, A. 1999. *Il cippo di Castelciès nell'epigrafia retica*. Rome: L'"Erma" di Bretschneider.

Pellegrini, G.B. and Prosdocimi, A.L. 1967. *La Lingua Venetica*. Padua: Istituto di glottologia dell'Università.

Penney, J.H.W. 1988. "The languages of Italy." In *Cambridge Ancient History* Vol. 4. *Persia, Greece and the Western Mediterranean*, 2nd edn, eds J. Boardman, N.G.L. Hammond, D.M. Lewis, and M. Ostwald, 720–38. Cambridge, Cambridge University Press.

Piana Agostinetti, P. 2004. *Celti d'Italia*. Vol. 1. *Archeologia, lingua e scrittura*. Rome: Spazio Tre.

Poccetti, P. 1979. *Nuovi documenti italici: a complemento del Manuale di E. Vetter*. Pisa: Giardini.

Prosdocimi, A.L. 1984. *Le Tavole Iguvini*, I. Florence: Olschki.

Prosdocimi, A.L. 1990. "La lingua." In *I Veneti antichi: lingua e cultura*, ed. G. Fogolari and A.L. Prosdocimi, 225–422. Padua: Editoriale Programma.

Ridgway, D. 1996. "Greek letters at Osteria dell'Osa." *Opuscula Romana* 20: 87–97.

Rix, H. 1991. *Etruskische Texte. Editio minor*, 2 vols. Tübingen: G. Narr.Heidelberg: C. Winter.

Sanpaolo Antonacci, E. 2001. "Landscape change. Romanisation and new settlement patterns at Tiati." In *Italy and the West: Comparative Issues in Romanization*, eds S. Keay and N. Terrenato, 27–38. Oxford: Oxbow.

Simone, C. de and Marchesini, S. 2002. *Monumenta Linguae Messapicae*. Wiesbaden: Reichert.

Solinas, P. 1994. "Il celtico in Italia." *Studi Etruschi* 60: 311–385.

Stoddart, S. and Whitely, J. 1988. "The social context of literacy in Archaic Greece and Etruria." *Antiquity* 62: 761–772.

Vetter, E. 1953. *Handbuch der italischen Dialekte*. Heidelberg: C. Winter.

Wallace, R.E. 1989. "The origins and development of the Latin alphabet." In *Origins of Writing*. Lincoln: University of Nebraska.

Wallace-Hadrill, A. 2008. *Rome's Cultural Revolution*. Cambridge: Cambridge University Press.

Woolf, G. 1996. "Monumental writing and the expansion of Roman society in the early Empire." *Journal of Roman Studies* 86: 22–39.

Woolf, G. 1998. *Becoming Roman. The Origins of Provincial Civilization in Gaul*. Cambridge: Cambridge University Press.

2.2 Greek Italy

CHAPTER 12

Roman Naples

Kathryn Lomas

12.1 Introduction

Naples provides an unusually complex and fascinating case study of the interactions between Roman and non-Roman cultures and populations from the period of first contact with Rome onwards. At the time of the Roman conquest, it was not an entirely Greek city, but one which included a substantial minority of people of Campanian origin amongst the population, and also traces of earlier Etruscan settlement. It enjoyed a close political and diplomatic relationship which was established between Naples and Rome in the fourth century BC, when it became a key Roman ally in Campania, and it also benefited from the complicated and sometimes ambivalent nature of Rome's relationship with the Greeks and their culture.

The Greek writers Strabo and Dio Cassius note the survival of Greek culture and the local pride in it, and Tacitus describes Naples as *quasi Graecam urbem* – "like a Greek city" (Strabo, *Geography*: 5.4.7; Dio Cassius: 55.10.5–6; Tacitus, *Annals*: 15.33). Epigraphic evidence suggests that Greek culture remained central to Roman Naples, and to its interactions with Rome. From the second century BC, Naples positioned itself as a significant cultural center, whose Greek past was instrumental in shaping its relationship with Rome, and in particular with the increasingly philhellene Roman elite. It successfully presented itself as having a mainly Greek public identity in dealing with Rome, and capitalized on the increasing Roman interest in hellenism to establish a uniquely privileged relationship with Rome. Accordingly, the culture of Roman Naples was a complex blend of Roman, Greek, and Campanian elements, which provides an excellent opportunity to study the interaction of three important cultures of Italy, how these developed and interacted, and how the various aspects of Naples' heritage became embedded in the culture of the Roman city.

The nature of Naples and its site poses its own problems for the historian and archaeologist. The Greek and Roman cities lie under the center of the later medieval and modern city, and are therefore largely inaccessible. There are relatively few visible remains of ancient Naples, and much of our knowledge of the ancient city depends on localized excavations where Greek and Roman remains have come to light beneath later structures or in the course of rebuilding work. There are also some descriptions by authors of the medieval period onwards of ancient structures which no longer survive. The whereabouts of the agora of the Greek city is, for

A Companion to Roman Italy, First Edition. Edited by Alison E. Cooley.
© 2016 John Wiley & Sons, Ltd. Published 2016 by John Wiley & Sons, Ltd.

instance, described by the fourteenth-century *Cronaca di Parthenope* and the sixteenth-century writer Fabio Giordano, and the temple of the Dioscuri, which was preserved as part of the church of S. Paolo but destroyed by an earthquake in 1631, is known mainly from engravings made in the sixteenth and early seventeenth centuries. Although our knowledge of the archaeology is patchy, it nevertheless adds up cumulatively to a substantial body of material from a variety of different contexts which can give us some insight into the physical development of ancient Naples, even if it cannot provide a complete overview of the city. In addition, a surprisingly large quantity of epigraphic evidence has survived, and we have a significant amount of literary evidence from ancient authors. This depth of evidence permits us to examine the ancient city in its transition from independence to part of the Roman state, and to use it as a way of examining the reception of Roman culture in Naples.

12.2   Naples: Greek, Campanian, and Roman

Paradoxically, Naples is better documented for the period after the Roman conquest than for its independent existence. It was a Greek settlement and was certainly in existence by the second half of the fifth century BC, but its earlier history is very unclear. A Greek city known as Palaepolis is said to have been established by people from Syracuse and Cumae, and Strabo mentions another Greek settlement called Parthenope (Livy: 8.22.5; Velleius Paterculus: 1.4.2; Pliny the Elder, *Natural History*: 3.62; Statius, *Silvae*: 5.3.104-6 and 109–11; Lutatius fr.7 (Peter, *HRF* 1.192); Pseudo-Scymnus: 251; Strabo, *Geography*: 14.2.10, Stephanus of Byzantium s.v. *Neapolis*; Frederiksen, 1984: 86–87; Raviola: 1995). The discovery of a Greek cemetery on Pizzofalcone which included archaic burials (De Caro, 1974) gives some archaeological support to the existence of an archaic settlement at Naples. The establishment of Naples itself, however, occurred in the fifth century BC (Strabo, *Geography*: 5.4.7, Scholia to Lycophron, *Alexandra*: 732 [= *FGrH* 566 Timaios F98]). There is circumstantial evidence suggesting a date of circa 450–430 BC, although it may have been as early as circa 470 BC (Rutter, 1979: 5–6, 45, 94–95; Lepore, 1967:179; Frederiksen, 1984: 103–05). Livy (8.22.5) describes a city which was physically divided into two distinct parts – Palaeopolis and Neapolis – in the fourth century BC, and which did not become a single settlement until 326 BC. This is not implausible, as similar divisions are known from other Greek settlements in the western Mediterranean, such as Emporion (Strabo, *Geography*: 3.4.8; Silius Italicus, *Punica*: 3; Livy: 34.9). The bipartite structure at Naples is sometimes associated with ethnic/cultural divisions between two sets of settlers, but there is no conclusive evidence for this (Lepore, 1967: 228–39).

Towards the end of the fifth century BC, Naples faced a significant threat from its Campanian neighbours and underwent some important cultural and ethnic changes. During the fifth century, there was a steady migration of Oscan-speaking peoples from the Samnite areas of the Apennines into Campania, and in particular into the area around Capua. By circa 430 BC this had reached a critical mass, and many Campanian cities fell under the control of these migrants. Sources describe this as a violent rampage, in which Samnite settlers rose against the local inhabitants, first at Capua in 423 BC, and massacred or enslaved many of them. This may be an oversimplification, as some communities, notably Paestum, show a lot of demographic and cultural continuity between the fifth and fourth centuries, but it undeniably changed the ethnic and cultural landscape of Campania. By the end of the century, most of Campania, Lucania, and Bruttium was overrun by Oscan-speaking migrants, including the Greek cities of Cumae and Paestum (Diodorus Siculus: 12.76.4, 16.15.1; Livy: 4.37.1–2, 4.44.12; Dionysius of Halicarnassus, *Roman Antiquities*: 15.1.3–6; Strabo, *Geography*: 5.4.7; Frederiksen, 1984: 117–32, 137–40).

Naples, however, took an alternative route. The Greek population was augmented by refugees from Cumae, who fled from the Oscan takeover of 421 BC (Diodorus Siculus: 12.76.4; Dionysius of Halicarnassus, *Roman Antiquities*: 15.6.4). More significantly, though, Naples also offered settlement rights and citizenship to the Oscans, including the right to hold political office. Strabo, who took a dim view of this, tells us that from the late fifth century the lists of the *demarchoi* – the chief magistrates of Naples – included both Greek and Oscan names (*Geography*: 5.4.7). By the time of the Roman conquest, Naples was, therefore, a mixed community. Culturally it seems to have been predominantly Greek, but with a substantial Oscan minority which exercised full political rights and influence. Regionally, it was a significant center, although not as powerful as Capua, the principal city of Campania.

The earliest information we have about connections between Rome and Naples concerns the Second Samnite War. It is likely, given that Rome already had contacts with other Campanian cities – especially Capua – that there were also earlier contacts with Naples, but the extent and nature of these (if they existed) is unknown. The war between Rome and Naples in 327–25 BC which brought Naples into alliance with Rome took place against the background of the wider conflict between Rome and the Samnites. This was triggered by Roman expansion in the Volturnus valley (Cornell, 1995: 352–55), in which the Campanians were mostly inclined to support the Samnites, perhaps unsurprisingly in view of the ethnic connections between the two and the rivalry between Rome and Capua (Salmon, 1967: 215–19; Frederiksen, 1984: 206–09; Dench, 1995: 53–54).

The specific cause of conflict with Naples was a series of Neapolitan raids on Roman settlers in the Ager Falernus in 326 BC (Livy: 8.22; Dionysius of Halicarnassus, *Roman Antiquities*: 15.5.1–2). This seems to have been an attempt to curb Roman influence in the hinterland of Naples, although Livy pins the blame on machinations by the Samnites and Campanians. When Rome declared war, Naples promptly received both Campanian support in the form of troops sent from Nola and a promise of assistance from Tarentum (Livy: 8.22.7, 23.1–3, 23.7; Dionysius of Halicarnassus, *Roman Antiquities*: 15.5.2–6.5). Dionysius, possibly following a source sympathetic to the Samnites, gives an account of negotiations between Naples and the Samnites, saying that the Samnites induced the Neapolitans to support them against Rome by offering to restore Cumae to the Greeks, thereby gaining the support of Cumaeans who had settled at Naples after 421 BC (Livy: 8.25.8; Dionysius of Halicarnassus, *Roman Antiquities*: 15.5.2; Frederiksen, 1984: 208–12; Lomas, 1993: 44–47). Frederiksen, (1984: 208–12) suggests, plausibly, that the central portion of the account, which gives details of the negotiations with the Samnite ambassadors, is probably drawn from a Greek source, while the later portions of the account follow the same source as Livy (Dench, 1995: 54–61).

The campaign itself was short and sharp. The Roman commander, Q. Publilius Philo, raided Neapolitan territory and laid siege to the city, setting up camp between the settlements of Palaepolis and Neapolis but the expected reinforcements from Tarentum failed to arrive, and the presence of Campanian troops was unpopular (Livy: 8.25). Early in 326 BC, a group of disaffected Neapolitans, led by a Greek, Charilaus, and an Oscan, Nympsius, staged a coup and opened the city gates to the Roman forces. Our sources imply that there were tensions between ethnic groups within the city, but the facts do not bear this out (Livy: 8.25.5–9; Dionysius of Halicarnassus, *Roman Antiquities*: 15.4.1–5; Frederiksen, 1984: 208–212; Lomas 1993, 44–47). The leaders of the coup which led to the surrender of Naples included both Greeks (Charilaus) and Oscans (Nympsius). Livy identifies the pro-Roman faction as members of the elite, and this seems likely to be correct. Dionysius's version is noticeably less anti-Greek, although it ultimately favors the Roman point of view, and, unlike Livy, places less emphasis on the division between "good" aristocrats and "bad" democrats. There were long-established contacts between the Campanian and Roman elites which might predispose the elite to support Rome, and the leaders of the revolt against the Samnites are described as *principes civitatis*, implying that they were of the elite (Livy: 8.25.9; cf. Dionysius of Halicarnassus, *Roman Antiquities*: 15.6.2).

The city, under its new pro-Roman regime, was rewarded for its timely change of heart by a treaty of exceptionally favorable terms, which became a byword in Roman history, being referred to by both Livy and Cicero as a *foedus aequissimum* – a most equal treaty (Livy: 8.26.6–7; Cicero, *In Defence of Balbus*: 8.21). The nature of these favorable terms has been much debated, with speculation that they may have involved some form of exemption from military service, but we have no information about the specifics of the treaty. The few Roman treaties for which we do have some evidence are mostly very general in their terms, so it is difficult to make any assumptions about what the favorable nature of Naples' treaty may have comprised.

Whatever the terms were, however, they formed the basis of a very strong and enduring alliance between Rome and Naples. This is particularly evident during the Punic Wars. Ships from Naples served as part of the Roman fleet in 264 BC (Polybius: 1.20.14), and played an important role during the early years of the First Punic War, when Roman naval capacity was limited. In the Second Punic War, there is no evidence that Naples was providing troops in support of Rome, but the city remained a Roman ally after the defection of Capua and many other Campanian cities in 216–15 BC. It strongly resisted attacks by Hannibal in 215–14 (Livy: 23.1.5–7, 14.5–9, 15.1–6) and donated 40 pieces of gold plate to help with Rome's war expenses in 216 BC (Livy: 22.32.4–9; Lomas, 1993: 64–8, 78–84; Fronda, 2010: 130–46).

We know relatively little about the relations between Rome and Naples between circa 213 BC and the Social War. A number of Neapolitan citizens crop up in the epigraphy of Delos and other major centers in the Greek East during the second century BC, suggesting that they were active players in the exploitation of the new economic opportunities offered by the Roman conquest of the region (Hatzfeld, 1912, 1919; Lomas, 1993: 191). This in turn implies that Naples itself was benefiting from the wider trading and economic opportunities. This was also the period in which interest in Greek culture began to take root amongst the Roman elite, and also the period at which Roman aristocrats began to build villas on the Bay of Naples, laying the foundations for something which was to become an important theme in the later history of Naples.

The privileged status of Naples in relation to Rome, whatever this might have consisted of, was not enough to protect the city from the Roman tendency to interfere in allied affairs during the second century. At some point, a boundary dispute occurred between Naples and Nola, and they requested Roman arbitration to solve it (Cicero, *On Moral Duties*: 1.33). Unfortunately, the commissioner, Q. Labeo, did so by confiscating the land on behalf of Rome. Cicero does not give a date, but 133–23 BC may be plausible. The Gracchan land commissioners were active throughout Italy at this date, and land tenure was a politically sensitive topic.

Despite this heavy-handedness, there is little evidence of friction between Naples and Rome during the second century BC, and Naples does not seem to have participated in the Social War. According to Cicero, Naples and Heraklea petitioned Rome to retain their status as autonomous allies after the war, rather than becoming Roman citizens, saying that many of their citizens "preferred the freedom of their treaties to citizenship" (Cicero, *In Defence of Balbus*: 21; Lomas, 1993: 92–94). Cicero's apparent reading of this was that the terms of Naples' treaty were so advantageous that Roman citizenship was seen as a potential backward step, but it could also imply that the Neapolitans' relationship with Rome had cooled somewhat over the course of the second century. Whatever the reason for this request, it was rejected, and from 89 BC Naples became a Roman *municipium*, along with the rest of peninsular Italy. It later became a colony, because of a settlement of army veterans there by the Flavians, and in AD 222 Pertinax conferred the honorific title upon it of *Colonia Aurelia Antoniana Felix Neapolis* (*Notizie degli scavi di antichità* 1890: 220; CIL 10.1492, *Liber coloniarum*: 235; Statius, *Silvae*: 3.7.78.).

12.3 Public Building and Civic Identities: The Reshaping of an Urban Environment

Pre-Roman Naples is not well documented. There is general agreement that the street plan was based on the Hippodamian model of two intersecting main thoroughfares and a grid of long narrow blocks of housing (Napoli, 1959; Greco, 1985a: 199–208, and 1985b: 132–39; see Figure 12.1). A sixteenth-century description by Fabio Giordano locates the agora, and later the forum, in an area bounded on one side by the Via del Duomo and transected by the Via dei Tribunali (see Figure 12.2). Greco identifies the area around the church of S. Lorenzo as Giordano's commercial forum and the area between the theater and the temple of the Dioscuri as the forum/agora proper, but little else is known about the Greek city, a fact which makes the transition from Greek to Roman difficult to trace (Greco, 1985a: 208–11; Greco, 1985b: 138; Baldassare, 1985: 227–28).

The Roman city is better understood, but it is difficult to arrive at anything more than a schematic urban plan. The Greek street grid remained the basis of the urban layout, but from the late first century BC there seems to have been an increasing amount of building in a Roman style. Much of this was private housing, such as the insula of Carminiello ai Mannesi, another example is near the church of S. Gregorio Armeno, or the area of Roman housing near the Palazzo Corigliano (Arthur, 1984; Pozzi, 1989; Bragantini, 1991). However, a number of public buildings have been excavated in the area around the churches of S. Paolo Maggiore and S. Lorenzo Maggiore, the location of the forum (see Figure 12.3). The four principal structures are the theater, an *odeion*, a temple of the Dioscuri, and a large and complex structure beneath the church of S. Lorenzo which was probably the *macellum* of the city.

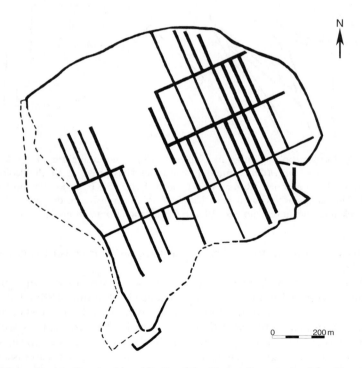

N

0   200 m

Figure 12.1   Naples: Street grid and limits of the Graeco-Roman city. After Napoli, 1959.

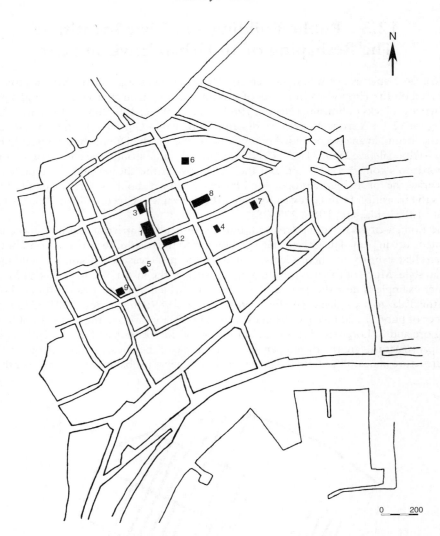

Figure 12.2 Major Roman buildings in Naples. 1. S. Paolo Maggiore (Temple of Dioscuri);
2. S. Lorenzo Maggiore (*macellum*, commonly known as "basilica"); 3. Via S. Paolo (theater and
odeion); 4. Carminiello ai Mannesi (Roman insula and baths); 5. S. Gregorio Armeno (possible site of
Caesareum); 6. Donnaregina Nuova (Roman baths); 7. Archivio di Banco di Napoli (Roman house);
8. Duomo (Greek and Roman remains); 9. Palazzo Corigliano (Roman houses).

All of these have been dated to the first century AD, on their construction technique and
architectural detail.

The building beneath S. Lorenzo was a rectangular structure with a mosaic pavement built on a terrace with a large cryptoporticus (De Simone, 1985: 185–95). It had
tabernae around three of the inner walls and an open central area containing a circular
tholos, and is very similar to the *macellum* of Pompeii. The two theaters are situated on
the north-east corner of the forum/agora area. Both probably existed in the Greek phase
of Naples' history, but the extant remains are entirely Roman. The theater is a semicircular

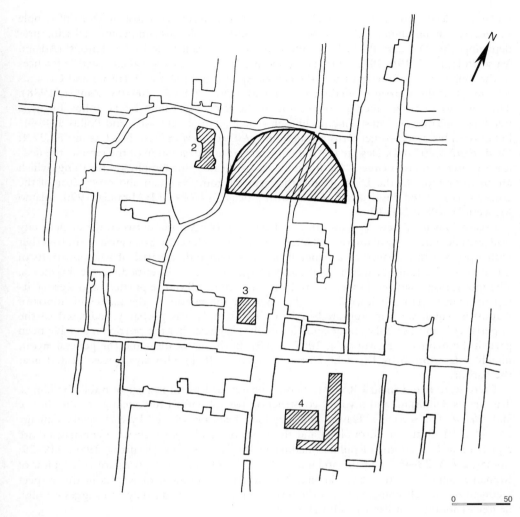

Figure 12.3 Area of the Roman Forum in Naples: 1. Theater; 2. *Odeion*; 3. Temple of the Dioscuri; 4. *Macellum*.

structure in *opus reticulatum* and is similar in style, construction technique, and date with other theaters in Campania, such as those of Nuceria and Beneventum (Johannowsky, 1976). The first phase is Augustan in date and may be associated with the establishment of a Greek athletic and artistic festival in honor of the emperor in 2 BC. The second phase, with a remodeled interior, and addition of a portico, and a bath building behind the *cavea*, dates to the Flavian period. The *odeion*, which is badly preserved, was a square structure decorated with pilasters and stucco facing, located on the east side of the theater and of similar date. Like the theater, it also has parallels from early imperial Campania (Johannowsky, 1976).

The temple of the Dioscuri does not survive, apart from the base of two pillars. It was incorporated into the church of S. Paolo and the facade is recorded in numerous drawings, but it was destroyed in an earthquake in 1631. It is depicted as a Roman form of temple *in antis* set on a podium, with a facade of six Corinthian columns and pedimental sculptures depicting the Dioscuri flanked by Apollo, Tellus, Oceanus, and two Tritons (Adamo Muscettola, 1985: 196–208). This may be specifically Augustan iconography, with references to the Tellus panel of the Ara Pacis, the cult of Apollo, and the use of Tritons and Oceanus to symbolize the victory of Actium (Adamo Muscettola, 1985: 204–05; Zanker, 1988). There is also a strong Tiberian connection, as the temple was built by Ti. Julius Tarsus, a freedman of Tiberius, whilst Tiberius himself rebuilt a temple of Castor and Pollux at Rome in honor of his dead brother Drusus (Suetonius, *Life of Tiberius*: 8.20; Dio Cassius: 55.27.4; Ovid, *Fasti*: 1.707–08). Despite the Roman structure and decoration of the temple, the dedicatory inscription is in Greek: "Ti. Julius Tarsus (dedicated) the temple and the things which are in the temple to the Dioscuri and the city. Pelagon, freedman and procurator of the emperor, completed this dedication at his own expense" (*IG* 14.714; Miranda, 1990; Adamo Muscettola, 1985: 200–01).

Excavations for a new Metro station at Piazza Nicola Amore, between the ancient city wall and the harbor, have uncovered a temple dating to the early first century AD, together with a portico and a paved area. Finds from the site include a statue of Nike, portraits of members of the Julio-Claudian family, and a large number of inscribed marble fragments. The inscriptions, written in Greek, are from the inner wall of the portico, and were written on marble slabs, at least 2 m high. They list the victors in the games in honor of Augustus which were inaugurated in 2 BC. The temple was probably dedicated to the imperial cult and the Nike statue and victory lists suggest that the portico may have been part of the gymnasium (Miranda, 2007; 2010). Both the location and the general layout match a description by Dio Chrysostom (*Orations*: 28.1) who says it was located near the harbor.

There were two principal Roman building phases, at least in respect of public buildings. The first is Augustan, and involves construction (or substantial remodeling) of the theatre and *odeion*. The second is Flavian and may have been occasioned by earthquake damage (*IG* 14.729). Both the chronology and the types of buildings which were constructed are typical of wider patterns of public building in Italy at this date (Jouffroy, 1986: 319–29; Lomas, 2002: 28–45), and the architectural forms and decorative styles are also typical of Roman Campania in the early Empire. The urban development of Naples in this respect seems to be entirely consistent with the rest of this area of Roman Italy and suggests a high degree of adoption of Roman cultural norms.

12.4   Institutions in Transition: The Municipal Administration of Roman Naples

Roman Naples is both unusual and very interesting as an examination of cultural change and the process of municipalization. In most Italian states, this seems to have involved the adoption of Roman law and a Roman form of administration based on a local council and annually elected boards of magistrates (on the complexities of municipalization, see Sherwin-White, 1973: 165–73; Bispham, 2007: 199–246). The actual process by which this happened was, inevitably, drawn-out and with a lot of local variation, and in some cases it is likely that the new Latin titles used by magistrates were simply a renaming of traditional offices and forms of government. The general pattern, however, is for a growing standardization of local administration, based on boards of *duoviri* or *quattuorviri* and a *cursus honorum* of junior magistrates, such as *quaestores*, and *aediles*, by the end of the first century BC.

At Naples, the pattern appears somewhat different. We know relatively little about its constitution before 90 BC, or whether the government of the city was democratic or oligarchic in nature (*IG* 14.737, 746, 758, 760; *CIL* 10.1489; *AE* (1954) 186; Sartori, 1953: 48–53). The main magistrates were known as *demarchoi* (Strabo, *Geography*. 5.4.7; De Martino, 1952; Sartori, 1953: 48–53; Lomas, 1993: 145, 149–52), and there seems to have been a council (*boule*) and assembly (*eskletos*) as in many other Greek cities, although we have no information about who was eligible to participate. The evidence for the constitution during the transitional period after the Social War is sparse, but a Greek inscription honoring one Seleukos, son of Seleukos, describes him as having been one of the *tessares andres* – a literal Greek translation of the Latin *quattuorviri*, the normal title of a chief magistrate of a *municipium* (*IG* 14.745). This points to a transition from a Greek political system to a more Roman one, in the same manner as other cities in Italy at this time (for the problematic nature of this, see Bispham, 2007). However, his civic offices also included the Greek posts of *archon*, *gymnasiarchos* and *laukelarchos*, which point to a more complicated situation than simply a Roman-style government with Greek titles.

Evidence from the early empire also shows a more complex picture. Latin inscriptions refer to the civic magistrates as *duoviri* or *quattuorviri*, in the usual Roman fashion, but there is evidence that quite a number of Greek magistracies still existed in the early empire, including the offices of *demarchos*, *laukelarchos*, *archon*, *antarchon*, *gymnasiarchos*, *agoranomos*, and *agonothetes*. Some of these can be explained as the normal Greek terms for Roman offices (*agoranomos*, for instance, is the usual translation of aedile). Others, such at the offices of *gymnasiarchos* and *agonothetes*, are well known from the Greek cities of the eastern empire but are not otherwise found in Italy. Other titles (*archon*, for instance) are so general that they could well be a Greek translation of a Roman magistracy, while others (*demarchos*, *laukelarchos*) have a long pre-Roman history and are very local to Naples.

Some insight into the civic culture of Roman Naples is offered by a group of decrees honoring prominent citizens or visitors, or expressing public condolence on their deaths (*IG* 14.757, 758, 760; *ILS* 6460; Miranda,1990, 114–30). These date to the first–third centuries AD and are issued in the name of the *boule* and *demos* of Naples, initiated by the *archon*, *antarchon*, or *demarchos*. The decrees are written in Greek and are of a type which is very common in the Greek East. The significance of these documents has been much debated. The fact that these Greek offices appear only in honorific or ceremonial contexts may be significant. They seem to be concerned with ceremonial aspects of civic life, not the day-to-day administration of the community. This suggests that the elite of Naples was privileging Greek aspects of the city's culture in certain contexts as a means of creating and maintaining a Greek civic identity. This divergence between practical administrative offices and ceremonial ones is perhaps reinforced by the fact that Hadrian, a notable philhellene was an honorary *demarchos* of Naples (*IG* 14.729, Scriptores Historiae Augustae, *Life of Hadrian*: 1.9.1).

The constitution and administration of Roman Naples seems to be a mixture of Roman elements coexisting with long-standing local offices and more generic Greek titles. It is far from clear whether this represents continuity of pre-Roman practice through the first and second centuries AD, gradually dying out in the third century, or a deliberate revival of hellenism in the early Empire. Some offices – notably those of *demarchos* and *laukelarchos* – are known from pre-Roman Naples, but others, such as *archon*, do not occur until after the municipalization of the city (Pinsent, 1969; Miranda, 1985a). Given the sparse nature of the evidence for Greek Naples, it is possible that they existed before 90 BC, but it is also possible that this was in part a process of deliberate archaization or hellenization. It seems very likely that the day-to-day running of Naples was undertaken according to the usual Roman municipal model, but that this coexisted with some of the pre-Roman Greek magistracies and titles which continued in use for largely ceremonial or honorific purposes. Nevertheless, it provides persuasive evidence that hellenism was an important part of the public culture of Roman Naples throughout the first and second centuries AD, and did not become eroded until at least the third century.

12.5   The Cultural Life of Roman Naples

Other aspects of Neapolitan life also reinforce the importance of hellenism in the early Empire. According to Strabo, "many traces of a Greek way of life are preserved there, [such as] gymnasia and ephebeia and phratries and Greek names, although they [the Neapolitans] are Romans" (*Geography*: 5.4.7). Dio Cassius goes further, emphasizing the enthusiasm of the Neapolitans for their Greek cultural heritage, and suggesting that they actively strove to promote this: "Sacred Games were voted to Augustus himself in Naples, in Campania, ostensibly because he had restored it when it had been demolished by an earthquake and a fire, but in fact because they alone of their neighbors strove, in a manner, after Greekness…" (Dio Cassius: 55.10.9–10). Although the evidence of public building does not seem to corroborate this, and the evidence for the organization of the city is mixed, the surviving epigraphy provides strong support for these statements.

   The subdivisions of the Greek city, known as phratries, are known from a series of inscriptions, mostly in Greek, recording their activities (Strabo, *Geography*: 5.4.7; Suetonius, *Life of Claudius*: 11.2; Varro, *On Latin Language*: 5.85; *CIL* 6.1851; *IG* 14.721, 722, 742, 743, 744, 748; Miranda, 1990: 61–74). The latest of these dates to the third century AD, implying that they remained an important part of civic life until well into the Empire. There were 12 phratries altogether, although one, the Antinoitoi, may be a Hadrianic renaming of an existing phratry. The archaic names suggest an ancient origin, and membership was probably originally based on kinship. Nothing is known of their role in the Greek city, but in Roman Naples, each had its own cults and meeting house, held meetings, and elected officers (Guarducci, 1936; Lomas, 1993: 166–68). Inscriptions describe gifts, often valuable, offered to phratries ranging from new buildings to smaller gifts such as statues, cups, and candelabra of precious metal (*IG* 14.715, 721–22, 728, 742, 748; *CIL* 10.1491; *SEG* 19.622; Maiuri, 1913). For example, the phratry of the Artemisioi conferred honors on Munatius Hilarianus, a benefactor of the phratry and the city, and conferred the status of hero, marked by a shrine and statue, on Hilarianus's deceased son (Maiuri, 1913; Miranda, 1990: 66–72). Many members of these Greek associations were members of the elite of Rome or Naples, and include Romans of senatorial rank. Phratry members or patrons include the consulars L. Munatius Hilarianus, L. Cresperius Proculus, and L. Claudius Arrianus, and the equestrians T. Julius Dolabella and P. Sufenatius Myron. An important role of the phratries was to exploit an aspect of the city's Greek heritage to attract high-level patronage and benefactions.

   A more spectacular example of the revival and manipulation of Greek culture is the creation of a Greek festival in honor of Augustus in 2 BC, touched on earlier in this chapter. It was called the *Sebasta Italica Rhomaia Isolympica*, a title which makes explicit its Roman and Italic background, and its imperial connections. There was a long tradition of games at Naples, including some dedicated to the local goddess Parthenope, which may have provided the basis for the *Sebasta*, although it is not clear whether it was a rededication and elaboration of an existing event or a new one inspired by the agonistic traditions of the city (Strabo, *Geography*: 5.4.7; Timaeus fr. 566 *FGrH* F98; Lycophron, *Alexandra*: 732–37. For argument against continuity between the Parthenope festival and the *Sebasta*, cf. Geer, 1935; Miranda, 1985b: 390). It was a panhellenic festival which attracted athletes and artists from all over the Greek world (Suetonius, *Life of Augustus*: 98; Velleius Paterculus: 2.123; Strabo, *Geography*: 5.4.7; Dio Cassius: 55.10.9, 56.29; Statius, *Silvae*: 3.5.91–92; Miranda, 1982: 165–81; Miranda,

1985b: 390–92; Hardie, 1983: 2–14.) and the rules and events were directly modeled on those of the Olympic games (Dittenberger and Pergold, 1896, no. 56). Greek commemorative inscriptions set up by victorious athletes demonstrate that it had wide international appeal.

A further distinctive aspect of Roman Naples, which has already been touched on several times, is the survival of the Greek language. This is significant because the use of Latin as a formal written language, particularly in inscriptions and even more so in inscriptions of a public or official nature, was an important marker of Roman culture (Woolf, 1996; Cooley, 2002). In many other areas of Italy, the adoption of Latin for inscriptions such as civic decrees, building inscriptions, and other inscriptions set up by the elite is a demonstration of the use of Roman cultural forms as means of displaying status, either by individuals or groups. Non-Latin languages, where they persisted, were more often found in inscriptions of a more private nature, such as ownership inscriptions and graffiti on objects (Häussler, 2002). In Naples, however, Greek persisted as an epigraphic language until well into the second century AD, and this raises some important questions about Neapolitan culture in the early Empire.

Greek inscriptions account for circa 25% of the body of epigraphic evidence from the city, which is an unusually high ratio of Greek to Latin by the standards of southern Italy (Miranda, 1990; 1995. For discussion, Lomas, 1993: 161–87; Leiwo, 1994: 133–56). The use of Greek is not universal, however, which suggests that it was chosen for specific purposes to make a specific point. More significantly, Greek was used in contexts such as civic decrees or other public and official documents – precisely those contexts in which Latin was adopted as the preferred language elsewhere in Italy. Many funerary inscriptions from Naples are, in contrast, written in Latin. The use of Greek seems, therefore, to be closely connected with civic activity rather than with private commemoration, and to be closely linked with the activities of the city's elite.

Epigraphy, of course, can only offer an insight into language choice in particular types of written document, which are intended for preservation and/or display. It cannot tell us what languages were spoken in Naples in the early Empire, nor in what contexts they were used. What proportion of the population were Greek speakers or Latin/Greek bilinguals is not known, although it seems likely that Greek was still used as a spoken language (Leiwo, 1994: 168–72). Greek was, of course, widely spoken by the elite of Rome and Italy (Adams, 2003: 9–18), and its high status as a language was undoubtedly a factor in its survival in parts of southern Italy. Its use as a written language for certain types of public document, however, seems to represent a deliberate choice designed to emphasize Greek aspects of civic culture.

12.6 Public and Private: Identities in the Funerary Record

The public culture of Roman Naples appears to include both Roman and Greek elements, with Roman influences predominating in public building and urban development, but with hellenism remaining strong in other aspects of public life. In order to place this public culture in context, it is useful to look at the culture of Roman Naples in a less public context by examining funerary inscriptions and monuments. These can give an insight into the demographic composition of Roman Naples, and also into the way in which Neapolitans viewed their individual or family identities. Inevitably, given that recorded burials cost money, the evidence mainly represents the higher socioeconomic groups, but it can nevertheless give some insight into culture beyond that of the collective civic identity.

One group of inscriptions is especially interesting. This is composed of 12 epitaphs from the first century BC, and is particularly relevant because it belongs to the period shortly after the municipalization of Naples. Several come from family chamber tombs of pre-Roman type, which were in use for many generations (Levi, 1926: 378–402; Greco Pontrandolfo and Vecchio, 1985), a fact which suggests that these were established elite families. The inscriptions were written in Greek (Miranda, 1995, nos 90, 95, 97, 104, 123, 135, 138, 142, 143, 149, 153, 181) and inscribed on Greek-style funerary stelae, most of which depict the deceased saying farewell to their relatives (Papadopoulos, 1985; Lomas, 2003). A number of plain stelae with Greek inscriptions from the same group of tombs have traces of painted decoration which appears to depict similar scenes, but in most cases the decoration survives only as slight traces. The personal names, however, are a mixture of Greek, Campanian, and Roman, although usually expressed in the Greek form (name + patronymic) rather than the Roman form. In other tombs, such as the Via Foria hypogaeum (Levi, 1926), the names of the deceased, which are a mixture of Campanian and Greek names which alternate within the family between generations, are incised into the plaster of the walls of the tomb. The list includes Epilytos Epilytou, Bibios Epilytou, Epilytos Trebiou and Epilytos Bibiou. The tomb seems to have been in use from the mid-late first century BC, but the latest epitaph, "Epilytos Epilytou, hiereus Sebastou Kaisaros" ("Epilytos, son of Epilytos, priest of Augustus Caesar") demonstrates that it was still in use in the first century AD. The emphasis in these families seems to be on continuity and preservation of Greek forms of commemoration.

The majority of funerary inscriptions from Naples is, in contrast, written in Latin, and commemorates people with Latin (or Latinized) names. Some of those which are in Greek are literal translations of the Latin *D(is) M(anibus)* type of epitaph, which suggests a high degree of Latinization of the epigraphic culture. This contrast may be partly the result of chronology, as these date to the second century AD or later, while the inscriptions from the hypogaea are somewhat earlier. It may also reflect socioeconomic status, as they commemorate people beyond the elite. Nevertheless, they reveal a division between the public culture of Naples, with its emphasis on hellenism, and the increasingly Roman culture of the mass of the population.

Onomastic practices are also revealing. From the Augustan period onwards, Greek names, where they occur, were mainly of a type which suggests slave origin. Most Neapolitans had adopted Roman names. Even the members of the elite who were commissioning public inscriptions in Greek, and of Greek type, had all adopted Roman names, expressed in Roman form. Much of the population, therefore, had adopted Roman naming practices – an important element in assessing cultural change (Leiwo, 1994; Lomas, 2003). This raises some important questions about demographic continuity. Studies of the onomastic history of Naples suggest that there was a fair amount of continuity until the first century AD, indicated by the survival of Greek and Campanian names. From the second century AD, Latin names became more predominant, which may point to the arrival of significant numbers of people from other areas of Campania, perhaps migrating following the eruption of Vesuvius (Leiwo, 1994: 171–72). As Leiwo himself recognizes, however, it can be difficult to distinguish between Neapolitan names and those of the rest of Campania. It should also be borne in mind that an increase in Roman names may be the result of a culturally driven change in naming practices rather than a change in population.

12.7   Conclusions

In conclusion, it may be useful to consider why Roman Naples developed such a unique hybrid culture, mixing Greek, Roman, and Campanian elements. Latin was widely adopted, as were many features of Roman administrative organization, and the urban landscape appears to have changed to embrace the building types and architectural styles of contemporary Italy. At the same time, Greek customs and language did not just persist, but were in some cases – such as the Greek games – actively reinvented and promoted. This trend appears to be the result of the cultural choices made by the inhabitants of the city, and in particular the elite. Even during the second century AD and later, when there may have been significant demographic change which diluted the original Graeco-Oscan population, some aspects of Greek culture were actively and enthusiastically promoted by the Neapolitans. It should also be noted that promotion of traditional culture was a selective process. Only the Greek aspects of Naples' heritage were actively promoted in the Roman period, despite the fact that Oscan/Campanian influence was also part of the city's history (Lomas, 1997; Lomas, 2015).

This opens up some important questions as to why Naples, in particular, retained such a strong Greek culture, and why the city developed along these lines. The answer may lie in the wider cultural context created by the Roman conquest and incorporation of Italy, and by the changes which took place in Roman culture in the second–first centuries BC. From the second century onwards, the Roman elite developed a strong – if ambivalent – interest in Greek culture (cf. Schultz, ch. 3 this vol.). Greek language and culture formed an important element in the education of upper class Romans, and aspects of hellenism became increasingly embedded in Roman culture (Wallace-Hadrill, 2008: 73–103). Naples and its surrounding area became very popular with the Roman elite from the second century BC onwards. The notoriously philhellene Scipio Africanus owned a villa at Liternum, on the north side of the Bay of Naples, and many wealthy Romans followed suit. By the early empire, a complex of imperial villas had grown up at Baiae, on the far side of the Bay (D'Arms, 1970). The Greek culture of the region was one of its attractions, and this undoubtedly benefited Naples. Its Greek festivals and games, and other ongoing Greek survivals attracted rich Romans and even secured it the patronage of philhellene emperors such as Nero and Hadrian.

Naples was also still a point of contact between the Greek world and Italy, and attracted Greek visitors to its games (Strabo, *Geography*: 5.4.7; Dio Cassius: 55.10.5). It was also used as a handy stepping-stone by some Greeks who aimed at a career in Rome. The Greek poet Archias, for instance, acquired Neapolitan citizenship (Cicero, *In Defence of Archias*: 5–6) and used this as a springboard to launch his career at Rome. A more successful example is the poet Statius, the son of an eminent grammarian from Velia who settled at Naples (Statius, *Silvae*: 5.3.103–94). His literary career, assisted by aristocratic connections and the patronage of Domitian, is a good illustration of the power of Greek culture and importance of its survival in this area of Italy. These were not trivial considerations. Greek culture conferred prestige, and after Hadrian's creation of the Panhellenion, a league of Greek cities which enjoyed significant privileges, it also conferred serious benefits and enhanced civic status on a community (Spawforth and Walker, 1985; Swain, 1996). By showcasing elements of Greek heritage, Naples was well placed to take advantage of this phenomenon, and before that, to benefit from the long-standing Roman admiration of Greek culture which gave rise to it.

Naples undoubtedly benefited from its Greek history and from embedding this in its contemporary culture, but there are still many unknowns about how and why this culture developed. The scarcity of evidence from the first century BC means that it is impossible to ascertain whether the hellenism of the early empire was a direct development from the culture of pre-Roman Naples or a revival of specific aspects of this. The fact that hellenism appears to be confined to elite culture and to certain aspects of civic culture suggests that it may have become a restricted area of high culture, mainly used for the more ceremonial and public aspects of civic life such as exchanges of honors and benefactions. It would be wrong, however, to interpret this as evidence for a lack of engagement by the rest of the population. Dio Cassius's references (55.10.5–6) to the enthusiasm of the Neapolitans for their Greek customs suggests both a level of nostalgia for the city's Greek past and a recognition that it conferred a distinctive cultural identity in the present.

FURTHER READING

There is currently no comprehensive work on ancient Naples available in English, although there is a wealth of material in Italian. Keppie 2009 provides an outline of the archaeological remains. Lomas 1993 discusses Roman Naples in the context of the conquest of southern Italy, and Arthur 2002 covers Naples in Late Antiquity. More detailed discussions of the culture of Roman Naples can be found in Lomas 1997 and in Leiwo 1994. The inscriptions are collected in Miranda 1990 and 1995. The catalog of an exhibition held in Naples in 1985, *Napoli Antica*, presents a wealth of information about the archaeology of the city, as well as articles (mostly in Italian) on many aspects of Greek and Roman Naples. Finally, there is a book, published in 2015, on the reception of the Greek past in Naples edited by Hughes and Buongiovanni.

REFERENCES

Adamo Muscettola, S. 1985. "Il tempio dei Dioscuri." In *Napoli Antica*, 196–208. Naples, Macchiaroli Editore.

Adams, J.N. 2003. *Bilingualism and the Latin Language*. Cambridge: Cambridge University Press.

Arthur, P., ed. 1984. *Il complesso archeologico di Carminiello ai Mannesi, Napoli (1983–83)*. Galantina: Congedo editore.

Arthur, P. 2002. *Naples. From Roman town to city-state*. London: Archaeological Monographs of the British School at Rome, 12.

Baldassare, I. 1985. "Osservazioni sull' urbanistica di Neapolis in età romana." In *Neapolis. Atti del 25° Convegno di Studi sulla Magna Grecia: 221–32*. Taranto: Istituto per la storia e l'archeologia della Magna Grecia.

Bragantini, I., ed. 1991. *Ricerche archeologiche a Napoli.Lo scavo di Palazzo Corigliano I*. Naples: Istituto Universitario Orientale.

Bispham, E.H. 2007. *From Asculum to Actium: the municipalization of Italy from the Social War to Augustus*. Oxford: Oxford University Press.

Cooley, A.E. 2002. "Introduction." In *Becoming Roman, writing Latin? Literacy and epigraphy in the Roman West*, ed. A.E. Cooley, 9–14. Portsmouth, RI: *Journal of Roman Archaeology* Suppl. 48.

Cornell, T.J. 1995. *The Beginnings of Rome: Italy and Rome from the Bronze Age to the Punic Wars (c. 1000–264 BC)*. London: Routledge.

D'Arms, J.H. 1970. *Romans on the Bay of Naples*. Cambridge, MA: Harvard University Press.

De Caro, S. 1974. "La necropoli di Pizzofalcone in Napoli." *Rendiconti dell'Accademia di Archeologia, Lettere e Belle Arti di Napoli* n.s. 49: 37–67.

De Martino, F. 1952. "Le istituzioni di Napoli greco-romana." *Parola del Passato* 7: 335–43.

Dench, E. 1995. *From Barbarians to New Men. Greek, Roman and modern perceptions of peoples from the central Apennines*. Oxford: Clarendon Press.

De Simone, A. 1985. "Il complesso monumentale di San Lorenzo Maggiore." In *Napoli Antica*, 185–89. Naples: Macchiaroli Editore.

Dittenberger W. and Pergold, K. 1896. *Die Inscriften von Olympia*. Berlin: A. Ashe & Co.

Frederiksen, M. 1984. *Campania*, ed. N. Purcell. London: British School at Rome.

Fronda, M. 2010. *Between Rome and Carthage. Southern Italy during the Second Punic War*. Cambridge: Cambridge University Press.

Geer, R.M. 1935. "The Greek games at Naples." *Transactions of the American Philological Association* 66: 208–21.

Greco, E. 1985a. "L'impianto urbano di Neapolis: aspetti e problem." *Neapolis. Atti del 25°Convegno di Studi sulla Magna Grecia, 187–220*. Taranto: Istituto per la storia e l'archeologia della Magna Grecia.

Greco, E. 1985b. "Problemi urbanistici." In *Napoli Antica*, 132–39. Naples: Macchiaroli Editore.

Greco Pontrandolfo, A. and Vecchio, G. 1985. "Gli ipogei funerarie." In *Napoli Antica*, 283–92. Naples: Macchiaroli Editore.

Guarducci, M. 1936. "L'istituzione della fratria nella Grecia antica e nelle colonie greche d'Italia. I." *Memorie della classe di scienze morali, storiche e filologiche dell' Accademia dei Lincei* 6.6.1.

Hardie, A. 1983. *Statius and the* Silvae. *Poets, patrons and epideixis in the Graeco-Roman World.* Liverpool: Francis Cairns.

Hatzfeld, M.J. 1912. "Les italiens résidant à Délos mentionnés dans les inscriptions de l'île." *Bulletin de correspondance hellénique* 36: 5–218.

Hatzfeld, M.J. 1919. *Les trafiquants italiens dans l'orient hellénique.* Paris: De Boccard.

Häussler, R. 2002. "Writing Latin – from resistance to assimilation: language, society and culture in N. Gaul and S. France." In *Becoming Roman, Writing Latin? Literacy and epigraphy in the Roman West,* ed. A.E. Cooley, 61–76. Portsmouth RI: *Journal of Roman Archaeology* Suppl. 48.

Hughes, J. and Buongiovanni, C., eds. 2015. *Remembering Parthenope. The reception of Classical Naples from Antiquity to the present.* Oxford: Oxford University Press.

Johannowsky, W. 1976. "La situazione in Campania." In *Hellenismus in Mittelitalien,* ed. P. Zanker, 267–99. Göttingen: Vandenhoeck und Ruprecht.

Jouffroy, H. 1986. *La construction publique en Italie et dans L'Afrique romaine.* Strasbourg: AECR.

Keppie, L.J.F. 2009. *The Romans on the Bay of Naples: an archaeological guide.* London: The History Press.

Leiwo, M. 1994. *Neapolitana: a study of population and language in Graeco-Roman Naples.* Helsinki: Societas Scientarum Fennica.

Lepore, E., 1967. "La vita politica e sociale." In *Storia di Napoli,* Vol.1: 139–372. Naples, Società Editrice Storia di Napoli.

Levi, A. 1926. "Camere sepolcrali scoperte in Napoli durante i lavori della direttissima Roma-Napoli." *Monumenti Antichi dell'Accademia dei Lincei* 31: 378–402.

Lomas, K. 1993. *Rome and the Western Greeks, 350 BC–AD 200. Conquest and acculturation in south Italy.* London: Routledge.

Lomas, K. 1997. "Graeca urbs? Ethnicity and culture in early imperial Naples." *Accordia Research Papers* 7: 113–30.

Lomas, K. 2002. "Public building and urban renewal in early imperial Italy." In *Euergetism and Municipal Patronage in Roman Italy,* eds T.J. Cornell and K. Lomas, 28–45. London: Routledge.

Lomas, K. 2003. "Personal identity and Romanization: funerary inscriptions and funerary iconography from southern Italy." In *Inhabiting Symbols: symbol and image in the ancient Mediterranean,* eds J.B. Wilkins and E. Herring, 193–210. London: Accordia Research Institute.

Lomas, K. 2015. "Colonising the past: cultural memory and civic identity in Roman Naples." In *Remembering Parthenope. The reception of Classical Naples from Antiquity to the present,* eds J. Hughes and C. Buongiovanni. Oxford: Oxford University Press.

Maiuri, A. 1913. "La nuova iscrizione della fratria napoletana degli Artemisi." *Studi Romani* 1: 21–36.

Miranda, E. 1982. "I cataloghi dei Sebastà di Napoli. Proposte ed osservazioni." *Rendiconti dell'Accademia di Archeologia, Lettere e Belle Arti di Napoli* n.s. 57: 165–81.

Miranda, E. 1985a. "Le magistrature." In *Napoli Antica,* 386–89. Naples: Macchiaroli Editore.

Miranda, E. 1985b. "Gli agoni." In *Napoli Antica,* 390–92. Naples: Macchiaroli Editore.

Miranda, E. 1990. *Iscrizioni greche d'Italia. Napoli* I. Rome: Quasar.

Miranda, E. 1995. *Iscrizioni greche d'Italia. Napoli* II. Rome: Quasar.

Miranda E. 2007. "Neapolis e gli imperatori. Nuovi dati dai cataloghi dei Sebastà." *Oebalus. Studi sulla Campania nell'antichità* 2: 203–15.

Miranda, E. 2010. "Consoli e altri elementi di datazione nei cataloghi agonistici di «Neapolis»." In *Le tribù romane: atti della XVIe « Rencontre sur l'épigraphie»,* ed. M. Silvestrini, 417–22. Bari: Edipuglia.

Napoli, M. 1959. *Napoli greco-romana.* Naples: F. Fiorentino.

Papadopoulos, J. 1985. "I rilievi funerary." In *Napoli Antica,* 293–98. Naples: Macchiaroli Editore.

Pinsent, J. 1969. "The magistracy at Naples." *Parola del Passato* 24: 368–72.

Pozzi, E. 1989. "L'attività archeologico in Campania; provincie di Napoli e Caserta." In *Un secolo di ricerche in Magna Grecia: Atti del 29° Convegno di studi sulla Magna Grecia.* Taranto: Istituto per la storia e l'archeologia della Magna Grecia.

Raviola, F. 1995. *Napoli origini*. Rome: «L'Erma» di Bretschneider.

Rutter, N.K. 1979. *Campanian Coinages, 475–380 B.C.* Edinburgh: Edinburgh University Press.

Sartori, F. 1953. *Problemi di storia costituzionale italiota*. Rome: «L'Erma» di Bretschneider.

Salmon, E.T. 1967. *Samnium and the Samnites*. Cambridge: Cambridge University Press.

Sherwin-White, A.N. 1973, 2nd edn. *The Roman Citizenship*. Oxford: Clarendon Press.

Spawforth, A.J.S. and Walker, S. 1985. "The World of the Panhellenion I." *Journal of Roman Studies* 75: 78–104.

Swain, S. 1996. *Hellenism and Empire. Language, classicism and power in the Greek world, AD 50–250*. Oxford, Oxford University Press.

Wallace-Hadrill, A. 2008. *Rome's Cultural Revolution*. Cambridge: Cambridge University Press.

Woolf, G. 1996. "Monumental writing and the expansion of Roman society in the early Empire." *Journal of Roman Studies* 86: 22–39.

Zanker, P. 1988. *The Power of Images in the Age of Augustus*, trans. A. Shapiro. Ann Arbor: The University of Michigan Press.

CHAPTER 13

Magna Graecia, 270 BC–AD 200

Kathryn Lomas

13.1 Introduction

Magna Graecia, as the area of Italy settled by the Greeks was commonly known, was a region of contrasting fortunes in the eyes of ancient authors. Sources for the pre-Roman history of the region characterize its cities as prosperous and luxurious to the point of decadence. The wealth and power of Sybaris, and later of Croton and Tarentum, was proverbial. Even the name, "Great Greece" (*Magna Graecia*, or *Megale Hellas* in Greek), given to the region by both Greeks and Romans, signifies magnitude in both geographical and economic terms. After the Roman conquest, however, this changed dramatically to an image of economic decline, depopulation, and barbarization. The Greek cities of Italy were said to have fallen from their former glory and to be depopulated and abandoned (Cicero, *On Friendship*: 13). Greek culture, it is implied, had disappeared and the Greek population was either driven out, or became barbarized (Aristoxenos, in Athenaeus, *Deipnosophists*: 16.632a). Strabo qualifies this, saying that: "apart from the Tarentines, Rhegines and Neapolitans, the Greeks have become barbarians; some have been captured and held by the Lucanians and Bruttians, and by the Campanians – in name, that is, but in reality by the Romans. For these have themselves become Romans" (*Geography*: 6.1.3) implying that there were some exceptions to the general barbarization, and that it was offset a little by Roman influence.

Needless to say, this is a huge oversimplification of Magna Graecia after the Roman conquest, but such a sweeping characterization of a large area of Italy and a disparate group of communities poses many challenges for the historian. One is to evaluate a sparse and difficult body of ancient sources, and to try to disentangle cultural prejudice from fact. Another is to integrate this with a body of epigraphic evidence which suggests that despite Cicero's gloom-laden picture, most of the Greek cities of Italy were still alive and well long after the Roman conquest. Finally, these written sources must be considered in the light of archaeological investigation, which has transformed the picture of decline, allowing a much more nuanced reconstruction of Hellenistic and Roman Magna Graecia. Although the Greek cities of southern Italy underwent major social, economic, demographic, and cultural changes, they did not disappear. This chapter will examine the evidence for Magna Graecia after the Roman conquest, a region of changing cultural identities where Greek,

A Companion to Roman Italy, First Edition. Edited by Alison E. Cooley.

Roman, and other Italian cultures interacted, and a region of contact and dialog between Italy, Rome, and the Greek world.

Firstly, something must be said about the definition of Magna Graecia and the nature of the region (see Figure 13.1). Some ancient authors used the term to refer to all Greek settlement outside Greece (Pindar, *Pythian Odes*: 1.146; Euripides, *Medea*: 439–40, *Trojan Women*: 1110–17, *Iphigenia in Aulis*: 1378), but it was more commonly used to refer to areas of Greek settlement in Italy. Most do not apply the term to Sicily, and some also exclude Campania, defining Magna Graecia as some or all of the Greek cities along the coast of Puglia, Basilicata, and Calabria (Polybius: 2.39.1; Pliny the Elder, *Natural History*: 3.38 and 95; Appian, *Samnite Wars*: 7.1; Servius, *On the Aeneid*: 1.569; Seneca, *On Consolation, to Helvia*: 7.2; Strabo, *Geography*: 6.1.2; Pseudo-Scymnos: 303. On the changing geographical definitions of Magna Graecia, see Maddoli, 1982; Musti, 1988: 78–94; Lomas, 1993: 8–13). This chapter will focus principally on Greek settlement south of Campania (see ch.12, this vol., for discussion of Roman Naples). It will be clear, given the wide area covered, that there was a

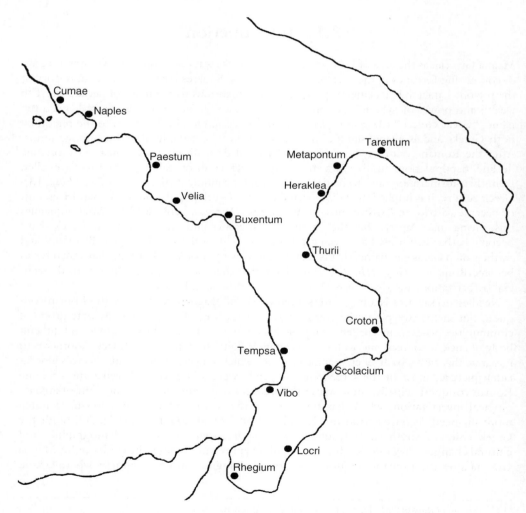

Figure 13.1   The major Greek settlements of Italy. Drawing: K. Lomas.

considerable amount of diversity between the Greek communities of Italy (Purcell 1994; Cerchiai, Jannelli, and Longo, 2002). They were originally settled by people from various different areas of Greece and, by the fourth century, they identified with many different Greek *poleis* as their founding cities. This was important as the relationship between founder and colony (even if that relationship rested largely on myth) was significant both to the cultural identities of the Italian Greeks and to political and diplomatic affiliations. There were also considerable variations in economic success. The cities of the south coast, such as Croton, Tarentum, and Metapontum, controlled large and fertile territories and were amongst the wealthiest in the Greek world. Others, such as the Greek communities of Calabria were much smaller, relying largely on fishing and exploitation of small strips of coastal territory. By the fourth century BC, Tarentum had established itself as the dominant city of much of Magna Graecia, but its influence over the northern part of the region, and especially the cities of Campania and Lucania, seems to have been very limited. They were, therefore, a disparate group of communities and their various relationships with Rome, and histories during the Roman period, must be understood in the context of this diversity.

13.2   Roman Conquest: Magna Graecia Before the Social War

The Roman conquest took place between 327 and 270 BC, and was largely a consequence of the Samnite wars and later the Pyrrhic war. A short war between Rome and Naples in 327–326 BC ended when a political faction sympathetic to Rome seized power and negotiated an advantageous peace settlement (Livy: 8.22.7–29.5; Dionysius of Halicarnassus, *Roman Antiquities*: 15.5.1–9.2; Cicero, *In Defence of Balbus*: 8.21; Lomas, 1993: 44–48). Following this, there were intermittent clashes with Tarentum, principally in 326 and 320 BC, followed by the Pyrrhic war of 281–270 BC. Discussion of this complicated period of history (for details, see Franke, 1989) is beyond the scope of this chapter, but an outline of Magna Graecia's relations with Rome between 270 and 90 BC may be useful.

It is likely that after 270 BC relations with Rome were governed by biliateral treaties with each individual city (Livy, *Summary / Periocha*: 15), as was the case elsewhere in Italy. However, Tarentum and its allies had come close to defeating Rome during the Pyrrhic war, and the region was perceived as troublesome. A Roman garrison was placed at Tarentum at the outbreak of the Hannibalic war, well before Hannibal's campaign in southern Italy, and hostages were taken from Tarentum and Thurii (Polybius: 3.75.4; Livy: 25.10.1–3). Roman uneasiness was justified in 215–209 BC, when a significant number of Greek cities rebelled and joined Hannibal (Fronda, 2010; Lomas, 1993, 66–72; 2011: 344–45, 351). Cumae, Naples, Paestum, Velia, and Rhegium all remained loyal to Rome, but Croton and Locri changed sides in 215 BC (Livy: 24.1.1–3) and Tarentum revolted in 212, taking Heraklea and Metapontum along with it (Livy: 24.13.1–9, 24.20.9–16; Polybius: 8.32–33; Appian, *Hannibalic War*: 6.32–36). All were recaptured by Rome in 210–209 BC.

The post-war settlements reimposed Roman alliances on the rebel cities (Livy: 27.25.1–5; 29.19.7–9, 21.7–8) but with added penalties. 30 000 slaves and 3000 talents of precious metal were seized from Tarentum (Livy: 27.16.7–9, 21.8, 25.1–5; Appian, *Hannibalic War*: 8.49; Plutarch, *Life of Fabius Maximus*: 8. 21–23; Suetonius, *Grammarians*: 18.1–3) and some parts of Magna Graecia were placed under direct Roman supervision (Livy: 27.25.1–5, 31.29.9–10, 38.42.5–6, 39.39.8–10, 41.6–7; Appian, *Syrian Wars*: 15; Plutarch, *Life of Flamininus*: 1.4). Pleminius, the Roman governor, was withdrawn from Locri in 208 BC following complaints about his conduct (Livy: 29.19.7–9, 21.7–8) but much of Puglia – including Tarentum– was governed by a Roman prefect until at least 186 BC, probably due to continued unrest and the strategic importance of the harbor of Tarentum. Livy (31.29.9–10, 38.42.5–6, 39.39.8–10) refers to brigandage and "conspiracies of shepherds" which resulted in 20 000 arrests in 186, suggesting ongoing instability. Although the basis of Roman relations with the region remained a series of alliances with individual states, Rome also founded a number of colonies in Magna Graecia (see Table 13.1), which also suggests an ongoing concern with the security of the region, and which tied the communities concerned more firmly to Rome.

Little is known about the role of Magna Graecia in the Social War or the civil wars of the first century BC. None of the Greek cities is known to have rebelled in 90 BC, and so far as we know, all were given Roman citizenship in 90 BC by the *Lex Julia Civitatis* apart from Cumae, which had possessed *civitas sine suffragio* since 338 BC and full Roman citizenship since 188 (Livy: 8.14; 40.42.13). The only insight is offered by Cicero's slightly odd statement that Naples and Heraklea petitioned Rome to retain their status as autonomous allies after the war, rather than becoming Roman citizens, saying that many of their citizens "preferred the freedom of their treaties to citizenship" (Cicero, *In Defence of Balbus*: 21; Lomas, 1993: 92–94). Cicero's apparent reading of this is that the terms of Naples' treaty were so advantageous that Roman citizenship was seen as a potential backward step, but it could also imply that these cities were trying to keep Rome at arm's length. Whatever, the reason for this request, it was rejected and, from 89 BC, all of Magna Graecia was incorporated into Roman citizenship, either as *municipia* or *coloniae*.

13.3 Reorganizing Magna Graecia

13.3.1 *Roman colonization and settlement*

An important factor in the transformation of Italy from the third century onwards was the foundation of numerous Roman colonies. As well as establishing a permanent Roman presence in a region, they also disseminated Roman-style urban development and many other Roman practices such as use of Latin and adoption of Roman forms of government. Magna Graecia, like many areas of Italy, experienced a significant level of Roman settlement and consequent reorganization (see Table 13.1).

The nature and purpose of these colonies varied. Buxentum, Tempsa, and Croton were small colonies (circa 300 settlers), designated as Roman citizen colonies. All were founded in coastal locations, possibly to protect the coast in case of invasion or raids by pirates, and to

Table 13.1 Roman colonization in Magna Graecia

Location	Date	Size and Status
Paestum	1. 273 BC	Latin, circa 4000 settlers
	2. circa 80 BC	Sullan veterans
Buxentum	194 BC	Roman Citizen, circa 200–300 settlers
Tempsa	194 BC	Roman Citizen, circa 200–300 settlers
Croton	194 BC	Roman Citizen, circa 200–300 settlers
Thurii	193 BC	Latin, circa 3000–5000 settlers
Vibo	192 BC	Latin, circa 3000–5000 settlers
Tarentum	1. 122 BC	Gracchan colony
	2. First century AD	Veteran settlement under Nero
Scolacium	1. 122 BC	Gracchan colony
	2. Early second century AD	Veteran settlement under Nerva

revive communities which had suffered from the Hannibalic war. Valentia, founded at Vibo, and Copia, founded near Thurii, were somewhat larger, with 4000 and 3300 colonists respectively (Livy: 39.53.2; Brunt, 1971: 281), and had the status of Latin colonies. Two further colonies were founded in 123/22 bc, as part of Gaius Gracchus's program of colonization, namely Minervia at Scolacium and Neptunia in the territory of Tarentum, almost certainly occupying land confiscated from the Tarentines after 209 bc (Plutarch, *Life of Gaius Gracchus*: 8; Velleius Paterculus: 1.14.7; Pliny *Natural History*: 3.99). Finds of Roman boundary markers also demonstrate that there was redistribution of land on an individual basis during the Gracchan period in some parts of the region, especially in Lucania and parts of Bruttium (Isayev, 2007: 178–85).

Colonization in Magna Graecia continued intermittently throughout the first century AD. From the 80s bc onwards, colonial foundation mostly involved the settlement of discharged soldiers, although some grants of colonial status during the Roman Empire were merely changes in legal status and privilege unaccompanied by any settlement. Inscriptions from Cumae containing the abbreviation *D(ecreto) D(ecurionum) C(oloniae) I(uliae)* suggest that there was an Augustan colony there, although the colonial status of the city has also been dated to the second century AD (*CIL* 10.3703–04; Keppie 1983, 148–50; Sartori 1953, 38–42). At Paestum, there is epigraphic evidence for a settlement of veterans from the fleet at Misenum in AD 71, while at Tarentum there is evidence of two post-Gracchan colonies, one in the first century bc consisting of a group of pirates pardoned by Pompey and the other in AD 60 and composed of military veterans (Tacitus, *Annals* 14.27; Gasperini 1968, 389–97 and 1971, 148; Mello and Voza 1968, nos 36, 37, 86; Mello 1974, 119–25).

The extent of demographic change is difficult to quantify, and its impact on the culture and ethnicity of Magna Graecia was complex. The evidence for both colonization and the settlement of individuals outside colonies suggests that by the first century AD there was a significant non-Greek element in the population of the region. We should, however, be wary of viewing this as a simple division between an ethnically Greek population in the pre-Roman period and, afterwards, an ethnically Italian one, with a sharply decreasing Greek element. The region was always ethnically mixed, with Lucanians, Campanians, and other Italic groups living in Greek communities and integrating with them. In addition, there is no easy equivalence between language, culture and ethnicity. In some parts of the region, the persistence of Greek culture and language was striking, despite demographic changes.

The foundation of a colony could, however, have a big impact on the surrounding area. A survey of the Bussento valley has shown that the foundation of a colony at Buxentum (previously the Greek city of Pyxous) strengthened the city significantly and changed patterns of settlement in the hinterland. The Lucanian site at Roccagloriosa, situated further up the Bussento valley, declined and other inland settlements were abandoned. A more intensive pattern of land use developed around Buxentum itself (de Polignac and Gualtieri, 1991; Fracchia, 2001; Isayev 2007: 170–78), suggesting that the foundation of the colony had strengthened the area around the new Roman settlement at the expense of the upper reaches of the valley. The urban center of Buxentum also underwent development, with the construction of a forum and market building, and new city walls (Jouffroy, 1986: 69, 86–88), over the period between the foundation of the colony and the end of the first century bc. Other changes to civic culture can also be traced in colonies. Roman forms of civic administration replaced those of the Greek past. Latin replaced Greek (and in the case of Cumae and Paestum, Oscan) as the official language of these cities. Latin personal names are found in inscriptions – especially those concerning the activities of the elite – reflecting the demographic changes and the increasing social dominance of the colonists at the expense of the previous population.

13.3.2   Municipal government: Magna Graecia
after the Social War

The municipal reorganization of Italy after 89 BC inevitably caused major changes in the Greek communities, as it did elsewhere in Italy. Magna Graecia poses some particularly fascinating problems in this respect, touching on the wider issues of civic and cultural identity as well as on the nuts-and-bolts mechanisms of municipal administration. Many aspects of Roman municipal government were adopted and in communities which had been colonized by Rome, city government seems to have been based closely on the usual Roman forms of elected boards of two or four magistrates (*duoviri* or *quattuorviri*), supported by junior magistrates, and a local senate (Bispham. 2007: 381–404). At Paestum, for instance, this type of constitution is established from the foundation of the Latin colony of 273 BC, as demonstrated by early inscriptions mentioning quaestors and *duoviri* (Mello and Voza, 1968: nos 139–48; Torelli, 1999: 89–95). The *Lex Tarentina*, a fragment of a municipal law or charter of the first century BC demonstrates that Tarentum had adopted a Roman type of constitution relatively soon after the Social War (Crawford, 1996: 301–12). In some communities, however, aspects of Greek civic government seem to survive alongside these Roman institutions, at least into the first century AD and possibly even later (Sartori, 1953: 17–27; Lomas, 1993: 143–58).

   The most complex case is Naples, where some civic inscriptions name the civic magistrates as Roman *quattuorviri* (or in Greek, as *tessares andres*) while others refer to Greek magistrates such as the *archon*, *demarchos* and *laukelarchos* (Sartori, 1953: 46–55; Lomas, 1993: 148–52. See also Lomas, ch. 12, this vol). However, this is not the only city which shows evidence of Greek survivals. At Velia, an epitaph of the first century BC commemorates Cornelius Gemellus who held the Roman-style offices of *duumvir*, *quaestor*, *quattuorvir iure dicundo* and the Greek post of *gymnasiarchos* (*ILS* 6461). Another Greek office, that of *pholarchos*, also continued to exist at least until the first century AD. This is unknown from anywhere else in the Greek world, and seems to be associated with the healing cult of Apollo Oulios, one of the main cults of Velia (*AE* (1966) 108; Ebner, 1962: 125–36; Pugliese Carratelli, 1970: 243–48; Ebner, 1970: 262–67). Two decrees of the local council, awarding honors to a local priest and a visiting Roman dignitary, are also presented in Greek terms. They date to the first or early second century AD, and are written in Greek – although the decree in honor of the Roman C. Julius Naso also has a Latin translation – and are closely modeled on the proxeny decrees conferring honors on prominent people which are found throughout the Greek world (*AE* (1959) 97; Pugliese Carratelli, 1970; Lomas, 1993: 156–58). There are also inscriptions from Rhegium which refer to the continuation of the office of *gymnasiarchos* and that of *prytanis* well into the early empire (*IG* 14.617–21; *SEG* 29.987–89; Costabile, 1979: 525–45). All these cities possessed constitutions largely based on Roman forms by the end of the Republic but also preserved some aspects of Greek practice in the continuation of Greek offices, some of which are of types common in the Hellenistic and Roman East, such as the *gymasiarchos*, while others seem to be very local, such as the *pholarchos* at Velia and the *laukelarchos* at Naples.

   None of these Greek institutions map easily onto Roman ones, so it is unlikely that these Greek elements are simply Greek terms for Roman offices. They are also unlikely to be straightforward survivals of pre-Roman forms of government (Sartori, 1953). At Naples, for instance, only the *demarchos* and *laukelarchos* are known from the Greek era. *Archontes* only appear in inscriptions from the first and second century AD (Lomas, ch. 12, this vol.). In addition, the Latin inscriptions from these cities, which form the bulk of our epigraphic evidence, demonstrate that the usual Roman civic organization was in place (Lomas, 1993: 143–58, 174–76).

Looking more closely, these Greek survivals seem to cluster into two main fields of activity. In many cases, Greek titles and offices, and the use of Greek language in official documents, only occurs in documents with a ritual or ceremonial function rather than in routine administrative inscriptions. The Greek decrees from Rhegium issued by the *Prytanis*, for instance are records of sacrifices to Apollo, a very ancient Greek cult, not records of civic administration. In this context, the use of traditional Greek titles and forms of recording may have been thought particularly appropriate (for similar examples at Naples, see Lomas, ch. 12, this vol.). Greek decrees from Velia and the Naples area were also largely ceremonial rather than administrative, conferring Greek types of honors on prominent citizens or visitors. Greek types of magistracy were peripheral to the day-to-day running of the city. Instead, the *gymnasiarchoi* at Naples, Rhegium, and Velia are primarily concerned with supervising the civic gymnasium (an important feature of the culture of Hellenistic cities), and the *pholarchos* at Velia and the *laukelarchos* at Naples seem to have been connected with Greek cults. The implications of this, and the cultural significance are discussed further in section 13.7 of this chapter, but in all these cases, the Greek survivals seem to have been embedded in largely Roman frameworks of government.

13.4 Economic Development

The economic history of Magna Graecia in the Roman period is a highly contentious area. One well-established view is that the region was in terminal economic decline from the end of the Hannibalic war onwards. On this interpretation, vast areas of southern Italy which had been devastated during the war never recovered (Appian, *Civil Wars*: 1.7; Kahrstedt, 1960; Toynbee, 1965; Brunt, 1971: 277). The damage to land and crops and the sacking of cities, combined with depopulation due to deaths, exile, and the continuing drain on manpower caused by Roman military demands, undermined the rural economy. Many small farms were abandoned and the land either fell into disuse or was absorbed into large estates which were exploited by largely absentee landlords, draining income and resources from the local area. This doom-laden picture has been modified, particularly in the light of the ever-increasing evidence of archaeological survey data. The depopulation and devastation of the south in the immediate post-war period may have been a relatively short-term problem (Garnsey, 1988: 188–97; Erdkamp, 1998: 270–96; for a restatement of Toynbee's view, see Cornell, 1996). Magna Graecia, in particular, has been assumed to have suffered a severe decline and become moribund, but we should beware of some of the sweeping statements to this effect in the sources. Many of these are making a moral rather than an economic point, contrasting previous glories with current status. Some areas of Magna Graecia recovered more quickly and completely than others, and it is possible that new developments in the agrarian economy of Italy were a change rather than a crisis. If examined closely, the epigraphic and archaeological evidence modifies this picture significantly.

It is undeniable that the structure of land ownership and agrarian production changed significantly in the period after the Hannibalic war, as did the economic relationship between city and territory. Surveys of the territories of Metapontum and Croton (Carter, 1984; 1990) demonstrate the rise of villa agriculture. The number of rural settlements and farms shows a slow decline from the end of the fourth century BC until the second century AD, followed by a more marked decline thereafter, but there is no sudden slump in productivity. Even at Metapontum, which suffered acutely from depopulation in the late third century, there is evidence of production of several types of pottery, tiles, and amphorae; a harbor which continued in use until Late Antiquity; and warehouses which could store a significant amount of grain (Crawford, 2003: 23–25). Archaeological evidence from Calabria also shows the growth of many villas in the late Republic and early Empire (Sangineto, 1994; Accardo, 2000). Of 168 securely identified villas in this region, 42% date to the late Republic and 32% to the early Empire, with a marked diminution from the third century onwards (Accardo, 2000: 206). Far from collapsing economically, the numbers of villas, and the production of items associated with the storage and trade in agrarian products, such as oil jars or wine amphorae, seem to indicate that the south Italian economy in this period was healthy. A similar pattern is found in Apulia, where the development of villa agriculture is associated with the production and export of olive oil in large quantities (Desy, 1993). This suggests that the land was productive from the first century BC to second century AD, although with signs of economic contraction in the third and fourth centuries AD. What is much less clear is who owned the villas and benefited from their produce, and how this affected the economic relationships between city and territory. Many leading Romans are known to have owned villas in various areas of southern Italy, including Crassus, Claudius Pulcher, and Cicero himself (Accardo, 2000: 49–51; Crawford, 2003: 18–22), so the profits from these estates were benefiting absentee landlords from outside the area, rather than the surrounding region. However, these developments were not necessarily at the expense of urban life. The known senatorial landowners cannot account for all the villas in the region, and it is likely that at least some were owned by members of the local elite (Accardo, 2000: 49–51). Despite the damage to the cities of Magna Graecia in the short term, most of the Greek cities continued to survive, and new urban centers began to develop in some parts of the region (see section 13.6 of this chapter; Accardo, 2000: 43–47). This argues that the development of a villa-based economy was not incompatible with the survival of urban life.

It is also clear that Magna Graecia was engaged in trade and manufacture. Inscriptions from Delos demonstrate that Velian merchants were involved in the olive oil trade, and there is circumstantial evidence that they may also have been involved in the slave trade (Leiwo, 1985). As well as olive oil, Velia also produced *garum* (Morel, 1976: 310). Tarentum was a noted producer of wool, fine textiles, and purple dye. The veracity of some of the poetic references to wool has been questioned (Morel, 1978: 94–110) but evidence of the high price of Tarentine products suggests that the industry was both real and profitable. Pliny the Elder cites the price of Tarentine dye at the considerable sum of 100 *denarii* per pound and notes a high demand for it, while Diocletian's prices edict quotes Tarentine wool at 175 *denarii* per pound for fleeces and weaving costs of 30 *denarii* per pound – much higher than for wool from other areas (Pliny the Elder, *Natural History*: 9.137; Diocletian's *Prices Edict*: 21.2, 25.1 = Graser, 1940). Ancient authors also describe wine, olive oil, and fruit from Magna Graecia as well regarded (Pliny the Elder, *Natural History*: 14.39, 14.69, 15.37, 15.55, 15.71, 15.90, 15.93–94; Athenaeus, *Deipnosophists*: 1.26–27), and Campana pottery was produced in large quantities in the northern part of the region (Morel, 1981).

Although some Greek cities struggled after 200 BC, many show signs of substantial economic activity. There is no doubt that centers such as Tarentum, Croton, and Rhegium had declined in power and prosperity from their fourth-century peak, but they remained viable and functioning cities, and some – such as Naples, Cumae, and Velia – did well out of the trading opportunities and Roman patronage made available by the expansion of Rome into the Greek world. Naples, Rhegium, and Tarentum remained important ports, although Naples and Tarentum were later overshadowed by the development of Puteoli and Brundisium. The development of the Roman road system undoubtedly impacted on the economy of Magna Graecia. The cities located on or near the *via Appia* and *via Annia Popilia*, the main arterial roads between Rome and Brundisium and between Rome and Rhegium, did better than those which were more isolated from the main transport network, with its flow of goods, information, and people. The structure of the agrarian economy changed significantly – as it did in many other areas of Italy – but there are signs that this was a process of change rather than terminal decline. Ultimately, some cities did vanish, but this took place much later. Paestum seems to have fallen into a decline in the fourth century AD and to have been largely abandoned in the seventh century AD because of climate changes which rendered the area malarial and less viable (Pedley, 1990: 163–65; Torelli, 1999: 165–69), while Velia was abandoned in the ninth century. Others, however, have been continuously occupied since their foundation, and continued to be viable into the Medieval period and onwards.

13.5   Magna Graecia and the Greek World

The Roman conquest of Magna Graecia inevitably shifted the attention of the Greeks of Italy towards Rome, but this did not mean that they lost their connections with the Greek world. Athletes and artists from Magna Graecia are found in lists of competitors and victors in local games and festivals in many parts of Greece. For example, a Neapolitan flute-player, Agathokles son of Theodosios (*IG* 7.540) won a contest at Oropus in Boeotia circa 80 BC, and a Tarentine actor, Dorotheos Dorotheou, won contests at Orchomenos and Argos around the same date (*IG* 7.3197; Gossage, 1984: 115–34). These examples do not just demonstrate the success of individuals, but also that Greeks from Italy were still participating in the circuit of Greek athletic and artistic festivals, which played an important role in fostering a shared Greek identity.

Greeks from Italy also turn up in diplomatic documents in the rest of the Greek world, and there are a number of funerary inscriptions indicating that some had died overseas, either as exiles or as travelers in the Greek world. The largest body of evidence, however, comes from Delos. From the mid-second century BC, it became a major hub for trade in the eastern Mediterranean, attracting a large number of merchants and bankers. Inscriptions from the island demonstrate that many people who took advantage of these trading opportunities were Italian, mainly from areas of Apennine and southern Italy. Around 20% of the Italians on Delos can be identified as from Magna Graecia, thanks to the Greek habit of adding an ethnic element to their personal name in inscriptions (Hatzfeld, 1912; Leiwo, 1985). Although this is not a huge proportion, it is still significant and demonstrates that Greeks from Italy were economically active in the Greek world. People from Velia and Tarentum form the majority of these, but individuals from Locri, Naples, and Heraklea are also known (Hatzfeld, 1912; Lomas, 1993: 191–94). Some maintained extensive contacts with the island. Herakleides of Tarentum, for instance, was a banker whose family connections with Delos can be traced over three generations (Hatzfeld, 1912: 42). Men from Heraklea and Velia invested in the building or repair of the agora of the Italians, which may give a clue as to the nature of their business, as the agora was the main slave market. The family of Hermon of Velia can be traced over four generations, and several of his descendants are named as oil-merchants (Hatzfeld, 1912: 84–85; Leiwo, 1985, 495–97). Some of the Italiotes (i.e., Greeks from Italy) found in the East, especially just after the Hannibalic war, may have been exiles from their home cities who never returned, but many are likely to have been visitors to the Greek world, not permanent emigrants. These individuals demonstrate that some cities of Magna Graecia, at least, were active participants in the trading and cultural networks of the Greek world throughout the second and first centuries BC. They also indicate a level of economic activity which may have benefited their home cities. Many cities in southern Italy show an increase in the building of elite private houses, and of public buildings and amenities at this point, as families which made money from the new trading opportunities invested it in new houses and public benefactions.

Connections with Greece were not a one-way process, however. As Roman interest in Hellenism increased during the second and first centuries (see Schultz, ch. 3 this vol.), the cities of Magna Graecia attracted Greek artists and intellectuals who traveled to Italy with a view to making a career there. The most notable example is Archias, the Greek poet defended by Cicero in 62 BC on a charge of illegally claiming Roman citizenship. He moved at first to Magna Graecia, where he received artistic acclaim and became a citizen of Tarentum, Rhegium, Naples, and Heraklea, before settling in Rome. It was at Heraklea and as a Herakleote citizen that he registered himself in order to gain Roman citizenship in 89 BC (Cicero, *In Defence of Archias*: 5–6). Greek visitors to Italy are also known from the first and second centuries AD. Epigraphic evidence indicates that a substantial number of Greek artists and athletes were attracted to Italy by the Greek games, the most famous of which were held at Naples from 2 BC onwards (Dio Cassius: 55.10.9; Strabo, *Geography*: 5.4.7; Geer, 1935: 208–22; Arnold, 1960: 241–51; Crowther, 1989). Although Magna Graecia was firmly part of the Roman world from 270 BC, it also remained part of a complex network of connections with the wider Greek world.

13.6   Cities and Urban Development

The impact of Roman culture on the physical layout of cities and on the urban environment is not easy to assess. Many cities of Magna Graecia have been continuously occupied since Antiquity and our knowledge of the layout and appearance of the ancient city has to be reconstructed from very fragmentary evidence, augmented by inscriptions. Other sites, however, were abandoned in Late Antiquity, and these provide more complete documentation.

The impact of Rome was most immediate in the cities which became colonies. There is epigraphic evidence for reconstruction of walls at Vibo in the second/first centuries BC, and for the addition of elite private houses in the late Republic and early Empire (*AE* (1973) 225; Jouffroy, 1986: 20; Sanfineto, 1989). Copia-Thurii also acquired new public buildings in the same period, including walls, gates, porticoes, a temple, and a basilica (*CIL* 10.123; Guzzo, 1976), some of them built over areas previously used for elite private housing. Paestum provides an earlier and even more graphic example of the impact of a Roman colony. The street plan of the Greek city, based on a grid of long narrow rectangular blocks, may have been modified after the colonial settlement of 273 BC, as the precinct of the two temples of Hera seems to have undergone some modification in the mid-third century (Pedley, 1990: 113–25). A large area in the center of the city was cleared to form a forum, lined with Roman-style buildings, which shifted the focus of public life away from the Greek agora. The earliest phases of the forum date to the third century, and early structures include the *comitium* and the *curia*, in which the popular assembly and senate met, and an Italic temple adjacent to it and dominating one side of the forum (Greco and Theodorescu, 1980; Greco, 1999). The temple was dedicated to the cult of Mens Bona, which became one of the most important Roman cults of the city. The forum continued to develop, with the addition of porticoes, a basilica, and other temples. Although some were not added until considerably later, the basic layout of the area and its imposition in the very center of the city seem to have been established from the third century (Pedley, 1990: 119–25).

In other cities of the region, it seems that the civic landscape was more gradually transformed by new buildings, or by refurbishment of existing ones, in Roman style. At Naples, for instance, the Roman forum seems to have occupied roughly the same area of the city as the Greek agora, but some of the Greek structures, such as the theater, *odeion*, and some of the temples, were rebuilt in a more Roman style in the early empire (see Lomas, ch. 12, this vol.). Tarentum seems to have undergone a similar process, with the rebuilding of the Greek theater in a Roman style and the addition of an amphitheater, baths, and aqueducts (Lo Porto, 1970; Lippolis, 1981). At Rhegium, little is known about the Roman public buildings from archaeology, although there are remains of baths and private houses (Michelini and Savelli, 2001: 26–45). Some public buildings are known from inscriptions, such as the construction of a temple of Isis and Serapis and building or refurbishment of a temple of Apollo (*CIL* 10.1, 6). Velia also acquired baths and there were repairs and rebuilding to some sanctuaries, especially the sanctuary of Asklepios, which was the site of a noted healing cult (De Franciscis, 1970; Greco, 1999; Tocco Sciarelli, 1999). For these cities, the impact of Rome on the civic environment seems to have been confined to the addition of some specifically Roman structures such as baths, and to the rebuilding of some existing buildings in a more contemporary Roman style.

Elsewhere, however, the impact of Rome seems to have been more drastic. Much of the Greek center of Metapontum was abandoned. The *castrum Romanum* (Roman camp), a rectangular area to the east of the Greek agora and main sanctuary, became the focus of a small nucleus of Roman habitation, and many of the Greek temples and public buildings fell into disrepair during the second and first centuries BC (Di Siena, 1999: 38–41; Crawford, 2003). The very low number of inscriptions from the city after the Roman conquest suggests that civic life may have declined considerably, although there is considerable evidence of habitation and economic activity in the areas of the *castrum* and the harbor until the fourth century AD (Crawford, 2003). Croton and Locri also appear to have undergone a major shrinkage of the inhabited areas in the post-Hannibalic period, with concentrations of Roman habitation in only one area of each site, and the development of villas in areas which had previously been part of the Greek cities (Giangiulio and Sabbaione, 1987: 488–500; Arias and Parra, 1993: 201–14). Inscriptions, however, demonstrate that both were still functioning cities in the second century AD, with active civic elites which donated money for public benefactions (Croton: *ILLRP* 575; *CIL* 10.107, 109–10. Locri: *CIL* 10.19–20; *AE* (1978) 273).

The extent of building activity is not just an indicator of change to the fabric of these cities, but an index of financial investment by each city or individual members of its elite, or of its ability to attract investment by patrons from beyond the city. Magna Graecia seems to have been weaker than some other areas of Italy in some crucial respects. Relatively few people from the region acquired senatorial status – only around 18 senatorial families are known – and this may have limited the influence of the Greek cities at Rome, as well as reducing the possibility of civic investment by local families who had achieved social promotion. Some inward investment took place, mostly by imperial officials of various sorts, but most buildings and other benefactions, such as provision of games and public meals, were undertaken by members of the local elite, or other prominent social groups such as *Augustales*. It is also undeniable that for much of Magna Graecia, levels of elite activity and public building were lower than in some other areas of Italy. It has been suggested (Crawford, 2003) that the region underwent a process of "de-urbanization" and that the cities of the region declined as the focus of economic activity moved to the villas in their territories. Despite this assertion, there is enough epigraphic and archaeological evidence to demonstrate that most of the former Greek colonies were still viable and functioning communities with independent municipal or colonial status. There is no denying that the long-term impact of Rome was significant, but exactly how dramatic it was depended very much on the circumstances of the individual community. Some seem to have a high degree of continuity, with change experienced as additions to, and restyling of, the urban environment over time, while others seem to have undergone rapid and radical transformation. One thing which is clear, however, is that with the possible exception of Metapontum, they all remained viable communities until well into the imperial era.

13.7 Urban Society and Culture: Cultural Identities Between Greece and Rome

The demographic and ethnic changes which took place in Magna Graecia had the effect of introducing many aspects of Roman culture, particularly after the Social War. Latin was widely used, Roman forms of personal name were adopted after the region gained Roman citizenship in 90 BC, the civic landscape became more Roman, and many aspects of Roman material culture were adopted. Nevertheless, Greek culture did not just disappear. The survival of Greek elements of civic life, such as Greek magistracies, has been mentioned above, and other aspects of Hellenism also persist. The survival of Greek culture in the region shows some interesting patterns.

Greek cults and priesthoods remained important in many cities. The cults of Apollo and Artemis at Rhegium, which had links to the foundation of the city, were still celebrated in the first century AD with traditional Greek rituals, which were recorded in Greek inscriptions (Costabile, 1979). Other important cult centers, such as the sanctuary of Juno Lacinia at Croton and the sanctuaries of Asklepios and Apollo Oulios at Velia, continued in use. Additions and extensions to the Asklepieion demonstrate its continued importance, and inscriptions and statues honoring *pholarchoi* – probably cult officials of Apollo – indicate that they continued to play a role well into the first century AD (Pugliese Caratelli, 1970; De Franciscis, 1970). Velia may have been a center of medical training, and enjoyed some fame as a spa town, much to the disgust of the poet Horace, who preferred the hot spring of the more fashionable Baiae (Horace, *Epistles* 1.15.1–2; Ebner, 1962). New cults – both Roman cults and new imports from elsewhere – were introduced into the region. Roman cults such as that of Iuppiter Optimus Maximus (Tarentum: *AE* (1896) 111; Locri: *CIL* 10.16) were particularly important as they symbolized Roman power, as did the imperial cult (*CIL* 10.2; Torelli, 1999: 108–19). The more unusual Roman cult of Mens Bona was prominent at Paestum as mentioned earlier in this chapter (Torelli, 1999: 64–68; *ILLRP* 8), and there is evidence of the importation of cults from the east in the form of a temple of Isis and Serapis at Rhegium (*CIL* 10.1). Many new elements of ritual and religious life were introduced to the region, but many Greek cults continued to be important.

There is evidence that the Greek language continued to be used. Clearly, our reliance on epigraphic documents means that we cannot know much about the relation between written and spoken languages in these communities, but it seems very probable – particularly given that Greek was a high status language in the Roman world – that it still remained widely spoken (Adams, 2003, 9–18). We have some corroborating evidence from Strabo, who says that Greek language, as well as Greek customs, survived at Naples, Tarentum, and Rhegium (Strabo, *Geography* 5.4.7, 6.1.3, 6.3.4), and the persistence of Greek is confirmed by epigraphic evidence. Greek inscriptions account for nearly 50% of those from Naples and Velia in the first century BC and first century AD, although it seems to die out in the second–third centuries AD (Leiwo, 1994: 167–73). This was not a case of a straightforward linear progression from Greek to Latin, however. As well as being very localized, Greek seems to have been used for very specific purposes. Most of the Greek inscriptions of Roman date come from only four cities – Rhegium, Naples, Velia, and Tarentum. At three of these, Greek was used mainly in high-status inscriptions connected with the public life of the community, such as the decrees and honorific inscriptions from Rhegium, Velia, and Naples, records of the Greek games at Naples, and other similar texts. If, however, we consider inscriptions which were not connected with public life, such as epitaphs, they were predominantly written in Latin (Lomas, 1993: 174–85; 1995: 353–62). Greek is used as the written language of choice for particular types of activity, mostly concerned with ceremonial and honorific aspects of civic life, long after Latin was widely used for other purposes. Honors offered to prominent citizens or to eminent visitors were not only recorded in Greek, but were carefully couched in Hellenistic conventions as well. When set against the strong evidence for widespread use of Latin and adoption of many aspects of Roman culture, this appears to be a very deliberate cultural choice.

At Naples, there even seems to have been an active revival of Greek culture in the early Empire. A Greek festival was established in 2 BC in honor of Augustus, but based on a traditional Neapolitan festival associated with the Greek cult of the siren Parthenope. The *Sebasta*, as it was known, based its rules and events on those of the Olympic games (Dio Cassius: 55.10.9; Strabo, *Geography*: 5.4.7; Geer, 1935: 208–222; Arnold, 1960: 241–51; Crowther, 1989). It became an important part of the circuit of games and festivals which developed throughout the Greek world at this date, and attracted competitors from all over the eastern empire (Miranda, 1990: 75–114). Other Greek institutions also continued to flourish, including the phratries. These traditional subdivisions within the city seem to remain active until the third century AD, recording some of their activities in inscriptions, almost all of them in Greek (Guarducci, 1938; Lomas, 1993: 166–67). Naples, Velia, and Tarentum also maintained their civic gymnasia (Strabo, *Geography* 5.4.7, 6.3.1; *ILS* 6461), an important feature of Greek culture in the Hellenistic and Roman worlds.

It is probably no accident that there was increased emphasis on Greek aspects of civic culture in this period. The revival of Greek language in civic inscriptions, and the use of Greek-style honors such as Greek decrees honoring prominent citizens or visitors, or the conferment of honorary Greek titles, are best documented at Naples, but are found elsewhere in Magna Graecia in the early Empire. It is all the more striking because many of the cities of the region were of mixed population by this date. The widespread adoption of Roman forms of personal names makes it difficult to assess the ethnic composition of the region, but the substantial level of Roman colonization, as well as immigration from other areas of both Italy and the Greek world is likely to have significantly changed or eroded the ethnic Greekness of the population (Lomas, 1993: 172–74; Leiwo, 1994: 171–72). Nevertheless, Greek culture remained an important part of the cultural identity of some, although not all, communities.

This renewal of Hellenism coincides with a period of intense interest in Greek culture by the Roman elite. From the second century BC onwards, there was an increasing trend for wealthy Romans to invest in villas on the Bay of Naples as luxury holiday homes, and one of the attractions of the region seems to have been its Hellenism. Its proximity to Rome enabled Roman aristocrats to indulge their fondness for Greek culture without incurring the stigma of becoming un-Roman. By the first century AD, the imperial villas at Baiae ensured a constant stream of high-level visitors to the area. The Greek culture of Naples attracted a lot of high-level Roman attention and patronage, including that of notable philhellenes such as the emperors Nero and Hadrian. Nero performed there as a musician, and Hadrian became an honorary magistrate (Suetonius, *Life of Nero*: 20–25; Augustan Histories, *Life of Hadrian*: 1.9.1). In the second century AD, Greek culture and institutions received a further boost from the emperor Hadrian. The Panhellenion, a body intended to provide a focus for all cities of proven Greek origin, provoked a great upsurge of interest in Greek culture and customs. This was particularly strong in cities on the periphery of the Greek world (Spawforth and Walker, 1985). As part of this initiative, an embassy led by Callicrates was sent by Sparta to Tarentum in AD 145–50, apparently to revive the traditional connection, and seems to have been received with enthusiasm, although the outcome of this venture is unknown (*SEG* 11.481; Spawforth and Walker, 1986: 91).

In this context, the survival – or even resurgence – of Hellenism becomes entirely comprehensible. Greek heritage could confer a considerable level of cultural cachet on cities of Greek background. Displays of Hellenism could have the effect of enhancing civic status and reputation in the eyes of both Romans and the Greek world. It could also help to maintain local identities and cohesion by invoking powerful cultural memories. This factor may have been important given that these cities had undergone a high degree of demographic disruption (Lomas, 1995) and had acquired large non-Greek populations.

In conclusion, the history of Magna Graecia in the Roman period is one of mixed fortunes. Some of the former Greek cities prospered reasonably well, while others struggled. The displacement of population after the Punic wars, and successive waves of colonization and migration placed considerable strains on cities, but almost all remained self-governing municipalities, and some retained considerable economic and cultural vigor. Cultural responses to Rome varied considerably. Some cities retained little of their Greek culture, but others seem to have actively promoted and revived this, very much to their benefit. The region undoubtedly declined from its fourth-century BC peak of prosperity and may have prospered less than some other areas of Italy, but for the most part it was very far from the economic and cultural desert described by Cicero and others.

FURTHER READING

The history of Magna Graecia in the Roman period is surprisingly poorly covered and many general accounts of the region end with the Roman conquest, or even earlier. The only full length work in English is Lomas 1993. Cerchiai, Jannelli and Longo 2002 is a lavishly illustrated introduction to the Greek cities of the West, and Pugliese Carratelli 1996 is a mine of information, although it focuses on the pre-Roman period. The proceedings of the annual Taranto conferences (published as *Atti dei Convegni di Studio sulla Magna Grecia* by the Istituto per la storia e l'archeologia della Magna Graecia, Taranto) include reports on new archaeological discoveries from all parts of the region.

REFERENCES

Accardo, S. 2000. *Villae romanae nell'Ager Bruttius. Il paesaggio rurale calabrese durante il dominio romano.* Rome: «L'Erma» di Bretschneider.

Adams, J.N. 2003. *Bilingualism and the Latin Language.* Cambridge: Cambridge University Press.

Arias, P. and Parra, M.C. 1993. "Locri." In *Bibliografia topografica della colonizzazione greca in Italia e nelle isole tirreniche*, vol. 9, eds G. Nenci and G. Vallet, 191–249. Pisa and Rome: Scuola normale superiore/École française de Rome.

Arnold, I.R. 1960. "Agonistic festivals in Italy and Sicily." *American Journal of Archaeology* 64: 241–51.

Atti dei Convegni di Studio sulla Magna Grecia. Taranto: Istituto per la storia e l'archeologia della Magna Graecia.

Bispham, E.H. 2007. *From Asculum to Actium: the municipalization of Italy from the Social War to Augustus.* Oxford: Oxford University Press.

Brunt, P.A. 1971. *Italian Manpower, 225 BC–AD 14.* Oxford: Clarendon Press.

Carter, J.C. 1984. "Crotone." In *Crotone. Atti di 23° Convegno sulla studi di Magna Grecia*: 169–77. Taranto: Istituto per la storia e l'archeologia della Magna Grecia.

Carter, J.C. 1990. "Metapontum – land, wealth and population." In *Greek Colonists and Native Populations: Proceedings of the First Australian Congress of Classical Archaeology*, ed. J.-P. Descoeudres, 405–44. Canberra, Oxford, New York: Clarendon Press.

Cerchiai, L., Jannelli, L., and Longo, F. 2002. *The Greek Cities of Magna Graecia and Sicily.* Los Angeles: Paul Getty Museum.

Cornell, T.J. 1996. "Hannibal's Legacy: the effects of the Hannibalic War on Italy." In *The Second Punic War: a reappraisal*, eds T.J. Cornell, P. Sabin and B. Rankov, 97–116. London: BICS Suppl. 67.

Costabile, F. 1979. "Il culto di Apollo quale testimonianza delle tradizioni corali e religiose di Reggio e Messana." *Mélanges de l'Ecole Française de Rome, Antiquité* 91: 525–45.

Crawford, M.H., ed. 1996. *Roman Statutes.* 2 vols. London: Institute of Classical Studies/*BICS Supplement* 64.

Crawford, M.H. 2003. "Brave new world: Metapontum after Metapontum." In *Les élites et leurs facettes: les élites locales dans le monde hellénistique et romain,* eds M. Cébeillac-Gervasoni and L. Lamoine, 1–17. Rome: Ecole française de Rome.

Crowther, N.B. 1989. "The Sebastan Games in Naples (IvOl. 56)." *ZPE* 79: 100–102.

De Franciscis, A. 1970. "Sculture connesse con la scuola medica di Elea." *Parola del Passato* 25: 267–84.

Desy, P. 1993. *Recherches sur l'économie apulienne au IIe et au Ier siècle avant notre ère.* Brussels: Latomus.

Di Siena, A. 1999. *Metaponto. Archeologia di un colonia greca.* Taranto: Scorpione.

Ebner, P. 1962. "Scuole di medicina a Velia e a Salerno." *Apollo* 2: 125–36.

Ebner, P. 1970. "Nuove iscrizioni di Velia." *Parola del Passato* 25: 262–66.

Erdkamp, P. 1998. *Hunger and the Sword: warfare and food supply in Roman Republican wars (264–30 B.C.).* Amsterdam: Gieben.

Fracchia, H. 2001. "The Romanization of the *Ager Buxentinus* (Salerno)." In *Modalità insediative e strutture agrarie nell'Italia meridionale in età romana,* eds E. Lo Cascio and A. Storchi Marino, 55–73. Bari: Edipuglia.

Franke, P.R. 1989. "Pyrrhus." In *Cambridge Ancient History,* vol. 7.2 (2nd edn), eds F.W. Walbank, A.E. Astin, M.W. Frederiksen, R.M. Ogilvie, 456–85. Cambridge: Cambridge University Press.

Fronda, M. 2010. *Between Rome and Carthage. Southern Italy during the Second Punic War.* Cambridge: Cambridge University Press.

Garnsey, P. 1988. *Famine and Food Supply in the Graeco-Roman World: responses to risk and crisis.* Cambridge: Cambridge University Press.

Gasperini, L. 1968. "Su alcune epigrafia di Taranto romana." *Seconda miscellenea greca e romana,* 379–98. RomeL Istituto italiano per la storia antica.

Gasperini, L. 1971. "Il municipio tarantino: ricerche epigrafica." *Terza miscellenea greca e romana,* 143–209. Rome: Istituto italiano per la storia antica.

Geer, R.M. 1935. "The Greek games at Naples." *Transactions of the American Philological Association* 66: 208–21.

Giangiulio, M. and Sabbaione, C. 1987. "Crotone." In *Bibliografia topografica della colonizzazione greca in Italia e nelle isole tirreniche,* vol. 5, eds G. Nenci and G. Vallet, 472–521. Pisa and Rome: Scuola normale superiore/École française de Rome.

Gossage, A.E. 1984. "The comparative chronology of inscriptions relating to the Boeotian festivals in the first half of the first century B.C." *Annual of the British School at Athens* 70: 115–34.

Graser, E.R. 1940. "The Edict of Diocletian on Maximum Prices." In *An Economic Survey of Ancient Rome,* vol. 5. *Rome and Italy of the Empire,* ed. T. Frank, 305–420. Baltimore: Johns Hopkins Press.

Greco, E. 1999. *Poseidonia-Paestum IV: Le Forum ouest-sud-est.* Rome: École française de Rome.

Greco, E. and Theodorescu, D. 1980. *Poseidonia-Paestum I: La "curia."* Rome: École française de Rome.

Guarducci, M., 1938. "L'istituzione della fratria nella Grecia antica e nelle colonie Greche d'Italia. II." *Memorie della classe di scienze morali, storiche e filologiche dell' Accademia dei Lincei* 6.8.2: 65–135.

Guzzo, P.G. 1976. "Epigrafi latine della provincia di Cosenza." *Epigraphica* 38: 129–43.

Hatzfeld, M.J. 1912. "Les italiens résidant à Délos mentionnés dans les inscriptions de l'île." *Bulletin de correspondance hellénique* 36: 5–218.

Isayev, E. 2007. *Inside Ancient Lucania: dialogues in history and archaeology.* London: Institute of Classical Studies.

Jouffroy, H. 1986. *La construction publique en Italie et dans L'Afrique romaine.* Strasbourg: AECR.

Kahrstedt, U. 1960. *Der wirtschaftsliche Lage Grossgriechenlands unter der Kaiserzeit.* Berne: Franke.

Keppie, L.J.F. 1983. *Colonisation and Veteran Settlement in Italy, 14–47 B.C.* London: British School at Rome.

Leiwo, M. 1985. "Why Velia survived through the 2nd century B.C. Remarks on her economic connections with Delos." *Athenaeum* 63: 494–99.

Leiwo, M. 1994. Neapolitana: *a study of population and language in Graeco-Roman Naples.* Helsinki:
Societas Scientarum Fennica.

Lippolis, E. 1981. "Alcune considerazioni topografiche su Taranto romana." *Taras* 1: 77–114.

Lomas, K. 1993. *Rome and the Western Greeks, 350 BC–AD 200. Conquest and acculturation in south
Italy.* London: Routledge.

Lomas, K. 1995. "The Greeks in the west and the Hellenization of Italy." In *The Greek World,* ed. C.A.
Powell, 347–67. London: Routledge.

Lomas, K. 2011. "Rome, Latins and Italians in the Second Punic War." In *Blackwell Companion to the
Punic Wars,* ed. D. Hoyos, 339–56. Oxford: Wiley–Blackwell.

Lo Porto, F.G. 1970. "Topografia antica di Taranto." *Taranto nella civiltà della Magna Grecia. Atti del
decimo Convegno di Studi sulla Magna Grecia,* 343–84. Naples: Arte Tipografica.

Maddoli, G. 1982. "Il concetto di Magna Grecia: gennesi di un realta storico-politiche." In *Megale
Hellas: Nome e immagine,* 9–30. Taranto: Istituto per la storia e l'archeologia della Magna Grecia.

Mello, M. 1974. *Paestum romana.* Rome: Istituto italiano per la storia antica.

Mello, M. and Voza, G. 1968. *Le iscrizioni latine di Paestum.* Naples: Università degli studi.

Michelini, C. and Savalli, I. 2001. "Reggio di Calabria." In *Bibliografia topografica della colonizzazione
greca in Italia e nelle isole tirreniche,* vol. 16, eds G. Nenci and G. Vallet, 1–77. Pisa and Rome: Scuola
normale superiore/École française de Rome.

Miranda, E. 1990. *Iscrizioni greche d'Italia. Napoli* I. Rome: Quasar.

Morel, J.-P. 1976. "Aspects de l'artisanat dans la Grande Grèce romaine." In *La Magna Grecia nell'età
romana: atti del quindicesimo convegno di studi sulla Magna Grecia, Taranto, 5–10 ottobre 1975,* 263–
324. Naples: Arte Tipografia.

Morel, J.-P. 1978. "La laine de Tarente." *Ktema* 3–4: 94–110.

Morel, J.-P. 1981. "La produzione della ceramica campana: aspetti economici e sociali, II." In *Merci,
mercati e scambi nel Mediterraneo,* eds A. Giardina and A. Schiavone, 81–98. Bari: Laterza.

Musti, D. 1988. *Strabone e la Magna Grecia: città e popoli dell'Italia antica.* Padua, Programma.

Pedley, J.G. 1990. *Paestum: Greeks and Romans in southern Italy.* London: Thames & Hudson.

Polignac, F. de and Gualtieri, M. 1991. "A rural landscape in western Lucania." In *Roman Landscapes.
Archaeological survey in the Mediterranean region,* eds G. Barker and J.A. Lloyd, 194–203. London:
British School at Rome.

Pugliese Carratelli, G. 1970. "Ancora su φωλαρχος." *Parola del Passato* 25: 243–48.

Pugliese Carratelli, G. 1996. *The Western Greeks: classical civilization in the Western Mediterranean.*
London: Thames and Hudson.

Purcell, N. 1994. "South Italy in the fourth century BC." In *Cambridge Ancient History* vol. 6. *The
fourth century BC* (2nd edn), eds D.M. Lewis, J. Boardman, S. Hornblower, M. Ostwald, 381–403.
Cambridge: Cambridge University Press.

Sangineto, B. 1989. "Scavi nell'abitato romano di Vibo Valentia." *Annali della Scuola Normale Superiore
di Pisa* 19: 833–43.

Sangineto, B. 1994. "Per la recostruzione del paesaggio agrario delle Calabrie romane." In *Storia della
Calabria antica. Età italica e romana,* ed. S. Settis, 559–93. Reggio Calabria: Gangemi Editore.

Sartori, F. 1953. *Problemi di storia costituzionale italiota.* Rome: «L'Erma» di Bretschneider.

Spawforth, A.J.S. and Walker, S. 1985. "The World of the Panhellenion. I. Athens and Eleusis. *Journal
of Roman Studies* 75, 78–104.

Spawforth, A.J.S. and Walker, S. 1986. "The World of the Panhellenion. II. Three Dorian cities. *Journal
of Roman Studies* 76, 88–105.

Tocco Sciarelli, G. 1999. "Spazi pubblici a Velia: L'Agora e un santuario." In *Neue Forschungen in Velia:
Akten des Kongresses "La Ricerca Archeologica a Velia,"* eds F. Krinzinger and G. Tocco Sciarelli, 61–5.
Vienna: Österreichischen Akademie der Wissenschaften.

Torelli, M. 1999. *Paestum romana.* Rome: Ingegneria per la cultura.

Toynbee, A. 1965. *Hannibal's Legacy: the Hannibalic War's effects on Roman life.* 2 vols. London:
Oxford University Press.

2.3 Case-study: Becoming Roman in *Cisalpina*

CHAPTER 14

The Changing Face of Cisalpine Identity

Clifford Ando

14.1 Gaul, Transapadana, Italy. What's in a Name?

The geographic area under study in this chapter might be defined in several ways, even as its changes in name might serve as an index, pointing both to the contingency of those definitions and to the historical issues raised by their shifting valence and usage. Thus, "Cisalpine Gaul," meaning "Gaul on this side of the Alps," emerges as a term to describe the area north of the Apennines and south of the Alps in part in consequence of increased Roman involvement in "Gallia citerior," "the Gaul that is further away" (see, e.g., Caesar, *Gallic War*: 1.24.3). (That the meaning of these terms is relational in respect to Rome as metropole is likewise an important pointer to the nature of the episteme at work; the same point is made within a different interpretive framework by Polybius: 2.15.9.) The name "Gaul" of course derives from the Roman name for the inhabitants of those regions, whom they (sometimes) understood to be types of a single ethnic group, the Gauls. But through complex processes related both to the classification of its residents and to political geography more abstractly, Cisalpine Gaul was ultimately designated part of Italy, and its residents, remarkably, came to be considered Roman. Hence it was possible for Tacitus, writing of political machinations during the wars after the fall of Nero, to describe the *regio Transpadana*, "the Transpadane region" or "the region across the river Po" (another relational term) as "that broadest part of Italy" (*Histories*: 1.70.1–2). His vocabulary reflects the end of the story I shall here unfold, namely, the drawing of the final ancient boundary for Italy by Augustus, the division of Cisalpine Gaul into four regions, and their inclusion in Italy (cf. Cooley, ch. 6.1, this volume). That said, unusually, Augustus did not have the final word in this matter: the great Florentine patriot and historian Leonardo Bruni, writing in the first half of the fifteenth century, described the Gallic migration that drove the Etruscans back across the Apennines as the Gauls "seizing from the Tuscans all that part of Italy which is now referred to as Cisalpine Gaul" (*History of the Florentine People*, 1.18: *eam omnem Italiae partem, quae nunc Gallia Cisalpina dicitur, Tuscis ademerunt*).

Inquiry into the history of Cisalpine Gaul brings one face to face with numerous problems of evidence, familiar in broad strokes to all students of ancient history. The nodal points in any narrative history must be those events rehearsed in surviving literary texts or, more rarely,

A Companion to Roman Italy, First Edition. Edited by Alison E. Cooley.
© 2016 John Wiley & Sons, Ltd. Published 2016 by John Wiley & Sons, Ltd.

those commemorated in monumental texts concerned with statal action. (This is obviously not true of all forms of historical inquiry as practiced on ancient evidence, nor even of all narrative history of the ancient world, but it is certainly true in respect to the west.) But the kinds of information literary historians in antiquity sought to record can only with difficulty be made to address the questions an historian of provincial contexts might wish to pose (and scarcely all of those!), nor of course is all the information that those historians provide accurate. That said, falsehoods, including errors and especially motivated distortions, are not simply an inescapable part of the historical record; they often tell as much as any truth. The same might be said of the patterned expressions of belonging or factual asides in literary texts outside historiography – not least where Cisalpine Gaul is concerned – as the participation of Gallic Romans in late Republican literary culture must figure in the telling of this tale.

Enormous amounts of information can also be gleaned from the material and epigraphic records, including privately generated documents. In a Republican Italian context, evidence of this kind is naturally limited in kind and occasional in quantity: it concerns roads, walls, and public monuments; the control and usage of the land within some narrow sphere (more on this later in this chapter); and, where one is lucky, patterns of practice in private commemoration, patterns in the use of certain non-perishable goods, and so forth. Such information is an essential ingredient to any modern social history. But it can only occasionally be correlated in a chronological or causal scheme with the information provided by literary texts. Their understanding of historical significance, like their notions of cultural or social history, was not ours.

One significant consequence is that one must tell different kinds of stories at different moments across any large historical period, of nearly any ancient context. In what follows, I shall seek to describe those actions and practices by which Cisalpine Gaul became Italian, which is a story at once of changes in Gaul itself, taken both by Romans and natives, and also of percipience and response at Rome. The disappearance from historical memory – the elision from recorded modes of identity construction – of any sense that (Cisalpine) Gallic constituted an identity apart from, rather than constituent of, Roman Italian, is necessarily reflected in our inability on the basis of surviving evidence to tell some other story, perhaps of resistance, or to recuperate some local hidden transcript. But in some other perspective, that inability is very precisely a provocation to inquiry.

14.2   The Archaic Background: The Arrival of the Gauls

As Jonathan Williams (2001) has shown, our ability to provide an historical demography of the Po Valley has been inexorably shaped by the Greek and Roman historiographic traditions of the late Republic, in two related ways. First, Greek and Roman authors describe the Gauls as having come from outside, which is to say, they depict the Gauls as migratory and as immigrants. Second, in their accounts, the Gauls encounter a landscape populated by communities organized along ethnic lines. The importance and effects of these historical claims need to be carefully unpacked.

As regards the historical situation of the Po Valley before the arrival of Roman arms, it must be emphasized that mere diversity of style in the material record whether between sites – or, for that matter, within a particular site – does not indicate, and cannot confirm, that the Iron Age population groups in the valley were articulated along ethnic lines, or even that they possessed self-understandings kindred to the framework visible in Greek ethnic thought and ethnographic literature, in which different peoples were understood as descending genealogically from common ancestors, and patterns in cultural practice are overdetermined by those lines of descent. Nor can the very limited pre-Roman epigraphic record afford any certainty in this regard. The ethnic groups famous in the Roman historical tradition – the Boii, the Senones, the Cenomani, what have you – may have some ontological integrity apart from that tradition, but their emergence and consolidation in history may well be due in part to their interpellation *as* ethnics under pressure from contact with imperial and colonizing powers that wanted to see them as such (Figure 14.1).

There is of course every reason to believe that population groups did descend over the Alps into the Po Valley, among which were no doubt some of those later described by Greek, Roman, and apparently Etruscan sources as Gallic. Certainly two universal features of ancient historiography on Cisalpine Gaul are first, that the Gauls are described as having arrived en masse, sometimes in waves, and second, that those migrations rapidly came into conflict with pre-existing populations: thus the Gauls are described as pushing the Etruscans back across the Apennines, for example, or as sacking and pillaging their way south to Rome (Cato, *Origins* frr. 1.13, 2.5 Beck and Walter, 2005 = Peter *HRR* frr. 36, 62 = FRHist frr. 27, 72; Polybius: 2.17–17; Dionysius of Halicarnassus, *Roman Antiquities*: 13.10–11; Livy: 5.33–34). What is more, the immigrating Gauls are of necessity seen as non-Roman (or non-Greek or non-Etruscan) in precisely their migratory lifestyle.

Hence, in these accounts pre-existing models and polarities are adduced to explain the movements of populations, which are, for the sake of narrative and cognitive simplicity, reduced to a single migration event or at most a series of such. Those models often find their roots in Greek historiography of the age of Greek colonization, even as Greek ethnographic models served to classify the Gallic form of migration as essentially barbarous or, at the very least, non-poliadic. In the tradition, the migration is therefore described as a response to overpopulation; but in contrast to civilized peoples, the migrating Gauls neither settle down nor found cities, nor do they practice cereal agriculture. Rather, they wander overland until they come upon populations higher than themselves along some index of civilization, at which point they either pillage the cities or are themselves rebuffed. (The Greek and Roman understanding of such cultures as fundamentally self-destructive finds articulation later in the standard historical accounts, too, when the Gauls allied with Hannibal inevitably die off in greater numbers than the Carthaginians, whether in battle or merely on the march.)

Please note, I do not claim that large-scale migrations did not occur into the Po Valley in the Bronze and Iron Ages. Indeed, Roman sources describe population groups continuing to descend from the Alps into Cisalpine Gaul in the historical period, and there is every reason to believe in their veracity. (Large-scale migration, and state-mandated resettlement, is a major theme in ancient history writ large and a very important component in the history of Cisalpine Gaul.) But those sources sing a different tune when they recount the later migrations than they did rehearsing the earlier ones. As we shall see, Gallic immigrant groups of the early second century BC are at least occasionally described as founding cities and as conducting themselves in other respects, too, as politically articulated societies.

Beyond the influence of Greek ethnography, extant accounts of the arrival of the Gauls display the influence of a second, enormous ideological pressure, namely, the construal of the Gauls as a truly existential threat to Rome. This construal was both a result of the sack of Rome by Gallic populations in the first decade of the fourth century BC, an event known today above all from the remarkable account in Livy's fifth book, and also a factor in the tradition that developed around that event. That is to say, the later construal of assorted Roman enemies in Cisalpine Gaul during the third and early second centuries BC, in the Cimbric wars of the late second century, and so forth, *as* Gauls naturally played into this fear, and much political work could be done through such acts of construal. In short, generals could elevate the importance of their achievements by assimilating their opponents to the great menace of the earlier war, even as ongoing claims that the Gauls were still a threat elevated the fourth-century sack to greater and greater cultural importance. As a result, in an oration of 56 BC, Cicero could say when describing Caesar's wars in Gaul that: "No one who has thought prudently about our state from the very beginning of this empire did not regard Gaul as the greatest source of fear for the empire. Because of the strength and greatness of its peoples, never before have we engaged with them all at once.

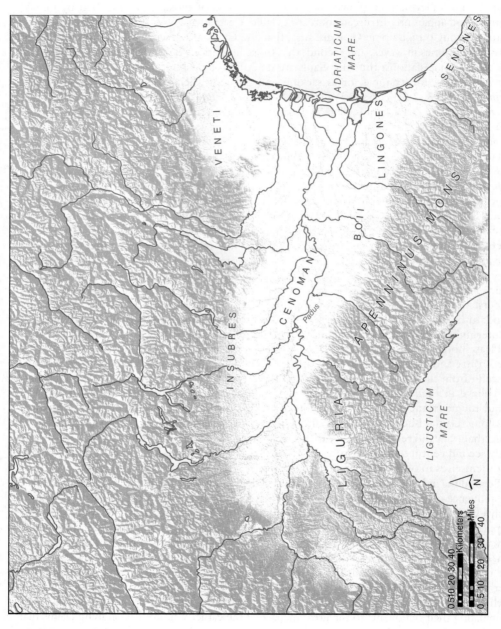

Figure 14.1 The distribution of population groups in the Po Valley on the eve of Roman intervention, circa 300 BC. Ancient World Mapping Center © 2012 (www.unc.edu/awmc).

When attacked, we have resisted. But now at last it has come to this, that the limits of our empire and their lands are one and the same" (Cicero, *On the Consular Provinces*. 33). Likewise, it remained a feature of Roman law on military service into the late Republic that a Gallic invasion, however improbable, would vacate the exemption from the draft otherwise granted to certain classes of colonists: even the colonists of the Caesarian colony at Urso in Spain were imagined as leaving their homes in defense of Rome itself (*Lex coloniae Genetivae* = Crawford, 1996: no. 25, ch.62, where further late Republican evidence is cited).

Again, the shape and tenor of the historical and ethnographic tradition ultimately took the form in which we have received it very largely as a result of the sack of Rome by Gauls in the first decade of the fourth century BC. Even Hannibal had not wreaked such terrible and humiliating harm on the fabric of the city itself. As a result, despite variations within extant accounts of the early history of both Gaul and the Gauls (on the question, for example, whether the Gallic invasion that produced the sack of Rome was their first entry into Italy, or but the latest wave among many), Roman enmity required the Gauls to be understood as non-Roman in essential regards: as lacking geographic fixity, with all that entailed as regards their capacity for culture and civilized deportment, and most importantly as invaders to Italy from outside. The subsequent history of Roman Gaul must be understood against this two-fold historical background, of the reality and memory of warfare, and of the ongoing power of those memories in late Republican political discourse.

14.3   First Roman Forays Across the Apennines, 290–218 BC

The history of Roman action in respect to Cisalpine Gaul between the Gallic sack and the Hannibalic war cannot be rehearsed as a continuous narrative. The defective condition of the surviving evidence does not permit us to fix in time (and often in space) even large battles, even those named for the site where they occurred. Indeed, even the date of the sack of Rome was contested already in antiquity. The earliest Roman narrative of the period, the history of Fabius Pictor, is lost. Pictor was himself involved in the Gallic wars of the mid-220s (Pictor fr. 30a, Beck and Walter, 2005 = FRHist fr. 21), and we might therefore lament all the more the disappearance of his History. That said, his narrative influenced most if not all later accounts, including that of Polybius, and careful reading in the tradition reveals the systematic operation of prejudice and error that likely derive from Pictor. What is more, beyond the operation of prejudice lie still other factors. Roman politics in the early third century BC was dominated by a small number of families, scattering homonymous individuals throughout the record, and numerous individuals held high office more than once. The extent and depth of confusion among readers of Pictor over the attribution of agency to individuals, and among individuals to particular terms of office, is most easily explained by reference to the defective condition of the records on which Pictor drew and his own incapacity to resolve the cruces before him.

Fortunately, the overall arc of this chapter does not require that we resolve any such problems. Our focus is rather on two themes. First, the information available to us suggests a pattern of interaction in Cisalpine Gaul itself (or between Romans and residents of Gaul during military action below the Apennines) in which the Romans devoted ever greater resources to ever more complex extensions of state infrastructural power into the Po Valley, while the Gauls for their part very gradually developed institutions and forms of social differentiation that echoed those of Rome. Such patterns of historical change in the shadows of empire or borderlands between discrepant cultural systems are by now well theorized: in an ancient context, they are visible in later periods across the Roman borders of the Rhine and Danube or again in the gradual artic-ulation and self-awareness of the early Islamic *umma* as a territorial state and, indeed, an empire.

The second theme of importance in this material is the understanding that later Romans assigned to the period – indeed, not only to their ancestors but also to their Gallic opponents – to the effect that the project of empire in Cisalpine Gaul was not simply one of conquest, but of demographic change effected across an increasingly Roman landscape.

After a long period characterized by intermittent hostilities involving Gallic raiding parties, Roman acts of revenge and deterrence, and shifting alliances on both sides with third parties, a crucial shift in the scale of their interaction took place in the second and third decades of the third century BC. Amidst a complex range of actions reaching across the Apennines at several points, the Romans established circa 289 BC a colony called Sena Gallica (modern Senigallia) in the territory of the Senones, in the fertile stretch of land that extends south from the plain of the Po along the Adriatic coast. In the very same years they also established a further colony on the Adriatic coast at Hadria (modern Atri), in the territory of the Praetuttii. The conditions under which the Senones ceded land for the colony are unclear. Whatever they were, hostilities rapidly erupted again. After what appear to have been particularly brutal battles located in the tradition at Arretium and by Lake Vadimon in 284/3 BC, the Romans formally annexed the territory of the Senones, which as a public property of the Roman people was named the *ager Gallicus*. At the level of warfare and diplomacy, there then followed a remarkably long peace – 45 years, according to Polybius (2.21.1) – during which Rome strengthened both its grip on the Adriatic coast and its claim on the southern plain of the Po through the founding of two further colonies, at Ariminum (modern Rimini) in 268 and at Firmum (modern Fermo) in 264 BC.

Because Polybius relies on a particularly partisan Roman source, he ascribes the 45-year peace to a waning in Gallic aggressiveness, and its end to a corresponding waxing in the natural restlessness and aggression of a new generation of Gauls. In fact, it must have owed its existence in large measure to Roman distraction during the First Punic War. (The apparent failure of the Carthaginians to exploit Gallic hostility to Rome during that war is a mistake Hannibal would not repeat.) What is clear is that Rome returned its attention to the north almost immediately upon the end of hostilities with Carthage in 241 BC: a colony was founded in that year at Spoletium in Umbria, on the route of the future *via Flaminia* from Rome across the Apennines to the *ager Gallicus* and on to Ariminum, and in 238 BC the two consuls launched campaigns of aggression north-west into Liguria and north-east against the Boii in the Po Valley proper (Zonaras: 8.18). When Polybius (2.21.1–6) records a Gallic attack on Ariminum in 237 BC as the first event in the new period of hostility, he would seem to betray a distinctly pro-Roman distortion of the historical record.

The sequence of actions undertaken in this period of renewed Roman action in the north – between 238 and 220 BC – represents a massive development upon earlier forms of Roman engagement in the area, which unusually betrays across some 12 years the continuous influence of a single guiding light, Gaius Flaminius. As tribune in 232 BC, Flaminius carried a bill later notorious in Roman domestic politics for the distribution of individual plots in the *ager Gallicus* (Cato, *Origins* fr. 43 Peter *HRR* = fr. 2.14, Beck and Walter, 2005 = FRHist fr. 46; Polybius 2.21.7-8). (Much is made by Roman sources of the novelty of *viritim* distribution, person by person, as opposed to the granting of a block of land to a colony. But colonial agricultural land was subsequently always shared out to individual freeholders. The practical difference in provincial contexts between *viritim* and colonial distribution was probably relatively small: it was the public and private law consequences at Rome of this new system that cause our sources to focus on the issue.)

This action appears to have been received by the Senones and other peoples of the Po Valley as a sign for what, frankly, it was, the first stage in a systematic attempt to settle Roman populations across the Valley, in order to exploit, control, and dominate social conduct and economic output throughout the territory. (The fact that the Senones are recorded by

Polybius *both* as having been expelled in the early third century *and* angry at the viritane settlement of Romans in their territory by Flaminius in 232 BC is a feature of Roman narrative to which we shall return.) Indeed, we might say that the view attributed by Polybius to the Boii in the aftermath of Roman appropriation of the *ager Gallicus* half a century earlier – "seeing the Senones expelled and fearing for themselves and their land" (2.20.1) – is much more naturally placed in the aftermath of 232 BC, when the Romans finally actualized a plan that had been merely potential in the 280s. In that later context Polybius attributes the same view again to the Boii and also to others in the aftermath of Flaminius's legislation: "For what prompted many of the Gauls, and especially the Boii, whose territory bordered on that of Rome, to take action, was the conviction that now the Romans no longer made war on them for the sake of supremacy and rule, but with a view to their wholesale expulsion and extermination" (Polybius: 2.21.9, trans. Paton, 1922, lightly modified).

The tensions aroused by the settlement of Romans in the *ager Gallicus* came to a head in 225 BC in a massive military confrontation. According to Polybius, enormous forces were then arrayed on each side: the peoples of the Po Valley tempted Gauls south across the Alps with images of easy plunder, while the peoples of the Italian peninsula perceived the coming war as an existential crisis and dropped, however momentarily, their animosity toward each other (Polybius: 2.22–31). The Romans even made a temporary peace with Carthage. Though the origins of the war lay in the Romans' seizure of land north of the Apennines in 232 BC, it is not implausible that both sides came rapidly to perceive that issues of great geo-political significance were at stake. The result in any event was a complex campaign involving several columns on each side, which culminated in a massive battle at Telamon (modern Talamone, on the Etruscan coast north of Monte Argentario). The defeat of the Gauls in that battle was so overwhelming, we are told by Polybius, that "the Romans hoped that they might be able to expel the Celts entirely from the areas around the Po" (2.31.7–10).

In keeping with that view, the Romans followed up on that victory with campaigns north of the Apennines for another half decade, their concentration on the area being so overwhelming that they sent both consuls to the area for the next several years, with Gaius Flaminius himself as one of the consuls in 223 BC. During this period the Romans made their first extended campaigns across the Po against the Insubres and north and west along the coast against the Ligurians. This sequence of campaigns culminated in major victories at Clastidium and Mediolanum in 222 BC (modern Casteggio and Milan, respectively); these towns came to anchor the Roman road that ultimately stretched north–south across the western end of the valley and passed on to Comum in the north. In 220 BC, Flaminius as censor seemingly put the seal on military action and opened a new phase in the transformation of Gaul when he let the contract for the construction of the *via Flaminia* (Livy, *Summary/Periocha*: 20), and he may likewise have been responsible for the legislation, passed in this year, that established the first Roman colonies in the central Po valley, at Cremona and Placentia (modern Cremona and Piacenza). These were established in 218 BC, on the eve of the Hannibalic War, and though they suffered greatly in the disastrous first years of that war, when Hannibal allied with Gauls ranged at will in Italy, they stayed loyal to Rome and figure prominently in the history of Roman action in the first decades of the second century (Livy: 27.10.8).

14.4   The Transformation of the Landscape, 201–148 BC

The needs of Roman narrative and Roman politics drove the Romans to represent the Gauls as ferocious but strategically incompetent, and hence to describe the Roman victory at Telamon in 225 BC as total. The seeming success of subsequent campaigns and Roman ability to commence the material transformation of the central valley support, at least, representations of that victory as significant. But the peoples of Cisalpine Gaul remained – and remained hostile. Thus when Hannibal appeared across the Alps, he found ready allies among the Celts, to use the name employed by Polybius. Indeed, in his initial northern campaigns, Hannibal was able to exploit Roman reluctance to close with Gallic warriors in the woods and so was able to bring them to battle in the open on his terms (Polybius: 3.71.2–3). That said, the Gallic troops allied with Hannibal suffered disproportionate casualties every step of the way: whether because of their own incompetence, or because in their greater anger they attacked the Romans more rashly, or because (mimicking the Romans' own practice) Hannibal positioned his forces so that foreign auxiliaries would bear the brunt of losses, we cannot say (Polybius: 3.74.10; 3.79.8; 3.85.5). The Romans were able to establish the northern Apennines and the Po Valley as a sphere for regular commands only late in the war (see, e.g., Livy: 28.38.13, in support of Ariminum). In the aftermath, Roman projects in north Italy had very nearly to begin anew.

Alas, extant sources do not allow for the drawing of any demographic portrait of the Po Valley at the conclusion of the war and turn of the century, but there can be no doubt that the pre-Roman populations had also suffered huge losses among adult males between 225 and 201 BC, even as the Roman colonies and the Roman presence overall must have been substantially diminished in reach and effectiveness during the years of war (for a rehearsal of the numbers provided in ancient narrative and an attempt to assess them see Brunt, 1971, 184–90). Autopsy is of highly limited value in demography; it nonetheless bears mention that Polybius himself travelled the valley and claimed on the basis of his own viewing that the Gauls "were wholly driven out from the regions around the Po, except for a few places lying close up under the Alps" (2.35.4).

The half century that followed the end of the second Punic War witnessed a wholesale transformation in northern Italy, with a concentration of activity in the decade and a half from 198 to 183 BC, but with warfare, forced resettlements, Roman foundations, and road-building on-going until 131 BC (for the data see A. Toynbee 1965, 654–57; Brunt 1971, 190–98, 570–76). Indeed, from the end of the Second Punic War down to 166 BC – when extant data cease to permit any specification – at least one and very often both consuls drew provinces in Liguria or Cisalpine Gaul (both consuls campaigned in northern Italy in 197–196, 194–192, 188–178, 176–175, 173–172 and 167 BC). The only breaks in this remarkable concentration of effort and resources came in years like 168 BC, when the eruption of hostilities with Perseus of Macedon drew Roman attention away. Even then, when word reached Rome of the victory over Perseus at Pydna, the consul Licinius Crassus, whose duty it had been to raise troops for the Macedonian war, dismissed the Macedonian levies and took himself off to campaign in Gaul (Livy: 45.1–2; 45.12.9–12). The full details of these actions cannot be rehearsed here. In what follows I describe the main military actions, colonial foundations, and infrastructural projects of the Roman state, alongside such reflections as the sources permit on the demographic history of the region.

The 190s BC were consumed almost wholly in warfare, with perhaps the notable battles bookending the decade. The first was the crushing of the Insubres north of the Po in 197 (Livy: 32.30–31): according to Livy, their capital was Brixia, modern Brescia, at the foot of the Alps between Lake Iseo and Lake Garda. Livy's testimony should be weighed against that of his rough contemporary Strabo, who observes by way of comparison with other peoples of the valley that the Insubres continued to exist, their metropolis being Mediolanum, with Verona, Brixia, Mantua, and Comum among their *poleis* (Strabo, *Geography*: 5.1.6). The second was a major victory over the Boii in 191 BC (Livy: 36.38.5–7). Livy refuses to credit the numbers of the slain reported by Valerius Antias (fr. 41 Peter *HRR* = fr. 42 Beck-Walter 2005 = FRHist fr. 45) but nonetheless observes that the Boian camp was captured and the Boii surrendered immediately thereafter. It is notable in the aftermath that Strabo records the Boii as having been forcibly relocated wholesale to regions around the Danube (Strabo, *Geography*: 5.1.6 and

10). It is certainly possible that they were ordered to relocate north of the Alps – forced resettlement was practised by Rome in just these years – and Boian populations are recorded both in Gaul and along the Danube in the late Republic. But Strabo might be drawing an inference from the mere presence of Boii along the Danube, and there are reasons to believe Gauls persisted among and assimilated with Roman colonial populations in subsequent generations, and likewise reasons to doubt Strabo's claims in regard to the total extirpation of other such peoples, not least the Senones and Gaesatae (Strabo, *Geography*: 5.1.6 and 5.1.10, advancing the claim that only Roman colonists and Ligurian tribes are left on this side of the Po). Writing demographic history on the basis of ancient literary evidence is fraught with peril.

The next decade witnessed efforts of two kinds to consolidate Roman gains in the Po Valley itself. On the one hand, Rome reinforced the colonies of Cremona and Placentia, which had been founded in 218 BC and which must have suffered greatly in the Hannibalic war and from local hostility during the campaigns that followed. Indeed, it is remarkable that they survived at all. Limited efforts to shore up their populations had already been made in 206 and 198 BC (Livy: 28.11.11 and 32.26.3). Nonetheless, embassies came to Rome from those cities in 190 to request additional settlers: they reported as the causes for their depopulation death by war and illness, as well as flight from the exhausting hostility of their Gallic neighbors. The consul Gaius Laelius was dispatched to tour the area, and the result of his inspection was a plan to enroll 6000 further settlers for Cremona and Placentia and to establish two new colonies "on land that had once belonged to the Boii" (Livy: 37.46.9–47.2). In the immediate aftermath, however, only one is known to have been founded, Bononia, modern Bologna, established as a Latin colony in 189 BC (Livy: 37.57.7–8).

The process of demographic transformation and the projection of Roman infrastructural power accelerated over the next few years. The consuls of 187 BC, Marcus Aemilius Lepidus and Gaius Flaminius, both campaigned in Liguria at the start of the year, but both undertook significant road-building projects in Cisalpina later in the season. Aemilius laid the great *via Aemilia* along the southern edge of the valley from Ariminum in the east (where it connected with the *via Flaminia*) through Bononia to Placentia, connecting the disparate Roman colonies into a network dominating the entire Cispadana (Livy: 39.2.9–10). Flaminius the consul of 187 BC was son to the homonymous censor of 220, and, like his father, he built a road across the Apennines, in this case from Bononia south to Arretium, modern Arezzo (Livy: 39.2.6).

The next year an exogenous force drew Rome's attention north across the Po: some Gauls descended from the Alps into Venetia "into the territory where Aquileia now is, without raiding or war, and seized land in order to found a town" (Livy: 39.22.6). Roman envoys were dispatched across the Alps and received the response that "they had set out without the permission of their tribe, nor did their tribe know what they were doing in Italy" (Livy: 39.22.7). It is surely notable that the Gauls found northern Venetia underpopulated; its condition may well have been an effect of the Roman campaigns against the Insubres in the previous decade. Likewise noteworthy is the explicit upending of ethnographic and historiographic commonplaces (which Livy treats simply as common-sense expectations): these Gauls did not come to raid, but to settle down and, indeed, found a city.

After some back-and-forth, the Romans ordered the Gauls to return back across the Alps. The process turned messy: the Romans on the ground deprived the Gauls of arms and seized their goods. In response, the Gauls sent an embassy to the senate. Livy seized the occasion of the senate's response to this embassy to voice some remarkable suppositions about both politics and political geography, which are naturally attributed in his narrative to the senate of 183 BC. The Gauls describe themselves as having found the land a solitude, while their founding of a city was proof of peaceful intention. The senate replied: "They had not acted properly when they came into Italy and tried to build a city on land not their own without the permission of the Roman magistrate who was in charge of that province." The Gauls were sent home with a warning: "The Alps were a nearly insuperable border between them: it would not go well for whosoever first rendered them easy of passage" (Livy: 39.54.3–12). Two years later Rome filled the vacuum that had drawn the Gauls and founded a Latin colony on the site. In being true to history, Livy's announcement of that event upended the new realities that Roman power had made and to which the senate had given notice in his own narrative a book earlier: "In the same year [181 BC], Aquileia, a Latin colony, was founded on land of the Gauls" (Livy: 40.34.2).

Like many colonies, Aquileia would ultimately require a second infusion of colonists. The second deduction, in 169 BC, is now known from a contemporary dedicatory inscription, erected by one of the board of three dispatched to settle the new colonists, Titus Annius Luscus: in his words, he donated and erected the temple, composed and delivered a charter to the town, and enrolled its senate (*AE* (1996) 685). The fact that Aquileia's early years were evidently difficult is not, however, representative of the broader trend of these years, which rather sees Rome surging forward along many fronts. In particular, the valley south of the Po was felt secure enough that Rome followed the foundation of new colonies in the late 180s BC (including Mutina and Parma along the *via Aemilia* in 183 BC (Livy: 39.55.7–8), Luna (Livy: 41.13.4–5), and very likely Dertona)) with a huge range of smaller conurbations classified as *fora*, nodal points for economic and administrative conduct in rural areas outside the catchment of a city proper (Brunt, 1971: 570–76). Finally, in 173 BC the Romans decided to allocate *viritim* broad swaths of land seized in war from the Ligurians and Gauls (Livy: 42.4.3–4): the result was a massive programme in centuriation and settlement along the *via Aemilia* (see esp. Ewins, 1952: 59–67). Indeed, it may have been to service this population that many of the *fora* were established.

It bears stressing that the processes of settlement and centuriation effected more than a demographic, ecological, and economic revolution. Centuriation was fundamentally a material process, in which a small range of techniques was used to mark boundaries between plots of land. In the Po Valley, which tends toward marsh, the delineation of plots was accomplished by digging drainage ditches along property divisions and lining them with stone. The scarring – the "Romanization" – of the land remains visible from the air today (Chevallier, 1983: 32–80; Bussi, 1983). What is more, two of the major infrastructural projects undertaken by the Roman state in Gaul in this period are related to drainage. The first was largely urban, namely that at Aquileia, in support of constructing a proper Roman urban core (Strazzulla, 1989); the second, apparently centered on Placentia, was largely rural (Strabo, *Geography*. 5.1.11; see Figure 14.2).

Three further aspects of the history of Cisalpine Gaul in the second century BC deserve consideration here. First, although it advanced more slowly and always at chronological remove compared with developments south of the Po, the extension of Roman power north of the Po, through settlement and the remaking of the terrain, proceeded apace. The first major east–west artery in Transpadana appears to have been laid in 148 BC by the consul Spurius Postumius Albinus Magnus, running from Dertona all the way to Aquileia (Radke, 1973: cols 1601–06).

Second, the history of northern Italy cannot be neatly separated into narrative nor analysed in webs of causation territory by territory. The Romans understood by the first decade of the second century, if not before, that their ability to exploit the resources of Cisalpina rested on the pacification of Liguria and the Apennines (see, e.g., Livy: 39.2). Roman action in those regions lies outside the scope of this chapter, but I observe that a significant weapon in Rome's arsenal was the forced resettlement of entire populations. At times, as was common elsewhere, the Romans simply moved groups from mountains to plain and, on one occasion at least, north to plains across the Po (see, e.g., Livy: 39.2.9, "from mountains into the plains";

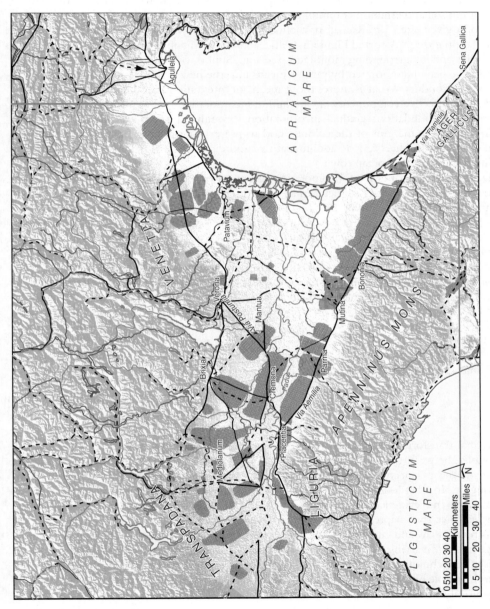

Figure 14.2 The landscape of Roman Cisalpina in the late second century BC. Hatchmarks indicate areas of centuriation. Ancient World Mapping Center © 2012 (www.unc.edu/awmc).

40.53.3, "into agricultural land"; and 42.22.5–6, "land was assigned to those led across the Po"). But sometimes the Romans moved resistant populations much, much further, including two resettlements from Liguria to Samnium (Livy: 40.38.1–9; 40.41.1–6).

Third, these tales of relocation recall our attention to the pre-Roman settlers of Cisalpina. We must not be distracted by ideal-type images of colonization, in which settlers from outside find virgin soil and establish communities *ex nihilo*. Nor should we be misled by the sterilization of a given site's pre-Roman past effected by the renewal of civic memory entailed by foundation *de novo*. Assorted Ligurian, Celtic, and Venetian populations persisted throughout the valley and its surrounding mountains (see, e.g., Strabo, *Geography*: 5.1.4, 5.1.6), and they must have been incorporated by various means into the new structures of Roman social and economic conduct. What is more, those means of integration had different legal, material, and social-affective components, including full incorporation into Roman settlements at the moment of foundation; gradual incorporation through intermarriage; allocation of land within or at the margins of the colonial grid to pre-existing populations; assigning of legal rank to pre-existing elites; or administrative subordination of a neighboring non-Roman polity to the nearest Roman town.

Detecting such patterns of incorporation of pre-existing populations into Roman foundations has proved immensely difficult in all areas of Roman Republican colonization (see, e.g., Fentress, 1996: 83–86; 2000: 13). Ideological pressure toward the depiction of colonies as wholly Roman militates against the inclusion of relevant information in contemporary records. In documentary material, it is rather in later legal texts that such histories protrude, when the results of intermarriage or simply commingling must be resolved (the problem is discussed in section 14.6, this chapter; see also Christol and Goudineau, 1987–88; Ando, 2011: 7). That said, information about indigenous populations was relevant to many discourses, nor did all non-Roman populations persist solely at the margin of Roman ones. Cato the Elder, writing in the first half of the second century BC, describes the ham produced by the Insubres "in Italy" as so high in quality, and their industry so great, that they salt three or four thousand legs a year (Cato, *Origins* fr. 2.9, Beck and Walter, 2005; cf. FRHist fr. 48). Their flourishing notwithstanding, the presence of non-Romans from the past in the Roman present remained an issue in Roman politics and memory into the first century AD. To that later history we now turn.

14.5   Citizenship and Belonging

The final transformative chapter in the ancient history of Cisalpine Gaul occurs in the late Republic, between the Social War and the age of Augustus. It might be told in at least two ways, in the perspective of law and citizenship and in that of the affective structures of belonging. In what follows, I take these in turn, thereby disaggregating for the sake of narrative issues and evidence that must have existed in complex relation to each other. The conclusion of this chapter attempts to weave these strands back together.

As regards law and citizenship, the story in brief is as follows: over some 50 years, Roman magistrates of varying political stripes, for wildly discrepant motives, employed a range of legislative techniques to extend first defective and then full citizenship rights to first parts and later the whole of Cisalpine Gaul. The steps by which this occurred naturally reflected matters of political interest, but they also reflected judgments at the metropole over the Romanness of the peoples – and Italianness of the land – south of the Alps. As a result, we should dearly like to know the evidence and arguments by which a given party justified full citizenship below this or that line but Latin rights above, and why the line was moved from this river system to that one on one or another occasion, and for that matter, what rivers were at stake on each occasion. But as so often in the late Republic, despite the existence of massive evidence, the details seem insecure in proportion to the partisanship of contemporary politics.

At the outbreak of the Social War in 90 BC, Rome passed a *lex Iulia*, granting citizenship to allies and Latins who stayed loyal (Cicero, *In Defence of Balbus*: 21; Appian, *Civil Wars*: 1.49.213–14). A year later, a law passed by the consul Gnaeus Pompeius Strabo gave Latin status to the Roman and Romanizing communities of Transpadana, to whom non-urbanized, non-Romanizing peoples were administratively and legally subordinated. (To be precise, Asconius says that Pompeius Strabo established "Transpadane colonies," not by founding them *ex nihilo* but by giving the *ius Latii* to the inhabitants who were already residing there (Asconius, *Against Piso*: 3).) The effects of the *lex Pompeia* seem clear enough on their own, but why had the *lex Iulia* not covered Cisalpina? And on what formal legal grounds was a boundary drawn at the Po? Finally, if, as seems probable, the same law granted citizenship to all those in Cispadana who did not already have it, did that law distinguish between Latins in that area whom it raised to full citizenship and the Ligurian tribes that Strabo described as still resident there in his day (Strabo, *Geography*: 5.1.10)?

Details aside, at stake clearly was the meaning of the term "Italy" and the potential for disjuncture between its popular, geographic, and political valences. Cato's inclusion of the Insubres and their ham production within the political economy of "Italy" gestures at one frame of reference. Livy's description of the senate as marking the edge of Italy at the Alps gestured at another, even as the language he attributed to the senate – referring to a supervisory magistrate – construed the region as provincial more than Roman in both cultural affairs and public law. And indeed, there are some who argue that the *lex Pompeia* should be understood as a provincial charter. Among many consequences of that position, it is urged by its advocates that references to "Italy" or, more commonly, "Italian land" in legal texts before the Social War must refer to Italy below the Apennines (most famously, *lex agraria*, Crawford, 1996: no. 2, lines 11, 21). In that case, the *lex Iulia* cannot have applied to Cispadana, either, unless perchance it contained some rider extending its field of application to that region. But if it did not, the conferral of citizenship on the residents of Cispadana must be imagined as a consequence of another piece of legislation contemporaneous with the *lex Pompeia*.

The legal situation was resolved in two dramatic actions 40 years later, one concerning persons, the other asserting a pure nominalism in respect to political language. First, in one of his earliest acts as dictator, on 11 March 49 BC, Caesar brought about the passage of a law proposed by Lucius Roscius Fabatus, one of the year's praetors, granting full citizenship to the *Transpadani*. (This was not the whole import of the law.) In Dio's narrative, which attributes all agency to Caesar rather than Roscius, the act was aimed precisely "at the Gauls below the Alps and above the Po, because [Caesar] had once governed them" (Dio Cassius: 41.36.3; for the date, see Crawford, 1996: no.16, line 13). That said, as a matter of public law, the region beyond the Po apparently remained a province, still named Gaul (Cicero, *Philippics*: 3.13). The second transformative act occurred seven years later, in 42 BC. During the negotiations with the Antonians in that year, Octavian urged the extension of Italy to the Alps, to prevent new troops being raised or stationed anywhere on the peninsula (Dio Cassius: 48.12.5; see also Appian *Civil Wars*: 5.3.12, 20.79–80, 22.86–87). Gaul was now Italy.

These separate acts of enfranchisement (the creation of Romans) and political geography (the expansion of Italy at the expense of Gaul by moving the boundary) are conflated by Strabo, who is at least aware that the Romans extended full citizenship to the "Gauls on this side of the Alps and the Veneti" only after they had granted citizenship to the Italians, but does not distinguish in time between that act and the Romans' redescription of the Gauls as both "Italians and Romans" (Strabo, *Geography*: 5.1.1). The same act of conflation might be said to occur – albeit knowingly – in the speech on citizenship attributed to the emperor Claudius in Tacitus's *Annals*. There, Tacitus's Claudius assimilates the taking-up of Italian notables into the senate as an act of political integration with the extension of Italy to the Alps. That latter act was undertaken "so that not only single individuals but lands and peoples might unite in our name: then there was unalloyed domestic calm, and in the face of things foreign we flourished when the *Transpadani* were received into the citizen body" (*Annals*: 11.24.2–3, trans. Woodman, 2004, with slight changes).

As regards the affective structures of belonging, the redescription of Gaul as Italy lived on in the national and literary imaginary long after the politics of that act had faded from relevance, for knowledge of it was necessary to a proper appreciation of Virgil's *Aeneid*. The first lines of that poem proclaimed Aeneas to have been the first to come from Troy to Italy, but that assertion appeared to be flat-out contradicted by the story of Antenor as related by Venus later in the first book (*Aeneid*: 1.242–52). Four resolutions to the apparent error circulated in late antiquity. The anonymous author of the *libellus* on the origin of the Roman people, which was transmitted with the history of Aurelius Victor, placed the onus of his explanation on the meaning of *primus*: comparing Virgil's usage elsewhere, he argued that *primus* at *Aeneid* 1.1 must have the meaning *princeps*, designating priority in significance and not in time (*The Origin of the Roman People*: 1.5–6). The fourth-century commentator Servius, on the other hand, offered three explanations, all of which depend ultimately on the meaning of *Italia*. Servius himself preferred merely to argue that Virgil wrote in a fashion most appropriate to the usage of his day, when (as he imagined) Italy had ended at the Rubicon: Antenor did not, therefore, reach Italy, but rather Cisalpine Gaul. When, afterwards, the borders of Italy were moved to the Alps, it was the innovation that created the error (Servius on *Aeneid* 1.1–2; see also on 1.13, as well as Cato, *Origins* fr. 42 Peter *HRR* = fr. 2.12, Beck and Walter, 2005 = FRHist fr. 58).

Virgil's interest in Antenor, legendary founder of Patavium, was neither innocent nor accidental. Virgil was born in 70 BC in Mantua, a Roman city on the Mincius, north of the Po. He was therefore not an Italian and, indeed, may not have been Roman at birth: those identities came to him and his native land in separate acts in his adulthood (see Toll, 1991; 1997). In positing a Trojan founder for Transpadane urbanism kindred to the Trojan founder of Rome itself, Virgil exploited a deeply contemporary mode of political recognition, which employed mythopoetic genealogies and foundation stories to establish kinship between regions and races. Nor was this Virgil's only poetic engagement with the Italian question. On the contrary, one can read the "Praises of Italy" in book 2 of the *Georgics* and the catalog of Italian allies in the *Aeneid* as advancing complex claims regarding the ecological and cultural unity of the Italian peninsula: Italy was not diverse, but constituted a single *patria* for plants; home to a single *durum genus*, Italy had but one *disciplina et vita*, a single way of life.

What is more, Virgil was hardly the first Transpadane Roman to thematize the Italianness of Gaul in his writing (Wiseman, 1979: 161–66; 1985: 107–15), nor, it should be noted, was his the only argument, or the only form of argument, on the Italian question circulating in late Republican and Augustan Rome (Ando, 2002: 123–42). The poet Catullus, born at Verona at the feet of the Alps, dedicated his book to a fellow *Transpadanus*, the polymathic historian Cornelius Nepos. Nepos, Catullus wrote, was the first of the Italians "to dare to explain all history in three books, learned and well-wrought" (Catullus 1.5–6). "Italians" is emphatic: by it, the achievement of Nepos is enhanced, even as the achievements of "Roman" authors are subsumed within a greater Italian whole.

Catullus dedicated his book to Nepos in the mid-50s BC; on these and other grounds, we should date Nepos's *floruit* prior to the triumviral removal of the boundary of Italy to the Alps. Nepos himself shared with Virgil an interest in the eastern origins of the Veneti, whom he traced to Paphlagonia (Pliny the Elder, *Natural History*: 6.5 = Nepos *Anecdotes* fr. 14 Peter *HRR* = FRHist fr. 7). To judge from the extant fragments of his works, they provided much detail on the history and geography of Transpadana, though of course it is likely that the selection is not random. Rather, Nepos was known to be *Transpadanus* and therefore achieved an authority in matters Transpadene that he did not achieve in other areas of inquiry.

It might be that Nepos rehearsed this information without partisan ambition. That said, one fragment hints at a more complex agenda. Concluding a list of vanished communities in Transpadana in the third book of his *Natural History*, Pliny the Elder writes: "Other communities that have perished [include] … the exceptionally wealthy town of Melpum, which is stated by Cornelius Nepos to have been destroyed by the Insubrians, Boii and Senones on the very day that Camillus took Veii" (*Natural History*: 3.125 = Nepos *Anecdotes* fr. 9 Peter *HRR* = FRHist fr. 10). Nepos here identifies a synchronism, the simultaneous occurrence of structurally similar events in contexts that one wishes to connect. The expulsion of the tyrants at Athens and the foundation of the Republic at Rome is one such (synchronisms in ancient culture are a major theme of Feeney, 2007: esp. 7–67). The synchronism between Transpadana and Rome should be understood as kindred to Virgil's redescription of the Veneti as Trojan. Writing well prior to the reclassification of his native land as Italian, Nepos instead asserted a cultural affinity between the land of his origin and the metropolitan center where he made his home and his name. Born circa 110, Nepos died in 24 BC. The juridical and political acts that transformed his homeland were thus a small part of the revolutions that he witnessed in a long and tumultuous lifetime.

14.6 Conclusion: An Epitaph for Cremona

In AD 46, the emperor Claudius was called upon to resolve two problems, one between the city of Comum and a neighboring people, the Bergalei, the other between the Tridentini and three neighboring peoples, the Anauni, Tulliassi, and Sinduni. The situation at Comum is mentioned without being further explained, but its appearance in the same edict with the Tridentini suggests the problem was the same.

   Among the Tridentini the problem was as follows: the chief city of the Tridentini, Tridentum (modern Trento) had been created *de novo* as a Roman municipality by Julius Caesar when he extended citizenship to Transpadana, and he had administratively subordinated to it several neighboring peoples. An appeal was made to Claudius because it had been discovered that many among those neighboring peoples had long acted as if they were Roman citizens. Indeed, they passed as such not only at Tridentum, but some had become citizen-soldiers in the praetorian guard and others had served as lay judges in Roman trials! Claudius was asked to regularize the situation by granting them citizenship, "since by long-standing legal usage they are said to be in possession of it and are so mixed up with the Tridentini that it could not be taken away from them without serious harm to that splendid municipality" (*ILS* 206). What is more, that commingling had occurred without respect to the niceties of administrative subordination: Claudius admits that the question of who was and who was not "attributed" to Tridentum is without import to the facts on the ground. Claudius granted the request.

   Later, in AD 69, the city of Cremona became embroiled in the civil wars that erupted after the death of Nero, being held first by troops of Vitellius against those of Otho. Later, troops loyal to Vespasian occupied the city and, motivated by sheer greed and spite, turned on the populace: the entire urban fabric of public and private buildings was destroyed. Only a single extra-urban temple survived (Tacitus, *Histories*: 3.26–33): "This was the end of Cremona, in the 286th year since its founding. It was founded when Tiberius Sempronius and Publius Cornelius were consuls, as Hannibal was entering into Italy, as a bulwark against Gauls acting across the Po and if some other force should cross the Alps. Thereafter, thanks to the number of colonists, the convenience of the rivers, the richness of its fields and association and inter-marriage with the indigenous peoples, it grew rich and flourished, untouched by foreign wars but unlucky in civil ones" (Tacitus, *Histories*: 3.34.1). These two narratives both contribute new perspectives on the histories we have rehearsed, and expose significant limitations in ancient narrative. Despite the generic and ideological claims made in ancient sources regarding the Romanness of Roman foundations; despite the essential and existential enmity ascribed to Roman-Gallic relations; and despite claims by Romans to have extirpated or expelled many indigenes from the Po Valley, complex patterns of social, economic, and cultural exchange took place between Romans and Gauls. Indeed, at Comum, they took place by design, within the urban fabric: an indigenous city, it had received several influxes of Roman colonists, starting with one implanted by Pompeius Strabo (Strabo, *Geography*. 5.1.6). What is more, not only is the existence and pattern of such exchanges now reasonably well understood in the historiography of the Roman west, there are very good reasons to believe the Roman colonization and administrative attribution were undertaken with such effects in mind (Ando, 2012).

That said, the complex interplay of myth and truism that seems to have shaped Roman policy and which structured historical narrative and contemporary percipience from Pictor down to Livy – precisely the claims of extirpation and expulsion as responses to essential enmity – must have factored heavily in those late Republican political decisions and administrative acts that created Romans and Italians from the residents of Cisalpina. That is to say, given Roman belief that the Gauls were their mortal enemies, it is hard to imagine passage of the *lex Pompeia* or *lex Roscia* apart from the myth that the valley had been cleared of Celtic peoples and the reality that Roman infrastructural power and agricultural practice penetrated throughout its landscape.

At the level of political geography, the ancient history of Cisalpine Gaul may therefore be said to have ended under Augustus, when Italy received its final ancient border and Cisalpina, Transpadana, and their environs were all reclassified as but regions of Augustan Italy (VIII Aemilia, IX Liguria, X Venetia et Histria, and XI Transpadana). Tacitus's epitaph for Cremona testifies to another form of knowledge, a persistent historical memory in which the non-Roman, even non-Italian contribution to Roman Italy was long commemorated. Indeed, as Leonardo Bruni attests, or the popularity of the Northern League, as the Anglophone press names the Italian political party *Lega Nord per l'indipendenza della Padania*, attests, those memories have remained available for recuperation and mobilization down to the present day.

FURTHER READING

There is no monographic treatment of the Po Valley in the Roman period to match Chevallier 1983 which is, alas, now 30 years out of date. In the meantime, epigraphic and archaeological discoveries have proceeded at an enormous pace. That said, in all regions of the empire, epigraphic and material evidence derives overwhelmingly from the age of Augustus and beyond, not the age of conquest. In provincial histories of the Republican period, the perspective and the agency are perforce nearly always Roman. A contemporary synthesis is badly needed, but it might not substantially revise the story rehearsed here.

Even with that caveat, up-to-date literature in English is wanting. Jonathan Williams 2001 is an elegant and informative study of the ancient historiographic tradition of the conquest period. Purcell 1990 remains one of the most exciting essays on the material transformations worked by Roman urbanism and agricultural practice in the west. In somewhat different fashion, Arnold Toynbee's analysis (1965) of Roman colonization in the second century BC remains without peer for its passion and analytic sweep. For assorted technical questions related to the history of colonization and enfranchisement in Gaul (for example, the foundation dates of second-century *fora* and the tribal affiliations of various settlements), Ursula Ewins' essays of 1952 and 1955 remain extremely useful, though they are naturally substantially out of date in their collation of epigraphic material.

REFERENCES

Ando, C. 2002. "Vergil's Italy: ethnography and politics in first-century Rome." In *Clio and the Poets. Augustan poetry and the traditions of ancient historiography*, eds D.S. Levene and D.P. Nelis, 123–42. Leiden: Brill.

Ando, C. 2011. *Law, Language, and Empire in the Roman Tradition*. Philadelphia: University of Pennsylvania Press.

Ando, C. 2012. "The Roman city in the Roman period." In *Rome, a City and its Empire in Perspective. The impact of the Roman world through Fergus Millar's research*, ed. S. Benoist, 109–24. Leiden: Brill.

Beck, H. and Walter, U., eds. 2005. (2nd edn). *Die frühen römischen Historiker*. 2 vols. Darmstadt: Wissenschaftliche Buchgesellschaft.

Brunt, P.A. 1971. *Italian Manpower, 225 BC–AD 14*. Oxford: Clarendon Press.

Bussi, R. 1983. *Misurare la terra: centuriazione e coloni nel mondo romano*. Modena: Panini.

Chevallier, R. 1983. *La Romanisation de la Celtique du Po. Essai d'histoire provinciale*. Rome: École française de Rome.

Christol, M. and Goudineau, C. 1987–88. "Nîmes et les Volques Arécomiques au Ier siècle avant J.C.," *Gallia* 45: 87–103.

Crawford, M.H., ed. 1996. *Roman Statutes*. 2 vols. London: Institute of Classical Studies/*BICS Supplement* 64.

Ewins, U. 1952. "The early colonisation of Cisalpine Gaul." *Papers of the British School at Rome* 20: 54–71.

Ewins, U. 1955. "The enfranchisement of Cisalpine Gaul." *Papers of the British School at Rome* 23: 73–98.

Feeney, D. 2007. *Caesar's Calendar. Ancient time and the beginnings of history*. Berkeley: University of California Press.

Fentress, E. 1996. "Saturnia: figures in a centuriate landscape." In *Splendidissima Civitas. Études d'histoire romaine en hommage à François Jacques*, eds A. Chastagnol, S. Demougin, and C. Lepelley, 79–99. Paris: Publications de la Sorbonne.

Fentress, E. 2000. "Frank Brown, Cosa, and the idea of a Roman city." In *Romanization and the city. Creations, transformations and failures*, ed. E. Fentress, 9–24. Portsmouth, RI: *Journal of Roman Archaeology* Suppl. 38.

Paton, W.R. 1922. *Polybius: The Histories*. Cambridge MA: Harvard University Press.

Purcell, N. 1990. "The creation of provincial landscape: the Roman impact on Cisalpine Gaul." In *The Early Roman Empire in the West*, eds T. Blagg and M. Millett, 6–29. Oxford: Oxbow.

Radke, G. 1973. "Viae publicae Romanae." In *RE* Supplement 13: cols 1417–1686.

Strazzulla, M.J. 1989. "In paludibus moenia constituta: problemi urbanistici di Aquileia in età repubblicana alla luce della documentazione archeologica e delle fonti scritte." In *Aquileia repubblicana e imperiale*, 187–228. Udine: Arti Grafiche Friulane.

Toll, K. 1991. "The *Aeneid* as an epic of national identity: *Italiam laeto socii clamore salutant*." *Helios* 18.1: 3–14.

Toll, K. 1997. "Making Roman-ness and the *Aeneid*." *Classical Antiquity* 16.1: 34–56.

Toynbee, A. 1965. *Hannibal's Legacy: the Hannibalic War's effects on Roman life*. 2 vols. London: Oxford University Press.

Williams, J.H.C. 2001. *Beyond the Rubicon. Romans and Gauls in Republican Italy*. Oxford: Oxford University Press.

Wiseman, T.P. 1979. *Clio's Cosmetics*. Leicester: Leicester University Press.

Wiseman, T.P. 1985. *Catullus and his World. A reappraisal*. Cambridge: Cambridge University Press.

Woodman, A.J. 2004. *Tacitus: The Annals*. Indianapolis: Hackett.

PART III

Town and Country

3.1 Settlement Patterns

CHAPTER 15

Urbanization

Joanne Berry

15.1 Introduction

The Roman Empire was characterized by its network of cities, which the Romans themselves saw as the social, political, and economic centers of their empire. According to Pliny the Elder (*Natural History*: 3.6.22), in the first century AD there were 400 cities in Italy alone, and it is clear from other ancient sources that cities were considered to be synonymous with civilization (for example, Tacitus, *Agricola*: 21; Procopius, *Gothic War*: 8.22; Strabo, *Geography*: 4.1.11). Those who did not live in cities were considered barbarians (Tacitus, *Annals*: 2.52). More importantly, by Pliny's time, cities were expected to have monumental public buildings, and those lacking certain amenities such as temples, baths, theaters, and government offices were scorned by contemporary observers (Pausanias, *Description of Greece*: 10.4.1). It has been estimated that, at the time of Augustus, 25% of the population of Italy lived in urban centers (40% if Rome is included), although, with the exception of a few regional centers and a small number of major cities, the majority of towns were probably quite small, with populations of between 1000 and 5000 people (Lo Cascio, 2009; Morley, 1996a: 181–83; Scheidel, 2004). Nevertheless, cities of all sizes, with their monumental public buildings, were the symbols of Roman civilization and power, and their remains can still be seen throughout the Mediterranean world today.

For this reason, the archaeology of individual urban centers has traditionally dominated the attention of both scholars and the general public (Keay *et al.*, 2004: 223). Yet urban archaeology is rarely straightforward, not least because the varying nature of preservation and survival of urban centers makes it difficult to make comparisons between sites. Cities like Pompeii and Herculaneum were destroyed in a natural disaster and – despite some post-eruption disturbance – survive to a much greater extent than cities which were slowly abandoned, like Ostia. Others, like the city of Rome itself, have been continuously occupied since Roman times, their structures built over or incorporated into later buildings. The excavation of a city is always limited or influenced by its later history, and conditions are rarely ideal. It is fair to say that our picture of cities in Roman Italy, and in the Roman Empire more generally, is far from complete.

A Companion to Roman Italy, First Edition. Edited by Alison E. Cooley.
© 2016 John Wiley & Sons, Ltd. Published 2016 by John Wiley & Sons, Ltd.

In recent years, scholars have begun to turn their attention to broader patterns of urbanization, studying cities within their wider environment, undertaking regional studies and examining the evidence for smaller urban sites. As our data grows, so does our understanding of the processes and extent of urbanization in the Roman period. The purpose of this chapter is to review our current state of knowledge, based on the extant archaeological and literary evidence, and then to examine some of the roles that the city played in the Roman period.

15.2   Defining Urbanization

Urbanization, or the growth of urban centers, is just one of a series of interconnected processes by which complex societies come into being, the others being the transformation of social institutions and practices, the establishment of social stratification, and the expansion of economic activity (Gordon Childe, 1950; discussed by Smith, 2009). Thus, the development of cities in Roman Italy was a result of changes in the society and economy of the Republican period rather than the agent of those changes (Morley, 1996a; 1996b; Cornell 1995a: 102–03). Cities reflect these wider changes: in addition to a certain level of population, attracted from the countryside, a city demonstrates complexity (in terms of administration, government, social hierarchies, uneven distribution of wealth and so on) and influence outside its urban boundaries (Smith, 2009). But it is important to note that the three elements of population, complexity, and influence can each vary considerably, which means that there can be significant differences between cities. Despite broad and recognizable similarities in architecture, amenities, and building types considered as typifying Roman cities, they were often different in terms of their development, status, and function. There is no simple "model" that can be applied to all Roman cities.

15.3   The Development of Cities in Italy

The earliest cities in Italy were Greek, not Roman. Greek colonists settled first at Pithecusae on the island of Ischia (circa 770 BC) and at Cumae in Campania (757 BC) and then spread out along the coast of southern Italy and into Sicily, founding their settlements on promontories or headlands that could be easily defended, or at places near rivers which formed natural lines of defense as well as providing routes into the interior (De Vita, 1996: 265–66). In this period the main aim of the colonists was to secure arable land. This can be seen at Metapontion (Metapontum), founded sometime in the eighth century BC. Strabo (*Geography*: 6.1.15) claims that Achaean settlers at nearby Sybaris sent for new colonists and persuaded them to settle at Metapontion, supposedly to stop the neighboring colonists of Tarentum from taking the land. Archaeological evidence from the Incoronata hilltop has shown that a thriving Iron Age settlement near Metapontion was wiped out in about the same period, and replaced by a Greek settlement, evidence that Greek colonization was not always peaceful and could involve the expulsion of indigenous inhabitants (Orlandini, 1998). In mainland Greece in this period, geographically close groups of villages were only just beginning to develop into coherent or unified settlements, so the new Greek colonists of southern Italy and Sicily brought with them no models of urban organization which they could use to plan their new cities (De Vita, 1996: 263). Instead, the new colonies initially employed a largely egalitarian division of arable land, needed to ensure the self-sufficiency of each family, along with common ground that was marked out from the start. At Metapontion and elsewhere arable zones were staked out, and surrounded by sanctuaries. Excavations by the École Française at Metapontion have uncovered regularly laid out farm-type lots with uniform one-room houses, and a demarcated central area that in the seventh century BC would develop into the agora (De Vita, 1996: 266–67). However, within two or three generations growing complexity in the social and political organization of these early colonies led to the creation of planned urban centers with much denser volume of building and increasing monumentality. By 600 BC orthogonal street grids are found at Selinunte and Megara Hyblaea in Sicily, which then spread to many other Greek colonies in Magna Graecia, like Neapolis (Naples) which was planned on virgin territory near the older Greek colony of Palaeopolis (Partenope) (Mertens and Greco, 1996: 258).

Other types of city in Italy also pre-dated the Romans. In Etruria and Latium large local centers began to appear from circa 1000 BC, often located in areas with strong natural defenses, although not always with fortification walls (Cornell, 1995b). For example, Etruscan cities such as Vulci, Tarquinia, and Veii in southern Etruria developed on the sites of earlier Villanovan settlements during the eighth century BC, at the same time that the first Greek colonies were being founded in southern Italy. During the seventh century BC the first evidence of the formal demarcation of space within these settlements appears. An early example is Tarquinia where areas of habitation and burial were marked out and separated (Spivey and Stoddart, 1990: 52). By the sixth century BC, Etruscan cities had fortification walls, monumental temples, and public buildings, as well as road systems, reflecting more complex social hierarchies (Torelli, 1986: 51). Other Etruscan cities in central and northern Etruria developed more slowly but followed the same pattern. Etruscan colonies were founded in Campania, at places like Capua and Pontecagnano, and in the Po Valley. The Etruscan city near Marzabotto, founded in the sixth century BC is a prime example of an Etruscan city that swiftly developed a clear orthogonal plan with formalized bounded areas for cemeteries and an acropolis, and regular blocks of houses grouped about a central courtyard (Spivey and Stoddart, 1990: 59; Torelli, 1986: 52–53).

The development of the city of Rome near the mouth of the river Tiber took place within this broader context of urbanization in Italy. Miniature objects found in ninth-century burials in what would later become the Roman Forum, and the remains of huts found on the Palatine Hill show that Rome was no different from other settlements in Latium in this period. At the end of the seventh century, at the same time that monumental building began to take place in other parts of Italy, Rome began to grow and develop, albeit in an unplanned and irregular fashion, partly dictated by its topography and partly by the speed at which it expanded. The archaeological evidence for both the foundation and development of Rome is fragmentary, since most of the structures dating to this period were either destroyed in antiquity or in more recent times, or today remain buried under later Roman or modern structures. However, excavations have established that from 630/620–580 BC there was a phase of systematic reorganization of the Forum area, including the earliest evidence of paving and the construction of public buildings (Tagliamonte, 1995). The Temple of Jupiter on the Capitoline Hill, large aristocratic houses built of stone, and a circuit of defensive walls were also constructed.

15.4 The Historical Context of Urbanization in Roman Italy in the Republican Period

What distinguished Rome from other Latin cities in this period was not how it developed but its exceptional size. It has been estimated that the city walls enclosed an area of 426 hectares, making Rome larger than any other city in Italy. In addition, by the fifth century it controlled a considerable part of Latium, as far as 100 km to the south (Claridge, 1998: 5–6). The territory under Rome's control continued to grow rapidly and it has been suggested that by 338 BC the *Ager Romanus*, or territory under direct Roman administration, covered an area of 5525 km^2; by 264 BC this had grown to 26 805 km^2 (Cornell, 1995a: 380).

As its sphere of influence grew within Italy, Rome chose to use a system of cities to administer its newly conquered territory. Initially, as the Romans conquered the areas around Rome itself, the larger Latin cities, starting with Tusculum, became independent *municipia* whose inhabitants obtained full Roman citizenship and were liable to Roman taxes and military service, but legally maintained their own laws and traditions (albeit heavily influenced by Rome). Other cities became *municipia sine suffragio*, with rights in Roman law but without the vote in Roman assemblies. Gradually other peoples of Roman Italy were conquered and some became "allies" of Rome. This meant that they had to give up some land and agree to supply soldiers to the Roman army, but they were not taxed and in theory remained independent. Some eventually were awarded Roman citizenship without the vote. Examples listed by the Roman historian Velleius Paterculus (1.14.2) include Acerra in 332 BC, and Fundi and Formiae in 338 BC (see also Livy: 8.14.10). All three cities were eventually upgraded to full citizenship, Fundi and Formiae in 188 BC, and Acerra at an unknown date. It was not until 90 BC that the *Lex Julia* made all the towns of Italy *municipia* with full civic rights.

The fact of Rome's extraordinary expansion into an empire is undisputed, but it should be noted that, particularly during the Republican period, the impact it had on settlement and urbanization in Italy was variable and subject to different influences. The Greek geographer Strabo (5.2.9) lists the cities of Roman Italy in the first century AD, "some of which exist in their original state, others have been colonized by the Romans, or partially ruined by them in their wars." Some cities fell under Roman influence, others were conquered and had their lands confiscated and eventually (within a generation or so) redistributed to new settlers (Laurence, 2001: 597), and some were destroyed or abandoned, such as Populonia in Etruria (Strabo, *Geography*: 5.2.6), or reduced to villages, such as the Greek/Etruscan city Spina (Strabo: 5.1.7). Strabo (5.4.12) describes how the Picentini who lived near the Adriatic were transplanted by the Romans to the Gulf of Paestum: "Picentia was formerly the capital of the Picentes; but they now dwell in villages, having been ejected by the Romans for taking part with Hannibal … To keep them in check, the Romans fortified Salernum, which is a little above the sea." Similar incidents are described by other ancient authors such as Livy (40.38.1–7) who describes how 400 000 Ligurians were resettled on part of the *ager publicus* near Beneventum that had been confiscated from the Taurasini in 180 BC.

A network of new Roman colonies was also established in newly conquered lands during the fourth and third centuries BC, initially close to Rome and settled by Latin peoples as well as Romans, but eventually being sent further afield throughout Italy, so that the number of urban centers increased dramatically and changed the landscape of Italy (Wallace-Hadrill, 2008: 79). Down to the Second Punic War (218–201 BC), a series of maritime colonies, located on the coast and containing small garrisons, were founded whose inhabitants had full citizen rights at Rome. Examples include Ostia and Antium (both established circa 338 BC). But these were the exception, and most colonists – even if they were Romans – usually had Latin rights. This meant that they did not have the right to vote at Rome. The Roman historian Velleius Paterculus (1.14.2) recorded the foundation of the following in this period: Setia (circa 383 BC), Sutrium (circa 382 BC), Nepi (circa 382 BC), Cales (334 BC), Tarracina (329 BC), Luceria (314 BC), Suessa Aurunca (313 BC), Saticula (313 BC), Interamna (312 BC), Sora (303 BC), Alba (303 BC), Carseoli (302 BC), Minturnae (296 BC), Sinuessa (296 BC), Venusia (291 BC), Cosa (273 BC), Paestum (273 BC), Ariminum (268 BC), Beneventum (268 BC), Firmum (264 BC), Castrum (264 BC; this is Castrum Novum), Aesernia (263 BC), Aefulum (247 BC; this is possibly Pyrgi, cf. Salmon, 1969: n.120), Alsium (247 BC), Fregenae (245 BC), Brundisium (244 BC), Spoletium (242 or 241 BC), Cremona (218 BC) and Placentia (218 BC) (cf. Salmon, 1969; Livy: 27.9.10 also gives a list of Latin colonies at the time of the Second Punic War and this is supplemented by references in Dio Cassius, Dionysius of Halicarnassus and Festus). Some of these colonies were intended to be large cities from the start, such as Cales in Campania which was founded with 2500 settlers, and Firmum in the Marche which had 6000 initial colonists. Some were founded on virgin land, but others were established in conquered cities in hostile territories. Often they were established as defensive strongholds in strategically important locations. A good example is the series of Latin and Roman colonies founded in the central Adriatic region in the late third and second century BC, including Potentia in 184 BC (Livy: 39.44). These colonies protected the Potenza Valley, a natural corridor linking the Adriatic area with the Tiber River (Vermeulen and Verhoeven, 2006: 396).

Subsequently, in the first century BC colonies of veteran soldiers were also established in Italy by the Roman general Sulla in some of the places that had fought against him during the Social War (91–88 BC), such as Pompeii and Praeneste. Later in the first century Julius Caesar also founded veteran colonies in Italy (and Gaul), such as Calatia in Campania where soldiers of the seventh legion were given land (Keppie, 2004: 71, 111–12), and after the Battle of Philippi (42 BC), Octavian organized veteran settlements throughout Italy, which involved the expropriation of land from 18 cities, selected for their prosperity (Appian, *Civil Wars*: 4.3; cf. Keppie, 1983: 61). These cities included Capua, Rhegium, Venusia, Beneventum, Nuceria, Arminum, and Vibo, and possibly Cremona, Concordia, Luca, and Bonomia). Some of these cities received the veterans from two legions. After the Battle of Actium in 31 BC, it is thought that Octavian had to settle a further 40 000–50 000 veterans (Keppie, 1983: 73–82). Some were given a cash payment, but others received land in cities from which some of the existing inhabitants were made to leave (they were compensated with either cash or land elsewhere). Augustus claimed that he founded 28 new colonies of veterans in Italy in this period (*Res Gestae*: 28; Suetonius, *Life of Augustus*: 46; Ateste is the only known example, cf. Keppie, 1983: 77–82), probably in the years immediately after Actium, but throughout Augustus's reign others, such as Capua, Castrum Novum, Minturnae, Nola, and Puteoli were also reinforced with veterans (Keppie, 1983: 80–82). Keppie (1983: 82) suggests that 50 or more colonies were likely to have been established in Italy in the period from the Battle of Philippi in 42 BC to the end of Augustus's reign in AD 14. In addition, many colonies were founded in the provinces during Augustus's reign, usually as part of his provincial reorganization, such as Augusta Emerita in Lusitania (Keppie, 1983: 82–86).

Some colonies flourished, but others were eventually abandoned or destroyed. Aquileia was founded as a colony in 180 BC to check northern barbarians (Strabo, *Geography*: 5.1.8) and eventually became an important harbor; Suessa Pometia, a Volscian city which later seems to have become a colony, revolted against Roman rule in 503 BC and was wiped out by the Romans (Pliny the Elder, *Natural History*: 3.5.9). Placentia and Cremona were besieged by a Gallic army in the aftermath of the Hannibalic Wars and their colonists had suffered from war and sickness, with the result that many fled (Livy: 28.11.10). Representatives of these colonies complained about depopulation to the senate at Rome, and a further 6000 families were sent out to be divided between the two cities (Livy: 37.46.9–11). Examples such as these reveal how precarious the early history of many colonies could be. Later, during the Social Wars of the first century BC, many cities in Samnium in particular, including some colonies, were destroyed by Sulla. Aesernia was a Roman colony captured by the Samnites in this period and eventually used as the headquarters of the Italic League. As punishment, it was completely razed by Sulla in 84 BC (Strabo, *Geography*: 5.3.10) – and it was not the only city to suffer this fate. Strabo (*Geography*: 5.4.11) claims that Bovianum, Panna, and Telesia were reduced to villages after Sulla's actions, and that only Beneventum and Venusia were spared from devastation (Dench, 1995: 128).

Laurence (1999: 27–38; 2001: 599) has shown that smaller urban nuclei known as *fora* (small settlements founded by a magistrate) were particularly important in the development of the Italian landscape in the third and second centuries BC. Some were deliberately established along major roads, such as Forum Flaminium, Forum Sempronium and Nuceria, all close to the *via Flaminia* and populous because of their location rather than political importance (Strabo, *Geography.* 5.2.10). Their role must have been primarily economic. Other *fora* were more urban in nature and may have developed into local centers where the Romans recruited soldiers and enforced the law. Laurence suggests that *fora* were often nucleated settlements on confiscated land in recently conquered territory (Laurence, 2001: 601–03), complementing the foundation of colonies. Some went on to develop into important places on the Italian road network, such as Forum Novum in the Sabina which later became a *municipium* with basilica, baths and a *campus* (Filippi, 1989) which explains why they were listed by the Elder Pliny alongside other towns. Others failed to develop distinctively urban features because of their proximity to major cities; one example is Forum Gallorum on the *via Aemilia* which lay only 11 miles from Mutina and 14 miles from Bononia and which is referred to as a *vicus* by Cicero (*Letters to his Friends.* 10.30.3; Laurence, 2001: 604).

15.5   Regional Diversity

The expansion of Roman power in Italy in the Republican period, along with the conquest of Italian cities and the foundation of Roman colonies, is clear to see, but, as we have seen, the process of urbanization was not uniform across Italy. Furthermore, it was not simply related to conquest alone. At times, urban populations seemed to have expanded during, rather than as a consequence of, war. At Pompeii, for example, a wave of new house construction in the third century BC has been attributed to an influx of refugees during the Hannibalic Wars (Nappo, 1997; Cornell, 1995b: 127). It is also the case that coastal cities developed much more quickly than inland ones, the cities of Latium and Campania leading the way. In these two regions many cities were already very prosperous by the first century BC, thanks to their effective exploitation of their hinterland and the wealth that came from the Roman conquests beyond Italy, and had begun to construct substantial public buildings (Patterson, 1987: 144). But the situation was different in other regions of Italy.

Indeed, recent archaeological investigation of some inland areas of Italy has revealed substantial differences from Latium and Campania. Despite being conquered by the Romans, parts of central Italy lagged behind in the development of urban centers. Archaeological surveys in Samnium in the Central Apennines (occupied in antiquity by the Pentri and Frentani) have revealed the predominantly rural character of this area until the first century BC (Barker, 1995; Patterson, 1987; 1991). Although there is some evidence of urbanization here from the late fourth century and early third century BC, particularly in lowland areas, revealed by both archaeological remains (for example, at Larinum where imported south Italian fine pottery was found during survey; cf. Lloyd, 1995a: 185) and by the Greek geographer Strabo's rather exaggerated claims that Samnite towns were reduced to villages by Sulla (Dench, 1995: 133; Lloyd, 1995b: 213), it was slower and on a smaller scale. Some sites dating to before the first century BC in this part of Italy cannot be considered to be urban settlements at all: fortified hill forts in Samnium and the Central Apennines were only occupied in times of emergency, the local populations preferring to live in the countryside (Cornell, 1995b: 124). Here administration was based on the *touto* (state), made up of *pagi*, territorially defined administrative units formed of one or more *vici* and administered by local magistrates (Dench 1995, 135; Lloyd 1995a, 207). The existing towns were small (such as Reate, which covered only eight hectares) and were not the focus of elite activities. Instead, local Samnite elites chose to embellish rural sanctuaries, which acted as regional cult-centers (probably with an additional economic role during festivals, cf. Barker, 1995: 209), rather than their settlements. The best example of this is at the sanctuary at Pietrabbondante, probably the center of the

Samnite League, which was lavishly reconstructed in the second century BC, with the addition of a theater and large temple built by the Staius family. Its architecture was derived from Hellenistic rather than Roman models, and many inscriptions from here relate to the construction and dedication of buildings by the local elite (Dench, 1995: 136–38; Poccetti, 1979; Strazzulla and De Marco, 1982). Towns did not benefit from elite building in these areas, except where Latin colonies had been founded by Rome, for example, at Beneventum and Aesernia (Patterson, 1987).

Patterson (1987) has argued that the *vicus* system continued into the first century BC because of the remoteness of the region and the suitability of the *vicus* for exploiting the plains, and because the Samnite elites had suffered so greatly in the aftermath of the Social Wars (see also Dench, 1995: 140). However, in low-lying areas close to major communication routes, changes had started to take place by the mid-first century BC (Lloyd, 1995b: 217–18), and by the imperial period hill forts and rural sanctuaries had largely been abandoned. It may be that the development of public buildings and the construction of city walls related to the extension of citizenship to the people here after the Social War (Gabba, 1971; cf. Cornell, 1995b: 126–27), that is to say, that a change in the political circumstances of the region was the impetus for urbanization and that the local Samnite elite began to adopt the more conventional Italian urban center as its political focus (Lloyd, 1995b: 249; Patterson 1991: 149–57). Saepinum became a *municipium* in this period (*CIL* 9.2451 and 2457), as did Bovianum (*CIL* 9.2563 and 2565), which developed on the site of the earlier Samnite town, close to the road leading from Aesernia to Beneventum (Lloyd, 1995b: 218). But more profound changes took place under Augustus, who systematically reorganized rural Italy, dividing the entire peninsula into separate municipal territories. Augustus raised some *vici* to the status of *municipia* and gave them control of the surrounding territory (Patterson, 1987: 145). Examples include Trebula Mutuesca and Amiternum. One impact of this was that local elites began to focus their activities on the new *municipia*, where they could compete for prestige and local office (eventually leading to a career in Rome itself), which by the early first century AD finally started to acquire monumental public buildings. At Saepinum, once a Samnite settlement, the majority of visible remains today date to the Augustan period or slightly later, including the city walls with its towers and gates (constructed 2 BC–AD 4; *CIL* 9.2443), a forum-basilica complex, temples, a theater, a *macellum* and a bath building (Lloyd, 1995b: 218). Yet this change in urban development was short-lived: by the end of the first century AD much of the Central Apennines had reverted to the *pagus-vicus* system (Dench, 1995: 140; La Regina 1968; 1970–71: 441 ff.; Frederiksen, 1976: 350).

15.6   Case Studies: Poseidonia/Paestum and Cosa

The variable fortunes and development of cities in Italy is best illustrated by case studies which serve to highlight some of the factors that influenced urban development.

The Greek and Roman city of Poseidonia/Paestum located in the Bay of Salerno in southern Italy is a good example of the development of a city over time in response to varying local and regional factors and political conditions. According to Strabo (*Geography:* 5.4.13), Poseidonia was founded by Greek colonists from Sybaris in the Gulf of Taranto; archaeological evidence (early Corinthian-style pottery found in tombs of the colonists) dates the foundation of the city to circa 600 BC (Pedley, 1990: 30). During the sixth century BC, an agora, *bouleuterion,* and two temples (to Hera and to Athena) were constructed, as were a series of rural sanctuaries that marked the limits of the city's territory. It is thought that the original grid layout of the city was similar to other Greek colonies, but this no longer survives (Pedley, 1990: 36). A third temple (also to Hera) followed in the fifth century BC.

Fortifications around the urban center were constructed in the fifth or fourth century BC. In 400 BC Poseidonia was occupied by Lucanians, a Samnite people, who held the city for around 150 years. Rather than a conquest, this period has been characterized as a fusion of peoples and ideas (Pedley, 1990: 97; Crawford, 2006) since the Greek sanctuaries and temples remained in use, as did the *bouleuterion*. The main difference was that density of settlement increased (based on the number and distribution of rural cemeteries) and that burial practices became more ostentatious, including lavish tomb paintings (Pedley, 1990: 97). Although no large-scale buildings were constructed, the city and its people seem to have flourished under Lucanian rule.

Radical changes instead came with the arrival of the Romans who conquered Campania in the third century BC and founded a colony – Paestum – at Poseidonia in 273 BC. The new Roman colonists changed the grid plan of the town, so that it was no longer oriented on the archaic Greek temples. Instead the new focus was the forum, located at the center of the city and completely separate from the existing agora (see Figure 15.1). In its initial phase, dating to the third century BC, the forum was surrounded by shops, all similar in layout and dimension. Two major Roman public buildings located to the north of forum, the *comitium* (for public meetings for the election of magistrates) and its attached *curia* (for senate meetings) were an integral part of the original design of the forum. A *capitolium* may lie beneath the modern road that covers part of the forum today. In the Augustan period the forum was embellished with a portico; the construction of an amphitheater to the north of the forum also dates to the first century BC. In the second century AD the amphitheater was expanded, and a *macellum* and a basilica were constructed (the former over the remains of a sixth-century BC sanctuary, the latter probably replacing an earlier basilica). Over the course of four centuries the Romans had transformed the Greek city of Poseidonia into a Roman city with the recognizable and expected

Figure 15.1   Paestum: the sixth-century Greek Temple of Athena behind the Roman temple in the Forum. Photograph: Francesca del Duca.

public buildings – but the older Greek buildings were not entirely destroyed by Roman occupation. The Greek sanctuaries and temples remained in use, as did the *bouleuterion*, and the Romans completed the Greek fortification walls. Roman elements were added to the pre-existing urban form; they did not replace it. Greek and Roman went side by side, creating a distinctive local character.

This contrasts with the situation at Cosa. The colony here, founded in 273 BC, was not imposed on the existing Etruscan city but built on a new, defensive, site and – given the drastic reduction in the number of farms in the surrounding territory – may have involved the elimination of the local Etruscan inhabitants (Fentress, 2000: 12–13). Cosa was a purely Roman foundation in a barren landscape, and its early years must have been ones of great hardship for its colonists. The Punic Wars probably caused the town to be depopulated, and during the third century BC there was almost a total lack of building on the site. In 197 BC a second wave of 2000 families was sent to Cosa, about 25% of whom lived in the town itself (based on archaeological remains of houses). The remainder lived on farms established on the land around the town, and identified through archaeological survey. By the mid-second century, Cosa had four temples, a basilica, a *comitium-curia* complex, a forum, a possible market and a rectangular forum. All were placed within a regular grid plan. The layout of the town must have been planned in Rome since other colonies of the second century, like Alba Fucens, have similar plans (Fentress, 2000: 22). Indeed, Zanker has argued for a state-sponsored notion of what a Roman city plan should be by the second half of the fourth century, which was applied to new colonial foundations (Zanker, 2000). This was then enlarged and embellished over time, although this does not mean that all cities were the same or developed at the same rate.

15.7   Patterns of Public Building

So far, we have concentrated on the variable and ongoing processes of urbanization in Roman Italy, highlighting both chronological and regional differences and touching on some of the factors that influenced these processes. However by the early empire, despite their different plans and history of development, Roman cities usually had a recognisable set of monumental public buildings, including forum, basilica and temples. This monumentalization was not a uniform process in each city but could take place over generations and be influenced both by the local context and by the culture of the local elite (Edmondson, 2006: 280; Nevett and Perkins, 2000: 214). Yet there are broad patterns to be identified in the development of the cities of Roman Italy from the late Republican period, both in terms of the buildings constructed and the financing of these buildings.

The second and first centuries BC were years of profound political and economic change in Italy, and the consequences of this change were that smaller towns began to grow in size and sophistication (Lloyd, 1995a: 210) and that many new towns were established, often planned from the outset to include particular types of building. For example, Julius Caesar (*Civil Wars*: 1.15.2; 49 BC) describes how Titus Labienus had given a constitution to the new municipality of Cingulum (in Picenum) and at his own expense provided for it to have a new monumental center (Edmondson, 2006: 251). Jouffroy has shown that, during the late Republican period, there was a high level of public building in central Italy, particularly in Latium and Campania, with an emphasis on fortification walls, either reconstructed with monumental gates or built from scratch; temples and sanctuaries; bath buildings; and basilicas (Jouffroy 1986; see also Lomas, 1997: 26–29). Political and religious buildings often clustered at the heart of a settlement around the forum (Wallace-Hadrill, 2011b: 157). In addition, large-scale public works such as road-building, harbors and aqueducts were undertaken, usually by Roman magistrates as part of broader schemes geared to the needs of Rome. Otherwise, most public building was undertaken by local magistrates as part of their official obligation to their cities, or was paid for from municipal funds, and before the Social War of 90 BC there was little private euergetism.

Once again, the Augustan period saw great changes (Cooley, ch.6, this vol.). Augustus himself boasted that he found Rome a city of brick and left her a city of marble (Suetonius, *Life of Augustus*: 28), and his contribution to the development of the urban environment is noted by ancient writers such as Vitruvius (*On Architecture*: 1, preface 2) who claimed that the Republic was as indebted to Augustus for the many grand public buildings he constructed as for the extension of its empire. This was the period when many cities in Italy, spurred on by developments in Rome, began to acquire additional public buildings such as theaters and porticoes, and palaestras, described by Vitruvius (*On Architecture*: 5) as part of a standard "set" of civic buildings, and amphitheaters. A good example is Puteoli, originally founded by the Greeks as Dicaearchia (circa 521 BC) and colonized by the Romans in 194 BC. By the Augustan period this bustling port had become one of the largest and most important cities in Italy, and was re-founded as the Colonia Iulia Augusta Puteoli, probably before 27 BC. Large numbers of inscriptions date to the early imperial period. Amongst other things, they reveal that a temple, probably the Capitolium, was rebuilt by a Calpurnius (*CIL* 10.1613), the forum was decorated with the *Ara Augusti Hordioniana*, and the *porticus Augusti Sextiana* was constructed (*AE* 1970, 94 and 1973, 139–42 (from Murecine); cf. Frederiksen, 1984: 332). Building activity continued into the Julio-Claudian period, and included a basilica, *chalcidica*, colonnades and altars, an amphitheater, and extensive public and private warehouses (Frederiksen, 1984: 352). A temple was also restored in this period. Another amphitheater and a stadium were built in the Flavian period.

The high point of private benefaction of public buildings throughout the Roman empire was the Julio-Claudian period, when most towns gained or completed their distinctive urban form. After this, the overall level of building began to decline, with the exception of certain types of building – bath buildings, amphitheaters, places of entertainment, and *macella*. At the same time feasts, distributions of money, food, and oil, became more important. As formal political participation declined, civic identity was maintained through sociable events that gathered citizens together (Patterson, 2006).

To a certain extent, the cities of Italy – particularly those in Campania and Latium – copied developments in the city of Rome itself where high levels of building took place. Architectural comparisons have been drawn, for example, between structures like the *Saepta Iulia, Porticus Octaviae*, and *Porticus Liviae* at Rome – open squares surrounded by colonnades – and the design of certain buildings in other cities, such as Eumachia's Building at Pompeii, the so-called Basilica in Herculaneum, and a porticoed structure at Cumae (Najbjerg, 2002: 154–55). This does not mean that all porticoes had the same civic or economic functions, or that the cities of Italy attempted to mimic the city of Rome, but rather that the architectural form was borrowed (Zanker, 2000: 26). Porticoed structures gained great popularity throughout the empire from the Augustan period as part of the wider urban renewal that was taking place (Najbjerg, 2002: 154–55).

The majority of these public buildings, or restorations of public buildings, were paid for by private individuals from their own funds, or by imperial benefaction (see Cooley ch.6, this vol.). Indeed, cities provided the perfect stage for local elites to highlight both their status and their loyalty to Rome (Edmondson, 2006). At Pompeii, for example, epigraphic evidence demonstrates that the Large Theater (*CIL* 10.833 and 834 = Cooley and Cooley, 2014: D54), amphitheater (*CIL* 10.852 = Cooley and Cooley, 2014: B12), Eumachia's Building (*CIL* X 810 = Cooley and Cooley, 2014: E56), and Temple of Augustan Fortune (*CIL* 10.820 = Cooley and Cooley, 2014: E44) were all constructed or reconstructed at private expense, and

Figure 15.2 The funerary altar and statue of Marcus Nonius Balbus, located outside the Suburban Baths of Herculaneum. Photograph: Brian Donovan/Herculaneum Conservation Project.

private benefactors were also responsible for facilities such as braziers and benches in the Forum Baths (*CIL* 10.818 = Cooley and Cooley, 2014: D123–24), awnings in the amphitheater (e.g. *CIL* IV 3884 = Cooley and Cooley 2014, D17), and a sundial in the Temple of Apollo (*CIL* 10.802 = Cooley and Cooley 2014: E2). In return, these benefactors were honored by the local community, for example, being awarded statues in prominent locations (e.g. the statue of Holconius Rufus outside the Stabian Baths, *CIL* X 830 = Cooley and Cooley, 2014: F93), or after their deaths with funerary plots on public land and contributions towards the cost of their funerals. For example, the Tomb of Marcus Tullius, who constructed the Temple of Augustan Fortune, was set up by decree of the town councillors (*EE* 8.330 = Cooley and Cooley, 2014: E46). At neighboring Herculaneum, the leading citizen and proconsul M. Nonius Balbus, who was originally from Nuceria but had adopted Herculaneum as his home town, repaired the city walls, monumentalized the southern wall towards the sea, possibly helping to improve the terraces beneath the walls, and constructed a basilica (*CIL* 10.1425 = Cooley and Cooley, 2014: F94; Wallace-Hadrill, 2011b). Statues of him were set up in the Theater, in a public square outside the theater, and in his basilica (*CIL* 10.1426, 1428–30, 1434 = Cooley and Cooley, 2014: F95–F99; see Figure 15.2). After his death, a funerary altar was set up in his honor that records the full text of an honorific decree passed by the town council (Wallace-Hadrill, 2011a: 133; *AE* 1976, 144 = Cooley and Cooley, 2014: F104); he was awarded a posthumous *bisellium* in the theater, an equestrian statue in the most crowded part of the town (presumably the forum), the marble altar that bears the inscription, and it was decreed that the Parentalia procession should start at the altar each year.

The social elite were not the only ones responsible for building. Again at Pompeii, the Temple of Isis was rebuilt after it was damaged in an earthquake by a freedman, Numerius Popidius Ampliatus. In return, his six-year old son was adlected to the town council

(*CIL* 10. 846 = Cooley and Cooley, 2014: C5). Similarly, at Herculaneum, a freedwoman Vibidia Sabina and her son(?) A. Furius Saturninus repaired and partly rebuilt the Temple of Venus and also contributed to the repair of the Capitolium. At the inauguration of the Temple of Venus they also made a cash distribution to members of the local council, to the *Augustales* and priestly college of Venus, and made a gift to the town of 54 000 sesterces (Wallace-Hadrill, 2011a: 168; Camodeca, 2008; *AE* 2008, 357 and 358 = Cooley and Cooley, 2014: E30–E31). In return they were probably elevated to equestrian rank, and, according to Camodeca (on the basis of a military diploma (*AE* 2003, 2061) dating to 7 November AD 88), Saturninus went on to command an auxiliary cavalry unit in Syria.

Public benefaction was a route to public recognition, influence, and status, even for the wealthy non-elite. Thus, although each city had its own revenues, generated from taxes and land rental, this income was heavily supplemented by members of its local elite, either in the form of monies or through the benefaction of buildings, facilities, or entertainments such as banquets or games.

15.8   The Role of the City in Roman Italy

The public buildings found in Roman cities reflected the roles of those cities. First and foremost, Rome administered its empire through its network of cities. Cities meant that local populations were settled in fixed locations, making them easier to control and tax, and making it easier to administer justice. In theory, cities were autonomous. Each had its own council and *ordo* with elected magistrates and officials, and was responsible for administering a clearly defined territory and for the upkeep of roads in that territory. The relationship between city and hinterland is illustrated in the edict of Claudius of AD 46 granting citizenship to the Alpine peoples of the Anauni, Sinduni and Tulliasses (*ILS* 206). These peoples lived in the territory around Tridentum (Trento) and already considered themselves to be citizens of this city because of their proximity to the city; the edict served to legalize their relationship with the *municipium* of Tridentum. This was the general pattern of administration in Italy. Smaller settlements, the *vici* (rural villages), *conciliabula* (meeting places) and *castella* (small nucle-ated communities) were included in the jurisdiction of the nearest major city and presumably did not have their own magistrates.

Thus cities were the focus of local and sometimes regional attention. In addition to their administrative roles, Roman cities were the focus of political, economic, and cultural activities, all of which had an impact on the physical development of the city. Local elections and legal cases took place here, commerce and trade took place throughout the city, and religious and cult activities were not limited to temple precincts but could involve processions and cere-monies at crossroads.

15.9   Conclusion

The number and legal rights of the inhabitants of the different types of urban settlements changed and developed over time. The *Lex Julia* of 90 BC gave the vote to citizens of those Italian cities who had not stood against Rome in the Social Wars, and this was subsequently extended to all of Rome's Italian allies, eventually leading to the establishment of *municipia* often based on existing settlements throughout Italy (see Bispham, ch. 4, this vol.); then, during the first century BC, colonies were founded to settle veteran soldiers. In theory there was a hierarchy of status between these cities. Colonies were the most important cities in a region, described by Aulus Gellius (*Attic Nights*: 16.13.8–9) as small-scale images of Rome.

Colonies were followed in status by *municipia* and then by *fora, conciliabula, pagi* and *vici*. That it was considered desirable for one's home city to rank as a *colonia* is shown by the fact that during the imperial period cities could be promoted to the status of *colonia* through imperial benefaction, which in turn could lead to the expansion and development of urban centers (Edmondson, 2006: 259). A good example is the *municipium* of Italica in Baetica, ancestral home of the families of Trajan and Hadrian, which was raised to the status of a colony during Hadrian's reign (Dio Cassius: 69.10.1), and more than doubled in size to include an amphitheater, new bath complex, Temple to Trajan, and *collegia* buildings along with more housing (Boatwright, 2000: 162–67).

However, in practical terms, the distinctions between the different types of city gradually began to fade, so that already by the time of the *Lex Rubria de Gallia Cisalpina*, which was enacted to limit the jurisdiction of magistrates in Gallia Cisalpina in circa 43 BC, the term *municipium* is used generically and covers both *munipicia* and *colonia* (and also *praefecturae*, although this is used in relation to the city of Mutina alone). Based on archaeological remains alone, it is impossible to identify the status of a particular city, since most cities had similar architecture and amenities. Pompeii and its neighbor Herculaneum both had a theater, baths, temples and other monumental public spaces, and a range of different types of housing, but, based on epigraphic and literary evidence, we know that Pompeii was a *colonia* and Herculaneum a *municipium*. In many other cases we remain uncertain about the status of a city.

What is clear is that cities were central to the Roman way of life. They were administratively, politically, socially, and economically fundamental, the focus of elite competition, the center of consumption and exchange, and the focus of the rural hinterland. In addition to having a constitution, laws, magistrates and local council, a city was expected to have an appropriate built environment in which the activities of all these different institutions could take place. It is clear from the ancient literary sources that there was an idea of what buildings a city was expected to have. By the imperial period most cities in Italy conformed to this expectation, despite having their own individual character and history, and even if only on a small scale.

FURTHER READING

The most recent analysis of the development of Italy's rural landscape and urban development is Patterson 2006. There is also a series of useful articles on urbanization in Italy by Kathryn Lomas (e.g. 1995 and 1997). The major study of patterns of public building in Italy is by Jouffroy 1986. For developments in different regions of Italy, see Barker 1995, Patterson 1987 and 1991, Lloyd 1995a and 1995b, and Dench 1995. The classic works on colonization are by Salmon 1969 and Keppie 1983.

REFERENCES

Barker, G. 1995. *The Biferno Valley Survey: the archaeological and geomorphological record*. Leicester: Leicester University Press.

Boatwright, M.T. 2000. *Hadrian and the Cities of the Roman Empire*. Princeton: Princeton University Press.

Camodeca, G. 2008. "Le iscrizioni di dedica del Tempio di Venere e delle imagines Caesarum ad opera di Vibidia Saturnina e di A. Furius Saturninus." In *Ercolano. Tre secoli di scoperte*, ed. M.P. Guidobaldi, 59–61 Milan: Electa.

Claridge, A. 1998. *Rome. An Oxford archaeological guide*. Oxford: Oxford University Press.

Cooley, A.E. and Cooley, M.G.L. 2014. *Pompeii and Herculaneum. A sourcebook*. London and New York: Routledge.

Cornell, T.J. 1995a. *The Beginnings of Rome: Italy and Rome from the Bronze Age to the Punic Wars (c. 1000–264 BC)*. London: Routledge.

Cornell, T.J. 1995b. "Warfare and urbanisation in Roman Italy." In *Urban Society in Roman Italy*, eds T. Cornell and K. Lomas, 127–40. London: Routledge.

Crawford, M.H. 2006. "From Poseidonia to Paestum via the Lucanians." In *Greek and Roman Colonization. Origins, ideologies and interactions*, eds G. Bradley and J.-P. Wilson, 59–72. Swansea: Classical Press of Wales.

Dench, E. 1995. *From Barbarians to New Men. Greek, Roman and modern perceptions of peoples from the central Apennines.* Oxford: Clarendon Press.

De Vita, A. 1996. "Urban planning in ancient Sicily." In *The Western Greeks. Classical civilization in the Western Mediterranean*, ed. G. Pugliese Carratelli, 263–308. London: Thames and Hudson.

Edmondson, J. 2006. "Cities and urban life in the Western provinces of the Roman Empire, 30 BC–250 AD." In *A Companion to the Roman Empire*, ed. D.S. Potter, 250–80. Oxford: Blackwell.

Fentress, E. 2000. "Frank Brown, Cosa, and the idea of a Roman city." In *Romanization and the City. Creations, transformations and failures*, ed. E. Fentress, 9–24. Portsmouth, RI: *Journal of Roman Archaeology* Suppl.38.

Filippi, G. 1989. "Regio IV. Sabina et Samnium, Forum Novum (Vescovio – I.G.M. 144, IV.NE)." *Supplementumi Italica nuova serie* 5: 146–237.

Frederiksen, M.W. 1976. "Changes in the pattern of settlement." In *Hellenismus in Mittelitalien*, ed. P. Zanker, 341–55. Göttingen: Vandenhoeck und Ruprecht.

Frederiksen, M. 1984. *Campania*, ed. N. Purcell. London: British School at Rome.

Gabba, E. 1971. "Urbanizzazione e rinnovamenti urbanistici nell'Italia centro-meridionale del I a.C." *Studi classici e orientali* 20: 73–112.

Gordon-Childe, V. 1950. "The Urban Revolution." *Town Planning Review* 21.1: 3–17.

Jouffroy, H. 1986. *La construction publique en Italie et dans L'Afrique romaine.* Strasbourg: AECR.

Keay, S., Millett, M., Poppy, S., Robinson, J., Taylor, J., and Terrenato, N. 2004. "New approaches to Roman urbanism in the Tiber Valley." In *Bridging the Tiber. Approaches to regional archaeology in the Middle Tiber Valley*, ed. H. Patterson, 223–36. London: Archaeological Monographs of the British School at Rome 13.

Keppie, L.J.F. 1983. *Colonisation and Veteran Settlement in Italy, 47–14 B.C.* London: British School at Rome.

Keppie, L.J.F. 2004. *The Making of the Roman Army from Republic to Empire.* London: Routledge.

La Regina, A. 1968. "Ricerche sugli insediamenti vestini." *Memorie dei Lincei* 13.5: 362–446.

La Regina, A. 1970–71. "I territori sabellici e sannitici," *Dialoghi di Archeologia* 4–5: 443–59.

Laurence, R. 1999. *The Roads of Roman Italy. Mobility and social change.* London: Routledge.

Laurence, R. 2001. "Roman Italy's urban revolution." In *Modalità insediative e strutture agrarie nell'Italia meridionale in età romana*, eds E. Lo Cascio and A. Storchi Marino, 593–611. Bari: Edpuglia.

Lloyd, J.A. 1995a. "Pentri, Frentani and the beginnings of urbanisation (500–80 BC)." In *A Mediterranean Valley: landscape archaeology and Annales history in the Biferno valley*, ed. G. Barker, 181–212. London: Leicester University Press.

Lloyd, J.A. 1995b. "Roman towns and territories (*c.*80 BC – AD 600)." In *The Biferno Valley Survey: the archaeological and geomorphological record*, ed. G. Barker, 213–53. Leicester: Leicester University Press.

Lo Cascio, E. 2009. "Urbanization as a proxy of demographic and economic growth." In *Quantifying the Roman Economy*, eds A.K. Bowman and A. Wilson, 87–106. Oxford: Oxford University Press.

Lomas K. 1995. "Urban elites and cultural definition: Romanization in southern Italy." In *Urban Society in Roman Italy*, eds T. Cornell and K. Lomas, 107–20. London: Routledge.

Lomas, K. 1997. "The idea of a city: elite ideology and the evolution of urban form in Italy, 200 BC–AD 100." In *Roman Urbanism. Beyond the consumer city*, ed. H. Parkins, 21–41. London: Routledge.

Mertens, D. and Greco, E. 1996. "Urban planning in Magna Grecia." In *The Western Greeks: Classical civilization in the Western Mediterranean*, ed. G. Pugliese Carratelli, 243–62. London: Thames and Hudson.

Morley, N. 1996a. *Metropolis and Hinterland: the city of Rome and the Italian economy, 200 B.C.–A.D. 200.* Cambridge: Cambridge University Press.

Morley, N. 1996b. "Cities in context: urban systems in Roman Italy." In *Roman Urbanism: Beyond the consumer model*, ed. H.M. Parkins, 42–58. London: Routledge.

Najbjerg, T. 2002. "The so-called Basilica in Herculaneum." In *Pompeian Brothels, Pompeii's Ancient History, Mirrors and Mysteries, Art and Nature at Oplontis, and the Herculaneum "Basilica,"* 123–65. Portsmouth RI: *Journal of Roman Archaeology* Suppl. 47.

Nappo, S.C. 1997. "The urban transformation at Pompeii in the late third and early second centuries BC." In *Domestic Space in the Roman world: Pompeii and beyond*, eds R. Laurence and A. Wallace-Hadrill, 91–121. Portsmouth, RI: *Journal of Roman Archaeology* Suppl. 22.

Nevett, L. and Perkins, P. 2000. "Urbanism and urbanisation in the Roman world." In *Experiencing Rome. Culture, identity and power in the Roman world*, ed. J. Huskinson, 213–44. London: Routledge and Open University.

Orlandini, P. 1998. *Scavi e scoperte all'Incoronata di Metaponto*, in *Siritide e Metapontino. Storia di due territori coloniali. Atti dell'incontro di Studio (Policoro 1991)*, (*Cahiers du Centre J. Bérard*, XX), 91–94. Naples-Paestum.

Patterson, J.R. 1987. "Crisis: what crisis? Rural change and urban development in imperial Apennine Italy". *Papers of the British School at Rome* 55: 115–46.

Patterson, J.R. 1991. "Settlement, city and elite in Samnium and Lycia." In *City and Country in the Ancient World*, eds J.Rich and A.Wallace-Hadrill, 147–168. London: Routledge.

Patterson, J.R. 2006. *Landscapes and Cities. Rural settlement and civic transformation in early imperial Italy*. Oxford: Oxford University Press.

Pedley, J.G. 1990. *Paestum: Greeks and Romans in southern Italy*. London: Thames & Hudson.

Poccetti, P. 1979. *Nuovi documenti italici: a complemento del Manuale di E. Vetter*. Pisa: Giardini.

Salmon, E.T. 1969. *Roman colonization under the Republic*. London: Thames & Hudson.

Scheidel, W. 2004. "Human mobility in Roman Italy, I: The free population." *Journal of Roman Studies* 94: 1–26.

Smith, M.E. 2009. "V. Gordon Childe and the urban revolution: an historical perspective on a revolution in urban studies." *Town Planning Review* 80.3: 3–29.

Spivey, N. and Stoddart, S. 1990. *Etruscan Italy: an archaeological history, 1280–400 B.C.* London: Batsford.

Strazzulla, M.J. and De Marco, B. 1982. *Il santuario sannitico di Pietrabbondante*. Rome: Centenari.

Tagliamonte, G. 1995. "Forum Romanum (fino alla prima età repubblicana). In LTUR vol. 2, D–G, ed. E.M. Steinby, 313–25. Rome: Quasar.

Torelli, M. 1986. "History: land and people." In *Etruscan Life and Afterlife: a handbook of Etruscan studies*, ed. L. Bonfante, 47–65. Deitroit: Wayne State University Press.

Vermeulen, F. and Verhoeven, G. 2006. "An integrated survey of Roman urbanisation at Potentia, Central Italy." *Journal of Field Archaeology* 31.4: 395–410.

Wallace-Hadrill, A. 2008. *Rome's Cultural Revolution*. Cambridge: Cambridge University Press.

Wallace-Hadrill, A. 2011a. *Herculaneum: past and future*. London: Frances Lincoln.

Wallace-Hadrill, A. 2011b. "The monumental centre of Herculaneum: in search of the identities of the public buildings." *Journal of Roman Archaeology* 24: 121–60.

Zanker, P. 2000. "The city as symbol: Rome and the creation of an urban image." In *Romanisation and the City*, ed. E. Fentress, 25–41. Portsmouth, RI: *Journal of Roman Archaeology* Suppl. 38.

CHAPTER 16

Urban Peripheries

Penelope J. Goodman

16.1 Introduction

A close look at Roman culture reveals some conflicting ideas about the relationship between city and country. On the one hand, cities across the Roman world were laid out with a view to creating a clearly marked urban center. This was usually achieved by building defensive walls, but other methods included choosing a topographically distinct site or using the orientation of the streets to highlight the city's entrances and exits (Goodman, 2007: 59–68). Legal practitioners sometimes used urban boundaries such as these when seeking technical definitions of the difference between city and country. The Severan-period jurist Julius Paulus, for example, claimed that "generally all cities are held to finish with the wall" (*Digest* 33.9.4.4). Meanwhile, literary texts asserted and reified the idea of a city–country divide. Horace's fable of the town mouse and the country mouse (*Satires*: 2.6.80–115) is just one of the most vivid examples. Authors everywhere treated "city" and "country" as distinct and mutually exclusive categories, although there was plenty of debate over the nature of the differences, and which was morally superior (Ramage, 1973; Braund, 1989; Goodman, 2007: 9–10).

On the other hand, the basic function of an ancient city was to act as a center for the shared activities of a single community, whose members were dispersed across the city itself and an associated rural territory (Nevett and Perkins, 2000: 213–18). Political debate, economic exchange, and religious observances might be concentrated in the city, but they reflected the concerns and activities of the community as a whole. Most laws were formulated and treaties struck at the level of the entire community, while individuals moved freely and regularly between urban and rural space (Reynolds, 1988; Wallace-Hadrill, 1991; Lintott, 1993: 129–53). Physically, too, the neat spatial divide between city and country was often blurred, inverted, or undermined (Esmonde Cleary, 1987; Purcell, 1987b; Bedon, 1998; Goodman, 2007). In fact, the immediate environs of cities throughout the Roman Empire were frequently characterized by buildings and activities which were obviously closely associated with the nearby city, and yet lay beyond the urban boundaries. The legal and symbolic significance of those boundaries should mean that such features were recognized as non-urban. Indeed, they were regularly described using words such as *suburbanus*, *extra urbem* and *proast(e)ion*, all of

---

A Companion to Roman Italy, First Edition. Edited by Alison E. Cooley.
© 2016 John Wiley & Sons, Ltd. Published 2016 by John Wiley & Sons, Ltd.

which acknowledge a connection with the city (*urbs* or *astu*), but signal a falling short of full urban status. At the same time, the use of these terms reveals that this type of occupation was not simply viewed as rural, either. It was something in between: neither fully urban, nor fully rural, but on the cusp between the two.

This chapter will explore the character of this type of space in Roman Italy, looking at its distinctive qualities, how and why it developed, and how it related to the city, the country-side, and the overall activities of the local community. It will be referred to here using the terms "urban periphery" and "periurban development", since these acknowledge its relationship with the city ("around" or "near" it), but avoid two problematic connotations of the English words "suburbs" and "suburban." Firstly, ancient authors usually employed the Latin terms *suburbium* and *suburbanus* to refer specifically to the environs of Rome, where the suburban landscape was dominated by the luxury villas of the wealthy elite on a scale which we would not expect at other, more ordinary, cities (Champlin, 1982; Morley, 1996; Witcher, 2005; Adams, 2008). When the term was applied elsewhere (e.g. Pliny the Younger, *Letters*: 1.3), it evoked an association with the metropolis, but this seems an unhelpful approach if we wish to explore the fringes of Italian cities in their own right. Secondly, modern suburban development has been profoundly shaped by factors such as industrialization and transport innovations which did not exist in the ancient world (Harris and Larkham, 1999). This means that we may risk slipping into anachronistic assumptions if we use the same term to describe development around ancient cities. The terms "periurban development" and "urban periphery" allow us to approach the edges of ancient Italian cities with fewer preconceptions.

16.2   The Urban Periphery in Roman Italy

16.2.1   Defining the urban periphery

We shall begin by thinking about how periurban development might be identified, either by ancient observers or by scholars today. We have already seen that Roman cities were usually defined by boundary markers, and that these markers – especially walls – were regarded as the technical limits of the city. In the ancient world, such cues were important because some activities, such as burial, were forbidden within the urban center. For us, too, the boundaries of an ancient city provide an essential starting-point for identifying any periurban development which might lie beyond. In Roman Italy, identifying urban boundaries is relatively easy, since they were usually marked by a walled circuit. Defensive walls were already a widespread feature of Italian urbanism before the rise of Rome (Dench, 1995: 131; Bradley, 2000: 77–80; Izzet, 2007: 182–89), and in the Roman period they continued to be added to existing cities or planned into new ones (Gros and Torelli, 2007: 158–98). Since defensive circuits tended to be large and solidly constructed, they have usually left at least some trace in the archaeological record. It is important, though, to be aware of the dating of the walled circuit if we are to understand individual buildings and quarters. The built development which had originally occurred outside one set of walls could be absorbed into the urban center via the construction of a new, larger circuit. Equally, existing walls could be breached or engulfed by new buildings, raising questions about whether or not they were still perceived as functional urban boundaries.

A clear example of boundary extensions is furnished by Minturnae (Minturno), a *colonia* founded in 296/95 BC in the territory of the Aurunci (see Figure 16.1). The original urban center consisted of a walled three-hectare *castrum* (Coarelli, 1989: 49–50), but this proved inadequate as the community grew. During the third century BC, structures including a temple

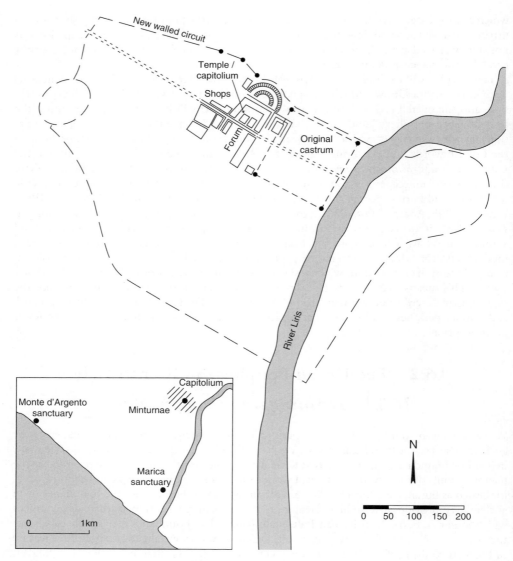

Figure 16.1 Urban development at Minturnae, with inset showing the locations of Auruncan coastal sanctuaries. Drawn by Alexander Santos.

and shops developed immediately to the west of the *castrum*, alongside the *via Appia* (Johnson, 1935: 16–17, 42–44; Coarelli, 1989: 51; Livi, 2006: 95–97). These buildings must originally have been understood as periurban, since they were obviously connected with Minturnae, but fell outside the *castrum*. But around the end of the third century, a new walled circuit was constructed. This enclosed all of the periurban structures, and would have made it clear that they were in fact urban. This resolved a growing disparity between theory and practice at Minturnae, which had developed into a large agglomeration but until this point still had only a very small explicitly demarcated urban center. Interestingly, around the same time as the new walls were built, the formerly periurban quarter to the west of the *castrum* also underwent redevelopment. The temple was replaced by a new tripartite Etrusco-Italic building, which has been identified as a *capitolium*, a structure which we would normally expect to find in the very center of a *colonia* (Johnson, 1935: 18–29; Coarelli, 1989: 50–52; Livi, 2006: 95–97). Meanwhile, the quarter around it on both sides of the *via Appia* was developed as a *forum*, thus becoming the chief monumental focus of the city (Coarelli, 1989: 53–66). The enclosure of this quarter within the new walled circuit, then, seems to have been only part of a wider process of change, during which Minturnae's center of gravity shifted from somewhere within the original *castrum* to an area just outside it. The new walls explicitly signaled that the temple quarter should now be regarded as urban. At the same time, its physical appearance also changed, so that it became more obviously and recognizably urban in character.

Other cities saw their boundaries breached without any new ones being established to replace them. From the Augustan period onwards, the state promoted a vision of *pax Romana* in which safety would be guaranteed by civil harmony and strong frontiers, rather than city walls (Dyson, 1992: 155; Haselberger, 2007: 222–37), and communities responded accordingly. Two examples from opposite ends of the Italian peninsula – Herdonia (Ordona) in the south-east and Albintimilium (Ventimiglia) in the north-west – attest to the widespread change in approach. Herdonia was enclosed by a ditch and rampart of the fourth century BC, to which a stone wall was added in the third century (Mertens, 1995: 139–49). But in the mid-first century AD, part of that wall was dismantled, and an amphitheater constructed in the hollow of the original ditch (Mertens, 1995: 207–10). At Albintimilium, a first-century BC circuit was breached when a theater of the late second or early third century AD was built over one corner of the walls (Lamboglia, 1964: 17–22, 46–68; see Figure 16.2). At both cities, the remainder of the walled circuit appears to have been left intact, and probably continued to function as an urban boundary.

Figure 16.2 The theater at Albintimilium, showing the remains of a dismantled section of the city wall passing under the building (bottom left). Photograph: Luca Colombo. Reproduced with permission.

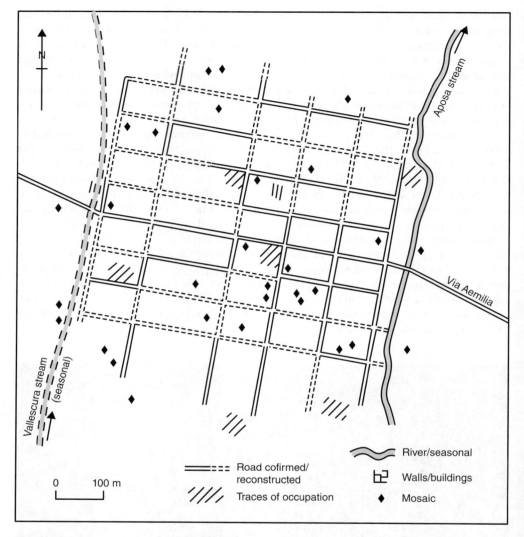

Figure 16.3 Bononia, showing the various features which served to mark out the urban center in the absence of a walled circuit. Drawn by Maura Pringle.

Other ways of marking urban boundaries also developed as an alternative to defensive walls. Some examples can be seen at Bononia (Bologna), a *colonia* of the early second century BC which seems never to have been walled (Scagliarini, 1991; Goodman, 2007: 62–64; see Figure 16.3). Here, the urban center could nevertheless be distinguished by its orthogonal street-grid and its position situated between two watercourses. The *via Aemilia*, which ran through the city, also changed orientation as it entered and left the grid, creating a distinct "kink" in the road on either side of the urban center. Elsewhere, monumental arches emphasized and adorned the entrances to Italian cities from the mid-first century BC onwards (De Maria, 1988: 53–54, 83–84, 162–63).

An example is Capua, where a freestanding arch was built at the eastern entrance to the city, probably in the Flavian period (Quilici and Quilici Gigli, 1991). Its location coincides with a change in the orientation of the *via Appia*, as described above at Bononia, suggesting that it served partly to mark out and monumentalize an existing point of transition between city and country.

A city's boundaries, then, might be marked by walls, orthogonal street-grids, watercourses, changes in the direction of major roads, or monumental arches. We can thus conclude that features lying outside those boundaries would have been understood in the past as something less than fully urban. But it is much harder to be certain that they were understood as *peri*urban, rather than rural. The difficulty is that even in the ancient world, the distinction between the two was very subjective. While the urban center was marked out with visible boundaries, there was no equivalent line to show where the urban periphery ceded to the countryside. Instead, individual observers must have drawn their own conclusions. Horace (*Letters*: 1.11.7–8) and Juvenal (*Satires*: 6.55–57), for example, speak of Fidenae as a rustic village, yet Martial considers it suburban to Rome (*Epigrams*: 4.64). These references are allusive and playful: but the scope for ambiguity means that we can never be completely certain what real-life features might once have been viewed as periurban. We can, though, construct our own model of what is *likely* to have been viewed as periurban by interrogating literary texts.

One factor to look for is references to physical distance from the city. Literary discussions of villas described as *suburbanus* reveal that most were located within a day's journey of Rome (e.g. Columella, *On Agriculture*: 1.1.19; Pliny the Younger, *Letters*: 2.17.2). This translates to a radius of some 30–37 km (Champlin, 1982: 98; Laurence, 1999: 82): an extremely large area which reflects Rome's status and influence, but would include the entire territory of many Italian cities. What may be more helpful are references to the *ways* in which the relationship with the city was sustained. Certainly, reports of regular journeys back and forth between Rome and its suburban villas (Champlin, 1982) or its shrines (Ovid, *Fasti*: 6.771–90, Cicero, *Philippics*: 12.24) are prominent in the literary tradition. An epigram by Martial about a relative's property on the Janiculum hill (4.64) also stresses its commanding views over Rome. Though Martial does not explicitly describe this property as *suburbanus*, he jokes that it is a *rus* (country place) which might as well be called a *domus* (town-house). This situates it on the ambiguous borderline between urban and rural: the very defining characteristic of the urban periphery.

These texts, of course, refer to the *suburbium* of Rome and especially its elite villas, but the principles which they imply can also provide a template for identifying periurban development elsewhere. We should look above all for features which appear to have been the focus of regular journeys to and from the city, and were connected to it by physical communication routes or direct lines of sight. In all cases, the intensity of the connection should be greater than we would expect for equivalent rural features, which had their own relationship with the urban center. It is also important to note that it may be unhelpful to limit our understanding of periurban development to those structures or activities which we have reason to suspect were consciously identified as periurban in the past. Literary texts tended to focus on the buildings and places of interest to the elite, such as villas, temples, funerary monuments, and small towns, rather than humbler features like kilns, quarries, or farms (Goodman, 2007: 20–22). The people who used these structures may have been little concerned about whether they should be classified as "urban," "rural," or "periurban." But our understanding of ancient society can still be enhanced by considering the extent and strength of the connections between these features and the nearby city, and thus deciding for ourselves whether or not they constituted part of an urban periphery.

16.2.2   The characteristics of the urban periphery

We can now move on to look at some examples of periurban development, establishing an overview of its relationship with the city and its typical characteristics. The range of available material is somewhat limited. As for urban centers, much periurban development is obscured by later occupation. Even on accessible sites, systematic excavations have traditionally focused on city walls, public buildings, and streets, extending beyond the urban boundaries only where surface remains are visible. Meanwhile, field survey campaigns do not generally focus on the urban periphery, aiming instead to sample land-use equally across an entire landscape. Between the two approaches, the urban periphery in its own right receives little systematic attention. Recent work at Falerii Novi provides a welcome sign of changing approaches. An initial campaign of geophysical survey was conducted here in 1997–98, chiefly within the city's visible walled circuit (Keay *et al.*, 2000). But the project team recognized that this method would leave the urban periphery unexplored, and have since devoted considerable attention to the extramural area. This has included geophysical survey across a total area of 14 ha. north of the walled circuit, revealing evidence for multiple funerary structures, minor roads, and a possible atrium house (Keay *et al.*, 2000: 64–69; Hay *et al.*, 2010). But this sort of approach remains all too rare, meaning that there are few places where a coherent overview of periurban development around a single city can be achieved.

One exception is Ostia (see Figure 21.1). Systematic excavations on the site in the twentieth century, combined with more recent surface survey, targeted excavations, and re-examinations of older documents, allow Ostia, its periphery, and the relationship between the two to be explored. Like Minturnae, Ostia began as a 2.5-hectare *castrum* founded in the fourth or early third century BC (Meiggs, 1973: 20–22; Martin, 1996). This was soon surrounded by periurban development, and the *castrum* wall either demolished or engulfed by new buildings. A second circuit was constructed in the mid-first century BC, now enclosing 69 hectares and completed along its northern perimeter by the course of the river Tiber (Zevi, 1997). This formalized the status of the development outside the original *castrum*, acknowledging its essentially urban character. But Ostia was still growing. On the western side of the city, buildings were already being constructed directly against the internal facade of the new wall by the Augustan period (Heinzelmann and Granino Cecere, 2001: 322). From the Flavian period onwards, they began to be constructed against its external facade (Heinzelmann and Granino Cecere, 2001: 322; Martin *et al.*, 2002: 269), while the Hadrianic Terme Marittime were built over a section which had been demolished altogether (Veloccia Rinaldi 1969–70). Yet recent work by the Deutsches Archäologisches Institut and the American Academy in Rome has identified phases of restoration or embellishment at two of the city's gates in the third century AD (Martin *et al.*, 2002: 265). This suggests that the late Republican circuit retained its significance as an urban boundary, despite its partial obliteration on the western side of the city.

Some of the land use outside the Republican circuit at Ostia was almost indistinguishable from that within. This is particularly clear on the western side, where development outside the Porta Marina included shops, houses, a temple, a public fountain, a porticoed square, and a set of baths (Ward-Perkins, 1981: 140–45; MacDonald, 1986: 263–66). These buildings, and the streets which served them, are very much consistent with those inside the walled circuit, suggesting that the area functioned as an extension of the urban center. Indeed, lawyers explicitly acknowledged the existence of such development, and the problems of classification which it posed. Ulpius Marcellus in the mid-second century explained that "As Alfenus said, '*urbs*' means '*Roma*' which was surrounded by a wall, but '*Roma*' also extends as far as there are continuous buildings: for it can be understood from daily use that Rome is not considered to extend only as far as the wall, since we say that we are going to Rome, even if we live outside the *urbs*" (*Digest*: 50.16.87). The Latin phrase used is *continentia aedificia* ("continuous buildings"), and it can be found in a wide range of legal texts applying not only to Rome but also to other cities in Italy and Spain (Goodman, 2007: 14–15). The Porta Marina quarter, then, was an extramural sector of the Ostian *continentia aedificia*: technically it was part of the urban periphery, but it was actually very similar in character to the urban center.

The resemblance was not perfect, though, because the Porta Marina quarter contained one type of structure *not* normally found within an urban center: the funerary monument. Two of these were erected in the late Republican period close to the Porta Marina itself, and remained in place as living occupation developed around them (Meiggs, 1973: 131–32; van der Meer, Stevens, and Stöger, 2005). Their presence would have made it clear that this area differed from the urban center proper, where burial was prohibited. On the other side of the city, the district outside the Porta Romana featured a similar mixture of funerary monuments and living occupation. Here, tombs dominated, but shops, domestic apartments, and what may have been stables have also been identified (Heinzelmann, 2000; 2001). Both quarters were thus recognizable as periurban not merely because they lay outside the city walls, but also from the structures encountered there.

Once we move beyond the *continentia aedificia*, we can no longer use the fact of physical continuity with the urban center to help us identify features as periurban. Nonetheless, many structures lying within the first mile or so of Ostia's boundaries were evidently so closely associated with the city that they can best be understood as part of its periphery. In addition to the Porta Romana cemetery, another burial area lay a short distance to the south-east of the Porta Laurentina (Heinzelmann, 2000; 2001; Graham, 2005). The close relationship between the tombs here and the nearby city is clear from their positions along a road leading into the urban center, from inscriptions and sculptural reliefs which show that they were the burial places of urban magistrates or traders, and from dining facilities for families visiting the graves. Meanwhile, another set of baths, some warehouses, and an unidentified round structure lay opposite the city on the right bank of the Tiber (Bertacchi, 1960; Pellegrino, Olivanti, and Panariti, 1995). The baths and warehouses are the direct equivalents of buildings located within the walls, so can also be identified as periurban, that is, essentially urban in character, but located beyond the city limits.

The seafront was dominated by luxury villas, two of which lay so close to Ostia that they effectively became part of the *continentia aedificia*. These include the villa of Perseus just south of the walls (Meiggs, 1973: 69), and another identified by the DAI-AAR project close to the Porta Marina quarter (Martin *et al.*, 2002: 265–69). Architecturally, these properties stand out from any within the urban center thanks to features such as an extensive bath-suite and a long seaward-facing stadium garden. They are not urban buildings, but their position on the very fringes of the city means that they can hardly be considered rural either. They are best understood as periurban, and indeed helped to characterize the surrounding quarters as periurban too, much like the tombs in the Porta Marina district. Further down the coast, an almost unbroken series of villas began about three km south-east of Ostia, and extended for another 15 (Claridge, 1998). This area, the *litus Laurentinum*, was used above all as a leisure retreat for the wealthy elite of Rome (Purcell, 1998). This is not to say that it had nothing to do with Ostia. Pliny the Younger, who owned a villa in the region, reports that he bought supplies from the nearby city (*Letters*: 2.17.26). But these villas belonged more to the *suburbium* of Rome than to the periphery of Ostia. Meanwhile, set back from the seashore itself, the Pianabella plain was populated by modest farms and – particularly within the first km from Ostia – more funerary monuments (Heinzelmann, 1998). Clearly, there would have been some interaction between this district and the nearby city: for example in the form of economic exchange or family visits to the tombs. But the built structures here are more sparsely situated, and the intensity of the relationship must have fallen off with increasing distance from the city. In fact, this sort of landscape encapsulates the impossibility of drawing a neat line to mark the outer edge of a city's periurban zone. Ostia's urban periphery simply merged gradually into the surrounding countryside.

16.3 Spurs for Periurban Development

At Ostia, one of the main causes of periurban development was clearly rapid growth. But although this was certainly a common spur for the usage of the urban periphery, it was not the only one. Structures or activities could be located outside urban boundaries for their own reasons: the most obvious example is tombs, which were forbidden from the urban center whether there was space available for them or not. This section explores the various factors which could prompt periurban development: both the negative reasons why particular features were *not* situated within the urban boundaries, and the positive reasons why they *were* situated in the urban periphery.

16.3.1 *Spatial overspill*

That there was pressure on space in some cities is without doubt. Vitruvius was conscious enough of the issue to offer it as a reason for the development of multistory apartment blocks in Rome (*On Architecture*: 2.8.17). We have already seen that some urban communities allowed their defensive walls to become engulfed under surrounding structures, or dismantled them in order to free up building space. Often, such decisions appear to have been made specifically for the sake of spectacle buildings: for example, theaters at Albintimilium (Lamboglia, 1964: 46–68) and Spoletium (Spoleto) (Ciotti, 1960), or amphitheaters at Herdonia (Mertens, 1995: 207–10) and Tuder (Todi) (Tascio, 1989: 67–68, 102). As some of the largest public monuments in Roman Italy, spectacle buildings must have posed particular problems for urban communities facing pressure on space. The issue was exacerbated by the fact that most were built in mature urban agglomerations, where their construction had not been anticipated. Some southern Italian cities built theaters between the fourth and second centuries BC (Sear, 2006: 48–50), and permanent amphitheaters began to be constructed in Campania during the first century BC (Welch, 1994; Bomgardner, 2000: 39–60). But it was not until the Augustan era that theaters became popular throughout Italy (Sear, 2006, 50–53), while the true hey-day of amphitheaters was the Flavian era (Golvin, 1988: 409–10; Patterson, 2006: 130–48).

A systematic study of theaters and amphitheaters by Frézouls (1990) revealed variant preferences in the locations of the two types of building, which may relate to issues of space. Frézouls found that only 20% of Italian theaters were located in the urban periphery, while the equivalent figure for amphitheaters was 35%. This might suggest that larger buildings were more likely to be built in the urban periphery. But Frézouls also points out that one side of a theater is rectilinear, making it easier to accommodate within the urban street network. The different periods when each of the two monuments tended to be constructed may also be significant. The first century AD saw intensive building activity throughout Italy (Gros and Torelli, 2007: 243–70), so that even a short time-lag between the construction of a theater at the start of that century and the construction of an amphitheater towards the end of it could mean that less space was available by the time the amphitheater was built. This means that we cannot be sure whether amphitheaters were more likely to be built in the urban periphery because they were larger, or simply because they were built later. In either case, though, the root cause would still be a lack of available space in the urban center.

On the other hand, 65% of amphitheaters *were* located within the boundaries of Italian cities, in spite of their size. This suggests that communities and benefactors were willing to overcome the problems involved in accommodating a large and awkwardly shaped structure within an existing urban center. This may be because of the status which an amphitheater could convey, and could also reflect the model of the Colosseum in Rome. As for circuses, very few were constructed in Italy outside Rome until late antiquity (Humphrey, 1986: 571–78). Those built in association with imperial palaces at Milan, Aquileia, and Ravenna in the fourth and early fifth centuries were constructed on the edges of the existing urban agglomerations, but generally within new defensive fortifications (Humphrey, 1986: 613–25 and 632–38). In relation to the old urban center, then, they did represent an overspill of new structures into the periphery. But their special role in the pageantry of the imperial court appears to have ensured that the urban boundaries were simultaneously redefined in order to include them.

16.3.2   *Exclusion*

The urban periphery could also be used for activities which were important to urban life, but considered inappropriate within the city boundaries (Patterson, 2000). The most straightforward example concerns burial and cremation, which were forbidden from an early period within the walled *urbs* at Rome (Twelve Tables 10.1 = Crawford, 1996: vol. 2, 704–05). The separation of living and dead was already practiced by most Italian peoples before they came under Roman rule (Gros and Torelli, 2007: 30), and became universal afterwards (Toynbee, 1971: 48–49). The principle probably derived mainly from fears about death-pollution (Hope, 2000; Lindsay, 2000), but may have been reinforced by an awareness of health risks and a desire to guard against fires caused by funeral pyres (Cicero, *On Laws*: 2.24.61).

Groups of living individuals were sometimes also barred from the urban center. Regulations for the contractors who handled burials, punishments, and executions at Puteoli (Pozzuoli) stated that their workers were forbidden to enter the town (*oppidum*) except in the course of their work, and to live either within or closer to Puteoli than a tower in the grove of the funerary goddess Libitina (Hinard and Dumont, 2003: II.3–4, 105–08). This restriction may have been intended to protect the urban center from the metaphorical pollution associated with individuals who handled corpses and executed criminals (Bodel, 2000; Lindsay, 2000). But it could also reflect concerns for public order (Belayche, 2003: 54), especially if the equipment used by the contractors for executions caused them to be viewed as armed men, equivalent to soldiers or *vigiles* in Rome.

There is also considerable evidence for the concentrated dumping of refuse immediately beyond urban boundaries. A series of Republican-era inscriptions from Rome forbids the dumping of *stercus* (refuse, especially faeces), the dumping of corpses, and the burning of funeral pyres immediately outside the city walls on the Esquiline hill (*CIL* 1^2.591, 838, 839, 2981). The fact that such legislation needed to be passed, though, suggests that it was common behavior to deposit unwanted waste immediately outside the city (Peña, 2007: 279). Excavations at Pompeii and Ariminum (Rimini) have revealed what appear to be refuse deposits immediately outside the walls of both cities (Peña, 2007: 279–82). Peña points out that several of the Pompeian deposits match up with points where internal city streets must have met the walled circuit, suggesting that local practice was to carry unwanted rubbish to the ends of the streets, climb the interior embankment, and tip it directly down the outside face of the defensive wall.

Principles of exclusion were clearly practiced in the cities of Roman Italy, then. But we should be cautious of turning to them too readily. The case of the amphitheater exemplifies the dangers of overemphasis. Some scholars have suggested that the association of gladiatorial games with death, violence, and barbarism meant that they were best suited to a location outside the urban center (e.g. Wiedemann, 1992: 46). But Frézouls (1990) showed that this did not prevent 65% of amphitheaters being built in the urban center all the same. Furthermore, gladiatorial games were regularly performed in the forum at Rome and other Italian cities, thus placing them at the very heart of civic life (Welch, 1994: 69–78; *CIL* 10.1074d = Cooley and Cooley, 2014: D11). The suggestion that amphitheaters were excluded from the urban center for ideological reasons therefore does not stand up. The temptation to make it means that other possible reasons for their construction in the urban periphery may be overlooked.

16.3.3   Creating an urban facade

In any case, the urban periphery was *not* simply a no man's land, where unwanted activities and materials could be banished far from human sight. It was also the aspect of the city which approaching visitors encountered first, and would shape their initial impressions of the community based there (Dyson, 1992: 147; Purcell, 1987a: 26–27; Zanker, 2000: 29–33). Viewed from this perspective, the urban periphery offered the opportunity to emphasize local wealth and status through the careful design and placement of prestigious monuments.

We have already seen that tombs were situated in the urban periphery primarily because it was Italian custom to exclude them from the urban center. If the sole concern had been to keep the dead apart from the living, we should expect to find cemeteries in isolated settings visited only on the occasion of a burial. Instead, they usually clustered along the major roads outside the urban center, with the most visible burial plots outside city gates being particularly highly prized (Dyson, 1992: 149; Hope, 2000: 110). This reflects an ongoing relationship between the tombs and the city, perpetuated through family visits during funeral ceremonies and festivals (Toynbee, 1971: 61–64; Hopkins, 1983: 233–35). It also meant that the tombs were well-placed to attract the attention of travelers moving along the roads (Purcell, 1987a). Viewed separately, the design of the tombs, their decorative sculpture and their inscriptions announced the aspirations and achievements of the deceased individuals and their families. Collectively, these same features expressed the values of the entire local community (Hopkins, 1983: 211–17; Dyson, 1992: 147–53; Zanker, 2000: 30–31; Graham 2005). The prime audience for these displays was probably the community itself, where the deceased's relatives could continue to benefit from the status conferred by their family monument. But many funerary inscriptions also solicit the attention of generic passers-by, suggesting that the impression which they made on outsiders was an important secondary concern.

A periurban location could also help to maximize the impact of monumental public buildings. In general, situations within the urban center appear to have been preferred by the individuals who paid for such buildings, as Frézouls' findings (1990) about theaters and amphitheaters suggest. Nonetheless, where public monuments *were* constructed in the urban periphery, they were often built in locations which ensured visibility and impact within the local landscape. An example is the amphitheater built 200 m to the east of the walled circuit at Luna (Luni) (Golvin, 1988: 166–67; see Figure 16.4). This building was sited on the *via Aurelia* as it approached from the south-west: probably the most prestigious approach to the city, since it would have been used by visitors from Rome. The orientation of the amphitheater may also have enhanced its impact. It was positioned with its longer axis at a right angle to the course of the road, meaning that travelers approaching from a distance would see it first width-ways on, and could thus appreciate the full extent of its widest dimension. As they passed the amphitheater, they could then turn and look in through its western entrance. Assuming that this was open, this would afford a view along the arena's longest axis, again giving every opportunity to appreciate its size. We should, of course, be wary of assuming that the amphi-theater at Luna would have been quite as visible from a distance as it appears now. Until recently,

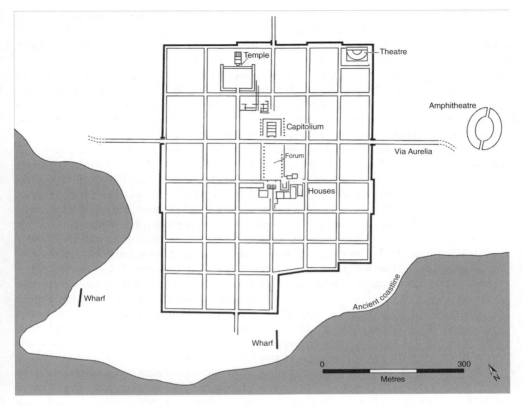

Figure 16.4 Luna, showing the periurban amphitheater. Drawing by Harry Buglass. Reproduced with permission of Simon Esmonde Cleary, Ray Laurence and Gareth Sears.

the amphitheater at Falerii Novi appeared to be separated from the nearby *via Amerina* by largely empty terrain: but survey work has now revealed periurban structures filling much of this space, thus potentially interrupting views from the road (Keay *et al.*, 2000: 64–69; Hay *et al.*, 2010). Nevertheless, periurban development was usually looser in structure than the urban center, and there were less likely to be other imposing public buildings close by. For a large structure like an amphitheater, then, the urban periphery may not have been the first choice of location, but it could compensate by offering better visibility than the urban center.

16.4   The Role of the Urban Periphery

We shall finish by considering the role which the urban periphery played in two particular spheres: the economic and the religious.

16.4.1   *Economic activity*

Scholars have now largely rejected Moses Finley's paradigm of the "consumer" city (1977), which rested on the assumption that cities and their rural hinterlands functioned as separate economic units. Today it is widely recognized that the two belonged to the same economic system, and that while that system certainly generated disparities in wealth and power, these cannot be mapped straightforwardly onto a city–country divide (e.g. Horden and Purcell, 2000: 89–122). The city served as a center for economic exchange, primarily for goods produced within its own territory, but also for those which circulated via long-distance trade (Wilson, 2009: 213–18). This means that all parts of a city's rural hinterland were connected to the urban center via this process. But because it lay physically closest to the city, the urban periphery offered different conditions from the more distant sectors of its hinterland, such as lower transport costs to market and easier access to a pool of consumers. We should therefore expect to see distinctive forms of economic activity being pursued there.

Field survey results show that villas generally clustered around three main attractors: Rome, the coast, and other Italian towns (Marzano, 2007: maps 2a, 19, 22, 23). Some, particularly around Rome and along the bay of Naples, are the elite villas which literary texts portray chiefly as leisure retreats (see also Pollard, ch. 17, this volume). But the same texts reveal that these were also agricultural estates which most owners sought to run at a profit (Goodman, 2007: 24–25). Meanwhile, studies of villas clustered around individual cities confirm that most were working farms, even when also equipped with leisure facilities (e.g. Brown, 1980: 69–70; Moorman, 2007). For those whose villas lay closest to the city, Cato (*On Agriculture*: 7–8), Varro (*On Agriculture*: 1.16.3) and Columella (*On Agriculture*: 3.2.1) offered advice on how to take advantage of this by specializing in the production of high-value perishable goods (Morley, 1996: 83–107). Work conducted in the context of the Tiber Valley Project has now provided archaeological support for this approach in the districts around Rome. The intensively cultivated landscape of south Etruria transpires to have been characterized by the presence of large cisterns, with a capacity better suited to the irrigation of perishable horticultural crops than staples like wheat and vines (Wilson, 2008).

Other forms of economic activity took place in the urban periphery partly because of the way in which cities were positioned with respect to the sea. Many Italian cities were located on the coast, but the harbor installations which served them were almost never incorporated into the urban center. To do so would conflict with the desire for clearly demarcated urban boundaries, since it would require that one side of the city opened directly onto the coast. Generally, cities developed on sites set back from the shoreline with a separate harbor just outside, as at Luna, Cosa, Ostia, Herculaneum, or Pompeii. The economic importance of the harbor facilities often also gave rise to related periurban development. The port installations at Cosa, for example, were situated in the shelter of cliffs below the promontory occupied by the city (Brown, 1980: 49–51). Next to the harbor, a commercial fishing lagoon was established, while *garum* manufacture and amphora production may also have been practiced nearby (McCann, 1979; 1987). Similarly, it is noticeable that some of the most vigorous periurban development at Ostia and Pompeii occurred on the coastal side of these cities. This probably reflects a combination of economic and aesthetic interests. For example, the shops lining the roads in the Porta Marina quarter at Ostia could attract customers approaching the city from the shore before they came to the commercial outlets of the urban center. The development of luxurious seaward-facing properties at both cities, however, clearly had more to do with the elite interest in spectacular views than practical economic factors (Martin *et al.*, 2002: 265–69; Tybout, 2007).

Finally, clusters of workshops, especially pottery kilns, have been identified just beyond the boundaries of various Italian cities. A well-known example is the *terra sigillata* industry of Arretium (Arezzo), which was chiefly concentrated within one km of the urban nucleus (Maetzke, 1958; Fülle, 1997; see Figure 16.5). Other similar cases include Pisa (Pasquinucci and Menchelli, 2006) or Ariminum (Giovagnetti, 1995). This type of development is often interpreted as evidence for the exclusion of workshops from the urban center, out of concern for noise, smells or fire (e.g. Dyson, 1992: 153; Patterson, 2000: 93). But the main ancient

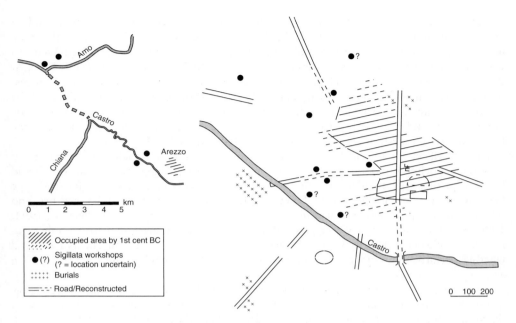

Figure 16.5 Arretium, showing the locations of the major *terra sigillata* workshops in relation to the urban nucleus and the course of the river Castro. Drawn by Alexander Santos.

evidence offered to support this idea is the colonial charter for Urso (Osuna) in Spain, which forbids the construction of "tile-kilns with a capacity of more than three hundred tiles or tile-like objects in the *oppidum* [i.e. urban center] of the colony" (ch. 76, ll.25–28 = Crawford, 1996: vol. 1, 25). This is the only surviving example of any such restriction, though, and does not prove that similar rules applied to industries other than tile production, at places other than colonies, or in regions other than Spain. The principle is also undermined by the presence of similar workshops *within* some urban centers, such as a pottery workshop on the via di Nocera at Pompeii (Peña and McCallum, 2009). This suggests that we should look for alternative factors behind the concentration of some industrial activities in the urban periphery. These might include cheaper rents outside the limited space of the urban center, or the attraction of features such as watercourses which could provide access to transport and the water required during the manufacturing process. Certainly, most workshops at Arretium cluster along the river Castro to the south-west of the city, suggesting that this was a key factor behind their distribution.

16.4.2 *The religious landscape*

The interface between city and country received plenty of religious attention. Rome itself was enclosed by a protective religious boundary known as the *pomerium*, which was reinforced by lustral processions in times of danger (Beard, North, and Price, 1998: 177–81). There is some debate over whether other Italian cities had a formal *pomerium* (Stevens, 2009: 16–47), but the boundaries of colonial foundations were certainly marked out using religious rituals (Varro, *On Latin Language*: 5.143), and there are also many examples of divinely protected city gates (Dyson, 1992: 155). The *Tabulae Iguvinae*, a series of bilingual bronze tablets from Iguvium (Gubbio) which date from the third to first centuries BC, reflect similar concerns

(Poultney, 1959; Devoto, 1962). They provide instructions for community rituals, including sacrifices performed "before" and "behind" three city gates (Ia 2–27, VIa 22–VIb 23), a lustral procession (Ib 19–22, VIb 56–65), and another procession to a place named Acedonia which probably lay in the urban periphery (Ib14–18, VIb 52–55; Poultney, 1959: 273). At Rome, too, literary texts and religious calendars attest numerous festivals involving processions between the city and the urban periphery (e.g. Strabo, *Geography*: 5.3.2). Some of the sanctuaries visited have been identified, and it is striking that they clustered in two concentric "rings": one a mile from the city (Colonna, 1991: 216–32), and the other between the fourth and sixth milestones (Alföldi, 1965: 296–304; Scheid, 1987).

This sort of activity should not be surprising: the boundaries of Italian cities were of great importance, helping to define them as urban as well as guaranteeing their safety. Nor should it be surprising that religious rituals connected cities with sanctuaries in the landscape beyond. An ancient city could only function effectively in symbiosis with its territory, and religious activity provided one medium for binding the two together (see de Polignac, 1994; 1995: 45–80 on the archaic Greek *polis*). But we might ask whether the urban periphery, as the closest element of a city's territory, had any special religious identity of its own, and whether periurban sanctuaries played a different role in local religious life from their urban and rural counterparts.

Some literary texts cast the urban periphery as a suitable location for cults which were important to the urban community, but associated with concepts which provoked anxiety. Such thinking is applied to foreign gods such as Aesculapius (Pliny the Elder, *Natural History*: 29.16), Isis, and Serapis (Dio Cassius: 53.2.4), but also to Italic deities such as Mars, Vulcan, and Venus out of fears concerning conflict, fire, and sexual license (Vitruvius, *On Architecture*: 1.7.1). Vitruvius, who offers the fullest discussion of temple locations, also allows for much local flexibility. His advice on the matter is expressed as suggestions rather than absolute rules, and he frequently offers alternatives to suit different urban landscapes. Indeed, after dealing with the best locations for the temples of 11 named deities, he concludes that "for the precincts of the other gods, suitable areas should be assigned on the basis of the sacrifices performed" (Vitruvius, *On Architecture*: 1.7.2). Vitruvius's perspective, then, appears to have been that communities should ultimately make their own judgments about what locations best suited their cult practices. The localized character of ancient religion means that he could hardly have advised otherwise. Religious priorities varied from community to community, and even deities with the same name could be understood quite differently in different contexts. Although Vitruvius clearly thought of Mars as a war-god, for example, Mars was also associated with agricultural fertility (Cato, *On Agriculture*: 141). This means that when we encounter a temple of Mars in the urban periphery, we should not assume that the cult has been excluded from the urban center because of its military associations. Another possibility might be that it was functioning as a place for city- and country-dwellers to come together in the expression of their shared concern over the crops (for similar ideas on the Greek Demeter: Cole, 1994: 204–05).

Some temple locations do appear to match up with the exclusionary principles voiced by ancient authors. At Rome, the *Campus Martius* area outside the *pomerium* was named after an altar of Mars with clear military associations (Festus p. 204L; *LTUR* vol. 3, 223–26). It also housed temples to the war-goddess Bellona and foreign deities such as Apollo, Isis, and Serapis (*LTUR* vol. 1, 190–92, 49–54 and vol. 3, 107–09). On the other side of Rome, a temple of Mars stood at the first mile on the *via Appia* (Colonna, 1991: 216–18), and a grove of the funerary goddess Libitina lay on the Esquiline hill outside the city wall (*LTUR* vol. 3, 189–90). Yet several foreign cults had temples within the *pomerium* at Rome, including Isis and Magna Mater (*LTUR* vol. 3, 112–13, 206–08), as did Venus in multiple different guises (*LTUR* vol. 5, 113–23), and two Augustan temples to Mars Ultor (*LTUR* vol. 2, 289–95 and vol. 3, 230–31). Other well-documented towns such as Ostia and Pompeii tell the same story. Temples of Bellona, Magna Mater, Serapis, Attis, and possibly Jupiter Sabazius were all built within the walled circuit at Ostia, as were at least 14 mithraea (Meiggs, 1973: 337–402; Mar, 1996). Similarly, the walls at Pompeii enclosed temples to Isis and probably Aesculapius (Ling, 2005: 109–10), while a major temple of Venus straddled a demolished section of the circuit (Carroll, 2010). Even Libitina, whose sacred grove was located outside the walls at Rome, was worshipped within the walls of the central Italian town of Anagnia (Anagni) (Castagnoli in *PECS*, 1976: 53).

These variations are perfectly in keeping with Vitruvius's recognition of local diversity. It is clear that some communities were happy to enclose temples within their urban boundaries for the same deities which the literary texts express concerns about, and it is hard to deduce any real consistency of practice in the placement of particular cults (Ziółkowski, 1992: 278–79; Orlin, 2002). As a result, we should be wary of interpreting *any* periurban sanctuary in terms of exclusion unless we have direct evidence that such principles were applied. A more rewarding approach may be to look instead for the positive attractions of a periurban location.

One may simply have been that the temple was associated with a place or activity itself situated in the urban periphery. Cosa provides an example in the form of a small temple on a rocky hill at the north end of the fishing lagoon, looking out over the lagoon and port beyond (McCann, 1987: 129–36). Although the deity housed there is unidentified, the temple's construction in the second century BC coincided with the beginnings of activity at the port, and its embellishment in the early first century occurred in the same period as the installation of full harbor facilities and the nearby fish-tanks. This suggests that it served to ensure divine protection for the port and related activities (on this principle in Gaul, see Derks, 1998: 142–44). Another attraction of the urban periphery may have been that it was accessible from the urban center, yet removed from the bustle of everyday life. Certainly, this sort of principle is voiced by Vitruvius. He advises that temples to Ceres "should be in a solitary spot out of the city, to which the public are not necessarily led except for the purpose of sacrificing" and adds that "this spot is to be reverenced with religious awe and solemnity of demeanor by those whose affairs lead them to visit it" (*On Architecture*: 1.7.2). A possible example might be the sanctuary of Dionysus established in the late third century BC at the mouth of the Sarno near Pompeii (Elia and Pugliese Carratelli, 1979). This temple stood on a small rise which would have made it visible from the urban center, but it lay half a kilometer south of the walls, creating the sense of distance from the city which Vitruvius evokes. Nevertheless, its connection with the urban center is clear from Oscan inscriptions which record the involvement of aediles in the provision of its altar and entrance ramp (Elia and Pugliese Carratelli, 1979: 448–49; Cooley and Cooley, 2014: A20–21).

Temples may also have been located in the urban periphery in order to achieve monumental impact. A study of mid-Republican Rome found that although consideration was given to religious factors when locating new temples, these were flexible enough to allow patrons to select positions which were also busy or highly visible, and especially ones which enhanced their own status or overshadowed the achievements of their rivals (Muccigrosso, 2006: 194–206). In most cases, locations within the city walls were favored, but some temple-builders chose periurban sites which better suited their personal agendas. The triumphal route across the *Campus Martius* was lined with victory temples which would serve as permanent reminders of their patrons' achievements, even while new victories were being celebrated (Favro, 1994). At other Italian cities, too, periurban sanctuaries were regularly situated on major routes or high ground, where they could dominate the experience of the approaching visitor (cf. Figure 3.2). At Tibur (Tivoli), for example, the sanctuary of Hercules Victor was rebuilt in monumental form in the early first century BC so that it literally straddled the *via Tiburtina*, which passed in a tunnel beneath the vast temple podium before continuing on into the city (Gros and Torelli, 2007: 195–96).

Along with the funerary monuments and other public buildings discussed earlier, temples of this sort formed another element in the urban facade. The road carefully channeled through the sanctuary of Hercules Victor was also the main approach from Rome, so that Tibur's powerful neighbors could not miss this testimony to the community's economic and cultural standing (Wallace-Hadrill, 2008: 112–116). Meanwhile, Horace's account of his journey to Brundisium offers a literary account of the role which a periurban temple could play in the experiences of an approaching traveler (*Satires*: 1.5.24–33). Horace relates that after disembarking from the canal which ran parallel to the *via Appia*, he and his companions stopped at a sanctuary of Feronia five km north-west of Tarracina (Terracina). Here, they washed in the goddess's stream and ate breakfast, before progressing onwards to Tarracina itself. The impression is of a sanctuary functioning as an intermediary stage on the journey into the city, offering practical facilities for travelers but also encouraging them to show their respect for the local gods before entering into the heart of the community which they protected.

Some cult structures also developed without reference to an urban center, but later became absorbed into the periphery of a city. An example can be seen at Minturnae, where the Roman *colonia* of the third century BC was established a short distance from two Auruncan coastal sanctuaries, both already in use since the seventh century (see Figure 16.1). One, at Monte d'Argento, is poorly documented, but appears to have remained active throughout the Roman era (Livi, 2006: 104–05). The other, at the mouth of the Liris, was dedicated to the Auruncan goddess Marica, and is better known (Livi, 2006: 105–13). The character of activity here altered with the establishment of the Roman colony, as would be expected given the local change which this entailed. But it remained in use, seeing several phases of new building work. In fact, work in the second century BC employed architectural terracottas which imitated decorative schemes from the archaic phase of the Marica sanctuary, but were produced using a mold also employed at the new *capitolium* in the urban center (Livi, 2006: 109–11). This reveals a close connection between sanctuary and city, with the urban *capitolium* drawing on the decorative schemes of the Marica sanctuary, and work at the sanctuary employing equipment also used in the urban center. It is not possible to be certain who was using the Marica sanctuary by this time, since the changes observed could reflect the activities of either Roman incomers or Auruncan locals who had adopted a new material culture (Livi, 2006: 114–16). But its continued development and direct links with the city do suggest a willingness on the part of the colonists to absorb existing cults into the religious landscape of their new territory.

16.5 Conclusion

In spite of their interest in the city–country divide, ancient authors also recognized that some buildings and activities did not fit neatly into either category. The archaeological evidence from Italy, too, confirms that the urban periphery was real and recognizable. While some forms of periurban development, like the Porta Marina quarter at Ostia, were almost indistinguishable from the urban center, even these reveal a different approach to the use of space through the presence of funerary monuments and seaside villas amongst the other buildings. This underlines the significance of urban boundaries in Roman Italy, and shows that it is unhelpful simply to treat the urban agglomeration as an undifferentiated mass. Distinct forms of land-use *can* be identified in different quarters of the city. Meanwhile, the urban periphery had a particular contribution of its own to make to the life of the local community. It could be used for practical purposes such as providing extra building space, burying the dead, or depositing urban refuse. But it could also make a striking first impression on approaching visitors, contribute to the local economy and help to sustain religious bonds between the city and the wider landscape. In doing so, it offered opportunities for civic display, the generation of wealth, and social interactions that neither the city nor the country proper could provide. If we wish to understand the communities of Roman Italy and the diverse range of activities which they engaged in, then, we cannot afford to overlook the urban periphery.

FURTHER READING

Rome's *suburbium* has been thoroughly treated by scholarship concerned with its role in elite lifestyles (Champlin 1982; Purcell 1987a), agricultural production (Morley 1996; Witcher 2005) and religious ritual (Scheid 1987; Colonna 1991). Periurban development outside other Italian cities remains under-investigated and under-analyzed, so there is little dedicated literature on the subject. Work on periurban development in other parts of the empire can provide some guide to the issues involved: e.g. Esmonde Cleary 1987; Bedon 1998; Goodman 2007 (with three chapters on the urban periphery as a general phenomenon). Only a small selection of publications deals directly with periurban development in Italy. For overviews of development at particular cities, there is Scagliarini 1991 on Bononia; Pellegrino, Olivanti, and Panariti 1995 and Heinzelmann 1998 on Ostia. For particular activities and their relationship with the city there are McCann 1987 on the port and fishery at Cosa, Graham 2005 on the cemeteries at Ostia, Livi 2006 on sanctuaries around Minturnae, Pasquinucci and Menchelli 2006 on *terra sigillata* production around Pisa, and Moorman 2007 on villas around Pompeii and Herculaneum. Stevens 2009 addresses the impact and significance of Italian urban boundaries, but is not yet available as a commercial publication.

REFERENCES

Adams, G.W. 2008. *Rome and the Social Role of Élite Villas in its Suburbs*. Oxford: Archaeopress.

Alföldi, A. 1965. *Early Rome and the Latins*. Ann Arbor: University of Michigan Press.

Beard, M., North, J., and Price, S. 1998. *Religions of Rome*. Vol. 1. *A History*. Cambridge: Cambridge University Press.

Bedon, R., ed. 1998. Suburbia: *Les faubourgs en Gaule romaine et dans les régions voisines (Caesarodunum* 32). Limoges: PULIM.

Belayche, N. 2003. "Pouzzoles: éléments d'histoire et de topographie." In Libitina. *Pompes funèbres et supplices en Campanie à l'époque d'Auguste. Édition, traduction et commentaire de la* Lex Libitinae Puteolana, eds F. Hinard and J.C. Dumont, 45–55. Paris : De Boccard.

Bertacchi, L. 1960. "Elementi per una revisione della topografia Ostiense." *Rendiconti della Reale Accademia dei Lincei, Classe di scienze morali, storiche e filologiche* 15: 8–32.

Bodel, J. 2000. "Dealing with the dead: undertakers, executioners and potter's fields in ancient Rome." In *Death and Disease in the Ancient City*, eds V. M. Hope and E. Marshall, 104–27. London: Routledge.

Bomgardner, D. 2000. *The Story of the Roman Amphitheatre*. New York and London: Routledge.

Bradley, G. 2000. *Ancient Umbria. State, culture and identity in Central Italy from the Iron Age to the Augustan Era*. Oxford: Oxford University Press.

Braund, S.H. 1989. "City and country in Roman satire." In *Satire and Society in Ancient Rome*, ed. S.H. Braund, 23–47. Exeter: Exeter University Press.

Brown, F.E. 1980. *Cosa: the making of a Roman town*. Ann Arbor: University of Michigan Press.

Carroll, M. 2010. "Exploring the Sanctuary of Venus and its sacred grove. Politics, cult and identity in Roman Pompeii." *Papers of the British School at Rome* 78: 63–106.

Castagnoli, F. 1976. "Anagnia (Anagni) Italy." In *The Princeton Encyclopedia of Classical Sites*, ed. R. Stilwell, 53. Princeton: Princeton University Press.

Champlin, E. 1982. "The *suburbium* of Rome." *American Journal of Ancient History* 7: 97–117.

Ciotti, U. 1960. "Il teatro romano di Spoleto." *Spoletium* 10: 9–26.

Claridge, A. 1998. "The villas of the Laurentina shore." *Rendiconti della Pontificia Accademia romana di archeologia* 70: 307–17.

Coarelli, F., ed. 1989. *Minturnae*, Rome: Nuova Editrice Romana.

Cole, S.G. 1994. "Demeter in the ancient Greek city and its countryside." In *Placing the Gods: sanctuaries and sacred space in Ancient Greece*, eds S.E. Alcock and R. Osborne, 199–216. Oxford: Oxford University Press.

Colonna, G. 1991. "Acqua Acetosa Laurentina, l'ager romanus antiquus e i santuari del I miglio." *Scienze dell'antichitá; storia, archeologia, antropologia* 5: 209–32.

Cooley, A.E. and Cooley, M.G.L. 2014. *Pompeii and Herculaneum. A sourcebook*. London and New York: Routledge.

Crawford, M. H., ed. 1996. *Roman Statutes*. 2 vols. London: Institute of Classical Studies/*BICS Supplement* 64.

De Maria, S. 1988. *Gli archi onorari di Roma e dell'Italia romana*. Rome: «L'Erma» di Bretschneider.

Dench, E. 1995. *From Barbarians to New Men. Greek, Roman and modern perceptions of peoples from the central Apennines*. Oxford: Clarendon Press.

Derks, T. 1998. *Gods, temples and ritual practices. The transformation of religious ideas and values in Roman Gaul*. Amsterdam: Amsterdam University Press.

Devoto, G. 1962. *Tabulae Iguvinae*. Rome: Istituto Poligrafico dello Stato.

Dyson, S.L. 1992. *Community and Society in Roman Italy*. Baltimore: Johns Hopkins University Press.

Elia, O. and Pugliese Carratelli, G. 1979. "Il santuario dionisiaco di Pompei." *La Parola del Passato* 34: 442–81.

Esmonde Cleary, A.S. 1987. *Extra-Mural Areas of Romano-British Towns*. Oxford: British Archaeological Reports, British Series 169.

Favro, D. 1994. "The street triumphant: the urban impact of Roman triumphal parades." In *Streets of the World. Critical Perspectives on Public Space*, eds D. Favro, Z. Celik, and R. Ingersoll, 151–64. Berkeley: University of California Press.

Finley, M.I. 1977. "The ancient city: from Fustel de Coulanges to Max Weber and beyond." *Comparative Studies in Society and History* 19: 305–27.

Frézouls, E. 1990. "Les monuments des spectacles dans la ville: théâtre et amphithéâtre." In *Spectacula* Vol. 1. *Gladiateurs et Amphithéâtres*, eds C. Domergue, C. Landes, and J.-M.Pailler, 77–92. Lattes: Éditions Imago.

Fülle, G. 1997. "The internal organisation of the Arretine terra sigillata industry: problems of evidence and interpretation." *Journal of Roman Studies* 87: 111–55.

Giovagnetti, C. 1995. "La ceramica di Rimini repubblicana. La vernice nera di produzione locale." In *Pro poplo Arimenese: Atti del Convegno Internazionale. Rimini antica: una respublica fra terra e mare*, eds A. Calbi and G. Susini, 437–68. Faenza: Fratelli Lega.

Golvin, J.-C. 1988. *L'amphithéâtre romain. Essai sur la théorisation de sa forme et de ses functions*. Paris: de Boccard.

Goodman, P.J. 2007. *The Roman City and its Periphery: from Rome to Gaul*. New York and London: Routledge.

Graham, E-J. 2005. "The Quick and the Dead in the extra-urban landscape: the Roman cemetery at Ostia/Portus as a lived environment." In *TRAC 2004. Proceedings of the Fourteenth Annual Theoretical Roman Archaeology Conference. Durham 2004*, eds J. Bruhn, B. Croxford, and D. Grigoropoulos, 133–43. Oxford: Oxbow.

Gros, P. and Torelli, M. 2007. *Storia dell'urbanistica: il mondo romano*. Rome: Laterza.

Harris, R. and Larkham, P. 1999. *Changing suburbs: foundation, form and function*. London: Spon.

Haselberger, L. 2007. Urbem adornare: *die Stadt Rom und ihre Gestaltumwandlung unter Augustus/ Rome's Urban Metamorphosis under Augustus*. Portsmouth, RI: *Journal of Roman Archaeology* Suppl. 64.

Hay, S., Johnson, P., Keay, S., and Millett, M. 2010. "Falerii Novi: further survey of the northern extra-mural area." *Papers of the British School at Rome* 78: 1–38.

Heinzelmann, M. 1998. "Beobachtungen zur suburbanen Topographie Ostias. Ein orthogonales Strassensystem im Bereich der Pianabella." *Mitteilungen des Deutschen Archäologischen Instituts, Römische Abteilung* 105: 175–225.

Heinzelmann M. 2000. *Die Nekropolen von Ostia. Untersuchungen zu den Graeberstrassen vor der Porta Romana und an der Via Laurentina.* Pfeil: Munich.

Heinzelmann M. 2001. "Les necropoles d'Ostie: topographie, developpement, architecture, structure sociale." In *Ostia, Port et porte de la Rome antique*, ed. J.-P. Descoeudres, 373–84. Georg: Geneva.

Heinzelmann, M. and Granino Cecere, M.G. 2001. "Ostia, Regio III. Untersuchungen in den unausgegrabenen Bereichen des Stadtgebietes. Vorbericht zur dritten Grabungskampagne 2000." *Mitteilungen des Deutschen Archäologischen Instituts, Römische Abteilung* 108: 313–28.

Hinard, F. and Dumont, J.C., eds. 2003. Libitina. *Pompes funèbres et supplices en Campanie à l'époque d'Auguste. Édition, traduction et commentaire de la* Lex Libitinae Puteolana. Paris: De Boccard.

Hope, V.M. 2000. "Contempt and respect: the treatment of the corpse in ancient Rome." In *Death and Disease in the Ancient City*, eds V.M. Hope and E. Marshall, 104–27. New York and London: Routledge.

Hopkins, K. 1983. *Death and Renewal.* Cambridge: Cambridge University Press.

Horden, P. and Purcell, N. 2000. *The Corrupting Sea.* Cambridge: Cambridge University Press.

Humphrey, J.H. 1986. *Roman Circuses. Arenas for chariot racing.* London: Batsford.

Izzet, V. 2007. *The Archaeology of Etruscan Society.* Cambridge: Cambridge University Press.

Johnson, J. 1935. *Excavations at Minturnae.* Vol. 1. *Monuments of the Republican Forum.* Philadelphia: University of Pennsylvania Press.

Keay, S. Millett, M., Poppy, S., Robinson, J., Taylor, J., and Terrenato, N. 2000. "Falerii Novi: a new study of the walled area." *Papers of the British School at Rome* 68: 1–93.

Lamboglia, N. 1964. *Ventimiglia romana.* Bordighera: Istituto internazionale di studi liguri.

Laurence, R. 1999. *The Roads of Roman Italy. Mobility and social change.* London: Routledge.

Lindsay, H. 2000. "Death-pollution and funerals in the city of Rome." In *Death and Disease in the Ancient City*, eds V.M. Hope and E. Marshall, 152–73. London: Routledge.

Ling, R. 2005. *Pompeii: history, life and afterlife.* Stroud: Tempus.

Lintott, A. 1993. Imperium Romanum: *Politics and Administration.* Abingdon: Routledge.

Livi, V. 2006. "Religious locales in the territory of Minturnae: aspects of Romanization." In *Religion in Republican Italy*, eds C.E. Schultz and P.B. Harvey, 90–116. Cambridge: Cambridge University Press.

MacDonald, W.L. 1986. *The Architecture of the Roman Empire.* Vol. 2. *An Urban Appraisal.* New Haven and London: Yale University Press.

Maetzke, G. 1958. "Arezzo." In *Enciclopedia dell'Arte Antica Classica e Orientale* Vol. 1, eds R. Bianchi Bandinelli and G. Becatti, 617–18. Rome: Istituto Poligrafico dello Stato.

Mar, R. 1996. "Santuarios e inversion inmobiliaria en la urbanística del siglo II." In *"Roman Ostia" Revisited. Archaeological and historical papers in memory of Russell Meiggs*, eds A. Gallina Zevi, and A. Claridge, 115–64. London: British School at Rome.

Martin, A. 1996. "Un saggio sulle mura del castrum di Ostia (Reg. I, ins. x, 3)." In *"Roman Ostia" Revisited. Archaeological and historical papers in memory of Russell Meiggs*, eds A. Gallina Zevi, and A. Claridge, 19–38. London, British School at Rome.

Martin, A., Heinzelmann, M., De Sena, E.C., and Granino Cecere, M.G. 2002. "The urbanistic project on the previously unexcavated areas of Ostia (DAI-AAR 1996–2001)." *Memoirs of the American Academy in Rome* 47: 259–304.

Marzano, A. 2007. *Roman Villas in Central Italy. A social and economic history.* Leiden and Boston: Brill.

McCann, A.M. 1979. "The harbor and fishery remains at Cosa, Italy." *Journal of Field Archaeology* 6: 391–411.

McCann, A.M., ed. 1987. *The Roman Port and Fishery of Cosa. A center of ancient trade.* Princeton: Princeton University Press.

Meer, L.B. van der, Stevens, N.L.C., and Stöger, H. 2005. "Domus Fulminata: The House of the Thunderbolt at Ostia (III, vii, 3–5)." *Bulletin Antieke Beschaving* 80: 91–111.

Meiggs, R. 1973. (2nd edn). *Roman Ostia*. Oxford: Clarendon Press.

Mertens, J., ed. 1995. *Herdonia: scoperta di una città*. Bari: Edipuglia.

Moorman, E.M. 2007. "Villas surrounding Pompeii and Herculaneum." In *The World of Pompeii*, eds J.J. Dobbins and P.W. Foss, 435–54. New York and London: Routledge.

Morley, N. 1996. *Metropolis and Hinterland: the city of Rome and the Italian economy, 200 B.C.–A.D. 200*. Cambridge: Cambridge University Press.

Muccigrosso, J. 2006. "Religion and politics: did the Romans scruple about the placement of their temples?" In *Religion in Republican Italy*, eds C.E. Schultz and P.B. Harvey, 181–206. Cambridge: Cambridge University Press.

Nevett, L. and Perkins, P. 2000. "Urbanism and urbanisation in the Roman world." In *Experiencing Rome. Culture, identity and power in the Roman world*, ed. J. Huskinson, 213–44. London: Routledge and Open University.

Orlin, E.M. 2002. "Foreign cults in Republican Rome: rethinking the pomerial rule." *Memoirs of the American Academy in Rome* 47: 1–18.

Pasquinucci, M. and Menchelli, S. 2006. "Pisa ed isola di Migliarino: città, territorio e produzioni di *terra sigillata*." In *Territorio e produzioni ceramiche: paesaggi, economia e società in età romana*, eds S. Menchelli and M. Pasquinucci, 217–24. Pisa: Pisa University Press.

Patterson, J.R. 2000. "On the margins of the city of Rome." In *Death and Disease in the Ancient City*, eds V.M. Hope and E. Marshall, 85–103. New York and London: Routledge.

Patterson, J.R. 2006. *Landscapes and Cities. Rural settlement and civic transformation in early imperial Italy*. Oxford: Oxford University Press.

Pellegrino, A., Olivanti, P., and Panariti, F. 1995. "Ricerche archeologiche nel Trastevere Ostiense." *Archeologia Laziale* 12: 393–400.

Peña, J.T. 2007. *Roman Pottery in the Archaeological Record*. Cambridge: Cambridge University Press.

Peña, J.T. and McCallum, M. 2009. "The production and distribution of pottery at Pompeii: a review of the evidence. Part 1: production." *American Journal of Archaeology* 112: 57–79.

Polignac, F. de. 1994. "Mediation, competition and sovereignty: the evolution of rural sanctuaries in Geometric Greece." In *Placing the Gods: sanctuaries and sacred space in Ancient Greece*, eds S.E. Alcock and R. Osborne, 3–18. Oxford: Oxford University Press.

Polignac, F. de. 1995. *Cults, Territory, and the Origins of the Greek City-State* (revised edition, trans. by Janet Lloyd). Chicago: University of Chicago Press.

Poultney, J.W. 1959. *The Bronze Tables of Iguvium*. Baltimore: American Philological Association.

Purcell, N. 1987a. "Tomb and suburb." In *Römische Gräberstraßen. Selbstdarstellung – Status – Standard*, eds H. von Hesberg and P. Zanker, 25–41. Munich: Bayerische Akademie des Wissenschaften.

Purcell, N. 1987b. "Town in country and country in town." In *Ancient Roman Villa Gardens*, ed. E.B. MacDougall, 185–203. Washington DC: Dumbarton Oaks.

Purcell, N. 1998. "Discovering a Roman resort-coast: the *litus Laurentinum* and the archaeology of *otium*". Laurentine Shore project website, 1–23. http://www.rhul.ac.uk/classics/laurentineshore/. Accessed January 20, 2011.

Quilici, L. and Quilici Gigli, S. 2002. "Sull'arco di Capua." In *Urbanizzazione delle campagne nell'Italia antica*, eds L. Quilici and S. Quilici Gigli, 205–31. Rome: «L'Erma» di Bretschneider.

Ramage, E.S. 1973. Urbanitas: *ancient sophistication and refinement*. Norman, OK: University of Oklahoma Press.

Reynolds, J. 1988. "Cities." In *The Administration of the Roman Empire, 241 BC–AD 193*, ed. D.C. Braund, 15–51. Exeter, University of Exeter Press.

Scagliarini, D. 1991. "Bologna (Bononia) and its suburban territory." In *Roman Landscapes: archaeological survey in the Mediterranean region*, eds G. Barker and J. Lloyd, 88–95. London: The British School at Rome.

Scheid, J. 1987. "Les sanctuaires de confins dans la Rome antique." In *L'Urbs. Espace urbain et histoire*, 583–95. Rome, École Française de Rome: Coll.EFR no. 98.

Sear, F. 2006. *Roman Theatres. An architectural study.* Oxford: Oxford University Press.

Stevens, S. 2009. *City Boundaries and Urban Development in Roman Italy: 4th century BC–AD 271.* Unpublished D.Phil. thesis, University of Oxford.

Tascio, M. 1989. *Todi: forma e urbanistica.* Rome: «L'Erma» di Bretschneider.

Toynbee, J.M.C. 1971. *Death and Burial in the Roman World.* London: Thames & Hudson.

Tybout, R. 2007. "Rooms with a view: residences built on terraces along the edge of Pompeii (Regions VI, VII and VIII)." In *The World of Pompeii*, eds J.J. Dobbins and P.W. Foss, 407–20. New York and London: Routledge.

Veloccia Rinaldi, M.L. 1969–70. "Scavi alle Terme Marittime." *Fasti Archaeologici* 24–25: 563–65.

Ward-Perkins, J.B. 1981. *Roman Imperial Architecture.* Harmondsworth: Penguin.

Wallace-Hadrill, A. 1991. "Elites and trade in the Roman town." In *City and Country in the Ancient World*, eds J. Rich and A. Wallace-Hadrill, 241–72. New York and London: Routledge.

Wallace-Hadrill, A. 2008. *Rome's Cultural Revolution.* Cambridge: Cambridge University Press.

Welch, K. 1994. "The Roman arena in late-Republican Italy: a new interpretation." *Journal of Roman Archaeology* 7: 59–80.

Wiedemann, T.E.J. 1992. *Emperors and Gladiators.* New York and London: Routledge.

Wilson, A.I. 2008. "Villas, horticulture and irrigation infrastructure in the Tiber Valley." In Mercator Placidissimus. *The Tiber Valley in Antiquity*, eds H. Patterson and F. Coarelli, 731–68. Rome: Quasar.

Wilson, A.I. 2009. "Approaches to quantifying Roman trade." In *Quantifying the Roman Economy: methods and problems*, eds A.K. Bowman and A. Wilson, 213–49. Oxford: Oxford University Press.

Witcher, R.E. 2005. "The extended metropolis: *urbs, suburbium* and population." *Journal of Roman Archaeology* 18: 120–138.

Zanker, P. 2000. "The city as symbol: Rome and the creation of an urban image." In *Romanisation and the City*, ed. E. Fentress, 25–41. Portsmouth, RI: *Journal of Roman Archaeology* Suppl. 38.

Zevi F. 1997. "Costruttori eccellenti per le mura di Ostia. Cicerone, Clodio e l'iscrizione della Porta Romana." *Rivista dell'Istituto nazionale d'archeologia e storia dell'arte* 19–20: 61–112.

Ziółkowski, A. 1992. *The Temples of mid-Republican Rome and their Historical and Topographical Context.* Rome: «L'Erma» di Bretschneider.

CHAPTER 17

Villas

Nigel Pollard

17.1 Introduction

A villa, on the most basic level, was a rural residence. However, beyond this fundamental criterion, the term carries other implications both in Roman culture and in modern scholarship. Roman villas in Italy were diverse, in terms of their architecture and functions. However, perhaps the most important unifying factors, beyond the simple fact of rural location, were productivity – all (or almost all) villas were, in some sense at least, productive centers, whether for export or local consumption; and status– the architecture, decor and productive capacity of a villa reflected its owner's elite status, or aspiration to elite status. The aim of this chapter is to provide an overview of the villa as a phenomenon in Roman Italy, and to give an indication of the range of evidence, written and archaeological, that can be deployed to study that phenomenon.

Villas dominated the study of the Roman countryside until the last decades of the twentieth century, for a number of reasons (overview in Dyson, 2003: 13–19). They were well known to scholars grounded in classical philology, who learned of villas and villa life from the letters of Cicero and Pliny the Younger as well as from the agricultural manuals of Cato, Varro, and Columella. Architectural and decorative features (such as mosaic floors) were substantial enough to survive to be excavated and studied, as interest in the remains of Roman antiquity developed through the early modern period. These factors, combined with the appeal of Roman villa life to contemporary upper-class tastes (in Italy and beyond) for "cultured rustication" (Dyson, 2003: 14) led to early topographical studies drawing on both texts and archaeology, as scholars sought to associate surviving remains with villa owners known from literature (such as the poetry of Horace) (Frischer and Brown, 2001; Frischer, Crawford, and De Simone, 2006) or to reconstruct and reflect the villa structures recorded in literature, such as Pliny's Laurentine and Tuscan villas (Du Prey, 1994). While developing methods and techniques of environmental and survey archaeology from the 1960s onwards meant that villas were no longer the sole focus of the study of the Roman countryside, these new approaches revitalized villa studies in that they enabled scholars to study villas within their broader rural contexts, and also to study individual villas (such as the Francolise villas – Cotton, 1979; Cotton and Metraux, 1985; and Settefinestre – Carandini, 1985) effectively and in detail, as ensembles of both production and residence.

17.2 Definitions

In ancient literature, the fundamental meaning of *villa* is a rural residence, in contrast to the urban *domus*. Cicero (*On his House*: 62), for example, contrasted his *domus* on the Palatine in Rome with his *villa* near Tusculum when complaining of their confiscation in 58 BC. Very often *villa* referred to the built portion of a farm rather than the land or the estate as a whole, which were termed *praedium*, *fundus*, or *ager*. This sense of *villa* is made explicit in some of the earliest uses of the word. Cato, for example (*On Agriculture*: 3.1, circa 160 BC), wrote that the *villa* (the residence and agricultural buildings) should be built in proportion to the *fundus* (the estate as a whole). Cato further distinguished (*On Agriculture*: 3.2) between the *villa rustica* (built structures for processing and storing crops, including facilities for wine and oil production) and *villa urbana* (residence – *On Agriculture*: 4.1 – see also Varro, *On Agriculture*: 1.13.6–7; 3.2.10). Columella (*On Agriculture*: 1.6.1, circa AD 60) divided the villa into *pars urbana* (residence), *pars rustica* (accommodation for slaves and other staff, stables, and animal stalls) and *pars fructuaria* (presses and storage vats for wine and olive oil production, along with granaries, haylofts, and similar). Cato placed little emphasis on luxury as a characteristic of a villa, but a speech of Scipio Aemilianus delivered circa 140 BC (quoted by Aulus Gellius, *Attic Nights*: 2.20.6) refers to *villae expolitissimae*, "very finely finished villas" suggesting that luxury was a characteristic of at least some early examples.

Certainly by circa 37 BC, when Varro wrote his dialog on the nature of a villa (*On Agriculture*: 3), his fictional characters could toy with various notions of what the word signified, applying it to suburban properties that were primarily luxurious residences as well as to austere working farms (*On Agriculture*: 3.2.3–10). They agreed that a structure was "no less ....a villa if it is purely agricultural (*simplex...rustica*) than something which is both rural and refined (*urbana*)," This has led some scholars (especially in Italian) to adopt the term *villa rustica* for an agricultural establishment lacking a developed *pars urbana* (see the Villa Regina site, section 17.7.3, this chapter; De Caro, 1994), although this is not a regular ancient usage. However, the terms *villa suburbana* for a specifically suburban villa, and *villa maritima* for a coastal one were used in antiquity, as neatly combined in a passage in Cornelius Nepos's biography of Atticus (14.3), in which he stated that Cicero's friend had "no luxurious suburban or coastal villa."

At the upper end of the villa spectrum, we find that something as vast as Hadrian's palatial residence at Tibur (modern Tivoli) could be defined as a villa in antiquity (Augustan Histories, *Life of Hadrian*: 23; 26: *villa Tiburtina*), but defining the lower end on the basis of literature alone is much more difficult. Accounts of supposedly small and humble villas associated with past Roman leaders, such as that of Scipio Africanus at Liternum (Seneca, *Letters*: 86.4–7), must be treated with some suspicion, as must those of writers like Horace or Martial (see later in this chapter). The estates and structures implied by Cato's account are less complex than Varro and Columella's, but even Cato's villa was a substantial slave-run establishment organized with an eye to profit, with a *pars urbana* attractive enough to encourage regular visits from an absentee landowner (*On Agriculture*: 4.1). Ancient writers sometimes used terms like *tuguria* (see Cicero, *In Defence of Sestius*: 43) and *mapalia* to denote sub-villa rural dwellings (the latter more typically outside Italy), but it is unclear how such terms map on to the surviving archaeological evidence, or where a Roman would draw the dividing line, and typically vaguer terms like *fundus* and *ager* are used to denote farms of various sizes, emphasizing land rather than structures. For example, the seven-*iugera* farm of Atilius Regulus, Roman general in the First Punic War, was described by Valerius Maximus (4.4.6) as an *agellum* ("little *ager*") rather than in terms of its structures.

Turning to surviving archaeological evidence, it would be uncontroversial to label excavated structures such as Settefinestre (see section 17.7.2) or the Villa San Marco at Stabiae (for example) as villas, and there is little problem identifying the upper end of the spectrum unless one seeks to sub-define on the basis of size or function. The primary issue, again, is distinguishing between villas and other kinds of rural dwelling, at the other end of the spectrum.

Most archaeological studies distinguish between villas and other, smaller and less elaborate, dwellings, examples of which existed in the Italian rural landscape before the emergence of the villa, and even before the spread of Roman power (Attolini and Perkins, 1992). The Albegna Valley survey project, for example, distinguished between villas and three classes of *case* ("houses," a deliberately neutral term) as well as villages, on the basis of the size and character of surface scatters (Fentress, 2002: 54–59). Villa sites were defined as substantial spreads of material (over 2500 m²) implying some level of architectural sophistication or decoration, such as marble, column fragments, mosaic *tesserae*, or fragments of painted plaster. Sites defined as "houses" were smaller and lacked such materials. As Fentress notes (2002: 54), this distinction between "house" and villa is a tangible one (Barker, Lloyd, and Webley, 1978: 42) and one with underlying social significance, since the luxury materials reflect construction by an individual who, on some level, shared the tastes of urban elites or at least sought to assimilate to them. Such criteria made it possible to define a rural site, such as the sample excavated farmstead at Giardino Vecchio (Cambi, 2002: 142–43), with its relatively small size (circa 500 m²) and functional architecture, as a "non-villa" or "sub-villa," like similar excavated sites elsewhere in Italy (at Monte Forco in the *Ager Capenas*, for example: Jones, 1962: 172–73; 1963: 147–58).

Fentress's characterization of a villa as a rural structure whose physical remains reflect elite status or aspirations is a useful one when one moves beyond the core areas of villa distribution (coastal Etruria, Latium, and Campania, and the *suburbium* of Rome). As she notes (using the *Ager Veientanus*, closer to Rome, as a point of comparison), the physical characteristics of villas vary in different parts of Italy. Nevertheless, physical evidence of the owner's elite status or aspirations provides a central theme linking rather different buildings. The Villa Regina site at Boscoreale (see section 17.7.3, this chapter), one of a number of small inland villas in the rural territory of Pompeii, is similar in size to the Giardino Vecchio farm, and similarly functional in its emphasis on agriculture rather than luxury. Nevertheless, it does have two rooms with wall paintings comparable to those of urban *domus* and larger villas, and these suggest elite connections (an owner based in the town, perhaps) or a level of aspiration perhaps lacking at Giardino Vecchio. This might lead us to define the Villa Regina site as a "small villa" rather than a "small farm." The sites characterized as villas in the Biferno valley survey area in Molise (central-southern Italy), such as the excavated example at Matrice, were comparable in size to those of the *Ager Cosanus*, but mostly relatively basic compared to Settefinestre (Lloyd, 1991: 181–85; Barker, 1995: 224–36). However, the evidence they *do* provide of luxury (some basic painted plaster and black and white mosaic tesserae; fragments of column and flue tiles), along with their size, relative to other rural sites in the area, suggests that their owners were local elites or wealthy absentee landlords. Their economic base was not the same as that of Settefinestre (for example), but the Biferno "villa" sites still reflect their owners' ability to exploit and manipulate reflections of metropolitan material culture as symbols of power, albeit on a local scale. The same is true of similar sites elsewhere in Italy, such as the Buccino villas in Lucania (Dyson, 1983), and these underlying social and economic criteria (rather than just their material manifestations) can even be applied to the diverse range of rural structures defined as villas beyond Italy, from Britain to Syria.

17.3 Origins, Chronology, and Development

17.3.1 General

The vast majority of evidence, written and archaeological, for villas in Italy suggests that they were predominantly a second-century BC to second/third century AD phenomenon, with archaeological evidence showing a peak in new constructions from the mid-first century BC through the early Julio-Claudian period.

Marzano (2007: 237–796) compiled the published chronological evidence for a large sample of villas in Lazio, Toscana and Umbria. Taking her data from her Fig. 20, the distribution of occupation start-dates is as shown in Table 17.1.

Her start date is an artificial one, omitting possible evidence before the second century BC (Marzano, 2007: 203 n. 9), and she notes the inadequacies and distortions of the published evidence for dating. Nevertheless, this shows in general terms what is true for the majority of sites excavated or defined by survey, that the peak of villa construction in Italy was the first century BC to first century AD, and particularly the period circa 50 BC–AD circa 50. Villa construction was largely a phenomenon of the triumviral to Julio-Claudian period. When it comes to the decline of villa construction and occupation, Marzano (2007: 210) acknowledges major change from the later first century AD onwards, but rejects the notion that "the crisis of the Italian villa-system was *total*," pointing to evidence of continued late occupation at many sites, despite the archaeological problems of studying this. The thoroughly excavated villa at Settefinestre shows the broad strokes of the chronology of the villa phenomenon in microcosm, with construction in the triumviral period and effective abandonment in the late second century AD (Carandini, 1985: 1.183–85).

17.3.2 In literature

The earliest literary use of the term *villa* is by Plautus, in the first decades of the second century BC, when the word already implies a productive farm of some size, with slaves (see *The Merchant*: 277; *The Three Pieces of Money*: 944). Cato's *On Agriculture* was written within a few decades, and depicts the villa as the center of a substantial agricultural estate with slave labor, with an owner seeking to profit from its production. While the scale of the estates which Cato described has been characterized variously by different modern scholars, ranging from "small estate" to "large industrial enterprise" (see White, 1970: 387, settling on the lower end of his "medium" category), his focus is very much on efficient production, with little about the villa's architecture or decoration. Nevertheless, Scipio Aemilianus's reference (Gellius, *Attic Nights*: 2.20.6) to *villae expolitissimae*, and Cato's own condemnation of such structures (Plutarch, *Life of Cato the Elder*: 4.4, "that none of his homes were plastered"; D'Arms, 2003: 23–24) suggests that luxury was as much a feature of some early villas as it was of some of their later counterparts. Later writers, referring back to the second century BC (D'Arms, 2003: 15–29) also imply that distinguished Romans had already acquired villas on the coast of Campania, in places like Misenum and Puteoli that became major centers of villa culture in the following centuries, suggesting the emergence of the *villa maritima* at that time. Certainly the works of Cicero and Varro's *On Agriculture* make it clear that, by the end of the Republic, the term *villa* could be applied to a wide range of rural residences, more or less agricultural or luxurious, located in suburbs, on the coast or in more distant, inland rural areas. It retained that range of meanings through into late antiquity, adding imperial rural

Table 17.1   Villa occupation start-dates in Lazio

Century	2nd BC	1st BC	1st AD	2nd AD	3rd AD	4th AD	5th AD
No. of villas	92	171	125	19	4	2	0

properties – as noted, Hadrian's palatial residence at Tibur could be defined as a villa according to its range of meanings.

Regardless of these implications of luxury, all three of the major agricultural writers, Cato (circa 160 BC), Varro (circa 37 BC), and Columella (AD circa 60), notionally at least, deal with the theme of intensive investment agriculture, making a villa estate as productive as possible (Varro, *On Agriculture*: 1.1.2 *"quem bene....fructuosum"*; Columella, *On Agriculture*: 1.*pr.*10; 1.1.3). The estate is assumed to be one in which the primary labor is provided by slaves supervised by a *vilicus*, although Cato, (*On Agriculture*: 136) and Columella (*On Agriculture*: 1.7) discuss cultivation by free tenants as an option. Discussion of the villa as a rural residence, particularly a luxurious one, is very much secondary, and largely negative.

All three authors provide some advice on how and where to build and equip the villa residence and its associated agricultural structures such as presses, wine and oil production, and storage areas, threshing floors, and mills. The later writers draw on the works of the earlier ones, but their emphases and the agricultural regimes discussed vary somewhat. While advocating a high degree of self-sufficiency for the villa estate (*On Agriculture*: 2.7), Cato focused on oil and wine production for investment, noting (*On Agriculture*: 1.7) that wine was the most profitable form of production and oil the fourth (after osier beds and horticulture, with arable and stock-raising less so). He specifically set out the equipment and personnel required for a 100-*iugera* farm estate with 16 slaves focused on wine production (*On Agriculture*: 11–14) and a 240-*iugera* estate with 13 slaves focused on olive production (*On Agriculture*: 10.1).

Varro did not specify size but assumed for his general discussion (*On Agriculture*: 1.13) a mixed farm with facilities for stock-raising, wine, oil, cereal crops, and legumes, and all of these topics are discussed at some length. However, he devoted a strikingly large part of his text (*On Agriculture*: 3.2.10–17) to asserting the profitability of *pastio villatica*, the raising of specialized "livestock" including poultry and exotic birds, dormice, boar, hares, bees, snails, and fish for specialized markets, including an (implausible) anecdote about the profits his maternal aunt made from fieldfares at her Sabine villa estate. The main focus of the modern scholarship on Columella's work has been on his lengthy discussion of viticulture and its profitability (in books 3–5, with discussion of profitability in *On Agriculture*: 3.3; see Duncan-Jones, 1982: 33–59; Carandini, 1983; 1985: 1.165–69; Tchernia, 1986: 209–15), although his discussion of the layout and equipment of the farm (*On Agriculture*: 2.6) assumed facilities for cereal, arable and livestock production too, and his lengthy (12-book) treatise included information on all of these things and more. Despite the problems in using them (in great part the result of their literary characteristics, and, in the case of Cato's text, its frequent incoherence) these manuals have served as the main sources for most of the literature-based scholarship on Roman villa-based agriculture, and have been used in conjunction (perhaps too much so – see Purcell, 1988: esp. 196–98; Marzano, 2007: 125–53) with archaeological evidence to reconstruct the agricultural regime at Settefinestre (section 17.7.2, this chapter).

17.3.3 Archaeology

Most modern scholarship presents the emergence of villas (alongside or in place of the small farms that had long been part of the Italian countryside – see Attolini and Perkins, 1992) as a late third/second century-BC development, associated with a range of interrelated economic factors such as:

- an influx of wealth from foreign conquests, particularly to the upper classes
- changes in land holding
- changes in agricultural practices, perhaps under Greek or Punic influence
- the development of agricultural slavery

and/or cultural developments such as:

- the influence of Greek architecture in general, and particularly of monumental public architecture or Hellenistic palatial architecture on elite domestic architecture
- the evolution of new methods of domestic decoration, again, perhaps, under the influence of the Greek world
- the use of domestic architecture to advertise social status

Certainly some of the moralizing criticism of luxurious villas presents them (like other contemporary changes in Roman culture) as intrusive and foreign, and even (superficially, at least), Greek (see Varro, *On Agriculture*: 2.*pr*.2), although indigenous architectural developments, particularly of concrete construction facilitating terracing of villas – a particular feature of coastal villas (see the Villa dei Papiri, section 17.7.1, this chapter) – was also crucial. In general it seems reasonable to argue that villas, defined broadly, emerged by the second century BC, and that their outward form, at least, related to other contemporary changes, as Roman/Italic material culture engaged with external, particularly Greek, influences (see Schultz, ch.3, this vol.). Clearly their emergence also related to economic change, perhaps specifically a less even distribution of wealth in Roman society. However, that relationship is perhaps a complicated one, and villas may have been more a result and a symbol of economic change rather than its cause (Terrenato, 2001: 27).

The main dissenter from the view that villas emerged in the Middle Republic under such external influences has been Terrenato (2001), who proposes that the villa (as monumental elite rural residence) was an indigenous Italian/Roman development, with roots in the archaic period. He argues this from the similarities of plan and scale between the excavated Auditorium site in Rome (which in antiquity lay within the city's rural territory) and later Republican villas. Indeed the Auditorium "villa" itself shows substantial continuity of form and occupation from the late archaic to the late Republican period. The principal objection to his argument, as Terrenato himself admits, is that there is only one other possible example (a site at Grottarossa, just north of Rome) known of such an early "proto-villa."

Whatever the weaknesses of his argument for the archaic and indigenous origins of the villa, Terrenato (2001: 18–24) does make an effective case against the view that villas in Italy underwent a general process of evolution (in terms of scale and complexity of architecture, plan and economic organization – see, for example, Carandini, 1985: 1.116–17) from the middle Republican to imperial period, from relatively simple "Catonian" structures, through "Varronian," "Columellan," and even "Plinian" forms (Carandini, 1985: 1.181). Archaeological evidence does show evolution in some individual cases. Excavation of the Posto villa at

Francolise in Campania revealed an early phase (originating circa 100–80 BC) with a small farmhouse and yard replaced by a more elaborate "classic" villa circa 30 BC (Cotton, 1979: 8–17). The villa at Matrice in the Upper Biferno Valley started as a late third/early second-century BC "peasant cottage," was reconstructed as a modest terraced villa in the second century BC and a "fully fledged, but somewhat plain, villa" in the early first century AD (Lloyd, 1991: 182–85). But these two examples do not fit the model of "Catonian" to "Columellan" in terms of date (Posto), location (Matrice is far from the core area of villa development – see later in this chapter), or complexity of the final structure (both). In general, villas of varied size, luxury, and complexity appear to have coexisted with one another and with smaller farms over several centuries rather than showing any single clear trajectory of development. "The villa" was a diverse phenomenon.

17.4   Geography

Villas owned by the ruling elite of the city of Rome, and the majority of the developed villas that emulated them, were concentrated in western-central Italy, particularly near Rome itself, on the Bay of Naples, and more generally along the coast of Etruria, Latium, and Campania.

Columella (*On Agriculture*: 1.1.19) noted the advantages of owning a villa close enough to the city for its owner to visit after completing *negotium* in the forum, and Pliny the Younger (*Letters*: 2.17.2) singled this out as one of the advantages of his coastal villa at Laurentum. Defining the *suburbium* of Rome as a day's travel from the city, circa 35 km, (Goodman, 2007: 20–21, 50; see also Morley, 1996: 91) circumscribes a zone including towns and areas such as the Alban Hills, Tibur, Praeneste, and the coast of Latium. Pliny the Younger (*Letters*: 2.17.27) suggested that villas along the coast near Laurentum formed "a façade resembling so many cities," and numerous remains are visible in the area even now (see Lafon, 2001: 348, Fig. 72, with relevant catalog entries). Tusculum, in the Alban Hills, was another prime location for senators' villas, and Pauly-Wissowa (*RE* 1487 s.v. *Tusculum*) records some 38 senatorial villa owners known from our very fragmentary literary and epigraphic evidence for the area, including Cato (who came from Tusculum), Lucullus, Crassus, Sulla, Varro, and, of course, Cicero.

Social and cultural functions may have predominated in elite villas so close to Rome (see later in this chapter), and, indeed, some authors suggested that economic motives were not of primary importance in their acquisition (Seneca, *On Benefits*: 4.12.3 on Tibur and Tusculum, citing their *salubritas* ("healthiness") and role as summer retreats instead; Pliny the Younger, *Letters*: 4.6 on Laurentum) in acquiring such properties. The agricultural writers, however, highlighted economic rather than the social advantages of proximity to cities and good transport infrastructure (Cato, *On Agriculture*: 1.1.3; Varro, *On Agriculture*: 1.16.1; Columella, *On Agriculture*: 1.3.3), and noted particular crops suited for production in suburban areas and consumption in the owner's urban residence or sale on nearby urban markets (Cato, *On Agriculture*: 7.1; Varro, *On Agriculture*: 1.16.3 on flowers). Both Varro and Columella paid considerable attention to *pastio villatica*, specialized production of luxury items (poultry and other birds, fish, game, dormice, honey) for such markets (Varro, *On Agriculture*: 3.2.10–3.17; Columella, *On Agriculture*: 8–9; Carandini, 1985: 1.125–26; Morley, 1996: 87–90; Purcell, 1995). Anecdotal evidence (compiled by Morley, 1996: 84, map 2; 107) shows that particular areas of Rome's *suburbium* were known for particular commodities like fruit, flowers, and vegetables.

The coast of the Bay of Naples, particularly places like Baiae, Cumae, and Stabiae, was another area with concentrations of villas belonging to the metropolitan elite, to the extent that Strabo (*Geography*: 5.4.8) wrote how these luxurious "palaces" were built "one on top of the other" at Baiae, giving an impression of the terracing of villas on hillsides overlooking the sea, a phenomenon demonstrated by the physical remains of (for example) the Villa dei Papiri at Herculaneum (see section 17.7.1, this chapter) and the Villa Arianna and Villa San Marco at Stabiae. The attractions of the area for Roman aristocrats were numerous. Besides its natural beauty and resources, Strabo cited its Greek cultural ambience but also its hot springs and thermal baths (surviving remains of which are prominent at Baiae – Yegül, 1996), and Baiae was also known for decadence and vice (Cicero, *In Defence of Caelius*: 35; Martial, *Epigrams*: 1.62). Cicero (*Letters to Atticus*: 2.8.2) refers to the Bay of Naples as *illum cratera delicatum*, "that 'crater' of luxury, probably punning on two different meanings of that word, denoting both the crater-shaped bay itself, and also a mixing bowl used at drinking parties. Construction of such villas by Roman aristocrats probably began in the second century BC, but the evidence, both written and archaeological, is much more substantial from the second quarter of the first century BC onwards (D'Arms, 2003: 15–29; Lafon, 2001: 83–99). D'Arms (2003: 48, 57–58) suggests that by 74 BC, at least, there was a regular spring "season," with senators migrating from Rome to Campania for a holiday during the senatorial recess in April–May each year.

Much of the readily accessible evidence, at least, suggests that these large, elite coastal villas were primarily centers of luxury, consumption, and display rather than of production. Cicero (*On the Agrarian Law*: 2.78) implied that such villas consumed rather than produced wealth when he claimed that the land commissioners would acquire farmland in Campania for themselves to subsidize their villas at Cumae and Puteoli. The agricultural writers discussed specifically coastal forms of production, notably fish-farming (Varro, *On Agriculture*: 3.17; Columella, *On Agriculture*: 8.16–17). Columella (*On Agriculture*: 3.17; 3.16.6) provided specific instructions for constructing fishponds, and rather grudgingly admitted that if a villa lacked good agricultural land, a profit (*quaestum villaticum*) could be made from fish and shellfish, as did Varro (*On Agriculture*: 3.17.2 on freshwater fishponds). However, the moralizing (see later in this chapter) won out, and both authors presented fishponds and their fish primarily as expensive luxuries for display by wealthy individuals such as Lucullus and Hortensius rather than for profit or even local consumption, as, for the most part, does Higginbotham (1997) in his study of Roman fishponds. Much of our knowledge of the ideology of fishponds derives from this strongly moralizing presentation by the agricultural writers, and Cicero's hostile allusions to *piscinarii* ("fish-breeders"; *Letters to Atticus*: 1.19; 1.20; 2.9). More recent works (Lafon, 2001: 127–86, esp. 158–81; Marzano, 2007: 47–75) place greater emphasis on production as a function of coastal villas in general, not just of fish and shellfish, but also from agricultural land, clay-pits, and quarries in their hinterlands.

While there was a notable concentration on the Bay of Naples and close to Rome, by the early imperial period villas were distributed along much of the west-central Italian coast, particularly between Monte Argentario (near Cosa) in Etruria, and Formiae in Campania (Marzano, 2007: 33), including places like Antium and Sperlonga. Other substantial villas (like Settefinestre, see later in this chapter) lay just inland from the western coast of Italy, in areas such as the *Ager Cosanus*, where they benefited from good agricultural land, relatively easy access by sea or overland for owners based in Rome, and convenient nearby port facilities for the movement of goods, like the port of Cosa (McCann, 1987), which amphora-remains show served as a conduit for wine produced in its hinterland.

Conversely, Campania was not just the preserve of large coastal villas. Just inland from the Bay of Naples there were numerous smaller villas and farms whose remains suggest more functional agricultural establishments, typically characterized as *ville rustiche* by Italian scholars. The best known are those around Pompeii (Rostovtzeff, 1926: 30, 551–53, n.26; Carrington, 1931; D'Arms, 2003: 351–83; De Caro, 1994. See discussion of the Villa Regina site, section 17.7.3, this chapter). However, similar structures have also been found inland from the grand coastal villas at Stabiae, where Camardo, 2004: 30–31 records more than 50 known smaller inland villas compared with the eight large coastal establishments. Ownership and occupation of these smaller villas appear to have varied. Some may have been farmed by tenants or dependents of the owners of the large coastal villas. Cicero's Cumae villa, for example, had *vilicos, procuratores* (*Letters to Atticus*: 14.16.1; "bailiffs and agents"), and the plural implies multiple farms associated with the main villa. Similarly one may take more-or-less literally Cicero's accusation (*On the Agrarian Law*: 2.78) that the land-commissioners would acquire Campanian land to subsidize their coastal villas, to support the idea of a pattern of landholding entailing a central, luxurious coastal villa with outlying smaller villas and other farms. Certainly Cicero's Arpinum estate (*Letters to Atticus*:13.11.1) and Pliny the Younger's Tifernum villa (*Letters*: 9.37) had rent-paying tenants who presumably occupied satellites of the main villa (see also Marzano, 2007: 107 on such networks around Tibur). But, returning to the smaller, inland villas and farms in the hinterland of the Bay of Naples, their owners and occupants may have been of many different statuses. For the villas around Pompeii, Carrington (1931; Rostovtzeff, 1926: 551–53, n.26), suggests (on the basis of seals, stamps and *dipinti* on their *instrumentum domesticum*) that some were owned by wealthy residents of Pompeii, perhaps farmed by bailiffs, while others were farmed by smallholders, including independent freedmen.

Wealthy members of the metropolitan elite typically owned multiple villas in different areas. Cicero's villas, for example, included properties at Tusculum, Arpinum, Formiae, and nearby Caieta, Astura (near Antium), Cumae, Puteoli, and Pompeii, while Pliny the Younger had villas in the Transpadane area of Italy, at Laurentum near Ostia, and (his favorite, Tuscan, estate) at Tifernum in the Upper Tiber Valley (*Letters*: 4.6; see Sherwin-White 1966: 329–30 on *Letters* 5.6.45, and 186–99 and 321–30 on his Laurentine and Tuscan villas). They owned villas in the same places as their friends, political allies, and enemies. For example, Cicero (*Letters to his Friends*: 5.15.2) noted that L. Lucceius was his neighbor in both Tusculum and Puteoli. Hortensius, Catulus, and Lucullus, the (historical) protagonists of the (fictional) dialog of Cicero's *Academy* (2.148) were all at Hortensius's villa at Bauli, yet indicated that they all owned properties near Tusculum too. The existence of networks of properties owned by individuals (and their friends), often quite close to one another, made it possible to undertake trips that entailed travel from one property to another, with social or political motives, to oversee economic activity on their villas or just for convenience of travel (Goodman, 2007: 23, 50). In April 59 BC, Cicero wrote to Atticus (*Letters to Atticus*: 2.8.2) from Antium that he intended to travel to Formiae, back to Antium, then on to Tusculum and Arpinum before returning to Rome, and he hoped that Atticus would be able to meet him at one of those places.

As noted already, the main areas of villa development were the west coast of Italy, particularly from Etruria to Campania, its hinterland, and the vicinities of major cities, particularly Rome itself. Villas were not confined to those areas, however, and establishments definable as villas (as noted earlier in this chapter) have been studied by excavation and survey in other regions of Italy, inland and coastal. The size, appearance, and luxury of such villas varied, but typically their size and complexity displayed their owners' wealth and power relative to the majority of the local population, and so (for the most part) their owners' status as members of local or external elite groups. There is no reason to assume that their economic bases were the same as those of villas on the west coast (themselves diverse), let alone corresponded to the Columellan model of the slave-run villa emphasizing cash-crop production that Carandini (for example – see section 17.7.2, this chapter) has applied to western villas like Settefinestre. The relative prosperity of the villas of the Biferno Valley (such as Matrice) suggests that they produced surplus for export, but the archaeological remains and environment suggest that this was based on arable production and pastoralism, and there is virtually no evidence of slave labor (Barker, Lloyd, and Webley, 1978: 41–42; Lloyd, 1991: 181–85; Lloyd in

Barker, 1995: 224–26, 232–36). In rural areas like this beyond the western "core" of villa development, structures definable as villas were fewer in number and related to smaller farm sites in different ways. We can see this in the hinterland of the *colonia* of Saturnia, for example, just some 40 km inland from Settefinestre and the coastal *Ager Cosanus* that was dominated by villas in the late first century BC/late first century AD. Around Saturnia, villas were fewer overall, coexisted with smaller farms to a greater extent, and survived longer (Regoli in Carandini and Cambi, 2002: 150–152). This was, perhaps, because of the area's relative remoteness and the more marginal nature of its agricultural land. Most villa owners in this area were probably local elites rather than absentee landowners, and both the distance from the coast (and thus from non-local urban markets) as well as the nature of the terrain favored extensive exploitation (livestock, for example) rather than intensive production for export.

The agricultural and socio-cultural landscapes of Roman Italy were diverse, and certainly no single agricultural regime or mode of production dominated the entire peninsula. Nevertheless, rural residences of some size, wealth, and complexity, whether the "classic" villas of central-western Italy or otherwise, from which we may surmise their owners' elite status, existed in many areas.

17.5 *Fructus* and *Luxuria*: Production and Luxury in the Italian Villa

Most villas fulfilled a range of economic and socio-cultural functions. On the one hand, even imperial residences like that at Villa Magna near Anagni (south-east of Rome; Fentress and Maiuro, 2011) and the vast and luxurious Villa dei Papiri near Herculaneum (see section 17.7.1 below) provide some evidence of productive activities, a theme emphasized in the recent synthesis by Marzano (2007). To a great extent, the "lack" of evidence for production on particular excavated villa sites reflects the quality and extent of fieldwork rather than the real absence of productive facilities (Carandini, 1985: 1.126). On the other hand, even some small and apparently functional structures like the Villa Regina farm at Boscoreale (see section 17.7.3, this chapter) also provide some evidence of elite pretensions.

Nevertheless, both the ancient literature and modern scholarship tends to focus on (and prioritize/prefer) one or the other of these strands of villa function. In antiquity, this was a product of literary genre and competing but coexisting ideologies that tended to set in rhetorical opposition rural with urban, *otium* (leisure) with *negotium* (business), production with consumption, and traditional virtue with luxury (Marzano, 2007: 82–101; Wallace-Hadrill, 2008: 196–208). The agricultural writers typically emphasized, on the surface at least, the productive role of the villa and expressed scorn for "modern" luxury and sophistication (e.g. Cato *On Agriculture*: 3–4; Varro, *On Agriculture*: 1.13.6–7; 2.*pr*.1; 3.2.1–10) in part because that was the stated purpose of their works (Varro, *On Agriculture* 1.1.2; Columella, *On Agriculture*: 1.*pr*.10) but also because they reflected a long-standing, moralizing ideology that harked back to a (constructed) past when the leaders of the state were simple farmers like Cincinnatus, cultivating their small and simple farms (Columella, *On Agriculture*: 1.*pr*. 13–18). This *topos* is widely expressed elsewhere in Roman literature, for example in Seneca's explicitly moralizing account (*Letters*: 86.4–7) of Scipio Africanus's small and dark retirement villa at Liternum, near Cumae. Writers' exploitation of this *topos* typically reflected contemporary aims and agendas. Even the agricultural manuals are not the straightforward practical handbooks that some modern scholars (White, 1970: 19–24; Dalby, 1998; Astin, 1978: 240–66) suggest. Cato's emphasis on production, self-sufficiency, and rural simplicity made a virtue of his *novus homo* status in contrast to the wealth of the *nobiles*

(D'Arms, 2003: 23–24; Terrenato, 2001: 24–25), and Plutarch's claim (*Life of Cato the Elder*: 21.5–6) that Cato himself in later life preferred other means of making money to agriculture, including maritime loans, perhaps undermines the image of rustic virtue. Varro was a wealthy and sophisticated writer whose own villas (at Tusculum, for example – see Cicero *Letters to his Friends*: 9.2.4) are unlikely to have been as basic as some of those described in his *On Agriculture*, and the dichotomy of degenerate luxury and rustic virtue which he presented in his discussion of villas (in *On Agriculture* 3) is a teasing rhetorical one adopted for satirical effect (Purcell, 1995: 151–54; Wallace-Hadrill, 2008: 197–98). Vitruvius, a technical writer of a different kind, also emphasized and advocated the rustic and productive aspects of the villa in that section of his architectural treatise explicitly dedicated to them (*On Architecture*: 6.5.2; 6.6 – see Wallace-Hadrill, 2008: 199–200), while at the same time admitting the possibility of luxury (and thus setting up an opposition between urban luxury and simple rural productivity) by referring the reader who seeks something "more refined" (*quid delicatius*) in his villa to his precepts on the architecture and decoration of town houses.

A similar taste for constructed rustic simplicity can be seen in Latin poetry, typically presented in opposition to urban life or (as in Varro's treatise) to more sophisticated forms of rural living. Horace (*Odes*: 2.18; *Satires*: 2.6) contrasted the rustic simplicity of his Sabine farm and Martial (*Epigrams*: 6.43; 12.57) that of his suburban villa near Nomentum (characterized as *parva rura*, "a little country place") with both the urban sophistication of Rome and the luxurious villas of the metropolitan elite at Baiae on the Bay of Naples. While poets and others may well have received smaller rural properties as gifts from patrons (Rawson, 1976: 93–94 on the "intellectual's farm") one should regard claims of simplicity with suspicion. Horace himself (*Epistles*: 1.14.3) implied that his estate was big enough to have five tenant families, and if the site in the Licenza valley traditionally identified as such really is Horace's Sabine villa (which is not particularly likely), then it was significantly larger and more luxurious than Horace's poems suggest (Frischer, Crawford, and De Simone, 2006).

The modern study of villas has also tended to emphasize one or the other of luxury or production (or socio-cultural versus economic significance), for a variety of disciplinary and methodological reasons. On the one hand, study of the villa lifestyles of individuals like Cicero, Horace, and Pliny the Younger remained attractive to scholars whose primary background was philological. The survival and selective excavation of architecture, mosaics, sculpture, and wall paintings, initially for collectors and the antiquities market, and subsequently for art historical study, encouraged a scholarly emphasis on villas as luxury residences. This is a strand of scholarship that has evolved and remains strong (see, for example, Mattusch, 2005).

On the other hand, developing trends in ancient economic history from the 1920s onwards led to studies that emphasized productive aspects of villas (for example, Rostovtzeff, 1926: 30 with 551–53, n. 26; Carrington, 1931), a development enhanced from the 1960s by new techniques in environmental and landscape archaeology. While the excavation, study, and publication of the villa of Settefinestre near Cosa in western Tuscany (Carandini, 1985) was also exemplary in its presentation of the architecture and decoration of the residence, its main emphasis was on the interpretation of its productive capacity as a model of the Marxist slave mode of production. Some recent studies of villas have continued to focus on the villa as a productive unit, but in a more nuanced and diverse way, notably the synthesis by Marzano (2007). As she demonstrates, one can generally point to some evidence for productive capacity in any particular villa. It need not be solely agricultural, and may extend to textiles (Marzano, 2007: 121–24; Roth, 2007: esp. 53–118), clay-pits, fish-farming, for example, and covers a spectrum from self-sufficiency (advocated by Cato, *On Agriculture*: 2.7) and production for the owner's consumption (whether on site or at an urban residence – see Horace, *Epistles*: 2.2.158–171) to large-scale production for the market, for profit, as envisaged by the agricultural writers and advocated in various interpretations of Settefinestre (Carandini, 1985: 1.165–69; Purcell, 1988: 196–97).

Some recent studies, while eschewing traditional philological and art historical approaches, have downplayed the idea of the villa as a predominantly economic phenomenon, emphasizing instead its role as elite symbol and center of consumption. Millett (discussing the western provinces, quoted in Morley, 1996: 130) sums up this approach, stating that "the opulent villa is not the result of a particular mode of production but of a decision to display existing wealth in a particular way," echoed by Terrenato (2001: 27): "there is little direct indication that [the villas] were what made their owners affluent."

While the nature of the evidence makes it convenient and perhaps even necessary to separate out, in the first instance, themes of production and luxury/consumption, in reality they both reflect status and power. Viewed from "inside" Roman culture, the important thing is how both aspects were balanced and reconciled (Purcell, 1995; Wallace-Hadrill, 2008: 204–08). Taking a view from "outside" Roman culture, we need not draw a distinction between production and luxury, but can consider them as slightly different manifestations of the same thing. The urban architecture and physical trappings of luxury seen in the *pars urbana* of Settefinestre (for example) can be read as cultural symbols of power (Wallace-Hadrill, 2008: 205 characterizes this as demonstrating "control of wealth and the ability to impose on the countryside an alien cultural language"); the productive aspects of the villa (the presses, the slave cells, and so on) and the control and ownership of land, labor, and surplus which they imply also represent power, the ability to exploit. This is clearly the case at Settefinestre, but also, for example, at a villa such as Matrice, where the overt luxury was on a lesser scale but still, even as a weak reflection of metropolitan elite culture, served to mark out the status of the owner in local terms, as did the size of the estate and its productive facilities and capabilities, whether for local consumption or the market, whether realized through the exploitation of slaves or social-political control of free labor. Villas may be different in functions, appearance, and complexity but fundamentally they reflected their owners' status and power, or at least their aspiration for these things.

17.6 *Otium* and *Negotium* in Villa Lifestyles: Literary Evidence

17.6.1 Otium

As already noted, some categories of written evidence, particularly the letters of Cicero and the Younger Pliny, emphasized the socio-cultural aspects of villas and villa life, and this evidence provides a vivid insight into some aspects of the uses to which villas were put, as well as the fabric of the villas themselves. Typically this evidence presented villas (the writers' own, and those of their friends) as venues for social and cultural gatherings, the exercise of *otium* in comfortable and pleasurable surroundings, literary, and philosophical activities, and the display of art. On the other hand, we also see villas performing some of the public (or at least semi-public) functions of the elite town house (*domus*), displaying the status and wealth of the owner and his family, acting as places to receive clients and guests, and even for informal political activity. On the surface, this appears to run contrary to the emphasis on the villa as a place of *otium* (leisure, or at least, freedom from public life), in contrast to the *negotium* that was the main focus of city life. However, in reality, the two were not incompatible.

Ancient writers often presented villas as places where their owners could escape the stresses of life in Rome (Horace, *Satires*: 2.6; Martial, *Epigrams*: 12.57) to enjoy *otium*. This encompassed both relaxation in the sense of rest (including rest and recuperation from illness – Cicero, *Letters to his Friends*: 7.26.1; 16.18), and also cultural activities that could be pursued free from the pressures of public life in Rome. Pliny the Younger (*Letters*: 2.2.3) recorded, "here in my villa, I enjoy both *desidia* (relaxation, laziness) and *studium* (intellectual activity), both of which are born of *otium*."

Cultural activities can be seen in the evidence for the literary production and philosophical activities undertaken in these rural retreats, as well as in their outfitting with libraries and works of art. Pliny the Younger (*Letters*: 4.6) playfully claimed that his Laurentine villa was the most productive of all his rural estates, although it only contained the house, a garden, and the sands of the coastal dunes (although in *Letters*: 2.17.15 and 2.17.28 he praised its productive garden, its milk and the fish to be had from the sea). For, he wrote, "there I have plenty of opportunity to write, and I cultivate not wide-ranging fields (which I don't have) but my intellectual output. I can show you full granaries elsewhere, but at Laurentum I can show you a desk piled high with writing….if you seek a sure and fruitful estate, buy one on this coast." Literary evidence shows that some villas were equipped to support their owners' cultural activities. Libraries, of course, were crucial. Cicero (*Topics*: 1.1), for example, referred to Trebatius consulting Aristotle's *Topics* in the *bibliotheca* of Cicero's Tusculum villa. The idea that a villa might include a philosophical library is, of course, borne out by the archaeological evidence from the Villa dei Papiri at Herculaneum (section 17.7.1, this chapter). Structures within Cicero's villa complex were also named to reflect and inspire such cultural activities. For example (*On Divination*: 1.18) the upper *gymnasium* of the villa was called the "Lycaeum" after the center of Aristotelian philosophy in Athens, and he also referred to an "Academy" (*Letters to Atticus*: 1.9.2). Many of Cicero's philosophical works were written or set in villas, including (of course) the *Tusculan Disputations*, and (as already noted) the *Academy*.

Villas, like urban *domus*, could house collections of art to display their owners' cultural taste and enhance their status in the eyes of visitors, as well as decorating the buildings in a more general sense. Varro and his characters were scornful of the *pinacothecae* (picture galleries) in the notoriously luxurious villas owned by Lucullus in Tusculum and on the Bay of Naples (*On Agriculture*: 1.2.10; on Lucullus's villas more generally, see Plutarch, *Life of Luculls*: 39; Cicero, *On the Laws*: 3.30). Over a century after Varro, Pliny the Younger (*Letters*: 2.7) emphasized the books and works of art kept in the numerous Campanian villas of Silius Italicus, the famous writer, orator, and politician. Some such works of art clearly were expensive masterpieces. Pliny the Elder (*Natural History*: 35.130) recorded that the orator Hortensius had Kydias's painting of *The Argonauts*, bought for 144 000 sesterces, set in its own shrine (*aedes*) in his Tusculum villa. In contrast, Cicero's numerous letters to Atticus in 68–65 BC (see, for example, *Letters to Atticus*: 1.8.2; 1.9.2; 1.10.1) and later letters to friends (*Letters to his Friends*: 7.23; 7.11.2) show a preoccupation with acquiring sculpture and paintings for his Tusculum villa, but largely as generic decor for particular parts of the villa (its *palaestra* and *gymnasium*, for the most part), rather than as individual masterpieces. As in urban *domus*, contemporary works of art in villas could be used to advertise an individual's status and achievements in a very direct way. Sulla, for example, had a painting done for his Tusculum villa (the villa later owned by Cicero) depicting himself being crowned by his army with the *corona graminea* ("grassy crown": Pliny the Elder, *Natural History* 22.12).

The *Villa dei Papiri* at Herculaneum provides excellent archaeological evidence for the display of sculpture in a villa setting (see later in this chapter; Mattusch, 2005), as does Sperlonga (Stewart, 1977), and wall paintings have survived to a greater or lesser degree at many villa sites, where they can sometimes be studied as ensembles within their urban contexts, with particularly fine examples from the (in antiquity) coastal villa at Oplontis near Herculaneum.

Besides such manifestations of high culture, literary descriptions of villas also depicted other luxuries that enhanced the status or the comfort of their owner. As noted above, while *piscinae* (fishponds) might have had productive potential, they were largely treated as "Lucullan" displays of status and luxury rather than profit, with colored and "dancing" fish providing spectacle, and tame fish feeding from their owners' hands (Varro, *On Agriculture*: 3.17.4–6). Varro was also, on the surface, scornful of the elaborate dining rooms, pavements, and floors of contemporary villas (*On Agriculture*: 2.*pr*.1; 3.1.10). Otherwise, literary accounts of villas (in particular Pliny the Younger's detailed descriptions of his Laurentum and Tifernum villas – *Letters*: 2.17; 5.6) emphasized things like gardens (von Stackelberg, 2009: esp. 125–34 on Pliny; MacDougall, 1987), fountains, promenades and exercise areas, baths, and heated rooms. Villas might also exploit views over the surrounding countryside, or particularly, in the case of coastal villas, seascapes. This is one of the things emphasized by Statius (*Silvae*: 2.2; Bergmann, 1991), whose account of a coastal villa near Surrentum emphasizes how nature was controlled and exploited by its terraces and colonnades built on the cliffs and rooms with views of both rising and setting sun, as well as the kinds of decor (marble veneer, sculpture) attested in other villas. Even agriculture could serve as a form of cultural entertainment (as well as "economic" activity) for the wealthy villa owner. He might himself engage in what Goodman (2007: 24) has characterized as "pastiche" agriculture, as the young Marcus Aurelius did at Villa Magna, and dine in sight of real agricultural labor undertaken by his dependents (Fronto, *Correspondence*: 4.5).

17.6.2 Negotium

Despite the emphasis on villas as venues for *otium*, to escape the pressures of urban life, and the opposition of urban *domus* and rural *villa*, it is clear that villa life might serve, in some ways, as an extension of urban life, a location for *negotium*, for receiving clients and political allies. In the Republican period, the concentration of senators' villas in particular areas facilitated their use as venues for informal political networking, meetings, and other activities. Cicero (*Letters to Atticus*: 5.2.1–2, May 51 BC), in his villa at Cumae, described a visit from Hortensius seeking instructions on what Cicero wanted his political allies to do while he was absent in Cilicia, as well as "a great crowd of others besides," to the extent that he described Cumae as *pusilla Roma*, "a little Rome." In the politically heated aftermath of Caesar's assassination, in the spring of 44 BC, Cicero was again at Cumae, surrounded by individuals plotting while Mark Antony was in control of Rome: "Balbus, Hirtius, and Pansa are with me here. Then Octavius (i.e. Octavian) came, and he's in Philippus' villa nearby, completely dedicated to me. Lentulus Spinther is here with me today. He's leaving tomorrow morning." (*Letters to Atticus* 14.11.2; see also 14.12.2; 15.1.2–3). He noted (*Letters to Atticus*, 14.16.1) that while his properties at Puteoli and Cumae were desirable places, they were "almost to be avoided because of the crowds of visitors' at that time. Cicero's *On Oratory*, an imaginary dialog set in the Tusculum villa of M. Antonius (the grandfather of the triumvir) in 91 BC, starts with a reference to heated political discussion between Antonius, L. Licinius Crassus, and other influential guests, but Cicero claimed that Crassus's charm was such "that what had seemed like a day in the senate-house turned into a social gathering at Tusculum." This reflects both the expected contrast between political activity in Rome and *otium* at Tusculum, and the real possibility of informal political activity even at the latter.

On the other hand, a rural villa in a location like Tusculum might be a place to lie low in times of political strife or under an unacceptable regime, despite the presence of numerous senatorial neighbors. In the aftermath of the Caesarian victory over the Pompeians at Thapsus in 46 BC, Cicero wrote (*Letters to his Friends*: 9.2.4) from Rome to Varro (the author of *On*

Agriculture) advising him to stay in his own Tusculum villa until it was clearer what might happen, and he characterized Varro's situation there as "in harbor" (*in portu*) while he himself was battered by political storms in Rome. Cicero himself fled proscription to his coastal villa at Caieta before he was caught and killed there (Plutarch, *Life of Cicero*: 47) in 43 BC.

Of course, villas were also venues for meeting clients and other dependents associated with one's rural estates. While Cicero's and Pliny's letters mostly focus on interaction with their peers, and their cultural lives, they sometimes shed light on estate business such as relations with tenants (Pliny, *Letters*: 9.37; Cicero, *Letters to his Friends*: 16.18.2; *Letters to Atticus*: 13.11.1. See also Wallace-Hadrill, 2008: 205 on access and villa architecture).

17.7   Villas in Archaeology: Case Studies (Villa dei Papiri; Settefinestre; Villa Regina)

The following case studies are provided to illustrate some of the main features of a selection of villas known (or rediscovered) from recent archaeological excavation. They cover a range of establishments: a large and luxurious coastal villa (the Villa dei Papiri at Herculaneum); a large villa that provides clear evidence that it served as the center of a large agricultural estate as well as a luxurious residence (Settefinestre); and a small, primarily agricultural, establishment at the lower end of the villa spectrum, in the territory of Pompeii (the Villa Regina site).

17.7.1   *The Villa dei Papiri, Herculaneum*

The Villa dei Papiri (Villa of the Papyri), buried in the eruption of Vesuvius in AD 79 (see Figure 17.1), provides a fine example of a coastal suburban villa, constructed on a huge scale with an emphasis on luxury. Past investigation of the site has provided an unprecedented knowledge of the villa's "cultural furnishings," including sculpture, painting, stuccowork and, exceptionally, its library, from which it takes its name. Recent excavation has also shown how the villa's architect adapted the natural topography of the site by terracing, to exploit its

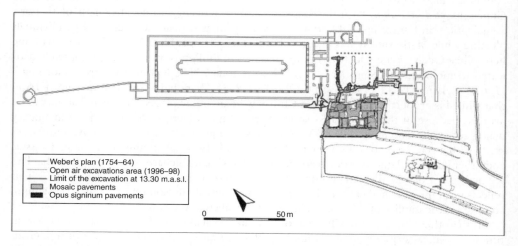

Figure 17.1   Plan of the Villa dei Papiri, Herculaneum. Drawn by Massimo Brizzi. By permission of Sarah Court, Herculaneum Conservation Project.

proximity to the sea and its sea views, a feature of coastal villas known from wall painting, literature (Statius, *Silvae*: 2.2; Bergmann, 1991), and from examples such as the Villa Arianna and Villa San Marco at Stabiae. In antiquity, the Villa dei Papiri lay by the sea (now receded) and just north-west of Herculaneum itself (see De Simone, 2010: 8–9). Until recently, much of what we knew about the villa derived from tunneling excavation undertaken by the Swiss engineer Karl Weber in 1750–1760 (Parslow, 1995: esp. 77–106), primarily to obtain arti-facts for his Bourbon patrons. This he did in spectacular fashion, including 68 bronze and 24 marble statues and some 1800 rolls of Latin and (mostly) Greek papyri (sculpture: Mattusch, 2005; papyri: Sider, 2005; Gigante, 1995).

Weber reconstructed the villa's plan from his tunneling. It was a huge structure, over 200 m by 70 m, its long axis parallel to the coast, rivaling the length of the seafront of Herculaneum itself. Its size is exceptional but not unprecedented. The Villa Arianna at Stabiae, for example, is of similar magnitude. In terms of plan, the Villa dei Papiri had a peristyle–*atrium* axis, with the peristyle preceding (from the land side) the *atrium*. This was the opposite of the usual sequence in a *domus*, as recommended for villas by Vitruvius (*On Architecture*: 6.5.3; see Wallace-Hadrill, 2008: 200–05). Other archaeologically attested examples of a peristyle–atrium plan include Settefinestre and the suburban Villa of the Mysteries at Pompeii. The *atrium* looked out to sea through a colonnaded facade. To the north-west side of the *atrium*–peristyle axis was a huge (circa 100 m by 30 m) colonnaded garden, and beyond that a passageway leading to a circular pavilion. The whole complex was lavishly decorated with Pompeiian Second Style (and some Pompeiian Fourth-Style) paint-ings, black and white and polychrome mosaics, and stuccoed ceilings. The scale and luxury of the villa has led scholars to assume, probably rightly, that the owner was a member of an established senatorial family from Rome, and perhaps L. Calpurnius Piso Caesoninus, consul in 58 BC, father-in-law of Julius Caesar, and target of Cicero's *Against Piso*. Much of the argument (summarized by Mattusch, 2005: 20–23) focuses on Piso's known adherence to Epicurean philosophy and on the fact that the majority of the papyri discovered contain works of the contemporary Epicurean Philodemos of Gadara. Besides the papyri, our knowledge of the sculptural ensemble of the villa in its contexts provides a unique concentration of material to complement written sources.

Of course, the Villa dei Papiri was destroyed in AD 79. New, open-air, excavations in 1991–1998 and 2007–2008 concluded (on the basis of construction techniques and decorative ensembles) that the villa was essentially planned and constructed in a single phase circa 60 BC (De Simone, 2010: 14; although Guidobaldi and Esposito, 2010: 57 date the original decoration to circa 40–30 BC). The most dramatic new insights produced by the recent exca-vations relate to the vertical dimension of the villa. Weber's plan implies that it was built on a single plane, whereas in fact it was built against a hillside on at least four terraced levels, with the main level comprising the *atrium* and peristyle set on a platform with a second level of finely decorated rooms; a third level with remains of curvilinear architecture and large win-dows; and a fourth level, nine metres below the *atrium* floor level, comprising a terrace with remains of a hall decorated with marble *opus sectile*, a swimming pool, and steps to the sea itself (De Simone, 2010: 11–18; Guidobaldi and Esposito, 2010: 33–50). This completely alters our image of the villa from that presented by Weber's plan. Clearly the terraces and colonnades of the villa presented a dramatic "scenographic" arrangement of carefully articu-lated levels when viewed from the sea, like the coastal villas known from Pompeian wall paint-ings. Conversely, the architecture was designed to enhance the views out to sea from the upper levels, and to provide direct access to the shoreline from the lower terrace. In these respects it was like other known coastal villas, such as the Villa Arianna and Villa San Marco at Stabiae, with their spectacular hillside sea views, and the villa attributed to Tiberius at Sperlonga, with its sea access (see Lafon, 2001 on coastal villa architecture).

While it would be easy to assume that leisure was the sole function of the Villa dei Papiri, some possible evidence of productive activity has been found even given the limited and selective excavation of the site, including concentrations of fish-hooks and grain. Typically this has been dismissed as evidence of a late (and negative) change in use of the villa (Mustilli, 1983; see Wallace-Hadrill, 2008: 205–07 on Maiuri's similar arguments for the press room of the Villa of the Mysteries at Pompeii), but it seems more likely that the villa exploited (at least for local consumption) the resources of the sea and an agricultural hinterland, perhaps through outlying smaller farms (see earlier in this chapter).

17.7.2   Settefinestre

The villa of Settefinestre, near the *colonia* of Cosa in western Etruria, provides a well-documented example of a "classic" villa of the imperial period, combining a luxurious *pars urbana* with a well-excavated *pars rustica* with evidence of intensive agriculture employing slave labor (Carandini, 1985; site summary in Marzano, 2007: 655–57; see Figure 17.2). The stratigraphic excavation of Settefinestre (1976–1981) was one of the earliest in Italy (besides the Francolise excavations) to employ a wide range of environmental archaeological techniques to help understand the agricultural and consumption economies of the villa. It shows that Settefinestre was built in the 40s–30s BC, with two main periods of use, the first from construction to the Flavian period, and the second in the Trajanic/Antonine period, before it fell out of use in the late second century AD.

The main focus of the villa estate was a rectangular block circa 45 by 75 m, set on a terrace. This included the *pars urbana*, a compact adjacent *pars fructuaria* with oil and wine processing facilities, and the *pars rustica*, a courtyard flanked by slave accommodation (in the first phase), stalls for livestock, and other agricultural buildings (see Figure 17.3). A larger rectangular block (circa 85 by 110 m) incorporated this main block along with a walled garden (with distinctive turreted dovecotes found on other villas in the area) in front, a porticoed garden adjacent to the *pars urbana* and additional structures (new slave quarters, a larger bath suite) added in the second period. There were other outlying elements of the villa estate beyond this, including a large granary and walled orchard, and, of course, the agricultural land of the estate, estimated (since there is no direct archaeological evidence) by the excavators as circa 500 *iugera* (Carandini, 1985: 1.168).

The *pars urbana* bears strong similarities to contemporary urban *domus*, but with the reversed peristyle–*atrium* axis advised by Vitruvius (*On Architecture*: 6.5.3) for country residences. This was flanked by rooms including a Corinthian *oecus* (dining room) to the west (Carandini, 1985: 1.153; 2.20–23). These residential quarters were finely decorated, with painted Second Style perspectival architecture comparable to that of the House of Augustus in Rome (Carandini, 1985: 1.81–89; 2.215–40), mosaic floors, stucco moldings, and some imported marble veneer. The luxurious nature of the residence was enhanced by its ornamental gardens, apparently modified into specialized exercise areas (*xystus* and *palaestra*) when a grander bath suite was added in the second period of use (Carandini, 1985: 1.173; 2.111–146).

The villa provides evidence for a mixed agricultural regime, with its large granary, animal stalls, orchard, and olive press (Carandini, 1985: 1.169–170; 1.164–65). However, Carandini (1985: 1.165–69), drawing heavily on Roman agricultural manuals, interprets the wine processing facilities (including three presses) at Settefinestre as the most profitable part of the villa estate. He argues that, while the acreage devoted to arable production was perhaps three times that of the vineyard (calculated from the capacities of the granary and the wine tanks), the grain was largely for local use while the wine produced could have been sold for circa

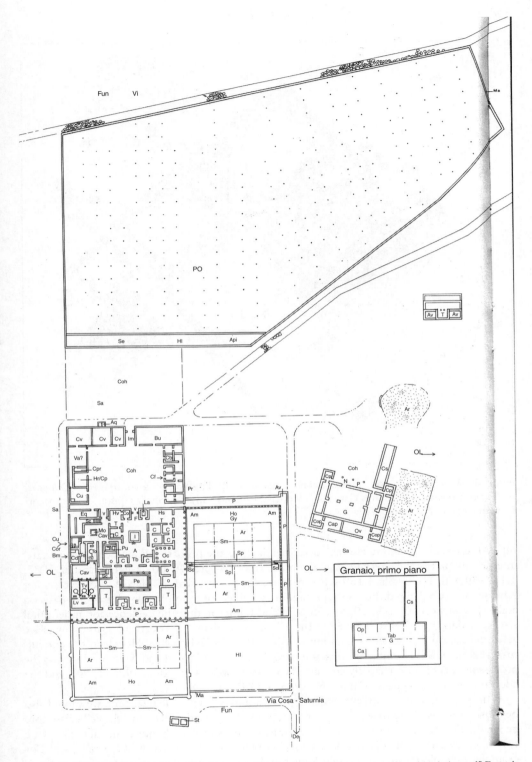

Figure 17.2 Plan of the Settefinestre Roman villa. From *Settefinestre: una villa schiavistica nell' Etruria romana*, ed. Andrea Carandini (Modena: Panini, 1985) 014: R. Caciagli e M. Rossella Filippi. By permission of Alessandro Vicenzi.

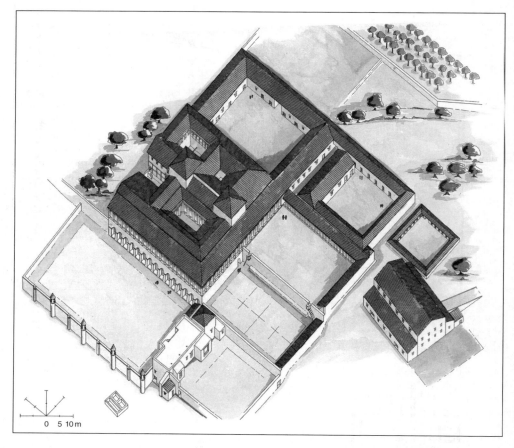

Figure 17.3 Reconstruction of the Settefinestre Roman villa. From *Settefinestre: una villa schiavistica nell' Etruria romana*, ed. Andrea Carandini (Modena: Panini, 1985) 011: Sheila Gibson - Maura Medri. By permission of Alessandro Vicenzi.

60 000 sesterces. Carandini also characterizes slaves as the primary labor force for the estate, interpreting part of the *pars rustica* as accommodation for circa 40–60 slaves (Carandini, 1985: 1.157–60 with 2.152–65; 1.159 sets out a possible scheme with 52 slaves). However, other scholars have challenged these interpretations, arguing, for example, for greater emphasis on arable production (Purcell, 1988: 196–97), and reinterpreting the evidence for agricultural slavery (Marzano, 2007: 125–53). In the second phase, a courtyard with new slave accommodation was added (Carandini, 1985, 1.175–78; 2.171–81). However, the agricultural regime in this second period changed too, with an end to oil and wine production (the processing facilities were largely converted to storage areas: Carandini, 1985: 1.180) and the addition of a large piggery (Carandini, 1985: 1.179; 2.182–88).

As noted, aspects of the excavators' interpretation have been challenged, and we should also be cautious in assuming that Settefinestre can be used as a model for even "classic" villas more generally. For example, excavation of the nearby (and superficially quite similar) villa of Le Colonne, revealed some distinct differences between the two villas as well as similarities. For example, Le Colonne shows a much longer and more complicated occupation history, with origins in the second century BC but little evidence of habitation in the late Republic.

Le Colonne was certainly occupied in the Julio-Claudian period, but that site reveals a hiatus in the later first century AD (probably due to evident structural damage, perhaps from an earthquake that affected Cosa in AD 51) and later periods of occupation in the second and fourth centuries AD (Marzano, 2007: 651–53; Dyson, 2002). Nevertheless, the excavation and publication of Settefinestre was a remarkable achievement, not least in the way it illuminated the agricultural activities of the villa as well as presenting the evidence for elite accommodation.

17.7.3   Boscoreale: The Villa Regina farm site

This site lies within the territory of Pompeii, about 1 km north-east of the suburban Villa of the Mysteries (see Figure 17.4). It contrasts with Settefinestre dramatically in its size and luxury, and in some respects is comparable to the Giardino Vecchio farm in the *Ager Cosanus*, cited earlier in this chapter as an example of a marginal "sub-villa" site. But its (modest) wine processing facilities perhaps suggest a degree of investment, and the Fourth Style wall paintings in some of its rooms perhaps imply that the owner was an occasional visitor of (probably local) elite status, or else a smallholder who sought to emulate local urban elites on some basic level, thus qualifying it as a villa in the terms set out above (see De Caro, 1994: 125–26 on ownership. Note that "Villa Regina" is a modern toponym). Its excavator De Caro (1994) characterizes it as a small *villa rustica*, and (following on from the discussion of Varro's use of the term above) it certainly lacks a developed *pars urbana* like Settefinestre's. In its agricultural emphasis it is similar to numerous other small inland villas in the territory of Pompeii

Figure 17.4   Overall view of Villa Regina, Boscoreale. Photograph: Nigel Pollard.

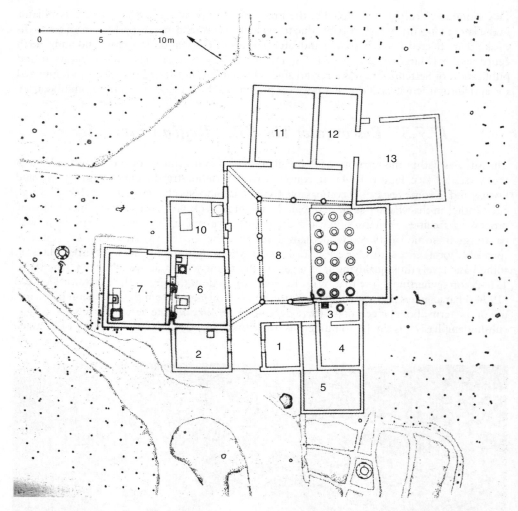

Figure 17.5 Plan of the Villa Regina, Boscoreale. From *Uomo e ambiente nel territorio vesuviano*, ed. G. Stefani, Marius edizioni, Pompei (2002): 122. By permission of Anna Maria Penna.

and beyond that were buried by the AD 79 eruption of Vesuvius (see De Caro, 1994, tav. A; Carrington, 1931), although there were also larger and grander villas with a greater emphasis on luxury, such as those attributed to Agrippa Postumus at Boscotrecase and P. Fannius Synistor at Boscoreale (Rostovtzeff, 1926: 551–53, n.26). However, the relatively recent (1977–1983) excavation and investigation of the Villa Regina site meant that more refined methodologies could be applied to its study than to many of the other sites, including proper study (and thus reconstruction) of collapsed upper stories, and detailed study of the agricultural facilities and adjacent garden and vineyard (by making casts of voids left by roots, directed by Wilhelmina Jashemski – De Caro, 1994: 95–114).

The villa buildings form a rough rectangle circa 25 by 20 m, arranged around a central courtyard (see Figure 17.5). Careful excavation showed that most of the villa was built on two stories, although most of the upper story was destroyed by the eruption. De Caro (1994: 116–22) argues from the excavated evidence that the villa originated in the late second/early first century BC, was expanded in the Augustan period, and achieved its definitive form in the Julio-Claudian period. Parts of the villa were undergoing restoration in AD 79, although it was still in use. The areas that provide evidence of luxury, on a basic level at least, are a room with remains of Third Style painting (black ground with white candelabrum motifs) in the south part of the villa that De Caro interprets (although room function is difficult to determine with any certainty) as a *cubiculum* (4 on plan; De Caro, 1994: 71–72; its floor had been removed and the level was being lowered in AD 79) and another room, interpreted as a *triclinium* (and probably a reception room of some sort, given its size and decor) on the east side (11 on plan; De Caro, 1994: 51–56). This also had remains of Third Style painted plaster, with red, yellow, and black panels, flimsy pseudo-architectural motifs, and birds.

The central courtyard (8 on plan) was clearly a functional area, flanked on three sides by a portico supported by brick columns plastered and painted white and red. To the north-west of the court is the wine pressing complex (6–7 on plan); De Caro, 1994: 35–46), whose structural elements (sockets for the press itself, waterproof cement flooring, a lead conduit and a sunken *dolium* for collecting the grape must) have survived, along with plaster-cast evidence for some wooden elements. Grapes could be fed into the pressing area from the vineyard outside through a window in the press room wall. On the opposite (south-east) side of the central court was the *cella vinaria*, a group of 18 sunken *dolia* for fermentation and storage of the wine (9 on plan; De Caro, 1994: 63–69; see Figure 17.6). The total capacity of the *dolia* was circa 10 000 litres, about a tenth of the estimated output of Settefinestre, with its three presses (Carandini, 1985: 1.167). Plaster-casting of root voids showed dense planting of vines around the Boscoreale villa, but also a functional garden area and some fruit,

Figure 17.6   *Cella vinaria*, Villa Regina, Boscoreale. Photograph: Nigel Pollard.

nut, or olive trees. A room to the east was interpreted as a store for grain, hay or legumes, with a large opening onto a yard paved with cocciopesto and low retaining wall (12–13 on plan; De Caro, 1994: 56–63) that could have served as (among other things) a drying and threshing floor. So crops besides wine may have been produced, for local consumption at least, and the body of a pig was also found (and cast in plaster – De Caro, 1994: tav. 12b) in the villa.

17.8   Decline?

The case studies presented here all conform to the general chronological trend discussed above, that presents villas in Roman Italy as predominantly a phenomenon of the first century BC to first century AD, although, of course, the lives of the Villa Regina site and the Villa dei Papiri were cut short by the eruption of Vesuvius in AD 79. Broadly speaking, this chronological model is a valid one. However, Marzano's (2007: fig. 19) compilation of chronological evidence discussed above shows 142 of her sample of central Italian villa sites still occupied in the third century AD, and 42 of them continuing into the fifth century (see Chapter 8 for more on villas in late antiquity). Thus while the number of new constructions plummeted after the first century AD, many villas continued to be occupied or re-occupied. Villa life remained an important phenomenon among the elite in late antique Italy, as demonstrated in the letters of the fourth-century senator Symmachus (e.g. *Letters*: 2.19; 7.18; 7.24), who, like his friends owned numerous suburban and rural villas in Italy. Seeck (1883: xlv–xlvi) lists 18 such properties, including examples at such familiar locations as Laurentum, Tibur, and Praeneste (see *Letters*: 7.15; 6.81; 3.50 respectively, to cite just a few references) along with Baiae and other sites on the Bay of Naples (e.g. *Letters*: 7.24; D'Arms, 2003: 214–16). We also have the remains of numerous grand sites of late antique date for which the term *villa* is perfectly appropriate, such as the Villa of the Quintilii on the outskirts of Rome (Frontoni, 2006), and the Casale Villa near Piazza Armerina in Sicily (Carandini, Ricci, and de Vos 1982).

FURTHER READING

Terrenato 2007 and Dyson 2003 are useful as general introductions to the concept of the villa in the Roman world, and in setting villas in the wider context of the Roman countryside. Marzano 2007 is of great value both in her discussions of crucial themes relating to villa culture and villa economies, but also as a source of data and bibliography for further study. Lafon 2001 provides a similar service focused on coastal villas, with both thematic discussion and useful data. The papers recently published in Becker and Terrenato 2012 explore in greater depth and from a number of perspectives some of the themes addressed in this chapter.

REFERENCES

Astin, A. E. 1978. *Cato the Censor*. Oxford: Clarendon Press.
Attolini, I., Perkins, P. 1992. "The Excavation of an Etruscan Farm at Podere Tartuchino." *Papers of the British School at Rome* 60: 1–76.
Barker, G. 1995. *The Biferno Valley Survey: the archaeological and geomorphological record*. Leicester: Leicester University Press.
Barker, G., Lloyd, J., Webley, D. 1978. "A Classical Landscape in Molise." *Papers of the British School at Rome* 46: 35–51.

Becker, J. and Terrenato, N., eds. 2012. *Roman Republican Villas: architecture, context and ideology.* Ann Arbor: University of Michigan Press.

Bergmann, B. 1991. "Painted perspectives of a villa visit: landscape as status and metaphor." In *Roman Art in the Private Sphere*, ed. E.K. Gazda, 49–70. Ann Arbor: University of Michigan Press.

Camardo, D. 2004. "Mount Vesuvius and human settlement in the Gulf of Naples in the first century AD." In *In Stabiano: exploring the ancient seaside villas of the Roman elite*, 25–33. Castellamare di Stabiae: Nicola Longobardi Editore.

Cambi, F. 2002. "La casa del Colono e il paesaggio (III–II secolo a.C.)." In *Paesaggi D'Etruria: Valle dell'Albegna, Valle d'Oro, Valle del Chiarone, Valle del Tafone*, eds A. Carandini and F. Cambi, 137–45. Rome: Edizioni di Storia e Letteratura.

Carandini, A. 1983. "Columella's vineyard and the rationality of the Roman economy." *Opus* 2: 177–204.

Carandini, A., ed. 1985. *Settefinestre: una villa schiavistica nell'Etruria romana.* 3 vols. Modena: Edizioni Panini.

Carandini, A., Ricci, A., de Vos, M. 1982. Filosofiana: *The Villa of Piazza Armerina. The image of a Roman aristocrat at the time of Constantine.* Palermo: S.F. Flaccovio.

Carandini, A.and Cambi, F. 2002. *Paesaggi D'Etruria: Valle dell'Albegna, Valle d'Oro, Valle del Chiarone, Valle del Tafone.* Rome: Edizioni di Storia e Letteratura.

Carrington, R.C. 1931. "Studies in the Campanian 'Villae Rusticae'." *Journal of Roman Studies* 21: 110–30.

Cotton, M.A. 1979. *The Late Republican Villa at Posto, Francolise.* London: The British School at Rome.

Cotton, M. A. and Metraux, G.R.P. 1985. *The San Rocco Villa at Francolise.* London: The British School at Rome.

Dalby, A. 1998. *Cato: On Farming/De Agricultura.* Totnes: Prospect Books.

D'Arms, J.H. 2003. *Romans on the Bay of Naples and Other Essays on Roman Campania.* Bari: Edipuglia.

De Caro, S. 1994. *La villa rustica in località Villa Regina a Boscoreale.* Rome: «L'Erma» di Bretschneider.

De Simone, A. 2010. "Rediscovering the Villa of the Papyri." In *The Villa of the Papyri at Herculaneum: archaeology, reception and digital reconstruction*, ed. M. Zarmakoupi, 1–20. Berlin: De Gruyter.

Duncan-Jones, R. 1982 (2nd edn). *The Economy of the Roman Empire: quantitative studies.* Cambridge: Cambridge University Press.

Du Prey, P. de la R. 1994. *The Villas of Pliny from Antiquity to Posterity.* Chicago: University of Chicago Press.

Dyson, S.L. 1983. *The Villas of Buccino.* Oxford: BAR International Series 187.

Dyson, S.L. 2002. "The excavations at Le Colonne and the villa culture of the Ager Cosanus." *Memoirs of the American Academy in Rome* 47: 209–228.

Dyson, S.L. 2003. *The Roman Countryside.* London: Duckworth.

Fentress, E. 2002. "Criteri tipologici." In *Paesaggi D'Etruria: Valle dell'Albegna, Valle d'Oro, Valle del Chiarone, Valle del Tafone*, eds A. Carandini and F. Cambi, 54–59. Rome: Edizioni di Storia e Letteratura.

Fentress, E. and Maiuro, M. 2011. "Villa Magna near Anagni: the emperor, his winery and the wine of Signia." *Journal of Roman Archaeology* 24: 333–69.

Frischer, B. and Brown, I. 2001. *Allan Ramsay and the Search for Horace's Villa.* London: Ashgate.

Frischer, B., Crawford, J., De Simone, M. 2006. *The Horace's Villa Project, 1997–2003.* Oxford: Archeopress.

Frontoni, R. 2006. "Quintiliorum, Praedium." In *LTUR: Suburbium*, vol. 4, ed. A. La Regina, 279–294. Rome: Quasar.

Gigante, M. 1995. *Philodemus in Italy: the Books from Herculaneum.* Ann Arbor: University of Michigan Press.

Goodman, P.J. 2007. *The Roman City and its Periphery: from Rome to Gaul.* New York and London: Routledge.

Guidobaldi, M.P. and Esposito, D. 2010. "New archaeological research at the Villa of the Papyri." In *The Villa of the Papyri at Herculaneum: archaeology, reception and digital reconstruction*, ed. M. Zarmakoupi, 21–62. Berlin: De Gruyter.

Higginbotham, J. 1997. *Piscinae. Artificial fishponds in Roman Italy*. Chapel Hill: University of North Carolina Press.

Jones, G.D.B. 1962. "Capena and the Ager Capenas I." *Papers of the British School at Rome* 30: 116–210.

Jones, G.D.B. 1963. "Capena and the Ager Capenas." *Papers of the British School at Rome* 31: 100–81.

Lafon, X. 2001. *Villa Maritima: Recherches sur les villas littorales de l'Italie romaine* (IIIᵉ siècle av. J.-C./ IIIᵉ siècle ap. J.-C.). Rome: École Française de Rome.

Lloyd, J.A. 1991. "Farming the Highlands: Samnium and Arcadia in the Hellenistic and Early Roman Imperial Periods." In *Roman Landscapes: archaeological survey in the Mediterranean region*, eds G. Barker and J.A. Lloyd, 180–93. London: The British School at Rome.

MacDougall, E. 1987. *Ancient Roman Villa Gardens*. Washington DC: Dumbarton Oaks.

Mattusch, C.C. 2005. *The Villa dei Papiri at Herculaneum: life and afterlife of a sculpture collection*. Los Angeles: The J. Paul Getty Museum.

Marzano, A. 2007. *Roman Villas in Central Italy. A social and economic history*. Leiden and Boston: Brill.

McCann, A.M., ed. 1987. *The Roman Port and Fishery of Cosa. A center of ancient trade*. Princeton: Princeton University Press.

Morley, N. 1996. *Metropolis and Hinterland: the city of Rome and the Italian economy, 200 B.C.–A.D. 200*. Cambridge: Cambridge University Press.

Mustilli, D. 1983 [1956]. "La villa pseudourbana ercolanese." In *La Villa dei Papiri*, 7–18. Second Supplement to *Cronache ercolanesi* 13: Naples.

Parslow, C. 1995. *Rediscovering Antiquity: Karl Weber and the excavation of Herculaneum, Pompeii and Stabiae*. Cambridge: Cambridge University Press.

Purcell, N. 1988. "Review of A. Tchernia, *Le vin de l'Italie romaine* and A. Carandini *et al.*, *Settefinestre: una villa schiavistica nell' Etruria romana*." *Journal of Roman Studies* 78: 194–98.

Purcell, N. 1995. "The Roman villa and the landscape of production." In *Urban Society in Roman Italy*, eds T.J. Cornell and Kathryn Lomas, 151–79. London, UCL Press.

Rawson, E. 1976. "The Ciceronian aristocracy and its properties." In *Studies in Roman Property*, ed. M.I. Finley, 85–102. Cambridge: Cambridge University Press.

Regoli, E. 2002. "Il paesaggio delle ville (II secolo a.C-metà I a.C.)." In *Paesaggi d'Etruria*, eds A. Carandini and F. Cambi, 145–54. Rome: Edizioni di Storia e Letteratura.

Rostovtzeff, M. 1926. *The Social and Economic History of the Roman Empire*. Oxford: Oxford University Press.

Roth, U. 2007. *Thinking Tools: agricultural slavery between evidence and models*. London: Institute of Classical Studies.

Seeck, O., ed., 1883. *Symmachi Opera. Monumenta Germaniae Historica. Auctores Antiquissimi* VI. Berlin: Weidmann.

Sherwin-White, A.N. 1966. *The Letters of Pliny: a historical and social commentary*. Oxford: Oxford University Press.

Sider, D. 2005. *The Library of the Villa dei Papiri at Herculaneum*. Los Angeles: J. Paul Getty Museum.

Stackelberg, K.T. von 2009. *The Roman Garden: space, sense and society*. London: Routledge.

Stewart, A.F. 1977. "To entertain an emperor: Sperlonga, Laokoon and Tiberius at the dinner-table." *Journal of Roman Studies* 67: 76–90.

Tchernia, A. 1986. *Le vin de l'Italie romaine*. Rome: École Française de Rome.

Terrenato, N. 2001. "The Auditorium site in Rome and the origins of the villa." *Journal of Roman Archaeology* 14: 5–32.

Terrenato, N. 2007. "(4b) The essential countryside: the Roman world." In *Classical Archaeology*, eds S. Alcock and R. Osborne, 139–61. Oxford: Blackwell.

Wallace-Hadrill, A. 2008. *Rome's Cultural Revolution*. Cambridge: Cambridge University Press.

White, K.D. 1970. *Roman Farming*. London: Thames and Hudson.

Yegül, Fikret K. 1996. "The Thermo-Mineral Complex at Baiae and the *De Balneis Puteolanis*." *Art Bulletin* 78: 137–62.

3.2 Case-studies of Towns and their Territories

CHAPTER 18

Republican and Early Imperial Towns in the Tiber Valley

Simon Keay and Martin Millett[1]

18.1 Introduction

The Roman towns of the middle and lower Tiber Valley have been a subject of study since at least the sixteenth century onwards, although it was not until the early 1800s that this knowledge began to be synthesized in general works on ancient settlement in the Roman Campagna to the north of Rome, by such scholars as Sir William Gell and Antonio Nibby, and followed in the early twentieth century by the syntheses of Tomassetti and Ashby (1927). These works have provided the framework for the accumulation of new knowledge about towns and rural settlement down to the present day, the objective implicit to all of them being a better understanding of the genesis and character of Roman towns and their relationship to the growing impact of the growth of Rome during the Republican and early Imperial periods.

Until recently, our understanding of urbanism in the region drew upon a range of fragmented evidence of differing origins and quality, such as the results of seventeenth- and eighteenth-century papal excavations that aimed at building up collections of sculpture in the Vatican, more recent work of limited scope that has aimed at understanding specific buildings, topographic studies of standing structures, and assorted analyses of the architectural fragments, sculptures, and inscriptions. By contrast, the evidence for the development of rural settlement in the hinterland of these towns has been much better served. The British School at Rome's South Etruria Survey (summarized in Potter, 1979) encompassed urban and rural settlements in the triangle of land between Rome, the *via Cassia*, the *via Tiberina* and Falerii Novi in the north, while parts of the Sabina and elsewhere along the east bank of the Tiber have been covered by a myriad smaller Italian surveys (the information from which has been re-analyzed in the Tiber Valley Project (H. Patterson, 2004; H. Patterson and Millett, 1998; H. Patterson *et al.*, 2000) leading to a complex mosaic of overlapping coverages employing a range of methodologies.

This paper builds upon the results of the Roman Towns in the Middle and Lower Tiber Valley Project (1998–2004) (Carlucci *et al.*, 2007; Hay *et al.*, 2008; Hay *et al.*, 2010; Hay, Keay, and Millett, 2013; Johnson, Keay, and Millett, 2004; Keay *et al.*, 2000; Keay *et al.*,

A Companion to Roman Italy, First Edition. Edited by Alison E. Cooley.

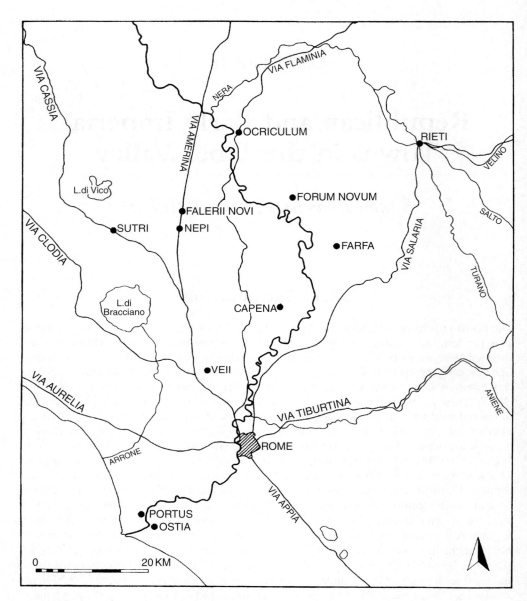

Figure 18.1 Map showing the distribution of towns studied in the course of the Roman Towns in the Middle and Lower Tiber Valley Project.

2004; Keay, Millett, and Strutt, 2006; Millett, 2007; Millett, 2013). It focuses upon towns in an area that lies between the Nera, near modern Orte and Rome itself (see Figure 18.1), a key part of the hinterland of Rome and its *suburbium* (Morley, 1996: 83ff.; Witcher, 2006) with much to teach us about the character and development of towns in Roman Italy as a whole. The towns were selected with a view to covering as representative a range as possible, notably the Iron Age settlement of Falerii Veteres (Civita Castellana), the major towns of Capena (La Civitucola), Falerii Novi (Santa Maria de Fàlleri) and Ocriculum (Otricoli), the lesser settlement of Forum Cassii (Santa Maria de Forcassi), the road station of Baccanae

(Campagnano di Roma), and the river port of Castellum Amerinum (Seripola) (the methods and preliminary results are summarized in Keay *et al.*, 2004); our work was complemented by survey and excavations at Forum Novum to the east of the Tiber (Gaffney, Patterson, and Roberts, 2004). The project also undertook survey at Portus, at the mouth of the Tiber, although the results of this lie outside the remit of this paper. The methodology adopted by the project was non-destructive with a view to understanding the sites as townscapes rather than fragments of urban landscapes or individual monuments (Keay *et al.*, 2004). In particular, it involved detailed topographical survey combined with a magnetometer survey of available areas, selective resistivity survey, and the collection of surface finds. The aim of this chapter is to focus upon a series of issues about the character of Roman towns that have emerged during the course of this research, rather than a summary of results.

18.2   Historical Background

The river Tiber acted as a route of communication and transport from north to south within central Italy and, by means of tributaries, provided access to the heartlands of the Umbrians, Faliscans, Capenates, Sabines, Etruscans, and Latins (for these peoples, see most recently Bradley, 2000; Ceccarelli and Stoddart, 2007; Izzet, 2007; Smith, 2007; Guidi and Santoro, 2004). It was navigable by large riverboats and barges as far as Rome and by smaller craft subsequently (Le Gall, 2005: 25–42). What readily distinguishes this part of Italy is that the Tiber, which rises in northern Umbria flows down to the Tyrrhenian Sea between a pre-littoral chain of extant volcanoes to the west, known today as the Monti Cimini and the Monti Sabatini, and the foothills of the Apennines that rise to the east. Very pronounced down-cutting by tributaries running eastwards from the former down into the Tiber basin, has created a very distinctive topography of volcanic plateaus dissected by deep gorges which are now heavily wooded. This stands in contrast to the rather hillier landscape leading to the Monti Sabini to the east of the river. Within these very contrasting landscapes, the Tiber also acted as a frontier, while the geographical differences between the land lying on either side of the river way conditioned the locations of the ancient towns themselves.

The study area was dominated in political, economic, and cultural terms by the development of Rome, particularly from the fifth century BC onwards. Since the Tiber effectively divides the valley into geographically distinct western and eastern sectors, it has tended to act as something of a barrier between east and west as well as a route of transport and communication (Cifani, 2003: 32ff.; H. Patterson, 2004, 62ff.), running from Umbria in the north down to the Tyrrhenian Sea in the south. The valley itself was both fertile and ecologically varied, producing a full range of Mediterranean crops such as grain, olives, and wine, as well as wood and other commodities. Inevitably, however, there was a tension in the consumption of these between the ongoing needs of regional communities and the growing requirements of Rome. From an early date, therefore, the middle and lower Tiber valley was supplemented by resources drawn from increasingly far afield, both in Italy and beyond.

The origins of Roman towns in the Tiber valley are a complex and polemical issue. The first proto-urban centers developed from out of the nucleation of a range of settlements between the eighth and seventh centuries BC (Guidi, 2004; Cifani, 2003). Those on the western side of the river tended to be larger and earlier than those to the east. By the sixth century, there had developed a clear hierarchy of settlements connected by roads (usefully synthesized by Potter, 1979: fig. 21). It comprised large centers such as Rome (circa 285 hectares) (Ampolo, 1988: 231ff.; Coarelli, 1988) and Veii (Bartoloni, 2004; Colonna, 2004); smaller centers (between 60 and 45 hectares), such as Falerii Veteres; lesser settlements (between 35 and 12 hectares) such as Cures, Narce, Poggio Sommavilla, and Eretum; and small settlements (between 10 and 1 hectares), such as Nazzano, Magliano Sabina, and Otricoli (Cifani, 2003: 175ff.). It has been suggested that this hierarchy formed the basis for some kind of state-system, with Rome, Veii, Cures, and Falerii Veteres usually being seen as the major centers of the Etruscans, Latini, Sabini, and Falisci respectively (Colonna, 1986; see alternatively Cifani, 2003). Some of these centers continued in occupation into the Roman Republican period and beyond, while others were eventually abandoned. Direct and indirect contact between these communities and major coastal centers mediated contacts with much broader Mediterranean networks. Hence links with Phoenician trade and Greek colonies in the Bay of Naples and beyond ensured the development of a rich orientalizing culture.

Internal dynamics within the region began to change in the sixth and fifth centuries BC with the emergence of Rome as the major urban center in the region. This has been discussed by Potter (1979), whose account is now outdated by more recent work, particularly in the context of the Tiber Valley Project (see the collected collected papers in H. Patterson, 2004, and H. Patterson and Coarelli, 2008). Recent excavations have shown with ever greater clarity that the sixth century BC saw the consolidation of Rome as a walled urban center with public areas, sanctuaries, aristocratic housing and infrastructure (Cristofani, 1990; Smith 2000; Cornell, 2002), while its growing military and political influence in Italy and beyond is well known from a plethora of historical and archaeological sources (see collected papers in Clemente, Coarelli, and Gabba, 1990). Culturally, Rome was a Latin city that drew upon a range of regional cultural influences, not least those of the Etruscans, as well as Hellenizing ideas similar to those current elsewhere in central and southern Italy. These became particularly marked after Rome's conquests of the Hellenistic kingdoms of the east Mediterranean from the third century BC onwards (Coarelli, 1996, 15–84; Schultz, ch. 3, this vol.). Rome's major competitor in the region was the Etruscan center of Veii. This controlled a very extensive territory between the Tiber to the north of Rome and Caere to the west, prior to its destruction by Rome in 396 BC.

The following period down to the beginning of the imperial era, saw an initial flurry of urban development followed by a progressive loss of municipal vigor in the face of the growth of Rome. Roman foundations appear from the third century BC, with a Latin colony at Narni, and foundations of a different kind at Falerii Novi (241 BC) and Forum Novum. Other communities, such as Capena were granted municipal status as early as the fourth century BC, with others like Ameria, Ocriculum, and Trebula Mutuesca were only enfranchised after the conclusion of the Social War in the earlier first century BC. The growing power of Rome in the region is also evident in the network of consular roads (*via Cassia*, *via Amerina*, *via Flaminia*, *via Tiberina*, and *via Salaria*) that were built in the course of the fourth and third centuries BC, radiating outwards from the City, connecting new foundations that were now central to Rome's interests, and isolating others that had been destroyed or sidelined, such as Veii and Narce (contrast Potter, 1979: figs 21 and 27). Archaeological evidence is patchy but suggests that the last two centuries BC also saw the main phase of topographical development of many settlements.

The mid-first century BC onwards saw the further transformation of this landscape in the context of the continued expansion of the population of the city of Rome, its growing economic and material needs, and its cultural redefinition in terms of a resurgent Hellenism under Augustus and his successors (most clearly discussed by Zanker, 1988, but also in collected papers in Lo Cascio, 2000). In terms of Augustan administrative districts, the study area encompasses the eastern sector of Etruria, the western sector of Sabina, and southern Umbria, with the Tiber forming the boundary between all three. Colonies were established at Lucus Feroniae and Sutrium (Keppie, 1983) within a road framework that was largely predicated on that established under the Republic, which continued to give prominence to Roman towns of Republican date, but also sidelined some earlier centers of importance such as Veii, which became a *municipium* under Augustus. Within the towns themselves the pace of development slowed considerably following the Augustan period (a subject addressed by J.R. Patterson, 2006: 88–183).

18.3   Settlement Patterns and Economy

By the early first century AD, the middle and lower Tiber Valley was one of the most intensely urbanized regions of central and southern Italy (Mattingly and Witcher, 2004: 182 and figure 13.6), at a level comparable to parts of Latium and Campania. However, it is important to note that there was very considerable variation in the size and character of the towns, a situation that is best in part explained by the very variable landscape of the region itself. So, for example, some towns like Lucus Feroniae, Falerii Novi, Forum Novum, and Forum Cassii were situated on flat, lower-lying land, while others like Capena, Ocriculum, Nepi, Veii, and Sutrium were situated on higher ground. Inevitably, therefore, the former, and particularly Falerii Novi, provided planners and engineers with the scope for more regularly planned settlements, while the latter had more organic layouts that represented a compromise between the difficulties of the terrain and Hellenistic and Roman planning ideals.

What is true of the towns themselves is also relevant to our understanding of the rural settlement that was focused upon them. We are fortunate that the archaeological evidence for this has been more intensively studied than most parts of Italy, most notably by Ashby (1927), Ward-Perkins, Potter (1979) and, most recently, the Tiber Valley Project. In general terms, this shows that there was a general decline in the density of rural settlement across the region during the Republican period (Witcher, 2006), even though this masks considerable variation from one town to another (see for example an analysis of rural settlement around towns in southern Etruria by Di Giuseppe, 2005). Furthermore, under the first two centuries AD there was a sharp increase in the numbers and range of rural settlements, with villas becoming prominent (Witcher, 2006; 2008). This pattern is different from that in other parts of Italy, in which the early Imperial period sees a period of relative decline. At the same time, however, the development of rural settlement in the northern end of the region around Falerii Novii (Cambi, 2004) and Ocriculum were marginally later than areas closer to Rome, while there were also differences in the density and character of rural settlement from one town to the next. Excavations at villa sites ranging from the great complex belonging to the Volusii Saturnini close to Lucus Feroniae, down to much smaller farms like Monte Forco to the west of Capena (Gazzetti, 1992: 39–47 and 67–68 respectively) emphasize the great variation in ownership, scope, and scale of rural settlements in different parts of the region. The influence of the city of Rome is apparent on settlement patterns throughout the area, with the economic demands for materials and produce combining with the political desirability of owning a residence near the center of power coming to have an impact which made the Tiber Valley unique (J.R. Patterson, 2008: 491–93).

While there is no doubt that the consular roads that traversed the region played an important role in connecting the Tiber Valley towns into close relationships with Rome and other parts of central Italy, it was the Tiber that was the single most important economic axis. The development of the towns and the exploitation of their agricultural resources need to be understood in terms of economic flows up and down the river between Umbria, Samnium, Etruria and Rome (H. Patterson, 2004). Towns and rural settlements throughout the region provide ample evidence for the movement of traffic southwards to Rome, such as the widespread distribution of wine amphorae from Spello in the upper Tiber valley (Fontana, 2008: fig. 5) and *terra sigillata italica* from Scopietto in southern Umbria (Bergamini, 2008). Goods also moved upriver, as reflected by a range of ceramics from southern Gaul, Baetica, north Africa and the eastern Mediterranean (Fontana, 2008: figs 8, 9). However, one should not forget that the river was also a key transport corridor for construction materials bound for Rome, with the town of Ocriculum playing a particularly important role in this traffic as its river port lay close to the confluence of the Tiber and the Nera. Bricks from production centers along the whole length of the Tiber between Fidenae and Ocriculum (Filippi and Stanco, 2005) were vital in the massive scale of public and private construction at Rome, Ostia and Portus. Another key commodity in this commerce was timber from forests in the Apennines which was also brought down via the Tiber (Diosono, 2008).

The evidence discussed suggests that it is difficult to make generalized statements about the location, size, and topography of the towns, or the character of economic development from one part of the Middle and Lower Tiber Valley to another during the late Republican and early Imperial periods. At another level it is clear that the region can be characterized as a region of Italy in which communities shared a floruit in urban development and a sharp increase in the number of rural settlements – a phenomenon that is to be explained by the expansion of Rome itself. It would be wrong, however, to imagine that this was in any way "typical" of developments elsewhere in Italy. Recent analysis has highlighted significant differences in the trajectories of urban development between this part of Italy and coastal and inland Etruria (Witcher, 2006), while one must expect an even greater contrast with parts of southern and northern Italy.

18.4 Key Issues in the Development of Roman Towns in the Middle and Lower Tiber Valley

The new data collected by the Roman Towns in the Middle and Lower Tiber Valley Project has complemented earlier work and has provided us with a much clearer understanding of the topography of the chosen settlements than before. It also makes it possible to think of them in terms of townscapes and, therefore, to raise a series of issues germane to the region as a whole, as well as to other parts of Italy.

18.4.1 *Urban planning and organization*

There is some inevitability that the study of Roman towns remains dominated by the image of the grid-planned site, and indeed the more spectacular results of our own surveys do tend to focus on these as revealed at Falerii Novi or as clarified further afield by our more recent work at Teanum Sidicinum (Hay, Keay and Millett, 2012) and Fregellae (Ferraby *et al.*, 2008). Although, as noted below, large-scale survey also contextualizes our understanding of these plans, it is important to recognize how exceptional orthogonally planned sites must have been. Not only are systematic grid plans absent from the smaller roadside and riverside settlements of Forum Cassii and Castellum Amerinum (Johnson, Keay, and Millett, 2004) and from the archaic sites of Capena and Falerii Veteres (Keay, Millett, and Strutt, 2006; Carlucci *et al.*, 2007), as might be expected, but they are also of only marginal importance at major centers like Ocriculum (Hay *et al.*, 2008; Hay, Keay, and Millett, 2013).

The explanation at Ocriculum may be the restricted topographical context, with the town built on a narrow ridge defined by steep slopes on three sides. However, its full development from the third century BC was a matter of choice, with the main focus perhaps transferred from the earlier Umbrian hilltop location under the modern village of Otricoli nearby to the ridge where there was a smaller area of pre-Roman settlement (see Figure 18.2). It is thus arguable that, had the ability to develop an orthogonally planned town been a priority, an alternative site

Figure 18.2   Photograph of the modern hilltop village of Otricoli. Photograph: Simon Keay.

on flatter ground easily available nearby might have been chosen. This implies that other factors were more important in the selection of the site and that the more topographically determined ridge-top location was a deliberate choice. It is arguable that this was a result of the long-standing significance of a settlement and sanctuary here (Hay, Keay, and Millett, 2013). The settlement had been in existence from the eighth century BC and was monumentalized during the Republican period; the identity of the deity that might have been worshipped here is unknown. This decision allowed the town to develop a particular form with a prominent external facade that dominated the route along the Tiber, which has some parallels with the enhanced and highly visible wall circuit developed at Falerii Novi (Keay *et al.*, 2000: 86).

In a broader context it may be appropriate to begin to consider when and where the use of the orthogonal grid was appropriate, bearing in mind that our best archaeological evidence for Italian urban sites tends to come from those without continuous occupation so that topographically determined irregular plans are arguably underrepresented and underestimated in importance. It is by no means clear that the form appropriate to Rome's new colonial foundations was seen as best for every urban community. This strongly suggests that we need to pay more attention to seeking to understand the organizational rules that determined the layout of towns without orthogonal plans.

Historical sources inform us that Falerii Veteres was sacked in the context of a Faliscan revolt against Rome in 241 BC (Polybius: 1.65; Livy, *Epitome*: 20), the presiding deity of Minerva was cast out in an act of *evocatio* (Carlucci *et al.*, 2007: 101), and that the displaced population was resettled at the new foundation of Falerii Novi (Zonarus: 8.18). One reading of this is to see the latter as symptomatic of Rome's harsh treatment of rebellious populations and the importance of Roman aggression in retaining control over the peoples of Italy, while another is to see it as a conscious re-foundation by surviving Faliscan elites (Keay *et al.*, 2004: 234). While strong objections can be raised against both of these, the position taken in that article is that Falerii Novi is best understood as a re-foundation expressed in terms of the architectural language of Roman colonies while consciously incorporating key points of reference to the earlier Faliscan settlement (Millett, 2007).

Falerii Novi lies a few kilometers to the west of Falerii Veteres, and can be reached from it by the Rio del Purgatorio, and it is also on the line of the *via Amerina*, which ran from Rome to Aemelia in the north. The position of the town is such that both Falerii Veteres and the Monte Soracte, sacred to Apollo, were visible to the east, providing an important visual reference point for the new foundation. The 30-hectare town was conceived as an artificially landscaped plateau that was enclosed within high walls that ran from east to west, and which was terraced from north to south in order to present a monumental facade to visitors approaching the town from the *via Amerina* to the south. It is possible that this was a deliberate attempt to recreate in a new environment the abrupt plateau-like settlement of Falerii Veteres from which the population was moved in 241 BC. Our understanding of its internal layout derives from a geophysical and topographic survey that reveals a complex orthogonal plan and a densely occupied townscape that incorporated a forum, theater, baths, temples, and a range of houses and buildings of less certain identification (Keay *et al.*, 2000; see Figure 18.3). It is important to remember that this plan is a palimpsest of street alignments and buildings ascribable to various periods during the Republican and Imperial periods. Current research suggests that there were at least four phases in the development of the street-plan of the town, ranging from a strict orthogonal grid at the time of the foundation of the town in the third century BC,

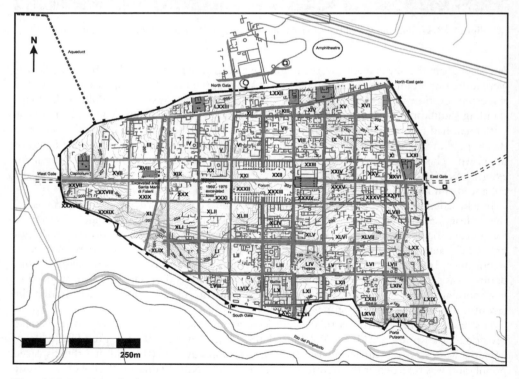

Figure 18.3 Plan of Falerii Novi based upon the interpretation of the geophysical results from the survey. From Keay *et al.*, 2000: fig. 7.

followed by some significant later modifications that date to some time in the later Republican and early Imperial periods: many of the visible buildings date to the Imperial period.

It is hard to deny major differences between the layout of Falerii Novi and its predecessor Falerii Veteres. The latter was a loosely organized settlement that extended over a number of adjacent plateaus, and the internal organization of which was articulated by major sanctuaries to Apollo Soranus, Minerva, Juno Curitis and Mercury (Carlucci *et al.*, 2007: 101–04; see Figure 18.4), while the former was an orthogonally planned lowland settlement that from an early stage incorporated houses laid out in a way which invites close parallels with contemporary Roman colonies, such as Cosa (273 BC) and Minturnae (296 BC). However, there are similarities too. A closer look at the plan of Falerii Novi points to the existence of what has been termed a "sacred way" that surrounds the orthogonal street grid and seems to have developed after its layout. It connected a series of temples to unknown deities that were located at the northern intersection of the north–south roads of the orthogonal grid and links them to the *capitolium* located on the highest point within the walls adjacent to the west gate. This would have facilitated processional movement around the perimeter, and into or out of the gates at the south-west and south-east corners of the town, and from thence along the Rio del Purgatorio to the still-functioning sanctuary of Juno Curitis at the foot of the abandoned site of Falerii Veteres (Keay *et al.*, 2000: 87ff.). This "sacred way" enabled the inhabitants of the town to relive a remote past that was already expressed in the position of the town in relation to the earlier site of Falerii Veteres and the sacred mountain of Monte Soracte. This interpretation suggests that Falerii Novi was a foundation that was expressed both in terms of contemporary Hellenistic and Roman architectural forms and pre-existing Faliscan religious traditions, the kind of cultural blend that was prevalent amongst Italian communities of the third and second centuries BC (issues discussed by Wallace-Hadrill, 2008: 71–143).

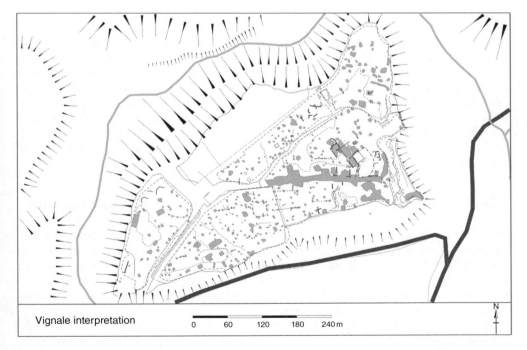

Figure 18.4   Plan of the settlement at Vignale, a key focus of occupation at Falerii Veteres (Civita Castellana), based upon geophysical survey results.

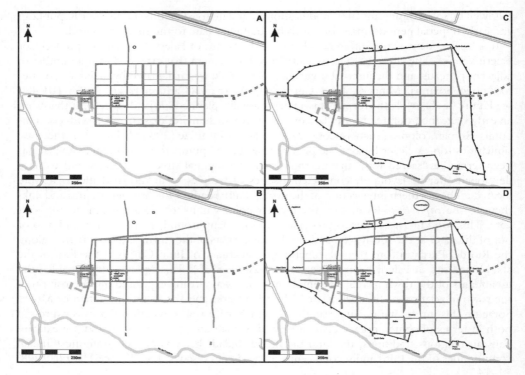

Figure 18.5   Plan showing the development of the street-grid at Falerii Novi.

Where we do have evidence for orthogonal planning across large parts of newly-founded cities, field survey can provide a key source for understanding land allotment, a topic which has recently received attention in the context of reconsidering early colonies (Fentress, 2000). The advantage of extensive survey in providing reliable new data is important, although it may undermine some common assumptions. For instance, there is reasonably clear evidence from the primary grid at Falerii Novi for the division of the site into units of two different sizes analogous to the scheme suggested at Cosa (Millett, 2007; see Figure 18.5). Such a system would conventionally be taken to imply a colonial deduction, but at Falerii the accepted historical reconstruction seems to rule out its interpretation as a colony (Keay *et al.*, 2000: 1–3). This is clearly a debate to develop further, but it does illustrate how new evidence may be of unexpected significance.

18.4.2   Urban continuity and geopolitical reorganization

One of the key characteristics of urban settlement in central Italy is the high degree of urban continuity. Many of those settlements that became integral to the conquered landscapes of central Italy had become established in the course of the earlier first millennium BC. At the same time, the results of recent excavations and field surveys have shown that the impact of the expansion of Roman power led to the abandonment of some settlements and significant changes in the regional importance of others.

This is particularly clear in terms of the changing relationships between Capena (La Civitucola) and Lucus Feroniae. Capena was the focal center of the Capenates, a people settled on land to the west of the Tiber. It was established in the eighth century BC and was located on a plateau that

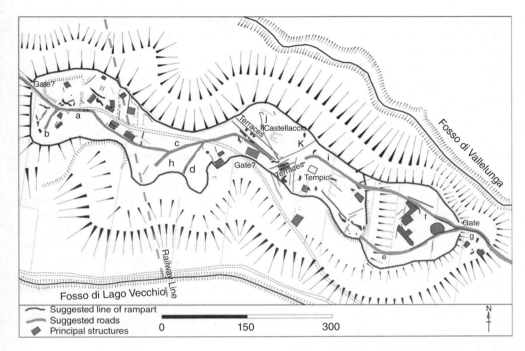

Figure 18.6   Plan of Capena based upon geophysical survey results. Keay, Millett, and Strutt, 2006: fig. 28.

overlooked the Fosso di San Martino, a tributary of the Tiber. The early material culture from the site has similarities with that from sites in Faliscan territory to the north, suggesting a degree of cultural affinity. A geophysical survey of the site (Keay, Millett, and Strutt 2006) suggests that by the fifth century BC the site had been walled and enclosed an area of circa 3 hectares (see Figure 18.6).

It is very likely that Capena played some kind of special role in relation to the neighboring great pan-Italic sanctuary of the goddess Feronia at Lucus Feroniae from around this time. This was located a few kilometers from Capena at a crucial junction close to where the Fosso di San Martino flows into the Tiber. It also lay on the line of the *via Tiberina* that connected it with Rome and Nazzano (Jones, 1962: 191ff. and fig. 22) and faced Cures Sabini on the east bank of the Tiber. Lucus Feroniae was a place of periodic meetings by devotees of Feronia from amongst the Faliscans, Etruscans, Sabines, and Latins (Strabo: 5, 2, 9; Livy: 1.1.30; see also Jones, 1962: 191ff) from the Archaic period onwards, a role that ensured it also acted as a center of regional commercial exchange. While the temple (Bartoccini, 1963), associated structures, and votive deposits (Moretti and Battaglia, 1975) are known from excavations undertaken in the 1970s, little is known about the extent or character of the sanctuary prior to the first century BC apart from the existence of a temple and adjacent house of Republican date (Moretti and Battaglia, 1975, 155–63). It is also unclear to what extent the pre-first century BC center could be described as "urban."

By the third century BC Capena had grown to 8.7 hectares and its topography conformed to the irregular topography of the site. Literary sources make it clear that it was a center of some importance, becoming a *municipium sine suffragio* by circa 270 BC (inscriptions from the town also refer to the *Capenates foederati*: Conti, 1932: 17; Keay, Millett, and Strutt 2006: 79), although it is noticeable that it was bypassed by the *via Flaminia* when it was built in the 220s BC and only connected to it by a minor road. The later Republican and early Imperial period saw the town shrink to circa 6 hectares, and a possible population of circa 1200 people (Keay,

Millett, and Strutt, 2006). The Castellacio temple complex and adjacent forum dominated the town and took up a considerable proportion of its ground area, while reasonably dense settlement of an indeterminate kind was scattered over the remaining area. It is unclear to whom the Castellacio temple complex was dedicated, although one clue comes from three statue pedestals from the site dedicated by the *municipium* of Capena to priestesses of Ceres (Conti, 1932: 16; Bartolini *et al.*, 1995: 49). Epigraphic fragments suggest that an *Augusteum* was also located in the vicinity (Papi, 2000: 30ff.). The temple and forum complex in turn overlooked other buildings of uncertain character terraced into the eastern facade of the town overlooking the Fosso di San Martino (Keay, Millett, and Strutt, 2006). Late Republican and early Imperial Capena, therefore, had become a small center in regional terms, suggesting that a substantial proportion of its population could have lived in the surrounding countryside: indeed the number of rural settlements in the vicinity of Capena increased under the early Empire (Jones, 1962; Keay, Millett, and Strutt, 2006). If this is the case, the surrounding population may have only frequented the town on special occasions, such as the *ludi victoriae Caesaris* that are recorded on inscriptions of second-century AD date (Jones, 1962: 194ff.).

A possible explanation for the apparent "non-development" of Capena as a regional urban center under the early Empire may be the transformation of the adjacent sanctuary of Lucus Feroniae. Since the character of the Republican sanctuary of Lucus Feroniae is unclear, it is not known whether this represents an earlier sanctuary being incorporated within the *colonia* or an earlier town with sanctuary focus being integrated within it. We may equally note that the development of the road system left Capena comparatively isolated whilst networking Lucus with other communities. In either case the key point is that urban trajectories of both Capena and Lucus were intimately linked.

The sanctuary at Lucus Feroniae must have been frequented continuously until circa 47/46 BC when its role was transformed by having to accommodate a colonial settlement by Caesar (Keppie, 1983: 168–69), even though its physical transformation may not have occurred until Augustus (Jones, 1962: 194ff.). The colony encompassed an area of circa 25 hectares and it would appear that the key known buildings of the sanctuary, the altar to Feronia and the Republican temple that stands immediately to the east of the forum, were deliberately incorporated at the heart of the new colony, while an adjacent house was demolished (Moretti and Battaglia, 1975: 155–56). It is noticeable that the colony does not appear to be orthogonally planned but it is uncertain how far this may reflect the persistence of an earlier street plan and the incorporation of this within the colonial street grid. The colony was also provided with a very small circular amphitheater, baths, and several other structures of uncertain nature. Lucus clearly receives all the patronage and building that early imperial Capena lacked, with the consular family of the Volusii Saturnini being amongst the main patrons (Papi, 2000: 67–80). In addition to this, the territory of the colony of Lucus was carved out of that of the southern part of that of Capena, with the settlement of veterans in 47/46 BC (Cicero, *Letters to his Friends*: 9.17.2), and again under Augustus (Frontinus, *On Land Disputes*: A.164). While survey has produced evidence for early Imperial rural settlement in the hinterland as one might expect, it is interesting to note that it is appears to be relatively light and does not attain the density of that closer to Capena. It is unclear whether this is a real difference or whether it is to be explained by the unevenness of survey coverage (Keay, 2010).

18.4.3   Public and private spaces

At a practical level, the extensive surveys of sites like Falerii Novi provide important new information about the internal organization and sequence of development of orthogonally planned sites in a way which is much more difficult to address in those towns whose shape seems topographically determined. Although we have already noted the difficulty presented by identifying the functions of less regular structures, such sites do enable us to distinguish broadly between residential and public spaces within the towns, and from this to move towards an assessment of population size (Millett, 2013).

The most common approach to the question of urban population size, which is central to debates in Roman history, is simply to take the occupied area and apply a multiple based on estimates for the average population density at other Roman urban sites. Our surveys are important in providing new and accurate estimates for the occupied areas of a series of sites in the Tiber valley. At the larger end of the spectrum the area within the walls at Falerii Novi is circa 30.6 hectares and this approximates to the maximum occupied area. The size of Ocriculum has also been estimated as circa 14.2 hectares. Neither site is thus very large by comparison with other Roman cities in northern Italy (de Ligt, 2008). The area occupied at Capena in the Imperial period was only circa 6 hectares, having declined from 8.7 hectares in the Republican periods (Keay, Millett, and Strutt, 2006). The roadside site at Baccanae and riverport at Castellum Amerinum are significantly smaller, in the range of circa 2–3 hectares (Johnson, Keay, and Millett, 2004; see Figure 18.7). An average population density of 120– 150 people per hectare has been suggested for those urban sites in northern Italy that do not contain multistory buildings (de Ligt, 2008: 153–54). Given the nature of our sites, the lower end of this range seems likely, providing the following population estimates for the early Imperial period: Falerii Novi 3672 people; Ocriculum 1704 people; Capena 720 people; Baccanae 240 people; and Castellum Amerinum 240 people.

A more nuanced approach is to work from the evidence of the geophysics surveys to identify building types or land uses, and hence to work upwards towards a site-based estimate. This is only possible for Falerii Novi, where following the suggested phasing of the town we can compare population numbers for two notional periods, that of the primary grid approximating to the second century BC, and that of whole walled area, arguably in the second century AD (Keay *et al.*, 2000: 85).

The primary grid (see Figure 18.5) comprises an area circa 460 by 270 m = 12.42 hectares. Using the average population density figures from above this suggests a population of 1490 people at a density of 120 per hectare. As only three of the 21 full *insulae* have any evidence of public buildings 18 full *insulae* (86%) appear to have been largely residential. This might suggest that the overall population estimate should be reduced proportionately to 1192. In a previous paper, one of us tentatively identified evidence for subdivision of the *insulae* into separate properties (Millett, 2007: 73–75). If these units were used regularly to fill the grid and each was used for individual houses then this provides an alternative basis for estimating the population. If regularized, three sizes of property can be identified: Type A (of which there are 33 potential examples) 60 by 22 m (1320 m²); Type B (18 examples) 40 by 40 m (1600 m²); Type C (12 examples) 30 by 4 m (1350 m²). This gives a total of 63 house units.

At Cosa it has been suggested that the larger houses (18 by 34.5 m. = 621 m²) might have been occupied by about 10–12 people (de Ligt, 2008: 148). Scaled up this suggests: Type A property = 21–25 people; Type B property = 25–31 people; Type C property = 22–26 people. This would give a total population of the 33 Type A properties as 693–825; the 18 Type B properties as 450–558; the 12 Type C properties as 264–312. This would imply a total population of 1407–1695 in the second century BC with an average density of 90–109 per hectare.

Within the total walled area which represents the full extent of the town in the early Imperial period, allowance should be made for the major public buildings and the apparently unoccupied zone beside the walls in Insula LXXI which totals circa 4.8 hectares, leaving a potential maximum area for residential occupation of 25.8 hectares. Using the figures derived

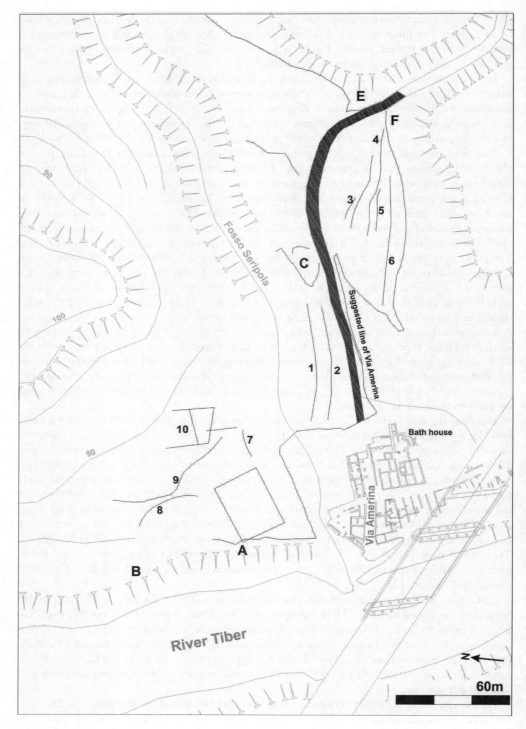

Figure 18.7   Plan of the river port of Castellum Amerinum based upon geophysical survey results. Johnson, Keay, and Millett, 2004: fig. 13.

from the calculations above this would suggest a population in the second century AD in the range of 2322–2812 as opposed to 3096 using the 120 persons per hectare range derived from general comparators.

18.4.4 Urban peripheries

Extensive urban surveys have also thrown new light on structures at the peripheries of urban centers, whether or not the towns show orthogonal planning (cf. Goodman, ch. 16, this vol.). This is partly simply a function of exploring zones which have too often escaped archaeological attention. The clearest example of this comes from Falerii Novi where the survey revealed a sequence of six temples all located along the irregular intramural street or "sacred way" in the northern half of the city, each one facing south at a street intersection (see section 18.4.1, this chapter). The interpretation of this pattern remains a matter of debate but in terms of overall understanding of a *de novo* urban foundation it has very important implications as it shows that the urban margins must have played a very significant role in town life. It is difficult to escape the conclusion that they relate to a processional route, perhaps part of that from the town to Falerii Veteres which features in Ovid, *Amores* 3.13 and which ended at the temple to Juno Curitis. In the same town, the survey also reveals a series of regular intramural plots running up to the walls which appear to have been used for cultivation (see Keay *et al.*, 2000; fig. 20). The character of these marginal areas is uncertain but given the absence of systematic exploration of similar areas in other planned towns, these features raise key questions about our knowledge of the full range and character of urban space.

The irregular intramural road around the orthogonal grid at Falerii Novi which provided access to these temples is also notable for the way in which it encompassed a series of substantial terraces just inside the South-East gate (the 'Porta Puteana'), where access is provided from the bottom of the adjacent river gorge. The substantial extent of civil engineering at this point is remarkable, not least because of the way in which the features have become naturalized over time. It is worth noting how in areas like South Etruria, such rock-cut features and similar ones at Falerii Veteres and to a lesser extent Ocriculum bear comparison with the more conspicuous Hellenistic-inspired concrete vaulted terraces at well-known sites like Praeneste and Terracina (Coarelli, 1987). In this sense the geophysical surveys have provided evidence of a mode of sculpting the landscape especially around access points to settlements which has perhaps elsewhere escaped notice. This may represent a key architectural characteristic of towns in this part of Italy (Millett, 2007: 79–81).

At Ocriculum survey has demonstrated another form of large-scale landscape modification, apparently a response to the limited land available for urban expansion. Early imperial builders responded to the limitations of building space on the narrow ridge occupied by the town by the piecemeal construction of retaining walls and concrete vaults which allowed building to extend out beyond the cliff edges. These sometimes monumental structures were complemented before AD 139 by a much bolder engineering project which involved largely backfilling the valley on the southern side of the city to create a platform on which new baths and other major buildings were constructed. This platform is now naturalized so that only the most inquisitive visitor will become aware of it. A key feature of this project was the canalization of the stream to run through an enclosed conduit which could be blocked-off, forcing the water upwards to supply a series of huge cisterns built into the valley fill (Hay, Keay, and Millett, 2013).

There seems little doubt that this engineering project at Ocriculum also fulfilled a role in displaying urban munificence to those arriving from Rome along the *via Flaminia* in much the same way as did the adjacent amphitheater and the magnificent temple and theater which will have dominated both the approach by road and the view from the Tiber. These features remind us that geophysical surveys of such centers offer the potential to understand the phenomenology of these urban centers in a way that is rarely possible through excavation.

18.4.5   Extramural areas

The importance of extramural areas of cities has often been underestimated or else treated in an entirely functionalist manner. What is clear from all our work is the way in which the visual impact of the approach to a city was fundamental. This can be seen in the deliberate displays that dominate urban approaches with monumentalized cemeteries along the roads at Falerii Novi and Ocriculum. The extent to which these were carefully designed to create an impression has often been overlooked. This is most clearly demonstrable on the southern approach to Falerii Novi where the straight course of the *via Amerina* runs through a deep cutting as it approaches the stream gorge immediately outside the walls. The effect will have been to emphasize the magnificence of the town walls and rock-cut tombs in the cliff beneath to the travelers as they exited from the cutting onto the bridge immediately outside the south gate (see Figure 18.8). Equally at Ocriculum, after a straight stretch flanked by mausolea, the route along the *via Flaminia* from the south descended into a valley turning left around the curve of the amphitheater until the facade of the town dominated by a temple came into view dominating the skyline above.

The other feature of the surveys we have undertaken is the variety in complexity of the non-funerary elements beyond town walls. At Falerii Novi the area to the north is marked by a complex set of land divisions which clearly linked urban and rural land allotments. At their intersection, we find major buildings and the amphitheater creating a rich and varied landscape (Hay *et al.*, 2010). Similar complexity is hinted at by the evidence from Ocriculum (Hay, Keay, and Millett, 2013; see Figure 18.9), whilst further afield at Teanum Sidicinum survey work has revealed new details of a major extramural sanctuary set around with funerary monuments (Hay, Keay, and Millett, 2012). The key point here again is the fact that by treating urban centers as landscapes we are opening up new and different aspects of their topography.

18.5   Discussion

The account above has highlighted the contribution of archaeological survey to the understanding of Roman towns in the Tiber Valley. Our work has brought a new dimension to a well-established field of study, using contemporary archaeological methods to elucidate aspects of urban topography. Whilst we are certain that these methods have a broader value and application (see Johnson and Millett, 2012) it would be a mistake to think that the results from the Tiber Valley can be generalized to other parts of Italy let alone to the Empire more generally. What our work here and elsewhere in Italy has shown (Vermeulen *et al.*, 2012) is that there is considerably more variety to Roman urban forms than has generally been assumed. One key challenge for the future is to move beyond the commonly received stereotypes to understand the nature of this variation in terms of the functions, histories, and geographical contexts of the different sites. Another is surely to integrate the study of different towns with that of their rural territories, thereby seeking to move beyond simple notions like centuriation or villa estates to embrace the infinite variety of forms of rural exploitation and land allotment. This is because they can only be understood in the context of a complex landscape history which encompassed both urban and rural dwellers and the range of economic and social institutions and interactions of which they were a part.

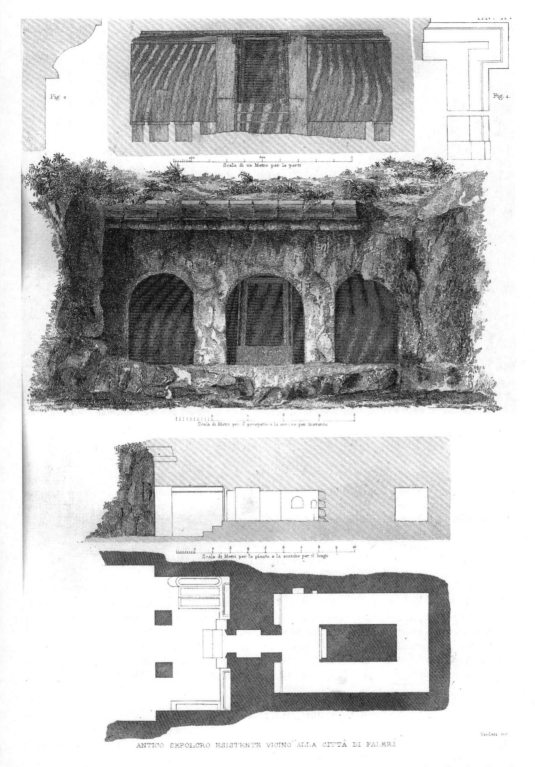

Figure 18.8 Rock-cut tombs on the south side of Falerii Novi. Canina, L. (1846–51) *L'antica Etruria marittima, compresa nella dizione pontificia / descritta ed illustrata con i monumenti dal cav. Luigi Canina.* Rome: Per i tipi della rev. Camera apostolica.

Figure 18.9   Photograph of the amphitheater at Otricoli. Photograph: S. Keay.

ENDNOTE

1 The authors gratefully acknowledge the support of the Arts and Humanities Research Council, the British School at Rome (Professor Andrew Wallace-Hadrill), the universities of Southampton, Cambridge and Durham, and the Soprintendenza Archeologica per l'Etruria Meridionale.

FURTHER READING

The results of the early field survey of south Etruria carried out under the auspices of the British School at Rome (BSR) can be found published in Potter 1979. In recent years, the BSR has continued to sponsor a major project reconsidering the settlement patterns that developed over time in the Tiber Valley. Archaeological reports on this project have been published in the *Papers of the British School at Rome*, whilst collected papers can be found in the volumes edited by H. Patterson 2004, and H. Patterson and Coarelli, eds 2008. Most recently, work from the Roman Towns in the Middle and Lower Tiber Valley Project has been published in Hay, Keay, and Millett 2013, Millett 2007 and Millett 2013.

REFERENCES

Ampolo, C. 1988. "La città riformata e l'organizzazione centuriata. Lo spazio, il tempo, il sacro nella nuova realta urbana." In *Storia di Roma. Volume primo. Roma in Italia*, 203–39. Turin: Einaudi.

Ashby, T. 1927. *The Roman Campagna in Classical Times*. London: Ernest Benn.

Bartoccini, R. 1963. "Il rinfornimento idrico della colonia Julia Felix Lucus Feroniae." *Autostrade* 7–8: 1–16.

Bartolini, F., Fei, F., Moscetta, M. P., Parenti, F., Toro, A., and Turchetti R. 1995. "I risultati delle ricognizione: catalogo delle presenze archeologiche." *Capena e il suo territorio*, 41–90. Bari, Dedalo.

Bartoloni, G. 2004. "Veio-Piazza d'Armi: campagne di scavo 1996–7". In *Bridging the Tiber. Approaches to regional archaeology in the Middle Tiber Valley*, ed. H. Patterson, 189–203. London: Archaeological Monographs of the British School at Rome 13.

Bergamini, M. 2008. "Scoppieto e i commerci sul Tevere." In Mercator placidissimus: *The Tiber Valley in antiquity*, eds H. Patterson and F. Coarelli, 285–321. Rome: Edizioni Quasar.

Bradley, G. 2000. *Ancient Umbria. State, culture and identity in central Italy from the Iron Age to the Augustan era*. Oxford: Oxford University Press.

Cambi, F. 2004. "Le campagne di Falerii e Capena dopo la romanizzazione." In *Bridging the Tiber. Approaches to regional archaeology in the Middle Tiber Valley*, ed. H. Patterson, 75–102. Rome: British School at Rome.

Canina, L. 1846–51. *L'antica Etruria marittima, compresa nella dizione pontificia / descritta ed illustrata con i monumenti dal cav.* Rome: Per i tipi della rev. Camera apostolica.

Carlucci, C., De Lucia Brolli, M. A., Keay, S., Millett, M., and Strutt. K. 2007. "An archaeological survey of the Faliscan settlement at Vignale, Falerii Veteres (Province of Viterbo)." *Papers of the British School at Rome* 75: 39–121.

Ceccarelli, L. and Stoddart, S. 2007. "The Faliscans." In *Ancient Italy. Regions without boundaries*, eds G. Bradley, E. Isayev and C. Riva, 131–60. Exeter: Exeter University Press.

Cifani, G. 2003. *Storia di una frontiera: dinamiche territoriali e gruppi etnici nella media Valle Tiberina della prima età del Ferro alla conquista romana*. Rome: Istituto Poligrafico e Zecca dello Stato.

Clemente, G., Coarelli, F., and Gabba, E., eds. 1990. *Storia di Roma. Volume secondo. L'impero mediterraneo I. La repubblica imperiale*. Turin: Einaudi.

Coarelli, F. 1987. *I santuari del Lazio in età repubblicana. Studi NIS archaeologia*. Rome: NIS.

Coarelli, F. 1988. "Demografia e Territorio". In *Storia di Roma. Volume primo. Roma in Italia*, 317–39. Turin: Einaudi.

Coarelli, F. 1996. Revixit Ars: *Arte e ideologia a Roma. Dai modelli ellenistici alla tradizione repubblicana*. Rome: Quasar.

Colonna, G. 1986. "Il Tevere e gli Etruschi". In *Il Tevere e le altre vie d'acqua del Lazio antico*, ed. S. Quilici Gigli, *Archeologia Laziale 7* (2). *Quaderni del Centro di Studio per l'Archeologia Etrusco-Italica* 12: 90–97. Rome: CNR.

Colonna, G. 2004. "I santuari di Veio: ricerche e scavi su Piano di Comunità". In *Bridging the Tiber. Approaches to regional archaeology in the Middle Tiber Valley*, ed. H. Patterson, 205–21. London: British School at Rome.

Conti, V. 1932. *Notizie storiche sulla ubicazione di Capena*. Rome: Poligrafico Salvuti.

Cornell, T.J. 2002. "La prima Roma." In *Roma Antica. Storia di Roma dall'antichità a oggi*, ed. A. Giardina, 3–22. Rome: Laterza.

Cristofani, M., ed. 1990. *La grande Roma dei Tarquini. Roma, Palazzo delle Esposizioni, 12 giugno–30 settembre 1990*. Rome: «L'Erma» di Bretschneider.

Di Giuseppe, H. 2005. "Villae, villule e fattorie nella Media Valle del Tevere." In *Roman Villas around the Urbs. Interaction with landscape and environment. The Swedish Institute in Rome. Projects and Seminars*, eds B. Santillo Fritzell and A. Klynne, 7–25. Rome: Swedish Institute.

Diosono, F. 2008. "Il commercio del legname sul fiume Tevere." In Mercator placidissimus: *the Tiber Valley in Antiquity*, eds H. Patterson and F. Coarelli, 251–83. Rome: Edizioni Quasar.

Fentress, E. 2000. "Frank Brown, Cosa, and the idea of a Roman city." In *Romanization and the City. Creations, transformations and failures*, ed. E. Fentress, 9–24. Portsmouth, RI: *Journal of Roman Archaeology* Suppl. 38.

Ferraby, R., Hay, S., Keay, S., and Millett, M. 2008. "Archaeological survey at Fregellae 2004–5." In *Dalle sorgenti alla foce. Il bacino del Liri-Garigliano nell' antichità: culture contatti scambi*, eds C. Corsi and E. Polito, 125–31. Rome: Quasar.

Filippi, G. and Stanco, E. 2005. "Epigrafia e toponomastica produzione laterizia nella Valle del Tevere: l'Umbria tra Tuder e Crustumerium; l'Etruria tra Volsinii e Lucus Feroniae." In *Interpretare i bolli laterizi di Roma e della produzione, storia economica e topografia*, ed. C. Bruun, 121–99. Rome: Institutum Romanum Finlandiae.

Fontana, S. 2008. "South Etruria revisited: le anfore, un tentative di analisi quantitative." In *Mercator placidissimus: The Tiber Valley in Antiquity*, eds H. Patterson and F. Coarelli, 655–69. Rome: Edizioni Quasar.

Gaffney, V., Patterson, H., and Roberts, P. 2004. "Forum Novum (Vescovio): a new study of the town and bishopric." In *Bridging the Tiber. Approaches to regional archaeology in the Middle Tiber Valley*, ed. H. Patterson, 237–51. London: Archaeological Monographs of the British School at Rome 13.

Gazzetti, G. 1992. *Il territorio capenate*. Rome: Quasar.

Guidi, A. 2004. "Modelli di occupazione del territorio tra l'eneolitico e la prima età del ferro nella media valle del Tevere". In *Bridging the Tiber. Approaches to regional archaeology in the Middle Tiber Valley*, ed. H. Patterson, 37–43. London: Archaeological Monographs of the British School at Rome 13.

Guidi, A. and Santoro, P. 2004. "Centri della Sabina Tiberina in epoca pre-romana." In *Bridging the Tiber. Approaches to regional archaeology in the Middle Tiber Valley*, ed. H. Patterson, 179–87. London: Archaeological Monographs of the British School at Rome, 13.

Hay, S., Johnson, P., Keay, S., and Millett, M. 2010. "Falerii Novi: further survey of the northern extra-mural area." *Papers of the British School at Rome* 78: 1–38.

Hay, S., Keay, S., Millett, M., and Sly, T. 2008. "Urban field-survey at Ocriculum (Otricoli, Umbria)." In *Mercator placidissimus: The Tiber Valley in antiquity*, eds H. Patterson and F. Coarelli, 797–809. Rome: Edizioni Quasar.

Hay, S., Keay, S., and Millett M. 2012. "Teano (Teanum Sidicinum), Campania." In *Urban Landscape Survey in Italy and the Mediterranean*, eds F. Vermeulen, G.-J. Burgers, S. Keay, and C. Corsi, 105–13. Oxford: Oxbow.

Hay, S., Keay, S., and Millett, M. 2013. *Ocriculum (Otricoli, Umbria): an archaeological survey of the Roman town*. London: British School at Rome.

Izzet. V. 2007. "Etruria and the Etruscans." In *Ancient Italy. Regions without boundaries*, eds G. Bradley, E. Isayev, and C. Riva, 14–30. Exeter: Exeter University Press.

Johnson, P., Keay, S., and Millett, M. 2004. "Lesser urban sites in the Tiber Valley: Baccanae, Forum Cassii and Castellum Amerinum." *Papers of the British School at Rome* 72: 69–99.

Johnson, P. and Millett, M. eds. 2012. *Archaeological Survey and the City*. Oxford: Oxbow.

Jones, G.D.B. 1962. "Capena and the Ager Capenas I." *Papers of the British School at Rome* 30: 116–210.

Keay, S. 2010. "Iberia and Italia: issues and challenges in the comparative study of Roman urbanism." In *Changing Landscapes. The impact of Roman towns in the Western Mediterranean. Proceedings of the International Colloquium Castelo de Vide, Marão 15–17 May 2008*, eds C. Corsi and F. Vermeulen, 27–45. Bologna: Antequeum.

Keay, S., Millett, M., Poppy, S., Robinson, J., Taylor, J., and Terrenato, N. 2000. "Falerii Novi: a new survey of the walled area." *Papers of the British School at Rome* 68: 1–93.

Keay, S., Millett, M., Poppy, S., Robinson, J., Taylor, J., and Terrenato, N. 2004. "New approaches to Roman urbanism in the Tiber Valley." In *Bridging the Tiber. Approaches to regional archaeology in the Middle Tiber Valley*, ed. H. Patterson, 223–36. London: Archaeological Monographs of the British School at Rome 13.

Keay, S., Millett, M., and Strutt, K. 2006. "An archaeological survey of Capena (La Civitucola, Provincia di Roma)." *Papers of the British School at Rome* 72: 73–118.

Keppie, L.J.F. 1983. *Colonisation and Veteran Settlement in Italy, 14–47 B.C.* London: British School at Rome.

Le Gall, J. 2005. *Il Tevere. Fiume di Roma nell'antichità*. Rome: Quasar.

Ligt, L. de 2008. "The population of Cisalpine Gaul in the time of Augustus." In *People, Land and Politics: demographic developments and the transformation of Roman Italy 300 B.C.– A.D. 14*, eds L. de Ligt and S.J. Northwood, 139–83. Leiden: Brill.

Lo Cascio, E., ed. 2000. *Roma Imperiale. Una metropoli antica*. Rome: Carocci.

Mattingly, D. and Witcher, R. 2004. "Mapping the Roman World: the contribution of field survey data". In *Side-by-Side Survey. Comparative regional survey in the Mediterranean world*, eds S. Alcock and J. Cherry, 173–86. Oxford: Oxbow.

Millett, M. 2007. "Urban topography and social identity in the Tiber Valley." In *Roman by Integration: dimensions of group identity in material culture and text*, eds R. Roth and J. Keller, 71–82. Portsmouth RI: *Journal of Roman Archaeology* Suppl. 69.

Millett, M. 2013. "Understanding Roman towns in Italy: reflections on the role of geophysical survey." In *Archaeological Survey and the City*, eds P. Johnson and M. Millett, 24–44. Oxford: Oxbow Books.

Moretti, A.M.S. and Battaglia, G.B. 1975. "Materiali archeologici scoperti a Lucus Feroniae." In *Nuove scoperte e acquisizioni nell'Etruria meridionale*, ed. M. Moretti, 93–175. Rome: Artistica.

Morley, N. 1996. *Metropolis and Hinterland: the city of Rome and the Italian economy, 200 B.C.–A.D. 200*. Cambridge: Cambridge University Press.

Papi, E. 2000. *L'Etruria dei Romani. Opere pubbliche e donazioni private in età imperiale*. Rome: Quasar.

Patterson, H., ed. 2004. *Bridging the Tiber. Approaches to regional archaeology in the Middle Tiber Valley*. London: Archaeological Monographs of the British School at Rome, 13.

Patterson, H. and Coarelli, F. eds, 2008. Mercator placidissimus: *the Tiber Valley in antiquity*. Rome: Edizioni Quasar.

Patterson, H., Di Gennaro, F., Di Giuseppe, H., Fontana, S., Gaffney, V., Harrison, A., Keay, S., Millett, M., Rendeli, M., Stoddart, S., Roberts, P. and Witcher, R. 2000. "The Tiber Valley Project: the Tiber and Rome through two millennia." *Antiquity* 284: 395–403.

Patterson, H. and Millett, M. 1998. "The Tiber Valley Project." *Papers of the British School at Rome* 66: 1–20.

Patterson, J.R. 2006. *Landscapes and Cities. Rural settlement and civic transformation in early imperial Italy*. Oxford: Oxford University Press.

Patterson, J.R. 2008. "Modelling the urban history of the Tiber Valley in the imperial period." In Mercator placidissimus. *The Tiber Valley in antiquity*, eds H. Patterson and F. Coarelli, 487–98. Rome: Edizioni Quasar.

Potter, T. W. 1979. *The Changing Landscape of South Etruria*. London: Elek.

Smith, C.J. 2000. "Early and Archaic Rome." In *Ancient Rome: the archaeology of the Eternal City*, eds J. Coulston and H. Dodge, 16–41. Oxford: Oxford University School of Archaeology.

Smith, C.J. 2007. "The hinterland of Rome: Latium and the Latins." In *Ancient Italy. Regions without boundaries*, eds G. Bradley, E. Isayev, and C. Riva, 161–78. Exeter: University of Exeter Press.

Vermeulen, F., Burgers, G.-J., Keay, S., and Corsi, C. eds. 2012. *Urban Landscape Survey in Italy and the Mediterranean*. Oxford: Oxbow.

Wallace-Hadrill, A. 2008. *Rome's Cultural Revolution*. Cambridge: Cambridge University Press.

Witcher, R.E. 2006. "Settlement and society in early imperial Etruria." *Journal of Roman Studies* 96: 88–123.

Witcher, R. 2008. "The Middle Tiber Valley in the imperial period". In Mercator placidissimus: *The Tiber Valley in antiquity*, eds H. Patterson and F. Coarelli, 467–86. Rome: Edizioni Quasar.

Zanker, P. 1988. *The Power of Images in the Age of Augustus*, trans. A. Shapiro. Ann Arbor: The University of Michigan Press.

CHAPTER 19

Cosa and the *Ager Cosanus*

Elizabeth Fentress and Phil Perkins

19.1 Cosa

19.1.1 Introduction

Widely cited as an exemplar of middle-Republican colonial urbanism (Brown, 1980), the status of the city of Cosa as the ideal type of a Roman colony has recently been called into question (Fentress, 2000; Dyson, 2005; Bispham, 2006). The faith of its excavator, Frank Brown, in its ability to represent Rome in terms of both its individual monuments and overall layout, led to its fame and to the assiduity with which it was excavated for 50 years (1948–1998) by the American Academy in Rome. In spite of the evident lacunae in our knowledge of the site (we know nothing of pre-imperial public baths or any market buildings), it still provides an interesting example of the subtlety with which Roman ideas of layout and urban structure were adapted to particular local contexts.

19.1.2 The colony of 273 BC

Settled as a *colonia Latina* in the thinly settled territory of the recently defeated Vulci in 273 BC (Velleius Paterculus: 1.14.7; Livy: Book 14 Summary/ *Periocha*; Strabo, Geography: 5.2.8), Cosa occupied a virgin site on a promontory between two fine natural harbors, the *Portus Cosanus* (McCann, 1987) and the *Portus Feniliae* (Calastri, 1999). It overlooked the fishing resources of the lagoon of Orbetello, where a subsidiary settlement was enclosed by polygonal masonry walls on an isthmus in the lagoon. This settlement was Etruscan in origin and may have been the major port of the colony in the third century BC, with its lagoon serving as a naval base in the Third Punic War (Ciampoltrini, 1995). Cosa dominates the coast from a hill rising some 110 m above the sea which creates a forced passage along the coast. This was later followed by the *via Aurelia*, built either in 241 or 201 BC (Fentress, 1984). We do not know much about the initial colony: it is possible that there was, in fact, not very much of it. Certainly the walls, in splendid polygonal masonry, were built in this period. These exploit the defenses provided by the natural terrain of the hilltop, encircling 14 hectares with an irregular shape. Towers were built at the four gates from which led roads to the *via Aurelia*, or its Etruscan predecessor, and to the ports on either side of the promontory. The only disadvantage of the site, and perhaps the reason why it was not occupied in the Etruscan period, was the lack of water: a small spring is found outside the town to the south-east, but the limestone formation of the hill means that the only reliable source of water is found at the *Portus Cosanus*, where there is a larger spring. This made the provision of adequate cisterns a prerequisite for the creation of a settlement on the hill.

It seems likely that the street grid was also created at the time of the foundation of the colony. Its layout is orthogonal, roughly parallel to the north-east wall and the coast. The small forum occupies the only available patch of relatively level ground, a saddle between the *Arx* and the Eastern Height. The *insulae* are of irregular widths and lengths, truncated by the even-more irregular walls. The plan of the town has been recently re-analyzed by Jamie Sewell, who proposes a radical alternative to the traditionally accepted arrangement (see Figure 19.1) (Sewell, 2010: 28–30). Focusing on the anomalous size and shape of the forum, and the fact that the public buildings on its north-east side actually block Street 7, whose existence is revealed by an early *cippus*, he suggests that in the original plan of the town the forum occupied the whole area between streets 5, O, 6 and Q, a layout in which street 6 would have continued across the north-east side of the forum. This arrangement would

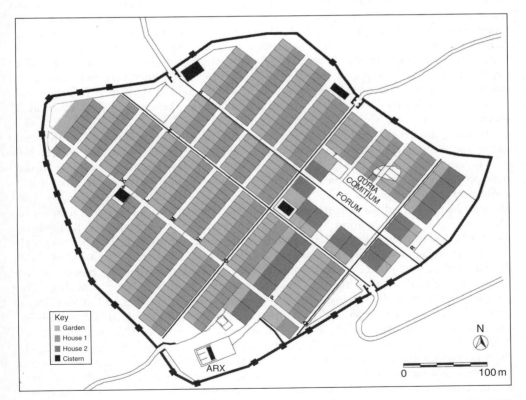

Figure 19.1   Reconstruction of the plan of the colony as it might have looked in around 150 BC with the larger plots darker grey and the smaller ones lighter. Sewell's hypothesis on the original plan of the forum and related roads is indicated by black lines. Drawing: E. Fentress.

have allowed the streets from three of the gates to pass along the sides of the forum, while the larger forum compares better with those of other mid-Republican colonies, measuring 360 × 200 ft, or 5 *actus quadrati*.

This proposal is attractive in that it creates a far more rational plan than that which we find today. However, there are various problems with it. Street 5 lies over 3 m higher than street 7. A stretch of preserved bedrock at the entrance to the forum, on the alignment of street P, shows that this difference in height is created by a sharp rise in the bedrock along the whole southern half of the proposed forum. This irregularity was not removed until the construction of the houses along the south side of the current forum, in the second quarter of the second century BC. Can we seriously imagine a forum that for 80 years remained unleveled, with a steep outcrop of bedrock along the whole of its southern edge? Further, there is very little evidence for any buildings that would have formed part of this early forum plan.

One solution to this issue lies in a reconsideration of our evidence for the third-century BC colony at Cosa. The only building we can certainly attribute to the earliest phase is the square structure on the *Arx*, apparently the predecessor to the Capitoline temple. This measured 7.5 × 7.5 m, or 25 × 25 Roman feet, and was oriented just east of north. To the north, and on axis with it, was a square hole, which was interpreted by Brown as the *mundus* of the colony, together with the *Cosa quadrata*, on the model of the elusive *Roma quadrata* (Brown, 1960: 9–17; 1980: 16–18). More recently, Rabun Taylor has suggested that, while the interpretation of the *mundus* remains plausible, at least as a votive deposit under an altar, the square structure must have been the original temple, some of whose terracottas were found under the later temples (Taylor, 2002: 66–80). Its date does not seem later than the early-third century BC, and its dedication remains unknown (Bispham, 2006: 98–99).

But there is precious little other evidence for early third-century activity on the site. The huge cistern at the south-east corner of Sewell's proposed forum may well belong to this period, but we have no direct evidence for this. We might imagine that the forum and the road network were laid out, but that major building works were not undertaken until much later in the century.

The *curia/comitium* complex on the north-east side of the forum seems to be firmly dated to the third century BC, in that it is abutted by a building which went out of use around 220 BC. The *comitium* consisted of a circular floor from which rose a set of eight or nine curved steps providing standing space for the assembly of the citizens: Brown has calculated that it could accommodate 600 individuals (Brown, Richardson, and Richardson, 1993: 26). This was inscribed in a roughly square podium built of mortared walls faced with thin rectangular blocks of stone, and measuring 16.20 × 17.50 m (Brown, Richardson, and Richardson, 1993: 13). A wide door opens onto the forum. Behind and bonded to it rose a hall on a high foundation whose door opened onto the *comitium*. This was covered with a tile roof and decorated in painted plaster in the Pompeian first style, with painted ashlar blocks, but we can say little else about the structure, which was largely obscured by later rebuilding. The complex, however, finds close parallels at Poseidonia, Fregellae, and Alba Fucens (Greco, 1988: 83; Brown, Richardson, and Richardson, 1993: 256–78; Coarelli, 1999: 31, 55–56; Mertens, 1968: 208–17; Sewell, 2010: 41). As both the *curia* and the *comitium* block Road 7, their construction seems to imply the redesign of the forum at this time, perhaps in the third quarter of the century, after the interruption of the First Punic War. A reduction in available manpower to carry out the massive amount of leveling necessary for the realization of the earlier forum plan might have caused the redesign. It seems certain that there were very few people in the colony at this time. To date, no private buildings have been found for this period (Fentress *et al.*, 2004: 13). We thus have no idea where the people who built the walls, the first temple, the *curia/comitium* or the large cistern actually lived.

The dimensions of the forum as it is seen today were thus established perhaps 40 years after the foundation of the colony, around 240 BC. Its sides were emphasized with eight planting pits in two rows on either side of the open space: the edges of the leveled open space were marked with trees rather than a portico.

19.1.3   *The deduction of 197 BC*

The lack of manpower was sufficiently acute at the end of the Second Punic War that the colony petitioned for new settlers in 199 BC, receiving them in 197. This was probably the point at which domestic architecture in stone began on the site. In all cases the construction of the houses started with the cistern, which was cut out of the limestone bedrock and plastered. The stone deriving from this excavation was then used to lay the foundations and first courses of the walls, which rose to around 50 cm above ground level. In the second century BC these were of drystone, with the stones carefully faced. Over these socles the walls were built of *pisé de terre*, pounded between shuttering. After the roof was tiled, the walls were plastered, producing a durable structure. Larger houses might have two cisterns, one receiving the rainwater from the roof at the rear of the house.

It seems clear from the plan of the colony that there were two standard sizes for the houses of the town (Fentress, 2000: 15–20). Around three sides of the forum and along the wider, "processional" streets were found houses with street frontages 60 Roman feet wide, using the canonical plan familiar from Pompeii and elsewhere: a vestibule flanked by *tabernae*, leading through a *fauces* into an atrium, with the *tablinum* on the axis of the door. *Cubicula* and *alae* were found on either side of the atrium, while behind the *tablinum* lay a garden with perhaps a small bath house. One of these, the "House of Diana," was entirely excavated between 1997 and 1999 (Fentress *et al.*, 2004: 14–23, 34–62).

Elsewhere in the town were found houses of an entirely different plan. Near the museum, north-west of the forum, Russell Scott excavated a long *insula* divided into house plots 8.5 m wide, or just under 30 Roman feet, around half the width of those on the forum plaza (Bruno and Scott, 1993: 13–63). On the south-west side of each plot was built a simple house, with a courtyard or atrium at the center. A *tablinum* and at least one *cubiculum* opened off this space. Behind the houses the plots were terraced at a lower level, with steps leading down to a garden and service areas. The basic layout here is similar to what we have seen on the forum, but on a smaller scale. The same hierarchy is inscribed in the streets, which were paved for the first time during this period. The ordinary streets are 6 m wide. However, the street leading from the forum to the *Arx*, and the street which leads from the south-west gate to the Eastern Height, are 9 m wide, and by the middle of the second century BC each of them led to a sacred area. Brown called these "processional streets." It is along these that further large atrium houses appear to have been built (Roca Roumens, 2007). It thus appears that there were houses for two classes of colonists, some of whom received plots exactly twice as large as the others. This scheme is suggested in Figure 19.1, where the smaller houses are shown as "house 1" and the larger as "house 2." The best estimate of their numbers is 21 larger houses, with around 238 smaller ones. These could have housed 259 of the 1000 new colonists, and the proportion between larger and smaller houses is slightly less than 1 to 10. These figures bear a close resemblance to those for a series of colonies sent out in the first two decades of the second century BC. At Thuri Copia and Castrum Frentinum in 193 BC, 300 *equites* received plots of 40 *iugera*, while 3000 *pedites* received 20 (Livy, *Epitome*: 35, 9, 7–8); at Vibo, in 192 BC, there were 300 *equites* and 3700 *pedites*, and again the *equites* received double-sized allotments (Livy, *Epitome*: 35, 40, 5–6); similar proportions applied at Bononia and Aquilea in 190 and 181 BC (Livy,

Epitome: 40, 34, 2–4). It seems that the Latin colonies of the period following the Second Punic War followed a consistent pattern, with colonies designed to accept two or three orders of colonists, and plots assigned by rank. The settlers, as we know from Livy, were drawn from the allies of Rome in the Second Punic War, and were in all probability veterans. The settlement, with its two orders of streets and two orders of houses, clearly reflects the difference in rank of its settlers. The forum would have been surrounded on three sides by the houses of the decurions, probably chosen from among the *equites*.

19.1.4   The forum

All of the principal public buildings were built, or rebuilt, beginning in the first quarter of the second century BC, around the same time as the construction of the houses. The architectural definition of the forum, and its related public buildings, seems to have been a primary concern (see Figure 19.2). On the three sides occupied by private houses and *tabernae* a portico was created, draining into a gutter around the open space, which seems to have been finally leveled at this time, and surfaced with beaten earth and small stone chips. The trees seem to have been eliminated at the same time.

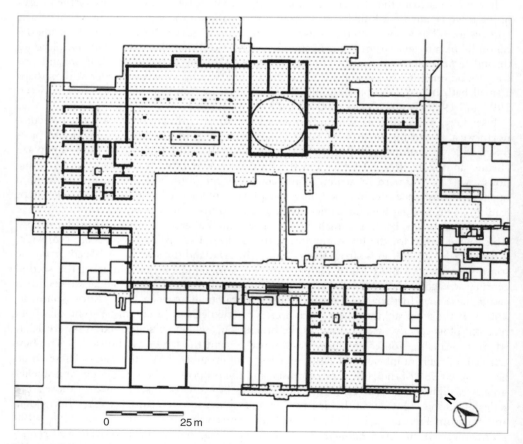

0   25 m

Figure 19.2   The forum at the end of the second century BC (stippling shows excavated area). Drawing: E. Fentress.

Along the north-east side of the forum a new set of public buildings was created, apparently at the expense of the private housing which previously occupied the spaces on either side of the *curia* (Fentress, *et al.*, 2004: 30–31). The *curia* was rebuilt, this time on a high podium of massive, irregular masonry. An amphora stamp of circa 180 BC gives a *terminus post quem* for the reconstruction, which we may date in the second quarter of the century (Brown, Richardson, and Richardson, 1993: 11, 227). Shortly thereafter the podium was expanded by two rooms flanking the original space, creating a building of three parallel halls facing onto the *comitium*. The new *curia* was abutted on its south-east side by a temple built slightly later, on a podium built of the polygonal masonry which would from this period mark the important buildings of the town. The temple, known as Temple B, took the place of a raised altar built against the *comitium* at the beginning of the second century BC, perhaps at the inception of the new deduction. The temple comprises a *cella* and a deep *pronaos* which is reconstructed by Brown as a distyle porch two columns deep, with Hellenistic Tuscan capitals (Brown, Richardson, and Richardson, 1993: 143–53). Brown, on the analogy of the Roman Forum, proposed that the temple was dedicated to Concord, a suggestion supported by an inscription to Concordia found built into a medieval grave (Brown, Richardson, and Richardson, 1993: 141; Brown, 1980: 31). However, the terracottas include two seated female figures which Richardson identifies as most likely to be Ceres and Proserpina. A third statue, apparently holding the piglet whose head is preserved, probably represents an offering to Ceres, support-ing this identification (Brown, Richardson, and Richardson, 1993: 184–206).

The final public building erected on the north-east side of the forum was the basilica, one of the earliest in Italy, dated by a coin in its foundation to some time after 157/156 BC (Brown, Richardson, and Richardson, 1993: 207–36). This was built in the space to the north-west of the *curia/comitium*, occupying the whole of the space between the facade of the forum and street 7, 35.89 m × 27.05 m, built on a rubblework foundation supporting a vault which terraced the building up to the level of the forum, and contained cisterns. A row of columns with Doric bases and capitals ran along the facade, while in the interior columns defined a rectangular space, which probably supported a clerestory with a smaller second order of columns. A flight of steps led to a terrace over the ambulatory, on the model of the *Basilica Aemilia* (*Paulli*) at Rome, built in 179 BC. To the rear of the building an *exedra* projects that was probably intended for a tribunal. The construction of the basilica in this period underlines the growing political and economic importance of Cosa in this period, after two generations of steady development since the end of the Punic Wars.

19.1.5   *The* Arx

A visual link between the forum and the hill to the south, referred to as the *Arx* by Brown, is formed by the broad street P, leading out of the center of the long side of the forum and climbing up towards the gateway in the wall which sets off the *Arx* from the rest of the town, forming a sort of extended *temenos*. Street P climbed directly towards the square structure at the top of the hill that Taylor (2002) interprets as the earliest temple of the colony. In the second quarter of the second century BC, at the same time as the work on the various buildings of the forum was beginning, this little temple was replaced with a far larger one which was interpreted by Brown as a *Capitolium*, the date based on coins found in the foundation and in the mortar of the mosaic flooring of the south *cella* (Buttrey, 1980: 32–33, 41). This is a large structure comprising the temple with a triple *cella*, a deep columnar *pronaos*, and a terraced forecourt. The *mundus* of the earlier temple, perhaps occupying the position of its altar, lies directly under the middle *cella*, but the orientation of the temple is very different, standing at an angle to the axis provided by street P. Its podium is, again, built of beautifully dressed polygonal masonry. Above this, the *cella* walls were built of concrete faced with small brick-shaped blocks of limestone, stuccoed white on the insides. On the outside of the building the podium was topped by a base and crown with a heavy, rounded Tuscan *torus*, over which was built the facing of squared ashlar blocks in sandstone. On the *pronaos*, four columns supported the roof, while *antae* formed by the prolongation of the walls of the *cella* flanked two further columns. Behind these, and parallel to the facade of the temple, was a deep cistern extending for the entire width of the building. This was evidently intended to collect the rainwater from the roof. The building's eaves were wide, as its drip lines show, and the elaborate terracotta decoration would have given it an archaic look, looming over the town from the top of the hill. Its attribution to the Capitoline triad is unproven, and would be anomalous for a Latin colony in this period; Bispham suggests that the temple was dedicated to Jupiter, Hercules, and Minerva (Bispham, 2006: 100–02; Crawley Quinn and Wilson, 2013).

Although the smaller Temple D, to the north of the large temple, has always been assumed to have preceded it there is in fact no evidence for this beyond the stylistic dating of the related terracottas (Taylor, 2002: 72; Brown, 1960: 182–98; Strazzulla, 1985; Scott, 1988). Indeed, the smaller temple seems placed to respect the position of the larger one, with its south corner on the axis provided by the front of the forecourt. Temple D is again tetrastyle on a polygonal podium, with a larger space between the middle two columns. The *antae*, with engaged columns at their ends, give the impression of a second row of columns, but the *pronaos* as a whole is proportionately much shorter than those of the *Capitolium* or Temple B. The Doric order of the columns will, again, have given a sober and rather archaic look to the whole. It is not clear to whom the temple was dedicated: Mater Matuta has been suggested, although Venus is also possible (Brown 1980, 47–49; Bispham 2006, no. 140).

19.1.6 The Eastern Height

A final religious building is represented by a small podium in polygonal limestone blocks on the Eastern Height (Fentress *et al.*, 2004: 29–30). Here the whole top of the hill was leveled to create an open space measuring circa 30 m, perhaps 100 Roman feet, by 23 m. The temple was situated in the center of the north-west edge of the sanctuary, looking out to sea, its axis exactly 14.78 m, or 50 Roman feet, from the north-east sanctuary wall. Its identification as a temple is based on the polygonal masonry of its foundation and on the few architectural terracottas found nearby: its outer dimensions of 6.25 × 11. 25 m. make it smaller than Temple D, although its masonry appears to have been directly comparable.

19.1.7 Cosa in the late Republic and early Empire

The half-century following 197 BC thus saw the construction of fully three temples, the rebuilding of the *curia*, and the construction of the basilica, as well as that of the atrium houses around the forum and probably a substantial amount of private building elsewhere in the colony. The prosperity which this indicates must have come from the countryside, whose farms were closely connected to the town and its port, and from the rich fisheries around the lagoon of Orbetello, whose products could have been salted near the ports and sold in Rome. During the next 70 years, however, we can see little activity beyond the inevitable changes to private houses, with some consolidation of smaller buildings into larger ones, as we can see in the case of the House of the Treasure, or new constructions occupying older gardens, like the House of the Skeleton (Brown, Richardson, and Richardson, 1993: 79–148). The town apparently filled out any empty spaces, and continued as a prosperous *municipium*. However, this prosperity came to a violent end in about 70 BC. There is evidence in various parts of Cosa for destruction and abandonment at that time: the skeleton in the eponymous house was thrown into a cistern of the building. The best evidence for the date of this event derives from a hoard found in the House of the Treasure (Bruno and Scott, 1993: 79, 147), and Brown's suggestion that the sack was an attack by pirates stands unchallenged. We have no evidence for any reoccupation of the site before circa 25 BC, although Scott suggests that it was garrisoned against Sextus Pompey from 40 BC (Bruno and Scott, 1993: 161).

The origins of the Augustan resettlement remain somewhat obscure. The coin evidence for the House of Diana shows a gap between 70 and 27 BC, while the stylistic evidence from painted plaster suggests a date for its decoration between 20 and 10 BC, which should give a *terminus ante quem* for the settlement as a whole (Fentress *et al.*, 2004: 154, 177). It may have been the object of veteran settlement, although we have no direct evidence for this. The resettlement of the colony would have provided services, a market, and a political base to the farmers that remained in the territory. The sample trenches indicate that the new town was smaller than the old, with only the forum and nine central *insulae* reoccupied. The new houses were generally bigger and better: the House of Diana was rebuilt with a loggia which occupied part of the old garden, while it used the ruins of the next-door house for a kitchen garden.

Some investment took place in public buildings: an altar from the *Arx* may record the *suovetaurilia* sacrifice at the lustral rites involved in the rededication of the temple (Brown, 1960: 518; Fentress *et al.*, 2004: 208–09), while one of the *tabernae* of the House of Diana appears to have been used as a little cult building, with a mosaic floor and a stuccoed ceiling (Fentress *et al.*, 2004: 36).

A new catastrophe struck the town in the middle of the first century AD. This took the form of an earthquake, which demolished the basilica and appears to have damaged the roof of the *Capitolium*. This earthquake, which may be associated with that which occurred the day Nero donned the *toga virilis* in AD 51 (Tacitus, *Annals*: 12.43.1; Fentress *et al.*, 2004: 55–62), apparently occasioned the appointment of a *curator* to manage the affairs of the ruined town: a number of dedications allow us to identify him as L. Titinius Glaucus Lucretianus (*AE* (2003) 632, 633–37; Fentress *et al.*, 2004: 56–62). Brickstamps show that he was involved in the replacement of the roof of the Capitoline temple, while a number of statue bases and statues found on the site of the old basilica show that he was active in its transformation into an *odeum*, with statues of Claudius and Nero: the latter is mentioned on two further inscriptions (*AE* (2003) 630, 631. Gros, 2000; Collins Clinton, 2000). He may have been the final owner of the House of Diana, where a little shrine to Diana ornamented with an inscription was built in the garden at this period. This, however, was almost the last sign of life in the town, which by the time of Trajan seems to have been prematurely deserted. A brief reoccupation took place under Caracalla, associated with the construction of granaries around the forum and the reconstruction of its portico, backed now only by ruins where there were no granaries (Fentress *et al.*, 2004: 63–69; see Figure 19.3). At the south-east end of the forum the former street was blocked by a shrine to *Liber Pater*, the tutelary deity of the Severan House (Collins Clinton, 1977). The site was now referred to in inscriptions dating from the reigns of Caracalla to Aurelian as the *Res Publica Cosanorum* (*CIL* 11.2633 and 2634; *AE* (1983) 325), but it seems to have been largely empty of *Cosani*, with only two *insulae* still occupied outside the immediate zone of the Forum. This occupation does not seem to have survived the third century, except for the occasional coin found at the shrine, perhaps traces of an annual festival. Rutilius Namatianus, who sailed past the site in AD 416, remarked on the ruins of the site, deserted because of a plague of rats (Rutilius Namatianus: 1.285–90; Cirelli and Fentress, 2012).

The last reoccupation before the middle ages seems to have begun around the middle of the fifth century, when a small settlement was created on the ruins of the basilica/*odeum*,

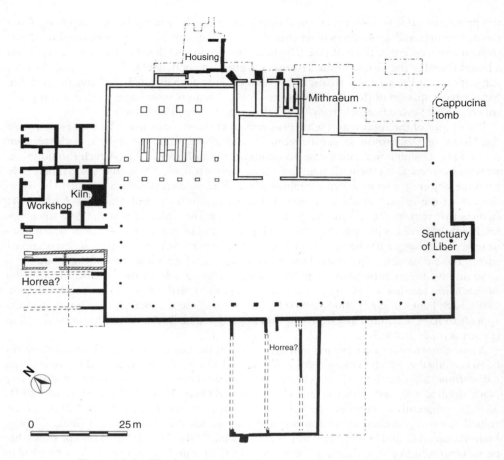

Figure 19.3   The forum in the third century AD. Drawing: E. Fentress.

and another on the Eastern Height (Fentress *et al.*, 2004: 72–86). The lower settlement was composed of two houses, a large oven, a small church, and a cemetery to the north of the church, as well as, perhaps, a few other buildings not yet discovered. A road along the line of street P linked this little settlement with the *Arx*, where a granary was built abutting the south side of temple D, using drums from its columns to support a wooden floor. Stabling seems to have been provided for horses to the north-east of the large temple, while there was certainly housing within the temple structure. It is probable that this settlement represents what remained of the imperial villa previously located at the *Portus Cosanus*, still managing the imperial properties in the area (Ciampoltrini and Notini, 1993). In the middle of the sixth century, after an incident in which the granary was burned, the *Arx* was refortified with a strong wall reinforced by towers on its east side. An inscription mentioning a [*ne*]*apolis* (*AE* (2003) 368) may suggest that this was a deliberate Byzantine foundation, aimed at the control of the *via Aurelia* and all traffic along the coast. Both amphorae and fine wares point to a well-established supply chain. It was probably this settlement that took the name of Ansedonia, the modern toponym, which has been plausibly explained as deriving from the *sitonia*, or granaries on the site (Patitucci, 2001: 199). If so, we can see here a recurrence of the function of the site as a point for tax-gathering which was first evidenced by the granaries of the Severan period: it may have remained on the imperial books since then. The settlement did not survive, however, and there is no evidence for occupation on the site from the seventh until the ninth century.

19.2   The *Ager Cosanus*

When the colony of Cosa, the first in Etruria, was founded it was given part of the land of the defeated Etruscan city of Vulci. The northern extent of the territory of Vulci is debated, but the boundaries of medieval dioceses have been used to reconstruct the hypothetical *Ager Cosanus* as contained by the River Albegna to the north-west, the River Elsa and Elsarella to the north and the River Tafone to the east (Perkins, 2010: 103–04). This area of 550 km² consists of thickly wooded limestone hills in the interior and about 220 km² of fertile (when drained) low-lying coastal plain of Pleistocene deposits with little transitional terrain. The Pleistocene deposits constitute the best arable lands. Closest to Cosa in the Val d'Oro and the coastal strip there are clayey sands and conglomerates deriving from marine deposits or erosion from the interior hills. In the lower Albegna valley the deposits form an extensive terrace at 15 m altitude running from the coast to Marsiliana along the southern bank of the River. In the western part of the *Ager* the lagoon of Orbetello survives whereas all the former lagoons on the coastal strip to the south have now been drained except the Lago Burano. The largely mountainous Monte Argentario is connected to the mainland by two sandbars and appears to have sustained little Roman settlement.

The *Ager* seems to have been centuriated at the time of the first foundation, given the rectangular module of 16 × 32 *actus*, and was aligned to 56°, unlike the city street plan. The *kardo* of the centuriation was drawn from the north-east gate of Cosa sighting towards the mouth of the river Albegna. At a distance of 16 × 16 *actus* (9.088 km) it intersects the orthogonal *decumanus maximus* that runs north-east along the 15 m Pleistocene terrace and appears to have been surveyed to intersect with the hill of Marsiliana by the River Albegna at the northern confines of the *Ager*. Conveniently, the *decumanus* that intersects the north-east gate of Cosa runs across the Val d'Oro; thus the three main axes of the centuriation traverse the best, and most densely settled agricultural land. These main axes appear to have been roads; the *kardo* partly coincides with the later *via Aurelia* perhaps dating to 200 BC, linking Rome to Pisa and eventually Liguria. The *decumanus maximus* continues to become, or at least join, the *via Clodia* at Saturnia, and the minor axes appear to have been stone walls. Surviving traces of the land division are largely confined to the flatter land below 50 m, coincident with the most fertile agricultural land. There are indications that the hills behind Orbetello to the north of Cosa were enclosed by a wall of polygonal masonry, perhaps separating the public grazing lands (*ager compascus*) from the centuriated areas (Celuzza, 2002a; Attolini, 2002).

19.2.1   *Settlement history*

Large-scale excavation and systematic field survey of approximatelty 100 km² in the 1970s and 1980s (Carandini and Cambi, 2002: 43–62) has provided a diachronic account of the development of the Roman settlement pattern enabling the archaeological study of the impact of the Roman conquest, centuriation, implantation of small farms, and the growth of the slave-powered villa system in central Italy (Dyson, 1978; Carandini, 1985a; 1985b; Carandini and Cambi, 2002). The Roman conquest of the area led to a generalized restructuring of the settlement pattern. Orbetello, the only Etruscan center of population in the *Ager*, survived the conquest and appears to have been fortified with walls identical to those of the colony. Centuriation of the land implies, at the least, a redefinition of the ownership of land parcels and probably an eviction of the previous Etruscan owners in the areas closest to the colony. However, in the third century, after the founding of the *colonia*, rural settlement is not extensive (see Figure 19.4). There is a cluster of sites in the Val d'Oro to the north of Cosa, a thin scatter in the lower Albegna Valley and a more consistent scatter in the valleys of the Chiarone and Tafone – the areas closest to Vulci and up to 15 km from Cosa (see Table 19.1). It may be the case that the early colonists – few in number – were largely settled in the Val d'Oro or Cosa itself and the more distant areas were retained by their Etruscan owners. There is good evidence for continuity of pre-conquest frequentation of the new Roman sites at only thirteen sites in the entire *Ager* (five cemeteries, one house/tomb, four houses, three villages). There is not good evidence for widespread building in all the centuriated land that might be interpreted as one farmstead for each of the colonists which would require a theoretical 2000 individual farmsteads (Rathbone, 1981: 17). There are methodological problems in interpreting the findings: fragments of Black Gloss tableware are not precisely datable and settlements from the third century BC may well be masked by later, larger settlements such as villas on the same site. Nevertheless 54 of the 89 sites are the smaller sites: house/tomb, house 1, and house 2. House/tomb sites are scatters of solely tile fragments covering less than 10 × 10 m where it was not possible to distinguish between burial or settlement use. House 1 sites are surface scatters less than 30 × 30 m with domestic refuse but no luxury items. House 2 sites are surface scatters larger than 30 × 30 m with evidence for stone buildings or substantial flooring such as *opus spicatum* or *cocciopesto* (Carandini and Cambi, 2002: 59). The early sites classified as villas, are most likely small settlements that only later developed into villas: the nature of surface scatters makes it difficult to tease out separate phases of occupation at the same site. Overall 70 rural settlement sites were located within the sampled transects that represent only 20% of the surface area of the *Ager*; multiplying this by five to represent 100% of the area would still only make 350 sites, far short of the theoretical maximum.

In this period up to four villages may have been occupied. They all lay on the coastal strip more than 10 km from Cosa. Two of these were ancient Etruscan settlements first occupied in the Archaic period and another was occupied in the fourth century. This class of site has not been explored by excavation but it would seem likely that these settlements, relatively remote from either Cosa or Vulci, would have performed some market or administrative functions. Another class of site that is distributed in the peripheries of the *Ager* are rural sanctuaries. Votive deposits dating from the third/second century have been recovered from Costa di Gherardino, near Marsiliana, and San Sisto in the lower valley. They consist of terracotta heads and body parts, *aes rude* and coins, and a statuette of a youth with a boar and a monkey on his shoulders, and so are typical of Etrusco-Italic and Campanian areas. Other votive finds, including a baby in swaddling, have been made near Orbetello but are poorly documented. In the north of the *Ager* just 1 km from Costa di Gherardino, a kiln site, possibly related to a villa, manufactured anatomical votives as well as other ceramics from perhaps the third century to the first century AD. The cults seem to be related to health, but may also perform a liminal role at the boundaries of the *Ager* (Camilli *et al.*, 2007: 356–57; Angás Pajas, 2005; Rendini and Firmati, 2003: 22–24; Rendini, 2009).

Some 30 inscriptions provide limited evidence for the people living in the *Ager Cosanus*. Nearly half of these are public inscriptions from Cosa and the remainder are funerary inscriptions of slaves and freedmen and women (Manacorda, 1979). Evidence from the field survey for burials in the *Ager Cosanus* is limited in its quantity and quality since it was not possible in surface survey always to be confident of separating tombs from settlements. However, the data table suggests that there was a significant degree of continuity in burial places between

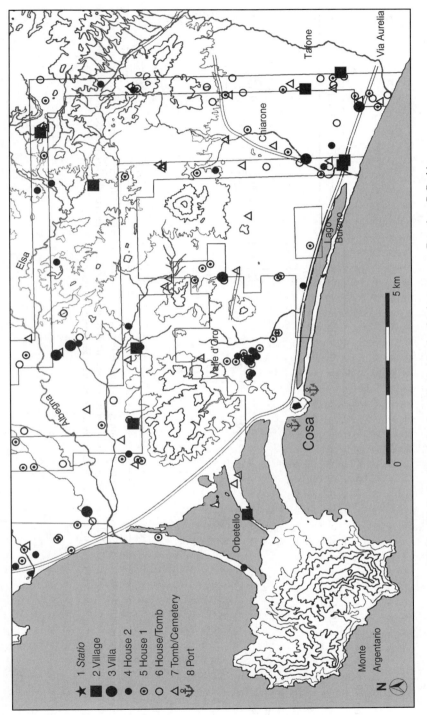

Figure 19.4 Settlement in *Ager Cosanus* in the third century BC. Drawing: P. Perkins.

1 Statio ★
2 Village ■
3 Villa ●
4 House 2 •
5 House 1 ⊙
6 House/Tomb ○
7 Tomb/Cemetery △
8 Port ⚓

Tafone

Via Aurelia

Chiarone

Elsa

Lago
Burano

Albegna

Valle d'Oro

Cosa

Orbetello

Monte
Argentario

N

5 km

0

Table 19.1 Sites within sample transects in the *Ager Cosanus* by type

Site type	4th C. BC	3rd C. BC	200–50 BC	50 BC–AD 100	2nd C. AD	3–4th C. AD	5–6th C. AD	7th C. AD
Statio	–	(1)	1	1	(1)	1	1	1
Village	(3)	(4) **1**	1 (3)	3	1 (1)	–	–	–
Settlement	(2)	(2)	–	–	–	–	–	–
Port	(1)	(2) **1**	(2)	2	1 (1)	1 (1)	(1)	–
Villa	(3)	(9) **6**	9 (20) **19**	41 **13**	22 (14) **1**	12 (4)	10 (3)	2 (4)
House 2	(3)	1 (13) **10**	10 (23) **19**	19 **3**	2 (3)	2 (2)	1 (1)	–
House 1	(1)	(26) **25**	(37) **13**	24 **4**	2 (6)	(2) **1**	1 (1)	–
House / Tomb	(6)	(14) **11**	3 (14) **5**	10 **1**	1 (3)	1	1	–
Cemetery	(8)	(12) **4**	(13) **4**	5 **1**	(5)	–	–	–
Tomb	(6)	(6)	1 (7) **3**	7 **4**	(1)	–	–	–
Dump	–	–	(3) **3**	1 (1)	(1)	1	–	–
Kiln	–	–	(3) **3**	2	1	1	–	–
Totals	(33)	1 (89) **58**	25 (125) **69**	117 (1) **25**	30 (36) **1**	19 (9) **1**	14 (6)	3 (4)

C. = century | Numbers indicate certain sites representing a minimum; numbers in brackets indicate uncertainly dated sites, adding the two provides a maximum number of sites. Numbers in bold indicate new foundations and are included in the certainly or uncertainly dated totals. Lack of certainty is caused by precision of dating of different types of ceramic in different periods. Source: Elizabeth Fentress.

the Etruscan and Roman periods. This is particularly notable in the eastern part of the *Ager Cosanus* in the valleys of the Chiarone and Tafone that are closest to Vulci: these are also the areas in which the two continuously occupied villages are found. Such continuity, often into the Augustan period, is common in the interior of Etruria, but is surprising in the *Ager Cosanus*, given the violent conquest of Vulci by the Romans. However, this continuity is limited to the eastern borders of the territory of Cosa.

The Punic wars and other unrest in the third century BC do not seem to have had a catastrophic impact on the settlement pattern. Only seven possible settlements do not continue to be inhabited in the second century suggesting only very limited decline in the rural population. However the arrival of 1000 new colonists in 197 BC marks the beginning of a period of intensification of rural settlement (Carandini and Cambi, 2002: 158–68).

The period from 200–150 BC is coincident with the period of greatest development and prosperity in Cosa when houses were built and the public buildings redeveloped (see Figure 19.5). After the injection of new colonists in 197 BC the rural settlement pattern develops considerably with the emergence of a dense, hierarchical settlement pattern in the Val d'Oro and the lower Albegna Valley whilst the more peripheral parts of the eastern and northern *Ager* are less intensively occupied. A small number of villas may have been developed at this time but the most common category of site is the house 2 (10–32 sites). In 1981–1982, a house 2 site was excavated at Giardino Vecchio 7.75 km to the north-east of Cosa (see Figure 19.6). Unfortunately, it has never been fully published, but a preliminary report and plan indicate that it was a well-built stone structure covering approximately 500 m². The farm focused on a 7.5 × 6.25 m internal courtyard entered from the north-east through a wide passage, with two large rooms with plastered walls and floors, a kitchen with a tile oven, and a workroom containing a loom on one side. Opposite these were a wine press and *dolium* for fermentation and store rooms with further stores on the fourth side. On the exterior of the south-east side were lean-to stables. Finds included ceramics and amphorae made at Cosa and numerous coins, including two in silver (Celuzza, 1985b). All in all, the farm forms a plausible home for a prosperous colonist and the evidence for wine and textile production along with the coins suggests the farm participated in the monetary economy of the region, perhaps contributing to Cosa's wine exports.

We know less about the smaller house 1 sites and the house/tomb sites. These could plausibly be the homes of free citizen farmers. The density of sites seems consistent with a land assignation of 16 *iugera* per (lower class) colonist (Celuzza, 2002a: 123). A small rectangular structure with stone foundations and associated hut at Casa Brancazzi, near the mouth of the Albegna, probably equate to a house 1 site. They were occupied through the first century BC and finds of lead weights and loom weights indicate fishing and textile manufacture. The structure is very basic, but finds of ceramics, bronze, and coins indicate engagement with the local economy (Ciampoltrini, 1984).

From the mid-second century BC into the first there is a generalized decline in the number of smaller rural settlements and a growth in the number of larger villas. This process coincides with the "agrarian crisis" of Rome, the rapid expansion of Roman power within and beyond Italy, the influx of slaves into Italy, and ultimately the Social War and Civil Wars (Launaro, 2011). According to Appian, writing much later, "The rich ... came to cultivate vast tracts instead of single estates, using slaves as laborers and herdsmen, lest free laborers should be drawn from agriculture into the army" (Appian, *Civil Wars*: 1.7). Within this turbulent context, the settlement pattern and economic basis of the *Ager* appears to have been transformed, and by the Augustan period the settlement in the areas closest to Cosa and the lower Albegna valley are entirely dominated by large, slave-powered villas. Smaller farms survive in peripheral areas, but in the core of the *Ager*, as at Giardino Vecchio for example, the small,

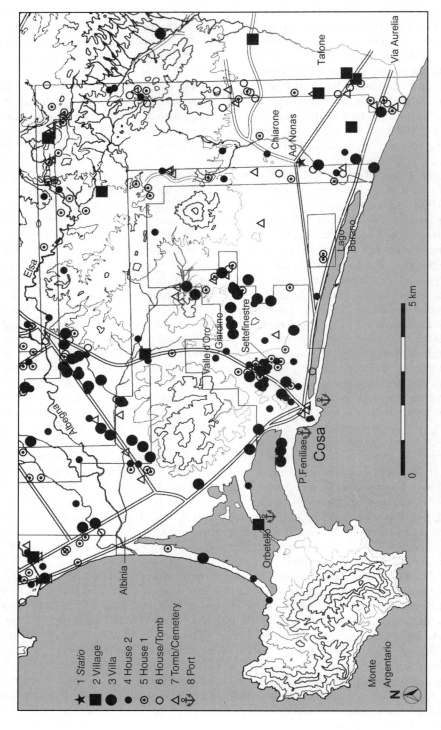

Figure 19.5 Settlement in *Ager Cosanus* 200–50 BC. Drawing: P. Perkins.

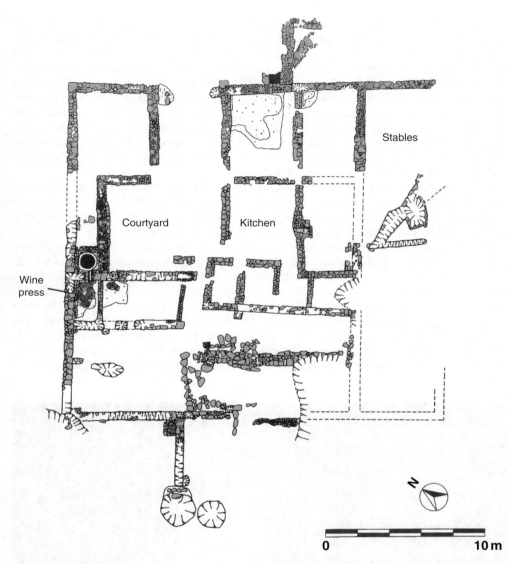

Figure 19.6   Plan of farm excavated at Giardino Vecchio. Drawing: P. Perkins after Carandini, 1985: fig. 113.

free landowner has almost entirely disappeared (Carandini, 1985; Carandini and Cambi, 2002: 158–96). None of the villas has been excavated in detail and so it is not possible to ascertain how many had developed from smaller, earlier farms. Equally, we cannot be sure that these villas conformed to the type of villa found in Cato, rather than being closer to the slave-run villa described by Varro (Regoli, 2002a). This general transformation has been taken as exemplifying the rise of externally financed, capitalist, slave-run estates designed to render income to the Roman elite at the cost of dispossessing free smallholders. This transformation is, however, only clearly visible in the good arable land closest to Cosa and in the lower Albegna valley; peripheral areas of the *Ager* and the territories of the neighboring colonies of Heba and Saturnia, surveyed using the same methodologies, do not appear to have undergone such an intense process of villa development at the expense of smaller sites.

Typically, in the surveyed areas, the villas were large surface scatters of tile, stone, and ceramics (greater than 2500 m²) with traces of architectural elaboration such as a cryptoporticus, column drums or mosaic tesserae. Many of the villas in the lower Albegna valley, around Orbetello and the Val d'Oro took the form of a *basis villa*: a concrete cryptoporticus substructure with working and living areas built above. These are typically fully integrated with the centuriation, with the walls following the same alignment and each occupying one *centuria*. In the lower Albegna valley these are remarkably evenly distributed along the *decumanus maximus*. The best known is Settefinestre in the Val d'Oro, although it is late in the sequence and was not constructed until around 40 BC.

At Settefinestre, on a small hill overlooking the *via Aurelia*, 4 km north-east of Cosa, a large villa was excavated in the late 1970s (Carandini, ed. 1985b; 1988, 109–224) (see also Pollard, ch. 17, this vol.). The villa and its gardens are enclosed by a wall with a turreted monumental facade resembling a city wall, an unusual feature shared with the nearby villas at La Provinca, Le Colonne, and Casa Marotti (Dyson, 2002; Calastri, 2004). The villa was entered from the top of the hill where a gate and a passage led into an open courtyard. To either side were stores, a cowshed, and kitchens. Twelve rooms each of about 3 × 3 m housed the estimated 52 slaves who worked the villa and its lands and tended the sheep, goats, and cattle that were housed in a separate animal house and granary to the west of the villa. The main block of the villa was large (44 × 44 m (150 × 150 Roman feet)) and set on the hillside on a concrete cryptoporticus (see Figure 19.7). It had two entrances from the courtyard: one led into the main living area, the *pars urbana*, and the other led into the working part of the villa, the *pars rustica* (cf. Figures 17.2 and 17.3). The axial layout of the *pars urbana* is arranged

Figure 19.7   View of the cryptoporticus and facade of the *basis villa* at Settefinestre. Photograph: P. Perkins.

around an *atrium* and a second set of rooms around a *peristyle*. Additionally the villa had rooms facing out from this central core towards the countryside. All of these rooms have remains of high quality wall and floor decorations.

The rooms in the north-east quarter of the building were linked to the main *atrium-peristyle* axis of the *pars urbana* by five different routes and so were closely integrated with the refined mosaic floors and painted walls of the living quarters. However, they held the agricultural machines of the estate: a donkey-powered olive mill, an oil press, and three wine beam-presses operated by a screw and linked by a hole in the floor to the vats (*dolia*) in the fermentation room below. Together these made up the heart of the *pars rustica* of the villa.

Andrea Carandini, the excavator of the villa, suggested that this building and its organization closely matched a villa of the type described by Varro (*On Agriculture* 1 written in about 37 BC) and Columella (circa AD 65) (*On Agriculture* 1). Combining the evidence from the villa and the ancient sources enables the estimation of the productive capacity of the villa. The excavator suggests that the villa could have produced about 100 000 liters of wine worth about 60 000 *sestertii*. Other produce of the villa such as cheese, eggs, poultry, game birds, geese, ducks, wild animals, snails, dormice, honey, and fish could have provided twice this sum bringing a considerable total of 180 000 *sestertii*. The sale of surplus olive oil and grain could have raised the income further (Carandini, 1988: 121, 173–77).

Settefinestre provides a detailed case study of the economic functioning of a villa producing wine at the end of the Republican period and through the first century AD. Yet earlier, the transformation in the settlement pattern that started in the second half of the second century BC, is paralleled by evidence for the large scale export of agricultural produce from the region (Attolini *et al.*, 1991). At both of the ports of Cosa, shards of amphorae, both Greco-Italic and Dressel 1, are abundant; they are even used to build walls. Although no actual kilns have been excavated, fire bricks have been found. The petrographic analysis of the amphora shards, the quantity of shards at the port, and the very high frequency of amphora stamps of the Sestius family all indicate that the amphorae were made at the port and that the port enabled the export of wine and possibly fish products in amphorae made by, or for, the Sestii. The earliest amphorae date to the end of the third century BC, but the period of major activity peaks at the end of the second century. Amphorae continue to be made despite the destruction of Cosa in circa 70 BC, although production of the Sestius amphorae does seem to cease around 40 BC (Manacorda, 1978; Will, 1987 and 2002; McCann, 2002: 28–30).

The infrastructure of the ports was also developed to support this economic activity: before the last quarter of the second century the port of Cosa had only a stone breakwater but in the next 50 years it was equipped with piers, wharves, a lighthouse, a fresh water spring house, and a fishery (Gazda and McCann, 1987: 137–55). Improvements were also made to the road system: south of Cosa the *via Aurelia* was built further inland and a *statio*, *Ad Nonas*, established at the crossing point of the river Chiarone, probably in 119 BC, creating a minor settlement, market and administrative center in the eastern part of the *Ager* furthest from Cosa (Fentress, 1984; Carandini and Cambi, 2002: 134–35, 159–60). North of Cosa the *via Aurelia* was rebuilt towards Pisa, probably in 115–09 BC (Fentress,1984; Coarelli, 1988) with a bridge, dock, and *mansio* built at Albinia, close to the mouth of the Albegna (Ciampoltrini, 1997). Here, a second large-scale amphora manufactory developed, producing Greco-Italic, Dressel 1, Dressel 2–4 and flat-bottomed amphorae. A wide variety of stamps name at least 14 individuals active between the last decades of the second century to the end of the first century BC. The SES and Albinia amphorae testify to the huge productive capacity of the new villa-based agricultural organization throughout the territory. These amphorae, presumably containing wine and perhaps also fish products, were widely exported from the *Ager Cosanus* across Etruria to southern and central Gaul (Bogdani, Calastri, and Vecchietti, 2009; Vitali *et al.*, 2007; Vitali, 2007).

The decline of Cosa after 70 BC does not seem to have directly impacted the development of the villas. It is likely that the villas grew on investment in the land by the Roman metropolitan elite rather than from the local elite in Cosa. A late Republican epitaph names a freedman, Lucius Domitius Papus, and so complements the literary evidence indicating that Lucius Domitius Ahenobarbus, a prominent opponent of Julius Caesar, owned land in the area which may, in due course, have become imperial property when the family's property passed to his great-grandson, Nero (Manacorda, 1979: 130; Celuzza, 1985a; 2002b: 202). Between 50 BC and AD 100 the villas, including the newly built Settefinestre and its monumentally walled neighbors, dominated the agricultural land in the coastal plain closest to Cosa and the lower Albegna valley. There was also an intensification of settlement, including villas on the sandbars joining Monte Argentario to the mainland. Smaller farms persisted only in the eastern part of the *Ager* where there were far fewer villas. The villas were presumably still dependent on the wine industry, although the evidence for amphora manufacture ceases in the early part of the first century AD, suggesting other agricultural produce, not exported in amphorae, may have grown in importance. By the imperial period, the harbor at Cosa seems little used for exports, although imported material is still found at the port. Estimates of the population based upon the field survey data suggest a density of 19–21 people per square km at this time (Fentress, 2009).

Later in the first century AD and in the early part of the next, the number of villas declined by perhaps a quarter, and only one new villa site was founded in the second century. The late Republican economic and settlement structure, based on slave-run villas producing wine and owned by cultivated, interested, and occasionally resident owners, appears to have become obsolete as competition from the provinces flooded the markets in Rome with provincial vintages and brought the export of Italian wine to an end (Tchernia, 1986; Carandini, 1989a; 1989b).

At Settefinestre the villa was reorganized at the beginning of the second century AD. The oil and wine presses in the *pars rustica* were dismantled and the rooms converted into stores. The *pars urbana* was redecorated, becoming less sumptuous, although a large complex of hot and cold baths was added. The rooms around the courtyard were reorganized and to the south west a second courtyard with rows of small rooms about 3×3 m^2 was built. Each room opened onto the courtyard, the walls were unplastered, and no flooring was found. This new block has been identified as a new set of cells and services for slaves that could have raised their total number to about 100 (Carandini, 1988, 173–77). However, in the absence of firm evidence, Marzano suggests that the rooms could also have had other uses, such as stables (Marzano, 2007: 130–38). Further to the south-west another similar structure was built with smaller cells arranged around a courtyard. The building matches the descriptions by Varro and Columella of a pigsty. The excavator suggests that these developments represent a fundamental shift in the economy of the villa, and that the villa had started "farming" slaves, with female slaves kept for breeding purposes and any children not required for labor sold at market. Alongside, there is the development of a pig farm, and possibly an increase in arable output (Carandini, 1989b; 1988: 185–219).

It is not known how typical Settefinestre is of the villas in the area, or whether it may have become part of a larger estate with merged infrastructure and services. Imperial estates may also have grown: in addition to the Neronian holdings, Vespasian was brought up on an estate near Cosa to which he frequently returned (Suetonius, *Life of Vespasian*: 2). There was a major reorganization of the port of Cosa which became dominated by a *villa marittima*, possibly in imperial ownership, dating from the Claudian period until the fifth century

(Gazda and McCann, 1987: 155–59; Ciampoltrini and Notini, 1993). In the second century small rural settlements were rare, their numbers were down from a maximum of 87 sites to only 17. This trend continues in the third to fourth century when the total of occupied sites is more than halved, despite a reoccupation of Cosa (Fentress *et al.*, 2004: 68–69). Settefinestre is abandoned in the Severan Period and it seems likely that after this there was a further transformation in the economic regime with the few surviving villas developing into *latifundia*, large estates with an economy oriented towards pastoralism and a population living an estate centers that had previously been villas. A halving in the number of settlements would imply a doubling in the average size of estates; however, it is also possible that less land was exploited or that malaria may have become established in coastal areas (Fentress, 2009). Unfortunately, no sites dating to this period have been excavated that might provide more detail about the nature of these late Roman settlements. In the Eastern part of the *Ager* the *statio* at *Ad Nonas* and two villages near the *via Aurelia* remain occupied, but we know nothing of their organization or economic functioning. The number of occupied sites reduces further in the fifth century and it seems likely that the Visigothic invasion will have disrupted life along the *via Aurelia* at least (Regoli, 2002b). In the sixth century, there is evidence for settlement on very few of the villa sites and otherwise at only the *Portus Feniliae*, the *statio*, and one village.

FURTHER READING

For the excavations at Cosa the synthetic account is still Brown (1980), although this has been subject to reinterpretation (Fentress 2000; Dyson 2005; Bispham 2006). The original excavation reports should be the starting point for any detailed investigation of Cosa (Brown 1960; Brown *et al.* 1993; Bruno and Scott 1993, Fentress *et al.* 2004, for the full details of the stratigraphy see http://press.umich.edu/webhome/cosa/home.html, accessed September 1, 2015). For the port of Cosa see McCann 1987. Many of the finds have also been well published: coins (Buttrey 1980); Black Gloss wares (Taylor 1957; Scott 2008); *terra sigillata* (Marabini Moevs 2006); coarsewares (Dyson 1976); thin walled wares (Marabini Moevs 1973 and 1980), lamps (Fitch and Goldman 1994), and amphorae (Will 1987).

For field survey in the *Ager Cosanus* the fundamental publication is Carandini and Cambi 2002 along with preliminary accounts in Carandini 1985a. The finds have not been published. Manacorda 1979 is the starting point for the epigraphy, though the inscriptions from Cosa itself are not yet published. For the Etruscan period sites and finds see Perkins 1999. For an analysis of the demography of the Albegna valley over time see Fentress 2009.

REFERENCES

Angás Pajas, J. 2005. "Santuarios como indicadores de frontera en el territorio noroccidental de Vulci (siglos VII–III a.C. Italia centro-tirrénica)." *Saldvie* 5: 65– 94.

Attolini, A., Cambi, F., Castagna, M., Celuzza M.G., Fentress, F., Perkins, P., and Regoli, E. 1991. "Political geography and productive geography between the valleys of the Albegna and the Fiora in northern Etruria." In *Roman Landscapes: archaeological survey in the Mediterranean region*, eds G. Barker and J. Lloyd, 142–52. London: British School at Rome.

Attolini, I. 2002. "La centuriazione di Heba." In *Paesaggi D'Etruria: Valle dell'Albegna, Valle d'Oro, Valle del Chiarone, Valle del Tafone*, eds A. Carandini and F. Cambi, 129–31. Rome: Edizioni di Storia e Letteratura.

Bispham, E.H. 2006. "*Coloniam deducere.* How Roman was Roman colonization during the Middle Republic?" In *Greek and Roman Colonization. Origins, ideologies and interactions*, eds G.J. Bradley and J.-P. Wilson, 73–160. Swansea: Classical Press of Wales.

Bogdani, J., Calastri, C., and Vecchietti E. 2009. "Lo scavo nelle fornaci romane di Albinia (Orbetello-GR)." In *Materiali per Populonia* 8, eds F. Ghizzani Marcìa and C. Megale, 255–68. Pisa: ETS.

Brown, F.E. 1960. *Cosa II, the Temples of the Arx.* Rome: *Memoirs of the American Academy in Rome* 26.

Brown, F.E. 1980. *Cosa: the making of a Roman town.* Ann Arbor: University of Michigan Press.

Brown, F.E., Richardson, E.H., Richardson, L. Jr. 1993. *Cosa III, The Buildings of the Forum.* Rome: *Memoirs of the American Academy in Rome* 37.

Bruno, V. J. and Scott, R. T. 1993. *Cosa IV, The Houses.* University Park, PA: *Memoirs of the American Academy in Rome*, 38.

Buttrey, T.V. 1980. "Cosa: The Coins." *Memoirs of the American Academy in Rome* 34: 11–153.

Calastri, C. 1999. "L'insediamento di Portus Fenilie nell'Agro Cosano." In *Campagna e paesaggio nell'Italia antica. Atlante tematico di topografia antica* 8, eds L. Quilici and S. Quilici, 127–36. Rome: «L'Erma» di Bretschneider.

Calastri, C. 2004. "Una nuova villa con fronte a torrette dall'agro di Cosa." In *Viabilità e insediamenti nell'Italia antica. Atlante Tematico di Topografia Antica* 13, eds L. Quilici and S. Quilici Gigli, 173–86. Rome, «L'Erma» di Bretschneider.

Camilli, A., Del Re, A., Sanchirico, C., Santoro, E., and Zifferero A. 2007. "Manciano (Gr). Nuove ricerche a Marsiliana d'Albegna: l'esplorazione archeologica della Tenuta Corsini." *Notiziario della Soprintendenza per i Beni Archeologici della Toscana* 2: 350–61.

Carandini, A. 1985. "Il sorgere delle ville." In *La Romanizzazione dell' Etruria: il territorio di Vulci,* ed. A. Carandini, 145–47. Milan: Electa.

Carandini, A. 1988. *Schiavi in Italia: gli strumenti pensanti dei romani fra tarda repubblica e medio impero.* Rome: La Nuova Italia Scientifica.

Carandini, A. 1989a. "Economia italica fra tarda repubblica e medio impero considerata del punto di vista di una merce: il vino." In *Amphores romaines et histoire économique: dix ans de recherche: actes du colloque de Sienne, 22–24 mai 1986,* eds M. Lenoir, D. Manacorda, C. Panella, 505–21. Rome : École française de Rome.

Carandini, A. 1989b. "La villa romana e la piantagione schiavistica in Italia (II secolo a.C.-IId.C.)." In *Storia di Roma IV,* 101–92. Turin: Giulio Einaudi editore.

Carandini, A., ed. 1985a. *La Romanizzazione dell' Etruria: il territorio di Vulci.* Milan: Electa.

Carandini, A., ed. 1985b. *Settefinestre: una villa schiavistica nell'Etruria romana.* 3 vols. Modena: Edizioni Panini.

Carandini, A.and Cambi, F., eds 2002. *Paesaggi D'Etruria: Valle dell'Albegna, Valle d'Oro, Valle del Chiarone, Valle del Tafone.* Rome: Edizioni di Storia e Letteratura.

Celuzza, M.G. 1985a. "La documentazione epigrafica." In *La romanizzazione dell' Etruria: il territorio di Vulci,* ed. A. Carandini, 102–04. Milan: Electa.

Celuzza, M.G. 1985b. "Un insediamento di contadini: la fattoria di Giardino." In *La Romanizzazione dell' Etruria: il territorio di Vulci,* ed. A. Carandini, 106–07. Milan: Electa.

Celuzza, M.G. 2002a. "Cosa, la centuriazione." In *Paesaggi d'Etruria,* eds A. Carandini, F. Cambi, M. G. Celuzza, and E. Fentress, 121–23. Rome: Edizioni di Storia e Letteratura.

Celuzza, M.G. 2002b. "Dalla riconversione delle ville alla crisi (50–200 d.C.)." In *Paesaggi d'Etruria,* eds A. Carandini and F. Cambi, 196–206. Rome: Edizioni di Storia e Letteratura.

Ciampoltrini, G. 1984. "Un insediamento tardo-repubblicano ad Albinia." *Rassegna di Archeologia* 4: 149–80.

Ciampoltrini, G. 1995. "Un pocolom e le mura di Orbetello." *Archeologia classica* 47: 289–302.

Ciampoltrini, G. 1997. "*Albinia, fluvius habet positionem.* Scavi 1983–1988 nell'approdo alla foce dell'Albegna (Orbetello, Gr)." *Rassegna di Archeologia* 14: 253–95.

Ciampoltrini, G. and Notini, P. 1993. "Castelli sul mare di Maremma. A proposito della 'Structure on the Eastern Height' di Ansedonia." *Archeologia Medievale* 20: 607–609.

Cirelli, E. and Fentress, E. 2012. "After the rats: Cosa in the Late Empire and Early Middle Ages." In *Urbes Extinctae: archaeologies of abandoned classical towns,* eds N. Christie and A. Augenti, 97–113. Aldershot: Ashgate.

Coarelli, F. 1988. "Colonizzazione romana e viabilità." *Dialoghi di archeologia* 3: 35–48.

Coarelli, F. 1999. "L'edilizia pubblica a Roma in età tetrarchica." In *The Transformations of* Vrbs Roma *in Late Antiquity*, ed. W.V. Harris, 23–33. Ann Arbor: *Journal of Roman Archaeology* Suppl. 33.

Collins Clinton, J. 1977. *A Late Antique Shrine of Liber Pater at Cosa*. Leiden: Brill/*Etudes prélimi-naires aux religions orientales dans l'empire romain*, vol. 64.

Collins Clinton, J. 2000. "The Neronian odeum at Cosa and its sculptural program: a new Julio-Claudian dynastic group." *Memoirs of the American Academy in Rome* 45: 99–130.

Crawley Quinn, J. and Wilson, A. 2013. "Capitolia." *Journal of Roman Studies* 103: 117–173.

Dyson, S.L. 1976. *Cosa, the utilitarian pottery*. Rome: *Memoirs of the American Academy in Rome* 33.

Dyson, S.L. 1978. "Settlement patterns in the Ager Cosanus: The Wesleyan University Survey, 1974–1976." *Journal of Field Archaeology* 5.3: 251–68.

Dyson, S.L. 2002. "The excavations at Le Colonne and the villa culture of the Ager Cosanus." *Memoirs of the American Academy in Rome* 47: 209–228.

Dyson, S.L. 2005. "Success and failures at Cosa (Roman and American)." *Journal of Roman Archaeology* 18: 615–20.

Fentress, E. 1984. "Via Aurelia, Via Aemilia." *Papers of the British School at Rome* 52: 71–76.

Fentress, E. 2000. "Frank Brown, Cosa, and the idea of a Roman city." In *Romanization and the city. Creations, transformations and failures*, ed. E. Fentress, 9–24. Portsmouth, R.I.: *Journal of Roman Archaeology* Suppl. 38.

Fentress, E. 2009. "Peopling the countryside: Roman demography in the Albegna Valley and Jerba." In *Quantifying the Roman Economy*, eds A.K. Bowman and A. Wilson, 127–62. Oxford: Oxford University Press.

Fentress, E. *et al.* 2004. *Cosa V: An intermittent town, excavations 1991–1997*, Ann Arbor: University of Michigan Press.

Fitch, C.R. and Goldman, N. 1994. *Cosa, the Lamps*. Ann Arbor: *Memoirs of the American Academy in Rome* 39.

Gazda, E.K. and McCann, A.M. 1987. "Reconstruction and Function: port, fishery and villa." In *The Roman port and fishery of Cosa*, ed. A.M. McCann, 137–59. Princeton: Princeton University Press.

Greco, E. 1988. "Archeologia della colonia latina di Paestum." *Dialoghi di Archeologia* series 3, 6.2: 79–86.

Gros, P. 2000. "L'odéon dans la basilique: mutation des modèles ou désagrégation des programmes? " In *Romanization and the City. Creation, transformations, and failures*, ed. E. Fentress, 211–20. Portsmouth RI, JRA Suppl. 38.

Launaro, A. 2011. *Peasants and slaves: the rural population of Roman Italy (200 BC to AD 100)*. Cambridge: Cambridge University Press.

Manacorda, D. 1978 "The Ager Cosanus and the production of the amphorae of Sestius." *Journal of Roman Studies* 68: 122–31.

Manacorda, D. 1979. "Considerazioni sull'epigrafia della regione di Cosa." *Athenaeum* 57: 73–97.

Marabini Moevs, M.T. 1973. *The Roman Thin Walled Pottery from Cosa (1948–1954)*. Rome: *Memoirs of the American Academy in Rome* 32.

Marabini Moevs, M.T. 1980. "Italo-Megarian ware at Cosa." *Memoirs of the American Academy in Rome* 34: 161–227.

Marabini Moevs, M.T. 2006. *Cosa. The Italian Sigillata*. Ann Arbor: *Memoirs of the American Academy in Rome* Suppl. Vol. 3.

Marzano, A. 2007. *Roman Villas in Central Italy. A social and economic history*. Leiden and Boston: Brill.

McCann, A.M., ed. 1987. *The Roman Port and Fishery of Cosa. A center of ancient trade*. Princeton: Princeton University Press.

McCann, A.M. 2002. *The Roman port and fishery of Cosa. A short guide*. Rome: American Academy in Rome.

Mertens, J. 1968. "Massa d'Albe (L'Aquila). Il foro di Alba Fucens." *Notizie degli scavi di antichità* 22: 205–17.

Patitucci S. 2001. "Evidenze archeologiche della Provincia Marittima bizantina in Toscana." In *Società multiculturali nei secoli V–IX. Scontri, convivenza, integrazione nel mediterraneo occidentale*, ed. M. Rotili, 191–222. Naples: Arte Tipografica.

Perkins, P. 1999. *Etruscan Settlement, Society and Material Culture in Central Coastal Etruria*. Oxford: BAR International Series 788.

Perkins, P. 2010. "The cultural and political landscape of the Ager Caletranus, north-west of Vulci." In *L'Étrurie et l'Ombrie avant Rome Cité et territoire*, ed. P. Fontaine, 103–22. Brussels / Rome: Brepols.

Rathbone, D.W. 1981. "The development of agriculture in the 'Ager Cosanus' during the Roman Republic: problems of evidence and interpretation." *Journal of Roman Studies* 71: 10–23.

Regoli, E. 2002a. "Dalla villa schiavistica al latifondo (III–IV secolo)." In *Paesaggi d'Etruria*, eds A. Carandini and F. Cambi, 218–27. Rome: Edizioni di Storia e Letteratura.

Regoli, E. 2002b. "Il paesaggio delle ville (II secolo a.C-metà I a.C.)." In *Paesaggi d'Etruria*, eds A. Carandini and F. Cambi, 145–54. Rome: Edizioni di Storia e Letteratura.

Rendini, P., ed. 2009. *Le vie del sacro. Culti e depositi votivi nella valle dell'Albegna*. Siena: Nuova Immagine.

Rendini, P. and Firmati, M. 2003. *Archeologia a Magliano in Toscana*. Siena: Nuova Immagine.

Roca Roumens, M. 2007. "Orbetello (GR). Excavación en la insula O-P/4-5 de ciudad romana de Cosa." *Notiziario della Soprintendenza per i Beni archeologici della Toscana* 3: 480–85.

Scott, A.R. 2008. *Cosa. The Black-Glaze Pottery 2*. Ann Arbor: *Memoirs of the American Academy in Rome* Suppl. Vol. 5.

Scott, R.T. 1988. "The Latin colony of Cosa." In *La colonizzazione di IV e III secolo a.C. Atti del Convegno (Acquasparta 1987), DArch*, s.III, 6.2: 73–77.

Sewell, J. 2010. *The Formation of Roman Urbanism, 338–200 B.C.: between contemporary foreign influence and Roman tradition*. Portsmouth, RI: *Journal of Roman Archaeology* Suppl. 79.

Strazzulla, M.J. 1985. "Le terrecotte architettoniche." In *La Romanizzazione dell' Etruria: il territorio di Vulci*, ed. A. Carandini, 79–100. Milan: Electa.

Taylor, D.M. 1957. "Cosa, Black-Glaze Pottery." *Memoirs of the American Academy in Rome* 25: 65–193.

Taylor, R. 2002. "Temples and Terracottas at Cosa." *American Journal of Archaeology* 106.1: 59–84.

Tchernia, A. 1986. *Le vin de l'Italie romaine*. Rome: École Française de Rome.

Vitali, D., ed. 2007. *Albinia I. Le fornaci e le anfore di Albinia: primi dati su produzioni e scambi dalla costa tirrenica al mondo gallico*. Bologna: Università di Bologna, Dipartimento di archeologia.

Vitali, D., Laubenheimer, F., and Benquet, L. 2007. "La produzione e il commercio del vino nell'Etruria romana. Le fornaci di Albinia (Orbetello, GR.)." In *Archeologia della vite e del vino in Etruria. Atti del Convegno internazionale di studi. Scansano, 9–10 settembre 2005*, eds A. Ciacci, P. Rendini and A. Zifferero, 191–200. Siena: CI.VIN.

Will, E.L. 1987. "The Roman amphoras." In *The Roman port and fishery of Cosa*, ed. A.M. McCann, 171–220. Princeton: Princeton University Press.

Will, E.L. 2002 "Defining the *regna vini* of the Sestii." In *New Light from Ancient Cosa*, ed. N.W. Goldman, 35–47. New York: Peter Lang.

CHAPTER 20

Pompeii and the *Ager Pompeianus*

Ray Laurence

20.1 Landscape History and Cultural Memory[1]

Pompeii was a city that was understood by later writers to have been founded by Hercules on his return from Cadiz driving in procession (*pompa*) the cattle of Geryon back to Greece. It is from the Latin word *pompa* (meaning procession) that Pompeii was seen to have taken its name (Servius, *Commentary on Virgil's Aeneid* 7.662 = **A4**; Isidore, *Etymologies* 15.1.51 = **A3**). Obviously, this does not mean that Hercules literally founded the city, but that later the city was understood to have its origins in this story from mythology. This is what should be described as a cultural memory about the past; it is something that was held to have been true by those living in antiquity. There were other similar stories found in the writers of antiquity in relation to the peoples who inhabited the city and its region: Oscans, Greeks, Umbrians, Etruscans, and Campanians in Pliny's *Natural History* (3.60–62 = **A8**) or Etruscans, Pelasgians, and Samnites in Strabo's *Geography* (5.4.8 = **A7**). The mapping of these peoples onto the archaeology of Pompeii and its hinterland is well-nigh impossible, because what Pliny and Strabo give us are sequences of unified groups who were thought to have inhabited the city in the past. These should be seen as memories of the past that were shared with others and understood as a cultural "common-sense." The form these take is to associate Pompeii with particular peoples, which successively occupied the city. For writers in the early Roman Empire, it provided a means of thinking about the antiquity of the past and also of associating that specific past of Pompeii with the past of other cities that may have been Etruscan or Pelasgian, or Samnite. It is a cultural logic that depends on the context of *tota Italia*, or a united Italy, in which all are Roman citizens, but the cultural pasts of these places was quite distinct and might be constructed via association with different generic groups or ethnicities that resided outside the region.

The view of the past as different from the Roman present was confirmed for visitors to Pompeii. Although Latin was the contemporary language of the city by the first century BC, it was still possible, even in AD 79, to find inscriptions in the Oscan language (Cooley, 2002). Those that survive (**A10–17, A20–21, A28, A30**) provide a view of the city prior to the settlement of Sulla's veterans in the city. Magistrates and their children were involved in the development of monuments and in road building. These inscriptions could be found in

A Companion to Roman Italy, First Edition. Edited by Alison E. Cooley.
© 2016 John Wiley & Sons, Ltd. Published 2016 by John Wiley & Sons, Ltd.

the Stabian Baths (a sundial: Crawford, 2011, Pompei 21 = **A13**); in the Samnite Palaestra (building-inscription of the palaestra: Crawford, 2011, Pompei 24 = **A12**); at the Stabian Gate (road building-inscription: Crawford, 2011, Pompei 13 = **A11**); at the Nolan Gate (building-inscription: Crawford, 2011, Pompei 8 = **A30**); in the temple of Apollo (pavement inscription: Crawford, 2011, Pompei 23 = **A15**); in the Triangular Forum (building-inscription: Crawford, 2011, Pompei 11 = **A14**); and (possibly) at the southern end of the forum (building of a portico: Crawford, 2011, Pompei 9 = **A28**). The Oscan language marks these inscriptions as different, but their content is almost identical to later Latin inscriptions in Pompeii. The inscriptions commemorate the same type of actions – the spending of money on the monuments of the city. Other Oscan inscriptions were plastered over, including those on street corners that gave direction on the defense of the city under siege (e.g. Crawford, 2011, Pompei 2 = **B6**), and also a painting within a house that identified one of the armed horsemen as Spartacus (Crawford, 2011, Pompei 45 = **B18a–b**). Outside the city, to the south, were three sanctuaries to the gods: Zeus Meilichios, Bacchus (Dionysus-Liber), and Poseidon (De Caro, 2007; Cooley and Cooley, 2014: 15–16). If these are indications of the nature of the non-Roman city, the *foci* of attention were very similar. It should also be pointed out that it is in the pre-Roman period that Pompeii developed a theater, bathing facilities, temples that included Egyptian deities, and a forum. The characteristics often picked out as those of the "Roman" city were in place at Pompeii prior to the settlement of Sulla's veterans following the Social War.

The revolt of the Italian Allies in 90 BC was an event to be recalled in centuries to come; interestingly, for Appian at least (*Civil Wars* 1.39 = **B1**), the list of peoples hostile to Rome, who revolted in that year, featured major groups such as the Samnites or the Lucanians, but also included the Pompeians – a people perhaps not just from the city of Pompeii and its territory, but of the entire valley of the Sarno that included the city of Nola – a conception of identity that is supported by Appian's account, which connects the two cities in discussion of military operations by Sulla that culminates in the destruction of the rebel army outside the gates of Nola (Appian, *Civil Wars*: 1.50; compare Strabo *Geography*: 5.4.8). More importantly, the revolt involved the region and included military action by the rebels against Nola, Nuceria, Surrentum, and Salerno – towns in close vicinity to Pompeii (Appian, *Civil Wars*: 1.42, note presence of factions in Nola). Both Pompeii and Nola had land confiscated and redistributed to Sulla's colonists, and subsequently the term Pompeians became associated not with a people inhabiting a number of cities but just one city (Cicero, *In Defence of Sulla*: 62–64 = **B19**; Berry, 1996: 250–57). The Pompeians, alongside the other allies who revolted, were to be constructed as in conflict with the Roman settlers and easily associated with plots such as that of Catiline against the Roman State – it was in Pompeii that a town councillor was struck by lightning, providing one of the portents for this conspiracy (Pliny, *Natural History*: 2.137 = **B20**). The Pompeians were to be remembered for their revolt against Rome.

The settlement of Sulla's veterans at Nola and Pompeii altered the social structure of these cities, and physically reshaped them. The process is most easily seen from the building of new monuments. Pompeii was one of the first cities known to have an amphitheater built for the display of spectacles (*CIL* 10.852 = **B12**), alongside a covered theater (*CIL* 10.844 = **B11**) – both buildings were constructed by the same persons, Gaius Quinctius Valgus and Marcus Porcius. The latter had also added a new altar in front of the temple of Apollo (*CIL* 10.800 = **B9**); the former was involved in construction at Casino, Aeclanum, and Frigento and was probably the father-in-law of P. Servilius Rufus, who proposed the agrarian law rigorously opposed by Cicero in 63 BC (Welch, 2009: 76–79). The forum was extended with the addition of a new *Capitolium*, and a new temple complex was dedicated to Venus with a sacred grove overlooking the walls just inside the Marine gate (Small, 2007: 186; Carroll, 2008; 2010).

To the north of the forum, a new set of baths was added and the Stabian Baths were altered. These changes effectively restructured the city: seen from the south, the landing point for ships, the skyline of the city would have been changed to include the new temple of Venus to the left and the amphitheater to the right, whilst in the center stood the temple of Hercules in the Triangular Forum. Within the city, the work of the colonists touched every point from the temples to the gods through to the baths in which people washed. The addition of the covered theater also, it is argued (see discussion in Laurence, 2007: 171) disrupted the traditional route of the procession of youths, since the steps leading up to the Triangular Forum became obstructed. What we do not see from the archaeological record is which houses in the city and what property in the countryside were taken from the Pompeians and given to the incoming veterans. However, all the evidence that we do have points to a fundamental change to the city over a relatively short period of time.

20.2   The Landscape of the City and the Country

Campania, the region in which Pompeii was situated, was famous for its productivity. Strabo (5.4.3) could see three crops grown on the same patch of soil; and Pliny the Elder (*Natural History*: 3.60) described a land of vine-clad hills, whose produce was drunk the world over (see Pliny the Elder, *Natural History*: 14.22, 35, 70 for examples) and was famous for cereal cultivation as well (Pliny the Elder, *Natural History*: 18.109–14). This productive landscape of grapes and cereals was destroyed by Vesuvius and recalled by Martial (*Epigrams*: 4.44 = **C25**). Fundamentally, this was a landscape of production and much of that produce (in the form of wine) was exported and became known by many in the Roman world. Productivity should not be underestimated: a minimal estimate for viticulture from Pompeii's hinterland would be in the region of 30 000 hectoliters per annum (Jongman, 1988: 132), but could be much higher than this to produce a considerable surplus, perhaps as much as 10 000 hectoliters for export (Banaji, 1988; Scheidel, 1992: 209; Senatore, 1998: 137). Such exports are attested by finds of amphorae marked with the stamp *L. Eumachi* finding their way not just to Rome, but also into southern Gaul and to Carthage in North Africa (Senatore, 1998: 141–42).

The extent of Pompeii's territory has been estimated at 20 000 hectares (80 000 *iugera* – Jongman, 1988: 107), that may have supported a population of 36 000 (Jongman, 1988: 110).With about a third of the population resident in the city or its vicinity, this would produce an overall population (it is calculated by Jongman, 1988: 110) of 180 persons per square kilometer. This is a far higher population density than we would expect to find elsewhere in Italy, and is also a factor that might be reflected in the size of Pompeii itself. With an urban area within its walls of 66 hectares, Pompeii is not the largest city in Italy by any means, but is significantly larger than other cities across the Italian peninsula. Moreover, an urban population of 12 000 is not insignificant – this might be seen as above average (the median) when compared to the other 430 or more towns in Italy. Hence, the city and region of Pompeii need not be greater than every other, but a much higher level of population was supported with the consequence that the higher population could be mobilized in times of crisis. However, only hard work could maintain such a high population density if it was to be maintained in the longer term (Jongman, 2007).

The relatively high population found in Pompeii and its region meant that the city could draw on its greater human resources, if required to do so. Just such an occasion was the aftermath of the major earthquake in AD 62. The scale of the damage caused by this event can be gauged from the account provided by Seneca (*Natural Questions*: 6 = **C1** for extracts; Tacitus

Annals. 15.22 = **C2**). The epicentre would appear to have been close to Pompeii with a section of Herculaneum experiencing considerable damage and Naples also experiencing considerable damage to private buildings, but Pompeii was described as simply "collapsed." Images of the public monuments of the forum depicted at a jaunty angle appear on reliefs from the *lararium* (household shrine) in the House of Caecilius Jucundus (**C3**, see Huet, 2007 for discussion). The scale of damage was higher and the scale of rebuilding work should not be underestimated; it was on a different scale from the run-of-the-mill earthquakes that affected Campania and was an event that might be included in Tacitus's *Annals* (Pliny *Letters*: 6.20.3 = **C11** on frequency of earthquakes in Campania). Not just the fabric of the city was affected: Seneca stresses that 600 sheep died as well (*Natural Questions*: 6.1.27) and we would expect the earthquake to have been associated with considerable damage to the agricultural resources of the region, as well as to the city itself. Looking at the buildings of the city and its associated villas, we can identify today patching to the walls, rebuilding using bricks (a new material that was beginning to be mass-produced in the first century AD) to patch up buildings in a concerted phase of mass-reconstruction of the city (see **C4** for example). Hard times meant that all resources needed to be mobilized regardless of the niceties of social position, age, or status – a freedman paid for the rebuilding of the temple of Isis but the inscription commemorated his six-year-old son undertaking the task; the young boy was rewarded for "his" generosity with a place on the town council (*CIL* 10.846 = **C5**). The freed slave, even in a crisis, could not be rewarded in this way due to his exclusion from the city council.

The scale of rebuilding was vast with new buildings under construction in AD 79, including a complete reconstruction of the forum that included some of the latest forms in terms of design technology (Dobbins, 1994; 1996) and the new Central Baths constructed in brick-faced concrete (Laurence, 2007: 34–38 for discussion). By analogy with other earthquake disasters found in Tacitus's *Annals* (2.47), Roger Ling (2007) has suggested the scale of development needed was far larger than the resources available locally, and he suggests that the emperor Nero and his Flavian successors were directly involved in supplying funding for the process of reconstruction. If this was the case, it occurred in a period of considerable instability. The Great Fire of Rome in AD 64 required a rebuild of a city that housed a far greater population, and reconstruction was far from complete when a further fire in AD 80 caused further damage in the capital. It needs to be remembered that the civil wars of AD 69 were the source of instability across the Italian peninsula (see Cooley, ch. 6, this vol.). There is some evidence of donations from Nero and his wife Poppaea (*AE* (1985) 283 and 284 = **E19, E20**), but the process was not smoothly carried out, with T. Suedius Clemens (a tribune) being sent on the orders of Vespasian to investigate amongst other things encroachment on public space (*CIL* 10.1018 = **F148**; Laurence, 2007: 35). Even so, what Pompeii provides us with is an example of what was possible after a seismic catastrophe, just as Rome's rebuild after the fire of AD 64 does in an almost identical context. The city could be rebuilt and it could be rebuilt on a more elaborate scale than before. In fact, what was produced was a quite unique structure, for its forum seems to have no actual parallels in other cities in Italy or elsewhere in the Roman Empire. Perhaps, where the money came from for the recovery of the city is not the most important question to ask. Pompeii, like other cities, was not so distant from Rome that there were no personal connections – the Sulpicii archive of documents points to links to Puteoli, the imperial household and regular appearances of the Sulpicii in Rome for legal reasons (Andreau, 1999: 71–79; Camodeca, 1999). The understanding of Pompeii's ability to rebuild itself needs to be seen not just in terms of the economic resource of its hinterland, but in terms of this economic resource and the ability to gain access to resources from other persons often located outside the region – particularly in Rome, the very center of the empire.

20.3   Emulation and Local Elite Identities

Pompeii, as we saw earlier, was located in Campania at the mouth of the river Sarno and was described separately as part of the region in revolt against Rome in the Social War. Although on the Bay of Naples, Pompeii sits in a unique position on relatively low-lying ground over-looking a river estuary. It is part of the culture of the Bay of Naples but is, in many ways, slightly separated from the elite culture of pleasure on its northern and southern shores. The northern shore of the Bay of Naples was associated with the villas and bathing facilities of Baiae (a place of leisure for those in Rome) and with Naples itself (Rome's Disney-esque Greek playground for those resident in the Capital) (cf. Lomas, ch. 12, this vol.); the southern shore of the Bay from Stabiae onwards was populated by villas constructed in the hills and on the cliffs overlooking the Bay (Laurence, 2009: 49–62; D'Arms, 2003). In contrast, Pompeii appears as a town amongst a landscape of villas overlooking the sea. It was part of the culture of the region, but seems on first sight geographically separated from it. This problem under-lines another: how do we read the remains of Pompeii? Should we see the city as emulating forms of housing and public buildings found in Rome and discussed in texts, such as *On Architecture* by Vitruvius?

John D'Arms (2003: 417) pointed out that in the Augustan Age "the chief interpreters of imperial ideology were a town's most eminent citizens," and that in Pompeii we are best able to see the process at work. In the forum, we find the public priestess constructing a *chalcidi-cum*, a crypt and a *porticus* all dedicated to Concordia Augusta and Pietas (*CIL* 10.810 = **E56**) in her own name and that of her son – significantly the *Porticus* of Livia in Rome was dedicated in the name of Livia and her son Tiberius (D'Arms, 2003: 421; Ovid, *Fasti*: 6.638–48; Dio Cassius: 55.8.1–2). The building has fewer parallels with the actual plan of that building and far more in common with the basilica in Herculaneum, or the *porticus* of Pompey's theater in Rome (Fentress, 2005). Yet, within this structure, there are parallels with other features of imperial ideology in Rome: statues of Romulus and Aeneas recalled similar ones set up in the Forum of Augustus (*CIL* 10.808 = **E58** and *CIL* 10.809 = **E59**). It is also worth mentioning at the outset that a mother in Pompeii could fund the largest building project of the Augustan age in the city.

The construction of the theaters of Pompey and of Marcellus (and to a lesser extent that of Balbus) in Rome created an impetus for the construction of theaters in the towns of Italy (Esmonde Cleary, Laurence, and Sears, 2011). Pompeii with its Hellenistic theater fits into this pattern of development. Two brothers – M. Holconius Rufus and M. Holconius Celer – constructed vaulted passageways, tribunal and an area of seating in 2 BC (*CIL* 10.833 = **D54**, see D'Arms, 2003: 422 for dating via *CIL* 10.890 and 837 = **E43** and **D56**) under the direction of a freed-slave architect (*CIL* 10.841 = **D55**). Significantly, perhaps, Marcellus had prior to his death been patron of the youths of Pompeii during his life time (*CIL* 10.832 = **F135**; D'Arms, 2003: 422 for interpretation). Two young men of the time (prior to Marcellus's death in 23 BC) were the Holconii brothers who in adulthood 20 years later would pay for the reconstruction of the theater, and one of them was named as patron of the colony with a suitably militaristic statue for a man who gained the symbolic title of military tribune on an arch at the intersection of the *Via di Stabia* and *Via dell'Abbondanza* adjacent to the Stabian Baths (*CIL* 10.830 = **F93a/b**; D'Arms, 2003: 426–27). The idiom of commemoration takes its cue from Augustan Rome and transposes that idiom to the context of Pompeii. One man connected to Rome with the aid of his brother could alter the very fabric of a city such as Pompeii. When combined with the actions of a few others, such as Eumachia, the city becomes transformed – but it needs to be remembered that the actions of the few shape the city for the many and bring forth from Rome the ideology of the Augustan capital to the small town setting.

Figure 20.1   Tomb of Eumachia, Pompeii – note the scale of the monument compared to the mature trees. Photograph: L.H. Davies.

Not surprisingly, perhaps, the money behind the building project of Eumachia also paid for her tomb, the most substantial monument of its kind from Pompeii (**E62–66**) (see Figure 20.1). There were tombs of other elite men and women found in the cemeteries in the Augustan period; for example, the priestess Mamia, who had built a temple (possibly) to the *Genius* of Augustus (*CIL* 10.816 = **E53**, *CIL* 10.998 = **E54**). This matching of building projects within the city and imposing tomb outside the city gates seems to have been a short-lived phenomenon associated with the Augustan period. For, as Henrik Mouritsen (2005) has stressed, it is only in this period that we find monumental tombs on this scale associated with the families of the city's elite found in such numbers in the cemeteries close to the city itself. Such structures had only begun to be built with the foundation of the Roman colony in 80 BC and included that of Marcus Porcius, one of the builders of the amphitheater and covered theater (*CIL* 10.997 = **B125**). However, Mouritsen (2005: 45) points out that of all the tombs known to have been constructed in the last 40 years of Pompeii's existence only five monuments can be associated with the elite of the city, whereas examples of tombs of a similar stature being built by freed slaves in the urban *necropoleis* can be found in abundance. The pattern needs explanation and the most convincing one would seem to be that the elite simply chose instead to commemorate their dead on lands adjacent to their rural estates rather than in the cemeteries adjacent to the city (Mouritsen, 2005: 45–55). Such a possibility has been substantiated by the excavation of a tomb in nearby Scafati that included the identification of its family – the very prominent late Pompeian family the Lucretii Valentes (*AE* (1994) nos 395–98 +*AE* (2008) 313 = **D16**, **F90**). This explains the phenomenon from the point of view of elite commemoration, but the appearance of large monumental tombs to dead freedmen in the cemeteries of the city needs further explanation. Freedmen were excluded from holding magistracies in the city, but they could serve as *Augustales* in the city and might in this capacity give *munera* (games – *CIL* 4.9962 = **D23**). Individual *Augustales* can be located in some of the largest marble-clad tombs in the cemeteries outside the gates of Pompeii (**F115–117**). The model used by historians to explain this phenomenon and that of the *Augustales* in general tends to be based on a form of emulation of the freeborn elite, which is said to cause the elite to abandon such forms of commemoration to ensure social distinction or separation from the freed slaves as a group (Mouritsen, 2005) (see also Perry, ch. 25, this vol.). It leads Mouritsen (2005: 57) to see a "distinct freedman community" and the monuments were set up, according to him, to celebrate their common achievement of transition from slavery to freedom *and* wealth and recognition of influence. This all seems to be true, but the reference point seems to be mistaken. Rather than looking to behavior of the elite of Pompeii, we should perhaps look to the recognition of the achievements of freed slaves in Rome, where the imperial freedmen under Claudius and Nero achieved recognition for their achievements and role in the state. Such a model integrates the freed slave into society, rather than excluding them into marginality. This social situation was not without its tensions: the aristocracy need not choose to build a tomb to commemorate its dead in close proximity to the tomb of a freed slave commemorated by a family of freed and freeborn Roman citizens. Overall, though, what we see in the cemeteries is the social recognition of freed slaves by society and that included the elite in the form of the *ordo* of decurions (or town council).

20.4   Homes in the City and the Countryside

The houses of Pompeii and the villas of its countryside excavated over the course of two centuries from its discovery have been objects of wonder for visitors to the site. However, their interpretation today is far from straightforward. In the nineteenth century, William Gell and John Gandy (1875: 78) could use the "assistance" of Vitruvius, the Augustan writer on architecture, to name each room: *atrium*, *peristylium*, *cubiculum* and so on. This was a straightforward and unproblematic reading of the text into the material culture of the city. This approach has been rightly questioned, not least by Penelope Allison. She finds such a reading less than useful and would reject the use of such nomenclature (Allison, 2004). It needs to be stressed that her analysis has a polemic to it: archaeology should be understood in its own right rather than as a process that is aided by texts. This process of textual rejection can be extended to discussion of the major earthquake in AD 62 and points instead to the likelihood of ongoing seismic activity from AD 62 to 79 (Allison, 1995). This possibility should not be rejected, but perhaps we would expect to find evidence of it in the well-studied Insula of the Menander (Ling, 1995).

Underpinning much of our interpretation of houses and villas in the region are the expectations of the modern observer of these houses and their material culture. Do we see these as the best-preserved Roman houses and read Vitruvius alongside our visits to them, or should we try to ignore Vitruvius and look at them from a different perspective? For example, Penelope Allison (1995: 183) begins her research from a premise that any "deviation" from an expected pattern, for example a "formally decorated room" being used for a "utilitarian" purpose or vice versa was a sign of the deterioration of domestic circumstances. There is an unstated correspondence between these signs of "downgrading" and a deviation from an expected pattern of usage derived from the texts of Vitruvius with regard to formal rooms such as the atrium and so on (Allison, 2004 for full analysis and discussion). It is almost impossible

Figure 20.2   Atrium in the House of the Ceii, Pompeii – a space roughly 10 m × 10 m. Photograph: R. Laurence.

to ignore texts on the Roman house, but perhaps it is better to realize that these texts, Vitruvius in particular, deliberately constructed an Italian architecture in opposition to that of Greece (Wallace-Hadrill, 2008: 208–10). Like all texts, Vitruvius's discussion of the Italian house was a representation of architecture that had a schematic relationship to his experience of seeing houses. Where many part company with Penelope Allison's views is that to use a text in explaining material evidence does not imply that the interpretation of the archaeological material is done in the manner of Gell and Gandy more than 100 years ago (1875). This could be described as the polemic or noise that distracts from the value of the study of artefacts in the understanding of domestic environments in Pompeii.

No one house is representative of all houses in Pompeii. However, to give a flavor of the nature of living conditions, I shall discuss one house specifically, the House of the Ceii, whose fabric dates from the second century BC with alterations ranging right through to the town's final phase (see Figure 20.2). The latter included the insertion of a staircase into the eastern side of the atrium (Michel, 1990 for full description of architecture and wall painting). The house covers an area of 300 m² (3200 ft²), and thus is larger than the average for Pompeian residences that could comprise simply a single room (Wallace-Hadrill, 1994: 72–82 on sizes of houses). However, it is also ten times smaller than the House of the Faun (3000 m² or 32 000 ft² in area). The decoration of the house is predominantly in the Third Style of painting characterized by chromatic blocks of color with intricate and, often, illusionary details) that dates from the first century AD. The facade of the house has stucco work to make it appear to be built from large blocks of masonry. Inside the entrance is an atrium about 10 m × 10 m with a roof supported on four columns. There are four rooms leading off from the atrium – a kitchen and three other rooms less defined by function. There is also a corridor leading to the rear, where there are a further three to four rooms arranged around a garden space that is dominated by a hunting scene. The upper floor probably contained a further three or four rooms. Overall the house would have contained 12 separate rooms arranged around the central atrium and garden to the rear. The distribution of artifacts in the house shows that items not in use on a daily basis were stored, for example a bronze brazier for heating or a water-heater. Equally, items used at different times of the day were put away, such as lamps in a cupboard under the stairs and kitchen utensils. What is clear is that the atrium was associated with storage as much as display, something that is a feature of other houses in Pompeii: where cupboards were located, there were concentrations of artifacts. Hence, what we find in Pompeii in the analysis of artifact studies are patterns of storage rather than of use. This is an important observation, since we should expect in the context of the eruption that other items might be taken by those leaving the city or in other cases simply left. However, for the most part the artifact assemblage of Pompeii is one that represents the actions of those experiencing a life threatening natural disaster – a pattern from which it is difficult to discern the activity patterns from the artifacts found in the domestic setting (Allison, 2004 for database, description, and analysis). The house had been subject to some changes, but perhaps this is normative of urban domestic space and should not be related to any general patterns of social change.

When looking at habitation outside the city, the archaeological evidence is biased towards larger, more monumental villas (Jongman, 2007a: 504–05; Moormann, 2007 for overview). They are easier to find in the endless redevelopment of the modern landscape of the Bay of Naples. In a recent publication, Eric Moormann sets out 103 sites in the valley of the river Sarno stretching from the slopes of Vesuvius at Boscotrecase in the north to the villas at Stabiae to the south (Moormann, 2007: 436–38). However, there is no single site amongst these that could be seen to be representative of all villas in the region. Nearly every site has signs of productive agriculture, alongside a greater or lesser degree of sophisticated facilities for the comfort of the inhabitants. A key feature found in villas in the rural hinterland that is mostly absent from the houses of the city is the private heated bath-house. Only the largest houses in Pompeii, such as the House of the Menander, had such a facility (Fabbricotti, 1976 gives 16 examples in Pompeii). In contrast, the bath-house can be found in some of the more modest villas from the hinterland, and was a feature of the more lavish villas such as that of San Marco at Stabiae (Fabbricotti, 1976: 109–11). Bathing was becoming not just a phenomenon associated with the city, but increasingly it was part of rural living in villas close to the city. This is important since it points to the widening of the availability of facilities for the elite, so that they might bathe wherever they were resident (compare Pliny the Younger, *Letters*: 2.17). The baths at the villas of the elite of Campania, with innovations such as window glass perhaps caused the city to become less attractive as the locale of residence. It is possible that this feature or change occurring in the rural domestic environments around Pompeii may, alongside the shift in commemoration of the dead to the rural setting of the villa, point not so much to a shift from the city to the countryside but to the urbanization of the countryside in the first century AD.

The fullest publication of a villa comes from the work of Stefano De Caro at the Villa Regina at Boscoreale (De Caro, 1994 for full description of structures, decoration, and finds). The villa is a prime example for the production of wine with its press, fermenting vats, and vineyard planted around it (Jashemski, 1993: 288–91; see also Pollard, ch. 17, this vol., with figures 17.4–17.6). It also provides the means to contrast life in the countryside with that of the city. The nine or so rooms are arranged around a courtyard with a colonnade with nine columns supporting the roof. The largest pair of rooms contained the wine press and the household's *lararium* (shrine) on the northern side of the courtyard, which was flanked on one side by a kitchen with bread oven and a further shrine close to the entrance to the kitchen. On the other side of the rooms with the wine press was a room that is described by the excavator as a storeroom for a range of materials, including a hammer, fish-sauce container, lamps, numerous vessels, and some glass bottles (De Caro, 1994: 31–32). On the eastern side of the courtyard, there was a purpose-built decorated dining room. The courtyard itself was for the most part dominated by jars for wine-making sunk into the ground. The inhabitants of this villa had a well that was accessed from a room off the courtyard. In addition to these utilitarian rooms, there were three ground-floor rooms that we could assume were bedrooms. The finds from this modest villa included 172 pottery vessels or containers; 11 amphorae or parts of amphorae; 14 lamps; two bronze vessels; 14 items made of glass; agricultural tools; hammers and nails. There was also a two-wheeled cart found on site. The material living conditions of the inhabitants of this small-scale wine production unit were not so distinct from life in the houses of the city of Pompeii. Their rooms were decorated, and there were shrines to the gods, and the inhabitants created artificial light by burning olive oil. What they did not have access to were bath facilities on site, but even today the site is only a 30-minute walk from the Herculaneum Gate (Keppie, 2009: 120). However, these rural residents did not have a different material culture from the inhabitants of the nearby city and had access to the city itself.

20.5   Urban Spectacle

Looking at Pompeii and the unique forms of evidence that it presents to us, in particular the *dipinti* – painted signs that were written by sign-writers – there is an opportunity to understand this city not so much in terms of the subcategories of "leisure," "religion," "politics" and so on, but as a place of spectacle (Figure 20.3). This allows us to see the city and understand its purpose as a place in which there were activities to be watched. These varied from the shows in the amphitheater, which was defined in its building-inscription as *spectacula* (*CIL* 10.852 = **B12**), through to the elections, the publicity for which survived until the modern day, painted on the plaster decoration of the external walls of houses.

Figure 20.3   Amphitheater at Pompeii. Photograph: R. Laurence.

Our attitude to these seemingly ephemeral forms of painted evidence needs some discussion. In AD 79, it was still possible to read a notice advertising a fight of 30 pairs of gladiators on five consecutive days in April in the reign of Nero provided by Decimus Lucretius Satrius Valens and his son (*CIL* 4.3884 = **D17**). There are other notices in the same wording with different dates found across the city referring to the shows of father and son in the amphitheater (*CIL* 4.1185, 7992, 7995 = **D18–19**). A notice of exactly this type can also be identified painted on the external wall of the Large Palaestra adjacent to the amphitheater in the famous fresco of a riot scene that decorated the peristyle of a Pompeian house (Clarke, 2003: 152–56 = **D41**). What this suggests about these "notices of games" is that they did not just announce an event in the future and subsequently the notice was erased. Instead, the notices announced the games and, if the games were memorable, the announcement was preserved as a reminder of that event. The majority refer to events from the past, rather than from the last decade of Pompeii's existence (Sabbatini Tumolesi, 1980). Intriguingly, none of these notices were dated by year but instead simply stated that an event would take place on a day in a month. For those unfamiliar with the city, reading these notices would not cause them to know whether a show was going to take place or had taken place in the past.

The amphitheater at Pompeii is an iconic monument in the study of Roman architecture. It is the earliest and best preserved example of such a monument, which may have been built together with the Large Palaestra adjacent to it, which served as a form of *Campus* (Welch, 2009: 72–74, 95–97). The location and area surrounding these two large structures were isolated from the main thoroughfares of the city and vehicle traffic was restricted from entry into the streets leading into the area. By AD 79, the watching of the action in the arena was regulated with larger seats (*bisellia*) for the town councillors and other city worthies, perhaps including freed slaves, whose right to these seats was duly noted in their tomb inscriptions (*CIL* 10.1026 = **F115**). The sections of seating were paid for by *duoviri* and also by magistrates of the *Pagus Augustus Felix Suburbanus* (the Fortunate Augustan Suburban Country District; *CIL* 10.854–857 = **D1–5**). This was a building that was duly restored after the earthquake of AD 62 and the *duoviri* who restored it were commemorated with statues in the forum (*CIL* 10.858–59 = **D6–7**; cf. *CIL* 10.790–91 = **D8–9**). The seating was separated from the arena by a two-meter high wall that was painted with life-size representations of gladiators that only survive in the form of copies (Mau, 1899: 208). The shows were to be remembered for posterity, as can be seen by the inclusion of scenes from the last day of Festius Ampliatus's games in stucco relief on his tomb (*CIL* 4.1182 = **D36a, 36b**). Drawings of gladiators are probably the most frequent figurative forms scratched into the plaster on the facades and inside houses across the city and are particularly prominent in the Large Palaestra and in the so-called House of the Gladiators (Langner, 2001; Garraffoni and Laurence, 2013). These were spectacles to be recalled and attracted visitors from the neighboring town of Nuceria, who were set upon by Pompeians in the famous riot that was recorded by Tacitus (*Annals*: 14.17 = **D39**) and proudly commemorated in frescoes and graffiti around the town (*CIL* 4.1293 = **D41–42**).

The observation that the painted notices "advertising" gladiatorial shows referred to past as well as future shows allows for the consideration that electoral notices, for which Pompeii is particularly famous, also had a similar ambiguity in terms of past, present, and future. There is much unresolved debate over the interpretation of these notices, or *programmata*, as evidence for how elections were conducted (Mouritsen, 1988; Biundo, 1996; Mouritsen, 1999; Chiavia, 2002). However, the electoral notices could be viewed in a similar way to the older announcements of gladiatorial games: these commemorated the action or spectacle of election of individual magistrates. This allows us to see a way into the memorialization of a spectacle in which the elite and their associates "requested" the support of the people in the streets of

Pompeii (for dated examples see Franklin, 2001). The medium by which this was done was via professionally painted letters that could name supporters of a candidate. When the election was over, the notices did not get painted over but survived as a tangible memory of the spectacle of toga-clad candidates seeking election to magistracies and also a memory of the support of a variety of persons, including women (Savunen, 1997).

The election to a magistracy was part of a process of communication by which magistrates were seen to take action on behalf of the community and for its benefit. It was these toga-clad members of the elite who organized sacrifices and placed themselves at the very center of the event with their toga drawn up over their heads (**E52a**). We can find images of processions of the elite leading animals to sacrifice (for example that found at Moregine, see Butterworth and Laurence, 2005: plate 10). These were the people who as *duoviri* provided the games or might replace their obligation to provide games with the renewal of parts of a building, for example the marble of the *orchestra* of the covered theater (*CIL* 10.845 = **D61**). However, we should not restrict our view of these games to just the performances provided by magistrates within the amphitheater itself. There were processions associated with the games that led bulls, bullfighters, their helpers, stage fighters, and various boxers through the city – the inhabitants of Pompeii and visitors from nearby had the opportunity in the town's narrow streets to see the animals, the fighters and their weapons close at hand (*CIL* 10.1074a = **D11**). The magistrate's role was defined as the performer of sacrifices and giver of games, and to perform this role a spectacle was created to be watched with the city as its backdrop.

The concept of the city as a spectacle in its own right extends to what has been described previously as "scenes from everyday life" that were found in the atrium of the Praedium of Julia Felix, famous for the rental notice that let out these premises composed of elegant baths, shops, and apartments (*CIL* 4.1136 = **H73**). Only 16 fragments of the frieze survive in the Naples Museum (published with photographs – Nappo, 1989; **H100–101**). These represent parts of a continuous frieze 3.1 m long by 0.7 m in height. It is difficult to place the location of the scenes, but the columns to the rear of the figures and association with statues would point to a real and/or imagined forum. There are scenes that include the transportation of goods either on pack animals or in a cart. There are representations of individuals selling goods, including shoes, containers, textiles, and utensils. In all cases, the people are staged. There are spaces around the people and items for sale. There is also an incident in which a stripped man is punished with a flogging, whilst children or young adults study – through the colonnade we can see onlookers watching not just the activity in the frieze but also in the room and the viewers of the frieze. There are also documents attached to a frame that attaches in turn to three equestrian statue bases being read by men and a boy in the foreground. The colonnades are decorated with garlands to denote a special occasion, rather than an "everyday" scene from the forum. Perhaps, this is most clearly denoted by a scene that Salvatore Nappo (1989: 88) suggests was that of a judicial decision made by a magistrate in a toga with regard to a young girl or woman accompanied by a man in a toga. This would suggest some specific commemorative purpose of the frieze, and perhaps we should see all of these 16 fragments as contributing to an understanding of the spectacle of Roman urbanism centered on the forum, a public square in which activity was staged with a backdrop of the architecture of public monuments. Few other cultures have a similar emphasis on this type of public space being fundamental to their definition of the city. This factor underlines the prevalence of the need for spectacle (whether a court case or the sale of shoes) to define the city and to combine with the monumental architecture that housed the gods in the creation of the central space of Roman urbanism – the forum: a place to mingle, to do public business, but above all a place to watch the activities of your fellow citizens and visitors to your city.

20.6   Pompeii and the History of Italy

A question that is often put to Pompeianists might allow us to reveal the significance of the evidence discussed above: is Pompeii representative of other developments in Italy? It is always tricky to answer this question. Unlike almost any other city (apart from Herculaneum of course), the evidence from Pompeii ends with its destruction in AD 79. The destruction of Pompeii by the volcanic eruption and, in particular, its pyroclastic surges disrupted the evidence that we see today. There is no "Pompeii premise" in which we may find all in situ (Binford, 1981). However, if we focus less on what is there in AD 79 and more on the micro-topography of change, it is possible to begin to understand the contribution of Pompeii to our understanding of Roman history and in particular to that of urban history. David Newsome (2009) has, through a detailed analysis of changes to the street pattern in the neighborhood of the forum, been able to demonstrate a fundamental shift in the nature of space and flow of movement from an east–west direction to a north–south orientation. This observation has implications for the interpretation of houses in the area. Those that had once been integrated with the main east–west traffic flow would have had little integration with the north–south flow during the final phases of Pompeii. The shift implies a major change to the lives of the inhabitants in these houses, but this change cannot be identified within the material forms of the houses themselves. In other words, the houses do not change but the integration of their owners and inhabitants with the flow of traffic of the city changed. What this makes clear is that the Roman city was far more dynamic and subject to change than might otherwise be expected. Importantly, these changes were caused in part by the transformation of the forum in the first century AD, but there were other interventions as well. The closing of streets to traffic created concentrations of flow across the city. What we see in these minor interventions was the adjustment of the grid of streets, so that traffic channeling might be created (Poehler, 2006). Some streets were associated with an intensification of activity, whereas others were deliberately isolated from the flow of traffic. This was an alteration to the cityscape as great as that of monument building in the forum, but does not seem to have been directly reflected in a uniform reorganization of private space in response to this change. What the understanding of traffic flow at Pompeii allows us to understand is that traffic flow and its intensity structures space, and that the interpretation of the domestic environment (houses) and public space needs to be contextualized with reference to such changes. The implication for the study of Roman Italy is clear: cities were environments that were dynamic and changing, but often these changes are invisible to us today – in Pompeii we have the means to glimpse some of the possible changes that may also have occurred elsewhere. Hence, the excavations at Pompeii and in the *ager Pompeianus* provide a reference point for all other studies of cities in Roman Italy.

ENDNOTE

1 References in bold are to entries in Cooley and Cooley, 2014.

FURTHER READING

Research on Pompeii went through something of a renaissance with a raft of publications in English in the late 1980s and through the 1990s into the twenty-first century. Most of these have stood the test of time and remain fundamental to understanding more recent work on the city and its hinterland. Thus, Mouritsen 1988 continues to be the fundamental starting point for the study of *programmata;*

Wallace-Hadrill 1994 on housing; Laurence 2007, a second edition of the original 1994 book, on the study of streets and space; Jashemski 1993 on gardens; Savunen 1997 on women; D'Arms 2003 on villas; Allison 2004 on artifact assemblages; and Mouritsen 2005 on freedmen. The *World of Pompeii* edited by Dobbins and Foss 2007 pulls together many areas of research. Traffic has become an area of considerable interest with the publication of a theory of circulation by Poehler 2006, built upon by Newsome 2009 and discussed recently in chapters in Laurence and Newsome, eds, 2011. It should be realized that research is ongoing and any list of further reading is of necessity preliminary – especially given publishers' knowledge that Pompeii books sell and more are produced each year.

REFERENCES

Allison, P.M. 1995. "On-going seismic activity and its effects on the living conditions in Pompeii in the last decades." In *Archäologie und Seismologie: la regione vesuviana dal 62 al 79 d.C.: problemi archeologici e sismologici*, 183–90. Munich: Biering & Brinkmann.

Allison, P.M. 2004. *Pompeian Households. An Analysis of Material Culture*. Los Angeles: University of California. Supported by website: http://www.stoa.org/projects/ph/home

Andreau, J. 1999. *Banking and Business in the Roman World*. Cambridge: Cambridge University Press.

Banaji, J. 1988 Review of Jongman 1988, *Journal of Roman Studies* 79: 229–31.

Berry, D.H. 1996. *Cicero Pro P. Sulla Oratio*. Cambridge: Cambridge Classical Texts and Commentaries 30: Cambridge University Press.

Binford, L.R. 1981. "Behavioural Archaeology and the "Pompeii Premise'." *Journal of Anthropological Research* 37: 195–208.

Biundo, R. 1996. "I rogatores nei programmata elettorali Pompeiani." *Cahiers Glotz* 7: 179–88.

Butterworth, A. and Laurence, R. 2005. *Pompeii: The Living City*. London: Weidenfeld & Nicolson.

Camodeca, G. 1999. Tabulae pompeianae Sulpiciorum (TPSulp.): *edizione critica dell'archivio puteolano deiSulpicii*. 2 vols. Rome: Vetera 12/Quasar.

Carroll, M. 2008. "*Nemus et Templum:* exploring the sacred grove of the Temple of Venus in Pompeii." In *Nuove ricerche archeologiche nell'area vesuviana*, eds P.G. Guzzo and M.P. Guidobaldi, 37–46. Rome: «L'Erma» di Bretschneider.

Carroll, M. 2010. "Exploring the sanctuary of Venus and its sacred grove: politics, cult and identity in Roman Pompeii." *Papers of the British School at Rome* 78: 63–106 and 347–51.

Chiavia, C. 2002. Programmata. *Manifesti elettorali nella colonia romana di Pompei*. Turin: S. Zamorani.

Clarke, J.R. 2003. *Art in the Lives of Ordinary Romans. Visual Representation and Non-Elite Viewers in Italy 100 B.C. – A.D. 315*. Berkeley: University of California Press.

Cooley, A.E. 2002. "The survival of Oscan in Roman Pompeii." In *Becoming Roman, Writing Latin? Literacy and Epigraphy in the Roman West*, ed. A.E. Cooley, 77–86. Portsmouth, RI: Journal of Roman Archaeology Suppl. 48.

Cooley, A.E. and Cooley, M.G.L. 2014. *Pompeii and Herculaneum. A Sourcebook*. London and New York: Routledge.

Crawford, M.H., ed. 2011. Imagines Italicae: *a Corpus of Italic Inscriptions*. London: BICS Supplement 110.

D'Arms, J.H. 2003. *Romans on the Bay of Naples and Other Essays on Roman Campania*. Bari: Edipuglia.

De Caro, S. 1994. *La villa rustica in località Villa Regina a Boscoreale*. Rome: «L'Erma» di Bretschneider.

De Caro, S. 2007. "The first sanctuaries." In *The World of Pompeii*, eds J.J. Dobbins and P.W. Foss, 73–81. London/New York: Routledge.

Dobbins, J. 1994. "Problems of chronology, decoration and urban design in the Forum at Pompeii." *American Journal of Archaeology* 98: 629–94.

Dobbins, J. 1996. "The imperial cult building in the Forum at Pompeii." In *Subject and Ruler. The Cult of the Ruling Power in Classical Antiquity*, ed. A. Small, 99–114. Ann Arbor: *JRA* Suppl.17.

Dobbins, J.J. and Foss, P. 2007. *The World of Pompeii*. Routledge: Abingdon.

Esmonde Cleary, A.S., Laurence, R. and Sears, G.M. 2011. *The City in the Roman West, c.250 BC–AD 250.* Cambridge: Cambridge University Press.

Fabbricotti, E. 1976. "I bagni nelle prime ville romane." *Cronache Pompeiane* 2: 29–111.

Fentress, E. 2005. "On the block: *catastae, chalcidica,* and *cryptae* in Early Imperial Italy." *Journal of Roman Archaeology* 18: 220–34.

Franklin, J.L., Jr. 2001. Pompeis Difficile Est. *Studies in the Political Life of Imperial Pompeii.* Ann Arbor: University of Michigan Press.

Garraffoni, R.S. and Laurence, R. 2013. "Writing in public space from child to adult: the meaning of graffiti." In *Written Space in the Latin West, 200 BC to AD 300,* eds G. Sears, P. Keegan, R. Laurence, 123–34. London: Bloomsbury Academic.

Gell, W. and Gandy, J.F. 1875. *Pompeiana: The Topography and Edifices, and Ornaments of Pompeii.* London: Chatto and Windus.

Huet, V. 2007. "Le laraire de L. Caecilius Iucundus: un relief hors norme ?" In *Contributi di archeologia Vesuviana* vol. 3, ed. M.-O. Charles, 142–50. Rome, «L'Erma» di Bretschneider / Studi della Soprintendenza archeologica di Pompei 21.

Jashemski, W.F. 1979/1993. *The Gardens of Pompeii: Herculaneum and the villas destroyed by Vesuvius.* 2 vols. New Rochelle, N.Y.: Caratzas Brothers.

Jongman, W. 1988. *The Economy and Society of Pompeii.* Amsterdam : J.C. Gieben.

Jongman, W. 2007. "The loss of innocence. Pompeian economy and society between past and present." In *The World of Pompeii,* eds J.J. Dobbins and P.W. Foss, 499–517. New York and London: Routledge.

Keppie, L.J.F. 2009. *The Romans on the Bay of Naples: An Archaeological Guide.* London: The History Press.

Langner, M. 2001. *Antike Graffitizeichnungen: Motive, Gestaltung und edeutung.* Wiesbaden: L. Reichert.

Laurence, R. 2007 (2nd edn). *Roman Pompeii: Space and Society.* New York and London: Routledge.

Laurence, R. 2009. *Roman Passions. A History of Pleasure in Imperial Rome.* London: Continuum.

Laurence, R. and Newsome, D. 2011. *Rome, Ostia, Pompeii: Movement and Space.* Oxford: Oxford University Press.

Ling, R. 1995. "Earthquake damage in Pompeii I.10: one earthquake or two?' in *Archäologie und Seismologie: la regione vesuviana dal 62 al 79 D.C. : problemi archeologici e sismologici* 201–09. Munich: Biering & Brinkmann.

Ling, R. 2007. "Development of Pompei's public landscape in the Roman period." In *The World of Pompeii,* eds J.J. Dobbins and P.W. Foss, 119–28. New York and London: Routledge.

Mau, A. 1899. *Pompeii: Its Life and Art* (trans. F.W. Kelsey). New York: The Macmillan Company.

Michel, D. 1990. *Casa dei Cei (I 6, 15).* Munich: Hirmer Verlag.

Moormann, E.M. 2007. "Villas surrounding Pompeii and Herculaneum." In *The World of Pompeii,* eds J.J. Dobbins and P.W. Foss, 435–54. New York and London: Routledge.

Mouritsen, H. 1988. *Elections, Magistrates and Municipal Élite: Studies in Pompeian Epigraphy.* Rome: «L'Erma» di Bretschneider.

Mouritsen, H. 1999. "Electoral campaigning in Pompeii: a reconsideration." *Athenaeum* 87: 515–23.

Mouritsen, H. 2005. "Freedmen and decurions: epitaphs and social history in Imperial Italy." *Journal of Roman Studies* 95: 38–63.

Nappo, S.C. 1989. "Fregio dipinto dal 'praedium' di Giulia Felice con rappresentazione del foro di Pompei." *Rivista di Studi Pompeiani* 3: 79–96.

Newsome, D.J. 2009. "Traffic, space and legal change around the Casa del Marinaio at Pompeii (VII 15.1–2)." *Bulletin antieke beschaving* 84: 121–43.

Poehler, E.E. 2006. "The circulation of traffic in Pompeii's *Regio VI." Journal of Roman Archaeology* 19: 53–74.

Sabbatini Tumolesi, P. 1980. Gladiatorum Paria: *annunci di spettacoli gladiatorii a Pompei.* Rome: Edizioni di storia e letteratura.

Savunen, L. 1997. *Women in the Urban Texture of Pompeii.* Helsinki: University of Helsinki.

Scheidel, W. 1992. "Neuen Wein in leere Schläuche: Jongman's Pompeii, Modelle und die kampanische Landwirtschaft." *Athenaeum* 80: 207–13.

Senatore, F., ed. 1998. *Pompei, il Sarno e la Penisola Sorrentina*. Pompei: Rufus.

Small, A. 2007. "Urban, suburban and rural religion in the Roman period." In *The World of Pompeii*, eds J.J. Dobbins and P.W. Foss, 184–211. New York and London: Routledge.

Wallace-Hadrill, A. 1994. *Houses and Society in Pompeii and Herculaneum*, Princeton: Princeton University Press.

Wallace-Hadrill, A. 2008. *Rome's Cultural Revolution*. Cambridge: Cambridge University Press.

Welch, K. 2009. *The Roman Amphitheatre*. Cambridge: Cambridge University Press.

CHAPTER 21

Ostia

Janet DeLaine

21.1 Introduction[1]

Ostia, as the port city of Rome, was neither a typical Italian town, nor an archetypical Roman colony. While tradition has it founded at the mouth of the Tiber in the seventh century BC by Ancus Martius, the fourth king of Rome, the present settlement can only be traced back to the start of the third century BC when, as a maritime colony, it had no independent political existence but was little more than a military outpost of Rome. During most of the Republic, Ostia served as coastal protection, naval base, and commercial entrepôt for the capital, and even under the Empire its history was tied very closely to that of Rome and the problems of supplying it with everything from grain to animals for the games. The closeness to the capital made it an attractive place for members of the Roman senatorial elite, and later the imperial circle, to own rural retreats, often acting as patrons and benefactors for the city. By the end of the first century AD it had become a substantial city, with its own particular political, religious, social, and economic structures and concerns, in which commerce played the most significant role; it continued to expand in the "boom" years of the second century, to which most of the extant structures belong. While the relationship with Rome will find its place, this chapter will concentrate mainly on Ostia as a city in its own right, in the context of its own territory and the neighboring *Ager Laurens* further to the south (see Figure 21.1).

Russell Meiggs' magisterial *Roman Ostia*, first published in 1960, still forms the starting point for all current interpretations of Ostia's history. More recent archaeological and epigraphical research has, however, inevitably superseded his account in many details and in some major aspects, but a complete new synthesis is still to be written. Although still awaiting final publication, the most dramatic addition to our knowledge comes from an extensive geophysical survey carried out in the late 1990s, which has shown that at its height the city was perhaps twice the size than had been previously thought (Martin *et al.*, 2002). While the precise dates of many of the key buildings, particularly from the Republican period, are still matters of debate, stratigraphic excavation is gradually clarifying many issues. Recent investigations have also transformed our understanding of Ostia's territory, embracing the imperial harbor of Portus to the north, the coastal villas and imperial *vicus* to the south, and the

A Companion to Roman Italy, First Edition. Edited by Alison E. Cooley.
© 2016 John Wiley & Sons, Ltd. Published 2016 by John Wiley & Sons, Ltd.

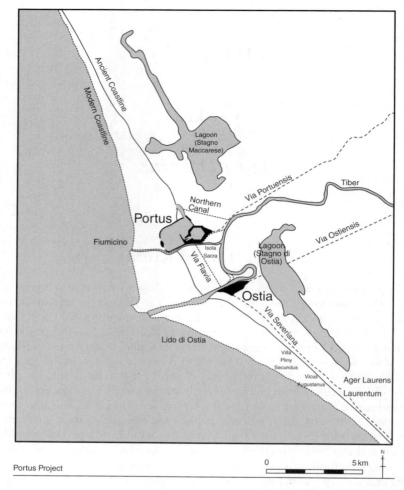

Figure 21.1 Map of Ostia and the surrounding area. After Keay and Parioli, 2011: fig. 1.1.

agricultural land to the east. This chapter represents a first attempt at integrating this material into a wider historical framework for an English-speaking audience.

21.2   The Foundation of Ostia

Ostia's early history has to be deduced from the limited written sources, and is still the subject of debate. Livy (1.33.9) associates three things with Ancus Martius's foundation: the extension of Roman territory to the sea, the taking of the Maesian forest from Veii, and the construction of saltworks on both sides of the river. Salt was a rare resource, early exploited; wood for timber and fuel an essential one; and access to the sea gave a strategic advantage, so that there is nothing inherently unlikely about the creation of a settlement to oversee these concerns. The main difficulty has been the absence of any archaeological evidence for such an early settlement at the current site. Meiggs' suggestion (1973: 479–82) that the original settlement may have been further north at the saltworks, has recently found support from geomorphological evidence for a change in the course of the Tiber around the fifth century BC, before which it most likely also discharged through two mouths near the saltworks, roughly where the imperial harbor was later situated (Giraudi, 2011). A settlement at the archaic Tiber mouth would also have been at the end of the ancient routeway which came down from Sabine territory to Rome and beyond it to the saltworks (the later *via Campana*). The few fragments of sixth- to fifth-century ceramics and architectural terracottas found on the later site of Ostia would then represent an early sanctuary, as Zevi has already suggested (2002).

Livy places the foundation of Ostia in conjunction with the defeat of Ficana, situated according to Festus (298L) on the left bank of the Tiber at the eleventh milestone of the *via Ostiensis*. This was valuable agricultural land, fertile and well-watered, which by the fourth century BC at least had become part of Ostia's territory. To the south beyond the lagoon of Ostia was Lavinium, already a walled settlement in the seventh century BC and a federal sanctuary of the Latin League from the sixth century onwards, associated with the legend of Aeneas. The early pathway which, scholars have argued, ran along the line of the coast between Lavinium and the Tiber mouth (Mar, 1991), would work equally well with a more northerly location for the original Ostia.

21.3 The *Colonia Maritima*

The political circumstances of the first half of the fourth century, with Etruscans, Gauls, and Greeks all making inroads on the saltworks and the coastal strip (Livy: 5.45; 7.17.6–9, 19.8, 25.3–4, 11–12, 26.13–15), together with the Latin War running into the 330s, would hardly have been conducive to the large-scale reorganization required following such a radical change in the Tiber's hydrological regime. Indeed, the available evidence points to the very end of the fourth century or to the beginning of the third not just for the new fortified settlement at the current mouth of the Tiber, the so-called "castrum," (Calza, 1953: 76–77; Martin, 1996; Zevi, 2002), but also for a general overhaul of the whole Ostian territory. The first formal road structures of the *via Campana* and nearly all traces of rural establishments, both north and south of the Tiber, are of this period (Serlorenzi and Di Giuseppe, 2011; Morelli *et al.*, 2011: 272–75; Pellegrino, 2004: 37–38). While some rural occupation does go back to the mid-fourth century (cf. Zevi, 2002: 16–17), it is notable that the one example on the north bank was abandoned at the end of the fourth century after a major flood, a reminder of the inherent instability of the river delta.

Livy (27.38; 36.3) lists Ostia among Rome's maritime colonies, which were arguably part of a contemporary Mediterranean-wide phenomenon of coastal fortresses intended to prevent enemies from establishing footholds at strategic locations. The *castrum* is indeed a small (circa 194 × 126 m) rectangular walled settlement, its two main roads (usually but inaccurately called the *decumanus* and the *cardo*) leading from four gates and crossing at the center in the manner of later military camps. Its implantation at the end of its own road from Rome, the *via Ostiensis*, but cutting across the ancient coastal road from Lavinium, certainly speaks more of military than of economic concerns. The construction of the fortress coincided with the development of Rome's navy, and from 267 BC Ostia was the base of one of the Roman *quaestores* with responsibilities for the fleet (Meiggs, 1973: 24–27).

As with other maritime colonies, Ostia may originally have had only 300 colonists, forming a permanent garrison generally exempt from other military service (Pohl, 1983). By the end of the century, however, there is evidence for a much larger population, albeit a temporary one. According to Livy (22.57) in 216 BC there were also 1500 men who had been enrolled in the fleet stationed at Ostia and available to send to the defense of Rome. In the period when Hannibal was in Italy, at least thirty warships were kept at Ostia (Livy: 27.22) which could be readied for the protection of the coast nearest to Rome, requiring at least 6000 men to man them fully (Meiggs, 1973: 580). In the same period, we hear of supplies arriving in Ostia and being sent out from there to other Roman coastal colonies (Livy: 25.22). Although there is no direct evidence for purely commercial activity at Ostia at this time, the Sardo-Punic and early Roman coins found in excavations just east of the *castrum* may be an indication (Carta *et al.*, 1987: 21–25). At the very least some sort of service or support sector for the fleet and colony can be postulated, and some of the trade heading for Rome would presumably have made landfall at Ostia rather than passing directly up the Tiber. This fits well with the Ostia of Ennius (*Annals*: 2 frag. 22), our earliest literary source writing at the end of the third century BC: a fortified site, with a harbor for ships and for sailors who make a living from the sea.

It is now clear that by the mid-third century Ostia had already expanded outside its walls on at least three sides. The limited excavations have all produced walls of squared stone blocks in *tufo*, suggesting reasonably substantial structures (Carta *et al.*, 1987: 12–48; DeLaine and Wilkinson, 1999; Kockel and Ortisi, 2000). This is also the period of the oldest of the four *tufo* altars in the *area sacra repubblicana*, located on the pre-existing Lavinium road just outside the *castrum*, the earliest locatable evidence for religious activity connected with the new settlement. Livy (32.1), however, reports for 199 BC that a temple of Jupiter at Ostia was struck by lightning, and this has sometimes been associated with very fragmentary remains at the heart of the *castrum* below the later forum temple. Opposite this possible colonial temple was a modest basilical hall, which Calza (1953: 71–72) argued was contemporary with the installation of the fortress; from its location and plan it appears to have served some civic function. Possibly from the start, and certainly by the end of the second century, Ostia had its own local magistrates, two *praetores* who presumably looked after the day-to-day running of the colony, leaving the *quaestores* to deal with matters relating to Rome and military affairs (Cébeillac-Gervasoni, 1996a). Signs of commercial activity appear by the mid-third century BC, in the form of rows of *tabernae* built against the outer face of the *castrum* wall.

After 191 BC, when it is mentioned incidentally among the maritime colonies (Livy: 36.3), Ostia falls out of the historical narrative, but this does not mean that it had become unimportant to Rome. In the later second century Gaius Caninius, the urban praetor, had a series of boundary stones set up which appear to identify the land north of the *via Ostiensis*, for at least 600 m east of the outer boundary road of the "castrum," as being in public ownership (*CIL* 14.4702). Although some scholars have assumed that the judgment first established the land as the public property of the Roman people and was intended to preserve the Tiber bank for essential shipping purposes connected with the grain supply to the capital (e.g. Coarelli, 1994: 39–40), others suggest that the judgement related to encroachment on existing public land (Zevi in Coarelli, 1994: 46; cf. Paribeni, 1918: 133). It is also possible that the area was not related to the *annona* but to the fleet, which would have required a considerable area of land, if only on an intermittent basis, for housing crews, and for storage and maintenance of the ships and their equipment and related supplies, which presumably would have included grain. Irrespective of the precise circumstances in which these markers were set up, by the start of the next century the *quaestor* for Ostia does seem to have become more concerned with the *annona* than the fleet (Cébeillac-Gervasoni, 2002: 63–67). Nevertheless, the main commercial port for Rome in this period remained Puteoli on the Bay of Naples, in addition to the Emporium district in Rome itself. It is in fact difficult to identify signs of significant storage facilities at Ostia before the middle of the first century AD, although there is evidence for imported goods, such as the Rhodian amphorae from the area of the *Quattro Tempietti* (Paribeni, 1916: 445–48), and the number of identifiable *tabernae* continues to increase.

There are other signs that Ostia was thriving in the late second and early first centuries BC. The sanctuary outside the west gate of the *castrum* acquired a substantial temple (probably to Hercules), and two smaller ones, one certainly to Aesculapius. The latter's fine marble cult statue, and important dedications including imported Greek sculpture (Zevi, 1976) and the earliest known marble inscription at Ostia (Cébeillac, 1971: 39–69), further point to the importance of the sanctuary. These signs of a political-religious life in the settlement have their counterparts in the very fragmentary remains of elegant wall and floor decoration (Mols, 2002: 152–53; Falzone, 2007: 30), comparable with second-century examples from Rome and Pompeii, which suggest the presence of a resident elite living in well-appointed *domus.* The same period also provides the earliest evidence for wealthy burials, in the monumental mausoleum or cenotaph opposite the area of the *Quattro Tempietti* (Sole, 2002), and in fragments of intricate bone and ivory funerary biers from graves near the east gate of the late Republican walls (Heinzelmann, 2000: 213–18).

Ostia thus appears to have been thriving when it was sacked by Marius in 87 BC (Appian, *Civil Wars*: 1.8.67), but it is hard to tell just how much destruction was caused. Subsequently there was a change in Ostia's political organization, with the establishment of a formal town council (*ordo*) with *duoviri*, perhaps in response to Ostia's loyalty to Sulla and the punishment it had received at the hands of Marius. While the first evidence for this appears only in the *fasti* of Ostia for 48 BC, the list clearly went back to the time of Sulla (Bargagli and Grosso, 1997: 8–9). The picture is complicated by the events of 67 BC, when pirates sailed into the Tiber and destroyed the fleet (Cicero, *In defence of the Manilian Law*: 33; *On the command of Cn. Pompeius*: 12). In response to this, and arguably at the instigation of Cicero during his consulship of 63 BC, Rome showed her concern for Ostia and the fleet by commissioning a new set of walls for the city (Zevi, 1997). Enclosing an area of some 69 ha, roughly 30 times that of the original *castrum*, they included the whole public area north of the main road, which was thus provided with the protection (at least from land) that it had lacked before.

The new walls aside, the existing archaeological evidence is rarely precise enough to assign other developments of the first half of the first century BC to the period before or after the sack by the pirates and the building of the walls. The replacement of the possible earlier temple at the center of the old *castrum* by two new ones, and the creation of an open space opposite, extending south from the *decumanus* to a new basilical hall just within the old inner circuit road of the *castrum*, provided the first identifiable forum space, and would fit very well with Ostia's acquisition of its own *ordo*, irrespective of exactly when the new buildings were completed. More problematic are the *Quattro Tempietti*, the four small temples built on a common podium east of the *castrum*, the suggested dates of which range from the time of Sulla to circa 50 BC and even as late as the early Augustan period. Whatever the actual date – and it is possible in fact that this structure had several phases between circa 80 and 25 BC – there is no real reason to assume that it would not have been built before the area was included in the new walls, as Ostia had by that time long existed as an essentially unwalled settlement.

The *Quattro Tempietti* have commonly been associated with P. Lucilius Gamala, the first member of the Ostian elite for whom we can flesh out something of his public career, thanks to a much debated, but no longer extant, inscription (*CIL* 14. 375; Gallina Zevi and Humphrey, 2004, with previous bibliography). Possibly of eastern origin, he was *pontifex* of Vulcan and *duumvir* with censorial powers, and at some point took charge of city finances and helped Ostia fulfill its financial promises in relation to a naval war, either Pompey's against the pirates, or Octavian's against Sextus Pompey. Although not recorded as being involved in politics at Rome, he (or his father) may very well have known Cicero (*Letters to Atticus*: 12.23.3). Certainly the list of Gamala's benefactions make it clear that he was a major figure in Ostian public life, and he was given a public funeral; scholars who favor the late chronology have attributed to him the substantial early Augustan mausoleum just outside the Porta Marina which included symbols of naval victory in its decoration (e.g. Pensabene, 2004).

In this same period there is a considerable increase in the evidence for high-status dwellings at Ostia and in the surrounding area. Richly appointed Pompeian-style atrium-peristyle houses, presumably housing Ostia's decurial families, proliferated both within the old *castrum* and along the main roads outside it, the greatest concentration being along the western extension of the *via Ostiensis* towards the sea. The most recently excavated of these, the *Domus aux Bucranes* of circa 60 BC, was a substantial house with wall decoration which can only be matched in quality by houses from the Palatine in Rome (Morard, 2007). At the same time, we know from Cicero of several members of senatorial families who owned property in Ostia's territory (Zevi, 2004), and in the area east of Ostia new rural establishments appear, much larger than, and in different locations from, those of the third century BC, which had been abandoned in the later second century (Pellegrino, 2004). South of Ostia along the coast of the *Ager Laurens* there is an emerging picture of the cult of *otium* in the form of maritime villas, such as the substantial residential structure of 150–50 BC excavated by Claridge (2008), with a colonnaded court associated with probable pisciculture.

It is again much more difficult to identify the commercial core we might have expected in this period if Ostia were a flourishing commercial center, but this may be the result of limited excavation. Fragmentary remains at lower levels, particularly east of the *castrum*, provide tenuous hints of storage buildings perhaps as early as the late second century BC. None of the three substantial commercial structures that can be positively identified before the middle of the first century AD – the so-called *mercato* at III.1.7, the *Horrea di Ortensio*, and the *Magazzini repubblicani* – has, however, to be earlier than the late Republican walls and all may in fact belong to the next main phase of development under Augustus.

21.4   The Creation of a *Façade Maritime*

Although the major development of Ostia is usually seen as consequent on the building of the harbors at Portus under Claudius and Trajan, it now appears that we should be thinking of Ostia, its harbors, and its territory as integrated developments in a long process of transformation which began under Augustus to create a *façade maritime* worthy of the capital of empire. It is easy to argue from hindsight that the building of Portus would inevitably lead to it taking over the role of Ostia as the harbor city of Rome, but until the end of the third century Portus was the harbor at the port city of Ostia, a city so successful that it more than doubled in size over the first two centuries AD.

The inadequacy of the river mouth as a harbor suitable for the world-power of Rome is said to have taxed Caesar (Suetonius, *Life of Claudius*: 20), particularly in comparison with Alexandria, the ultimate touchstone (cf. Purcell, 1998). Strabo (5.3.5) describes Ostia as harborless because of the silting up of the Tiber, forcing larger ships to ride at anchor and transfer their cargoes to smaller boats, allowing them to run up to Rome, or reloading without even entering the river. Since Strabo associates Ostia with the Roman navy (5.2.1) but does not mention the fleet when he talks of Misenum (5.4), he seems to be writing about the situation in the early years after Actium. Dionysius of Halicarnassus (3.44) gives a much more positive picture, even though he still says that the largest ships have to unload and reload at the river mouth. While some scholars have argued that the two pictures are not incompatible (e.g. Meiggs, 1973: 51–52), what we may be seeing are the results of active intervention by Rome in the river channel. Early in the first century AD there was reclamation work in the tongue of land on the north side of the Tiber enclosed by the meander just east of the *Porta Romana*, where a terminal *cippus* of Tiberius's Tiber commission was found (Arnoldus Huyzendveld and Parioli, 1995; Pellegrino, Olivanti, and Panariti, 1995). This commission was established in response to an unprecedented sequence of serious floods which afflicted

Rome at least nine times from 44 BC to AD 15 (Aldrete, 2006: 242–43). The sharp bend of the Tiber at Ostia must have made this last section of the river particularly prone to serious flooding, and the earliest structures in this area, of commercial nature, appear only in the first half of the first century AD. There was more land reclamation in the territory south of Ostia in the same period, including work to the boundaries of the *stagnum* and the reorganization of the land based on an orthogonal road grid, presumably for agriculture (Heinzelmann, 1998). Even further south, the development of coastal luxury villas in the *litus Laurentinum* was given a boost by the arrival of Augustus among their owners, and the foundation of a small nucleated settlement, the *Vicus Augustanus Laurentinus*, perhaps to serve the imperial and other estates in the district.

The most important development was, of course, the creation of the imperial harbor north of Ostia, the *portus Ostiensis* or *Augusti* as it came to be known, with its three-story lighthouse rivaling that of Alexandria. It may not be coincidental that Claudius chose some of the most ancient territory of Rome, possibly even the original site of Ostia, for his project, where it could also take advantage of the already established communications route to the saltworks, the *via Campana*. Large-scale channels and dikes in this area going back at least to the start of the first century AD suggest its continuing importance. Part of Claudius's harbor works involved cutting two canals, one south of the new harbor basin improving connections to Rome by cutting off the bend of the river at Ostia, and the other to the north designed as a flood relief measure, primarily for Rome but also of enormous potential benefit to Ostia itself (*CIL* 14.85; Keay *et al.*, 2005: 271–78).

At the same time, work was done on the river harbor at Ostia, cut into the south bank of the Tiber near the river mouth, which provided a safe anchorage away from the heavy river traffic (Heinzelmann and Martin, 2002). The large terraced structure with shipsheds on its east side acted as a platform for a new marble temple, probably to Castor and Pollux, emphasizing the formality of this river harbor as a companion, albeit on a smaller scale, to the great new basin to the north. While the precise chronological relationship between the building of the river basin and the much larger project at Portus is not clear, together they successfully addressed the problem of the Tiber mouth as the prestigious and functional gateway to Rome. Despite the oft-repeated anecdote concerning 200 ships that sank in the Claudian harbor in a storm in AD 62 (Tacitus, *Annals*: 15.18.2), it is now clear that this remained a major part of the harbor complex, which continued to develop throughout the rest of the first century AD, and even after the more visually impressive hexagonal inner basin was built under Trajan, itself only the start of a process of building and rebuilding which continued throughout the second century (Keay *et al.*, 2005: 271–90, 297–305).

21.5   The Formation of the Imperial City

The attention given to the Tiber harbors and the wider territory of Ostia in the first century of the Principate is mirrored in the development of the urban center itself. After Actium, the Roman fleet was no longer a major factor in Ostia's life, even if detachments remained to police the harbors, and this, together with the later creation of the harbor at Portus, opened up the whole public area north of the eastern *decumanus* for development. This was the location chosen for Ostia's first monumental civic complex, the theater and open square behind it provided by Agrippa about 18–17 BC (Cooley, 1999), alongside the existing sanctuary of the *Quattro Tempietti*, itself refurbished in the mid-20s BC. By the end of the Augustan period Ostia must have started to look like a real city, as the forum was extended further south to end in a lavish marble temple to Roma and Augustus, comparable with the finest in Rome and almost certainly an imperial gift (Pensabene, 2007: 135–36). The Claudian temple at the river harbor was of similar quality, and this is also the period for which we have the first evidence for the temple in the sanctuary of the *Magna Mater* (Mar et al., 1999), another possible imperial intervention. Remains of a colonnaded portico in travertine along the southern *cardo* leading down to the sanctuary of the *Magna Mater* and the *Porta Laurentina*, can now be matched with similar remains under the Garden Houses in the west of the city; it is tempting to parallel these with the well-known portico which formed part of the display element at Claudius's harbor. More of the public land north of the *decumanus* was developed, with the construction of a public bath building east of the theater, the earliest for which we have any remains. This presumably drew water from the aqueduct added in the first half of the first century AD (Bukowiecki et al., 2008: 56–57), although the city always had access to an abundance of fresh water from wells. This is also the most likely period for the construction of the *Grandi Horrea*, one of the largest ever built at Ostia.

All together, the evidence suggests an even more extensive development of Ostia in the first half of the first century AD than has generally been thought. The level of some main roads was raised, and the late Republican wall circuit became more permeable, with the *Porta Laurentina* absorbed into the urban fabric and a new opening created to the east, linking to the newly reorganized territory south of the city. The ground level was raised by up to a meter in various parts of the city even in the Augustan period, and then even further under Claudius, when, for example, the *porticus* behind the theater was rebuilt, and new constructions added to the adjacent public area to the east (see e.g. Heinzelmann et al., 1999); these too may have been in response to recurrent flooding. Already in the middle of the century an almost continuous necropolis occupied the swathe of land from the bend in the river westwards outside the city walls. Tombs were constructed along many of the rural roads, as in the well-preserved section outside the old *Porta Laurentina* (Heinzelmann, 2000).

The main development of Ostia as we know it, however, began in the later first century AD and continued throughout the second century. Many of the older *domus* were replaced by commercial and residential *insulae*, and new warehouses (*horrea*) appeared especially towards the new harbor at the mouth of the Tiber. The city also expanded greatly, progressively filling in the area north of the road from Rome, and extending east and south well beyond the Late Republican walls and incorporating the necropoleis (Martin et al., 2002). The geophysics shows these areas also to be densely packed with commercial and residential *insulae*, although no new public buildings have been identified. The continued raising of the ground level, generally on a piecemeal basis with each new building project, may reflect continued problems with flooding (four major events are recorded at Rome between AD 69 and 107) which led to renewed efforts by Trajan to relieve the situation by building canals at Portus as part of the harbor expansion; if so, this seems only to have given further impetus to Ostia's development.

By the middle of the second century Ostia had gained almost a full complement of public buildings, several constructed with the support of the emperors or high-ranking officials at Rome (see Figure 21.2). Both Trajan (in AD 106) and Hadrian (for the second time in 126) accepted the honorific position of one of the two *duumviri* of the colony with censorial powers, a tradition which can be traced back at least to Agrippa Postumus in AD 6 (Bargagli and Grosso 1997: 21, 35, 43) and may go back to Agrippa. Each of these arguably resulted in the gift of a major building, Agrippa with the building of the theater, while in Trajan's case his contribution was probably the lavish set of baths just outside the *Porta Marina*. Hadrian most likely funded the construction of Ostia's largest temple, the so-called *Capitolium* (Pensabene, 2007: 250–63), as well as (almost certainly) paying for another bath building (*CIL* 14.98), usually identified with the *Terme di Nettuno* but possibly to be linked to the little-known baths under the *Foro della Statua Eroica*. Other individuals closely linked to the emperors also provided major benefactions, such as Gavius Maximus, the praetorian prefect of Antoninus Pius, who provided the most luxurious of all the baths, the *Terme del Foro* (Cicerchia and Marinucci, 1992; see Figure 21.3).

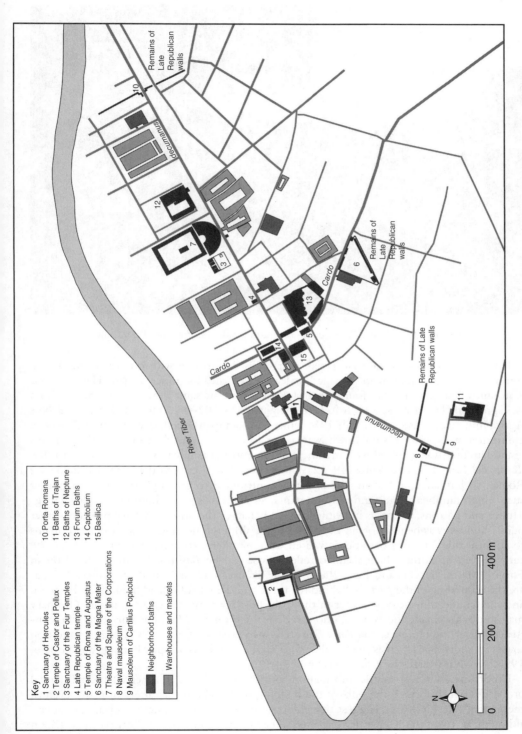

Figure 21.2 Ostia: schematic plan of the city at the end of the second century AD, showing main roads, public buildings, neighborhood baths, and warehouses and markets. Drawing: J. DeLaine.

Key
1 Sanctuary of Hercules
2 Temple of Castor and Pollux
3 Sanctuary of the Four Temples
4 Late Republican temple
5 Temple of Roma and Augustus
6 Sanctuary of the Magna Mater
7 Theatre and Square of the Corporations
8 Naval mausoleum
9 Mausoleum of Cartilius Popicola

10 Porta Romana
11 Baths of Trajan
12 Baths of Neptune
13 Forum Baths
14 Capitolium
15 Basilica

Neighborhood baths

Warehouses and markets

Figure 21.3   Ostia: Terme del Foro, south facade. Photograph: J. DeLaine.

It may be no coincidence that Trajan shared his duumvirate with one of the senatorial Egrilii, an Ostian family who provided at least three consuls under Trajan, Hadrian, and Antoninus Pius, and three or four patrons for the city in the same time period, one of whom was apparently Hadrian's substitute in 126 (Meiggs, 1973: 502–07). Another Ostian, C. Fabius Agrippinus, was suffect consul in 148, while Q. Asinius Marcellus, consul in 97, whose connection with the city is unknown, was patron of Ostia around the time of Trajan, and his granddaughter was involved with members of the imperial family in supplying bricks for the *Terme del Foro* (DeLaine, 2002: 49–52). These close links between the highest echelons of Roman society and the Ostian elite arguably contributed to the city's success in acquiring such a high number of prestigious monuments. Some of these same high-ranking local magistrates and patrons, acting as individuals or on behalf of the *ordo*, may have provided other public buildings as benefactors in their own right, although no epigraphic evidence remains to confirm this. The fine basilica, decorated with marble reliefs depicting episodes from the early history of Rome which seem to reflect those on the *Basilica Aemilia* in the Roman Forum (Marini Recchia and Zevi, 2008), is one likely candidate (Pensabene, 2007: 217), as are the rebuilding of the *porticus* behind the theater under Claudius and then under Hadrian, and the temple added in the center of the space possibly at the time of Domitian. Ordinary magistrates also made their contribution, such as the *duumvir* Maecilius Furranius who constructed a second temple to the *Bona Dea* at his own expense (Calza, 1942: 152), in addition to private individuals such as the Caltilius who built a temple to Serapis (Bargagli and Grosso, 1997: 43), but overall the evidence is limited.

Unfortunately we have little information about who built the commercial and residential properties which formed the bulk of the building stock. The sheer variety of plans, even of the *horrea*, does, however, suggest that these were largely the product of private initiatives, although the town council may have erected some buildings, such as the Portico of Pius IX, on land belonging to the colony to profit from urban rents (DeLaine, 2002; Heinzelmann,

2002). The larger of the many *collegia* (guilds) known from inscriptions also contributed to the urban fabric with their temples and headquarters, and possibly also through providing rental property or facilities such as smaller baths, as has been argued for the Baths of Buticosus constructed as a dependency of the sanctuary of Hercules (Mar, 1990).

Much of this was aimed at the needs not only of the permanent residents of the city, whether of long-standing Ostian origins or the recent immigrants well-attested from the Flavian period onwards, but also of the sizeable temporary population we can reconstruct for this harbor city. These included merchants and shippers, those working for the *annona*, those in transit to or from other parts of the empire, contingents of the *vigiles* and the Roman fleet stationed at Ostia in rotation, and crews of merchant vessels. Two of the smaller baths were located with visitors in mind, just inside the Late Republican city walls by major gates, while the more luxurious baths outside the *Porta Marina* and those of the "*Palazzo imperiale*" beside the river harbor were close to major landing stages for water transport. Others formed integral parts of residential *insulae*, providing focal points for neighborhoods as well as facilities for visitors.

The religious needs of this diverse population were well served. Epigraphic, literary, and archaeological evidence combine to show that the traditional cults of Vulcan, Capitoline Jupiter, Hercules, Venus, *Bona Dea, Pater Tiberinus*, Aesculapius, and Castor and Pollux at least, all arguably established in the Republican period and having close associations with Rome, were still the object of active interest under the Empire (Rieger, 2004). The temple of the *Magna Mater*, which cannot be dated before the mid-first century AD but may have replaced an earlier shrine, flourished in the imperial period, attracting the cults of Attis and Bellona; its precinct is the largest known for any cult in the city. In the later second century bull sacrifices (*taurobolia*) were made for the preservation of emperors and the imperial family, just one of the ways in which the new political situation affected the religious landscape of Ostia beyond the establishment of the cult of Roma and Augustus. There were certainly priests (*flamines*) chosen from the highest levels of society for all the deified emperors from at least the Flavian period onwards, although their temples have not been identified. The other change was the increased presence of cults from the eastern end of the empire, although by the time the temple of the Hellenistic Egyptian deity Serapis was dedicated in January AD 127 neither he nor Isis, whose temple at Ostia has never been identified, were exactly strangers to Rome and Italy. More significant, perhaps, are the 15 excavated *mithraea*, the earliest datable being as early as AD 162 (White, 2012). These are distributed fairly evenly around the excavated area, and while most have quite discreet access, they are not necessarily any more hidden away than, for example, the shrine of Silvanus entered through the large bakery on the *via dei Molini*. Many of these temples were connected with religious associations (*collegia*), most notably in cults connected to the *Magna Mater* (*dendrophori* and *cannophori*), Bellona (*hastiferi*), and possibly Serapis; there is even a group of members of an unidentified *collegium* who contributed financially to the enlargement of a temple under Antoninus Pius (*CIL* 14.246). Religion also formed an important part of those *collegia* relating to occupations, whose main functions were social and funerary. In the few cases where the focus of cult can be identified, the emperor predominates, although one at least, probably the *stuppatores* (caulkers), had a *mithraeum*.

Ostia is particularly rich in inscriptions relating to the various *collegia*, throwing light on those responsible for much of the day-to-day operation of Ostia's economy, many – but by no means all – of whom appear to have been freedmen or their descendants. Most *collegia* were concerned with commerce, from shipowners and bankers, to merchants, grain measurers, and shipbuilders. The rest either supported mercantile activities (salvage divers, rope-makers, caulkers) or serviced the city itself, from bakers to fullers, leather-workers, painters, lime-burners and builders (Hermansen, 1982: 55–61; Bollmann, 1998). The *collegium* of the *fabri tignuarii* (builders) was the largest known in Ostia, with over 300 members at the end of the second century AD (DeLaine, 2003). All the known members were most likely contractors or skilled specialists; many of their officers were men of considerable standing, including the *eques* Sex. Carminius Parthenopeus (*CIL* 14.314) and M. Licinius Privatus (*CIL* 14.374) who was given a special seat at the theater and made an honorary member of the town council, and whose descendants were *decuriones* and Roman equestrians. Privatus was also involved in the *collegium* of the bakers, and others can be identified as *Augustales* and members of other religious *collegia*.

Several attempts have been made to identify the headquarters of these associations, not always convincingly. The so-called *Caseggiato dei Triclini* next to the forum, based around an open court with a sanctuary on axis with the entrance, certainly housed the *fabri tignuarii* in the late second century AD, and they may also have used the temple they built to the Divine Pertinax opposite the theater for some of their activities. The seat of the *fabri navales* (ship-builders) along the western *decumanus* also combined a temple structure with a porticoed forecourt, but with a second court behind suitable for meetings. Other reasonably secure identifications are the *mensores frumentarii* (grain measurers) along the *Via della Foce* leading to the river harbor, and the *schola* (hall) of the *hastiferi* in the precinct of the Temple of Bellona. Several of those identified as headquarters of *collegia* are, however, more simply to be understood as rich *domus*, such as the so-called seat of the *Augustales* near the theater (Laird, 2000). An association of merchants met at the temple of the *Forum Vinarium*, yet to be identified, and there is no reason to believe that other *collegia* did not meet in various established temples in Ostia such as that behind the theater, or used temporary venues of other kinds, rather than having their own permanent headquarters.

21.6   Commercial City

Ostia in the imperial period was thus a city in its own right, but one whose prime interest was in commerce. Its rich commercial landscape is one of the most developed and best preserved in the Roman world (DeLaine, 2005), particularly noted for its large number and wide range of *horrea* and market buildings. In the past the focus has tended to be on the major warehouses and their possible function in providing storage for the city of Rome, particularly in relation to the state-controlled *annona* (Meiggs, 1973: 272–88; Rickman, 1971; Pavolini, 1986a: 76–117), but it is becoming increasingly clear that this is more to be associated with Portus. Ostia is therefore best seen as an entrepôt based on private enterprise serving other markets of the empire as well as Rome (Heinzelmann, 2010).

In addition to the 16 previously excavated (Rickman, 1971), the recent geophysical survey of Ostia has added as many more *horrea*, mostly in the area around the river harbor (Heinzelmann, 2002: 112–4, taf. IV.2). These display a wide range of sizes and layouts, with many arranged around a central courtyard, emphasizing the variety of needs that they served. Several of the excavated examples have fine entrance-ways designed to attract customers, and many of the smaller *horrea* have the same kind of access and circulation patterns as buildings, such as the *Caseggiato del Larario*, that are usually labeled markets or bazaars, reminding us that distribution was as important as storage, as we know to have been the case in Rome (Rickman, 1980: 141–42). The act of enclosure both provided security and allowed for the frequenters to be static and cut-off from other street activities, making them well-suited to auction. Among these are the *Horrea Epagathiana*, the only *horrea* in Ostia firmly identified as such. Security seems to have been an issue in this particular building, leading to suggestions that it dealt in high status and expensive merchandise such as precious metals and gems, luxury textiles, or spices.

Goods came to Ostia from all over the Mediterranean. Transport amphorae, coarse cooking pots and fine tablewares (Carandini and Panella, 1981; Panella, 1986; Pavolini, 1983 and 1996; Martin, 2006; Widemann and Naciri, 1989), quarry-state marble blocks (Pensabene 2007), inscriptions, and mosaic depictions, all contribute to understanding the origins of goods, the way these changed over time, and the presence of the merchants and shippers who made this commerce function. One major source is the *Piazza delle Corporazioni* (Calza, 1915). In this colonnaded *porticus* behind the theater, sometime before the mid-third century AD, associations of shippers and merchants from all over the empire, and others connected with servicing the shipping, advertised their activities by text and image in a series of floor mosaics. The traditional identification of these as formal offices has gradually given way to a more nuanced reading, in which the various associations were granted the right to this form of self-promotion thanks to their contributions to the embellishment of this important public space, subsequent perhaps to the restoration of the theater itself by Commodus (Pavolini, 2006, 70–72). While both the west and the east are represented, North Africans predominate, just as their olive oil amphorae and red gloss tablewares dominate the archaeological record from the end of the second century onwards, and their names appear increasingly in the epigraphy (cf. Cebeillac-Gervasoni, 1996b). In the late first and early second centuries, however, the evidence suggests that more goods were imported from the western provinces such as Spain, which provided bulk olive oil, and southern Gaul, particularly Narbonensis, which supplied wine; the latter also supplied some tablewares. Other tablewares came from the east, along with more wine from the Aegean, and we know of an association of shippers from the Adriatic from this period (Pellegrino, 1987).

While the wholesale distribution of these goods can be associated with the *horrea*, markets, and auction houses, small-scale retail most likely took place in one- or two-roomed units (*tabernae*) which were also used for small-scale production and services, including bars for the sale of food and drink. Over 800 have been excavated and the geophysical survey suggests that we should at least double that. Most of the excavated examples are concentrated in long rows of units flanking the busy main streets, with further clusters around public buildings such as the theater, the *forum*, important temples and the various baths, all areas of high social activity. While all of these would have served the whole population, there are also small groups of *tabernae* fronting minor streets and interior piazzas which seem more designed to provide for local neighborhoods.

As well as these outlets supplying the daily needs of the inhabitants, there are also several large bakeries and fulleries on an almost industrial scale, suggesting that they served more than just local domestic needs. We know from Strabo (5.1.7) that ships came to Ostia laden with black Spanish wool, and even after the building of the harbors at Portus, there is no reason to imagine that these cargoes necessarily ceased to arrive at Ostia; the large-scale *fullonicae* at Ostia might suggest that such material was processed in the town before being sold on (de Ruyt, 2002; Flohr, 2011). Other Ostian products include ceramics, particularly brick, lamps and possibly some finewares, although the volume of such produce seems to have remained small.

21.7 Housing

By the middle of the second century, commercial properties dominated the street frontages of most buildings. Many of the rich houses of the late Republic and Augustan periods had been replaced by three- to five-story *insulae*, although others, such as the Augustan successor to the *Domus aux Bucranes*, continued to function until at least the end of the second century (Perrier, 2007) and some new *domus* were also built, notably the original *Casa della Fortuna*

Annonaria (DeLaine 2012). In addition the German geophysical survey has revealed two very large *domus* in the unexcavated area, built in the Flavian period around large central courts and apparently without *atria* (Bauer, Heinzelmann, and Martin, 2000: 394–410; Martin *et al.*, 2002: 265–69; Heinzelmann, Mols, and McKinnon, 2002: 233–39). That in the east of the city was richly decorated with *opus sectile* and marble veneer, and, at roughly 4,300 m², was larger than any of the known earlier Ostian residences, and one of the best contenders for the previously vexed question of where the elite of Ostia lived in the mid-imperial period. The other lavish residence is a vast suburban villa just outside the late Republican *Porta Marina*, covering roughly 9,500 m² and comparable with the luxury villas on the Bay of Naples. This is the first of a long line of villas extending south along the coast, which included that owned by Pliny the Younger (*Letters*: 2.17.15), who says that the shoreline was so thickly occupied by the roofs of villas as to make it look like many cities. Augustus's villa remained in imperial hands (Claudius kept elephants there), and was particularly redeveloped under the late Antonines.

Ostia itself is more associated with the combined residential and commercial *insulae* from the first half of the second century. Contrary to general opinion, these include a small number of ground-floor dwellings arranged around their own internal courtyards with very high-quality decoration, most easily categorized as luxury town-houses, or "modern" versions of the atrium houses of the preceding centuries. The *Insula delle Muse* (3.9.22), the *Insula di Giove e Ganimede* (1.4.2), and the rich dwelling which preceded the *Casa di Diana* (1.3.3–4) were clearly high status dwellings, possibly for members of Ostia's elite who had country estates elsewhere in the area, or made their money from commerce or associated trades further afield (DeLaine, 1999: 175–87; Ceci, Falzone, and Marinucci, 2013).

More common are the so-called "*medianum*" apartments, residential units of regular plan typified by one or two large reception rooms usually of different sizes at either end of a long rectangular hall, all of which took light through large glazed windows opening onto the street or onto an internal courtyard or garden, and two or more private rooms or *cubicula*, often poorly lit, opening off the other side of the hall; many also had combined latrines and kitchens, often separated from the main living spaces by a corridor, while the largest also had extensive integral upper floors (Hermansen, 1982; DeLaine, 2004). This type of apartment was, in fact, well suited to insertion into long narrow blocks the width of either one or two rows of *tabernae*. While the surviving ones generally occupy the ground level, they were once presumably far more common on upper floors. Many of the 40 known examples were built together as part of groups of similar apartments, as in the *Casette Tipo* and the *Case a Giardino*, but often showing variations in layout or in numbers of rooms, presumably aimed at the needs of particular prospective tenants or at a rental market which was interested in the specific variants. While the *Casette Tipo* at least have generally been regarded as examples of lower class, multiple-occupancy accommodation, their overall size, level of decoration, and provision of facilities such as kitchens and latrines, suggest that the *medianum* apartments served rather for long-term rentals to an economically comfortable clientele. Specific evidence is lacking, but we might see these as including the more prosperous members of the many *collegia* which serviced the city and its commerce. At the upper end of the range at least, there are large, well-appointed and even luxurious apartments which are in many ways comparable with the smaller *domus*, while even the smaller ones could hardly be categorized as "lower class."

Although our understanding of apartment living comes mainly from the well-preserved ground-floor apartments, upper-floor ones were certainly far more numerous in the ancient city. Often all that survives of them are doorways to staircases at street level, often located amid rows of *tabernae* in otherwise entirely commercial street frontages. The late Antonine phase of the *Casa di Diana* preserves a rare arrangement of rooms on the first floor, and the remains of staircases at this level confirm that there was at least one, and most probably two, further floors. The layout suggests that many of these upper-floor apartments were small, only two to four rooms. On the same floor of this *insula* there is a rather different arrangement, a row of narrow, poorly lit cells off a corridor with a larger, presumably shared, single living room at the far end. While all of this was presumably rental accommodation, the two- to four-room apartments could have been rented on a monthly or yearly basis by respectable but lower-class elements of society. The group accommodation was more likely rented by the day or week, particularly by the transient or seasonal populations we might expect in a harbor city like Ostia, a type of boarding house or *pensione*. We have, however, no direct evidence of this, nor of how many individuals occupied each apartment. Equally impossible to identify are examples where a small apartment was actually shared by a number of unrelated individuals, rather than the small nuclear family we might assume, although the legal sources strongly suggest that this was a common occurrence.

21.8   From the Third Century to Late Antiquity

There is ample evidence that Ostia was still thriving throughout the Severan period, despite some arguments to the contrary (Pavolini, 2002). The town council was able to elicit imperial funding for the extension of the theater, begun under Commodus and dedicated by Septimius Severus and Caracalla (*CIL* 14.114), building an arch in Caracalla's honor beside the theater in return (Zevi and Pensabene, 1971). The last major new public building before the fourth century was the so-called Round Temple, a Pantheon-like structure erected under Severus Alexander or the Gordians, and most likely dedicated to the imperial house. The amount of new infill and adaptation in the residential and commercial building stock, and the rich epigraphic record relating to the *collegia*, all support this picture. Indeed, Ostia is described as *amoenissima civitas* – a most pleasant city – in the introduction to Minucius Felix's *Octavius*, written in the early years of the third century.

Nevertheless, in common with many communities in Italy, we hear nothing of local magistrates after the middle of the third century. Exceptionally, at Ostia it was the *praefectus annonae* who took charge of the city as *curator*, presumably reflecting its continuing role in relation to the grain supply to Rome. The silting of the river mouth appears, however, to have been increasingly a problem, and there may have been a concomitant shift of more commercial interest to Portus, which was finally made a city in its own right independent of Ostia by Constantine I in the early fourth century. Over the same period, inscriptions relating to the *collegia* at Ostia all but disappear, while some can still be found at Portus even a century later. While these indications of contraction are arguably also reflected in the abandonment of some commercial and residential *insulae* at Ostia, as well as one of its bath buildings, there are signs that some of this may have been partly the result of natural disaster, especially earthquake, as was apparently the case with the large suburban villa beyond the *Porta Marina*.

The fourth century at Ostia was a period of renewed vigor if with a smaller demographic, characterized by the selective embellishment of public places and the division of the city into discrete zones, created by the blocking off of roads and the demolition or boarding up of unwanted or damaged residential and commercial structures (Gering, 2004). The public face of the city was adorned with fountains and new public plazas, including the *Foro della Statua Eroica*, which replaced a substantial bath building of the Hadrianic period. Recent excavations are beginning to show that the main forum was given a facelift, including a new marble colonnade to the south, while the nearby *Terme del Foro* were restored and embellished under Constantine and his sons (Cicerchia and Marinucci, 1992). Overall, most of the remaining public and private baths were maintained if at a reduced scale, while at least 11 new bath buildings were added, generally small in scale but rich in decoration (Poccardi, 2006).

One of the best-known aspects of late Roman Ostia are the luxury residences, noted for their lavish marble decoration and fountain courts, originally seen as reflecting a very different way of life in a very different city from that represented by the multistory apartments of the second century AD (Becatti, 1948; see Figure 21.4). More recent studies, however, have shown that many, if not most, of these were merely elaborations of earlier elite houses. New creations of the fourth century are relatively few, even if we include the only two, the *Domus di Amore e Psiche* and the *Domus del Ninfeo*, which appear to have originated in the late fourth to early fifth centuries (Pavolini, 1986b). The transformation was clearly a gradual process over the third and fourth centuries, with the late antique *domus* even covering a similar size range to the second-century elite housing. These luxury *domus* appear to have been focal points for the new residential zones or neighborhoods of the late antique city. They are usually to be found in close proximity to one or more sets of baths, and some of the late small baths may have been situated with the presence of rich houses in mind (DeLaine, 2006). These nuclei are linked by the main roads into and through the city, the routes most lavishly embellished with new colonnades, squares and fountains. The seashore was another focus of interest, with a notable concentration of late small baths along the *via Severiana* and facing the sea providing further argument for the importance of Ostia as a coastal resort in the fourth century. Nevertheless, the placement of one of the new bath buildings next to the river basin suggests some continued maritime activity here, and it should not be forgotten that it was at Ostia that St Augustine was staying while awaiting a ship to Africa when his mother, St Monica, died in AD 388 (Augustine, *Confessions*: 9.10–13).

Figure 21.4 Ostia, Domus delle Colonne: view from the main reception room to the fountain court. Photograph: J. DeLaine.

The importance of Christianity in late antique Ostia is still the subject of debate (Boin, 2013). There is epigraphic evidence that traditional cults were active until – or had been revived in – the late fourth century, and that these were being promoted by high-ranking officials including the *praefectus annonae* (cf. Boin, 2010) Against this are to be set the large palaeo-Christian basilica to the apostles Peter, Paul, and John which Constantine I built at Ostia together with a certain Gallicanus (*Liber Pontificalis*: Vol. 1, 183–84), identified only at the end of the twentieth century in the south-east of the unexcavated area (Bauer and Heinzelmann, 1999; see Figure 21.5), and the impressive late-fourth century funerary basilica constructed over a pre-existing necropolis at Pianabella south of the city (Paroli, 1999), both suggesting involvement of Ostia's elite on the Christian side as well. Other indications of Christianity in the wider urban fabric, such as the elite Christian *domus* once believed to be a church and the Christianization of the Baths of Mithras (Brenk, 2001), are, however, rare, and now generally assigned to the fifth century rather than the fourth, as are most likely the excavated remains of the small basilica built over the tomb of St Aurea, in the region of which St Monica was also buried.

Ostia's real period of rapid and definitive decline seems to have begun in the fifth century, perhaps following Alaric's occupation of Portus and the Vandal sack of 455. Constantine's basilica continued, however, to function into the seventh century AD when it underwent some restoration, serving a much reduced city that may have consisted of only a limited settlement

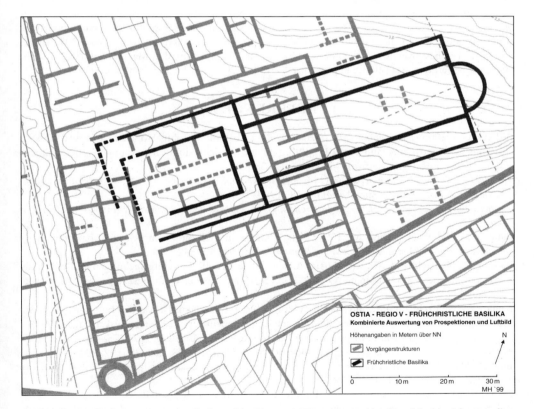

Figure 21.5 Ostia, Regio V: overall plan of the Constantinian episcopal basilica (black) with preceding second century AD structures (grey), as revealed by geophysics, aerial photography, and limited excavation. From Bauer, *et al.*, 1999. "Untersuchungen im Bereich der konstantinischen Bischofskirche Ostias. Vorbericht zur ersten Grabungskampagne." *RM* 106: 289–341.

around the basilica and other small Christian shrines, and it was only finally abandoned in the ninth century, at roughly the same time as the funerary basilica at Pianabella also fell out of use (Paroli, 1999).

ENDNOTE

1 For ease of reference, all extant buildings and streets are given their Italian names (in italics) and/ or addresses as used in Gismondi's 1:500 plan (Calza, 1953) and the Laterza guide to Ostia (Pavolini, 2006).

FURTHER READING

The best comprehensive historical study of Ostia remains Meiggs 1973 (2nd edn), to be read in conjunction with Calza 1953, which includes the 1:500 detailed plan still in use today, and Pavolini 1986a. Much has, however, changed since these were written, and for an up-to-date introduction to the site and the latest scholarship Pavolini 2006 is essential. The Ostia web-site (www.ostia-antica.org) provides a very accessible introduction to the site and its monuments, and is also valuable for its exhaustive, up-to-date, and searchable bibliography. Important new scholarship can be found in a number of conference proceedings: Gallina Zevi and Claridge eds 1996; *Atti del II Colloquio Internazionale su Ostia Antica (Roma, 8–11 novembre 1998)* 1999; Descoeudres ed. 2001, catalog of an exhibition in Geneva, which includes a small-scale updated version of the 1:500 plan; Bruun and Gallina Zevi eds 2002; Nicolet ed. 2002. The best overview of the new geophysical survey can be found in Martin *et al.* 2002. For the latest on the territory of Ostia see in particular Keay *et al.* 2005 and Keay and Paroli eds 2011.

REFERENCES

Aldrete, G.S. 2006. *Floods of the Tiber in Ancient Rome*. Baltimore: Johns Hopkins University Press.
Arnoldus-Huyzendveld A. and Paroli L. 1995. "Alcune considerazioni sullo sviluppo storico dell'ansa del Tevere presso Ostia." *Archeologia laziale* 12: 383–92.
Atti del II Colloquio Internazionale su Ostia Antica (Roma, 8–11 novembre 1998), Mededelingen van het Nederlands Instituut te Rome, Antiquity, 58 (1999)
Bargagli B. and Grosso C. 1997. *I fasti ostienses: documento della storia di Ostia*. Rome: *Itinerari ostiensi* 8.
Bauer F.A. and Heinzelmann M. 1999. "The Constantinian Bishop's church at Ostia: preliminary report on the 1998 season." *Journal of Roman Archaeology* 12: 342–54.
Bauer F.A., Heinzelmann, M., and Martin, A., and Schaub, A. 1999. "Untersuchungen im Bereich der konstantinischen Bischofskirche Ostias. Vorbericht zur ersten Grabungskampagne." *RM* 106: 289–341.
Bauer F.A., Heinzelmann, M., and Martin, A. 2000."Ostia. Ein urbanistisches Forschungsprojekt in den unausgegrabenen Bereichen des Stadtgebietes. Vorbericht zur 2. Grabungskampagne 1999." *Mitteilungen des Deutschen Archäologischen Instituts, Römische Abteilung* 107: 375–416.
Becatti G. 1948. "Case ostiensi del tardo impero." *Bollettino d'Arte* 33, 102–28; 197–224.
Boin D. 2010. "A hall for Hercules at Ostia and a farewell to the late antique 'pagan revival'." *American Journal of Archaeology* 114: 253–66.
Boin, D. 2013. *Ostia in Late Antiquity*. Cambridge: Cambridge University Press.
Bollmann, B. 1998. *Römische Vereinshauser: Untersuchungen zu den* Scholae *der römischen Berufs-, Kult- und Augustalen-Kollegien in Italien*. Mainz: von Zabern.
Brenk, B. 2001. "La christianisation d'Ostie. " In *Ostia. Port et porte de la Rome antique*, ed. J.-.P Descoeudres, 262–71. Geneva: Georg: Musée d'art et d'histoire.

Bruun, C. and Gallina Zevi, A. eds. 2002. *Ostia e Portus nelle loro relazioni con Roma*. Rome: Istitutum Romanum Finlandiae.

Bukowiecki, E., Dessales, H., and Dubouloz, J. 2008. *Ostie, l'eau dans la ville. Châteaux d'eau et réseau d'adduction*. Rome: École Française de Rome.

Calza, G. 1915. "Il Piazzale delle Corporazioni e la funzione commerciale di Ostia." *Bullettino della Commissione archeologica Comunale di Roma* 43: 178–206.

Calza, G. 1942. "Il tempio della Bona Dea." *Notizie degli Scavi*, 152 ff.

Calza, G. 1953. *Scavi di Ostia I. Topografia generale*. Rome: Libreria dello Stato.

Carandini A. and Panella C. 1981. "The trading connections of Rome and Central Italy in the late second and third centuries: the evidence of the Terme del Nuotatore excavations, Ostia." In *The Roman West in the Third Century. Contributions from archaeology and history*, eds A. King and M. Henig, vol. 2, 487–503. Oxford: BAR International Series 109.

Carta, M., Pohl, I., and Zevi, F. 1987. "Ostia. La Taberna dell'invidioso. Piazzale delle corporazioni, portico ovest. Saggi sotto i mosaici." *NSc Supplement* 32, 167–443.

Cébeillac, M. 1971. "Quelques inscriptions inedites d'Ostie: de la République à l'Empire." *Mélanges de l'Ecole Française de Rome, Antiquité* 83: 39–125.

Cébeillac-Gervasoni, M. 1996a. "Deux préteurs, magistrats de la colonie romaine d'Ostie avant la guerre sociale: Publius Silius et Marcus Critonius." In *"Roman Ostia" Revisited. Archaeological and historical papers in memory of Russell Meiggs*, eds A. Gallina Zevi and A. Claridge, 91–101. Rome: British School at Rome.

Cébeillac-Gervasoni, M. 1996b. "Gli 'Africani' ad Ostia ovvero 'Le Mani sulla citta'." In *L'Incidenza dell'Antico. Studi in memoria di E. Lepore*, eds A. Storchi Marino, L. Breglia Pulci Doria, C. Montepaone, 557–67. Naples: Luciano.

Cébeillac-Gervasoni, M. 2002. "Les rapports institutionnels et politiques d'Ostie et de Rome de la république au IIIe siècle ap. J.-C." *Mélanges de l'Ecole Française de Rome, Antiquité* 114, 58–86.

Ceci, M., Falzone, S., and Marinucci, A. 2013. *L'insula ostiense di Diana*. Fiumicino: Fondazione Portus.

Cicerchia P. and Marinucci A. 1992. *Le Terme del Foro o di Gavio Massimo*. Rome: *Scavi di Ostia* 11.

Claridge, A. 2008. "The evolution of Rome's maritime facade: archaeology and geomorphology at Castelporziano, 2.0.0 Excavation Report April 2008." http://archaeologydataservice.ac.uk/catalogue/adsdata/arch-968-1/dissemination/pdf/2_0_0_Excavation_reports/2_0_4_Archaeological_excavation_report_April_08.pdf. Accessed August 10, 2015.

Coarelli, F. 1994. "Saturnino, Ostia e l'annona. Il controllo e l'organizzazione del commercio del grano tra II e I secolo a.C." In *Le ravitaillement en blé de Rome et des centres urbains des débuts de la République jusqu'au haut empire*, 35–46. Naples/Rome: Collection du Centre Jean Bérard 11/Collection de l'École française de Rome 196.

Cooley, A.E. 1999. "A new date for Agrippa's theatre at Ostia." *Papers of the British School at Rome* 67: 173–82.

DeLaine, J. 1999. "High status insula apartments in early imperial Ostia – a reading." *Meded* 58: 175–89.

DeLaine, J. 2002. "Building activity in Ostia in the second century AD." In *Ostia e Portus nelle loro relazioni con Roma*, eds C. Bruun and A.G. Zevi, 41–102. Rome: Istitutum Romanum Finlandiae.

DeLaine, J. 2003. "The builders of Roman Ostia: organization, status and society." *Proceedings of the First International Congress on Construction History*, ed. S. Huerta, vol. 2, 723–32. Madrid: Juan de Herrera.

DeLaine, J. 2004. "Designing for a market: 'medianum' apartments at Ostia." *Journal of Roman Archaeology* 17: 146–76.

DeLaine J. 2005. "The commercial landscape of Ostia." In *Roman Working Lives and Urban Living*, eds A. MacMahon and J. Price, 29–47. Oxford: Oxbow.

DeLaine J. 2006. "Baths and Bathing in Late Antique Ostia." *Proceedings of the XVIth International Congress of Classical Archaeology*, eds C.C. Mattusch, A.A. Donohue, A. Brauer, 338–43. Oxford: Oxbow.

DeLaine J. 2012. "Housing Roman Ostia." In *Contested Spaces: houses and temples in Roman Antiquity and the New Testament*, eds D. L. Balch and A. Weissenrieder, 327–51. Tübingen: Mohr Siebeck.

DeLaine, J. and Wilkinson D. 1999. "The House of Jove and Ganymede." *Meded* 58: 77–79.

Descoeudres, J.-P., ed. 2001. *Ostia. Port et porte de la Rome antique*. Geneva: Georg: Musée d'art et d'histoire.

Falzone, S. 2007. Ornata aedificia. *Pitture parietali delle case ostiensi*. Rome: Libreria dello Stato.

Flohr, M. 2011. "Exploring the limits of skilled craftsmanship. The *fullonicae* of Roman Italy." In *Les savoirs professionnels des gens de métier. Etudes sur le monde du travail dans les sociétés urbaines de l'empire romain*, eds N. Monteix, N. Tran, H. Dessales, 87–100. Naples: Centre Jean Bérard.

Gallina Zevi, A. and Claridge, A. eds. 1996. *"Roman Ostia" Revisited. Archaeological and historical papers in memory of Russell Meiggs*. Rome: British School at Rome.

Gallina Zevi, A. and Humphrey, J. eds. 2004. *Ostia, Cicero, Gamala, Feasts, and the Economy: papers in memory of John D'Arms*. Portsmouth, RI: *Journal of Roman Archaeology* Suppl. 57.

Gering, A. 2004. "Plätze und Strassensperren an Promenaden. Zum Funktionswandel Ostias in der Spätantike." *Mitteilungen des Deutschen Archäologischen Instituts, Römische Abteilung* 111: 299–382.

Giraudi, C. 2011. "La geologia dell'Agro Portuense nell'ambito dell'evoluzione del delta del Tevere." In *Portus and its Hinterland*, eds S. Keay and L. Paroli, 21–30. London: Archaeological Monographs of the British School at Rome 18.

Heinzelmann, M. 1998. "Beobachtungen zur suburbanen Topographie Ostias. Ein orthogonales Strassensystem im Bereich der Pianabella." *Mitteilungen des Deutschen Archäologischen Instituts, Römische Abteilung* 105: 175–225.

Heinzelmann, M. *et al.* 1999. "Rialzamenti dei livelli delle strade e quartieri urbani ad Ostia," *Meded* 58: 61–97.

Heinzelmann, M. 2000. *Die Nekropolen von Ostia. Untersuchungen zu den Graeberstrassen vor der Porta Romana und an der Via Laurentina*. Pfeil: Munich.

Heinzelmann, M. 2002. "Bauboom und urbanistische Defizite – zur städtebaulichen Entwicklung Ostias im 2. Jh." In *Ostia e Portus nelle loro relazioni con Roma*, eds C. Bruun and A.Gallina Zevi, 103–22. Rome: Istitutum Romanum Findlandiae.

Heinzelmann, M. 2010. "Supplier of Rome or Mediterranean marketplace? The changing economic role of Ostia after the construction of Portus in the light of new archaeological evidence." *Bollettino di Archeologia on line* 1: 5–10.

Heinzelmann M. and Martin A. 2002. "River port, *navalia* and harbour temple at Ostia: new results of a DAI-AAR Project." *Journal of Roman Archaeology* 15: 5–19.

Heinzelmann M., Mols S.T.A.M., McKinnon M. 2002. "Ostia, Regionen III und IV. Untersuchungen in den unausgegrabenen Bereichen des Stadtgebietes. Vorbericht zur vierten Grabungskampagne 2001." *Mitteilungen des Deutschen Archäologischen Instituts, Römische Abteilung* 109: 225–42.

Hermansen, G. 1982. *Ostia. Aspects of Roman City Life*. Alberta: University of Alberta Press.

Keay, S., Millett, M., Paroli, L., and Strutt, K. 2005. *Portus. An Archaeological Survey of the Port of Imperial Rome*. London: Archaeological Monographs of the British School at Rome 15.

Keay, S. and Paroli, L. eds. 2011. *Portus and its Hinterland*. London: Archaeological Monographs of the British School at Rome 18.

Kockel, V. and Ortisi, S. 2000. "Ostia. Sogenanntes Macellum (IV 5,2). Vorbericht über die Ausgrabungen der Universität Augsburg 1997/1998." *Mitteilungen des Deutschen Archäologischen Instituts, Römische Abteilung* 107: 351–64.

Laird, M.L. 2000. "Reconsidering the so-called 'Sede degli Augustali' at Ostia." *Memoirs of the American Academy in Rome* 45: 41–84.

Mar, R. 1990. "El santuario de Hercules y la urbanistica de Ostia." *Archivo español de arqueologia* 63: 137–60.

Mar, R. 1991. "La formazione dello spazio urbano nella città di Ostia." *Mitteilungen des Deutschen Archäologischen Instituts, Römische Abteilung* 98: 81–109.

Mar, R., Nolla, J.M., Ruiz de Arbullo, J., and Vivo, D. 1999. "Santuarios y urbanismo en Ostia. La excavacion en el campo de Cibeles." *Meded* 58: 20–22.

Marini Recchia F. and Zevi F. 2008. "La storia più antica di Roma sul fregio della Basilica di Ostia." *Rendiconti della Pontificia Accademia romana di archeologia* 80: 149–92.

Martin, A. 1996. "Un saggio sulle mura del castrum di Ostia (Reg. I, ins. x, 3)." In *"Roman Ostia" Revisited. Archaeological and historical papers in memory of Russell Meiggs*, eds A. Gallina Zevi and A. Claridge, 19–38. London, British School at Rome.

Martin, A. 2006. "Sigillata and Red-Slip Ware at Ostia. The supply to a consumption center." In *Territorio e produzioni ceramiche. Paesaggi, economia e societa in eta romana*, eds S. Menchelli and M. Pasquinucci, 381–88. Pisa: Pisa University Press.

Martin, A., Heinzelmann, M., De Sena, E.C. and Granino Cerere, M.G. 2002. "The urbanistic project on the previously unexcavated areas of Ostia (DAI-AAR 1996–2001)." *Memoirs of the American Academy in Rome* 47: 259–304.

Meiggs, R. 1973. (2nd edn) *Roman Ostia*. Oxford: Clarendon Press.

Mols, S.T.A.M. 2002. "Ricerche sulla pittura di Ostia. Status quaestionis e prospettive." *Bulletin Antieke Beschaving* 77, 151–74.

Morard, T. 2007. "Le plan de la Domus aux Bucranes et son système décoratif: pavements – parois peintes – stucs – plafonds." In *Villas, maisons, sanctuaires et tombeaux tardo-republicains*, eds A. Gallina Zevi and B. Perrier, 55–80. Rome : Quasar.

Morelli, C., Carbonara, A. Forte V., Grossi, M.C., and Arnoldus-Huyzendveld, A. 2011. "La topografia romana dell'agro portuense alla luce delle nuove indagini." In *Portus and its Hinterland*, eds S. Keay and L. Paroli, 261–85. London: Archaeological Monographs of the British School at Rome 18.

Nicolet, C. ed. 2002. *Villes et avant-ports: l'exemple de Rome et Ostie. Actes de la table ronde des 29 et 30 novembre 1994, Mélanges de l'École française de Rome, Antiquité* 114.1.

Panella, C. 1986. "Oriente et Occidente: considerazioni su alcune anfore 'egee' di età imperiale a Ostia." *Recherches sur les amphores grecques*, eds J.-Y. Empereur and Y. Garlan, 609–36. Athens/Paris : BCH Suppl. 13.

Paribeni, R. 1916. "I Quattro Tempietti di Ostia," *Monumenti Antichi* XXIII.2: 442–84.

Paribeni, R. 1918. "Ostia – scavi e restauri nei mesi ottobre 1917–marzo 1918." *NSc* 128–38.

Paroli, L. 1999. "La basilica paleocristiana di Porto: scavi 1997–1998." *Meded* 58: 45–47.

Pavolini, C. 1983. "I commerci di Roma e di Ostia nella prima eta imperiale: merci d'accompagno e carichi di ritorno." In *Misurare la terra: centuriazione e coloni nel mondo romano. Città, agricoltura, commercio: materiali da Roma e dal suburbio*, 200–07. Modena: Edizioni Panini.

Pavolini, C. 1986a. *Vita quotidiana a Ostia*. Rome: Laterza.

Pavolini, C. 1986b. "L'edilizia commerciale e l'edilizia abitativa nel contesto di Ostia tardoantico." In *Società romana e impero tardoantico* II, ed. A. Giardina, 255–69. Rome-Bari, Laterza.

Pavolini, C. 1996. "Mercato ostiense e mercato romano: alcuni contesti ceramici a confronto." In *"Roman Ostia" Revisited. Archaeological and historical papers in memory of Russell Meiggs*, eds A. Gallina Zevi and A. Claridge, 223–42. Rome: British School at Rome.

Pavolini, C. 2002. "La trasformazione del ruolo di Ostia nel III sec. d.C." *Mélanges de l'Ecole Française de Rome, Antiquité* 114: 325–52.

Pavolini, C. 2006 (revised edn). *Ostia*. Rome-Bari: Laterza.

Pellegrino, A. 1987. "I navicularii maris Hadriatici ad Ostia." *Miscellanea greca e romana* 12: 229–36. Rome.

Pellegrino, A. 2004. "Il territorio ostiense nella tarda età repubblicana." In *Ostia, Cicero, Gamala, Feasts, and the Economy: papers in memory of John D'Arms*, eds A. Gallina Zevi and J. Humphrey, 32–46. Portsmouth, RI: *Journal of Roman Archaeology* Suppl. 57.

Pellegrino, A., Olivanti, P., and Panariti, F. 1995. "Ricerche archeologiche nel Trastevere Ostiense." *Archeologia Laziale* 12: 393–400.

Pensabene, P. 2004. "Marmi e classi dirigenti a Ostia tra la tarda repubblica e la prima eta augustea." *Ostia, Cicero, Gamala, Feasts, and the Economy: papers in memory of John D'Arms*, eds A. Gallina Zevi and J. Humphrey, 99–108. Portsmouth, RI: *Journal of Roman Archaeology* Suppl. 57.

Pensabene, P. 2007. Ostiensium marmorum decus et decor. *Studi architettonici, decorative e archeometrici*. Rome: *Studi Miscellanei* 33.

Perrier, B. 2007. "Les trois edifices successifs: Schola du Trajan, Domus à Peristyle, Domus aux Bucranes." In *Villas, maisons, sanctuaires et tombeaux tardo-republicains*, eds A. Gallina Zevi and B. Perrier, 15–32. Rome : Quasar.

Poccardi, G. 2006. "Les bains de la ville d'Ostie à l'époque tardo-antique (fin IIIe – début VIe siècle). " In *Les cités de l'Italie tardo-antique (IVe – VIe siècle)*, eds M. Ghilardi, C. Goddard, P. Porena, 167–86. Rome : Collection de l'École française de Rome 369.

Pohl, I. 1983. "Was early Ostia a colony or a fort? " *Parola del Passato* 38: 123–30.

Purcell, N. 1998. "Alla scoperta di una costa residenziale romana: il *litus Laurentinum* e l'archeologia dell'*otium*," in *Castelporziano III*, ed. M.G. Lauro 11–32. Rome: Viella.

Rickman, G.E. 1971. *Roman Granaries and Store Buildings*, Cambridge: Cambridge University Press.

Rickman, G.E. 1980. *The Corn Supply of Ancient Rome*. Oxford: Clarendon Press.

Rieger, A.-K. 2004. *Heiligtümer in Ostia*. Munich: Pfeil.

Ruyt, C. de. 2002. "Boulangers et foulons d'Ostie à l'époque impériale. Quelques réflexions sur l'implantation de leurs ateliers et sur leurs fonctions précises dans la ville portuaire." In *Les artisans dans la ville antique*, eds J.-C. Béal et J.-C. Goyon, 49–53. Lyon/Paris: Collection de l'Institut d'archéologie et d'histoire de l'antiquité 6.

Serlorenzi, M. and Di Giuseppe, H. 2011. "La Via Campana. Spunti di riflessione sul contesto topografico e ambientale." In *Portus and its Hinterland*, eds S. Keay and L. Paroli, 287–300. London: Archaeological Monographs of the British School at Rome 18.

Sole, L. 2002. "Monumenti repubblicani di Ostia Antica." *Archeologia classica* 53: 137–81.

White, L.M. 2012. "The changing face of Mithraism at Ostia. Archaeology, art, and the urban landscape." In *Contested Spaces. Houses and temples in Roman antiquity and the New Testament*, eds D.L. Balch and A. Weissenrieder, 435–92. Tübingen: Mohr Siebeck.

Widemann, F. and Naciri, A. 1989. "Analisi delle anfore galliche d'Ostia. Variazione delle origini del vino gallico consumato a Roma nelle diverse epoche." In *Amphores romaines et histoire économique. Dix ans de recherche*, 285–96. Rome: Collection de l'École française de Rome 114.

Zevi, F. 1976. "Monumenti e aspetti culturali di Ostia repubblicana,." In *Hellenismus in Mittelitalien*, ed. P. Zanker, 52–63. Göttingen: Vandenhoeck und Ruprecht.

Zevi, F. 1997. "Costruttori eccellenti per le mura di Ostia. Cicerone, Clodio e l'iscrizione della Porta Romana." *Rivista dell'Istituto nazionale d'archeologia e storia dell'arte* 19–20: 61–112.

Zevi, F. 2002. "Origini di Ostia." In *Ostia e Portus nelle loro relazioni con Roma*, eds C. Bruun and A.Gallina Zevi, 11–32. Rome: Istitutum Romanum Finlandiae.

Zevi, F. 2004. "Cicero and Ostia." In *Ostia, Cicero, Gamala, Feasts, and the Economy: papers in memory of John D'Arms*, eds A. Gallina Zevi and J. Humphrey, 15–31. Portsmouth, RI: *Journal of Roman Archaeology* Suppl. 57.

Zevi F. and Pensabene P. 1971. "Un arco in onore di Caracalla ad Ostia." *Rendiconti della Reale Accademia dei Lincei, Classe di scienze morali, storiche e filologiche* 26: 481–525.

PART IV

Economy and Society

CHAPTER 22

Regional Interaction

Rebecca R. Benefiel

22.1   Regional Interaction and Local Networks

At about the same time from a trivial dispute there sprang up between the Nucerian and Pompeian colonists a frightful slaughter at a gladiatorial spectacle… (*sub idem tempus levi initio atrox caedes orta inter colonos Nucerinos Pompeianosque gladiatorio spectaculo*…Tacitus, *Annals*: 14.17; trans. Woodman, 2004)

Thus Tacitus began his account of the riot that took place in the amphitheater of Pompeii in AD 59. The results were worthy of national attention. The Nucerians lost lives and limbs. The Pompeians were banned from holding similar spectacles for ten years, certain associations were dissolved, and leading figures were sent into exile (Galsterer, 1980; Moeller, 1970). While the riot was something that the cities of Italy had never seen the likes of, the occasion itself, an event that had drawn numbers of spectators from the larger region, was not all that unusual. Across Roman Italy, residents of different communities came together for a number of reasons, local travel was facilitated by social and economic networks, and the early empire in particular was a time of significant mobility. This chapter explores the nature of regional interaction in Roman Italy, a subject that illuminates the activities of the broader population and members at every level of society and illustrates communities working in cooperation.

Schooling was one motivation for heading to a nearby town. On a trip to his hometown of Comum, Pliny the Younger discovered that adolescents were traveling to the neighboring city of Mediolanum, some 30 km away, in order to pursue their education (Pliny the Younger, *Letters*: 4.13). He offered to help endow a teaching position so that there might be suitable teachers in Comum, if students' parents could come up with the rest of the cost. Having to go outside Comum was expensive, Pliny pointed out. Parents paid for lodging and travel; in fact, one had to pay for everything away from home. He suggested that parents pool their resources, using what they were already paying to send their sons to Mediolanum to provide instead for the stipend of a teacher at Comum.

Rome, as a capital city, may have been equipped with an enviable number of services, retail, and infrastructure to meet its residents' needs, but inhabitants of other cities throughout

Roman Italy had at times to venture beyond their hometown for goods, services, and opportunities. Regional networks aided such excursions by connecting the towns of Roman Italy. These networks supported individual towns working together. If Comum did not have sufficient numbers of teachers, at least another town in the region did. On other occasions when residents of different communities came together, however, such as at the gladiatorial spectacle mentioned at the beginning of this chapter, individual identities might clash and bring people into conflict. The subject of regional interaction allows us to look at activity outside the capital and provides a wider perspective on the Roman world, the functioning of the economy, and the culture of daily life.

Roman Italy provided an environment that encouraged local travel and promoted regional interaction. The road system that allowed the movement of troops and goods throughout the empire branched across the length and breadth of the Italian peninsula, connecting city and countryside, and linking towns of all sizes. Political stability contributed to safety on the roads, while general prosperity permitted people the means and opportunities to move around the region. The dense urbanization of Italy also fostered local travel, with communities situated in proximity to each other. If engagements in the region did preclude returning home the same day, inns and numerous eating establishments in the cities catered to travelers (Casson, 1994 163–218).

Since regional travel generally involved far more than the elite population, however, and occurred at a remove from life in Rome, we might not expect to have more than glimpses of these people and activities who tend to fly under the radar in any society. Yet two developments working in tandem pull the curtain back on this world: the rise of the epigraphic habit and the destruction of Pompeii. These developments have resulted in rich archaeological material, especially from the first century of the Roman Empire, which illustrates lively regional interaction in Roman Italy.

In a groundbreaking article of 1982, Ramsay MacMullen identified a strong adoption of the epigraphic habit during the Roman Empire. He pointed out "a pronounced increase in the number of all varieties of inscription in … the Latin-speaking world" up to the late second century, at which point there followed a marked decrease (MacMullen, 1982: 244). This phenomenon of increased production of inscriptions has left us the names of hundreds of thousands of individuals we might otherwise not have known had they not been carved into stone, often along with the length of their life or details of their career. In Roman Italy, the tendency to monumentalize the written word affected the survival of other types of information as well. Much of what is known about the system of market-days, or *nundinae*, in central Italy derives from adoption of the epigraphic habit.

The epigraphic habit was in full swing when the town of Pompeii was destroyed by the eruption of Mt Vesuvius in AD 79. Indeed, it is possible to see on the wall plaster preserved by the volcanic debris that text was not just carved into stone; it was also posted in less permanent media in abundant measure. As a result, Pompeii offers a unique look into regional interaction with material such as advertisements for gladiatorial games that were to be held in different towns around the region of Campania.

These two contexts for regional interaction – local market-days and gladiatorial games – are the focus of this chapter. Events like these involved inhabitants travelling locally and contributed to the economic and social dynamism of the larger region.

22.2　Market-Days in Roman Italy

If you visit Lake Garda in Italy today, you may see a sheet of A4 paper taped to a lamppost, listing the names of a number of towns around the lake and the day that each holds an open-air market. That system is the direct descendant of the Roman market-day, or *nundinae*.

Throughout much of classical antiquity, notices regarding the day of a town's market were probably posted in a similar manner. A notice may have been painted on wood or some other support and posted in the town's forum where people would see it. In the early Empire, however, the burgeoning epigraphic habit and a growing tendency to monumentalize information led certain towns to post market-day schedules by inscribing them in stone. Such schedules are known from five towns in central Italy. All date to the first century of the empire (Degrassi, 1963 [= *Inscr. It.*, vol. 13.2, 49–53]). These inscriptions demonstrate communities working in cooperation to establish a calendar of market-days around the region, much like the schedule in place today for the communities around Lake Garda.

As the etymology of the word *nundinae* implies (that is, *novem* and the adjectival form of *dies*), the market-day of a town was held every eight days, or nine, when counting inclusively. This eight-day cycle of time between market-days was the Roman equivalent of a week and served as a main unit of time through the Republic and early Empire. The *nundinae* were in place already by the third century BC, but may have come into being even earlier. Roman tradition placed the institution of the *nundinae* in the period of the monarchy. Macrobius (*Saturnalia*: 1.16.31–33) preserves the testimonies of Tuditanus, who attributed the *nundinae* to Romulus, and of Cassius Hemina who assigned them to Servius Tullius (De Ligt, 1993: 112–13). Roman calendars represent the days of the year within this repeating eight-day cycle, assigning to each day a letter of the alphabet from A to H (*Fasti Praenestini*: Degrassi, 1963, *Inscr. It.*, vol. 13.2.17. Cf. *Fasti Allifani* – *Inscr. It.* vol. 13.2.24, *Fasti Amiterni* – *Inscr. It.* vol. 13.2.25, and *Fasti magistrorum vici* – *Inscr. It.* 13.2.12).

From their beginnings, the *nundinae* were an important link between town and countryside. The occasion of the market-day gave those who lived in the countryside the opportunity to sell their surplus produce in the city and to purchase necessities. According to Festus, "The ancients wanted this to be a holiday, so that the country dwellers could come together for the sake of buying and selling…" (176L, s.v. *nundinas, feriatum diem esse voluerunt antiqui, ut rustici convenirent mercandi, vendendique causa…*). A passage in the pseudo-Vergilian poem, *Moretum*, presents the schedule of a rural peasant, characterized as a backwoods farmer of a tiny plot of land (*exigui cultor… rusticus agri*), who takes his produce to town on the *nundinae*. Columella's handbook on agriculture illustrates the utility of the *nundinae* not only for the small farmer but also for those working on large, productive villa estates. Cautioning that *vilici*, the overseers of slave-staffed villas, should not spend more time than necessary away from the estate, Columella (*On Agriculture*: 1.8.6; 11.1.23) did allow that an approved excursion was to the *nundinae* in order to purchase supplies.

The *nundinae* continued to function well into the imperial period, even with the explosion of urban expansion that took place in Italian towns during the late Republic. This survival was aided by the fact that the market-day also came to serve other purposes. The swell in population and increased activity on these days provided numerous opportunities, not only for merchants. Livy refers to political candidates using the *nundinae* to campaign for votes (Livy: 7.15.13). Livy mentions this practice in the context of the mid-fourth century, but it more likely reflects the situation of the Gracchan period (De Ligt, 1993: 112). New legislation was posted on market-days, and during the late Republic and early Empire auctions came to be held on the day of the *nundinae* (Andreau, 2000, updating his 1976 article; De Ligt, 1993: 114). It was at an auction during the *nundinae* in Arpinum, for example, that Cicero purchased an estate for his brother (Cicero, *Letters to his brother Quintus*: 3.1.3).

Since many cities and towns held their own *nundinae*, a market-day might be held in a different town within a particular region every day of the eight-day cycle. The *nundinae* held in individual towns were thus each a part of a larger market system (Storchi Marino, 2000; Frayn, 1993). The density of communities holding local markets and the complexity of the market system varied according to region. In North Africa, for example, cities were farther apart and *nundinae* were held less frequently: rather than an eight-day cycle, *nundinae* in the north African provinces were held twice a month (De Ligt, 1993: 119–22; Nollé, 1982: n.3–8). Areas such as central Italy, however, presented a very dense network of cities, many of which held weekly markets. Since so many communities were located in close proximity to each other and so many of them held markets, the system of weekly markets became very complex. This complexity may have necessitated documents such as the *indices nundinarii*, or market-day schedules.

The modern label of *indices nundinarii* refers to a class of inscribed documents that present information relevant to the Roman calendar. The main function of these documents was to keep track of multiple systems of time, including the days of the month and schedules recording when *nundinae* were held in various cities. Examples come from five different locations, all of which are in southern Latium and Campania: Allifae, Suessula, Pausilypon, Pompeii, and an unknown town in Latium. All together these lists name more than 20 towns in central Italy that held periodic market-days.

Latium and Campania may have had greater potential for a more intricately designed market system precisely because there were so many cities holding *nundinae* in this region. As a result, it appears that a certain amount of choice was available for selecting which cities in central Italy would be posted on the *nundinae* lists. Five of the seven cities on the list from Allifae, for example, appear also on the lists from Suessula. The list from Pompeii has four and five cities in common with the Allifae and Suessula lists, respectively, while only three cities are shared among all three lists. Cities common to both the Allifae and Suessula lists are Atella, Suessula, Nola, Cumae, and Cales, whilst all three lists from Allifae, Suessula, and Pompeii include Atella, Nola, and Cumae. The Pompeii list also shares Capua with the Allifae list, and Puteoli and Nuceria with the Suessula list. The list posted in each town did not need to be comprehensive for areas beyond its own region or micro-region. More distant cities may have been listed because they offered particular specialties (e.g. Saepinum for sheep or woollen products) or because they could serve as points of transfer to another market network (e.g. Capua or Luceria in Apulia). These inscriptions thus yield useful information about the role of local markets in the Roman economy.

These *nundinae* schedules also point to the functioning of regional networks and, in their inscribed (and thus monumentalized) form, the importance of such networks to the inhabitants of a region. A closer look at one of these *indices nundinarii* reveals how this information might be put to practical use.

None of the *indices nundinarii* is preserved in its entirety, but the format of the *index* from southern Latium permits a likely reconstruction of the whole. Roughly one-third of the index has been preserved (see Figure 22.1). This corresponds to the right third of the stone and includes the lower right hand corner and portions of the top, bottom, and right edges. The central portion of the inscription consisted of a series of interlocking circles created by a compass. By moving the central point of the compass to the outer edge of a circle, additional circles (or portions of circles) were created as well as six petal designs within each circle. These petals were each marked with a Roman numeral from I to XXX. At the top and bottom corners framing the circle design, there stand three-line captions that summarize the length of the seasons. The caption in the upper right corner explains summer: *Summer, from eleven days before the kalends of May until ten days before the kalends of August. 94 days in length (Aestas • ex • XI • K(alendas) • Mai(as) / in • X • K(alendas) • August(i) / Dies • LXXXXIIII)*. At the top edge of the stone a horizontal row of text names the planetary days of the seven-day week. Portions of three days have been preserved: [*Merc*]*ur(i)* • *Iovis* • *Ve*[*ner(is)*]. The right edge, the best preserved section of the stone, holds a list of eight cities below the heading *NUNDINAE*.

The existence of holes for movable pegs illustrates that a practical solution had been reached for keeping track of an increasingly complicated calendar. The inscription contains three

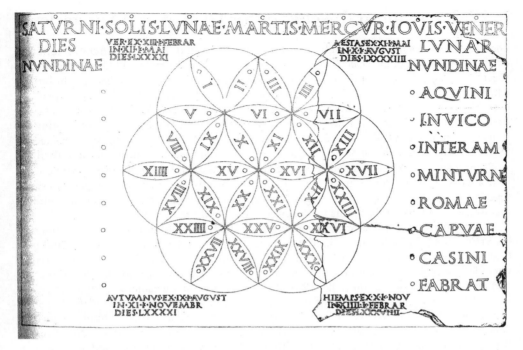

Figure 22.1 *Index nundinarius* from southern Latium. Source: *Index Nundinarius vici cuiusdam Latii* (*Inscr. It.* vol. 13.2, no. 49) from *Inscr. It.*, vol. *XIII fasc. 2, Fasti et Elogia*, ed. Attilio Degrassi, Rome: Istituto Poligrafico e Zecca dello Stato, 1963.

separate calendrical systems: the 30 days of the month, the eight-day cycle of *nundinae*, and the seven-day week. These three systems all ran concurrently and independently of each other. One hole stood beside each individual data point. Three simple pegs, then, were all that was needed to identify the day in any and all calendrical manners. This inscription was therefore a flexible mechanism to coordinate multiple systems of time for the wider population. By instituting a movable marker, it was possible to keep track of the day in each system simply by moving the three pegs one spot each day. And if a city did change the day on which it held its market, the information did not need to be recut. The peg could just as easily be moved to the appropriate spot and in the usual way broadcast the relevant information to the public.

The presence of the list of cities holding the *nundinae* alongside the other calendar information suggests that the market-day was economically and socially relevant. It also suggests that there was utility in knowing when the market-day would fall not just in one's own town but in other nearby towns as well. The *nundinae* have generally been understood as a system that was advantageous to itinerant merchants who would travel the circuit to sell their wares.

This type of regional schedule, however, also benefited local producers by allowing them additional opportunities to sell their items on different occasions, not just in the town closest to one's farm or fields but in other towns of the region too. Nor was the benefit restricted to producers. Consumers too gained by having additional opportunities to attend market. A resident of one town would not regularly attend the market in every other neighboring town, but, should a need or desire arise, there was the possibility of filling it sooner than waiting another seven days until the next market-day. The coordination of these market schedules and the publication of them for the benefit of the public points to regional cooperation at work.

22.3   A Cultural Network for Gladiatorial Spectacles

Gladiatorial games likewise brought together residents from different communities, offering entertainment on a grand scale. The Flavian Amphitheater at Rome could hold some 50 000 spectators, just a fraction of the city's residents, but towns outside Rome had amphitheaters whose capacity often exceeded their entire population. The amphitheater at Pompeii, for example, could hold up to 20 000 spectators (Mau, 1899: 212; for its measurements, see Tosi, 2003: 162–63; Golvin, 1988: 33–37), although the population of the town is estimated to have been between 8000 and 12 000 residents (Jongman, 1988: 108–12; Wallace-Hadrill, 1994: 95–98). There and in other Italian cities the amphitheater could hold more than the city's population, a feature explained by the fact that games in the amphitheater would draw in residents of the nearby countryside as well. Evidence from the city of Pompeii, however, reveals that gladiatorial spectacles might attract residents from both town and surrounding countryside, and even inhabitants from neighboring communities as well.

The enthusiasm for gladiatorial spectacles during the Roman Empire was overwhelming. In his *Satires* (6.82–113), Juvenal offered the account of a senatorial woman who had abandoned husband, home, and children to run off with a gladiator. Although they might be maimed, wounded, or otherwise deformed, these men were the stars of their day and the crowd was full of their fans (Ewigleben, 2000; Ville, 1981: 334–39). Critics of the games were in the minority. Even the emperor was often one of the biggest fans (cf. Suetonius's *Lives of the Emperors*, passim; Köhne, 2000: 16–30). Martial's *Liber Spectaculorum* served to commemorate 100 days of games that inaugurated the Flavian Amphitheater (Coleman, 2006). Nearly every Roman town of any size had its own amphitheater. Games were commemorated in permanent media, either in mosaic pavements or painted frescoes, and on tombs belonging to the sponsors of games. Gladiators themselves often highlighted their occupation on their own tombs (Hope, 2000). Images of gladiators were also integrated into the daily life of Romans. Gladiatorial imagery adorned lamps, pottery, and other household items from knife handles to mirrors to perfume bottles (Köhne and Ewigleben, 2000). Gladiator figurines provide further evidence of a flourishing souvenir industry. The mania for gladiators was not only a matter for public consumption; the populace produced evidence of this fascination as well. At Pompeii gladiators were one of the most popular images to draw on the walls (Langner, 2001).

The site of Pompeii also offers a unique insight into certain logistics for gladiatorial games, namely, how these events were advertised to potential spectators. The wall-plaster preserved by volcanic debris has yielded numerous painted inscriptions that publicly advertised gladiatorial games. These include advertisements for games that were to be held in Pompeii, as well as notices for games that would take place in other cities across the region. These documents reveal that traveling to attend games in another town was not an uncommon practice. The number of announcements that have been preserved and the various towns advertising their games point to the expectation of sponsors and advertisers that they would find a potential audience among the residents of other cities. These documents furthermore testify to the large social network in which almost every community in Campania took part.

In appearance the advertisements for gladiatorial games resemble the thousands of electoral *programmata* posted at Pompeii (Chiavia, 2002; Franklin, 2001; Mouritsen, 1988; Franklin 1980; Castrén, 1975; see also Laurence, ch. 20, this vol.). They were large, prominently displayed inscriptions of a public nature, painted in red or black paint and in capital letters by teams of *scriptores* (signwriters) whose responsibility it was to post these inscriptions on building facades and other major supports. From the signatures sometimes included in their work, it can be determined that the same *scriptores* were responsible for painting both electoral *programmata* and advertisements for gladiatorial games. Publius Aemilius Celer, for example, painted numerous electoral *programmata* as well as at least one advertisement for games sponsored by the Decimi Lucretii Satrii Valentes (*CIL* 4.3884; Franklin 1978; Magaldi, 1930: 49–76). It is evident from their placement and prominent locations, the standard format contained therein, and the consistent paleography of these inscriptions that these advertisements were an official communication.

More than 80 gladiatorial advertisements, or *edicta munerum*, have been discovered at Pompeii (Sabbatini Tumolesi, 1980 + *AE* (1990) 177b–177c; D'Ambrosio and De Caro, 1987). Many examples are fragmentary but can be identified from brief but key characteristics such as the mention of *glad(iatorum) par(ia)* ("pairs of gladiators"), a series of dates, or even a standard formula such as *pro salute* ("on behalf of the welfare of…"). The *edicta* that are better preserved supply a number of details that were once useful for spectators deciding to attend the games and now provide assistance to scholars attempting to reconstruct the overall system of gladiatorial entertainment. The typical *edictum muneris* supplies the following information:

1. the motivation for the spectacle (*optional*)
2. the type of entertainment that will be presented
3. the name of the individual sponsoring the games
4. the abbreviation *pugn(abunt)* ("they will fight")
5. the location of the spectacle
6. the date(s) of the spectacle.

Sabbatini Tumolesi created a typology of three categories to account for the occasional shifts in the order in which these elements appear (Sabbatini Tumolesi, 1980: 116–19).

The games sponsored by a certain Marcus Tullius were advertised in this way (*CIL* 4. 9979–81). The motivation for the event was not always provided and was not included in his announcements, but all other information was supplied. At least three separate advertisements, and probably more that have not been preserved, were posted to attract potential spectators. The advertisement reads (*CIL* 4.9980):

> "A beast-hunt and twenty pairs of gladiators – sponsored by Marcus Tullius –
> will fight at Pompeii, on November 4th, 5th, 6th, and 7th."

> [2] *Venat(io) et glad(iatorum) par(ia) XX* [3] *M(arci) Tulli*
> [4] *pug(nabunt)* [5] *Pom(peis)* [6] *pr(idie) Non(as) Non(is) VIII VII Idu(s)*
> *Novembr(es)*

The same manner employed for advertising games in Pompeii was also used for the announcements of gladiatorial spectacles that would take place in other towns. This standard format makes it clear that spectacles were taking place within a larger, well-defined system of cultural entertainment. Most of the *edicta munerum* that are preserved advertise games taking place in Pompeii, but nearly one quarter (22 of 83) advertise games that were to be held in other cities of Campania. The number of advertisements for games in other towns reveals that this system reached well beyond the city of Pompeii. So too does the fact that advertisements never neglect to mention the location of the games, even when the sponsor was a well-known magistrate of the city and it could have been taken for granted that Pompeii was the default location. Rather, the *edicta* for games to be held in Pompeii consistently specify the location of those spectacles as "at Pompeii" (*Pompeis*) (e.g. *CIL* 4.3884 = Sabbatini Tumolesi, 1980: 5 = Cooley and Cooley 2014, D17: *D. Lucreti / Satri Valentis flaminis Neronis Caesaris Augusti fili / perpetui gladiatorum paria XX et D. Lucreti{o} Valentis fili / glad. paria X pug. Pompeis VI, V, IV, III pr. idus Apr. venatio legitima / et vela erunt. CIL*

4.7993 = Sabbatini Tumolesi, 1980: 12 = Cooley and Cooley 2014, D26: *Dedicatione / operis tabularum Cn. Allei Nigidi Mai Pompeis idibus Iunis: / pompa, venatio, athletae, vela erunt. CIL 4, 9962* = Sabbatini Tumolesi 1980, 27: [---]r[---] / glad. pa[r(ia) ---] / L. Valeri Primi augustalis pugn. Pomp[eis IV] III [pr(idie) ---] / Februarias: venatio m(a)tutin[a et vela erunt]).

Advertisements for gladiatorial games were posted in conspicuous locations where passers-by were most likely to come across them. Most were painted on the outside walls of buildings along busy streets; others were painted on tombs along the streets leading into the city. One advertisement was posted in the courtyard of the Forum Baths, a high-traffic location where the announcement would have caught the attention of numerous visitors to the baths (*CIL 4. 1177* = Sabbatini Tumolesi, 1980: 11 = Cooley and Cooley, 2014: D27).

The location and distribution of these posters suggest that advertisers knew how to reach their intended audience. The advertisements for games at Pompeii were painted on walls all over the city, as well as on the roads leading into town. The densest concentration of advertisements occurred in the area of the amphitheater. Here, posters promoting games appeared near the amphitheater and the *campus* next door, as well as among the nearby city blocks that housed numerous bars and hospitality establishments with large, open gardens and dining facilities. Establishments like the Garden of Hercules, located at Regio II.8.6 in Pompeii, and the Inn of the Gladiator, at Regio I.20.1–3, were capable of serving large groups and must have catered heavily to spectators and fans of the games (Jashemski, 1979: esp. 172–78).

Advertisements appeared along smaller streets too, resulting in gladiatorial games being advertised in virtually every corner of the city. The main goal of advertising was to reach a wide audience, and this was achieved by posting multiple advertisements in different areas of the town. Games featuring the gladiatorial troupe of Aulus Suettius Certus, for example, were advertised near the amphitheater, but also right off the forum on the building of Eumachia, and along the Street of the Brothel in the middle of town. The games sponsored by Gnaeus Alleius Nigidius Maius were likewise advertised near the forum and at various points along the Street of Abundance, the road leading toward the amphitheater. The father–son pair of the Decimi Lucretii Satrii Valentes advertised the games which they sponsored in similar locations. It should be remembered that the advertisements we have documented were only a portion of those that initially graced the walls of the city. Even this portion, however, aptly demonstrates how painted advertisements were commonly used to announce and promote gladiatorial spectacles.

Pompeii also features numerous advertisements for gladiatorial games that were to take place in other towns in the region. These advertisements appeared both within the city and in larger numbers on the tombs lining the streets immediately outside the city walls. Such a location targeted individuals on the move, those who were already coming and going between countryside and town, or traveling between towns in the region.

Those advertising games in other towns shared the same goal of reaching a broad audience and so likewise posted multiple announcements. A set of gladiatorial games to take place in the city of Nola (roughly 25 km away) for example, sponsored by Quintus Monnius Rufus, was publicized with advertisements at either end of Pompeii. These appeared along the roads just outside the town's walls, both to the north and to the south of the city outside the Herculaneum Gate and the Nucerian Gate (*CIL* 4.1187 and 3881 = Cooley and Cooley, 2014: D30).

Yet, the individuals sponsoring games elsewhere achieved an advertising blitz not only with posters in multiple locations. They also used concentrated marketing strategies and the intensive use of available real estate. The tomb-lined road outside the Nucerian Gate in the south-western part of the city offers an illustrative example, revealing how intensely the funerary monuments of the roads leading into town were used for public notices (D'Ambrosio and

De Caro, 1983; 1987). The necropolis outside the Herculaneum Gate has been the subject of an excellent study of its funerary monuments (Kockel, 1983), but its early excavation means that its painted inscriptions were not as well recorded. The painted inscriptions on tombs outside the Nucerian Gate, however, present a dense assemblage of advertisements along with a concentrated use of space. Most of the tombs here display at least one advertisement, while many tombs feature several. One tomb (tomb 12 according to Della Corte's numbering (*CIL* IV Supp. 3, 1970) – tomb 10 EN according to the current numbering system – (D'Ambrosio and De Caro, 1983, the page preceding the plan of tomb 19 ES)) presents as many as six different advertisements for gladiatorial spectacles all crammed onto it (*CIL* 4.9971–9976). Although we do not have comparable preservation of the tombs outside the other city gates, it is likely that the other roads leading into Pompeii displayed a similar scene. This was clearly a good location in which to advertise.

Why would someone travel the 20 kilometers or more from Pompeii to Nola, or indeed even as many as 80 kilometers to Cales or Forum Popilii to attend gladiatorial spectacles in another town? The games were certainly popular, but were they popular enough to merit a full day's journey (or more)? The advertisements for gladiatorial games in other towns promise a variety of entertainments. While it does appear that 20 gladiators was the minimum size that would be advertised, the spectacles varied in all other aspects: the total number of gladiators presented, the length of the games, and the other entertainments that were included. No two spectacles were the same, and this variety, along with the universal enthusiasm for the sport, may have attracted spectators to travel to other towns in order to attend them.

Some advertisements for gladiatorial shows in other towns offered special features to attract the crowds. One set of games at Cumae also featured, in addition to the standard 20 pairs of gladiators and their *suppositicii* (gladiators who entered as replacements for those who had been defeated), a beast-hunt, awnings, and *cruciarii*, or prisoners condemned to crucifixion (Sabbatini Tumolesi, 1980: 107–08). Crucifixion was one of the punishments available for convicted criminals. Sponsors of games could bid for those sentenced to capital punishment. The deaths that would take place in any case were then incorporated into the spectacle (Coleman, 1990; Wiedemann, 1992, 68–101). At Paestum, for example, an inscription honored an individual who had put on a display of 20 pairs of gladiators and a beast-hunt, "enhanced with convicts" (*noxii*) (*AE* (1975) 256). A set of games in Nola also included capital punishment. The advertisement for these games listed the special entertainments that would take place during the games: on one day, free or freedmen would enter the arena; on another day slaves would be killed by the sword (*CIL* 4.9978 = Sabbatini Tumolesi, 1980, 72: [--- *glad*(*iatorum*) *par*(*ia*) --- *pu*]*gn*(*abunt*) *Nolae XIIII, XIII, XII k*(*alendas*) [---]: *uno die li*[*beri –berti*] / [*poste*]*ro servi ferro s*[*anguinari iussi* ---]). Outside Rome relatively few gladiatorial matches appear to have ended in death, (the fatality rate did increase significantly in the later Empire (Ville, 1981: 318–25; Junkelmann, 2000: 142–45)) so it is likely that these spectacles, where deaths were guaranteed, generated even greater levels of enthusiasm.

In addition to capital punishment, the promise of particular performers may have increased the appeal of the games. A few advertisements seem to promise particular performers by name. Ellios and Sabinianus are two specified among the advertisements at Pompeii (*CIL* 4. 1179 = Sabbatini Tumolesi, 1980: 10; *CIL* 4.9975 = Sabbatini Tumolesi, 1980: 52). That the audience knew the names of favorite gladiators is demonstrated by the number of drawings of gladiators at Pompeii, which are labeled with the gladiators' names and often with their records of wins (Langner, 2001: 111, Abb. 61, and tables 5 and 6 (on accompanying CD-ROM) for the popularity of gladiator images among Pompeian figural graffiti overall). An advertisement for games in Puteoli announces the participation of *Herculanei*, a group of gladiators who took their name from Hercules, an extremely popular figure in the gladiatorial world (*CIL* 4.9969 = Sabbatini Tumolesi, 1980: 77; cf. Angelone, 1990). Other gladiators were similarly identified by group affiliation. The most famous group of this period were the gladiators of the imperial training school at Capua, called *Neroniani* during the reign of Nero, a number of whom performed in gladiatorial spectacles at Pompeii. Several spectacles at Pompeii featured these gladiators who were presumably contracted out from the training school at Capua. Sometimes they fought against each other (*CIL* 4.1182; on the subject of gladiators fighting against their own comrades, see Coleman, 2005); at other times a mix of imperially owned gladiators and others entered the arena (cf. *CIL* 4.2508 = Cooley and Cooley, 2014: D37, a *libellus* that lists the participants of at least nine matches, which include *Iuliani*, *Neroniani*, and gladiators of free status).

Advertisements for games outside Pompeii also generally promised longer spectacles consisting of three or four days of games, or even more. Several days of games might have helped to make the trip worthwhile if one were traveling a distance to attend games in a different town. Since each day's entertainment continued from morning to late afternoon, however, the games would have been a significant event for any spectator. At Rome, it appears beast-hunts were generally offered in the morning, followed by public executions, when some spectators would leave for lunch. Seneca (*Letters*. 7.5) criticizes those who stayed. Suetonius marked this as one example of the emperor Claudius's bloodthirsty nature (Suetonius, *Life of Claudius*. 34). Gladiatorial combats would take place in the afternoon (Wiedemann, 1992: 67). Numerous spectacles of a single day were held at Pompeii, and were probably held in other towns as well. It appears, however, that sponsors who wanted to attract a larger crowd, and aimed to do so by broadly advertising their games, would generally offer games of several days' duration.

In addition to longer shows of three days or more, several advertisements for games outside Pompeii announced larger shows with higher numbers of gladiators. Twenty pairs of gladiators facing off appear to have been the standard size for an exhibition. No announcement for games either in Pompeii or elsewhere advertised fewer than 20 pairs. Several of the games outside Pompeii, however, offered more than the standard: 24 pairs, 30, 36, and for one set of games at Capua, no fewer than 40 pairs of gladiators. The largest event was a spectacle held at Puteoli for four days in May that featured a staggering 49 pairs of gladiators and was held somehow in association with the imperial family (*CIL* 4.7994 = Sabbatini Tumolesi, 1980: 74 = Cooley and Cooley 2014: D35: *Par(ia) XLIX. Familia Capiniana muneri[bus] Augustorum pug(nabit) Puteol(is): a(nte) d(iem) [IV idus maias] pr(idie) id(us) mai(as) et XVII, XV k(alendas) iu[n(ias)]. Vela erunt. Magus* (sc. scripsit). The phrase *muneri[bus] Augustorum* is puzzling. Sabbatini Tumolesi, 1980: 103 suggests that the spectacle was held at the request of the imperial family and was financed by them). This spectacle was "super-sized" in both the number of gladiators presented and the length of the entertainment. Whereas gladiatorial games were usually held for a number of days in succession, this

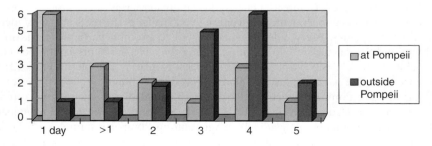

Chart 22.1   Length of spectacles.

announcement shows that it was possible, although extremely uncommon, to present entertainment over an extended period of time. These games were lengthened to last a full week, since the four days of entertainments took place every other day (May 12, 14, 16, and 18). Only one other *edictum* appears to announce games that were not held on consecutive days. It announces games to be held over three days: January 13, 23, and 24 (*AE* (1990) 177b: *Glad(iatorum) par(ia) XL P(ublii) Furi(i) et L(ucii) R[---]ami pug(nabunt) / Cap(uae) d(ie) eid(ibus) X IX k(alendas) Februar(ias) vela et / erunt / aqua…* The final line is unclear. D'Ambrosio and De Caro, 1987: 206 suggest the supplement *aqua(tica?)*, and record a few other letters at the end of the line that may not belong to the *edictum*). No other spectacle advertised at Pompeii lasted as long or featured as many gladiators.

Despite all of the special features advertised for games outside Pompeii, it does not seem that games in other towns *had* to promise things that were not offered in local, standard entertainments in order to attract spectators from different cities. Of the 21 wall-inscriptions that advertise "away" games, most did not promise entertainment that was not commonly found in the advertisements for games at Pompeii. In fact, the games that were held in the cities of northern Campania, the cities farthest from Pompeii, appear less likely to offer special enticements. A set of games at Cales, for example, lasted only two days and featured the standard 20 pairs of gladiators. Games at Atella also exhibited 20 pairs of gladiators. These were relatively small towns and even the wealthiest citizens may not have had the resources (or the need) to offer larger entertainments. Still, the sponsors of these games were evidently interested in publicizing them in many cities across the region. The farthest distant city that advertised games at Pompeii is Forum Popilii, a town located some 80 km away to the north. The individual responsible for that advertisement even seems to be aware that Pompeians might not be too familiar with this distant town. Directions, as it were, were therefore included in the announcement, which directed interested parties to "the Falernian territory, to Forum Popilii" (*AE* (1990) 177c: *Glad(iatorum) par(ia) XXIIII et venatio pug(nabunt) / in Falerno Foro Popili(i) L(uciorum) Attiliorum / a(nte) d(ies) XIII XII XI X k(alendas) iuni(as)*.) The *ager Falernus* would have been familiar; Falernian wine was a well-known specialty. One inscription advertising wine in Pompeii offers wine for 1 *as*, better wine for 2 *asses*, and Falernian for 4 (*CIL* 4.1679 = Cooley and Cooley, 2014: H20). It is also possible that "*in Falerno*" was added to distinguish this Forum Popilii from the town of the same name in Lucania.

Another reason why cities could confidently expect visitors from other communities to attend their games may be related to the frequency with which gladiatorial spectacles were offered. The fascinating details contained in these advertisements tend to obscure the fact that the spectacles themselves appear to have taken place on a relatively infrequent basis. The best-preserved announcements at Pompeii comprise 27 inscriptions that included the name of the sponsor. These inscriptions altogether advertised 13 or 14 distinct sets of games. The infrequency of the games is further highlighted when it becomes apparent that these games took place over several generations, from the Augustan period to the eruption of Mt Vesuvius (see Table 22.1).

A closer look highlights the gratitude that the populace expressed for those who sponsored games. Gnaeus Alleius Nigidius Maius, for example, was acclaimed *princeps munerariorum*, "the leader of those who sponsor games," and indeed he does appear among the gladiatorial advertisements more often than any other sponsor. Seven inscriptions announced games that he sponsored: two advertised games that took place most likely during his term as quinquennial *duovir* in AD 55/56; four announced his dedication of a group of *tabulae*; and a final poster announced one day of games that he held in honor of the emperor (probably Vespasian) and his sons (*CIL* 4.7990 = Cooley and Cooley 2014: D29: *Cn(aeo) Alleio Maio / principi munerarior[um] / feliciter*. Maius was also acclaimed *princeps coloniae* elsewhere (*CIL* 4.7989b).

Table 22.1 Dates of known sponsors of Pompeii's gladiatorial shows

Sponsor	Number of edicta munerum	Number of games	Chronological period
A. Clodius IIvir	0	1 (commemorated on tomb)	Augustan
M. Tullius IIvir	3	1	Augustan
DD. Lucretii Satrii Valentes flamen	4	3	AD 50–54
Cn. Alleius Nigidius Maius IIvir quinq.	7	3 or 4	2 games under Nero 1 under Vespasian
Ti. Claudius Verus, IIvir	3	2?	Neronian (duovir in AD 61/62)
A. Suettius Certus aedilis	4	1	Neronian
N. Popidius Rufus	2	1	AD 72–79
L. Valerius Primus, augustalis	1	1	Unknown

Games sponsored by Gnaeus Alleius Nigidius Maius: Sabbatini Tumolesi, 1980: no. 9–15; Cooley and Cooley 2014: D24–29). Thus, even this leader among sponsors, whose career can be charted over at least 20 years, is known to have offered only three sets of games, which altogether presented only five days of entertainment.

After Maius, the most prolific sponsors of games are Decimus Lucretius Satrius Valens and his son (Cooley and Cooley, 2014: D16–20). They too received an acclamation for their munificence in sponsoring games (*CIL* 4. 1084: *Satrio Lucretio Valenti munifico / IV sibi liberis feliciter. Pro Valente ex rog*[---]; Franklin, 2001: 102). Four advertisements related the details of the games they offered on at least three separate occasions. The fact that the father was identified as a perpetual priest of "Nero Caesar son of the emperor" (*flamen Neronis Caesaris Augusti f(ili) perpetuus*) in each suggests that these games should be dated to the period AD 50–54, the years in which Nero could be called "the son of the emperor" (Franklin, 2001: 101–02, n.3, with Sabbatini Tumolesi, 1980: 24–32, *contra* Mouritsen and Gradel, 1991). This father and son offered shows that lasted longer than those of Nigidius Maius. At least one set of games offered by the Lucretii Valentes lasted a full five days. The activity of the Lucretii Valentes in sponsoring games, however, can only be dated to these few years. Close relations between this family and Nero may account for the fact that the pair is not known to have sponsored any games after his reign (Franklin, 2001: 104–06). Nor is there any later evidence for the son's presence in Pompeian politics.

One final individual to be singled out and praised for his sponsorship of games is Numerius Popidius Rufus, who is acclaimed *invictus muneribus*, "unsurpassed in (offering) games" (*CIL* 4.1094). His family, the Popidii, appear to have gained leading roles in Pompeii during the last decades of the city (Castrén, 1975: 207–09; Franklin, 2001: 165–74). This sobriquet has led scholars (Sabbatini Tumolesi, 1980: 54) to suppose that he must have offered additional games, since he is only known from one definite gladiatorial advertisement (*CIL* 4.1186). Popidius attained municipal magistracies during the last decade before the eruption, as aedile in 72 and *duovir* in 76 or 77 (Sabbatini Tumolesi, 1980: 54–55). Only two sets of spectacles can be dated to this time period, namely his games and the show which Nigidius

Maius held in honor of Vespasian. If games were being held so infrequently during those years, Popidius may well have been viewed as *invictus*, even for sponsoring a single, crowd-pleasing event.

Even during the earlier reigns of Claudius and Nero, however, when it appears that gladiatorial games were taking place more frequently, Pompeii was not Rome, where inhabitants could count on the regular presentation of games and on their lavish scale. At Rome, gladiatorial games were offered by "officers of the state as part of their political careers, as an official obligation." Additional games were presented by the Emperor. The number of spectacles was by no means excessive, but Keith Hopkins draws a parallel with Christmas coming only once a year and affirms: "Gladiatorial shows were always something special" (Hopkins, 1983: 6–7). In the towns of Italy, games may have been offered by magistrates discharging their *summa honoraria* (fee for holding office), or by wealthy individuals hoping to profit politically, but the schedule of games appears not to have been standard in any way (cf. Cooley and Cooley, 2014: 68: figure 4.1, a table presenting the dates that games were offered both at Pompeii and in other Campanian towns. The wide variety of dates, with games offered in every month of the year except September, would appear to suggest that there was no set schedule for offering them.). Magistrates could offer other public works in the place of games: the seating in the amphitheater, for example, was constructed by *duoviri* and *magistri pagi Aug(usti)* in lieu of games (*pro ludis*) (*CIL* 10.853–57 = Cooley and Cooley 2014, D1–5). As a result, the population may not have counted on even the regular performance of two gladiatorial spectacles each year. Along the same lines, wealthy citizens took the initiative to offer games when it seemed expedient, but they were by no means required to do so. If games were offered only sporadically, fans of the sport may have jumped at the chance to attend games when they were offered, even if some travel was required.

The variety of cities advertising gladiatorial spectacles at Pompeii points to an extensive network of communities, one which covers the region of Campania (see Figure 22.2). Advertisements for games in as many as eight different cities have been discovered so far; two cities – Capua and Forum Popilii – were added to this list as recently as the 1980s, when excavations in the Nucerian Gate necropolis brought to light additional advertisements (*AE* (1990) 177b–c; D'Ambrosio and De Caro, 1987; D'Ambrosio and De Caro; 1983). The tombs outside the other gates of the city, which have not been excavated as fully, may hold similar numbers of announcements. These eight cities were located across the entire breadth of the region of Campania, from north to south, coast to hinterland. The cities that were situated closer to Pompeii do appear in greater numbers of advertisements; the number of announcements for each city decreases as the distance from Pompeii increased (see Table 22.2).

Pompeii's closest neighbor, Nuceria, appears most often among the advertisements for gladiatorial games. The other major cities of southern Campania – Nola, Puteoli, and Cumae –appear in multiple notices as well. Gladiatorial games, however, were not offered simply for one's fellow townsmen and the immediate surrounding areas, as the variety of cities listed in these advertisements illustrates. The announcements for the games in the cities of northern Campania – Atella, Capua, Cales, and Forum Popilii – confirm that this area too, though rather distant from Pompeii, was fully integrated into this cultural network.

Each of the cities advertising their gladiatorial spectacles at Pompeii, with the single exception of Forum Popilii, was equipped with a permanent amphitheater. These amphitheaters varied in size and features. Awnings, for example, provided shade for spectators at the amphitheaters in Puteoli, Cumae, Capua, Cales, and Pompeii, but not at Nuceria, Nola, or Atella. Still, an amphitheater was virtually required for a Campanian town of any substantial size (Tosi, 2003: 121. Welch (1994) observes a correlation between amphitheaters and colonial status.). The town of Herculaneum (a *municipium*), by contrast, does not appear to have been a part of this circuit. Evidence for gladiatorial activity at Herculaneum does exist. Pieces

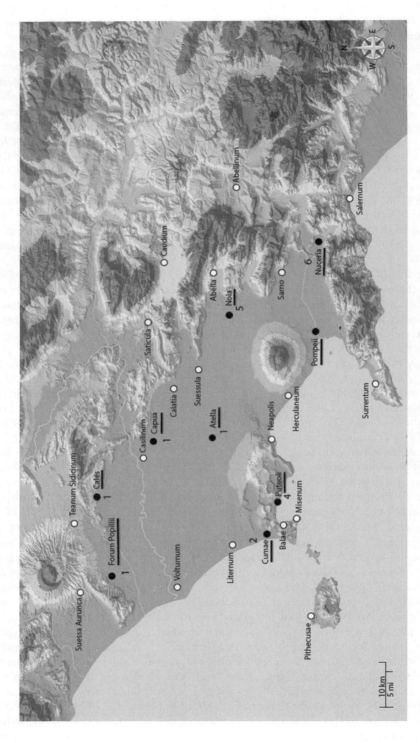

Figure 22.2 Map of Campania. The number beside each city denotes how many advertisements were posted at Pompeii for gladiatorial games in those cities. Map by Rebecca Benefiel, Map tiles © 2015 Ancient World Mapping Center.

Table 22.2 Host cities represented among the *edicta munerum*

City hosting games	Number of *edicta* preserved	Km from Pompeii
Nuceria	6	14
Nola	5	25
Puteoli	4	40 (faster by sea)
Cumae	2	45 (faster by sea)
Atella	1	40
Capua	1	55
Cales	1	70
Forum Popilii	1	80

of gladiatorial equipment were discovered there during early excavations, and a graffito on a column in the House of the Corinthian Atrium (Ins. 5 n.30) mentions a one-day spectacle at Herculaneum that exhibited 10 pairs of gladiators: "On the eighth day before the Kalends of March (i.e. around February 22nd), ten pairs of gladiators from the troupe of Numisius Genialis [fought] at Herculaneum," *VIII K(alendas)* • *Martias / Numisii Genialis / gladiatorum paria X / Herculani* (*CIL* 4.10579). On the basis of this equipment and graffiti, Angelone (1990) proposes that Herculaneum too was equipped with an amphitheater. Smaller spectacles, however, could have taken place in alternate venues such as the forum or palaestra. There is similarly scattered evidence for gladiatorial entertainment taking place in Surrentum and Calatia, although neither city has yielded traces of an amphitheater. Gladiatorial entertainment, therefore, does not appear to have been restricted to the larger towns of a region. It is likely that smaller shows took place on occasion, but that only shows of a particular standard, featuring 20 pairs of gladiators or more, would be sufficiently significant to be advertised in neighboring towns.

For events such as gladiatorial spectacles, then, one might be expected to travel significant distances. An 80 km journey would have required at least two days, but several days of games might have made the trip worthwhile. Certain extravagant spectacles, such as those presented at Puteoli, would probably draw especially large crowds, but the games themselves might have been enough to attract spectators, as the advertisements for towns in northern Campania illustrate.

Within Campania, it is clear that there was a strong appetite for gladiatorial games. These advertisements attest to popular interest in the games, and reveal that gladiatorial spectacles were one context in which residents of various communities would come into contact with each other. Gladiatorial spectacles were a costly production, and for this reason magistrates, who might be expected to discharge their *summa honoraria* (the payment rendered to a city by magistrates and certain types of priests upon taking office, cf. Duncan-Jones, 1982: 82–89, 141–56) by sponsoring games, sometimes offered other public works instead. Even considering that games would also be offered by wealthy individuals, it appears that gladiatorial spectacles in Campanian cities took place relatively infrequently and on an irregular basis. The act of advertising games to the populations of other cities resulted in a benefit for both the sponsor, who could more confidently expect a large crowd and a farther-reaching reputation, and the spectators who thereby had additional opportunities to attend the games. These advertisements demonstrate that, by the first century AD, there had developed in Campania a region-wide network of interaction in which almost all communities participated.

Discussions of Campania in ancient literature highlight the region as a destination and a setting for travel. The advertisements for gladiatorial spectacles, addressing the populations of the towns of the region, reveal that travel was not an activity limited to the Roman elite who had the time and the means for excursions from the capital. Mobility was a part of life for the inhabitants of Campania as well. Whereas the elite traveled primarily to and along the coast, where they enjoyed luxurious maritime villas, a larger network of interaction served the inhabitants of Campania and included cities both large and small, on the coast and in the hinterland, near and far.

FURTHER READING

On Campania as a region, Frederiksen/Purcell 1984 remains fundamental. Economic networks are discussed by De Ligt 1993. Wiedemann 1992 offers a general introduction to gladiatorial spectacle in the Roman world, whilst Jacobelli 2003 deals specifically with gladiatorial shows at Pompeii, with good illustrations. The second edition of the sourcebook by Cooley and Cooley 2014 includes translated documents from Herculaneum as well as Pompeii. The definitive edition of the gladiatorial notices from Pompeii is Sabbatini Tumolesi 1980.

REFERENCES

Andreau, J. 1976. "Pompéi: enchères, foires, et marchés." *Bulletin de la Société Nationale des Antiquaires de France*, 104–07.

Andreau, J. 2000. "Les marchés hebdomadaires du Latium et de Campanie au Ier siècle ap. J.-C." In *Mercati permanenti e mercati periodici nel mondo romano*, ed. E. Lo Cascio, 69–90. Bari: Edipuglia.

Angelone, R. 1990. "Spettacoli gladiatori ad Ercolano e gli edifici da essi postulati." *Rendiconti della Accademia di Archeologia, Lettere, e Belle Arti* n.s. 62: 215–43.

Casson, L. 1994 (rev. edn). *Travel in the Ancient World*. Baltimore and London: Johns Hopkins University Press.

Castrén, P. 1975. Ordo Populusque Pompeianus. *Polity and Society in Roman Pompeii*. Rome: Bardi.

Chiavia, C. 2002. Programmata. *Manifesti elettorali nella colonia romana di Pompei*. Turin: S. Zamorani.

Coleman, K.M. 1990. "Fatal charades: Roman executions staged as mythological enactments." *Journal of Roman Studies* 80: 44–73.

Coleman, K.M. 2005. *Bonds of Danger: communal life in the gladiatorial barracks of ancient Rome*. Sydney: University of Sydney.

Coleman, K.M. 2006. *Martial, Liber Spectaculorum: text, translation, and commentary*. Oxford: Oxford University Press.

Cooley, A.E. and Cooley, M.G.L. 2014. *Pompeii and Herculaneum. A sourcebook*. London and New York: Routledge.

D'Ambrosio, A. and De Caro, S. 1983. *Un impegno per Pompei. Vol. 1: Fotopiano e documentazione della necropoli di Porta Nocera, Vol. 2: Studi e Contributi*. Milan: Touring Club Italiano.

D'Ambrosio, A. and De Caro, S. 1987. "La necropoli di Porta Nocera. Campagna di scavo 1983." In *Römische Gräberstraßen. Selbstdarstellung – Status – Standard*, eds H. Von Hesberg and P. Zanker, 199–228. Munich: Verlag der Bayerischen Akademie der Wissenschaften.

Degrassi, A. 1963. *Inscriptiones Italiae* vol. XIII, *fasc.* 2. Rome: Istituto Poligrafico dello Stato.

De Ligt, L. 1993. *Fairs and Markets in the Roman Empire. Economic and social aspects of periodic trade in a pre-industrial society*. Amsterdam: Dutch Monographs on Ancient History and Archaeology, 11/ J.C. Gieben.

Duncan-Jones, R. 1982 (2nd edn). *The Economy of the Roman Empire: quantitative studies*. Cambridge: Cambridge University Press.

Ewigleben, Cornelia. 2000. "'What these women love is the sword': the performers and their audiences." In *Gladiators and Caesars. The power of spectacle in Ancient Rome*, eds E. Köhne and C. Ewigleben, 125–39. Berkeley-Los Angeles: University of California Press.

Franklin, J.L., Jr. 1978. "Notes on Pompeian prosopography: *programmatum scriptores.*" *Cronache Pompeiane* 4: 54–74.

Franklin, J.L., Jr. 1980. *Pompeii: the electoral Programmata, campaigns and politics, A.D. 71–79.* Rome: Papers and Monographs of the American Academy in Rome 28.

Franklin, J.L., Jr. 2001. Pompeis Difficile Est. *Studies in the Political Life of Imperial Pompeii.* Ann Arbor: University of Michigan Press.

Frayn, J.M. 1993. *Markets and Fairs in Roman Italy: their social and economic importance from the second century BC to the third century AD.* Oxford: Clarendon Press.

Frederiksen, M. 1984. *Campania*, ed. N. Purcell. London: British School at Rome.

Galsterer, H. 1980. "Politik in römischen Städten: die 'seditio' des Jahres 59 n. Chr. in Pompeii." In *Studien zur antiken Sozialgeschichte. Festschrift Friedrich Vittinghoff*, 323–38. Cologne/Vienna: Böhlau Verlag.

Golvin, J.-C. 1988. *L'amphithéâtre romain. Essai sur la théorisation de sa forme et de ses functions.* Paris: de Boccard.

Hope, V.M. 2000. "Fighting for identity: the funerary commemoration of Italian gladiators." In *The Epigraphic Landscape of Roman Italy*, ed. A.E. Cooley, 93–113. London: BICS Suppl. 73.

Hopkins, K. 1983. *Death and Renewal.* Cambridge: Cambridge University Press.

Jacobelli, L. 2003. *Gladiators at Pompeii.* Rome: «L'Erma» di Bretschneider.

Jashemski, W.F. 1979/1993. *The Gardens of Pompeii: Herculaneum and the villas destroyed by Vesuvius.* 2 vols. New Rochelle, NY: Caratzas Brothers.

Jongman, W. 1988. *The Economy and Society of Pompeii.* Amsterdam: J.C. Gieben.

Junkelmann, M. 2000. *Das Spiel mit dem Tod: so kämpften Roms Gladiatoren.* Mainz am Rhein: von Zabern.

Kockel, V. 1983. *Die Grabbauten vor dem Herkulaner Tor in Pompeji.* Mainz: Zabern.

Köhne, E. 2000. "Bread and circuses: the politics of entertainment." In *Gladiators and Caesars. The power of spectacle in Ancient Rome*, eds E. Köhne and C. Ewigleben, 8–60. Berkeley-Los Angeles: University of California Press.

Köhne, E. and Ewigleben, C. eds. 2000. *Gladiators and Caesars. The power of spectacle in Ancient Rome.* Berkeley-Los Angeles: University of California Press.

Langner, M. 2001. *Antike Graffitizeichnungen: Motive, Gestaltung und Bedeutung.* Wiesbaden: L. Reichert.

MacMullen, R. 1982. "The epigraphic habit in the Roman empire." *American Journal of Philology* 103: 234–46.

Magaldi, E. 1930. "Le iscrizioni parietali con particolaro riguardo al costume." *Atti della Reale Accademia di archeologia, lettere e belle arti, Napoli*, n.s. 11: 13–160.

Mau, A. 1899. *Pompeii: its life and art* (trans. F.W. Kelsey). New York: The Macmillan Company.

Moeller, W.O. 1970. "The riot of A.D. 59 at Pompeii." *Historia* 19: 84–95.

Mouritsen, H. 1988. *Elections, Magistrates and Municipal Élite: studies in Pompeian epigraphy.* Rome: «L'Erma» di Bretschneider.

Mouritsen, H. and Gradel, I. 1991. "Nero in Pompeian politics: *edicta munerum* and imperial flaminates in late Pompeii," *Zeitschrift für Papyrologie und Epigraphik* 87: 145–55.

Nollé, J. 1982. Nundinas instituere et habere. *Epigraphische Zeugnisse zur Einrichtung und Gestaltung von ländlichen Märkten in Afrika und in der Provinz Asia.* Hildesheim: Georg Olms.

Sabbatini Tumolesi, P. 1980. Gladiatorum Paria: *annunci di spettacoli gladiatorii a Pompei.* Rome: Edizioni di storia e letteratura.

Storchi Marino, A. 2000. "Reti interregionali integrate e circuiti di mercato periodico negli indices nundinarii del Lazio e della Campania." In *Mercati permanenti e mercati periodici nel mondo romano, Atti degli Incontri capresi di storia dell'economia antica (Capri 13–15 ottobre 1997)*, ed. E. Lo Cascio, 93–130. Bari: Edipuglia.

Tosi, G. 2003. *Gli edifici per spettacoli nell'Italia romana*. Rome: Quasar.

Ville, G. 1981. *La gladiature en occident des origines à la mort de Domitien*. Rome: École Française de Rome.

Wallace-Hadrill, A. 1994. *Houses and Society in Pompeii and Herculaneum*. Princeton: Princeton University Press.

Welch, K. 1994. "The Roman arena in late-Republican Italy: a new interpretation." *Journal of Roman Archaeology* 7: 59–80.

Wiedemann, T.E.J. 1992. *Emperors and Gladiators*. New York and London: Routledge.

Woodman, A.J. 2004. *Tacitus: the Annals*. Indianapolis: Hackett.

CHAPTER 23

Agricultural Production in Roman Italy

Robert Witcher

23.1 Introduction

Some beliefs about the ancient world are so commonplace that they appear unquestionable, and beliefs about agricultural production in Roman Italy are no exception: farming formed the principal source of wealth; the countryside produced whilst the cities consumed; the majority of the population lived in the countryside; peasant farmers worked on family farms. This chapter discusses the character, organization, and scale of agricultural production in Roman Italy, drawing on new approaches to texts and recent archaeological discoveries in order to challenge some of these widespread beliefs. It is, however, impossible to encompass the full breadth and complexity of Roman agricultural production in the space available. Recent contributions by Becker (2013), Goodchild (2013), and Kron (2012) provide wide-ranging and complementary overviews of agriculture in Roman Italy and therefore this chapter takes a selective sample of material to provide a flavour of recent and emerging debates.

23.2 Ancient Texts and Archaeology

Until quite recently, textual evidence was the dominant source of information about agriculture in the ancient world. Authors such as Cato, Varro, Columella, and Pliny the Younger were scrutinized for details of the practice of plant and animal husbandry; broader agrarian relations were illuminated through the works of historians such as Livy and Appian. Together, these texts have been used to create powerful narratives about the significance and organization of agriculture in Roman Italy. For example, a key theme is agrarian crisis in the form of access to land. During the second century BC, the great influx of wealth, ideas, and slaves resulting from Rome's East Mediterranean conquests led to a radical transformation in the scale and organization of agriculture. Roman aristocrats invested their new wealth by buying land (including *ager publicus*) and developing commercial farms based on the intensive application of slave labor for the production of wine and oil to feed expanding urban markets. However, the cumulative effects of continual overseas warfare and the growth of slave estates

A Companion to Roman Italy, First Edition. Edited by Alison E. Cooley.

came at the expense of the small farms of Roman citizens; these peasant families were pushed from the land, into the growing towns, helping to further expand the market for the produce of the aristocrats' estates (Hopkins, 1978).

The component parts of this interpretation draw in particular on the text of Cato for details of these new aristocratic farming methods and on Appian for the tensions between aristocratic slave estates and peasant farmers. This chapter will touch on debates which have developed around this traditional text-based narrative. A key part of its reassessment has been critical new approaches to the texts and, in particular, to the works of the so-called agronomists: Cato, Varro, and Columella. Most scholars have rejected the idea that these texts can be treated as farming manuals or descriptions of actual agricultural practice. Instead, these works are now generally approached as literature, and attention has turned to the motives of the authors and consideration of their intended audiences (e.g. Doody, 2007; Reay, 2005; Terrenato, 2001; 2012).

Varro's *On Agriculture* provides an example. This text has been widely cited as illustrative and supportive of the development of a "modern" or "rational" approach to agriculture in late Republican Italy, striving above all for the best yields at the least cost. But what was Varro's purpose in writing? He clearly states that his aim is to provide a manual for his wife, so that she may continue to manage the farm after his death (*On Agriculture*: 1.1.1–2). But how else might his work have been intended or have been understood? The text takes the form of a dialog between the agronomist Scrofa, arguing for a new approach to agriculture, and the more traditional Stolo. The advice of Scrofa, a figure also mentioned by Columella and Pliny the Elder, has often been accepted as evidence for the sophistication of agricultural theory and its practical application. Kronenberg (2009: 76ff.), however, argues that rather than accepting Scrofa as an historical figure and taking his advice at face-value, he can be re-read as a fictionalized character engaging in, and satirizing, Ciceronian-style debate: Scrofa/*ratio* versus Stolo/*consuetudo*. She suggests that Varro's aim was not to promote Scrofa as a progressive model, but to parody both Stolo and Scrofa, who are more concerned with debate than the advance of knowledge – and still less with a description of farming as actually practiced. This reminds us of the need for attention to the wider context of the gobbets of agricultural advice gleaned from the historical texts and liberally cited in discussions of Roman agriculture.

For a long time, archaeological evidence was cast in the role of providing the material evidence with which to demonstrate the veracity of the agricultural details derived from these texts. For example, White's (1970) important volume on Roman farming is based primarily on historical texts and, though it makes frequent reference to the excavation of Pompeian villas, this evidence is conceived largely in terms of the support it can provide for a predetermined textual narrative. This approach is problematical for a number of reasons. For example, isolating snippets of agricultural advice and successfully "testing" their accuracy against the archaeological (or ethnoarchaeological) record has sometimes been taken to imply that the wider interpretation of these texts as manuals for progressive agriculture should therefore be accepted. For example, Spurr (1986) stresses the reliability of Varro on points of agricultural detail. However, demonstrating that specific examples of arable cultivation were practical does not mean that Scrofa's advice was implemented, let alone universally.

Another reason why testing the texts against the archaeological record can be problematical is because the texts have often exerted a strong influence on the collection and interpretation of the archaeological evidence. For example, Terrenato (2001 and 2012) has argued force-fully that these texts have been used to create idealized villa types – Catonian, Varronian, Columellan – which have then profoundly influenced the way in which archaeologists have gone about selecting sites to excavate and how they have interpreted their findings (see Figure 23.1). He argues that the interpretation of a villa as "Catonian" represents an *a priori*

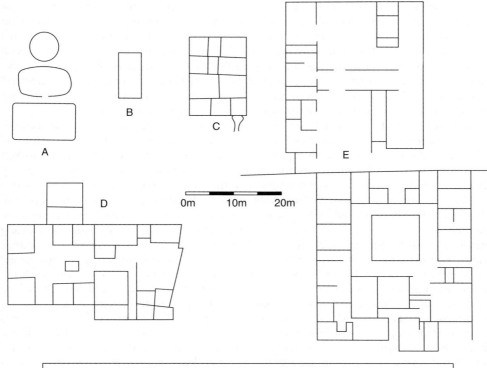

A. Round, oval and quadrangular early twentieth-century shepherd huts from the Roman Campagna (based on Erixon, 2001: fig 7)
B. Monte Forco, ager Capenas, late first century BC (based on Jones, 1963: fig. 18)
C. San Biagio, near Metaponto, second century AD (based on Carter, 2006: fig. 4.8)
D. Villa of the Auditorium, Rome, phase 4, second century BC (based on Carandini, D'Alessio, and Di Giuseppe, 2006: fig. 138
E. Francolise, Campania, first century BC (based on Cotton and Métraux, 1985: fig. 7)

Figure 23.1 Comparative plans of rural site types from Roman Italy.

reading of the archaeology; once the label has been applied, understanding of the site is then guided by a predetermined interpretation (see also Witcher, 2012). As a result, testing the reliability of the texts against this archaeological evidence becomes an exercise in circular reasoning. Terrenato presents a critical reassessment of the archaeological evidence for Republican villas demonstrating the lack of known sites of the appropriate date or form to be associated with the "Catonian" ideal. Although some newly discovered sites in the *suburbium* of Rome might buck this trend (see later in this chapter), the broad pattern is clear. Further, it is important to note that villa buildings are primarily evidence for the consumption rather than the production of wealth; the growing luxury of residential buildings is only indirectly linked to the agricultural output of an estate; the production and distribution of amphorae, which receive limited attention in the texts, are a better indicator of the intensification of agricultural production than mosaic floors (though see later in this chapter for caveats).

In sum, although the texts remain central to the interpretation of rural sites in Italy (e.g. Villa of the Auditorium: Carandini, D'Alessio, and Di Giuseppe, 2006; Villa della Piscina: Gioia and Volpe, 2004; Volpe, 2007), there has been a general shift away from the assumption of any simplistic correlation between texts and archaeological evidence. Still less can the accounts of Cato, Varro, and Columella be treated as consecutive snapshots which document the evolution of Italian agriculture. Instead, the most reasonable approach is to accept that the writers had broad familiarity with agricultural practice, and that we can recognize details of specific agricultural tasks, such as vine pruning, but that knowledge of these processes does not imply that they were practiced in pursuit of the wider objectives promoted by "characters" such as Scrofa. Rather, these details are embedded within texts which were written for particular literary and political reasons within specific social and cultural contexts.

If such texts must be subject to such critical reassessment, it is also important that archaeological evidence is similarly scrutinized. In contrast to the textual evidence, the quantity of archaeological material is constantly expanding and varied techniques (e.g. geophysical survey, archaeobotany, zooarchaeology, isotope analysis) continue to add to our understanding. There is obviously much that does not survive in the archaeological record, such as wooden barrels, sacks, and other perishable farm equipment, or that only survives in the rarest of conditions such as at Pompeii and Herculaneum. The archaeological record is therefore no more comprehensive than the textual evidence. In particular, whilst it is very suited to tackling questions about technology, such as olive oil processing, it is less well adapted to address issues concerning the organization of labor which are often equally influential on agricultural productivity (see Erdkamp, 2005: 7); indeed, a common criticism of archaeology is that it cannot tell us about the social status of sites' inhabitants (though see later in this chapter).

To some degree, the strengths and weaknesses of the textual and archaeological evidence are complementary: hence Cato's neglect of marketing can be addressed by archaeology's ability to trace amphorae distributions; conversely, archaeology's limitations in elucidating labor relations, are mitigated by the textual evidence for slavery and tenancy. The following sections put special emphasis on the archaeological evidence but will also draw attention to some of the difficulties of interpretation which arise; as with the texts discussed earlier in this chapter, the archaeological evidence cannot always be taken at face value.

23.3 Animals: The 'Other' Mediterranean Triad

Nearly all accounts of Greek and Roman agriculture start with discussion of the so-called Mediterranean Triad – cereals, olive trees, and grapevines – before considering if and how animals were integrated into this primarily arable economy. In recognition of the rapid expansion of zooarchaeological data, this chapter starts with consideration of animal husbandry and then turns to the evidence for the cultivation of crops.

In the pre-industrial economy, animals provided much more than just meat and dairy products; they also supplied traction and manure, as well as products such as wool, leather, horn, and bone which were far more important than today. Compared with the cultivation of crops, much less attention has been devoted to the role of animals in ancient farming, but recently a number of studies have examined the importance of animal husbandry, drawing in particular on the growing body of zooarchaeological evidence. In a synthesis of samples from almost 100 sites, Mackinnon (2004) has demonstrated that, with one or two exceptions, cattle, pigs, and sheep/goats comprise the vast majority of animal species (wild and domestic) found on sites of all types across Italy, from the pre-Roman period through to late antiquity; they might therefore be considered the "other" Mediterranean Triad.

From the perspective of understanding agricultural production, the zooarchaeological data present a challenge because most of these bone assemblages derive from rubbish deposits at urban centers and residential villas, and relate to the consumption of meat and, to a lesser degree, the processing of bone and hides. Our data are therefore biased in composition and most directly informative about meat consumption rather than offering a more rounded understanding of the role of animals on the farm and how they were husbanded before they were eventually consumed. However, embedded within this evidence for meat consumption there are clues about the organization of the husbandry practices which supplied these consumers.

The percentage of cattle bones represented in samples varies according to region, over time, and by site type; for example, cattle are more abundant in northern Italy compared with the center and south; they are also much more common at small urban centers than rural sites (MacKinnon, 2004: 77–100). There are also differences in the size of cattle; for example, cattle in the north of Italy were consistently smaller than animals in the center and south. All of this variation notwithstanding, two general trends are a) increased average height of cattle as measured at the withers, and b) the generally mature age of cattle at death.

The increased average height of cattle has been argued to relate to selective breeding to increase body size in order to supply growing urban demand for meat (Kron, 2002; but see later in this chapter). The overall range of animal sizes is also significant, with cattle in late antique central Italy varying in height by up to 35 cm; this may be partly explained by sexual dimorphism, but MacKinnon (2010) argues it may also indicate the presence of two or more breeds of cattle. Indeed, the ancient texts describe a number of distinct breeds (e.g. Columella, *On Agriculture*: 6.1.1–3). Hence, even if the average height of animals increased, smaller breeds were maintained. In this context, it is worth stressing that bigger is not always better when it comes to animal husbandry; farmers may prefer smaller animals which mature more rapidly, require less fodder or are easier to handle; or they may breed for characteristics such as milk which are not directly correlated with height.

Of all domestic animals, cattle in particular might also be expected to provide labor before their eventual consumption. The fact that most cattle bones derive from mature animals of three years of age or more, and many over five years, suggests the consumption of former plough animals; similarly, the high ratio of male animals supports the idea that traction was the primary function and that meat and/or milk was only secondary. In turn, such demand for traction is arguably indicative of increased cereal production. These "second-hand" cattle may be one reason why beef was a relatively inexpensive meat compared with pork (see later). Nonetheless, as the funerary monument of C. Valerius Faustus indicates, there was money and status in the marketing of cattle; the marble tombstone from the *ager Faliscus* north of Rome records that he was a freedman, official of the imperial cult, and a successful cattle merchant (*AE* (1991) 682c; Gilliver, 1997: 202–03; see also Chioffi, 1999).

Pigs receive limited attention from the agricultural writers, but pig bones frequently comprise over half of all mammalian bones in zooarchaeological samples (MacKinnon, 2004, 139–62). As with cattle, the percentage of pig bones varies across regions, over time and by site type, with particular abundance on urban sites and, though pig comprises a consistently lower percentage in southern Italy than in the center and north, during the imperial period there was a universal increase in the percentage of pig bones across the peninsula. MacKinnon (2004: 154) suggests that the significant range of height at the withers might correlate with the two distinct breeds described by the agricultural writers: a smaller bristly dark pig and a larger smooth white pig. The former may have been kept free-range in large herds, whilst the latter may been selectively bred and stall-fed, perhaps even in urban environments. Pigs breed prolifically and mature quickly and, unlike cattle and sheep/goats, they do not provide any significant secondary products. The only purpose for keeping a pig is to eat it. It is therefore no surprise that most animals were slaughtered young, with only 1% of animals reaching maximum breeding age (MacKinnon, 2004). Unlike the cheaper beef from old plough cattle, pork was a premium product. Nonetheless, pigs have the attraction that they can be left to forage on scrubland or in woods, or fed on scraps, and small herds are therefore more easily integrated into arable farms than cattle or sheep. In other words, although pigs did not provide farmers with any additional value beyond their meat, as long as there was a market, raising a few pigs was not a difficult or costly venture.

Completing the trio of principal farm animals, is sheep/goat. Although it is possible to differentiate between the bones of sheep and goats, it is not always easy and many studies do not make a reliable distinction. However, where the difference can be observed in Roman Italy, sheep are always more abundant, often 4:1 or higher (MacKinnon, 2004: 104). Unlike pigs, sheep/goats provide not only meat, but also milk, wool, and manure. A high percentage of sheep bones in Roman Italy relate to mature animals, with a high ratio of females, suggesting that it was wool and milk rather than meat which was valued (MacKinnon, 2004: 101–38). Indeed, wool remained the most important textile throughout the Roman period. The presence of spindlewhorls and loomweights on rural sites indicates that wool was both spun and woven in the countryside, and Roth (2007) has recently argued that textile production was a core economic activity undertaken by female slaves on commercial farms. As with cattle, therefore, the consumption of sheep may have followed productive earlier lives.

Cato (e.g. *On Agriculture*: 10.1) and Varro (e.g. *On Agriculture*: 1.19.3) provide insights into the importance of sheep for arable practices, especially through grazing stubble and manuring, but flocks of any significant size required the movement of animals during the year to maintain adequate grazing. The existence and organization of transhumance in Roman Italy is much debated, with discussion heavily informed by comparison with early modern practices and ethnoarchaeological studies of twentieth-century shepherds (see Gabba and Pasquinucci, 1979; Pasquinucci, 2002). There are two types of transhumance; most attention has concentrated on the long-distance movement of animals over hundreds of kilometers in search of summer grazing in the mountains. For example, Varro (*On Agriculture*: 2.1.17; 2.2.9) describes the annual relocation of his flock of 700 animals from Apulia to Sabina. Such transhumance would have been associated with large-scale, commercial enterprises producing wool and, though economically important, was probably exceptional. Short- to medium-distance movement was probably much more common. It is widely assumed that, during the spring and summer, agricultural communities on the coastal plain and lowland hills would send their flocks up into the mountains. However, analogy to traditional practices in Lazio which continued well into the second half of the twentieth century suggests movement in the opposite direction is also possible; that is, communities in the uplands sent their flocks down to the coastal plain to overwinter before returning home during the spring. These shepherds constructed temporary wooden huts and carried limited material culture (see Figure 23.2); the chances of detecting these shepherds' ancient predecessors in the archaeological record are therefore low. However, survey of upland landscapes has identified large stone enclosures intended to corral animals (Barker and Grant, 1991) and zooarchaeological analysis has begun to provide further insights. For example, MacKinnon (2004: 216) notes that sheep bones from large urban sites cluster in the 7–12 month bracket (lamb) and over 36–48 months (mutton). Such patterns point towards careful control of breeding and the timing of slaughter to provide meat (and dairy products) for urban populations which were concentrated in the lowlands. Isotope analysis of animal bones promises to add much more detail to understanding of transhumance, such as the timing and the geographical range of seasonal movement.

Cattle, sheep, and, to a lesser extent, pigs all appear to demonstrate increases in average height at the withers during the Roman period. This trend has been taken as evidence for the selective breeding of animals in response to growing market demand for meat (Jongman, 2007; Kron, 2002; 2004). However, this interpretation is not straightforward. The computation of animal height is complicated by poor publication of both critical base measurements and details of the extrapolation methods used. Moreover, the number of samples is still comparatively limited and coverage is uneven; individual assemblages are also

Figure 23.2 Twentieth-century shepherd hut. © British School at Rome, Ward-Perkins Collection, wpset-08135.

often very small. As the database grows and the standard of publication improves, the scale and significance of increased height will become clearer. A more complex problem is the relationship between animal height and weight; this is not fixed and it is noticeable that those arguing for the importance of meat in animal production (rather than wool or dairying) tend to assume more generous proportional increases in carcass weight (cf. cattle – Kron, 2004: 400 kg; MacKinnon, 2004: 200 kg).

If animal height as an indication of increased consumption of meat currently remains unclear, another approach is to assess chronological variation in the number of animal bones in the archaeological record. Jongman (2007: 191–92) provides a graph of the numbers of animal bones deposited between circa 500 BC and circa AD 100. He argues that a significant increase in the numbers of bones over time reflects a rise in the consumption of meat, resulting from increased economic prosperity and leading to improved nutrition. Convincing though this increase may appear, caution is needed. Firstly, the larger number of bones deposited must to be set against any change in the number of consumers; an increase in population – as suggested independently by census figures – would produce an increase in the number of animal bones with no change in per capita consumption, wealth, or health. Secondly, the graph shows numbers of bones deposited over time, but this assumes that archaeologists have excavated a standard number of deposits from each time period; this is probably untrue and the bias is likely to be towards imperial period sites. Not least, the late Republic and early Empire was a time of rapid urbanization which generated large, well-preserved rubbish deposits of a type which were previously rare. In other words, the graph could simply be demonstrating an increase in the visibility of meat consumption rather than absolute change.

A final approach to the issue of higher per capita meat consumption comes through the proxy of increased human stature. Height is closely associated with improved nutrition and

Kron (2005; see also Jongman, 2007) directly ascribes a "peak" in the average height of Italian males during the Roman period at 168.3 cm to increased meat consumption. But yet again, caution is necessary. Firstly, the majority of skeletal samples relate to urban populations whose stature and diet may not be representative of the wider rural population; secondly, it is far from clear that human stature really did increase during the Roman period, and other studies suggest this may not have been the case (see Gowland and Garnsey, 2010: 150).

On the basis of the available evidence, it is impossible to be certain that there was per capita increase in meat consumption with associated improvements in health and nutrition. More representative samples are required and the data need to be carefully calibrated; isotope analysis provides another method for assessing meat consumption and its variability (Killgrove, 2013; Prowse *et al.*, 2004). Nonetheless, one striking result of zooarchaeological studies is that although cattle bones represent on average one-sixth to one-fifth of those identified, when converted into meat weight, the larger size of cattle compared with sheep and pigs means that the relative contribution of beef to the Roman diet rises to as much as one-third; this is emphatically not the impression given by the ancient texts (MacKinnon, 2004: 217). Apicius's cookery book may be filled with recipes for pork, but many made do with the cheap beef of old plough animals.

Before turning to crop cultivation, it is important to mention briefly some of the other animal species which were also raised on farms (see also Kron, 2008a). Chicken (*Gallus gallus*) and other domestic fowl are well-attested (e.g. Mola di Monte Gelato: West, 1997), but as their bones are less robust than those of mammals, and those that survive are more easily missed during excavation, their prevalence is probably underestimated. The bones of smaller songbirds such as thrushes (*Turdus* sp.) are also attested and these may relate to the practice of *pastio villatica*, that is, the intensive production of high-value, gourmet foods; Varro (*On Agriculture*: 3.3–5) provides discussion of highly profitable aviaries. Other species raised for market included the dormouse (*Glis glis*; Varro, *On Agriculture*: 3.15); bones have been recognized on a number of sites (e.g. Settefinestre and Mola di Monte Gelato: King, 1997: 392) as have *gliraria*, the terracotta jars for fattening the animals. By definition, however, such products were restricted to a small and wealthy section of society, and production was highly specialized, often requiring capital investment. This practice is epitomized by fish-farming at villas along the coast of Latium and Campania. Brizzi and Marzano (2009) have quantified the capacity of these installations, arguing that production exceeded the immediate needs of the villa owners and could therefore have been marketed to cities. Certainly tanks could have been used to transport live fish, but it is far from clear that there was significant market demand for such a costly product; aristocratic display may well have been the primary motivation for such cultivation of fish.

Finally, as noted above, cattle were raised primarily as plough animals, but though oxen are powerful, they are also slower and less sure-footed than donkeys and mules for transporting goods, especially on unpaved or steep roads. Varro (*On Agriculture*: 2.1.17) discusses the breeding of mules on the Reate (Rieti) plain in the mountains north-east of Rome. These animals would have been a common sight on the roads of Roman Italy, transporting agricultural produce to urban centers (Laurence, 1999: 123–35). However, equid bones comprise only a small percentage of zooarchaeological samples, probably reflecting the fact that, unlike cattle, their meat was not consumed once their working lives were over.

23.4   Plants: The Original Mediterranean Triad

Animals were an integral part of the rural economy, but plant crops were the mainstay of agricultural production and diet. This section turns to the "original" Mediterranean Triad of cereals, olives, and vines, before considering the evidence for the wide variety of other plants which added nutritional and culinary diversity. The ancient texts again provide information about the range of crops and their cultivation (e.g. Pliny the Elder, *Natural History* books 12–22). Alongside these texts, the study of botanical remains from archaeological deposits provides an important and rapidly expanding resource. As with animal bones, botanical remains such as charred seeds derive overwhelmingly from contexts associated with consumption (e.g. urban, domestic) rather than production (e.g. rural sites). Conversely, pollen evidence, usually from lakes, is rarely associated with individual sites and tends to provide an indicator of general background flora.

As in all pre-industrial Mediterranean societies, cereals were the dietary mainstay. The significance of grain production, however, has been neglected for a number of reasons. First, drawing on Roman texts, the traditional narrative has emphasized the decline of peasant farmers and the rise of villas producing wine and oil; second, and consequently, the massive importation of grain from the provinces was assumed to have supplied urban demand. However, Spurr's (1986) re-analysis of the texts combined with ethnoarchaeological insights, argued that cereal production remained central to Italian agriculture throughout the Roman period. Nonetheless, a significant problem is that cereals leave few archaeological traces of cultivation, processing, or transportation compared with oil and wine, and the evidence we do have is biased to urban contexts, such as granaries and grain mills (on cultivation and harvesting, see Spurr, 1986; White, 1970: 173–89; on processing, see Thurmond, 2006: 20–72).

Pliny the Elder (*Natural History*: 18.83) observes that the early Romans ate porridge (*puls*) made of emmer wheat (*Triticum dicoccum*), rather than the bread which was the norm in his own day (Purcell, 2003, on social symbolism). Breadmaking requires wheat with high gluten content and we might envisage a shift in production from emmer to common (*Triticum aestivum*) or hard wheats (*Triticum durum*). However, the archaeobotanical evidence does not demonstrate any such simple chronological transition; indeed, most assemblages contain a variety of wheats, as well as other cereals such as six-rowed barley (*Hordeum vulgare*) and common millet (*Panicum miliaceum*).

Alongside rising demand for breadwheats, the strategies used by farmers to decide which cereals to plant will have been influenced by additional considerations, such as soils, rainfall, and reducing the risk of crop failure by sowing a range of different cereals. Rural households may also have grown different crops for household consumption and market sale (see later in this chapter).

The cultivation of olives (*Olea europaea*) and grapevines (*Vitis vinifera*) is archaeologically much more visible than cereals. In particular, the evidence for presses, settling tanks, *dolia*, and amphorae makes it much easier to trace the processing, storage, and distribution of oil and wine (see Thurmond, 2006: 73–110, 111–64). Equally, it is important to recognize that the high visibility of these processes is related to the intensification and specialization of production associated with capital-intensive commercial farming. Olive oil and wine can be produced without the need for such elaborate presses and transported without amphorae.

In addition to the well-known evidence for the processing of oil and wine, excavation has also revealed details of cultivation. For example, in the area of Centocelle (circa 6 km east of the center of Rome), extensive excavations have identified 10 systems of parallel trenches of rectangular profile, circa 85–90 cm wide, spaced circa 10 m apart; these have been interpreted as vine trenches intended to promote root growth (Cato, *On Agriculture*: 1; Columella, *On Agriculture*: 3.12.6, 11.2.28). In some areas, new trenches were cut at 90 degrees presumably when the vineyards were replanted. The spacing between the trenches is wide (especially compared with Columella's recommendation of 4–10 feet (1.2–3 m), though he wrote centuries after the vineyards at Centocelle were laid out). This wide row-spacing points to intercultivation (Italian *coltura promiscua*) with vines interspersed with other crops such as cereals or beans. This method of mixed cultivation diversifies the farmer's produce and reduces the risk associated with specializing in a single crop, though the overall returns are often reduced. Hence, these farms may have specialized in producing wine (even table grapes) for the market at Republican Rome, but they did not abandon their basic self-sufficiency. Excavation of an urban vineyard at Pompeii (II.v) reveals a different method of cultivation, with 2014 vines supported on stakes spaced four feet apart (circa 1.2 m; coinciding with Pliny the Elder's advice, *Natural History*: 17.171), interspersed with fruit trees, and possibly inter-cultivated with broad beans (*Vicia faba*) (Jashemski and Meyer, 2002: 21–22).

The Republican vineyards at Centocelle also provide a good example of how the high visibility of amphorae has encouraged archaeologists to regard them as a direct proxy for wine production, so that their absence can be easily misinterpreted as a lack of production. R. Volpe (2009: 379–81) notes that amphorae at imperial-period Rome regularly comprise 30% or more of the total ceramic assemblage; in contrast, the figure from Republican Rome rarely exceeds one or two percent. She argues that the clear evidence for Republican viticul-ture at Centocelle and elsewhere around the *suburbium* indicates large-scale production for the market, but that the short distance from the vineyards to the city did not require the wine to be packaged in the heavy amphorae required for sea-transportation; instead archae-ologically invisible skins or barrels could have been used. R. Volpe (2009: 380) uses the Centocelle vineyards to estimate the potential wine production of the Republican *suburbium* as a whole, suggesting that it could have met the demand from Rome's population 10 times over (see later in this chapter for discussion of the implications of this and similar estimates of very high Republican agricultural output). The low visibility of local wine production also helps to explain why imported wine dominates amphorae assemblages in the northern *suburbium* from as early as the second century BC, when Tunisian amphorae appear in significant numbers (Fontana, 2008: 660–62). This dominance does not indicate that local production had already been displaced by imports from an early date, but more probably that local production is under-represented. Similarly, the sharp increase in the percentage of amphorae at Rome during the imperial period does not represent new demand for wine, but a switch to provincial imports which were packaged in a more archaeologically visible way. In summary, when markets were in close proximity to production sites, the absence of amphorae precludes neither small-scale production (see earlier in this chapter) nor commer-cialized production. Amphorae provide unparalleled insights into the complexities of pro-duction, exchange, and consumption but like all our sources, their evidence cannot always be taken at face value.

Although the Mediterranean Triad tends to dominate attention, a wide range of other crops were cultivated. Legumes were an important group of plants which provided a significant source of protein for both humans and animals and could be conveniently dried and stored; they were also valued as an integral part of crop rotation because of their nitrogen-fixing qualities. Broad beans (*Vicia faba*) are commonly found in archaeobotanical samples and occur more frequently than any other food plant at Pompeii and Herculaneum (Jashemski and Meyer, 2002: 169) though the large seeds are particularly robust and easy to identify compared with the seeds of many other plants (see also Spurr, 1986: 105–12). Other common legumes include chickpeas (*Cicer arietinum*) and lentils (*Lens culinaris medikus*).

As well as the olive, a wide range of fruit and nut trees were cultivated. The archaeobotanical evidence suggests the fig (*Ficus carica*) was particularly common; as with legumes, this crop can be dried and stored, providing a significant calorific contribution. Fruit and nut trees might be planted in regular orchards, but also interspersed with other crops; the excavated farmland adjacent to the Villa Regina at Boscoreale has revealed a vineyard dotted with trees such as olive and almond (*Prunus dulcis*; Jashemski and Meyer, 2002: 24–25).

Alongside fields, vineyards, and orchards, there is also evidence for intensively worked vegetable gardens. The Pseudo-Virgilian *Moretum* describes the peasant Symilus working his small but productive plot of beets, parsnips, leeks, and a wide variety of herbs. Pointedly, however, these are crops destined for the market, and Symilus's hunger is sated by a "pesto" of cheese, garlic, oil, and vinegar. A significant difference between urban and rural diet, and the crops grown for household and market consumption, is entirely plausible (see earlier) though the simple but honest rustic Symilus is also a literary *topos* to be treated with circumspection. Archaeologically, such vegetable plots are very difficult to document, though the excavation of a market-garden attached to the House of the Ship *Europa* (I.xv) at Pompeii incorporated a vineyard, intercultivated with broad beans, and two small vegetable plots, defined by furrows and interspersed with trees (Jashemski and Meyer, 2002: 23–24; see Figure 23.3).

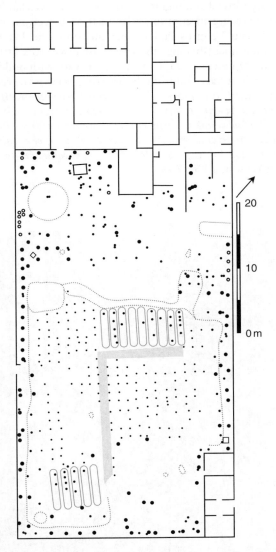

Figure 23.3   Market-garden, House of the Ship *Europa* (I.xv), Pompeii (based on Jashemski and Meyer 2002: 24). ● Trees; • Vines; ˙Vegetable plots, connected by a path.

Field crops in Roman Italy relied on rainfall, but gardens and orchards might also be irrigated. A recent study of water cisterns in the middle Tiber valley identifies 26 examples with particularly large capacity (>200 m³) beyond any individual site's domestic needs; many of these were also open to the sky, making the water unfit for consumption or bathing. Wilson (2008: 735) argues that these cisterns were used to irrigate vegetables, flowers, and fruit trees (see Figure 23.4).

A specific category of garden cultivation was the tomb garden (Purcell, 1987). Funerary enclosures could be planted with fruit trees and utilized as vegetable plots. Some, though certainly not all, of the burnt fruits and nuts offered at Pompeian tombs might have derived from such planting (Matterne and Derreumaux, 2008). Such small tomb gardens, located in the immediate vicinity of the city, could have provided urban families with welcome dietary variety or income. They were also integrated into the productive landscape of rural estates, as illustrated by the following inscription: "To Lictoria Chaerusa, who lived 15 years 7 months and 5 days, Lucius Veturius Pudens, her husband, and Larcia Aucta, her mother [made this]. To this monument belongs the rose garden with the little vineyard, and from the area of the pool and channel up to the yard, and the yard with buildings and the granary, and the cisterns on the sun terrace and from the area of it as far as the reed bed with the paths that are marked out; in total, one *iugerum*" (*Lictoriae Chaerusae vixit annis XV / mensibus VII diebus V fecer(unt) L. Veturius Pudens / vir et Lacia Aucta mater. huic monumento / cedit rosarium cum viniola (et) sola(rio) suo, fine viniae, / et e region(e) piscinae et canalis usque ad ariam, et area cum (a)edificiis et horreo, et cisternae in solar(io) et e regione eius usque <at> ad arundinetum cum itin(eribus) qu(a)e sunt determinata; et collige iug(erum).*) (*CIL* 9.3895 = *ILS* 8347, translation Wilson, 2008: 743).

Figure 23.4 Double vaulted water cistern at Vicus Matrini, South Etruria. Photo: R. Witcher.

As well as plant cultivation, gathering or foraging for wild fruits, nuts, herbs, vegetables, and fungi on common and uncultivated land may have been a significant activity (e.g. Evans, 1980: 138–39; Frayn, 1979: 57–72). Peasants may have collected plants such as caper, samphire, strawberry, and almond for household consumption, or even for sale at market. Cato (*On Agriculture*: 149.2) and Columella (*On Agriculture*: 12.7.1) discuss a wide range of wild plants such as asparagus, mulberry, fennel, and blackberry in the context of domestication, that is, transplanting and improving wild species. As a result, the distinction between cultivated and wild plants may have been quite blurred in practice, and is often impossible to distinguish via the archaeobotanical record. We therefore have no appreciation of the nutritional contribution of such gathered foods to the peasant diet. Nonetheless, it would be easy for this cornucopia of sustainably foraged plants, alongside cereals, olive oil, and wine, to be seen to reflect the healthy, varied "Mediterranean diet" we are often encouraged to eat today. However, caution is required before transforming the Roman peasantry and its diet into a paradigm of healthy living, in the same way that the hard toil of the peasant has been repeatedly idealized by political regimes. For example, it is unclear whether the consumption of foraged foods should be understood as the welcome diversification of diet or as a necessity brought about by insufficient farmland or crop failure. Indeed, as with the wider study of Roman agriculture, interpretation of the evidence is informed by powerful prior assumptions about whether peasants were impoverished rustics on the threshold of starvation due to their risk-averse strategies and under constant threat of eviction from the land or, conversely, resilient yeomen able to adapt their strategies to the prevailing economic and political environment, and to benefit accordingly. In short, were they stuffed or starved? Are they to be pitied or admired?

An example of how such assumptions can influence the interpretation of the archaeobotanical evidence is provided by the suggestion that an assemblage of grass pea (*Lathyrus sativus*), broad bean, barley, and acorns (*Quercus* sp.) from a reoccupation phase at an earlier villa near Rome is indicative of a sharply reduced standard of living during late antiquity (Sadori and Susanna, 2005). However, the association of such "famine foods" and socio-economic decline is far from straightforward. Firstly, there is no assemblage from the site's earlier phase against which to assess any reduction in the standard of living. Secondly, the character of occupation during late antiquity (a wooden lean-to) clearly indicates inhabitants of very modest status compared with the site's previous residents. Even if the late antique inhabitants did eat grass peas, it is not clear that their ancestors, who presumably lived elsewhere, did not share the same diet; without samples from earlier sites of comparable socio-economic status, we are not comparing like with like. Finally, the overwhelming dominance of one species (grass pea) may suggest that we are not looking at a representative cross section of diet, but one particular store of food. Perhaps this cache was one of several stores of different foodstuffs, or was intended for emergency rations, or even for animal feed. The archaeobotanical sample from this site raises interesting questions, but in isolation it cannot be taken to support a prior assumption about the declining standard of living in late antique Italy.

Finally, although all the crops discussed above relate to consumption by either humans or animals, plants were also grown and used for many other purposes. Such plants would have included willow for basketry (*Salix* sp.; Cato, *On Agriculture*: 31.1) and flowers for religious festivals. Such cultivation has left limited traces, but a couple of archaeological examples point to the scale and variety to be expected. Recent work at Lakes Albano and Nemi, south of Rome, has identified very high levels of hemp (*Cannabis sativa*) pollen which may indicate the cultivation and processing ("retting") of hemp fibers for textile production (Mercuri, Accorsi, and Bandini Mazzanti, 2002). Meanwhile, it has been suggested that the ton of unripe pomegranates, rich in tannin, discovered at the villa of L. Crassus Tertius at Oplontis was intended for use in leather tanning (Jashemski and Meyer, 2002: 153–54). This was a manufacturing process which was concentrated in towns (Flohr, 2013), but which made use of another agricultural product, animal hides; the higher than expected percentage of "extremities" (e.g. foot bones) in zooarchaeological assemblages from urban sites points towards the importation of animal hides, feet still attached, for central processing (MacKinnon, 2004: 244).

23.5   Aristocrats and Agrobusiness

The final two sections of this chapter turn from the products of agricultural estates to the agrarian relations within which they were produced. The first section examines the involvement of aristocrats in commercial agriculture; the second considers smallholder farming. Both aim to question some of the key assumptions which underpin widespread beliefs about social and economic relations.

As noted earlier, a central tenet of the traditional narrative of Roman agricultural production is the development of intensively farmed villa estates producing food for urban populations. There has been much debate about the origins of the villa and the associated new methods of farming: there is a general presumption that the concept, along with many of the slaves used for labor, was imported from the Hellenistic East, though influence has also been identified in relation to archaic Etruria (Terrenato, 2001) and North Africa and Sicily (Fentress, 2003). In contrast to origins, however, there has been less critical attention to the centrality of these agrobusinesses to the achievement and maintenance of aristocratic wealth and status. In particular, was agriculture as profitable as Cato and Varro suggest, and as the traditional narrative assumes?

One problem in assessing this question, as Rosenstein (2008) has recently argued, is the lack of attention to demand. There is an assumption that the market would buy whatever these estates could produce, thus guaranteeing large profits for their aristocratic owners and promoting their increasingly lavish lifestyles. However, production and supply can only be understood in the context of demand; to evaluate the scale and profitability of agriculture it is necessary to understand the size and nature of the market. Rosenstein therefore estimates the number of potential urban consumers and their demand for cereals, oil, and wine, sharing the resulting market between the number of producers (senators, equestrians, and decurions). The model makes generous assumptions: large urban populations with high per capita consumption and few producers with no competition from peasant farmers (i.e. maximum demand and the fewest suppliers). The resulting average market shares are, nonetheless, extremely modest (Rosenstein, 2008: table 1). For example, circa 200 BC, the average market share per producer would be just 6867 l of wine and 1288 l of oil, quantities which could be produced on just 26 *iugera* (6.5 ha) of land in total. This is far smaller, for example, than Cato's model 240-*iugera* oliveyard or 100-*iugera* vineyard (*On Agriculture*: 10–11).

Mid-Republican prices are poorly documented, but Rosenstein calculates that 1288 l of oil might be sold for 216–1796 *sesterces* (54–449 *denarii*). This is an extremely modest figure, which is even further reduced once production costs are considered. In reality, prices will have varied across time and space, but even if the figure is multiplied several times, the average market share does not appear to have provided great profits for producers. The average share of the wheat market was more significant at 8600–11 400 kg, equivalent to 85–114 *iugera* (21.25–28.5 ha) of land. However, the profit margin on cereals was much lower than that on wine or oil; indeed, it is precisely wine and oil production which supposedly underwent radical transformation through capital investment in technology (e.g. presses) and labor (i.e. slaves). By circa 50 BC, the population had risen, so the market was larger, but Rosenstein's estimates suggest the average market share was still comparatively low at 14 531 l of wine and 2725 l of oil, the equivalent of 54 *iugera* (13.5 ha). Late Republican wine prices suggest an average gross income of HS 4769–8416, still far short of the enormous profits assumed by the traditional narrative. Obviously some producers may have cornered a larger market share, especially those close to the cities, but assuming these figures are of the correct order of magnitude, total market demand was insufficient to sustain the economic fortunes of the mid and late Republican aristocracy as a whole.

This conclusion is in line with a number of other studies which have questioned the extent to which commercial agriculture spread across Republican Italy. For example, it is widely assumed that these estates were formed through the purchase or confiscation of extensive swathes of *ager publicus*, but Roselaar (2010) concludes that the availability of this public land was much more limited than commonly believed. Further, re-evaluation of the distribution of villas and the evidence for wine and oil production demonstrates distinct concentrations, notably along the coast, especially of western central Italy, in the *suburbium* of Rome, and in areas of former colonization (e.g. Marzano 2007; Witcher 2006). Indeed, rather than the norm, Terrenato (1998) has characterized these areas as "pockets of hyperactive economic activity" which existed alongside more traditional, peasant agriculture.

The implications of Rosenstein's analysis extend beyond balancing the supply and demand equation, and stress the necessity of relating agricultural innovations to their wider social and cultural context. Discussing olive oil production in the Greek world, Foxhall (2007) has stressed that this context is vital for understanding changing production strategies. Technology such as the oil press was not adopted because its higher productivity was superior, but because it was (or was not) useful for achieving wider social and economic objectives. So, if the market in Republican Italy was too small to provide significant profit for the Republic's aristocrats, their ownership of land and participation in agriculture point to reasons other than purely economic. The social, political, and cultural centrality of land and agriculture to aristocratic identity has long been recognized and perhaps the powerful aristocratic insistence on land-ownership and agriculture as the only appropriate means of producing wealth belies the fact that income increasingly came from other sources such as urban rents or money-lending. Even later emperors maintained this ideology; recent excavations at the site of Villa Magna, south of Rome, may have identified the villa described by the young Marcus Aurelius in a letter to Fronto (Fentress and Maiuro, 2011). A wine-pressing installation with a vat for treading grapes, *dolia* and an *opus spicatum* floor extravagantly and uniquely finished in white and colored marble may have been where the future emperor joined the vintage, having read Cato's *On Agriculture* the previous night (Fronto, *Letters*: 4.6). Just as Marie-Antoinette played at being a milkmaid, in many pre-industrial societies the relationship between aristocrats and agriculture was richly symbolic.

Rosenstein's calculations notwithstanding, those estates which did manage to compete effectively are likely to have been those which were located close to their markets. New evidence from the *suburbium* of Rome adds to the debate. The area of Centocelle, already mentioned earlier in this chapter, was well placed to respond to urban demand. During the third century BC, the plain was comprehensively reorganized; new sites were founded and new agricultural practices introduced (Volpe, 2004: 447–60). Later phases of Roman construction over these sites have made it difficult to establish the exact character of the earlier structures, but the stone (*tufo*) walled structure beneath the later Villa della Piscina covered circa 900 m² with rooms arranged around a central courtyard. These sites were associated with estates of circa 50–70 *iugera* (12–18 ha) and practiced mixed agriculture including vine cultivation (see earlier). At the end of the second century BC, these sites were rebuilt and greatly increased in size and comfort; for example, the Villa *ad duas Lauros* now comprised an atrium-peristyle complex with mosaic floors. Although estate sizes must have remained broadly stable, there were some changes in agricultural organization; for example, at the Villa della Piscina, a large new water tank possibly associated with irrigation was installed and the vineyard was reoriented and extended in size from 1.6 *iugera* to 8.8 *iugera* (0.39–2.2 ha; cf. Rosenstein's hypothetical estate sizes, earlier).

R. Volpe (2004) suggests that the evidence for modest third-century BC farms evolving into luxurious rural palaces provides new support for the reality of the "Catonian" villa; specifically, it provides the missing evidence for the existence of "transitional villas" which bridge the problematic gap – identified by Terrenato (2001) – between small yeoman farms of the archaic period and Republican slave-based villas. The evidence is particularly interesting because of the association of increased agricultural production (e.g. larger vineyards) with more elaborate villa architecture. Nonetheless, this model still requires significant assumptions about the association between the architecture of residential buildings and the organization of labor, specifically the use of slaves, which ultimately rests on Cato and Varro. Moreover, even if we accept these villas as examples of successful agrobusinesses growing rich on profits from the Roman market, their proximity to the city means they are probably not representative of the organization of Republican agriculture in general.

By the imperial period, the villas at Centocelle had been transformed again, developing into substantial rural palaces (Volpe, 2007). Even though market demand from Rome was higher than ever, land was taken out of cultivation and covered by luxurious residential structures. A reduction in agricultural output and an increase in the consumption of wealth may be another indicator that social and cultural considerations might take priority over the economic. Indeed, the proliferation of wealthy villa buildings on such small estates, particularly to the south and east of Rome, raises the question of whether the agricultural output of individual properties could have funded the construction of the associated buildings and maintained their owners' extravagant lifestyles. Put simply, did these villa estates come to consume more than they produced? Arguably, these villa buildings were not solely funded by their surrounding estates, but also drew on wealth derived from their owners' provincial properties and other investments. Proximity to Rome meant that the suburban villa was well positioned to corner the market during the Republican period, but by the time of the Principate the social and political importance of owning an appropriate rural retreat close to Rome exerted such a powerful influence that parts of the countryside began to consume more than they produced.

23.6   On the Family Farm

Under the influence of the historical texts and a heavy bias towards the excavation of villas, studies of Roman agriculture have been dominated by discussion of large, slave-based estates, rather than small family farms. Drawing in particular on Appian and Plutarch's biography of Tiberius Gracchus, the traditional narrative has cast these modest family farms as victims of an aristocratic monopolization of land, being comprehensively wiped out by the expansion of large estates during the second century BC. One of the key achievements of the many survey projects conducted across Italy since the 1960s has been the demonstration that small farm sites were not only ubiquitous but also, in contrast to the narrative of peasant decline, persisted throughout the Roman period, with the usual caveat of regional and chronological variation. Indeed, Launaro (2011) demonstrates that, in many areas, the number of small peasant farms actually increased during the early imperial period indicating an expanding free rural population.

Nonetheless, there is increasing consensus that such surveys may miss a significant percentage of sites, and hence, a large part of the rural population (Witcher, 2011). This problem is particularly clear in colonial contexts, where the historical texts provide a guide to the likely number of small farm sites. Only a minority of colonists could have been based in the new urban centers of the middle Republic, but surveys have consistently struggled to find evidence for sufficient numbers of contemporary farms to accommodate these rural colonists. This is often explained by the reduced archaeological visibility of early colonists due to their low standard of living. However, Pelgrom (2008: 348–54) has recently argued that this interpretation is based on the assumption that the colonists were settled as individual families in dispersed farms on individual plots of land; instead, he argues that early colonists were based in village settlements. In other words, small colonial farms are not archaeologically invisible; they did not exist in first place. The presumption that colonists, like peasant farmers more generally, would live in dispersed farms has a powerful influence on the narrative of Roman agriculture and its archaeological investigation. Villages, for example, remain a highly neglected category of settlement (though for recent work, Il Monte – Schörner, 2013; Falacrinae – Coarelli, Kay, and Patterson, 2008).

A number of similar powerful assumptions still color the way in which the Roman peasantry and its agricultural strategies are interpreted. These assumptions are related to wider beliefs about the ancient economy as primitive or modern and concepts such as progress and decline (see earlier in this chapter). Discussion of Roman peasants is particularly influenced by three key beliefs which have dominated the study of Mediterranean smallholders through history: self-sufficiency, self-determination, and immemorial stability (Horden and Purcell, 2000: 270–78; Roman Italy specifically: Witcher, 2007). Each of these is closely tied to issues of agricultural production and agrarian relations. For example, the belief that the wider political and economic developments of history washed over peasant communities with limited impact on their traditional lifestyles can predispose interpretation of agricultural strategies, social relations, and cultural identities towards a static vision, where any change is dismissed as a superficial "veneer," leaving the Roman countryside little different from its Iron Age predecessor (e.g. Frederiksen and Ward-Perkins, 1957: 117; Terrenato, 2007). However, this makes it difficult to explain developments such as tenancy, and fails to recognize the defining role of markets and social hierarchies in shaping peasant societies (e.g. Erdkamp, 2005: Redfield, 1955).

The assumption of self-sufficiency has particular implications for understanding agricultural production. The historical texts, especially those deriving from the specific social and political conditions of the late Republic, provide a powerful stereotype of the Roman peasant as a self-contained social and economic unit (Garnsey, 1980: 35–36; Horden and Purcell, 2000: 270) which has been translated into an assumption of small family farms providing for their own subsistence independently of neighbors and markets. However, this is highly questionable. Horden and Purcell (2000: 271) stress that the Mediterranean ecology makes self-sufficiency inherently risky; for example, unpredictable weather can ruin crops. This means that small farms need to produce a good surplus as insurance against bad years and to be more, not less, connected to the wider world through social and economic networks.

Even basic agricultural strategies, such as the decision to use oxen for ploughing, might involve small farms in varied social and economic interactions. Cattle require grazing land and fodder management; a yoke might also provide more capacity than a smallholding required. In such circumstances, a farmer might therefore come to an agreement with a neighbor to share a plough-team (cf. Jongman, 1988: 152–53; Lirb, 1993). Small numbers of animals also make it difficult to maintain a sustainable population, and new animals might have to be bought at market or borrowed from neighbors. Social and economic independence (*autarkeia*) may have been an ancient ideal, but was impractical. Archaeologically, the pottery and other artifacts recovered from small farm sites bear witness to their close connections with urban markets.

Far from being isolated from and unaffected by the wider world, peasants are defined by these relations. Erdkamp (2005: 60) demonstrates that it was the "imperfect market" conditions of antiquity – the lack of credit, volatile prices, inflexible labor – which shaped the peasantry. Further, the regional variability of these market conditions defined different peasantries in different places. Hence, the agricultural strategies of peasants in the more densely urbanized parts of Italy are likely to have differed from those in less urbanized areas (for the example of Etruria, see Witcher, 2006); as noted earlier in this chaper, this might involve growing different combinations of crops or, as discussed below, radical shifts in social relations, such as the emergence of tenancy. As a result, there is no such thing as "the" Roman peasant or a "typical" Roman farm; peasants and their agricultural strategies existed in complex networks of relations which, alongside the variation caused by the diverse physical geography of the peninsula, were defined by social, political and economic considerations which extended well beyond individual peasant households.

Histories of Roman agriculture also betray a strong presumption that peasant farming was unproductive and therefore vulnerable to failure and replacement with more intensive commercial farming. For example, rather than plough the fields, a peasant farmer might dig them with a spade or hoe. Such reliance on human labor is widely perceived as indicative of the primitive economic behavior which allowed the more progressive production of villa estates to expand. However, the high input of human labor can be seen as logical in the context of large families and an economy which provided few alternatives to agricultural work (see Erdkamp, 1999, on structural overmanning). Indeed, the absorption of surplus labor by "primitive" strategies such as hand-digging and intensive weeding can significantly increase yields and, although productivity may drop (i.e. more labor is used to produce the same amount of food), overall production may rise. Indeed, the ability of peasants to act in "economically irrational" ways may have allowed them to out-compete larger commercial farms which were more vulnerable to shifts in labor and commodity costs.

Hence, peasant farmers can be remarkably resilient. Indeed, despite the connectivity and technological complexity of the modern world, in the year 2000 just 3% of global wealth was generated by farming, but 22% of the world's population (40% of the labor force) worked in agriculture, many of them as subsistence farmers (Lang, 2010: 93). To be sure, they are poor, but they have been able to adapt their agricultural strategies to survive the changing economic and political conditions. As the examples cited throughout this chapter have suggested, the narrative of the noble but vulnerable citizen-farmer, pushed from the land by commercial farms is a simplification, underwritten by the notion of primitive versus progressive farming.

Finally, it is worth cautioning that the rehabilitation of peasant agriculture as resilient and rational within its own terms does not mean that it differed only in scale from the agriculture of larger commercial estates (for such a revisionist approach, see Kron, 2008b). Peasant strategies were defined by connections with wider social and economic networks including markets, but this does not mean they aimed to implement the advice of Cato or Varro; for all but a few, the overwhelming objective will have remained the retention of maximum flexibility in order to satisfy household needs rather than the achievement of maximum profit; how those needs were met might have changed, perhaps dramatically, but the objective remained broadly the same.

One example of a radical change in agrarian relations is the emergence of tenancy. It is during the late Republican period that references to tenancy begin to appear in the textual sources (De Neeve, 1984a), becoming more common during the early imperial period; Pliny the Younger's letters provide detailed insights into the labor arrangements on his estates, and are particularly valuable for references to his tenants (for archaeological investigation of Pliny's Umbrian villa, see Branconi and Uroz Sáez, 2008). Growth in the use of farm tenants broadly coincides with the so-called "crisis of the slave mode of production" and the shift away from the use of slave labor. There has been much discussion about why aristocratic landowners would have made the transition from slave to free (dependent) labor, and this has usually concentrated on the spiraling costs of maintaining slaves and the growing competition for urban markets from provinces such as Baetica. However, just as the origins and organization of the

Republican slave estate has been critically reassessed (see earlier), so its subsequent decline has been similarly re-evaluated (e.g. Marzano, 2007). If these estates were not as numerous and geographically widespread as previously assumed, the explanation for decline and its significance also needs reconsideration. McKeown (2007) reminds us that large-scale chattel slavery is historically unusual and he sees the rise of labor arrangements such as tenancy as a return to the long-term historical norm. Importantly, tenancy was a potentially attractive option for both tenant and landowner. During times of growing population, the balance between land and labor shifts, and would-be farmers find it harder to access land, and wages are depressed; tenancy therefore secures land to cultivate. The landowner also had an interest in the success of tenants and might provide patronage and capital. Of course, the landowner can also take advantage of the reduced cost of free labor in order to demand rent and, unlike slaves, tenants have every incentive to work hard (see de Neeve, 1984a; Erdkamp, 2005: 32–39; Foxhall, 1990) and to provide political support to their landlords.

As noted ealier, it a truism that archaeology cannot identify the legal status of a site's inhabitants. Establishing whether a particular farm was worked by an owner-occupier or by a tenant on a five-year lease is archaeologically problematical (for an attempt, see Foxhall, 1990). However, a recent synthesis of early imperial settlement patterns across Etruria (Witcher, 2006), including the northern *suburbium* of Rome, suggests that the significant rise in the number of small farm sites around Rome at this time cannot be easily explained as tenacious peasant farmers managing against the odds, not only to survive ferocious competition from land-hungry aristocrats, but also to increase in number. Growing demand pushed up the price of property, making it harder than ever to gain access to land; it was therefore argued that these sites might be better understood as the farms of dependent laborers, or tenants.

Support for this interpretation has emerged using a very different approach, namely the modeling of agricultural production and demography using Geographic Information Systems (GIS). A recent study integrated settlement patterns in the *ager Veientanus* in southern Etruria with ancient and comparative evidence for crop yields to estimate the potential agricultural productivity of Roman estates and the size of population which could be supported (Goodchild and Witcher, 2009). It has long been argued that the rise of large villa estates in this area pushed small farms onto the most marginal land (e.g. de Neeve, 1984b; Erdkamp, 2005: 42). However, the results of the GIS model indicate that, far from occupying the least productive land, newly founded farm sites occupied land which had greater productive potential than the land associated with either existing farms or newly founded villa sites.

One possible explanation for the successful acquisition of the best land by the most modest sites is tenancy. During the Republican period, the landscape was divided into large estates, the full extent of which could not be intensively exploited, but to which others were denied access. By the early imperial period, these estates were divided into smaller properties and rented to tenants who were prepared to pay for access because growing population had reduced their social and economic status. The effect may have been a shift from small pockets of intensive agricultural production towards a more continuous distribution of extensively cultivated farms. Overall production is likely to have increased (perhaps significantly), though productivity may have remained static or even declined because the replacement of slaves with peasant families led to the structural overmanning of agricultural production.

The switch to tenancy might suggest that early imperial landowners traded higher profits for a reliable income; as at Centocelle, they may have placed increasing value on the creation of an appropriate rural retreat rather than on farming the landscape to its full potential. The *ager Veientanus* study examines only one small area of the *suburbium* and further research is required to establish whether similar patterns can be found elsewhere. However, the GIS methodology illustrates one way in which archaeological data can be used to address not only the scale and organization of agricultural production, but also wider agrarian relations.

23.7 Conclusions

Interpretations of Roman agricultural production have been too generalized. For too long they relied on literal readings of the ancient writers and on generalizing the results of a few well-known sites to the peninsula as whole. In recent years, more critical approaches to the texts and a wealth of new archaeological evidence have emphasized the variability of agricultural strategies as practiced over time, in different regions, and by different types of farmer. This wealth of diversity makes it difficult to summarize Roman agricultural production; should we emphasize the technological and organizational innovations, which were significant, but arguably far from dominant? Or should we focus on adding ever more detail to the mosaic? Should we stress the continuities which characterized agricultural life (e.g. the cycle of seasons; the continuing importance of the Mediterranean Triads)? Or should we stress the changing context in which those farmers worked (e.g. growing urban markets, provincial imports)? There are no simple answers to these questions, but in order to provide a rounded approach, it is important to balance these different perspectives. For example, we must acknowledge the regional variability of agricultural production, but we also need to explore the connections between these regional economies, whether through the movement of people (as laborers), animals (transhumance), or goods (exchange). Agricultural production and agrarian relations lay at the heart of Roman society and were as ideologically potent as they were economically important. Revised understanding of these topics has implications which extend far beyond the farm gate.

FURTHER READING

The only English language monograph dedicated to agriculture in Roman Italy is White 1970; it is based mainly on texts and obviously lacks insights of the subsequent four decades of archaeological fieldwork. This is a period which has witnessed a major shift in the focus and method of archaeological study to include rural archaeology and techniques designed to illuminate Roman farming practices. In Italian, see Forni and Marcone, eds 2002; Marcone 1997; papers in Carlsen, ed. 1994; Carlsen and Lo Cascio, eds 2009.

Papers in Becker and Terrenato, eds 2012 present critical new approaches to Republican villas, building on recent excavations such as the Villa of the Auditorium (Carandini, D'Alessio, and Di Giuseppe, 2006). Marzano 2007 presents a comprehensive study of villas in the imperial period. For comparative studies of regional landscape surveys, see J.R. Patterson 2006 and Witcher 2006. Frayn 1979 addresses subsistence farming; see also Erdkamp 2005 on the relationship between peasant farmers and the grain market.

For the hinterland of Rome, Morley 1996 provides an overview; a sense of the wealth of evidence collected in advance of recent development projects around Rome can be found in volumes such as Gioia and Volpe 2004 and Musco, Petrassi, Pracchia 2000; also conference proceedings such as Jolivet *et al.* 2009. Major projects building on the long traditions of field survey in these areas include Attema, Burgers, and van Leusen 2010, and Patterson and Coarelli 2008.

For animal husbandry, MacKinnon 2004 provides a comprehensive study of the zooarchaeological, textual and iconographical evidence. There is no equivalent synthesis of the archaeobotanical evidence; Jashemski and Meyer 2002 on the natural history of Pompeii provides a sense of the richness of the data.

Spurr 1986 provides an ethnographically informed interpretation of the texts on arable cultivation. White 1975 provides a study on farm equipment and Rossiter 1978 addresses farm buildings. But all of these are inevitably dated. The wealth of recent archaeological evidence awaits synthesis.

REFERENCES

Attema, P.A.J., Burgers, G.-J.L.M., and van Leusen, P.M. 2010. *Regional Pathways to Complexity: Settlement and Land-use Dynamics in Early Italy from the Bronze Age to the Republican Period.* Amsterdam: Amsterdam University Press.

Barker, G. and Grant, A. 1991. "Ancient and modern pastoralism in Central Italy: an interdisciplinary study in the Cicolano mountains." *Papers of the British School at Rome* 59: 15–88.

Becker, J.A. 2013. "Villas and agriculture in Republican Italy." In *A Companion to the Archaeology of the Roman Republic*, ed. J. DeRose, 309–22. Chichester: Wiley-Blackwell.

Becker, J. and Terrenato, N., eds. 2012. *Roman Republican Villas: Architecture, Context and Ideology.* Ann Arbor: University of Michigan Press.

Branconi, P. and Uroz Sáez, J. 2008. "La villa di Plinio il Giovane a San Giustino." In Mercator Placidissimus: *The Tiber Valley in Antiquity. New Research in the Upper and Middle River Valley*, eds H. Patterson and F. Coarelli, 105–21. Rome: Quasar.

Brizzi, G. and Marzano, A. 2009. "Costly display or economic investment? A quantitative approach to the study of Roman marine aquaculture." *Journal of Roman Archaeology* 22: 215–30.

Carandini, A., D'Alessio, M.T. and Di Giuseppe, H., eds. 2006. *La fattoria e la villa dell'Auditorium nel quartiere Flaminio di Roma.* Rome: «L'Erma» di Bretschneider.

Carlsen, J. ed. 1994. *Landuse in the Roman Empire.* Supplementum 22. Rome: Analecta Romana Instituti Danici.

Carlsen, J. and Lo Cascio, E., eds. 2009. *Agricoltura e scambi nell'Italia tardo-repubblicana.* Bari and Rome: Edipuglia.

Carter, J.C. 2006. *Discovering the Greek Countryside at Metaponto.* Ann Arbor: University of Michigan Press.

Chioffi, L. 1999. *Caro: il mercato della carne nell'occidente romano. Riflessi epigrafici ed iconografici.* Atlante Tematico di Topografia Antica IV Supplementum. Rome: «L'Erma» di Bretschneider.

Coarelli, F., Kay, S., Patterson, H. 2008. "Investigations at Falacrinae, the Birthplace of Vespasian." *Papers of the British School at Rome* 76: 47–73.

Cotton, M.A. & Métraux, G.P.R. 1985. *The San Rocco Villa at Francolise.* London: British School at Rome.

Doody, A. 2007. "Virgil the Farmer? Critiques of the Georgics in Columella and Pliny." *Classical Philology* 102: 180–97.

Erdkamp, P. 1999. "Agriculture, underemployment, and the cost of rural labour in the Roman world." *Classical Quarterly* 49(2): 556–72.

Erdkamp, P. 2005. *The Grain Market in the Roman Empire: A Social, Political and Economic Study.* Cambridge: Cambridge University Press.

Erixon, S. 2001. "The shepherd's huts in the Roman Campagna and the characteristics of their construction." In *From Huts to Houses: Transformations of Ancient Societies*, eds J.R. Brandt and L. Karlsson, 451–58. Stockholm: Svenska Institutet i Rom.

Evans, J.K. 1980. "*Plebs rustica*. The peasantry of classical Italy." *American Journal of Ancient History* 5: 19–47 and 134–73.

Fentress, E. 2003. "Stately homes: recent work on villas in Italy." *Journal of Roman Archaeology* 16(2): 545–56.

Fentress, E. and Maiuro, M. 2011. "Villa Magna near Anagni: the emperor, his winery and the wine of Signia." *Journal of Roman Archaeology* 24: 333–69.

Flohr, M. 2013. *The World of the Fullo: Work, Economy, and Society in Roman Italy.* Oxford: Oxford University Press.

Fontana, S. 2008. "South Etruria revisited: le anfore, un tentative di analisi quantitative". In Mercator Placidissimus: *The Tiber Valley in Antiquity. New Research in the Upper and Middle River Valley*, eds H. Patterson and F. Coarelli, 655–69. Rome: Quasar.

Forni, G. and Marcone, A., eds. 2002. *Storia dell'agricoltura italiana.* I. *L'età antica.* 2 *Italia romana.* Florence: Polistampa.

Foxhall, L. 1990. "The dependent tenant. Land leasing and labour in Italy and Greece." *Journal of Roman Studies* 80: 97–114.

Foxhall, L. 2007. *Olive Cultivation in Ancient Greece: Seeking the Ancient Economy.* Oxford: Oxford University Press.

Frayn, J.M. 1979. *Subsistence Farming in Roman Italy.* London: Centaur Press.

Frederiksen, M.W. and Ward-Perkins, J.B. 1957. "The ancient road systems of the central and northern Ager Faliscus (Notes on Southern Etruria 2)." *Papers of the British School at Rome* 25: 67–204.

Gabba, E. and Pasquinucci, M. 1979. *Strutture agrarie e allevamento transumante nell'Italia romana (III–I a.C.).* Pisa: Giardini.

Garnsey, P. 1980. "Non-slave labour in the Roman world." In *Non-Slave Labour in the Greco-Roman World,* ed. P. Garnsey, 34–47. Cambridge: Cambridge Philological Society.

Gilliver, K. 1997. "The inscriptions." In *Excavations at the Mola di Monte Gelato,* eds T.W. Potter and A. King, 201–07. London: Archaeological Monograph of the British School at Rome 11.

Gioia, P. and Volpe, R., eds. 2004. *Centocelle I. Roma S.D.O. Le indagini archeologiche.* Rome: Rubbettino.

Goodchild, H. 2013. "Agriculture and the environment of Republican Italy." In *A Companion to the Archaeology of the Roman Republic,* ed. J. DeRose, 198–213. Chichester: Wiley-Blackwell.

Goodchild, H. and Witcher, R.E. 2009. "Modelling the agricultural landscapes of Republican Italy." In *Agricoltura e scambi nell'Italia tardo-repubblicana,* eds J. Carlsen and E. Lo Cascio, 197–220. Bari and Rome: Edipuglia.

Gowland, R. and Garnsey, P. 2010. "Skeletal evidence for health, nutritional status and malaria in Rome and the Empire." In *Roman Diasporas. Archaeological Approaches to Mobility and Diversity in the Roman Empire,* ed. H. Eckardt, 131–56. Portsmouth, RI: *Journal of Roman Archaeology* Suppl. 78.

Hopkins, K. 1978. *Conquerors and Slaves.* Cambridge: Cambridge University Press.

Horden, P. and Purcell, N. 2000. *The Corrupting Sea.* Oxford: Blackwell.

Jashemski, W.F. and Meyer, F.G., eds. 2002. *The Natural History of Pompeii.* Cambridge: Cambridge University Press.

Jolivet, V., Pavolini, C., Tomei, M.A., and Volpe, R., eds. 2009. *Suburbium II: il Suburbio di Roma dalla fine dell'età monarchica alla nascita del sistema delle ville (V–II sec. a.C.).* Rome: École française de Rome.

Jones, G.D.B. 1963. "Capena and the Ager Capenas, Part 2." *Papers of the British School at Rome* 31: 100–58.

Jongman, W. 1988. *The Economy and Society of Pompeii.* Amsterdam: Gieben.

Jongman, W. 2007. "Gibbon was right: the Decline and Fall of the Roman economy." In *Crises and the Roman Empire,* eds O. Hekster, G. de Kleijn, D. Slootjes, 183–99. Leiden: Brill.

Killgrove, K. 2013. "Biohistory of the Roman Republic: the potential of isotope analysis of human skeletal remains". *Postclassical Archaeologies* 3: 41–62.

King, A. 1997. "Mammal, reptile and amphibian bones." In *Excavations at the Mola di Monte Gelato,* eds T.W. Potter and A. King, 383–403. London: Archaeological Monograph of the British School at Rome 11.

Kron, G. 2002. "Archaeozoological evidence for the productivity of Roman livestock farming." *Münstersche Beiträge zur Antiken Handelsgeschichte* 21(2): 53–73.

Kron, G. 2004. "Roman livestock farming in southern Italy: the case against environmental determinism." In *Espaces intégrés et ressources naturelles dans l'empire romain,* eds M. Clavel-Lévêque and E. Hermon, 119–34. Besançon: Presses Universitaires de Franche-Comté.

Kron, G. 2005. "Anthropometry, physical anthropology, and the reconstruction of ancient health, nutrition and living standards." *Historia* 54: 68–86.

Kron, G. 2008a. "Animal husbandry, hunting, fishing, and fish production." In *The Oxford Handbook of Engineering and Technology in the Classical World,* ed. J.P. Oleson, 175–222. Oxford: Oxford University Press.

Kron, G. 2008b. "The much maligned peasant. Comparative perspectives on the productivity of the small farmer in Classical Antiquity." In *People, Land and Politics. Demographic Developments and the Transformation of Roman Italy, 300BC–AD14,* eds L. de Ligt and S. Northwood, 71–119. Leiden: Brill.

Kron, G. 2012. "Food production." In *Cambridge Companion to the Roman Economy,* ed. W. Scheidel, 156–74. Cambridge: Cambridge University Press.

Kronenberg, L. 2009. *Allegories of Farming from Greece and Rome. Philosophical Satire in Xenophon, Varro and Virgil.* Cambridge: Cambridge University Press.

Lang, T. 2010. "Crisis? What crisis? The normality of the current food crisis." *Journal of Agrarian Change* 10(1): 87–97.

Launaro, A. 2011. *Peasants and Slaves: the Rural Population of Roman Italy (200 BC to AD 100).* Cambridge: Cambridge University Press.

Laurence, R. 1999. *The Roads of Roman Italy. Mobility and Social Change.* London: Routledge.

Lirb, H.J. 1993. "Partners in agriculture. The pooling of resources in rural *societates* in Roman Italy." In *De Agricultura. In Memoriam Pieter Willem De Neeve (1945–1990)*, eds H. Sancisi-Weerdenburg, R.J. Van der Spek, H.C. Teitler, and H.T. Wallinga, 263–95. Amsterdam: Gieben.

MacKinnon, M. 2004. *Production and Consumption of Animals in Roman Italy: Integrating the Zooarchaeological and Textual Evidence.* Portsmouth, RI: *Journal of Roman Archaeology* Suppl. 54.

MacKinnon, M. 2010. "Cattle 'breed' variation and improvement in Roman Italy: connecting the zoo-archaeological and ancient textual evidence." *World Archaeology* 42(4): 55–73.

Marcone, A. 1997. *Storia dell'agricoltura romana. Dal mondo arcaico all età imperiale.* Rome: La Nuova Italia Scientifica.

Marzano, A. 2007. *Roman Villas in Central Italy. A Social and Economic History.* Leiden and Boston: Brill.

Matterne, V. and Derreumaux, M. 2008. "A Franco-Italian investigation of funerary rituals in the Roman World: 'Les rites et la mort à Pompéi.' The plant part: a preliminary report." *Vegetation History and Archaeobotony* 17(1): 105–12.

McKeown, N. 2007. *The Invention of Ancient Slavery?* London: Duckworth.

Mercuri, A.M., Accorsi, C.A. and Bandini Mazzanti, M. 2002. "The long history of cannabis and its cultivation by the Romans in central Italy, shown by pollen records from Lago Albano and Lago di Nemi." *Vegetation History and Archaeobotany* 11(4): 263–76.

Morley, N. 1996. *Metropolis and Hinterland: the City of Rome and the Italian Economy, 200 B.C.–A.D. 200.* Cambridge: Cambridge University Press.

Musco, S., Petrassi, L., and Pracchia, S., eds. 2000. *Luoghi e paesaggi archeologici del suburbio orientale di Roma.* Rome: Ministero per i beni e le attività culturali / Soprintendenza archeologica di Roma.

Neeve, P.W. de. 1984a. Colonus. *Private Farm Tenancy in Roman during the Republic and Early Principate.* Amsterdam: Gieben.

Neeve, P.W. de. 1984b. *Peasants in Peril. Location and Economy in Italy in the Second Century BC.* Amsterdam: Gieben.

Pasquinucci, M. 2002. "L'allevamento." In *Storia dell'agricoltura italiana. I. L'età antica. 2. Italia romana*, eds G. Forni and A. Marcone, 157–224. Florence: Polistampa.

Patterson, H. and Coarelli, F., eds, 2008. Mercator Placidissimus: *The Tiber Valley in Antiquity. New Research in the Upper and Middle River Valley.* Rome: Quasar.

Patterson, J.R. 2006. *Landscapes and Cities. Rural Settlement and Civic Transformation in Early Imperial Italy.* Oxford: Oxford University Press.

Pelgrom, J. 2008. "Settlement organization and land distribution in Latin colonies before the Second Punic War." In *People, Land and Politics. Demographic Developments and the Transformation of Roman Italy, 300BC–AD14*, eds L. de Ligt and S. Northwood, 333–72. Leiden: Brill.

Prowse T., Schwarcz H., Saunders S., Bondioli L., and Macchiarelli R. 2004. "Isotopic paleodiet studies of skeletons from the Imperial Roman cemetery of Isola Sacra, Rome, Italy." *Journal of Archaeological Science* 31 (3): 259–72.

Purcell, N. 1987. "Tomb and suburb." In *Römische Gräberstraßen. Selbstdarstellung – Status – Standard*, eds H. von Hesberg and P. Zanker, 25–41. Munich: Bayerische Akademie des Wissenschaften.

Purcell, N. 2003. "The way we used to eat: diet, community, and history at Rome." *American Journal of Philology* 124: 329–58.

Reay, B. 2005. "Agriculture, writing, and Cato's aristocratic self-fashioning." *Classical Antiquity* 24: 331–61.

Redfield, R. 1955. *The Little Community and Peasant Society and Culture.* Chicago: University of Chicago Press.

Roselaar, S.T. 2010. *Public Land in the Roman republic. A Social and Economic History of* Ager Publicus *in Italy, 396–89 BC*. Oxford: Oxford University Press.

Rosenstein, N.S. 2008. "Aristocrats and agriculture in the Middle and Late Republic." *Journal of Roman Studies* 98: 1–26.

Rossiter, J.J. 1978. *Roman Farm Buildings in Italy*. Oxford: BAR International Series 52.

Roth, U. 2007. *Thinking Tools: Agricultural Slavery between Evidence and Models*. London: Institute of Classical Studies.

Sadori, L. and Susanna, F. 2005. "Hints of economic change during the Late Roman Empire period in central Italy: a study of charred plant remains from "La Fontanaccia", near Rome." *Vegetation History and Archaeobotany* 14(4): 386–93.

Schörner, G., ed. 2013. *Leben auf dem Lande: 'Il Monte' bei San Gimignano: Ein römischer Fundplatz und sein Kontext*. Vienna: Phoibos.

Spurr, M.S. 1986. *Arable Cultivation in Roman Italy c.200 BC–AD 100*. London: *Journal of Roman Studies* Monograph 3.

Terrenato, N. 1998. "The Romanization of Italy: global acculturation or cultural *bricolage*?" In *TRAC 97: Proceedings of the Seventh Annual Theoretical Roman Archaeology Conference. Nottingham 1997*, eds C. Forcey, J. Hawthorne and R. Witcher, 20–27. Oxford: Oxbow Books.

Terrenato, N. 2001. "The Auditorium site in Rome and the origins of the villa." *Journal of Roman Archaeology* 14: 5–32.

Terrenato, N. 2007. "The clans and the peasants. Reflections on social structure and change in Hellenistic central Italy." In *Articulating Local Cultures. Power and Identity under the Expanding Roman Republic*, eds P. van Dommelen and N. Terrenato, 13–22. Portsmouth, RI: *Journal of Roman Archaeology* Suppl. 63.

Terrenato, N. 2012. "The enigma of 'Catonian' villas: the *De Agricultura* in the context of the second-century BC Italian architecture." In *Roman Republican Villas: architecture, context, and ideology*, eds J.A. Becker and N. Terrenato, 69–93. Ann Arbor: University of Michigan Press.

Thurmond, D.L. 2006. *A Handbook of Food Processing in Classical Rome: For Her Bounty No Winter*. Leiden: Brill.

Volpe, R. 2004. "Lo sfruttamento agricolo e le costruzioni sul pianoro di Centocelle in età repubblicana." In *Centocelle I. Roma S.D.O. Le indagini archeologiche*, eds P. Gioia and R. Volpe, 447–62. Rome: Rubbettino.

Volpe, R. 2007. *Centocelle II. Roma S.D.O. Le indagini archeologiche 2*. Rome: Rubbettino.

Volpe, R. 2009. "Vino, vigneti ed anfore in Roma repubblicana." In *Suburbium II: il Suburbio di Roma dalla fine dell'età monarchica alla nascita del sistema delle ville (V–II sec. a.C.)*, eds V. Jolivet, C. Pavolini, M.A. Tomei and R. Volpe, 369–81. Rome: École française de Rome.

West, B. 1997. "The bird bones." In *Excavations at the Mola di Monte Gelato*, eds T.W. Potter and A. King, 403–04. London: Archaeological Monograph of the British School at Rome 11.

White, K.D. 1970. *Roman Farming*. London: Thames and Hudson.

White, K.D. 1975. *Farm Equipment of the Roman World*. Cambridge: Cambridge University Press.

Wilson, A.I. 2008. "Villas, horticulture and irrigation infrastructure in the Tiber Valley." In Mercator Placidissimus: *The Tiber Valley in Antiquity. New Research in the Upper and Middle River Valley*, eds H. Patterson and F. Coarelli, 731–68. Rome: Quasar.

Witcher, R.E. 2006. "Settlement and society in early imperial Etruria." *Journal of Roman Studies* 96: 88–123.

Witcher, R.E. 2007. "Agrarian spaces in Roman Italy: society, economy and Mediterranean agriculture." *Arqueología espacial (Paisajes agrarios)* 26 [2006]: 341–59.

Witcher, R.E. 2011. "Missing persons? Models of Mediterranean regional survey and ancient populations." In *Settlement, Urbanisation and Population*, eds A. Bowman and A.I. Wilson, 36–75. Oxford: Oxford University Press.

Witcher, R.E. 2012. "'That from a long way off look like farms': the classification of Roman rural sites." In *Comparative Issues in the Archaeology of the Roman Rural Landscape. Site Classification Between Survey, Excavation and Historical Categories*, eds P.A.J. Attema and G. Schörner, 11–30. Portsmouth RI: *Journal of Roman Archaeology* Suppl. 88.

CHAPTER 24

Local Elites

John R. Patterson

24.1 Introduction

The history of local elites is fundamental to the history of ancient Italy: in fact, it is little exaggeration to say that the history of Roman Italy *is* the history of the Italian elites. They provided military and political leadership for their communities as these came into contact with Rome; their accumulation of resources, whether as a result of agriculture, overseas commerce, or both, allowed them to construct monumental sanctuaries, provide developing urban centers with public buildings, and build often grandiose tombs for themselves; their ambitions, whether for local autonomy or personal advancement at Rome, lay behind the Social War of 91–89 BC (see Bispham, ch.4, this vol.). Subsequently, and especially under Augustus, wealthy men of Italian origin came to form a significant element within the ruling class of Rome itself, as senators and equestrians. By the second century AD the ruling classes of the Italian cities had acquired legal privileges as well as social and political pre-eminence. The flourishing and engagement of local elites was crucial to the prosperity of their communities, and recruiting new blood to replace those whose political ambitions had taken them to careers beyond the confines of their local community came to be a major preoccupation for the cities of Italy.

Despite their central historical importance, it is not easy to write the history of the Italian elites over the long term. The indigenous elites of Italy before the advent of Roman rule are largely seen through the distorting filter of Greek or Roman ethnographic writing, whether – like the Sabines – as examples of commendable frugality or – like the Etruscans – of deplorable luxury (Dench, 1995; Farney, 2007). The ruling classes of the peoples of Italy appear as protagonists in the narrative histories of republican Rome only occasionally, and usually in time of war – for example, in Livy's accounts of Rome's conquest of Italy in the fourth and early third centuries BC, or the defection of allied communities in southern Italy following Hannibal's victory at the battle of Cannae. Appian provides a narrative of the Social War, as does Velleius Paterculus, and a range of anecdotes about these various conflicts is preserved in the writings of Valerius Maximus and others. Many of these stories carry a strong ideological charge, reflecting Roman disapproval of disloyal allies or clients, and the view, prevalent under the early Principate, that the Social War should be seen as a kind of civil war. Several of the speeches of Cicero, himself born in Arpinum and with strong continuing links to the local

A Companion to Roman Italy, First Edition. Edited by Alison E. Cooley.

elites of southern Latium, reveal the concerns and preoccupations of the Italian aristocracies in the latter years of the Republic. In particular, his *In Defence of Cluentius*, delivered in 66 BC, casts a lurid light on a complex network of family relationships and antagonisms in the Samnite town of Larinum, during the years which followed the Social War (Lomas, 2004: 108–10; Fronda, 2010: 320). Cicero's writings, like those of Sallust, are similarly a fundamental source for the ambitions and ideologies of the men of Italian origin who aspired to public office at Rome. Under the Principate, the affairs of the Italian communities and their leading men impinged only occasionally on the broader narratives of imperial rule (Millar, 1986: 295): this might be the result of major calamities such as the eruption of Vesuvius in AD 79, or more minor disturbances which nevertheless attracted the attention of the emperor, such as the episode under Tiberius, when the inhabitants of Pollentia, a town in the Ligurian Appennines, refused to let the burial of a *primus pilus* (chief centurion) take place until his heirs had organized funerary games (Suetonius, *Life of Tiberius*. 37).

Inscriptions in a range of local languages do, however, cast light on the administrative frameworks and political institutions of the Italian peoples before their incorporation within the Roman state after the Social War (Crawford, 2011; cf. Lomas, ch.11, this vol.), while from the late Republic onwards, epigraphic documents in Latin become available in much greater numbers than before. For the imperial period, honorary decrees, statue bases, funerary monuments, and building inscriptions provide a wealth of information on the various acts of generosity bestowed on the towns of Roman Italy by members of the municipal elites, and their other activities while holding local magistracies: this documentation can be seen as providing the authentic voice of the local aristocracies, their families, and the other inhabitants of their communities, to complement the perspective of the Roman elite mediated through the literary texts.

Archaeology, too, has an important role to play in our understanding of local elites, as the excavation of cemeteries and of individual tomb monuments may allow a reconstruction of the hierarchies and organization of otherwise poorly understood aristocracies. The contents of the "tombe principesche" at Praeneste of the eighth to the sixth centuries BC, and the *cistae* (bronze vessels) of the fourth and third centuries found in the La Colombella cemetery there, for example, illustrate the contacts of the Praenestine elites with Magna Graecia, Etruria, Rome, and the Mediterranean world more generally. Similarly, the public monuments which they constructed, and the artifacts and styles of decoration which they favored in the domestic context, illustrate that the cultural horizons of the Italian elites extended well beyond the confines of the peninsula. Although the phenomenon is not discussed here in detail, it is worth stressing that in many cases the allied elites were well ahead of their Roman counterparts in adopting features of Greek culture (Wallace-Hadrill, 2008: esp. 106–11).

What follows draws on this range of evidence to explore three selected but central issues. It sketches out the various ways in which Roman and Italian elites came into contact during the process which led over several centuries to the Roman hegemony over the Italian peninsula; the increasing involvement of the Italians in public life at Rome during the years after the Social War; and patterns of mobility within the Italian elites under the Principate. A fundamental question, though, is how the term "local elite" should be defined. For our purposes, the discussion centers on the free-born, landed aristocracies of the Italian communities: in essence those families whose members, under the late Republic or the Principate, served in municipal senates and took on the role of magistrates in their communities. Ex-slaves, in particular those who served as *Augustales*, and the magistrates and members of *collegia*, had important roles to play in the towns of Italy too, but these are discussed under the heading of "sub-elites" in chapter 25 of this volume. It is worth stressing, however, that there was considerable mobility between these different groups, particularly in the imperial period: as at Rome itself, a potential openness to outsiders was arguably one of the key defining features of the elites of Italy under Roman rule.

24.2   The Roman Conquest and the Italian Elites

As underlined elsewhere in this volume, the cultural, political, and institutional history of Italy in the period before the Roman conquest was strikingly diverse, and the same can be said of the elites of the different communities. Etruria, for example, characterized by urban settlement from an early date, was also known for the highly stratified nature of its society, with clear distinctions between ruling and subordinate classes (Harris, 1971: 114–29). Settlement in Samnium, by contrast, was largely structured around sanctuaries, villages, and hillforts, and there are some indications that Samnite society may have been less economically and socially polarized than elsewhere in Italy (Dench, 1995: 144–53).

Even within individual Italian communities, there were frequently internal divisions, whether between rich and poor or between rival factions of the wealthy. The Romans were well aware of these tensions within the societies of their opponents, and exploited them in various ways. In dealing with the Greek *poleis* of southern Italy, in which the citizen bodies tended to be divided according to oligarchical or democratic ideologies, the Romans usually sought the support of the elites, while their opponents appealed to the *demos*. In an account apparently derived originally from a Greek source, Dionysius of Halicarnassus records how at Naples in 328 BC the Romans sought to cultivate the "leading men;" however, in a debate in the popular assembly, the "worse element" prevailed and the Neapolitans decided to join the Samnites in a war against Rome (Dionysius of Halicarnassus, *Roman Antiquities*: 15.5–6, with Oakley, 1998: 640–42). Eventually, so Livy relates, two of the leading citizens organized the surrender of the city to the Romans (Livy: 8.25–26, with Frederiksen, 1984: 209–11; Lomas, 1993: 45). Discussing the siege of Croton by the Bruttian allies of Hannibal over a century later, Livy observes that at this time, the senates of the towns of Italy in general favored the Romans, while the plebeians tended to be sympathetic to the Carthaginians. According to his – perhaps too schematic – account of events at Croton in 215 BC, the *plebs* eventually admitted the Bruttians to the city, while the elite took refuge on the citadel (Livy: 24.2.8, 24.3.9 with Fronda, 2010: 171–72).

Once the Romans had conquered a community and brought it into an alliance, they were keen to support those elements in that community which were loyal to them. On several occasions we find the Romans intervening to support the local elites against the subordinate classes. At Arretium in 302 BC, the Romans intervened on behalf of an aristocratic family called the Cilnii who were about to be expelled from the city "because of envy for their wealth;" Livy records that as a result of the Roman intervention the upheavals were resolved and the Cilnii "reconciled with the *plebs*" (Livy: 10.3.1, 10.5.13). A few years later, a similar episode took place in Lucania, where an uprising led by "the poor and their impoverished leaders" was put down by the Romans "with the full support of the ruling class" (Livy: 10.18.8).

In other cases the Romans exploited (or perhaps in some cases created) splits within the local elites. Livy's narrative of the aftermath of the battle of Cannae in 216 BC illustrates that individual communities might contain factions which owed their position to Roman support, and whether a town remained loyal to Rome or deserted to Hannibal at that crucial point could well be related to the respective strengths of the pro-Roman faction and their opponents. Compsa, for example, was handed over to Hannibal at the initiative of Statius Trebius, who (according to Livy) was a *nobilis* of the town but had lost influence there because of the ascendancy of the family of the Mopsii, who "had become powerful as a result of the favor of the Romans" (Livy: 23.1.1–4 with Fronda, 2010: 31–32). Following Rome's victory over the Carthaginians, the punitive measures taken by Rome tended to reinforce the elements in the community which had remained loyal: at Locri, the property of the pro-Carthaginian faction was handed over to those who had supported Rome (Livy: 29.8.1–2). The elite of

Capua, which had deserted the Roman cause in 216 BC, was treated with particular severity: 70 leading senators were executed, 300 imprisoned, and others sold into slavery (Livy: 26.16.5–8, 26.34.2–13). While the physical structures of the city were not destroyed, the community's governmental structures were abolished, thus eliminating the stage on which the local elites were active (Cicero, *On the Agrarian Law*: 2.88–89; Farney, 2007: 188). The Capuan elite had previously had a privileged status – Livy tells us that the knights of that city had been granted Roman citizenship in 340 BC (Livy: 8.11.13–16 with Oakley, 1998: 513–55) – which may help to explain the exemplary nature of the punishment inflicted there. By contrast, the family of Minatius Magius, who was the great-great-grandfather of the historian Velleius Paterculus, but also descended from the pro-Roman Decius Magius of Capua, is at the time of the Social War found living at Aeclanum, where the Magii presumably relocated after the surrender of Capua to the Romans (Velleius Paterculus: 2.16.2).

During the second century BC, close links continued to be maintained (and indeed further developed) between Italian and Roman elites, at the individual as well as the collective level, and these relationships are well attested in the decades leading up to the Social War. Several cases are known of ties of *hospitium* (guest friendship) between Romans and Italians, for example (Badian, 1958: 154–55; Wiseman, 1971: 33–38; Patterson, 2006b: 140–43). Such "horizontal" relationships between elites of different communities existed in Italy, as well as in Greece from the archaic period onwards, and are reflected (for example) in the international character of the funerary assemblages discovered at Praeneste: many of these artifacts were apparently brought here as a result of gift-exchange. *Hospitium* relationships were characteristically established between men of elite status in different communities, and entailed the obligation to provide each other with hospitality and if appropriate other forms of assistance. The relationship could be symbolized by the casting of a bronze plaque known as a *tessera hospitalis*. Several of these survive: a particularly good example comes from Trasacco in the territory of the Marsi, which consists of half a ram's head, cast in bronze and inscribed with the names of the two partners in the relationship, T. Manlius M.f. (perhaps to be identified with a consul of the late third century BC) and T. Staiodius T.f. (*CIL* 1².1764 = *ILLRP* 1066) (Figures 24.1 and 24.2). Passages in Plautus and Cicero suggest that the artifact (one of a pair) would be produced when visiting one's opposite number, as a token of the connection between the two parties, or on other occasions as necessary (Plautus, *The Young Carthaginian*: 1046–50; Cicero, *In Defense of Balbus*: 41). Providing accommodation was an important element in the relationship, particularly so given the difficulties involved in travel at the time. According to Livy, L. Rammius, a leading citizen of Brundisium, was in the 170s BC accustomed to entertain not only Roman commanders and ambassadors, but also distinguished foreigners, since the port occupied a key position on the route from Rome to Greece. As a result, Persius, king of Macedon, tried to persuade him to poison important Romans staying with him (Livy: 42.17.3–9). Cicero tells us that Sex. Roscius of Ameria, father of the man he defended on a charge of parricide in 80 BC (Dyck, 2010: 1–2; Lomas, 2004: 104–06) had ties of *gratia* and *hospitium* with the most eminent Romans of the time, including the Metelli, the Servilii, and the Scipiones (*In Defense of Roscius of Ameria*: 15). He owned 13 farms, most of them close to the Tiber, which no doubt served as a regular stopping-off point for his Roman friends when they headed northwards along the *via Flaminia* (*In Defense of Roscius of Ameria*: 20). Equally, leading Italians might be entertained at the houses of the Roman aristocracy: we hear from Valerius Maximus and Plutarch that in 91 BC the Marsian Q. Poppaedius Silo, soon to be a leader of the Social War rebels, spent time at the house of his Roman *hospes* M. Livius Drusus discussing the concerns of Rome's Italian allies (Plutarch, *Life of Younger Cato*: 2.1; Valerius Maximus: 3.1.2a with Patterson, 2006b: 139–40). There were other occasions when members of Roman and Italian elites might meet informally: one favored location for such gatherings was the Bay of Naples, where members of the Roman aristocracy were accustomed to spend their leisure time, and might encounter leading Italian intellectuals (Rawson, 1985: 20–25).

Marriage-relations, too, are attested between individual members of Roman and Italian elites (Patterson, 2006b: 147–51). We are told by Livy that one factor which (for a while) restrained the Capuans from abandoning the Roman cause in 216 BC was the fact that many of them were married into Roman families (Livy: 23.4.7). One of these was their leader, Pacuvius Calavius, whose wife was a daughter of the Roman Appius Claudius, while his daughter was married to another Roman, M. Livius. When the Romans re-established control over Capua in 210 BC, the Campanians appealed for mercy on the grounds that "they were Roman citizens, related to them in many cases by marriage" (Livy: 26.33.3). Diodorus's narrative of the Social War records how, when the Roman army under the command of C. Marius and the Marsian force under Poppaedius Silo were fighting, "the soldiers on both sides recognized many personal friends, recalled not a few fellow-soldiers, and identified numerous kinsmen and relations, men who had been joined together in this friendly relationship by the law relating to marriage" (Diodorus Siculus: 37.15.2). How extensive marriage-relations between Roman and Italian elites were at this time is, however, hard to assess: in theory Romans were only allowed to marry another Roman, someone from a community possessing the right of *conubium*, or an individual who had received this right. It may be significant that many of the examples known concern Marsians, whose territory was close to Rome, and Capuans, who, as we have seen, seem to have had a particularly privileged status before 210 BC.

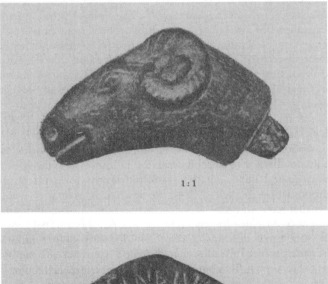

Figures 24.1 and 24.2   Inscribed *tessera hospitalis* from Trasacco. From F. Bernabei, "Trasacco: di una rarissima 'tessera hospitalis' con iscrizione latina." *Notizie degli scavi di antichità* 1895: 86 –87.

A further context in which Romans and Italians came into contact – and arguably one of particular importance – was military service (Pfeilschifter, 2007). As part of the obligations to Rome imposed by their alliance, Italian communities, together with Latin colonies, sent military contingents to serve in the Roman-led army; however, the allied soldiers, rather than being deployed in the legions alongside their Roman counterparts, served in auxiliary *turmae* or cohorts under the command of a *praefectus* drawn from their own community. While this man will have been in close contact with his superior officer, the Roman *praefectus sociorum*, and other Roman commanders, the experience of the rank-and-file soldiers may have served to consolidate their links with their fellow allies, rather than encouraging solidarity with the Roman legionaries, who would have been stationed in another part of the camp. It is worth highlighting the importance of the *extraordinarii* in particular. This was an elite corps of cavalrymen and infantry of particular ability drawn from the allied contingents (Polybius: 6.26.9), some of whom provided close support for the commander on the march, while others were located in the vanguard or the rear of the army, closest to the direction from which an attack was anticipated (Polybius: 6.31.2–3, 6.40.4–8). The predominance of cavalrymen in the unit, drawn from the most affluent families, suggests that its members had a social as well as a military prestige, and service in the *extraordinarii* may well have served as a means by which social contacts might have been established or consolidated between young men of the leading families of the allied communities (Patterson, 2012: 216–18).

These connections might help to explain why, in the years between the defeat of Hannibal and the Social War, we can detect increasingly close links developing not only between Romans and Italian allies, but also between the elites of the various allied communities, which (among other things) enabled them to make collective representations to Rome when they felt that their interests were being threatened. In 177 BC we hear that the Latin colonies complained to Rome about the problems they were suffering as a result of the migration of their citizens to Rome (Livy: 41.8.6–12): Cicero tells us that L. Papirius of Fregellae gave a speech *pro Fregellanis colonisque Latinis*, apparently on that occasion (Cicero, *Brutus*: 170). Similarly, representations were made by the Italian allies collectively to Scipio Aemilianus about the impact of Tiberius Gracchus's land reforms (Appian, *Civil Wars*: 1.19). This pattern of communication and collaboration is all the more striking given the traditional antagonisms and rivalries known to have characterized the various communities of Italy. For example, the tendency of the Samnites and Lucanians to invade the nearby lowlands, given the recurrent problems of overpopulation in their own territories, meant that they were uncomfortable neighbors; on a smaller scale, disputes about territorial boundaries could poison the relationships between neighboring cities for generations. Besides the internal tensions already discussed, traditional solidarities or long-standing enmities with local communities also had an impact on whether the peoples of southern Italy joined Hannibal or maintained their loyalty to Rome, as Fronda has shown. By contrast, these local resentments appear to have played a much smaller role in determining whether a community joined or opposed Rome in the Social War, and the increased level of interaction between Italian communities in the second century BC was arguably an important element in reducing these traditional hostilities (Fronda, 2010: 319–20; 327–29; Patterson, 2012).

Instead, the grievances of the Italian elites played a significant part in the growth of tension between Italy and Rome in the late second and early first centuries BC. Leading Italians were unhappy about the impact on their interests of Tiberius Gracchus's land bill, the Roman attempts to clamp down on those falsely claiming Roman citizenship, in particular through the *Lex Licinia Mucia* of 95 BC (Asconius: 67C), and the maltreatment of local magistrates, such as M. Marius, the *quaestor* of Teanum who was beaten in his own forum because the city baths were not clean enough for the consul's wife, or his counterpart at Ferentinum who threw himself off the city wall in similar circumstances (Gellius, *Attic Nights*: 10.3). Whether or not an ambition on their part to be involved in politics at Rome was also a significant motivation behind the conflict (Mouritsen, 1998: 94–99), the Italian elites did however come to play a significant role in the political scene at Rome in the decades which followed the Social War.

24.3 "Dim Characters with Fantastic Names": The Roman Revolution and the "Victory of the Italians"

The life-story of P. Ventidius Bassus is a striking one. Bassus, a man of humble origin (according to Aulus Gellius) was, as a child, captured at the siege of Asculum in the Social War with his mother, and the pair was led in the triumphal procession of Cn. Pompeius Strabo. After military service he went into business hiring out mules and carriages to magistrates, and accompanied Julius Caesar to Gaul, subsequently carrying out various tasks for him in the Civil War. On returning to Rome he entered the Senate, became a tribune, and was designated by Caesar as *praetor* for the year 43 BC. During the upheavals of that year he raised military forces in Picenum for Mark Antony, and was even declared a public enemy, but with the creation of the Triumvirate took on the role of consul in succession to Octavian himself. Subsequently he commanded an army against the Parthians and celebrated a triumph – the first Roman to do so over that people (Gellius, *Attic Nights*: 15.4; Velleius Paterculus: 2.65).

Bassus's career was by any standard exceptional: Valerius Maximus and Pliny the Elder highlighted the role of *fortuna* in the life of a man who was both led as a captive in another man's triumph and celebrated one himself (Valerius Maximus: 6.9.9; Pliny the Elder, *Natural History*: 7.135). Nevertheless it does highlight some recurrent features of the social mobility which characterized the period of Rome's Civil Wars (Patterson, 1993: 101–04): the acquisition of citizenship by the Italians following the Social War; the importance of patronage of leading men, in this case Caesar and then Antony; and the breakdown of normal constraints of office-holding.

Some individual Italians had already reached the Senate in Rome by the first century BC (Wiseman, 1971: 13–19; Farney, 2007: 180–90). These were, however, few in number, and tended to be drawn from a limited range of backgrounds. Often they originated in Latium, in the Sabine territory, or other areas close to Rome; others who reached the Senate at an early stage came from communities linked with Rome by the consular roads, which saw regular visits by members of the Roman elite, illustrating the potential political importance of *hospitium* (Wiseman, 1971: 28–32). It was the century from the conclusion of the Social War to the death of Augustus, however, during which the grant of citizenship to the former Italian allies enabled more of the affluent and ambitious among their number to become involved in Roman politics. The process was not an instantaneous one. Even after the *Lex Julia* of 90 BC enacted that the Italians who had remained loyal should be granted citizenship, and most of the others received it the following year, disputes about their registration in the voting tribes meant that it was only with the census of 70/69 BC that the Italians can be said to have become properly enfranchised. Furthermore, analysis of patterns of office-holding suggests that the Roman nobility reinforced its hold on the highest magistracies in the 20 years leading up to Caesar's crossing of the Rubicon in 49 BC (Badian, 1990). Nevertheless, there are indications that men of Italian origin did become increasingly involved in Roman politics during the same period, at various levels, even if others preferred to continue to give priority to local affairs (Lomas, 2004: 110–11).

C. Marius, who came from Arpinum and, despite his lack of senatorial background, held the consulship seven times in all, could perhaps be seen as a role model for Italians (Brunt,

1988: 129); Cicero, his fellow Arpinate, was another. In their political rhetoric, these "new men" tended to stress their own achievements and their adherence to traditional Roman virtues, in order to counter the emphasis placed by the nobility on their family heritage of service to Rome (Cicero, *Against Piso*: 2; Sallust, *Jugurthine War*: 85; Wiseman, 1971: 107–16; Flower, 1996: 60–90). They were also keen in practice to draw support from the cities of Italy. Cicero, defending Cn. Plancius in 54 BC against a charge of electoral bribery at the aedilician elections, claimed that citizens from Arpinum, Sora, Casinum, Aquinum, Venafrum, and Allifae, all towns close to his native Atina, had come to support him at the vote (*In Defense of Plancius*: 22 with Mouritsen, 2001: 119–20; Lomas, 2004: 102–04). It was clearly in Cicero's interest to suggest that Plancius could easily have won the election without recourse to illegal means, but the *Commentariolum Petitionis*, supposedly written by Cicero's brother Quintus, advised cultivating influential men in Italian towns (24) and building up a body of support from across the peninsula (31–32). This was a particularly appropriate strategy in Cicero's case, given his background, and in his speeches he frequently stressed how first his election to the consulship in 63 BC, and then the vote in favor of his restoration from exile in 57 BC, were achieved with the support of the "whole of Italy" (e.g. *Against Piso*: 3; *In the Senate after his Return*: 25). The patronage of influential men could also play a significant part in advancement to public office: during the 60s BC a significant number of men of Picene origin reached the Senate, including L. Afranius from Cupra Maritima, who became consul in 60 BC. The support of Pompey was no doubt important in this case, as allegedly was electoral bribery (Cicero, *Letters to Atticus*: 1.16.12; Wiseman, 1971: 32; Farney, 2007: 190). It is interesting to note that a shared Picene background did not necessarily mean that the individuals concerned were supportive of each other: Afranius was ridiculed by his fellow Picene M. Lollius Palicanus (Cicero, *Letters to Atticus*: 1.18.5). Local rivalries and antagonisms had not entirely disappeared from politics, and were to persist into the Principate.

It was, however, the Civil War period, the dictatorship of Caesar, and the Principate of Augustus, which were most central to the process by which the "flower of colonies and municipalities, good and wealthy men" (emperor Claudius's phrase: *ILS* 212) were brought into the Roman Senate. Many of the Roman nobility died in battle or in the proscriptions of the triumvirs; conversely, men of Italian origin gained the patronage of Caesar, Antony, or Augustus, as Ventidius Bassus had done, through serving alongside them in the army, or otherwise operating on their behalf. Several key men in the Augustan regime were of Italian descent: C. Maecenas, Horace's literary patron, was thought to have been descended from Etruscan kings (Horace, *Odes*: 1.1.1); Tacitus believed Maecenas was a member of the family of the Cilnii, who had been restored to power at Arretium by the Romans in the late fourth century BC (*Annals*: 6.11). Others were of more obscure origin, such as M. Agrippa. Q. Salvidienus Rufus, who was designated consul for 39 BC, despite not having held any magistracies previously, but then put to death for allegedly plotting against Octavian, was thought to have been a shepherd-boy in his youth (Velleius Paterculus: 2.76.4; Dio Cassius: 48.33). Collectively Syme described these men as "dim characters with fantastic names," and characterized the Principate as "in a sense the victory of Italy over Rome" (Syme, 1939: 361, 453). It was only under Augustus that the elites from some Italian communities first came to be represented in the Senate: the funerary monument of Q. Varius Geminus of Superaequum, who served as governor of two provinces under Augustus, records that he was the "first of all the Paelignians to become a senator" (*CIL* 9.3306 = *ILS* 932). The advent in the Senate of men of Italian origin did not mean, however, that they relinquished a sense of their family's heritage or their place of origin. Torelli has linked the "Corsini throne," a Roman copy in marble of a fifth-century BC Etruscan throne found on the Lateran Hill in the eighteenth century, with Urgulania, a friend of Livia, who married M. Plautius Silvanus, a Roman senator, and whose granddaughter in turn married the emperor Claudius (Torelli, 1999: 150–64). The throne is thought to have been displayed in the *tablinum* of Plautius's house, recalling Urgulania's distinguished Etruscan ancestry. Similarly we find examples, in the triumviral era and under Augustus, of senators of Italian origin bearing the same names as ancestors who were rebel leaders at the time of the Social War – Poppaedius Silo and Vettius Scato, for example (Farney, 2007: 220–22). Italian ancestry was now a matter of pride, rather than a social liability (D'Arms, 1984).

The grant of citizen rights to the former allies after the Social War also had a significant impact at the local level, as communities of Italians acquired the institutions and superstructure characteristic of municipalities of Roman citizens. In many parts of Italy, we can see extensive building programs taking place during the generation after the Social War, with the construction of city walls and other public monuments. At Aeclanum, for example, walls, towers, and gates were constructed by two magistrates and by C. Quinctius Valgus, the town's patron, whom we also know to have been active at Pompeii in this period (*CIL* $1^2.1722$ = *ILS* 5318 = *ILLRP* 523; Gabba, 1994: 63–103). The local elites were central to this process, either in their role as magistrates, or using their own resources in ways which would enhance their prestige and visibility in their own and in neighboring communities, and thus potentially contribute also to their advancement in public life at Rome (Torelli, 1995: 200–01). However, significant numbers of communities in some regions, in the mountainous center and south of the peninsula in particular, did not finally acquire municipal status until the reign of Augustus, and this may be one reason, we might suspect, why the pattern of advancement of local elites into the Senate varied so significantly from region to region (Bispham, 2007: 409). The new political structure provided a mechanism by which the local elites were able to maintain their authority locally, and it also enabled them to convey to Rome the collective view of their towns on issues of the day (Gabba, 1994: 123–32; Bispham, 2007: 425–27). Leading individuals could similarly use their own networks of friendship at Rome to exert influence on behalf of the community, as we can see happening in the case of Volaterrae, where the political connections of the Caecina family with Cicero and others were able to ward off the threat of colonial settlement from the town (Terrenato, 1998: 106–09). Contacts of hospitality and marriage continued to develop between Italian and Roman elites as the distinctions between the two increasingly became elided (Wiseman, 1971: 33–64). As political tensions led to the collapse of the Republican system, however, friendships and family relations led to individuals and communities having to choose one side or another in a civil war (Bispham, 2007: 428–29).

More generally, the Civil Wars had a major impact on the towns of Italy and their elites: disaster for some brought benefits for others, locally as well as at Rome. Where a colony of veterans was established in a town – whether by Sulla, Caesar, the triumvirs, or Augustus – this would inevitably be extremely disruptive. We know from Cicero that at Pompeii, where a Sullan colony had been established in 80 BC, there were ongoing tensions between the colonists and the indigenous inhabitants in relation to local politics (*In Defense of Sulla*: 60–61, with Berry, 1996: 254–56). In some places, tensions persisted for generations: at Arretium, where another colony of Sullan veterans had been founded, and more settlers were established by Julius Caesar, the indigenous population (*Arretini veteres*), the Sullans (*Arretini fidentiores*), and Caesar's veterans (*Arretini Iulienses*) were all separately identifiable even in the first century AD (Pliny the Elder, *Natural History*: 3.52 with Keppie, 1983: 54, 102). The ruling class would be affected too, with many landowners in the city's territory losing their property and their status, while incomers took their properties. It was customary in the late Republic for demobilized legions to be settled together as a whole, which meant that ex-tribunes and ex-centurions would accompany the rank-and-file veterans. These would be wealthier than the ordinary soldiers, and their rank enabled them to take on positions of authority in the civilian context. Tribunes, centurions, and even in some cases former legionaries are found serving as magistrates or local senators in the late first century BC (Keppie, 1983: 107–09).

The Social and Civil Wars can thus be seen to have had a significant impact on the elites of Italy, both at the local level, where communities were physically transformed by building projects associated with their new status as municipalities of Roman citizens, and by the arrival of large numbers of veterans in the newly founded colonies, but also at Rome, where the ruthless, the well-connected, or the fortunate among the Italian elites began to enter the ruling class in significant numbers.

24.4   The Italian Elites Under the Principate

In the Julio-Claudian period the Italian aristocracies maintained and extended this involvement at the center of the developing imperial elite (Patterson, 2006a: 191–96). The process of turnover in the Senate was an ongoing one, as was inevitable, given the generally low life expectancy in the Roman world (estimated to be of the order of 20–30 years at birth) and the nature of Roman inheritance law, which meant that children inherited wealth equally. This had the effect of discouraging affluent individuals from having large families, in case their resources were so subdivided as to diminish the family's senatorial status. The cost of the senatorial lifestyle was itself considerable, and the risk of incurring imperial displeasure made public life at Rome under the Principate a particularly risky business. Significant numbers of Italians continued to enter the Senate under the Julio-Claudians: it has been estimated that even during the reign of Vespasian over 80 percent of senators whose origin is known came from the peninsula. Thereafter, however, senators began to be drawn increasingly from the provinces, from the western half of the empire in the first instance (Hopkins, 1983: 200). Italians were predominant in the equestrian order, too, which became increasingly important because of the emperors' willingness to deploy *equites* in key administrative positions both at Rome and in the provinces. Out of the 547 equestrians from the Julio-Claudian period whose origin is known, 366 came from Italy (Demougin, 1988: 191). L. Aelius Seianus, Tiberius's notorious praetorian prefect, was born at Volsinii, so Tacitus disparagingly referred to him as a "municipal adulterer," despite the evident distinction of his family (Tacitus, *Annals*: 4.3 with Demougin, 1992: 234–37). His replacement as praetorian prefect, Q. Naevius Cordus Sutorius Macro, was likewise an Italian, from Alba Fucens (Demougin, 1992: 276–77).

At the local level, the elites continued to take the leading role in the running of the cities: after Augustus, the "municipal voids" where urban centers had previously been lacking had now been filled, and the whole of Italy was under the control of cities, with local aristocrats acting as magistrates and councillors, in a more-or-less standardized system which in broad terms reflected the constitution of republican Rome (Abbott and Johnson, 1926: 56–68). The *curia* or *ordo* (local senate) was composed of *decuriones* (councillors) who were drawn from the local landholding class. Members had to be residents of the town, have a specified level of wealth and have reached a specified age: they entered the local senate either by virtue of being elected to a specific magistracy, or by being "adlected," individually chosen to join that body. The size of the local senate, and the property qualification required for an individual to join it, varied according to the size and wealth of the community. At Tarentum after the Social War, the required wealth was defined in terms of numbers of roof-tiles on the councillor's house, but more commonly it was expressed as a cash sum (*Lex Tarentina*: 26–29 with Crawford, 1996: 310). Alongside the *curia*, the administration of the town was entrusted to a group of magistrates elected by popular vote, typically consisting of *IIviri* and aediles, or *IIIIviri*; every five years, *quinquennales* would be appointed, whose role, like that of the censors at Rome, was to choose new members of the *curia*, though given the importance of maintaining their number, it seems likely that vacancies would be filled more rapidly than that if necessary (Patterson, 2006a: 184–91).

Besides their responsibility for governing their community and maintaining order in its territory, the municipal elites also had a key role in financing their city. The towns had limited regular sources of income, and hence looked directly to the elites for assistance. Newly elected magistrates were expected to contribute a cash sum to the town on taking office, which would characteristically be spent on holding games, but it was also hoped that in due course they might also support their towns with benefactions, whether in the form of a public building project, a banquet for the town's population (or some of them) or a distribution of food or money. The well-being of the local elite, and its commitment to the local community, was thus of fundamental importance to the well-being of the town, and the status of the local elites was consequently reinforced by the public display of privilege, whether in the form of the special seats allocated for councillors at the theatre or at the games, the lavish provision made for them at public banquets, or the special dress they wore on formal occasions (Abbott and Johnson, 1926: 66; Garnsey, 1970: 243–44).

The local *curiae* had, however, the same problem of turnover of membership as the Roman Senate. Indeed they occupied a pivotal position in the complex nexus of upward and downward mobility which characterized Roman society in the early Principate. Although the risk of upsetting the emperor was less substantial in an Italian town than at Rome, the local councils, like the Roman Senate, needed to recruit new blood in order to fill the gaps left by those who had died, or whose family resources were no longer sufficient to finance their service on the local *curia*, and therefore dropped out of local politics. But there was the additional problem that ambitious and well-connected men in the local councils might be promoted upwards, to join the equestrian order and eventually the Senate. Some men of municipal background, such as Vespasian, whose family came from Reate, might even reach the imperial throne (Levick, 1999: 4–13); his rival Otho, whose family came from Ferentium, claimed descent from Etruscan kings (Suetonius, *Life of Otho*: 1.1). As under the Republic, and under Augustus, there are significant variations identifiable between different regions of Italy in terms of the pace of promotion of local elites, depending on issues such as the resources, location, and status of their home towns. The patronage of an emperor was potentially of particular significance: for example, the support given by Capua to Vitellius during the civil war of AD 69 seems to have been detrimental to the promotion of notable families from that city under the Flavians; the city of Puteoli, which had a long-standing rivalry with Capua, had by contrast supported Vespasian (Tacitus, *Histories*: 3.57 with Cébeillac-Gervasoni, 1982: 66–67). Even in this period, rivalries between neighboring cities were still of consequence. At least one family from Sabine territory appears to have benefited from the support of that Sabine emperor: Sex. Vettulenus Cerealis and his brother from Reate both reached the consulship in the AD 70s (Torelli, 1982: 194–95).

From many points of view, the promotion of members of the ruling class to the Roman Senate or equestrian order could be seen as a good thing for their home towns: such men were by definition wealthy and successful, and reaching the highest political levels brought them closer to the central structures of power, which was an undoubted benefit in a society so reliant on patronage as that of Roman Italy. Many honorary inscriptions express the gratitude of local communities to senators of local origin, such as the (anonymous) man from Beneventum who was touchingly thanked for the "exceptional affection he displayed towards his *patria* and its citizens" (*CIL* 9.1592 = *ILS* 1126 with Patterson, 2006a: 208). Some senators were undoubtedly generous towards towns with which they had close connections: the younger Pliny, for example, provided Comum with a library, baths, and an alimentary scheme for the maintenance of poor children (Duncan-Jones, 1982: 27–31). There was always a risk, however, that senators' new responsibilities on a broader stage might divert their attention from their home towns, and some anxiety must have been felt when senators of provincial origin began to acquire landholdings in Italy, as instructed by the emperors Trajan and Marcus Aurelius (Pliny the Younger, *Letters*: 6.9; Augustan History, *Marcus Aurelius*: 11.8).

The cities of Italy were thus potentially affected by both the upward and the downward mobility of their curial class, and needed constantly to look for replacements. Younger members of the families of existing *decuriones* were an obvious source of potential recruits; at Canusium, as we know from the "album" listing members of the local elite in AD 223, these were categorized as *praetextati* and given special privileges (Salway, 2000: 126–27). New *decuriones* might also be recruited from other free landowners in the territory, such as military veterans who had settled in the city's territory, perhaps after service in the praetorian guard. The towns frequently needed to look beyond these groups, though. Sons of freedmen who, unlike their fathers, were allowed to enter the *ordo*, were another potential source of recruits, especially in locations where commercial activities allowed resources to be acquired beyond the immediate territory of the city. For example, N. Popidius Celsinus was adlected into the

Figure 24.3 Rock-cut monument in honor of A. Quinctilius Priscus at Ferentinum. Photograph: J.R. Patterson.

council at Pompeii even though aged only six, following the rebuilding of the Temple of Isis by his father, a freedman (*CIL* 10.846 = *ILS* 6367; Patterson, 2006a: 221–41).

Another possible strategy was to seek to ensure the loyalty of those with connections to the city by granting them honorific statuses, or by seeking the support of influential outsiders. Actual or potential benefactors might formally be designated as patrons of the community: the album of Canusium lists no fewer than 39 patrons of equestrian or senatorial rank (Salway, 2000: 133–48). One such example is Pliny the Younger, who was appointed patron of the town of Tifernum Tiberinum on inheriting his uncle's estates there, even though he was still very young. As the town must have hoped, he expressed his gratitude for the honor by building a temple there (Pliny the Younger, *Letters*: 4.1; Nicols, 1980). Another is A. Quinctilius Priscus, who in the early second century AD held municipal magistracies at Ferentinum, was honored with a statue in the forum, and in return for the honor set up a foundation to finance an annual distribution of cakes and wine to citizens and *decuriones* on his birthday. The monument set up to commemorate this exchange of honors and benefactions survives, inscribed on a rock-face just outside the city walls (see Figure 24.3); a statue-base was also found nearby designating Quinctilius as *patronus municipii* (*CIL* 10.5852; 5853 = *ILS* 6271 with Lomas, 1996: 233–34; Pasqualini, 1992).

24.5   Conclusion

The degree to which communities succeeded in reinforcing their curial class, and gaining the support of senators and *equites*, clearly varied from place to place, but the scale of the efforts devoted to the task is very striking, and highlights the perceived importance of civic identity and institutions in Roman Italy (also reflected in the frequent appearance in the historical record of local antagonisms). The emperors, too, were aware of the central role of the municipal elites in the running of the Empire, and by the time of Hadrian *decuriones*, now subsumed in the superior social category of *honestiores*, had acquired significant legal privileges, including exemption from capital or other harsh punishments (Garnsey, 1970: 154–62 and 242–45). Behind these measures lay a concern to ensure that men could be found to serve their cities and take on the responsibilities of councillors or magistrates. In the long term, however, "local elites" increasingly became "regional elites": as, characteristically in oligarchic societies, wealth became concentrated in fewer hands, as a result of intermarriage, adoption, and inheritance within the landed aristocracy. The property portfolios of the wealthy now extended beyond individual urban territories, across Italy and even beyond. At the same time, new routes to social advancement – in the army, increasingly professionalized in the third century AD, in the growing imperial bureaucracy of late antiquity, and ultimately the Church – provided new means of access to power and influence, which tended to marginalize the cities of Italy.

FURTHER READING

A great deal has been written about the local elites of Italy, and the references deployed in this chapter are inevitably selective, and particularly highlight work published in English. For the mobility of the Italian elites from the Republican period up to Augustus, Wiseman's classic study (1971) remains fundamental; Hopkins (1983) sketches out the broader processes behind patterns of upward and downward mobility within the senatorial elite. The articles in the *Epigrafia e ordine senatorio* volumes (e.g. Torelli 1982) provide a wealth of material on the senatorial elite and the origins of its members, which are complemented by Demougin (1988) and (1992) for the equestrian order. On the "victory of the

Italians," see the memorably hostile comments of Syme (1939). Chapter 3 of Patterson (2006a) explores in more detail the patterns of elite mobility under the Principate discussed here.

Important recent publications dealing with the Italian elites under the Republic include Fronda (2010), looking at the varied reactions of the allied elites of southern Italy to Hannibal's victory at Cannae; Bispham (2007), with a wealth of analysis and comment on the history of Italy from the second century BC to Augustus, focusing in particular on the issue of municipalization; and Farney (2007), on the use of ethnic identity in the politics of the late Republic and early Principate. Pfeilschifter (2007) highlights the role of military service in the Roman-led army in the development of allied solidarity before the Social War; Wallace-Hadrill (2008) looks at various aspects of cultural change in this period, and the central role in this process played by the Italian elites.

REFERENCES

Abbott, F.F. and Johnson, A.C. 1926. *Municipal Administration in the Roman Empire*. Princeton: Princeton University Press.

Badian, E. 1958. *Foreign Clientelae, 264–70 BC*. Oxford: Clarendon Press.

Badian, E. 1990. "The consuls, 179–49 BC." *Chiron* 20: 371–413.

Bernabei, F. 1895. "Trasacco: di una rarissima 'tessera hospitalis' con iscrizione latina." *Notizie degli scavi di antichità*: 85–93.

Berry, D.H. 1996. *Cicero Pro P. Sulla Oratio*. Cambridge: Cambridge Classical Texts and Commentaries 30: Cambridge University Press.

Bispham, E.H. 2007. *From Asculum to Actium: the municipalization of Italy from the Social War to Augustus*. Oxford: Oxford University Press.

Brunt, P.A. 1988. "Italian aims at the time of the Social War." In *The Fall of the Roman Republic and Related Essays*, 93–143. Oxford: Clarendon Press.

Cébeillac-Gervasoni, M. 1982. "Ascesa al senato e rapporti con i territori d'origine. Italia: regio I (Campania: la zona di Capua e Cales)." In *Atti del colloquio internazionale AIEGL su Epigrafia e Ordine Senatorio (Roma, 14–20 maggio 1981)*, vol. 2, 59–99. Rome: Edizioni di storia e letteratura.

Crawford, M.H., ed. 1996. *Roman Statutes*. 2 vols. London: Institute of Classical Studies/BICS Supplement 64.

Crawford, M.H., ed. 2011. *Imagines Italicae: a corpus of Italic Inscriptions*. London: BICS Supplement 110.

D'Arms, J.H. 1984. "Upper-class attitudes towards *viri municipales* and their towns in the early Roman Empire." *Athenaeum* 62: 440–67.

Demougin, S. 1988. *L'ordre équestre sous les Julio-Claudiens*. Rome: Collection de l'École française de Rome 108.

Demougin, S. 1992. *Prosopographie des chevaliers romains julio-claudiens (43 av. J.-C.– 70 ap. J.-C.)*. Rome: Collection de l'École française de Rome 153.

Dench, E. 1995. *From Barbarians to New Men. Greek, Roman and modern perceptions of peoples from the central Apennines*. Oxford: Clarendon Press.

Duncan-Jones, R. 1982 (2nd edn). *The Economy of the Roman Empire: quantitative studies*. Cambridge: Cambridge University Press.

Dyck, A.R., ed. 2010. *Cicero, Pro Sexto Roscio*. Cambridge: Cambridge University Press.

Farney, G. 2007. *Ethnic Identity and Aristocratic Competition in Republican Rome*. Cambridge: Cambridge University Press.

Flower, H.I. 1996. *Ancestor Masks and Aristocratic Power in Roman Culture*. Oxford: Clarendon Press.

Frederiksen, M. 1984. *Campania*, ed. N. Purcell. London: British School at Rome.

Fronda, M. 2010. *Between Rome and Carthage. Southern Italy during the Second Punic War*. Cambridge: Cambridge University Press.

Gabba, E., ed. 1994. *Italia Romana*. Como: Edizioni New Press.

Garnsey, P. 1970. *Social Status and Legal Privilege in the Roman Empire*. Oxford: Oxford University Press.

Harris, W.V. 1971. *Rome in Etruria and Umbria*. Oxford: Clarendon Press.

Hopkins, K. 1983. *Death and Renewal.* Cambridge: Cambridge University Press.

Keppie, L.J.F. 1983. *Colonisation and Veteran Settlement in Italy, 47–14 B.C.* London: British School at Rome.

Levick, B. 1999. *Vespasian.* London: Routledge.

Lomas, K. 1993. *Rome and the Western Greeks, 350 BC – AD 200. Conquest and acculturation in south Italy.* London: Routledge.

Lomas, K. 1996. *Roman Italy, 338 BC – AD 200. A sourcebook.* London: UCL Press.

Lomas, K. 2004. "A Volscian Mafia? Cicero and his Italian clients in the forensic speeches." In *Cicero the Advocate*, eds J. Powell and J. Paterson, 97–116. Oxford: Oxford University Press.

Millar, F. 1986. "Italy and the Roman Empire: Augustus to Constantine." *Phoenix* 40: 295–318.

Mouritsen, H. 1998. *Italian Unification. A study in ancient and modern historiography.* London: *BICS Supplement* 70.

Mouritsen, H. 2001. Plebs *and Politics in the Late Roman Republic.* Cambridge: Cambridge University Press.

Nicols, J. 1980. "Pliny and the patronage of communities." *Hermes* 108: 365–85.

Oakley, S.P. 1998. *A Commentary on Livy, Books VI–X. Volume II: Books VII-VIII.* Oxford: Clarendon Press.

Pasqualini, A. 1992. "Sul testo dell'iscrizione rupestre di Ferentino (*CIL* X 5853)." In Rupes loquentes. *Atti del convegno internazionale di studio sulle iscrizioni rupestri di età romana in Italia*, ed. L. Gasperini, 385–405. Rome: Istituto italiano per la storia antica.

Patterson, J.R. 1993. "Military organization and social change in the later Roman Republic." In *War and Society in the Roman World*, eds J. Rich and G. Shipley, 92–112. London: Routledge.

Patterson, J.R. 2006a. *Landscapes and Cities. Rural settlement and civic transformation in early imperial Italy.* Oxford: Oxford University Press.

Patterson, J.R. 2006b. "The relationship of the Italian ruling classes with Rome: friendship, family relations and their consequences." In *Herrschaft ohne Integration? Rom und Italien in republikanischer Zeit*, eds M. Jehne and R. Pfeilschifter, 139–53. Frankfurt am Main: Verlag Antike.

Patterson, J.R. 2012. "Contact, co-operation, and conflict in pre-Social War Italy." In *Processes of Integration and Identity Formation in the Roman Republic*, ed. S.T. Roselaar, 215–26. Leiden: Brill.

Pfeilschifter, R. 2007. "The allies in the Republican army and the Romanisation of Italy." In *Roman by Integration: dimensions of group identity in material culture and text*, eds R. Roth and J. Keller, 27–42. Portsmouth, RI: *JRA* suppl. 66.

Rawson, E. 1985. *Intellectual Life in the Late Roman Republic.* Baltimore, Maryland: Johns Hopkins University Press.

Salway, B. 2000. "Prefects, *patroni* and *decuriones*: a new perspective on the album of Canusium." In *The Epigraphic Landscape of Roman Italy*, ed. A.E. Cooley, 115–71. London: *BICS Supplement* 73.

Syme. R. 1939. *The Roman Revolution.* Oxford: Oxford University Press.

Terrenato, N. 1998. "*Tam firmum municipium*: The Romanization of Volaterrae and its cultural implications." *Journal of Roman Studies* 88: 94–114.

Torelli, M. 1982 "Ascesa al senato e rapporti con i territori d'origine. Italia: regio IV (Samnium)." In *Atti del colloquio internazionale AIEGL su epigrafia e ordine senatorio (Roma, 14–20 maggio 1981)*, vol. 2, 165–99. Rome: Edizioni di storia e letteratura.

Torelli, M. 1995. *Studies in the Romanization of Roman Italy*, ed. and trans. by H. Fracchia and M. Gualtieri. Edmonton, Alberta: University of Alberta Press.

Torelli, M. 1999. Tota Italia. *Essays in the Cultural Formation of Roman Italy.* Oxford: Clarendon Press.

Wallace-Hadrill, A. 2008. *Rome's Cultural Revolution.* Cambridge: Cambridge University Press.

Wiseman, T.P. 1971. *New Men in the Roman Senate.* London: Oxford University Press.

CHAPTER 25

Sub-Elites

Jonathan S. Perry

25.1 Introduction

The final chapter of this volume poses significant challenges immediately from the outset: to what extent can we discern an identifiable, describable "sub-elite" in Roman Italy and, if such can be defined, how far down into that substratum should we drill for information? Alternatively, might it have been the case that just beneath the "frozen waste" (in John North's memorable phrase) of elite social and political maneuvering there existed only a formless mass of those who were fundamentally "not-elite," and thus not worthy of the attention of those privileged dwellers upon the surface? Perhaps one should revert to Sir Moses Finley's image, in *The World of Odysseus*, of "A deep horizontal cleavage [that] marked the world of the Homeric poems." "Above the line," he observed, "were the *aristoi*, literally the 'best people', the hereditary nobles who held most of the wealth and all the power, in peace as in war. Below were all the others, for whom there was no collective technical term, the multitude" (Finley, 1979: 53).

If, however, we were to examine those whose status seemed to place them *just below* the fault line that separated the elite from the multitude, a different dynamic might be detected. In recent decades, extensive work has been done on two sizable groups that are attested, principally in epigraphic sources, in both large and small cities throughout Roman Italy. Mining the inscribed references to *Augustales* and to members of *collegia* (associations of various types identified by these or similar terms), scholars have sifted out any traces of "social mobility" they contained. If these groups served as engines by which a non-elite person could launch himself toward — and occasionally breach — the ranks of a closed municipal aristocracy, then they would certainly seem worthy objects of study. However, as will become apparent throughout this chapter, the degree to which social mobility was desirable, feasible, and attainable by these groups may have been overstated in recent analyses.

Comprehensive new studies of the *Augustales*, particularly those by Duthoy (1978), Ostrow (1985), Abramenko (1993), and Demougin (1994), have underscored the significance of this "second *ordo*," lying just beneath the elite *ordo* of municipal decurions (Patterson 2006, 245). The political role of the *Augustales* should be seen within the scope of the "municipalization" of Roman Italy, identified by Bispham as a long process that culminated

A Companion to Roman Italy, First Edition. Edited by Alison E. Cooley.
© 2016 John Wiley & Sons, Ltd. Published 2016 by John Wiley & Sons, Ltd.

in the reign of Augustus (Bispham, 2007: 446). The "social potential" of the *Augustales*, identified by Abramenko (1993: 43) and others, also raises inevitable questions of status, and whether service of this sort was a means of social mobility, particularly for newly freed individuals aspiring to recast their ambitions into "social goods."

In the most insightful and thorough-going investigation of Roman Italy's cities now available (Patterson, 2006), John R. Patterson interpreted both the *Augustales* and collegial associations in this light, particularly in his chapter entitled "Social Mobility and the Cities of Italy". Introducing a section on the *Augustales* with the comment that, "The cities needed the continuing support of the upwardly mobile as well as the existing elites," Patterson argues that offices like these represented "a goal which could be reached not only by the sons of freedmen, but in many cases by the ex-slaves themselves" (Patterson, 2006: 242). Noting that some 80–90% of those attested as *Augustales* and *seviri Augustales* were freedmen, he concludes that "upwardly mobile ex-slaves" – and even some freeborn individuals – seem to have considered the status of *Augustalis* "worth acquiring" and that social mobility was "a significant dynamic force within civic life" (Patterson, 2006: 247, 251). Accordingly, Patterson sees in the gradual incorporation of freedmen into the civic aristocracy a reflection of the same "considerable degree of social mobility" uncovered by Mouritsen in the electoral behavior and shifting hierarchy of Pompeii. In Mouritsen's conceptualization, "[t]he heavy turnover in the Pompeian ordo" suggests that the Pompeian elite could "satisfy or conciliate the ambitions of underprivileged groups by external advancement," while still leaving "the underlying power structure intact" (Mouritsen, 1988: 118, 123; 1997).

Having established his points regarding sub-elite social mobility, Patterson goes on to examine "the complex network of institutions and offices that characterized the *collegia* of the Italian towns." By no means merely private, small-scale, and isolated communities, *collegia* "had an important role to play in the Italian cities of the high Empire," specifically by "supporting and helping to maintain their civic institutions" (Patterson, 2006: 252). Because the *collegia* have also received significant scholarly attention, at various points in previous centuries but especially in the past two decades (see Perry, 2006 and 2011, for these investigations and their wider intellectual contexts), the bulk of this chapter will focus upon their activities, at least as preserved in inscribed documents. While these texts raise many intriguing questions, I shall examine the assertion that they reveal a high degree of social mobility afforded to those sub-elite individuals aspiring to the higher reaches of municipal society. By investigating two smaller sets of *collegia* inscriptions from northern Italy, I also hope to illustrate some of the perils of interpreting the evidence in these terms, and then to propose an alternative reading for their function in civic society.

A key element of Patterson's argument concerns the "increasingly respectable" standing of *collegia*, which allowed their membership, like the *Augustales*, to be more "directly integrated into the civic life of the towns" over time (Patterson, 2006: 258). Thus, the *collegia* "acquired an established role in the city" and their presence – and their implicit endorsement of the civic order – contributed substantially to propping up existing institutions. While they could have fostered loyalties and crafted social hierarchies *outside* and independently of the city, they chose instead to make *the city* the focus of their social engagement. In short, their presence demonstrated "collective goodwill towards the town" and strengthened, rather than undermined, civic identity (Patterson, 2006: 267).

Scholarship since the 1990s has generally stressed the tangible benefits the *collegia* offered in terms of social mobility, particularly to those of recently freed status, as well as the attractive prospect of their engagement with a broader, more elevated, community. Patterson's earlier analyses (e.g. Patterson, 1994) accorded with those of Kathryn Lomas, who observed that the *collegia* and similar institutions "could confer status and give a stake in society to freedmen of less exalted status," providing "both a form of social cohesion and some essential services" (Lomas, 1996: 223–24). In several important studies, Onno van Nijf pointed to the tendency of *collegia* members to demonstrate their "solidarity with the essential values of the city," their loyalty to the existing order, and their sense of place within the civic hierarchy (van Nijf, 1997; 1999; 2003: 215–16).

The most recent studies of *collegia* have continued to reinforce the notion of the relative benefits of social mobility within a civic context. Nicolas Tran has offered an exhaustive study of "le rang social des *collegiati*," with sections entitled, for a few examples, "La dignité de *collegiatus*: l'acquisition de la respectabilité et du prestige" and "Le collège, l'aspiration au prestige et à une forme de mobilité sociale." Moreover, the ambitions of a *collegium* member could extend to intergenerational social mobility, and a few at least hazarded a savvy and determined social ascent up the various rungs of the civic ladder (Tran, 2006: 43, 61, 459). While she draws principal attention to the (surprisingly sparse) indications of the economic and professional aspects of collegial life, Francesca Diosono notes that the *collegia* were an expression of the "lower-middle classes" of the Roman world in respect to their will, their sense of possibilities and their culture (Diosono, 2007: 8). Finally, Koenraad Verboven has accentuated the essential identification of *collegiati* as "businessmen," for whom these institutions furnished "the platform and social capital they needed to acquire public esteem and in some cases to push through into the civic elites" (Verboven, 2007: 872).

The emphasis, therefore, has been on the positive, aspirational, and civic-minded aspects of collegial organization. But can one detect a more sinister visage behind this hopeful scenario? Might the elite have donned a mask of encouragement toward their more humble neighbors, only in order to restate and reinforce their dependence upon the elite – while also reminding them, perhaps subtly, of the *impossibility* of their actually rising into the ranks of the civic aristocracy? Two sets of inscriptions from Roman Italy, attesting associations of wool-workers and transport workers, demonstrate that this could have been the case. In other words, the repeated insistence upon the interests and concerns of elite patrons could have widened an effective distance, if not a "deep horizontal cleavage," between the "best" and the "multitude."

25.2   Working in Wool and Working for Status?: *Lanarii*

A survey of the mammoth collection of roughly 1500 *collegia* inscriptions compiled by J.-P. Waltzing (1895–1900) – now supplemented by Mennella and Apicella (2000) for Italy – yields seven inscriptions referring to associations of *lanarii*, or wool-workers. These texts are distributed among four cities in Augustan Regions VIII and X, specifically Altinum and Brixia (in the Veneto in the Roman era) and Brixellum and Regium Lepidum in Reggio Emilia. In his "Index Collegiorum" (4th volume), Waltzing noted that northern Italy was famous for wool, and Joan Frayn, drawing on scientific and literary sources, has concurred that "the ample plains of the Po basin and the lowlands of the Veneto offered the basis for highly productive sheep-farming and for the development of a complex textile industry" (Frayn, 1984: 25). However, Waltzing also found *lanarii* in Gaul and North Africa, together with two remarkable examples recovered in Asia Minor. At Ephesus and Thyatira there are honorary dedications by a συνεργασία τῶν λαναρίων (association of wool-workers) and by, simply, λανάριοι (wool-workers) (Waltzing, 1895–1900: III, 47, 60; IV, 95). Where one might expect to find the Greek equivalent ἐριουργοί, there is instead a transliteration from the Latin *lanarius*. This perhaps indicates a transferal of Italian personnel, together with their attendant professional terminology to the province of Asia. This, at least, seemed likely to

Carl Curtius, in the original publication of the Ephesian inscription in 1873. While the word is also known in Greek in scholiasts and Byzantine writings, Curtius felt confident in identifying them as "an association of wool-workers" (Curtius, 1873: 34).

A difficulty arises, however, when one asks what, precisely, is indicated by the seemingly simple term *lanarius/lanarii*. While one might conclude with Waltzing that they were "ouvriers en laine," at what stage of production should we place them? Curtius compared similar groups of *lanarii* in Italy, observing that some carry a more precise nomenclature, perhaps equivalent to "die Krempler" (carders), but *also* to "die Wollhändler" (merchants or dealers in wool) (Curtius, 1873: 34). Waltzing hedges this a bit by translating the Thyatira inscription with "wool-carders" while noting that the Ephesus dedication must refer to "the corporation of wool-merchants (carders)"(Waltzing, 1895–1900: IV, 60, 47). The *Dizionario Epigrafico* comments merely that "they refer in general to wool-work" and then goes on to explore the "two following types of small manufacturers" (*lanarii carminatores/pectinarii* and *lanarii coactores*) that were known at that time (De Ruggiero and Mazzarino, 1946: 361). H. von Petrikovits has observed that, because Latin terms do not always distinguish "producers" and "salesmen" in a particular industry, a given group of *lanarii* could have played either role (von Petrikovits, 1981: 69, 100) and Suzanne Dixon explains more succinctly, "The word tells us only that they did something with wool" (Dixon, 2000–01: 9).

Dixon and L.L. Lovén (1998) noted this obstacle but then went on to "count," or at least to account for the possibility of, female workers in wool production and/or the wool trade (challenging Moeller, 1969). Nevertheless, the class issues involved are at least as significant as gender considerations. The basic impression given in the literature to date is that the manufacture of woolen clothing would have been the preserve of the more "humble" and "modest" elements of Italian society. In her study of "lower class" occupations, Mima Maxey commented, "Another group of occupations in which we find humbler folk engaged is centered about clothing" (Maxey, 1938: 31–32). While the textile industry may have been, in Dennis Kehoe's valuation, "a basic component of the economic life of many ancient cities," the fundamental unit of production in the industry was small-scale and within the reach of many civic entrepreneurs. "The major capital outlay for this industry, the purchase of a loom, was relatively modest, and it seems likely that many weaving establishments consisted of little more than a space within a private house" (Kehoe, 2007: 564–65). Peter Garnsey also drew attention to the small-scale nature of this industry, hypothesizing that "independent freedmen" could have been involved in the manufacture of textiles more often than is generally supposed, since self-employed artisans could have employed small teams of craftsmen, of either freed or enslaved status. However, he adds, this could have been a means of accumulating wealth for a freed "investor." In short, he asks, "are those who ran or controlled a profitable business to be seen as mainly foremen and agents, or independent entrepreneurs?" (Garnsey, 1998: 146–47).

The degree to which *lanarii* were able to realize a profit from their industry is a crucial consideration, especially in terms of the space allowed for their social ambitions. "Spaces" may be a more apposite beginning point, since one of the best known of the *lanarii* inscriptions, from Brixellum, reads, *D(is) M(anibus). Haec loca sunt lanariorum carminator(um) sodalici(i) quae faciunt in agro p(edes) C ad viam p(edes) LV* ("To the gods of the dead. These are the plots that are used by the *sodalicium* of the *lanarii carminatores...*") (*CIL* 11.1031). The text has normally been interpreted as a marker of a common graveyard or "cemetery" (e.g. Waltzing, 1895–1900: I, 285–86; Patterson, 2006: 254) of a group of *lanarii carminatores*, specifically described as a *sodalicium*, demarcated within certain dimensions, and further subdivided (?) into individual burial plots. Their identification explicitly as *sodales* – which can be replicated in another *lanarii* inscription discovered at Brixia (see later in this chapter) – may suggest that they were "membri di un sodalizio di tipo religioso" (Garzetti, 1973: 57).

Nevertheless, the seemingly "professional" marker "*carminatores*" in the text has drawn the most comment. Many stages of the process of wool production in Roman Italy are known from a wide range of literary sources, primarily Varro and Pliny, and these have been helpfully detailed by Frayn and by W.O. Moeller in his study of the wool industry of Pompeii (Moeller, 1976). After its initial washing and before it can be spun, raw wool must have its "knots, tangles and residual impurities such as burrs removed and it had to be worked into a fluffy state by separating the fibers" (Moeller, 1976: 14–15). In modern times this was performed with a carding instrument, one that was unavailable in antiquity. Thus, it is perhaps inappropriate to label the *carminatores* "carders", and "wool-combers" might be a more accurate rendering (Frayn, 1984L: 159, nos 10 and 11). Some of the same sense clings to the term *pectinarii*, which is also mentioned in inscriptions (see later in this chapter) and sometimes jointly with *lanarii*. Several Roman wool-combs, made of iron and called *pectines*, have been recovered, and a painting from the shop of a Pompeian felter seems to depict three *pectinarii* seated behind workbenches (Moeller, 1976: 15).

While the specific trade performed here may seem labor-intensive and fundamentally "low," I would caution that we risk importing a class bias into our consideration of the evidence. Did this group band together to purchase a common cemetery because they feared that they were, individually, too poor to afford one on their own? Alternatively, these may have been highly specialized workers, proud not to be merely unspecified "*lanarii*" and even more proud of the creation of their quasi-religious "*sodalicium*." Might they, therefore, have purchased desirable property for their graveyard, commemorating for all time the important role they played in civic life?

Yet another explanation can be adduced by comparing another *lanarii* inscription discovered in 1971, to the north-east of Altinum in a necropolis along the *via Annia*. (The text is now Mennella–Apicella #3 (2000: 2).) Dating to the first half of the first century AD, the stone, described by Ezio Buchi as "a distinct inscription" (and accompanied by a clear photograph to prove the point) records a funerary dedication of burial property by a freedman for himself, his wife, and *colleg(iatis) gentilib(us) lanar(iorum) purg(atorum)*. The dimensions of the plot (45 × 18 feet) are listed, together with the note that he has performed this task in his lifetime (*vivus*). Buchi concludes that allowance is made here for "the hangers-on, perhaps freedmen or slaves" of a *collegium* of *lanarii purgatores*, who would seem to have performed specialized work in the "cleaning up and the purification of the raw product" (Buchi, 1987: 137). Such an interpretation would accord with other details concerning the washing or more likely the "washings" of wool, from its initial shearing to the ministrations of *lanilutores* and *polientes* among other groups known from literary sources (Frayn, 1984: 148–49; Moeller, 1976: 74–75).

The living dedicator here describes himself as a freedman, and his wife was likely, though not explicitly, a freedwoman. But need this inscription prove that he "cared for" or had even been "a member of" the group? I would argue that one cannot be as confident as Buchi was, in naming the recipients of the burial plot (though even their receipt of the arrangements is merely a supposition) "perhaps freedmen or slaves." Indeed, this text may furnish small evidence of Garnsey's hypothetical scenario of the independent freedman entrepreneur. Buchi reminds us that, regardless of how low-level this particular employment might seem, the dedicator must have reached a level of economic well-being (Buchi, 1987: 138). Did the man hire the members of this *collegium* to perform a service and then feel obliged to bury them within his plot? Or was he treating them as he would his other dependents, that is, virtually as members of his own enslaved household? One might compare here another collegial inscription from Altinum, a dedication of "gardens with a building, adjoining his tomb" to a local *collegium centonariorum*. There were terms attached to this endowment: roses and other provisions from the yield of the gardens should be rendered to the dedicator and to his patron (*CIL* 5.2176). Accordingly, it may have been the case that the *lanarii* dedication, and its apparent generosity, was actually a subtle means of reinforcing the dependence of the workers upon a higher-status individual.

Four of the seven *lanarii* inscriptions originated in Brixia, and these also seem to contain further markers of specialized labor, i.e. *lanarii carminatores, lanarii coatores* [*sic*: probably an error for *coactores*] and *lanarii pectinarii*. First published in *Notizie degli scavi* in 1925, a fragmentary text recovered in the outskirts of Brixia reads: *M. Domitio Fi[rm]o lana[r(ii) carmi]nator(es) so[dal]es* (Patroni, 1925: 342–43, now Mennella–Apicella #18 (2000: 35)). Because the center of the text has been obliterated by a round hole and the "*carminatores*" is a restoration, though, comparisons were immediately made to the Brixellum document which also referred to a *sodalicium*.

The *lanarii coatores* of Brixia made at least two dedications, and here again the details are frustratingly inadequate. *CIL* 5.4504 records an offering, *d(e) p(ecunia) s(ua)* ("at their own expense"), by the *lanari(i) coatores* in honor of C. Cominius Successor, and the following published text, *CIL* 5.4505, acknowledges the burial site of L. Cornelius Januarius, who lived 17 years, and of his father, L. Cornelius Primio (whose age at death is not specified), with a record that the deed was performed by the *lanari(i) coator(es)*. In both cases, the group would appear to have made a decision collectively and expended resources in order to make one or more dedications. Of course, we do not know for what reasons the dedications were made, or what sort of call either Cominius or the Cornelii might have had upon the *coatores'* purse. We cannot assume that either was himself a member, or even a patron, of the organization, but neither is there any indication that the group is rendered more socially mobile as a result of their actions.

Lanarii coactores would presumably have used wool and other animal fibers in a felting enterprise (or merely supervised its being done?). Moeller explains that, "To felt is *cogere* from the fact that the felter — *coactor* or *coactiliarius* — forced the wool together with his hands" (Moeller, 1976: 27). The resulting mass of fibers, held together with a gluey or greasy binding agent, would have made a strong material that was, as today, useful for making hats, boots, overcoats, and so on. *Coactiliarii* played a prominent role in Pompeian political maneuvering, and Moeller devotes substantial attention to their activities (1976: 27, 80–81, 100). Throughout the book Moeller notes that, given the self-advertisement of local fullers – and the many indications of other prominent aristocrats in the wool trade – there were, at least at Pompeii, "no social or political disabilities attached to engaging in industry" (Moeller, 1976: 106–07). While the physical process of felting might *seem* to belong to those on the lower rungs of the social ladder, we cannot discern from the inscriptions themselves whether this was the case. More fundamentally, we cannot know for certain whether the *coactores* were the laborers themselves or the entrepreneurs, owners, or beneficiaries of the labor of others.

The final *lanarii* inscription from Brixia is a funerary dedication by the *lanari(i) pectinar(ii) sodales* in honor of Acceptus, "the slave of Chia" (*CIL* 5.4501). Yet again, the designation *sodales* may indicate a religious resonance to this collegial organization, at least in the context of its funerary services, and *pectinarii* would seem, as mentioned earlier in this chapter, to link the membership to the specialized trade of wool combing. Frayn (1984: 150) observes that "the *lanarius pectinarius* [*sic*: she appears to assume that Acceptus was a member of the *sodales*?] of *CIL* 5.4501 must surely be a wool-worker who uses a comb", and she compares a *faber pectinarius* in Pola (*CIL* 5.98), whose inscribed monument appears to contain actual images of wool-combs. Moreover, there is another mention of a self-styled *pectinarius* at Brixia from a tombstone discovered there in 1970. In this text, a L. Cornelius Labeo, who marks himself as freeborn, makes provision while still alive for himself, his wife Antistia Tertia, who is also freeborn, and perhaps for some other individuals (the stone seems to break off after mentioning another female name). In the original publication of the text, A. Albertini linked this inscription with other references to the *lanarii* of Brixia (Albertini, 1971: 133–38).

Reinforcing the notion that this wider region was strongly identified with wool-production and wool-finishing, the occupational marker *pectinarius* alone appears on several tombstones, including both a *pectinator* and a *pectinarius* in Ateste (*CIL* 5.2538 and 5.2543) and a *refector pectinar(ius)* in Hasta (*CIL* 5.7569). The latter text seems to preserve an image of the deceased at work, as the commentary in *CIL* refers to an image, placed above the text, of a man sitting at a table "holding a mallet or some similar item in his right hand" and another unidentified object (perhaps a *pecten?*) in his left. The fact that he is freeborn may also indicate a higher status for this craft than has otherwise been supposed. Jones (1960: 190) was, thus, simply mistaken in claiming that, "No one calls himself a carder or spinner on his tombstone, or registers himself as such in the census, and no guilds of carders or spinners are known." He noted two "apparent exceptions" to this rule, the *lanarii carminatores* of Brixellum and the *lanarii pectinarii* of Brixia, but he suspected "that these did not card raw wool, but teased woven fabrics." Jones was determined to demonstrate that spinning was mainly done, "as today in the Nearer East", by women in their homes "in their spare time." However, he ignored much relevant evidence that indicates a more organized, male-centered, and potentially higher-status occupation than might be assumed.

For one example of this sort of assumption, when describing his newly discovered document in which a *pectinarius* seems unashamed of his profession, Albertini suggests that the *lanarii* in the area were of humble status whether technically freeborn, freed, or enslaved; in his judgment, the *pectinarii* must have been only "only a little more prosperous" than other artisans in general (Albertini, 1971: 138–40). If, however, the *pectinarii* at Brixia were not themselves enslaved, and perhaps not even *liberti*, why would they have facilitated the burial of a slave? Frayn may be correct in assuming that Acceptus was a member of the *sodales*, but an alternative explanation would be that organizations of this sort only "buried down" the social ladder. In other words, while they dedicated inscriptions of praise to individuals of a *higher* status than themselves, they may characteristically have preferred to fund the burial only of those of *lower* status, perhaps as an expression of the dependence of the deceased. By this interpretation, Acceptus may have been hired out by his mistress for specialized service to the *pectinarii,* and then upon his death they felt obliged to acknowledge that connection – while respectfully naming the actual owner of the slave in the offering.

Some of this subtle gradation of status seems apparent in another inscription naming *lanari(i) pect(inarii) et carmin(atores)*, a first-century AD text discovered at Regium Lepidum and published in 1940 (and now Mennella–Apicella 2000: 62, #73). The stone records the gratitude of this group to C. Pomponius Felix, a freedman and *sevir Augustalis Claudialis,* for the terms of his testament, arranging for gifts of clothing and funeral expenses for those lacking sufficient means. Another Pomponius is known from inscriptional evidence at Regium Lepidum, though this man was freeborn, a military tribune in the 10th Legion and had served as local aedile and *duumvir,* among other offices (*CIL* 11.969). Accordingly, it appears that a member of the civic elite has made provision for the more impoverished members of this order, in certain specific respects, including clothing and burial. In the original publication of the text, Aurigemma claimed that Pomponius here aimed "to benefit with his will the members of a corporation of which he had evidently been a part" (Aurigemma, 1940: 269).

Comparing the *lanarii purgatores* inscription from Altinum, I would suggest there is a very different dynamic at work here. Pomponius may be demonstrating, with his largesse, his more elevated status vis-à-vis the wool-combers. The *lanarii* were expected to acknowledge the gift, but this may be nothing more than an acknowledgment of their dependence upon a local aristocrat, even one who had himself been freed at some earlier point in his lifetime. Following the logic that one makes burial provision only for those who are in a position of dependence, the testament may have been a reinforcement of the hierarchical order to be found in the town when the *sevir* and the *lanarii* were all alive.

25.3 Getting from Point A to Point B and Getting Ahead?: *Muliones* and *Iumentarii*

The hierarchical order of the town of Regium Lepidum also contained a group of *muliones*, muleteers or mule-drivers, who appear to have been acting in a funerary capacity alongside a family member of the deceased. Another wide range of inscriptions attests the presence and activities of transport workers – primarily *muliones, asinarii,* and *iumentarii* – in the cities of northern Italy. While one may presume, with M. Maxey (1938: 67), that transportation workers plied a "group of occupations that required the service of humbler men," I hope to demonstrate that the precise social standing of these individuals is difficult to determine and that, as a result, it is also difficult to measure how much social mobility their association afforded them vis-à-vis the town's "less humble" classes.

CIL 11.962 records the delineation of a burial plot of 15 × 12 feet by Magia Macella, a freeborn woman, for herself and her dependents. The beneficiaries of the plot also included L. Magius Rufio, P. Magius Cato (presumably her father and uncle, since they share filiation) and Vettia, her freeborn mother. Between the mention of the two men and the mother can be read, *muliones hic.* This would appear to indicate that the *muliones* were a professional association, acting in this capacity as a burial society in conjunction with a living relative of the deceased. This, at least, was Waltzing's interpretation of the text, who followed earlier commentators in identifying these *muliones* as a *collegium salutare* or burial society (Waltzing, 1895–1900: IV, 100 and I, 262). If this is correct, it suggests that the "*muliones* here" (?) in Regium agreed to contribute to the burial of the two freeborn men, perhaps with their relative's assistance; notice that there is no indication that the men were members of the organization, nor that they were its patrons.

The phenomenon of *muliones* acting in a funerary capacity can be detected in at least three other texts, and these strengthen the interpretation of collegial involvement in commemorating the dead. Among the epitaphs in a cemetery of the *officiales* of Carthage's procurator was found a commemoration of an imperial slave called Felix, who died aged 18. As published in *Revue archéologique* in 1898, the inscription labels Felix a *cursor* and notes that the burial has been performed by a *colleg(ium) mulion(um) ob merit(a)* (Delattre, 1898: 348 #43). The conjunction of *cursor* and *muliones* suggests that the slave was employed in transportation work, perhaps in specific regard to the *vehiculatio*, a possibility that will be explored below. Within Italy itself, in Lucanian Potentia, there is a text recording the death of another 18-year-old who was buried by a *coll(egium* or *egia?) mul(ionum) et asinar(iorum)* (*CIL* 10.143). Burial by a *collegium* is also indicated by three other inscriptions from Potentia (*CIL* 10.142, 174 and 8340b), though this is the only explicit mention of this specific group (or groups).

For northern Italy, our main area of attention, there exists a fascinating archaeological discovery, together with an inscription, that may help to flesh out the lives of associated muleteers (Mennella–Apicella 2000, 64, #77). In the course of excavations at Sarsina in Emilia Romagna (Roman Sassina, Augustan Region VI) in 1981–1982, a cemetery with individual burial plots and an *ustrinum* (cremation site) was identified along the road leading from the town. In use from the middle of the first through the middle of the second centuries AD, the cemetery seems to contain at least eight individual burials of incinerated remains, four of them clustered around a *stele* reading, simply, *Loc(us) col(legii) mulionum* (Ortalli,1982: 201-05). In one of the plots, the nearest to the inscription, the excavators uncovered a little iron whip, perhaps designed for driving mules, the pieces of which were sketched for its publication in *Epigraphica*. Ortalli concludes that while this is the first attestation of the existence of a *collegium* of *muliones* in Sassina – supplementing the many references to *collegia* of *centonarii* and *fabri* in the town – it underscores "la posizione itineraria di Sarsina" and the significance of a vocation of this type. In fact, he suggests, the presence of such a college contributed to enrich the entire city (Ortalli, 1982: 207).

If a *mulio* was indeed buried with one of the "tools" of his craft, this would seem to confirm a close identification between the deceased and his profession, as well as between himself and the larger organization. Collective burial may thus suggest close relationships in life but the positioning of the cemetery within its wider geographic context suggests even more about the group's collective status and ambitions. Compiling evidence from the 1980s excavations in the general area, Ortalli (1987) reconstructed a road stretching from Sassina into the Pian di Bezzo. In his estimation (and in a series of sketches based on the archaeological evidence), this road would have contained an extensive series of funerary monuments and cemeteries, very much like the city of the dead to be found along the *via Appia*. Ortalli surmised that a rush on burial property in the area and "the practice of undifferentiated burials" had prompted the *muliones* to secure a small area, reserved to themselves, and then to codify their claim with "una semplice stele" centralized on their property (Ortalli 1987, 163).

This reconstruction presumes that the individuals buried in the plot were members of the *collegium* itself or at least that the *muliones* could enforce their decisions concerning those to be buried within their acquired property. Notice, however, that the stone does not specify the dimensions of their plot, nor does it seem to have identified the individuals actually buried within it. Perhaps, comparing evidence to be adduced below, they were instead *speculating* in burial property and selling off the plots as a land-rush gathered momentum in the town? Who better than a group of transportation workers to spot a property-buying trend, along the roads they traveled in their daily work, and then to profit from that information? Alternatively it could be argued that, if the *muliones* buried their own membership here, with their small plot jostling alongside those of local grandees (some of the 50+ monuments detailed by Ortalli are impressive in size and sophistication), might this be evidence of a subtle "grab" for *status* as well as for land?

Other associations of transport workers may help us to speculate on the social dynamics at work in both large and small towns, and especially in northern Italy. Other organizations of *asinarii* can be found in Numidia (*AE* (1898) 86), and *cisiarii*, apparently carriage-makers or carriage-drivers, are particularly well attested in the vicinity of Rome and in Campania (Tibur, *CIL* 6.9485; Praeneste, *CIL* 14.2874; Pompeii, *CIL* 10.1064; Cales, *CIL* 10.4660; together with the "Baths of the Cisiarii" at Ostia Antica). In some of these cases the *cisiarii* [or *gisiarii* in the inscription from Cales] appear alongside a particular city-gate, and this can be duplicated in several inscriptions naming *iumentarii* in Mediolanum, Verona, and Forum Sempronii (Fossombrone).

Extrapolating from his title, a *iumentarius* would seem to have been a handler of beasts of burden and inscriptional evidence suggests that *iumentarii* were most often associated, in a more or less official capacity, with the *cursus publicus* established by Augustus and reconfigured periodically throughout the Principate. The abundance of epigraphic references to their activities led Werner Eck to locate the *superiumentari(i) et muliones* named in a votive inscription in Carnuntum within imperial service, specifically as the slaves or freedmen of a legate in Pannonia (Eck, 1992: 209–10).

Similar groupings of *iumentarii*, including explicit *collegia* of them, often appear in funerary inscriptions and in this respect can be compared with the *muliones* mentioned above. An epitaph found at Vicus Martis Tudertium (modern Santa Maria in Pantano in Umbria) honors a soldier who served 14 years and lived only 32. According to the text on the stone (*CIL* 11.4749), he left the *sodales Martenses* 2000 sesterces to tend to his remains; however, a *collegius [sic] iumentariorum* is noted to have offered the stone itself. The interesting element here is probably that the named *collegius*, rather than the recipients of the legacy, have acted in a corporate capacity specifically to honor the deceased. Corporate behavior and a public purse are also indicated by another inscription from Tibur, the text mentioned earlier in this chapter as *CIL* 6.9485. The donor here stipulates that, if anyone outside the ring of his heirs and descendants should attempt to detach any property from the site, he must pay a fine of 50 000 sesterces to the *collegium iumentariorum qui est in cisiaris Tiburtinis Herculis*. The complex verbiage may point to an arrangement between *iumentarii* and *cisiarii* in Tibur. In any case, it is striking that a group that might be presumed to be of low status – transport workers who managed animals and/or light carriages – is here the guarantor of responsible behavior and the thwarting of *dolus malus* (deceit), as indicated in the remainder of the text.

Like their counterparts in the *muliones*, *iumentarii* are also attested as the managers of common graveyards in various cities of Roman Italy. At Forum Sempronii (Fossombrone in Umbria) a man donated a burial place, *loc(um) sep(ulturae)*, to a *conlegio iumentarior(um) Portae Gallicae*, as well as to all their heirs, wives, and concubines (*CIL* 11.6136). The fact, though not the purpose or justification, of the gift is thereby acknowledged, though it is also important to note that the previous item in *CIL* (11.6135) simply marks the *loc(us) sep(ulturae)* of a *sodalicium fabr(um) tig(nuariorum)* together with its dimensions. This latter text does not connect the graveyard with a specific donor, but it does suggest that corporate burial was at least feasible in this town. The unusual feature of the inscription is the specific identification of the college with a city-gate, perhaps but not necessarily within Forum Sempronii itself.

This is not the only association of *iumentarii* connected by their nomenclature to one or more city-gates, as one other is mentioned in Mediolanum and excavations at Verona in recent decades have added two more items to this evidence. In spite of a few missing letters on its left-hand side, the Milanese document (*CIL* 5.5872) seems to record an honor rendered to a Metilius [M]essor by a *[c]ollegium [iu]mentario(rum) Portae [Ve]rcellinae [e]t Ioviae*. The title hints that *iumentarii* could congregate at, and thus come to be associated with, one or more city-gates, and, noticing the tendency of *cisiarii* also to be associated with city-gates, Maxey compared the presence of "cab-stands" at established locations (Maxey, 1938: 71). Nonetheless, this text also suggests that a group of presumably low status could honor an elevated individual. Although his full nomenclature is fragmentary, it is clear that this Metilius Messor was freeborn. In any event, the five central lines of the 13-line inscription are taken up with the full title of the *collegium*, and this may reflect the true intentions of those who granted the honor.

Two further inscriptions, discovered at Verona in 1968 and 1986, made reference to the *iumentarii Port(ae) Iov(iae)*, and, despite extensive previous commentary on them, much remains to be explained. The first text, although badly damaged and fragmentary on the bottom, appears to be datable on the basis of its letter formation to the first half of the second century (Ramilli, 1969: 5–6; Mennella–Apicella, 2000: 69, #87). This tombstone, dedicated *D(is) M(anibus)*, reads, *Permiss(u) manc(ipum) iumentarior(um) port(ae) Iov(iae)* and then becomes illegible, save for the name "Sosius". Ramilli compared many other epigraphic sources and reference works to link these *mancipes* with the *cursus publicus* and to specific reforms of the service mounted by Hadrian (Ramilli, 1969, 7–13). He did not, however, attempt to explain why "permission" was needed from this group for a burial, nor did he consider the possibility that *mancipes* may have been officers or agents of these *iumentarii*.

Even before the recovery of another text in the 1980s mentioning a dedication *ex permissu colleg(ii) iumentarior(um) port(ae) Iov(iae)*, the main point of controversy seems to have been the precise identification of this "*Porta Ioviae*," that is, was it a city-gate within Verona or was it a subsidiary of, or directly connected with, the similar-sounding association in Milan? Challenging a theory that the *Porta Ioviae* was a station along the *via Postumia* radiating from Verona, Alfredo Buonopane linked it directly to the group in Mediolanum, rendering it unnecessary to locate a city-gate or other landmark within the town itself (Buonopane, 1985: 21–22). With the announcement of another inscription the following year, acknowledging Q. Spurius Senecio's creation of a burial space for himself and his son and daughter by permission of this association, Lanfranco Franzoni believed that this new text furnished proof of the existence of a local gate named in honor of Jove. This was the first document from Verona to mention the nomen Spurius, which is not rare in Regions X and XI and, in his publication of the text, Franzoni recapitulated the arguments of Ramilli concerning *iumentarii* in the *cursus publicus*. However, he argued that the *mancipes* of the previous inscription should be considered as roughly equivalent to the *collegium* of this text, that is, the "prestanome [figurehead]" or agents of a society rather than "small independent contractors" (Franzoni, 1986: 617–22).

Nevertheless, Franzoni does not pursue the "permission" angle of the inscription further, devoting the bulk of the article merely to arguing that a *Porta Ioviae* could be found in Verona. (Perhaps the *iumentarii* of the Milan gate "franchised" their operation in Verona, along the lines of a Western Union or Southeastern Van Lines, that is, entities notionally associated with one geographic entity that acted in a professional capacity elsewhere?) In any event, I would argue that the stated "permission" constitutes the most significant element in both inscriptions. Its presence suggests that, following the analogy of the communal graveyards owned by *muliones* at Sassina and *iumentarii* at Forum Sempronii, this group has allowed individuals to be buried in their own plot. The recipients of the permission need not have been extraneous to the association, but perhaps the *iumentarii* who gathered or plied their trade in the vicinity of a particular gate had also noticed a scramble – and rising prices – for burial land just outside the city. Determined to make a profit, perhaps the *iumentarii* bought a plot of land and then doled it out, as they saw fit, with exchange of cash or, more interestingly, in the pursuit of further connections with their more elevated neighbors.

This hypothesis can be strengthened with recent commentary on two more *iumentarii* inscriptions found at Brixia. One (*CIL* 5.4211) is merely an honorary and fragmentary dedication to the *Genius* of a *coll(egium) [i]umentarior(um)*, but the other (5.4294) records an offering to Vulcan by three men and the arrangements to be made for the monument's celebration and future upkeep. According to this text P. Antonius Callistio, a *sevir Augustalis*, joined with C. Clodius Comicus and P. Postumius Agatho to make the dedication, while also arranging for *sportulae* (food and drink to celebrate the occasion) and depositing 400 sesterces with a *coll(egium) iument(ariorum)* in trust, *in tutel(am)*, for its maintenance. C. Clodius Comicus, likely the same man, appears in another dedication to Silvanus (*CIL* 5.4288) and a wide range of Postumii and Postumiae, both freed and freeborn, are known from Brixian epigraphy.

Nevertheless, the same P. Antonius Callistio was offered an honor by another *collegium* at Brixia, a *coll(egium) aen(eatorum)*, and his agent Thallus contributed *sportulae* and 1000 sesterces in trust to the college, from whose proceeds annual offerings were to be made (Mennella–Apicella, 2000: 36, #22). In a recent article on the *iumentarii* in the Roman Veneto, Filippo Boscolo links the texts in an imaginative way, asking whether *both* the *aeneatores* and the *iumentarii*, with their service on behalf of Vulcan, could be tied to the transport industry in Brixia. He brings forth a small, but potentially a very significant detail, in support of this conclusion, noting that the site of discovery of the original text in 1831 was actually at Brescia's Porta Torrelunga. If the cities of Brixia and Verona were dependent on important roads like the *via Postumia* and contained *iumentarii*, he argues, we should not be surprised that they were clustered at the points of entry to their respective cities (Boscolo, 2006–07: 358–61). Boscolo ends with a vivid evocation of the "chaotic" scene that must have confronted the visitor to a city gate in Roman Italy, with animals and choking dust on the city's outskirts in the interest then, as today, of thinning traffic flow into the city center. Despite the essential reasonableness of this image, I would argue that a more basic "traffic pattern" is at work here, that is, the "avenues" by which various collegial members attempted to secure status, relative to their social betters, and the "roadblocks" that were placed on their way to this destination.

25.4   Conclusion: Revisiting Two Models of Urban Development

The evidence examined here has originated from a wide variety of town settings, ranging from prominent, highly developed towns like Mediolanum and Verona to tiny hamlets like Brixellum and Forum Sempronii. Patterson concluded his book by setting out the parameters of two "ideal cities" as models of urban development in Roman Italy, essentially "a large town" and "a small town, with a population of less than 1000" (Patterson, 2006: 270–71). To examine these models in depth, perhaps we should review two cities, large Brixia and small Regium Lepidum, since both boasted associations of wool-workers and transport workers.

Among the characteristics of the "large town" model would be a complex economy that offered *Augustales* and *collegiati* the prospect that they "would in due course be able to enter the *ordo*" (Patterson, 2006: 270), thereby complementing and supporting existing civic structures. The inscriptions from Brixia examined here suggest a complex economy but, as I have explained earlier, the civic standing of *lanarii carminatores, coatores,* and *pectinarii* may have been higher than is normally surmised. From their more elevated status – or on the strength of their perception of the same – they may have decided to bury less fortunate members of their own or of the surrounding community, essentially "burying down" in terms of social hierarchy. At the same time, the members of *collegia* may have "honored up" the social scale, as the *iumentarii* inscription could be interpreted as a means of reinforcing their inferior standing at least in respect to a local *sevir Augustalis*.

In a small town like Regium Lepidum, where the ability of *Augustales* and *collegiati* to support the *ordo* was viable only "to a limited extent," the lines of these status divisions may have been even sharper. In a dynamic that reverses the one in Brixia, the transport workers (*muliones*) appear in a burial inscription and the *lanarii* feature in an honorary document. Nevertheless, as I have attempted to suggest with reference to common graveyards and "permissions" offered by similar organizations of laborers, these plots may have resulted from land speculation. Accordingly, financial, as well as status-driven, considerations may have motivated their behavior. The *lanarii pectinarii et carminatores* text, in which another local *sevir Augustalis* is thanked for his generosity, could have been the result of a more calculated thwarting of social mobility than might at first appear. Was Pomponius actually underscoring the dependence and financially lower position of the *lanarii* by means of his benefaction of food, clothing, and burial?

Here one might compare a provocative parallel case that van Nijf addressed in a 2002 article: the Dutch civic guards ("schutters") of the sixteenth and seventeenth centuries.

Although the civic guards may have felt that they were garnering respectability, they were effectively frozen out of the higher reaches of the civic aristocracy and, in a telling point, city authorities offered them subsidies for clothes, sashes, and drink during their parades (van Nijf, 2002: 321). Was the institutional *collegium* itself a means by which the elite consigned restless members of the "multitude" firmly to their own groups, tacitly stressing in the process their subordinate position? Returning to the geological image with which the chapter began, the "sub-elite *ordines*" may have served as a mere safety valve, releasing the roiling ambitions of those just below the fault line – all in the greater interest of keeping the "frozen waste" glacially undisturbed.

FURTHER READING

The fundamental starting place for an investigation of sub-elite orders in Roman Italian cities, and especially of the roles of the *Augustales* and the *collegia*, is Patterson, 2006. While some of my conclusions here differ from Patterson's, he has established in a lucid, straightforward style the main parameters of debate concerning the acquisition and maintenance of "social mobility" by means of these institutions. For further insight on a specific *collegium* at work, in both a practical and a status-gathering sense, see Liu 2009 on the *collegia centonariorum*, which are attested in several Italian towns in the Principate. For the role of *Augustales* within the larger Augustan program see especially Ostrow, 1990, and for a summary of the major controversies concerning the interpretation of *collegia* in the twentieth century, chiefly in terms of the "Corporativismo" lauded in Fascist Italy, see Perry, 2006.

REFERENCES

Abramenko, A. 1993. *Die munizipale Mittelschicht im kaiserzeitlichen Italien: Zu einem neuen Verständnis von Sevirat und Augustalität*. Frankfurt am Main: Peter Lang.
Albertini, A. 1971. "Iscrizioni romane rinvenute a Brescia (1970)." *Epigraphica* 33: 105–46.
Aurigemma, S. 1940. "Reggio Emilia". *Notizie degli Scavi* ns. 1: 255–301.
Bispham, E.H. 2007. *From Asculum to Actium: the municipalization of Italy from the Social War to Augustus*. Oxford: Oxford University Press.
Boscolo, F. 2006–07. "Gli *iumentarii* e il sistema dei trasporti in area Veneta in età romana." *Atti e memorie dell'Ateneo di Treviso* 24: 345–61.
Buchi, E. 1987. "Assetto agrario, risorse e attività economiche." *Il Veneto nell'età romana*, ed. E. Buchi. Verona: Banca Popolare di Verona.
Buonopane, A. 1985. "Testimonianze epigrafiche dal territorio di Villafranca." In *Contributi per lo studio di Villafranca e del suo territorio*, ed. L. Antonini, 11–22. *Studi Villafranchesi* 1.
Curtius, C. 1873. "Inschriften aus Kleinasien." *Hermes* 7: 28–46.
Delattre, A.-L. 1898. "Les cimetières romains superposés de Carthage (1896)." *Revue archéologique* 33: 337–50.
Demougin, S. 1994. "À propos des élites locales en Italie." In *L'Italie d'Auguste à Dioclétien*, 353–76. Rome: École française de Rome.
De Ruggiero, E. and Mazzarino, S. 1946. "Lanarius." *Dizionario Epigrafico*, vol. 4, fasc. 12: 361–63.
Diosono, F. 2007. Collegia. *Le associazioni professionali nel mondo romano*. Rome: Quasar.
Dixon, S. 2000–01. "How do you count them if they're not there? New perspectives on Roman cloth production." *Opuscula Romana* 25–26: 7–17.
Duthoy, R. 1978. "Les *Augustales*." *Aufstieg und Niedergang der römischen Welt* II.16.2: 1254–1309.
Eck, W. 1992. "*Superiumentari et muliones* im privaten Personal eines römischen Statthalters." *ZPE* 90: 207–10.
Finley, M.I. 1979 (2nd edn). *The World of Odysseus*. London: Penguin Books.

Franzoni, L. 1986. "*Collegium iumentariorum portae Ioviae* in una nuova iscrizione veronese." *Aquileia nostra* 57: 617–32.

Frayn, J.M. 1984. *Sheep-Rearing and the Wool Trade in Italy during the Roman Period.* Liverpool: Francis Cairns.

Garnsey, P. 1998. "Non-slave labour in the Roman world". In *Cities, Peasants and Food in Classical Antiquity: essays in social and economic history*, ed. W. Scheidel, 134–50. Cambridge: Cambridge University Press. [Reprint of original 1980 publication].

Garzetti, A. 1973. "Epigrafia e storia di Brescia romana." In *Atti del Convegno internazionale per il XIX centenario della dedicazione del "Capitolium" e per il 150° anniversario della sua scoperta.* Vol. 1, 53–61. Brescia: Ateneo di Brescia.

Jones, A.H.M. 1960. "The cloth industry under the Roman Empire." *The Economic History Review* 13: 183–92.

Kehoe, D.P. 2007. "The early Roman empire: production." In *The Cambridge Economic History of the Greco-Roman World*, eds W. Scheidel, I. Morris and R. Saller, 543–69. Cambridge: Cambridge University Press.

Liu, J. 2009. Collegia centonariorum: *the guilds of textile dealers in the Roman West.* Leiden: Koninklijke Brill NV.

Lomas, K. 1996. *Roman Italy, 338 BC – AD 200. A sourcebook.* London: UCL Press.

Lovén, L.L. 1998. "Male and female professions in the textile production of Roman Italy." In *Textiles in European Archaeology*, eds L.B. Jørgensen and C. Rinaldo, 73–78. Göteborg: GOTARC.

Maxey, M. 1938. *Occupations of the Lower Classes in Roman Society.* Chicago: University of Chicago Press [Arno Press reprint, New York, 1975].

Mennella, G. and G. Apicella. 2000. *Le corporazioni professionali nell'Italia romana. Un aggiornamento al Waltzing.* Naples: Arte Tipografica.

Moeller, W.O. 1969. "The male weavers at Pompeii." *Technology and Culture* 10: 561–66.

Moeller, W.O. 1976. *The Wool Trade of Ancient Pompeii.* Leiden: E.J. Brill.

Mouritsen, H. 1988. *Elections, Magistrates and Municipal Élite: studies in Pompeian epigraphy.* Rome: «L'Erma» di Bretschneider.

Mouritsen, H. 1997. "Mobility and social change in Italian towns during the principate." In *Roman Urbanism: beyond the consumer city*, ed. H.M. Parkins, 59–82. London: Routledge.

Nijf, O.M. van 1997. *The Civic World of Professional Associations in the Roman East.* Amsterdam: J.C. Gieben.

Nijf, O.M. van 1999. "Verenigingsleven en stedelijke identiteit: de rol van *fabri, centonarii* en *dendrophori*." *Lampas* 32: 198–210.

Nijf, O.M. van 2002. "*Collegia* and civic guards: two chapters in the history of sociability." In *After the Past. Essays in ancient History in Honour of H.W. Pleket*, eds W. Jongman and M. Kleijwegt, 305–39. Leiden: Brill.

Nijf, O.M. van 2003. "Les élites comme patrons des associations professionnelles dans l'Orient romain". in *Les élites et leurs facettes. Les élites locales dans le monde hellénistique et romain*, eds M. Cébeillac-Gervasoni and L. Lamoine, 307–21. Rome: École française de Rome.

Ortalli, J. 1982. "La stele sarsinate dei *muliones.*" *Epigraphica* 44: 201–07.

Ortalli, J. 1987. "La via dei sepolcri di Sarsina. Aspetti funzionali, formali e sociali." In *Römische Gräberstraßen. Selbstdarstellung – Status – Standard*, eds H. von Hesberg and P. Zanker, 155–84. Munich: Bayerische Akademie der Wissenschaften.

Ostrow, S. 1985. "*Augustales* along the Bay of Naples: a case for their early growth." *Historia* 34: 64–101.

Ostrow, S. 1990. "The *Augustales* in the Augustan scheme." In *Between Republic and Empire: interpretations of Augustus and his Principate*, eds K.A. Raaflaub and M. Toher, 364–79. Berkeley: University of California Press.

Patroni, G. 1925. In *Notizie degli Scavi di Antichità* ns. 1: 342–43.

Patterson, J.R. 1994. "The *collegia* and the transformation of the towns of Italy in the second century AD." In *L'Italie d'Auguste à Dioclétien*, 227–38. Rome: École française de Rome.

Patterson, J.R. 2006. *Landscapes and Cities. Rural settlement and civic transformation in early imperial Italy.* Oxford: Oxford University Press.

Perry, J.S. 2006. *The Roman Collegia: the modern evolution of an ancient concept.* Leiden: Brill.

Perry, J.S. 2011. "Organized societies: *Collegia.*" In *The Oxford Handbook of Social Relations in the Roman World*, ed. M. Peachin, 499–515. Oxford: Oxford University Press.

Petrikovits, H. von 1981. "Die Spezialisierung des römischen Handwerks." In *Das Handwerk in vor- und frühgeschichtlicher Zeit*, ed. H. Jankuhn, W. Janssen, R. Schmidt-Wiegand and H. Tiefenbach, I, 63–132. Göttingen: Vandenhoeck und Ruprecht.

Ramilli, G. 1969. "Un'iscrizione veronese sul 'cursus publicus'." *Archivio Veneto* 88: 5–13.

Tran, N. 2006. *Les membres des associations romaines. Le rang social des collegiati en Italie et en Gaules, sous le Haut-Empire.* Rome: École française de Rome.

Verboven, K. 2007. "The associative order: status and ethos of Roman businessmen in [the] Late Republic and Early Empire." *Athenaeum* 95: 861–93.

Waltzing, J.-P. 1895–1900. *Étude historique sur les corporations professionnelles chez les romains, depuis les origines jusqu'à la chute de l'empire d'occident.* Louvain: Peeters.

Index

A Companion to Roman Italy, First Edition. Edited by Alison E. Cooley.
© 2016 John Wiley & Sons, Ltd. Published 2016 by John Wiley & Sons, Ltd.